CompTIA A+ 220-801 and 220-802 Authorized Cert Guide

Third Edition

Mark Edward Soper
David L. Prowse
Scott Mueller

800 East 96th Street
Indianapolis, Indiana 46240 USA

CompTIA A+ 220-801 and 220-802 Authorized Cert Guide, Third Edition

ISBN-13: 978-0-7897-4850-8

ISBN-10: 0-7897-4850-9

Library of Congress Cataloging-in-Publication data is on file.

Printed in the United States of America

Fourth Printing: January 2014

Trademarks

All terms mentioned in this book that are known to be trademarks or service marks have been appropriately capitalized. Pearson IT Certification cannot attest to the accuracy of this information. Use of a term in this book should not be regarded as affecting the validity of any trademark or service mark.

Warning and Disclaimer

Every effort has been made to make this book as complete and as accurate as possible, but no warranty or fitness is implied. The information provided is on an "as is" basis. The authors and the publisher shall have neither liability nor responsibility to any person or entity with respect to any loss or damages arising from the information contained in this book or from the use of the CD or programs accompanying it.

Bulk Sales

Pearson IT Certification offers excellent discounts on this book when ordered in quantity for bulk purchases or special sales. For more information, please contact

U.S. Corporate and Government Sales

1-800-382-3419

corpsales@pearsontechgroup.com

For sales outside the United States, please contact

International Sales

international@pearsoned.com

Associate Publisher
Dave Dusthimer

Acquisitions Editor
Betsy Brown

Development Editor
Andrew Cupp

Managing Editor
Sandra Schroeder

Senior Project Editor
Tonya Simpson

Copy Editor
Apostrophe Editing Services

Proofreader
Megan Wade

Technical Editor
Chris Crayton

Editorial Assistant
Vanessa Evans

Media Producer
Tim Warner

Book Designer
Gary Adair

Compositor
Bronkella Publishing

Contents at a Glance

Table of Contents

About the Authors

Mark Edward Soper has been working with PCs since the days of the IBM PC/XT and AT as a salesperson, technology advisor, consultant, experimenter, and technology writer and content creator. Since 1992, he has taught thousands of students across the country how to repair, manage, and troubleshoot the hardware, software, operating systems, and firmware inside their PCs. He has created many versions of his experimental computer known as "FrankenPC" for this and previous books. Mark earned his CompTIA A+ Certification in 1999 and has written four other A+ Certification books covering previous and current versions of the A+ Certification exams for Pearson imprints.

Mark has contributed to many editions of *Upgrading and Repairing PCs*, working on the 11th through 18th and 20th editions; co-authored *Upgrading and Repairing Networks*, Fifth Edition; and has written two books about digital photography, *Easy Digital Cameras* and *The Shot Doctor: The Amateur's Guide to Taking Great Digital Photos*.

In addition, Mark has contributed to Que's *Special Edition Using* series on Windows Me, Windows XP, and Windows Vista and to Que's *Windows 7 In Depth*. He has also contributed to *Easy Windows Vista* and has written two books about Windows Vista: *Maximum PC Microsoft Windows Vista Exposed* and *Unleashing Microsoft Windows Vista Media Center*. Mark has also written two books about Windows 7: *Easy Microsoft Windows 7* and *Sams Teach Yourself Microsoft Windows 7 in 10 Minutes*. Mark has also created a number of hardware tutorial videos available from the OnGadgets&Hardware podcast channel at www.quepublishing.com.

Mark has also written many blog entries and articles for MaximumPC.com and *Maximum PC* magazine. He has taught A+ Certification and other technology-related subjects at Ivy Tech Community College in Evansville, Indiana. See Mark's website at www.markesoper.com for news and information about upcoming projects.

David L. Prowse is an author, a computer network specialist, and a technical trainer. Over the past several years he has authored several titles for Pearson Education, including the well-received *CompTIA A+ Exam Cram*. As a consultant, he installs and secures the latest in computer and networking technology. Over the past decade he has taught CompTIA A+, Network+, and Security+ certification courses, both in the classroom and via the Internet. He runs the website www.davidlprowse.com, where he gladly answers questions from students and readers.

Dedication

For Mayer and Naomi.

Acknowledgments

After more than 12 years as a full-time technology content provider, I'm more conscious than ever of two things—how richly I have been blessed by God in my family and in the team of technology experts I get to work with.

Thanks first and foremost to Almighty God. He gives gifts and strives earnestly to help us discover them.

Thanks also to my family, PC and Mac users alike, whose good-natured discussions keep everybody looking for the perfect technology. Thanks especially to Cheryl for her love and patience. A big thanks as well to Jeremy, for performing laptop teardowns and assisting with system builds.

As always, Pearson has put together an outstanding team for this edition, and I especially want to thank the two Daves: Dave Dusthimer for his vision of becoming the leading provider of A+ study material and Dave Prowse, my co-author, for helping make this book the best edition yet.

Thanks again to Scott Mueller, whose original edition of *Upgrading and Repairing PCs* was the impetus for taking my tech career to the next level, and for the opportunity to work with him on many projects over the years, including this one.

Thanks also to Betsy Brown, Andrew Cupp, Sandra Schroeder, and Tonya Simpson for keeping this process rolling along. And a big thank-you to technical editor Chris Crayton for great suggestions and tips along the way.

Finally, a thank you to Vanessa, Tim, and Gary.

All of us want to see you, our readers, succeed both in passing your exams and in your IT careers. We all wish you the very best.

About the Technical Editor

Chris Crayton is an author, technical editor, technical consultant, and trainer. Formerly, he worked as a computer and networking instructor at Keiser University; as network administrator for Protocol, a global electronic customer relationship management (eCRM) company; and at Eastman Kodak headquarters as a computer and network specialist. Chris has authored several print and online books on PC repair, CompTIA A+, CompTIA Security+, and Microsoft Windows. Mr. Crayton has also served as technical editor and contributor on numerous technical titles for many of the leading publishing companies. He holds MCSE, A+, and Network+ certifications.

We Want to Hear from You!

As the reader of this book, you are our most important critic and commentator. We value your opinion and want to know what we're doing right, what we could do better, what areas you'd like to see us publish in, and any other words of wisdom you're willing to pass our way.

As an associate publisher for Pearson IT Certification, I welcome your comments. You can email or write me directly to let me know what you did or didn't like about this book—as well as what we can do to make our books better.

Please note that I cannot help you with technical problems related to the topic of this book. We do have a User Services group, however, where I will forward specific technical questions related to the book.

When you write, please be sure to include this book's title and author as well as your name, email address, and phone number. I will carefully review your comments and share them with the authors and editors who worked on the book.

Email: feedback@pearsonitcertification.com

Mail: David Dusthimer
         Editor in Chief
         Pearson IT Certification
         800 East 96th Street
         Indianapolis, IN 46240 USA

Reader Services

Visit our website and register this book at www.pearsonitcertification.com/register for convenient access to any updates, downloads, or errata that might be available for this book.

It Pays to Get Certified

In a digital world, digital literacy is an essential survival skill.

Certification proves you have the knowledge and skill to solve business problems in virtually any business environment. Certifications are highly-valued credentials that qualify you for jobs, increased compensation and promotion.

LEARN		CERTIFY		WORK
IT is Everywhere	**IT Knowledge and Skills Get Jobs**	**Job Retention**	**New Opportunities**	**High Pay-High Growth Jobs**
IT is mission critical to almost all organizations and its importance is increasing.	Certifications verify your knowledge and skills that qualifies you for:	Competence is noticed and valued in organizations.	Certifications qualify you for new opportunities in your current job or when you want to change careers.	Hiring managers demand the strongest skill set.
• 79% of U.S. businesses report IT is either important or very important to the success of their company	• Jobs in the high growth IT career field • Increased compensation • Challenging assignments and promotions • 60% report that being certified is an employer or job requirement	• Increased knowledge of new or complex technologies • Enhanced productivity • More insightful problem solving • Better project management and communication skills • 47% report being certified helped improve their problem solving skills	• 31% report certification improved their career advancement opportunities	• There is a widening IT skills gap with over 300,000 jobs open • 88% report being certified enhanced their resume

Certification Advances Your Career

- The CompTIA A+ credential—provides foundation-level knowledge and skills necessary for a career in PC repair and support.
- Starting Salary—CompTIA A+ Certified individuals can earn as much as $65,000 per year.
- Career Pathway—CompTIA A+ is a building block for other CompTIA certifications such as Network+, Security+ and vendor specific technologies.
- More than 850,000—Individuals worldwide are CompTIA A+ certified.
- Mandated/Recommended by organizations worldwide—Such as Cisco and HP and Ricoh, the U.S. State Department, and U.S. government contractors such as EDS, General Dynamics, and Northrop Grumman.

Some of the primary benefits individuals report from becoming A+ certified are:

- More efficient troubleshooting
- Improved career advancement
- More insightful problem solving

CompTIA Career Pathway

CompTIA offers a number of credentials that form a foundation for your career in technology and allows you to pursue specific areas of concentration. Depending on the path you choose to take, CompTIA certifications help you build upon your skills and knowledge, supporting learning throughout your entire career.

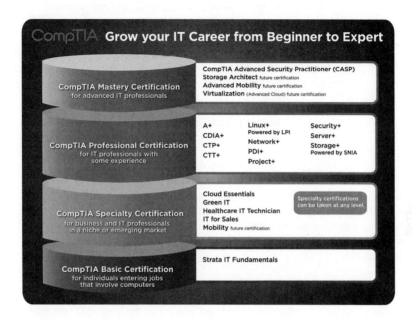

Steps to Certification

Steps to Getting Certified and Staying Certified	
Review Exam Objectives	Review the certification objectives to make sure you know what is covered in the exam. http://www.comptia.org/certifications/testprep/examobjectives.aspx
Practice for the Exam	After you have studied for the certification, take a free assessment and sample test to get an idea what type of questions might be on the exam. http://www.comptia.org/certifications/testprep/practicetests.aspx
Purchase an Exam Voucher	Purchase your exam voucher on the CompTIA Marketplace, which is located at: www.comptiastore.com.
Take the Test!	Select a certification exam provider and schedule a time to take your exam. You can find exam providers at the following link: http://www.comptia.org/certifications/testprep/testingcenters.aspx

Join the Professional Community

Join IT Pro Community
http://itpro.comptia.org

The free IT Pro online community provides valuable content to students and professionals.

Career IT Job Resources

- Where to start in IT
- Career Assessments
- Salary Trends
- US Job Board

Forums on Networking, Security, Computing and Cutting Edge Technologies

Access to blogs written by Industry Experts

Current information on Cutting Edge Technologies

Access to various industry resource links and articles related to IT and IT careers

Content Seal of Quality

This courseware bears the seal of **CompTIA Approved Quality Content**. This seal signifies this content covers 100% of the exam objectives and implements important instructional design principles. CompTIA recommends multiple learning tools to help increase coverage of the learning objectives.

Why CompTIA?

- **Global Recognition**—CompTIA is recognized globally as the leading IT non-profit trade association and has enormous credibility. Plus, CompTIA's certifications are vendor-neutral and offer proof of foundational knowledge that translates across technologies.

- **Valued by Hiring Managers**—Hiring managers value CompTIA certification because it is vendor- and technology-independent validation of your technical skills.

- **Recommended or Required by Government and Businesses**—Many government organizations and corporations either recommend or require technical staff to be CompTIA certified. (For example, Dell, Sharp, Ricoh, the U.S. Department of Defense, and many more.)

- **Three CompTIA Certifications ranked in the top 10**—In a study by DICE of 17,000 technology professionals, certifications helped command higher salaries at all experience levels.

How to obtain more information

Visit CompTIA online: www.comptia.org to learn more about getting CompTIA certified.

Contact CompTIA: Call 866-835-8020 ext. 5 or email questions@comptia.org

Connect with us :

Introduction

CompTIA A+ Certification is widely recognized as the first certification you should receive in an information technology (IT) career. Whether you are planning to specialize in PC hardware, Windows operating system management, or network management, the CompTIA A+ Certification exams measure the baseline skills you need to master to begin your journey toward greater responsibilities and achievements in IT.

CompTIA A+ Certification is designed to be a vendor-neutral exam that measures your knowledge of industry-standard technology.

Goals and Methods

The number one goal of this book is a simple one: to help you pass the 2012 version of the CompTIA A+ Certification exams 220-801 and 220-802.

Because CompTIA A+ Certification exams now stress problem-solving abilities and reasoning more than memorization of terms and facts, our goal is to help you master and understand the required objectives for each exam.

To aid you in mastering and understanding the A+ Certification objectives, this book uses the following methods:

- The beginning of each chapter defines the topics to be covered in the chapter; it also lists the corresponding CompTIA A+ objective numbers.

- The body of the chapter explains the topics from a hands-on and a theory-based standpoint. This includes in-depth descriptions, tables, and figures geared to build your knowledge so that you can pass the exam. The chapters are broken down into several topics each.

- The key topics indicate important figures, tables, and lists of information that you should know for the exam. They are interspersed throughout the chapter and are listed in table format at the end of the chapter.

- You can find memory tables and lists on the disc as Appendix A, "Memory Tables," and Appendix B, "Memory Tables Answer Key." Use them to help memorize important information.

- Key terms without definitions are listed at the end of each chapter. Write down the definition of each term, and check your work against the complete key terms in the glossary.

- Hand-on labs test you on your knowledge of key concepts. Develop possible solutions and check your work against the answers at the end of the chapter.

- Each chapter includes review questions meant to gauge your knowledge of the subjects. If an answer to a question doesn't come readily to you, be sure to review that portion of the chapter. The answers with detailed explanations are at the end of each chapter.

What's New?

You'll find plenty that's new and improved in this edition, including

- Updated coverage of motherboard features
- New coverage of custom system configurations
- Updated processor coverage
- Updated BIOS dialogs including UEFI BIOS examples
- USB 3.0
- SATA 6.0Gbps
- SSDs and how to fine-tune them for best performance
- Laptop teardown procedures
- Updated display technologies
- Video and display troubleshooting
- New seven-step laser printing process
- Better coverage of color laser printers
- New coverage of dealing with prohibited content/activity
- Enhanced coverage of Windows features
- Enhanced discussion of Windows upgrade paths and methods
- Windows 7 Enterprise features
- Virtualization
- Windows Virtual PC and Windows XP Mode
- Improved Control Panel discussion
- New Mobility domain covering iOS and Android devices

- Best practices for security (physical, digital, wireless network, wired network, and workstation folders)
- Drive wiping and destruction methods
- Security troubleshooting
- Wireless network troubleshooting

For a number of years, the CompTIA A+ Certification objectives were divided into a hardware exam and an operating systems exam. Starting with the 2006 exam, the exams were restructured so that knowledge of hardware and operating systems were needed for both exams. With the 2012 edition, the exams have been restructured again in a way that, we believe, will help you prepare more easily and avoid duplication of information. 220-801 covers hardware topics and operational procedures, whereas 220-802 covers operating systems, security, a brand new mobile devices domain, and troubleshooting.

For more information about how the A+ certification can help your career, or to download the latest official objectives, access CompTIA's A+ webpage at www.comptia.org/certifications/listed/a.aspx.

One method used by many A+ certification authors is to simply follow the objectives step by step. The problem is that because different parts of the computer—such as hard disk, display, Windows, and others—are covered in many different objectives, this approach creates a lot of overlap between chapters and does not help readers understand exactly how a particular part of the computer fits together with the rest.

In this book, we have used a subsystem approach. Each chapter is devoted to a particular part of the computer so that you understand how the components of each part work together and how each part of the computer works with other parts. To make sure you can relate the book's contents to the CompTIA A+ Certification objectives, each chapter contains cross-references to the appropriate objectives as needed, and we provide a master cross-reference list later in this introduction.

Who Should Read This Book?

The CompTIA A+ exams measure the necessary competencies for an entry-level IT professional with the equivalent knowledge of at least 500 hours of hands-on experience in the lab or field. This book is written for people who have that amount of experience working with desktop PCs and laptops. Average readers will have attempted in the past to replace a hardware component within a PC; they should also understand how to navigate through Windows and access the Internet.

Readers will range from people who are attempting to attain a position in the IT field to people who want to keep their skills sharp or perhaps retain their job due to a company policy that mandates that they take the new exams.

This book is also aimed at the reader who wants to acquire additional certifications beyond the A+ certification (Network+, Security+, and so on). The book is designed in such a way to offer easy transition to future certification studies.

Strategies for Exam Preparation

Strategies for exam preparation will vary depending on your existing skills, knowledge, and equipment available. Of course, the ideal exam preparation would consist of building a PC from scratch and installing and configuring the operating systems covered including Windows 7 (Ultimate edition is recommended), Windows Vista (Ultimate edition is preferred), and Windows XP Professional. To make things easier for the reader, we recommend that you use Microsoft's Windows Virtual PC (which works with Windows 7 Professional, Ultimate, and Enterprise) or Virtual PC 2007 (which works with other Windows 7 editions, Windows Vista, and Windows XP). Either program enables you to run virtual operating systems from within your current operating system without the need for an additional computer and can be downloaded for free from Microsoft's website. We also recommend that you have access to a laptop, a laser printer, and as many peripheral PC devices as possible. This hands-on approach will really help to reinforce the ideas and concepts expressed in the book. However, not everyone has access to this equipment, so the next best step you can take is to read through the chapters in this book, jotting down notes with key concepts or configurations on a separate notepad. Each chapter contains a quiz that you can use to test your knowledge of the chapter's topics. It's located near the end of the chapter.

After you have read through the book, look at the current exam objectives for the CompTIA A+ Certification Exams listed at http://certification.comptia.org/home.aspx. If there are any areas shown in the certification exam outline that you would still like to study, find those sections in the book and review them.

When you feel confident in your skills, attempt the practice exams included on the disc with this book. As you work through the practice exams, note the areas where you lack confidence and review those concepts or configurations in the book. After you review the areas, work through the practice exam a second time and rate your skills. Keep in mind that the more you work through the practice exam, the more familiar the questions will become.

After you have worked through the practice exams a second time and feel confident with your skills, schedule the real CompTIA A+ 220-801 and 220-802 exams through either Sylvan Prometric (www.2test.com) or Pearson Vue (www.vue.com).

To prevent the information from evaporating out of your mind, you should typically take the exam within a week of when you consider yourself ready to take the exam.

The CompTIA A+ Certification credential for those passing the certification exams is now valid for 3 years (effective January 1, 2011). To renew your certification without retaking the exam, you must participate in continuing education (CE) activities and pay an annual maintenance fee of $25.00 ($75.00 for 3 years). To learn more about the certification renewal policy, see http://certification.comptia.org/getCertified/stayCertified.aspx.

CompTIA A+ 220-801 and 220-802 Exam Objectives

Table I-1 lists the objectives and the chapters where they are covered. Be sure to check http://certification.comptia.org/home.aspx for any updates to the objectives.

Table I-1   CompTIA A+ 220-801 and 220-802 Exam Objectives

Objective	Chapters
220-801	
1.0 PC Hardware	
1.1 Configure and apply BIOS settings.	1, 3
1.2 Differentiate between motherboard components, their purposes, and properties.	1, 2
1.3 Compare and contrast RAM types and features.	1, 5
1.4 Install and configure expansion cards.	7, 8
1.5 Install and configure storage devices and use appropriate media.	1, 12
1.6 Differentiate among various CPU types and features and select the appropriate cooling method.	1, 2
1.7 Compare and contrast various connection interfaces and explain their purpose.	1, 6, 7
1.8 Install an appropriate power supply based on a given scenario.	1, 4
1.9 Evaluate and select appropriate components for a custom configuration, to meet customer specifications or needs.	8
1.10 Given a scenario, evaluate types and features of display devices.	1, 7
1.11 Identify connector types and associated cables.	1, 6, 7
1.12 Install and configure various peripheral devices.	6, 8
2.0 Networking	
2.1 Identify types of network cables and connectors.	16
2.2 Categorize characteristics of connectors and cabling.	16

Table I-1 Continued

Objective	Chapters
2.3 Explain properties and characteristics of TCP/IP.	16
2.4 Explain common TCP and UDP ports, protocols, and their purpose.	16
2.5 Compare and contrast wireless networking standards and encryption types.	16
2.6 Install, configure, and deploy a SOHO wireless/wired router using appropriate settings.	16
2.7 Compare and contrast Internet connection types and features.	16
2.8 Identify various types of networks.	16
2.9 Compare and contrast network devices their functions and features.	16
2.10 Given a scenario, use appropriate networking tools.	16
3.0 Laptops	
3.1 Install and configure laptop hardware and components.	9
3.2 Compare and contrast the components within the display of a laptop.	9
3.3 Compare and contrast laptop features.	9
4.0 Printers	
4.1 Explain the differences between the various printer types and summarize the associated imaging process.	11
4.2 Given a scenario, install, and configure printers.	11
4.3 Given a scenario, perform printer maintenance.	11
5.0 Operational Procedures	
5.1 Given a scenario, use appropriate safety procedures.	18
5.2 Explain environmental impacts and the purpose of environmental controls.	4, 18
5.3 Given a scenario, demonstrate proper communication and professionalism.	18
5.4 Explain the fundamentals of dealing with prohibited content/activity.	18
220-802	
1.0 Operating Systems	
1.1 Compare and contrast the features and requirements of various Microsoft Operating Systems.	14
1.2 Given a scenario, install, and configure the operating system using the most appropriate method.	13
1.3 Given a scenario, use appropriate command line tools.	14
1.4 Given a scenario, use appropriate operating system features and tools.	13, 14
1.5 Given a scenario, use Control Panel utilities (the items are organized by "classic view/large icons" in Windows).	14

Objective	Chapters
1.6 Setup and configure Windows networking on a client/desktop.	16
1.7 Perform preventive maintenance procedures using appropriate tools.	15
1.8 Explain the differences among basic OS security settings.	17
1.9 Explain the basics of client-side virtualization.	14
2.0 Security	
2.1 Apply and use common prevention methods.	17
2.2 Compare and contrast common security threats.	17
2.3 Implement security best practices to secure a workstation.	17
2.4 Given a scenario, use the appropriate data destruction/disposal method.	17
2.5 Given a scenario, secure a SOHO wireless network.	17
2.6 Given a scenario, secure a SOHO wired network.	17
3.0 Mobile Devices	
3.1 Explain the basic features of mobile operating systems.	10
3.2 Establish basic network connectivity and configure email.	10
3.3 Compare and contrast methods for securing mobile devices.	10
3.4 Compare and contrast hardware differences in regards to tablets and laptops.	10
3.5 Execute and configure mobile device synchronization.	10
4.0 Troubleshooting	
4.1 Given a scenario, explain the troubleshooting theory.	1
4.2 Given a scenario, troubleshoot common problems related to motherboards, RAM, CPU and power with appropriate tools.	1, 2, 3, 4, 5, 6
4.3 Given a scenario, troubleshoot hard drives and RAID arrays with appropriate tools.	1, 12
4.4 Given a scenario, troubleshoot common video and display issues.	7
4.5 Given a scenario, troubleshoot wired and wireless networks with appropriate tools.	1, 16
4.6 Given a scenario, troubleshoot operating system problems with appropriate tools.	15
4.7 Given a scenario, troubleshoot common security issues with appropriate tools and best practices.	17
4.8 Given a scenario, troubleshoot, and repair common laptop issues while adhering to the appropriate procedures.	9
4.9 Given a scenario, troubleshoot printers with appropriate tools.	1, 11

Pearson IT Certification Practice Test Engine and Questions on the Disc

The disc in the back of the book includes the Pearson IT Certification Practice Test engine—software that displays and grades a set of exam-realistic multiple-choice questions. Using the Pearson IT Certification Practice Test engine, you can either study by going through the questions in Study Mode or take a simulated exam that mimics real exam conditions.

The installation process requires two major steps: installing the software and then activating the exam. The disc in the back of this book has a recent copy of the Pearson IT Certification Practice Test engine. The practice exam—the database of exam questions—is not on the disc.

NOTE   The cardboard disc case in the back of this book includes the disc and a piece of paper. The paper lists the activation code for the practice exam associated with this book. Do not lose the activation code. On the opposite side of the paper from the activation code is a unique, one-time use coupon code for the purchase of the Premium Edition eBook and Practice Test.

Install the Software from the Disc

The Pearson IT Certification Practice Test is a Windows-only desktop application. You can run it on a Mac using a Windows Virtual Machine, but it was built specifically for the PC platform. The minimum system requirements are

- Windows XP (SP3), Windows Vista (SP2), or Windows 7
- Microsoft .NET Framework 4.0 Client
- Microsoft SQL Server Compact 4.0
- Pentium class 1GHz processor (or equivalent)
- 512MB RAM
- 650MB disc space plus 50MB for each downloaded practice exam

The software installation process is pretty routine compared with other software installation processes. If you have already installed the Pearson IT Certification Practice Test software from another Pearson product, there is no need for you to reinstall the software. Simply launch the software on your desktop and proceed to activate the practice exam from this book by using the activation code included in the disc sleeve.

The following steps outline the installation process:

Step 1.   Insert the disc into your PC.

Step 2.   The software that automatically runs is the Pearson software to access and use all disc-based features, including the exam engine and the disc-only appendixes. From the main menu, click the option to **Install the Exam Engine**.

Step 3.   Respond to windows prompts as with any typical software installation process.

The installation process gives you the option to activate your exam with the activation code supplied on the paper in the disc sleeve. This process requires that you establish a Pearson website login. You need this login to activate the exam, so please do register when prompted. If you already have a Pearson website login, there is no need to register again. Just use your existing login.

Activate and Download the Practice Exam

After the exam engine is installed, you should then activate the exam associated with this book (if you did not do so during the installation process) as follows:

Step 1.   Start the Pearson IT Certification Practice Test software from the Windows **Start** menu or from your desktop shortcut icon.

Step 2.   To activate and download the exam associated with this book, from the **My Products** or **Tools** tab, select the **Activate** button.

Step 3.   At the next screen, enter the Activation Key from the paper inside the cardboard disc holder in the back of the book. When entered, click the **Activate** button.

Step 4.   The activation process downloads the practice exam. Click **Next** and then click **Finish.**

After the activation process finishes, the **My Products** tab should list your new exam. If you do not see the exam, make sure you have selected the **My Products** tab on the menu. At this point, the software and practice exam are ready to use. Simply select the exam, and click the **Open Exam** button.

To update a particular exam you have already activated and downloaded, simply select the **Tools** tab, and select the **Update Products** button. Updating your exams will ensure you have the latest changes and updates to the exam data.

If you want to check for updates to the Pearson Cert Practice Test exam engine software, simply select the **Tools** tab, and select the **Update Application** button. This will ensure you are running the latest version of the software engine.

Activating Other Exams

The exam software installation process, and the registration process, must happen only once. Then, for each new exam, only a few steps are required. For instance, if you buy another new Pearson IT Certification Cert Guide or Cisco Press Official Cert Guide, extract the activation code from the disc sleeve in the back of that book—you don't even need the disc at this point. From there, all you need to do is start the exam engine (if not still up and running), and perform Steps 2–4 from the previous list.

Premium Edition

In addition to the two free practice exams provided on the disc, you can purchase two additional exams with expanded functionality directly from Pearson IT Certification. The Premium Edition eBook and Practice Test for this title contains two additional full practice exams as well as an eBook (in both PDF and ePub format). In addition, the Premium Edition title also has remediation for each question to the specific part of the eBook that relates to that question.

If you have purchased the print version of this title, you can purchase the Premium Edition at a deep discount. There is a coupon code in the disc sleeve that contains a one-time use code as well as instructions for where you can purchase the Premium Edition.

To view the premium edition product page, go to www.informit.com/title/978078978492.

This chapter covers the following subjects:

- **The Essential Parts of Any Computer**—In this section, you learn the most important features of desktop and laptop computers and where to find more information.

- **Hardware, Software, and Firmware**—A computer is built from many hardware components, but without instructions in the form of software and firmware, it's just a useless collection of parts. This section helps you understand how hardware, software, and firmware work together.

- **Points of Failure**—Computers contain many components. In this section you discover how component failures can affect a system.

- **The CompTIA Six-Step Troubleshooting Process**—Learn this process, apply it, and you're well on the road to solving computer problems of all types.

- **PC Tools**—Discover the hand tools you need to assemble, disassemble, and rebuild computers, test power supplies, and build a wired network.

- **Important Websites**—As you prepare for your exams and learn more about Microsoft Windows, the websites in this section are essential.

This chapter covers the **CompTIA A+ 220-801 objectives 1.1, 1.2, 1.3, 1.5, 1.6, 1.7, 1.8, 1.10, 1.11** and the **CompTIA A+ 220-802 objectives 4.1, 4.2, 4.3, 4.5, 4.9**.

CHAPTER 1

Technician Essentials and PC Anatomy 101

Before you start to work on a defective computer, it's important to understand the essential parts of any computer. These include the different hardware components found in desktop and laptop computers and the roles played by software and firmware to make hardware function. It's also helpful to be introduced to the most common types of computer failures, how to troubleshoot computer problems, the tools you need to make repairs, and some great websites to use as you prepare for the CompTIA A+ Certification exams. This chapter introduces you to most of the objectives found in 220-801 Domain 1 and 220-802 Domain 4, and provides a guide to where to find more detailed information elsewhere in this book.

Foundation Topics

The Essential Parts of Any Computer

220-801

Objectives:
220-801: 1.2,
1.3, 1.5, 1.6, 1.7,
1.8, 1.10, 1.11

What makes a computer a computer? After all, some furniture stores put 3D cardboard facsimile computers on computer desks so you can see that the furniture really will hold a computer. But what makes a real computer different from the cardboard phony?

Real computers contain a variety of components and subsystems, including

- Storage devices
- Motherboards
- Power supplies
- Processors/CPUs
- Memory
- Display devices
- Input, multimedia, and biometric devices
- Adapter cards
- Ports and cables
- Cooling systems

This section describes the components of a desktop PC and contrasts the features of a desktop with those of a laptop, or notebook, computer.

Front and Rear Views of a Desktop PC

Many of these components are visible in the front and rear views of a desktop computer. Figure 1-1 shows the front view of a typical desktop computer, and Figure 1-2 shows the rear view of the same computer.

NOTE   The system shown in Figure 1-2 lacks legacy ports such as serial and parallel ports. For a look at a system with these ports, refer to Figure 2-3 in Chapter 2, "Motherboards and Processors."

Some components, such as RAM, disk drives, and the CPU, are only visible when you remove part of the cover. Figure 1-3 shows the interior of a typical desktop computer, which, as you can see, is a pretty crowded place.

1. Empty 5.25-inch drive bay
2. Rewritable DVD drive
3. Flash memory card reader
4. Activity lights
5. Reset switch
6. Power switch
7. USB port
8. Microphone jack
9. Speaker/headset jack
10. IEEE-1394a (FireWire 400) port

Figure 1-1   The front of a typical desktop computer.

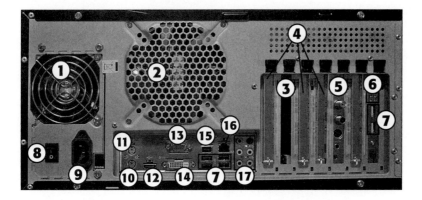

1. Power supply fan
2. Case fan
3. Empty expansion slot without slot cover
4. Empty expansion slot with slot cover
5. TV tuner card
6. Motherboard diagnostic lights
7. USB port
8. Power supply on/off switch
9. AC power connector
10. PS/2 keyboard port
11. PS/2 mouse port
12. HDMI audio/video port
13. VGA video port
14. DVI-D video port
15. IEEE-1394a (FireWire 400) port
16. Ethernet (RJ-45) port
17. 1/8-inch mini-jack audio port cluster

Figure 1-2   The rear of a typical desktop computer.

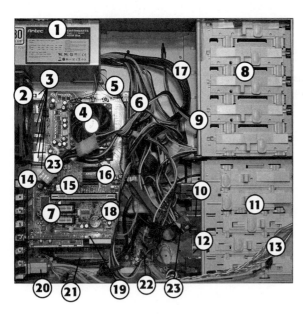

1. Power supply
2. Case fan
3. Rear port cluster
4. Active heatsink over CPU
5. Memory modules
6. Power cables for drives and fans
7. PCI Express x1 expansion slots
8. Empty 5.25-inch drive bay
9. Rewritable DVD drive in 5.25-inch drive bay
10. PATA drive in 3.5-inch drive bay
11. Empty 3.5-inch drive bay
12. SATA hard disk in 3.5-inch drive bay
13. Front panel cables
14. Expansion slot covers
15. PCI Express x16 video card slot
16. Passive heatsink over North Bridge chip
17. Power cable to motherboard
18. CMOS battery (CR-2032)
19. TV tuner card
20. Rear header cable
21. PCI expansion slot
22. Front header cable
23. Unused drive/fan power connector

Figure 1-3   The interior of a typical desktop computer.

All Around a Notebook (Laptop) Computer

Notebook computers use the same types of peripherals, operating system, and application software as desktop computers use. However, notebook computers vary in several ways from desktop computers:

- Most notebook computers feature integrated ports similar to those found in recent desktop computers (such as USB 2.0 or USB 3.0 ports and 10/100 or Gigabit Ethernet network ports) as well as one ExpressCard slot and a 56 kilobits per second (Kbps) modem.

- Some notebook computers support swappable drives, but less-expensive models require a trip to the service bench for a drive upgrade.

- Most notebook computers don't have an internal floppy drive, but rely on USB, rewritable DVD, or combo CD-RW/DVD-ROM drives to transfer or back up data.

- Notebook computers have integrated pointing devices built into their keyboards; most use a touchpad, but a few business-oriented models have a pointing stick instead of or in addition to a touchpad (which type is better is a matter of personal preference).

Figures 1-4, 1-5, and 1-6 illustrate the ports on a typical notebook computer, an HP dv4 series. Note that this computer lacks rear-mounted ports, while some other portable computers have ports on the rear as well.

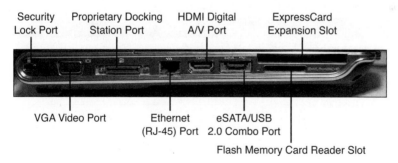

Figure 1-4   Left view of an HP dv4 series notebook computer.

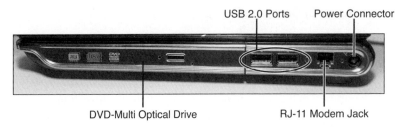

Figure 1-5   Right view of an HP dv4 series notebook computer.

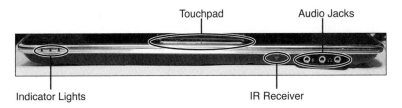

Figure 1-6   Front view of an HP dv4 series notebook computer.

Quick Reference to PC Components

Use Table 1-1 to learn more about many of the components and devices shown in Figure 1-1 through Figure 1-6.

Table 1-1   Where to Learn More About PC Components and Devices

Component/Device	Chapter
Audio jacks (microphone, speaker, headphone, and so on)	6
Case fan	4
CMOS battery	3
Drive bay	12
DVD drive	12
DVI-D video port	7
eSATA port	12
Ethernet network port	16
Express Card slot	9
Flash memory card reader	12
HDMI port	7
IEEE-1394 port	6
Memory module	5

Component/Device	Chapter
Modem port	16
Motherboard and its components	2
PATA hard disk drive and interface	12
PC Card/CardBus slot	9
PCI Express x1 slot	2
PCI Express x16 slot	2
PCI slot	2
Power supply	4
PS/2 keyboard and mouse ports	6
SATA hard disk drive and interface	12
S-video port	7
TV tuner card	8
USB port	6
VGA video port	7
Video card	7

Hardware, Software, and Firmware

220-801

Objective:
220-801: 1.1

The components seen in Figures 1-1 through 1-6 represent the hardware portion of the computer. Of these, the processor, or central processing unit (CPU), is king: Other components interact with the processor to create and modify information. However, the CPU relies on other components to receive instructions, store new and updated information, and send information to output or display devices. These essential parts can be broken down into three categories: hardware, software, and firmware. Components in all three categories are necessary to the operation of any computer.

Hardware

Hardware is the part of the computer you can pick up, move around, open, and close. Although hardware might represent the glamorous side of computing—whose computer is faster, has a larger hard disk, more memory, and so on—a computer can do nothing without software and firmware to provide instructions. Hardware failures can take place because of loose connections, electrical or physical damage, or incompatible devices.

Software

Software provides the instructions that tell hardware what to do. The same computer system can be used for word processing, gaming, accounting, or Web surfing by installing and using new software. Software comes in various types, including operating systems, application programs, and utility programs.

Operating systems provide standard methods for saving, retrieving, changing, printing, and transmitting information. The most common operating systems today are various versions of Microsoft Windows. The 2012 version of the A+ Certification exams focuses on recent 32-bit and 64-bit desktop versions of Windows (for example, Windows XP, Windows Vista, and Windows 7). Because operating systems provide the "glue" that connects hardware devices and applications, they are written to work on specified combinations of CPUs and hardware.

Operating system commands come in two major types: internal and external. Internal commands are those built into the operating system when it starts the computer. External commands require that you run a particular program included with the operating system.

Application programs are used to create, store, modify, and view information you create, also called data. Because an operating system provides standard methods for using storage, printing, and network devices to work with information, applications must be written to comply with the requirements of an operating system and its associated CPUs. A+ Certification does not require specific knowledge of application programs, but to provide the best technical support, you should learn the basics of the major applications your company or clients use, such as Microsoft Office, Corel WordPerfect Suite, OpenOffice, Adobe Creative Suite, and so on.

Certifications are available for major operating systems and applications, and seeking certifications in these areas can further improve your chances of being hired and promoted.

Utility programs are used to keep a computer in good working condition or to set up new devices. In the chapters related to operating systems, you'll learn how to use the major utilities included with Windows.

Because utilities included in Windows have limited capabilities, you might also want to invest in other utility programs, such as disk imaging, file backup, partition management, and others, for use in your day-to-day work; however, only standard Windows utilities, such as CHKDSK, Disk Management, Defrag, and others, are covered on the A+ Certification Exams.

Firmware

Firmware represents a middle ground between hardware and software. Like hardware, firmware is physical: a chip or chips attached to devices such as motherboards, optical drives, video cards, mass storage host adapter (RAID, PATA, SATA, and SCSI cards), network cards, modems, and printers. However, firmware is also software: Firmware chips (such as the motherboard BIOS) contain instructions for hardware testing, hardware configuration, and input/output routines. In essence, **firmware** is "software on a chip," and the software's job is to control the device to which the chip is connected. Because firmware works with both hardware and software, changes in either one can cause firmware to become outdated. Outdated firmware can lead to device or system failure or even data loss. Most firmware today is "flashable," meaning that its contents can be changed through software. You'll learn more about the most common type of firmware, the motherboard's BIOS, in Chapter 3, "BIOS."

Why Hardware, Software, and Firmware Are Important to Understand

As a computer technician, you will deal on a day-to-day basis with the three major parts of any computing environment. Whether you're working on a computer, printer, or component such as a video card, you must determine whether the problem involves hardware, software, firmware, or a combination of these three.

Points of Failure

> **220-801**
>
> **Objectives:**
> **220-801: 1.2, 1.3, 1.5, 1.6, 1.7, 1.8, 1.10, 1.11**

The phrase point of failure identifies components and accessories that can fail on a desktop or portable computer. This section describes points of failure on desktop and laptop computers.

Points of Failure on a Desktop Computer

A desktop computer can fail for a variety of reasons, including

- **Overheating**—Failure of the fans in the power supply or those attached to the processor, chipset, or video card can cause overheating and can lead to component damage. Some fans plug into the motherboard, while others plug into a lead from the power supply.

- **Add-on cards**—A loose add-on card or card that is not connected to additional power might not be detected by plug-and-play or Windows Device Manager, or might have intermittent failures after installation. An add-on card with a short might prevent the system from booting.

- **CPU**—A loose or defective CPU can prevent the computer from starting or cause erratic operation.

- **Motherboard components**—Failing capacitors, voltage regulators, and other components built into the motherboard can cause a system to not start or to lock up after being in use for some time.

- **Memory modules**—If memory modules are not installed properly or are damaged, they will work erratically at best and could cause data loss.

- **Drives**—If internal drives are not properly connected to power or data cables, or are not properly configured, they will not work properly.

- **Front panel cables**—The tiny cables that connect the case power switch, reset switch, and status lights are easy to disconnect accidentally if you are working near the edges of the motherboard, preventing the system from being turned on or from displaying activity.

- **CMOS Battery**—The battery maintains the system settings that are configured by the system BIOS. The settings are stored in a part of the computer called the CMOS, more formally known as the nonvolatile RAM/real-time clock (NVRAM/RTC). If the battery dies (average life is about two to three years), these settings will be lost. After you replace the battery, you must re-enter the CMOS settings and save the changes to the CMOS before you can use the system.

- **BIOS chip**—The system BIOS chip can be destroyed by ESD or lightning strikes. However, BIOS chips can also become outdated. Although some systems use a rectangular socketed BIOS chip, others use a square BIOS chip, which might be socketed or surface-mounted. In both cases, software BIOS upgrades are usually available to provide additional BIOS features, such as support for newer processors and hardware.

Points of Failure on a Notebook Computer

As with desktop computers, cabling can be a major point of failure on notebook computers. However, notebook computers also have a few unique points of failure. PC Card (PCMCIA card) or Express Card slots represent a significant potential point of failure for the following reasons:

- If a PC Card or Express Card is not completely pushed into its slot, it will not function.

- If a PC Card or Express Card is ejected without being stopped by using the Safely Remove Hardware system tray control, it could be damaged.

- Some older PC Cards designed as 10/100 Ethernet network adapters or 56Kbps modems use dongles (see Chapter 16, "Networking"). If the dongle is damaged, the card is useless until you get a replacement dongle.

Although a notebook computer's drives are much more rugged than those found in desktop computers, they are more expensive to replace with an equivalent or larger sized drive if damaged. Although some mid-range and high-end notebook computers offer swappable drives, most lower-priced models do not. Depending upon the specific notebook computer model, you can often perform an upgrade to a hard disk without special tools, but replacement of other types of drives on systems that don't support swappable drive bays can be expensive.

Drives are expensive to replace on notebook computers, but the biggest potential expense is the LCD display. Although some vendors provide user-replaceable LCD display modules, you should carefully consider the cost of replacing the LCD versus replacing the entire computer if the display is damaged. If an equivalent notebook computer is available new for less than twice the cost of replacing the display on an existing notebook computer, it usually makes sense to replace the computer instead of the display module.

The CompTIA Six-Step Troubleshooting Process

220-802

Objective:
220-802: 4.1

As you can see from the previous sections, any given computer problem could have multiple symptoms and several possible causes. To solve computer problems, PC technicians need a proven and effective troubleshooting theory. CompTIA has included a six-step process within the 2012 A+ objectives. As Table 1-2 indicates, the steps help you to find the source of a problem, find the solution, and help prevent recurrences.

Table 1-2   The Six-Step CompTIA A+ Troubleshooting Theory

Step	Description
Step 1	Identify the problem.
Step 2	Establish a theory of probable cause (question the obvious).
Step 3	Test the theory to determine the cause.
Step 4	Establish a plan of action to resolve the problem and implement the solution.
Step 5	Verify full system functionality and, if applicable, implement preventative measures.
Step 6	Document findings, actions, and outcomes.

As you attempt to troubleshoot computer issues, think in terms of this six-step process. Plug the problem directly into these steps. If you test a theory in Step 3, and the theory is disproved, return to Step 2 and develop another theory. Continue in this manner until you have found a theory that points to the problem. After you solve the problem (Steps 4 and 5), be sure to document what happened (Step 6) so you can more quickly solve a similar problem in the future.

PC Tools

220-802

**Objectives:
220-802: 4.2,
4.3, 4.5, 4.9**

A technician's best tools are his or her senses and hands. However, a technician needs hardware tools to open the personal computer (PC) and to install and replace components. Several categories of tools should be a part of every technician's toolkit.

Basic Tools for Assembly/Disassembly of Computers

Use the following tools when you assemble or disassemble desktop or laptop computers.

- **Phillips and straight-blade screwdrivers**—Used when hex drivers are not compatible; nonmagnetic preferred

- **Torx drivers**—Required for some Compaq models; nonmagnetic preferred

- **Hex drivers**—Used for opening and closing cases and securing and removing cards and motherboards; nonmagnetic preferred

- **3-claw parts retrieval tool**—Retrieves loose parts from computer interior; prevents lost parts, which can lead to dead shorts

- **Hemostat clamps**—Replaces tweezers for inserting and removing jumper blocks and cables

- **Needle-nose pliers**—Straightens bent pins

- **Eyebrow tweezers**—Replaces normal tweezers in toolkit for removing and replacing jumpers

- **Penlight**—Illuminates dark cases

- **Magnifier**—Makes small parts and markings easier to read

- **Jeweler's screwdriver set**—Enables repairs to devices that use small screws

You can buy toolkits that contain many of these items, but don't hesitate to supplement a kit you already have with additional items from this list or other items you find useful. Figure 1-7 illustrates some important tools.

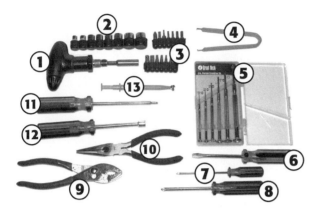

1. Screwdriver with removable tips (shown in #2 and #3)
2. Hex driver tips
3. Screw and Torx tips
4. Chip puller (also useful for removing keytops)
5. Jeweler's screwdriver set
6. Flat-blade screwdriver
7. Small Phillips-head screwdriver
8. Phillips-head screwdriver
9. Pliers
10. Needle-nose pliers
11. Torx driver
12. Hex driver
13. 3-claw parts retrieval tool

Figure 1-7   Typical tools used by computer technicians.

ESD Protection

Electrostatic discharge (ESD) can damage computer components during installation or removal processes. Even if you don't feel a shock when you touch a component, ESD could damage it. If your toolkit does not include an antistatic wrist strap (see Figure 1-8), you should add one to your kit and be sure to use it when you work inside a desktop or laptop computer. As Figure 1-8 demonstrates, you clip the wire to an unpainted metal part of the chassis. The metal plate on the wrist strap should make firm contact with the skin on your wrist. By using the strap properly, you equalize static charges that may build up in your body with the equipment, preventing a damaging discharge.

NOTE   See Chapter 18, "Operational Procedures and Communications Methods," for more information about how to prevent ESD.

System and Electrical Testing Tools

To help determine whether a component is defective, you should test it. Use the following tools to help test power supplies, cables, and ports on the motherboard or on add-on cards:

- **Multimeter**—Checks AC and DC voltage levels, resistance (Ohmns), continuity, amperage, diodes

- **Power supply tester**—Tests power supply operation without the need to install the power supply in a system

- **Loopback plugs**—Checks for correct input/output from serial, parallel, network, and USB ports

Attaching cable with alligator
(grounding) clip to wrist strap

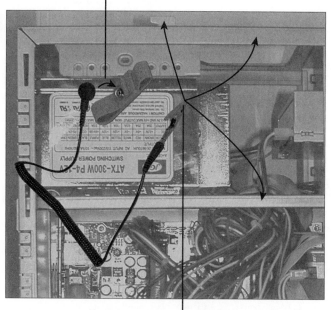

Bare metal parts of chassis that are suitable
locations to attach the grounding clip

Figure 1-8   A wrist strap and some suitable places to clip it inside the system.

> **NOTE**   Learn more about using a multimeter and a power supply tester in Chapter 4, "Power Supplies and System Cooling." Learn more about using loopback plugs in Chapter 6, "I/O and Input Ports and Devices," and Chapter 16, "Networking."

Network Installation and Configuration Tools

The tools in the following list help you install network cabling and check for correct operation of the physical components in a wired network:

- **Cable tester**—Checks cable continuity and twisted-pair configuration

- **Punch down tools**—Use for installation of UTP cable into a wall jack

- **Loopback plug**—Checks for correct input/output from various types of Ethernet cables

- **Toner probes**—Used to determine the patch panel port that matches a particular network wall socket

- **Wire strippers**—Removes cable shielding for installation of RJ-11, RJ-45, or coaxial cable connectors

- **Crimper**—Attaches connectors to cable

> **NOTE**   Learn more about using these tools in Chapter 16.

Printer Maintenance Tools

To help maintain printers, use the following tools:

- **Maintenance kit**—Most laser printers require the periodic replacement of certain components; contents vary by printer model.

- **Toner vacuum**—Laser printer toner particles are too small to be contained by conventional vacuum cleaner bags; use a toner-rated vacuum cleaner to pick up spilled or leaked toner.

- **Compressed air**—Blows dust and debris out of all types of printers.

> **NOTE**   Learn more about these tools in Chapter 11, "Printers."

Important Websites

There are several websites that we will refer to in this book; you will access these websites frequently when working in the field. They include

- **Microsoft's TechNet**—http://technet.microsoft.com. This site includes highly technical information about all of Microsoft's products.

- **Microsoft Help and Support**—http://support.microsoft.com (previously known as the Microsoft Knowledge Base or MSKB). This site has thousands of articles that show how to configure Windows and troubleshoot Windows problems such as STOP (BSOD) errors, registry problems, and others.

- **CompTIA's A+ web page**—http://www.comptia.org/certifications/listed/a.aspx. This site describes the CompTIA A+ certification and how the exam works, and it has downloadable objectives that show exactly what is on the exam.

Exam Preparation Tasks

Review All the Key Topics

Review the most important topics in the chapter, noted with the key topics icon in the outer margin of the page. Table 1-3 lists a reference of these key topics and the page numbers on which each is found.

Table 1-3 Key Topics for Chapter 1

Key Topic Element	Description	Page Number
List	The components and subsystems real computers contain	4
Table 1-2	The six-step CompTIA A+ troubleshooting theory	14
Figure 1-8	An antistatic wrist strap and common places to put it	17

Complete the Tables and Lists from Memory

Print a copy of Appendix A, "Memory Tables" (found on the CD), or at least the section for this chapter, and complete the tables and lists from memory. Appendix B, "Memory Tables Answer Key," also on the CD, includes completed tables and lists to check your work.

Define Key Terms

Define the following key terms from this chapter, and check your answers in the glossary.

hardware, software, firmware

Complete Hands-On Labs

Complete the hands-on labs, and then see the answers and explanations at the end of the chapter.

Lab 1-1: Determine the External Equipment Available on a Desktop or Laptop Computer

Scenario: You are examining a computer that has been stored for a few months with the objective of returning it to active service. You are looking for the presence of certain components needed for a particular use.

Procedure: Look for the components listed in Table 1-4. Use the photos earlier in this chapter or elsewhere as references. Use the table to indicate the number and location of each component listed.

Table 1-4   Determining External Equipment on a Computer (Lab 1-1)

Component/Device	Yes/No	How Many	Where Located*
Audio jacks (microphone, speaker, headphone, and so on)			
BD (Blu-ray) drive			
Case fan			
5.25-inch drive bays			
DVD drive			
DVI-D video port			
DVI-I video port			
eSATA port			
Ethernet network port			
Express Card slot			
Flash memory card reader			
HDMI port			
IEEE-1394 port			
Modem port			
Parallel port			
PC Card/CardBus slot			
PS/2 keyboard and mouse ports			
S-video port			
Serial port			
TV tuner card			
USB port			
VGA video port			

*F (front), B (back), L (left side), R (right side), CLUSTR (port cluster), BRKT (expansion slot or port bracket).

Lab 1-2: Determine the Tool(s) to Use for Performing Specified Service on a PC

Scenario: You are preparing to perform several tests and service procedures on a laptop computer.

Procedure: The procedures you are preparing to perform are listed in Table 1-5. Identify which tool or tools you will use to perform each procedures. Choose from the following list:

- Multimeter (MMTR)
- Driver equipped with hex, screw, and Torx bits (DRV)
- Compressed air (AIR)
- Loopback plugs (LOOP)
- Microsoft Knowledge Base website (KB)

Table 1-5   Selecting Tools for PC Repair and Testing Procedures (Lab 1-2)

Procedure	Tools Needed
Verify correct voltage from power supply	
Clean power supply and case fans	
Test I/O ports	
Research BSOD (STOP) error	
Test network cable	

Answer Review Questions

Answer these review questions and then see the answers and explanations at the end of the chapter.

1. Which of the following features are found almost exclusively on laptop computers? (Choose all that apply.)

   a. PCIe slot

   b. ExpressCard slot

   c. USB ports

   d. DVD drive

   e. port cluster

   f. touchpad

2. Which of the following features may be visible from the front of a desktop computer? (Choose all that apply.)

   a. Card reader

   b. DVI-D port

   c. USB ports

   d. DVD drive

   e. port cluster

   f. audio ports

3. You are preparing to upgrade the firmware in a system. Which of the following devices are likely to include a firmware chip? (Choose all that apply.)

   a. DVD drive

   b. USB card

   c. RAID host adapter

   d. motherboard

   e. port cluster

   f. touchpad

4. You are examining a possibly failed motherboard to determine whether the motherboard itself or a component connected to it has failed. Which of the following points of failure are likely to be found on the motherboard? (Choose all that apply.)

   a. CMOS battery

   b. DVD drive

   c. capacitors

   d. SATA cable

   e. Power supply

   f. ROM BIOS

5. You are evaluating a collection of add-on cards to determine which cards should be retained as spares. Obsolete cards that will be discarded include ISA cards and EISA cards for desktops and, for laptops, PC Cards that must use a special device to enable a network or modem cable to be connected to the card. The extension is known as a

   a. header cable

   b. gender changer

   c. port adapter

   d. Express Card

   e. dongle

   f. PCMCIA Card

6. The CompTIA six-step troubleshooting process includes a step in which you "verify full system functionality and, if applicable, implement preventative measures." Which number is this step?

   a. Step 2

   b. Step 1

   c. Step 6

   d. Step 5

   e. Step 4

   f. Step 3

7. You are checking the contents of your computer toolkit before performing internal upgrades on a desktop computer. Which of the following tools in your toolkit should be used to prevent ESD damage to internal components?

   a. Cable tester

   b. Wrist strap

   c. Loopback plugs

   d. Torx drivers

   e. multimeter

   f. Crimper

8. You are checking the contents of your computer toolkit before performing upgrades on a desktop computer. Which of the following tools in your toolkit should be used to verify proper operation of the power supply?

    a. Cable tester

    b. Wrist strap

    c. Loopback plugs

    d. Torx drivers

    e. multimeter

    f. Crimper

Answers to Hands-On Labs

Lab 1-1: Determine the external equipment available on a desktop or laptop computer.

Answer: For this lab, there are no right or wrong answers because the answers depend upon the exact equipment used in the exercise. However, Table 1-6 is an example of how you might complete this exercise when inspecting a desktop computer.

Table 1-6 Determining External Equipment on a Computer (Desktop Example)

Component/Device	Yes/No	How Many	Where Located*
Audio jacks (microphone, speaker, headphone, and so on)	Yes	2 sets	F, B
BD (Blu-ray) drive	No	—	—
Case fan	Yes	2	F, B
5.25-inch drive bays	Yes	3	F
DVD drive	Yes	1	F
DVI-D video port	No	—	—
DVI-I video port	Yes	2	BRKT
eSATA port	Yes	1	CLUSTR
Ethernet network port	Yes	2	CLUSTR
Express Card slot	No	—	—
Flash memory card reader	No	—	—
HDMI port	No	—	—

Component/Device	Yes/No	How Many	Where Located*
IEEE-1394 port	Yes	2	F, CLUSTR
Modem port	No	—	—
Parallel port	No	—	—
PC Card/CardBus slot	No	—	—
PS/2 keyboard and mouse ports	Yes	1 each	CLUSTR
S-video port	Yes	1	BRKT
Serial port	Yes	1	CLUSTR
TV tuner card	No		
USB port	Yes	8	F, CLUSTR, BRKT
VGA video port	No		

*F (front), B (back), L (left side), R (right side), CLUSTR (port cluster), BRKT (expansion slot or port bracket).

Table 1-7 is an example of how you might complete this exercise when inspecting a laptop computer.

Table 1-7   Determining External Equipment on a Computer (Laptop Example)

Component/Device	Yes/No	How Many	Where Located*
Audio jacks (microphone, speaker, headphone, and so on)	Yes	1 sets	F
BD (Blu-ray) drive	No	—	—
5.25-inch drive bays	No	—	—
DVD drive	Yes	1	F
DVI-D video port	Yes	1	B
DVI-I video port	No		
eSATA port	No	1	CLUSTR
Ethernet network port	Yes	2	L or R or B
Express Card slot	Yes	1	L
Flash memory card reader	Yes	1	L
HDMI port	Yes	1	L or R or B
IEEE-1394 port	Yes	1	L or R or B
Modem port	Yes	1	L or R or B
Parallel port	No	—	—

Table 1-7   Continued

Component/Device	Yes/No	How Many	Where Located*
PC Card/CardBus slot	No	—	—
PS/2 keyboard and mouse ports	Yes	1 combo	L or R or B
S-video port	No	—	—
Serial port	No	—	—
TV tuner card	No	—	—
USB port	Yes	3	L or R or B
VGA video port	Yes	1	L or R or B

*F (front), B (back), L (left side), R (right side), CLUSTR (port cluster), BRKT (expansion slot or port bracket).

Lab 1-2: Determine the tool(s) to use for performing specified service on a PC.

Answer: See Table 1-8.

Table 1-8   Answers for Lab 1-2

Procedure	Tools Needed*
Verify correct voltage from power supply.	DRV, MMTR
Clean power supply and case fans.	DRV, AIR
Test I/O ports.	LOOP
Research BSOD (STOP) error.	KB
Test network cable.	MMTR

*Multimeter (MMTR), Driver equipped with hex, screw, and Torx bits (DRV), Compressed air (AIR), Loopback plugs (LOOP), Microsoft Knowledge Base website (KB)

Answers and Explanations to Review Questions

1. **B, F.** Although a few desktop computers include an ExpressCard slot and a touchpad, these components are typically found on laptop computers. Both desktop and laptop computers typically include DVD drives and USB ports, while desktop computers include PCIe slots and port clusters.

2. **A, C, D, F.** Card readers and DVD drives are found on the front of desktop computers that include these components. USB and audio ports might be on the front as well as the rear of typical desktop computers.

3. **A, C, D.** While the ROM BIOS on the motherboard is the most common location for firmware, almost all rewritable DVD drives and RAID host adapters also include firmware.

4. **A, C.** The CMOS battery (maintains BIOS settings) and capacitors (used for the voltage regulator components for the CPU) are located on the motherboard.

5. **E.** A dongle is the special cable that enables standard cables to connect to PC Card and CardBus cards. PC Cards that use dongles are mainly obsolete today.

6. **D.** The step that includes "verify full system functionality and, if applicable, implement preventative measures" is the fifth step of the six steps in the process.

7. **B.** The wrist strap, which is worn on the wrist so that the metal plate on the band touches the user's skin and the other end is locked around bare metal components, helps prevent damage from ESD.

8. **E.** The multimeter is used to test the power supply by checking the actual output against the rated voltage for the various wires in the power supply connection to the motherboard.

This chapter covers the following subjects:

- **Motherboards and Their Components**—Form factors, integrated I/O ports, memory slots, expansion slots, chipset components, jumpers and jumper blocks, fan connectors, audio connectors, and front panel connectors are the component categories you discover in this section.

- **Installing Motherboards**—The A+ Certification exam doesn't require it, but we think you'll want to know, sooner or later, how to remove and install a motherboard.

- **Troubleshooting Motherboards**—Motherboards and their onboard components can fail. In this section, you learn what can go wrong and how to fix it.

- **Processors and CPUs**—Intel makes processors. AMD makes processors. What sockets do they use, and how can you tell what processors fit in a different socket? You learn the answers in this section.

- **CPU Technologies**—32-bit? Hyperthreading? L3 cache? Learn what these and other CPU technologies mean to system capabilities and performance in this section.

- **CPU Cooling**—Keeping the CPU cool is vital to a reliable system, and this section explains the major methods used.

> This chapter covers **CompTIA A+ 220-801 objectives 1.2 and 1.6** and portions of **CompTIA A+ 220-802 objective 4.2**.

CHAPTER 2

Motherboards and Processors

In this chapter we'll talk about some of the core components of the computer—the guts of the computer—including the motherboard and CPU. Everything connects to the motherboard, so it stands to reason that proper planning and design of a PC, to a certain degree, starts with this component. The CPU is just as important.

The **CPU** (or processor) is the "brain" of the computer and takes care of the bulk of the PC's calculations. Deciding on a CPU and motherboard should be the first tasks at hand when building a PC. Within these pages you learn how to specify, install, and troubleshoot motherboards and processors and discover some of the considerations to take into account when building the core of a PC.

Foundation Topics

Motherboards and Their Components

220-801

Objective:
220-801: 1.2

The motherboard represents the logical foundation of the computer. In other words, everything that makes a computer a computer must be attached to the motherboard. From the CPU to storage devices, from RAM to printer ports, the **motherboard** provides the connections that help them work together.

Figure 2-1 shows an example of a typical ATX motherboard. The various components of the motherboard are called out in the figure. We refer to this figure throughout the chapter.

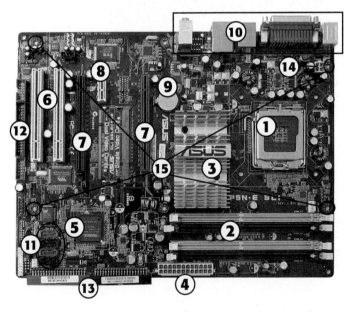

1. Socket 775 processor socket
2. Dual-channel DDR2 memory slots
3. Heat sink over northbridge
4. 24-pin ATX v2.0 power connector
5. Southbridge chip
6. PCI slot (2)
7. PCI Express x16 slot (2)
8. PCI Express x1 slot
9. CMOS battery
10. Port cluster
11. SATA host adapter (4)
12. Floppy drive controller
13. PATA host adapter (2)
14. 4-pix ATX12 power connector
15. Mounting holes

Figure 2-1   A typical motherboard.

The **form factor** is the design of the motherboard, with which the case and power supply must comply. Motherboards can come with integrated I/O ports; these are usually found as a rear port cluster and as headers on the motherboard for use by ports on the front of the system or on brackets occupying unused expansion slots. The motherboard also has memory slots, which enable a user to add sticks of RAM, thus increasing the computer's total resources. Of course, the motherboard also has expansion slots most commonly used by audio and video cards, although the slots can be used by many other types of cards as well. You can also find mass storage ports for hard drives, CD-ROMs, and DVD-ROMs on the motherboard. After covering all these concepts, you see how to select, install, and troubleshoot the motherboard. The motherboard is the central meeting point of all technologies in the computer.

NOTE Some motherboard features are covered in other chapters. For information about onboard host adapters for floppy drives, optical drives, and hard disks (PATA and SATA), see Chapter 12, "Storage Devices." For information about power connectors, see Chapter 4, "Power Supplies and System Cooling." For information about SCSI host adapters, see "SCSI," in Chapter 6, "I/O and Input Ports and Devices," for details.

Form Factors

Although all motherboards have some features in common, their layout and size vary a great deal. The most common motherboard designs in current use include ATX, microATX, and Mini-ITX. The following sections cover the details of these designs and some other motherboard designs in the same families.

NOTE You need to know ATX, microATX, and ITX (on which mini-ITX is based) for the exams.

ATX and microATX

The ATX family of motherboards has dominated desktop computer designs since the late 1990s. **ATX** stands for Advanced Technology Extended, and it replaced the AT and Baby-AT form factors developed in the mid-1980s for the IBM PC AT and its rivals. ATX motherboards have the following characteristics:

- A rear port cluster for I/O ports
- Expansion slots that run parallel to the short side of the motherboard
- Left-side case opening (as viewed from the front of a tower PC)

There are four members of the ATX family, as listed in Table 2-1. In practice, though, the Mini-ATX design is not widely used.

Table 2-1 ATX Motherboard Family Comparison

Motherboard Type	Maximum Width	Maximum Depth	Maximum Number of Expansion Slots	Typical Uses
ATX	12 in.	9.6 in.	Seven	Full tower
Mini-ATX	11.2 in.	8.2 in.	Seven	Full tower
microATX	9.6 in.	9.6 in.	Four	Mini tower
FlexATX	9.0 in.	7.5 in.	Four	Mini tower, small form factor

ITX

The ITX family of motherboards was originally developed by VIA Technologies in 2001 for use with its low-power x86 C3 processors. The original ITX motherboard form factor was about the same size as the FlexATX motherboard form factor and was quickly superseded by the smaller Mini-ITX form factor.

Mini-ITX measures 6.7 × 6.7 inches and has been adopted by many vendors for use with AMD and Intel processors. Original designs featured a single PCI expansion slot, but many recent designs include a PCIe x16 expansion slot instead. A Mini-ITX motherboard can typically fit into a case made for ATX-family motherboards and uses a similar port cluster. Mini-ITX motherboards are used in small form factor PCs and in home theater applications.

Pico-ITX and Nano-ITX motherboards are smaller than Mini-ITX and are used primarily in computing appliances. Figure 2-2 compares the general layout of Mini-ITX to ATX, microATX, and FlexATX motherboards.

NOTE In 2004, a new form factor called BTX was developed to help improve cooling because of the hot-running CPUs, such as the Intel Pentium 4, that were common at the time. BTX motherboards locate the CPU at a 45-degree angle and cover it with a thermal module with a horizontally mounted fan. Other changes in layout include the port cluster being relocated to the rear-left corner of the motherboard and the grouping of the CPU, memory, chipset, and voltage regulator next to each other. A BTX tower case opens on the right side rather than the left, as with ATX and mini-ITX.

BTX never became popular in the retail market, with only a few motherboard designs and retail systems using this form factor.

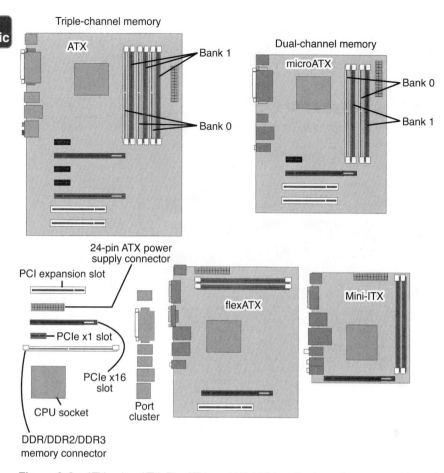

Figure 2-2   ATX, microATX, FlexATX, and Mini-ITX motherboard component layouts compared.

Integrated I/O Ports

Motherboards covered on the A+ Certification exams feature a variety of **integrated I/O ports**. These are found in as many as three locations: all motherboards feature a rear port cluster (see Figure 2-3 for typical examples), and many motherboards also have additional ports on the top of the motherboard that are routed to header cables accessible from the front and rear of the system.

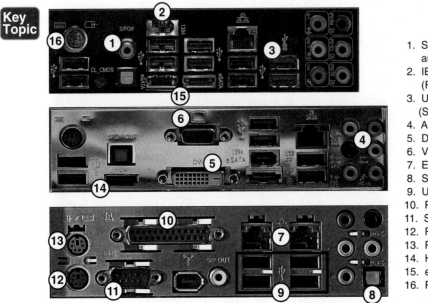

1. SPDIF coaxial audio
2. IEEE 1394a (FireWire 400)
3. USB 3.0 (SuperSpeed USB)
4. Analog audio
5. DVI-D digital video
6. VGA video
7. Ethernet RJ45
8. SPDIF optical audio
9. USB ports
10. Parallel (LPT) port
11. Serial (COM) port
12. PS/2 keyboard
13. PS/2 mouse
14. HDMI digital A/V
15. eSATA ports
16. PS/2 combo port

Figure 2-3 Typical port clusters on ATX motherboards.

More recent motherboards include the following ports in their port cluster:

- PS/2 mouse
- PS/2 keyboard
- USB 2.0 (Hi-Speed USB)
- 10/100 or 10/100/1000 Ethernet (RJ-45)
- Stereo or surround (5.1 or 7.1) audio

Additional ports you might find on most recent systems include

- USB 3.0 (SuperSpeed USB)
- FireWire 400 (IEEE 1394a)
- eSATA
- SPDIF coaxial digital audio
- SPDIF optical digital audio

Systems with integrated video include one or more of the following:

- VGA
- DVI-D
- HDMI

Systems with legacy ports typically include some or all of the following:

- Serial (COM)
- Parallel (LPT)
- Game port

Most of these ports are shown in Figure 2-3.

Most motherboards also include header cables to provide additional outputs. Headers for additional USB ports are the most common example (see Figure 2-4).

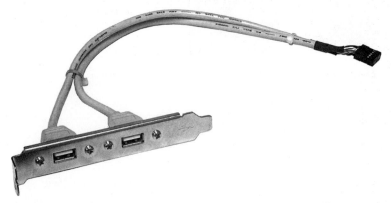

Figure 2-4   This header cable provides two additional rear-mounted USB 2.0 ports.

Memory Slots

Most modern motherboards, with the exception of some Mini-ITX and smaller motherboards, include two or more memory slots (refer to Figures 2-1 and 2-2). At least one memory slot must contain a memory module or the system cannot start or function.

Memory slots vary in design according to the type of memory the system supports. Older systems that use SDRAM use three-section memory slots designed for 168-pin memory modules. Systems that use DDR SDRAM use two-section memory slots designed for 184-pin memory modules. Systems that use DDR2 SDRAM use two-section memory slots designed for 240-pin modules. DDR3 SDRAM also uses two-section 240-pin memory slots, but the arrangement of the pins and the keying of the slot are different than in DDR2. DDR2 and DDR3 modules cannot be interchanged.

Each memory slot includes locking levers that secure memory in place. When memory is properly installed, the levers automatically swivel into place (see Figure 2-5).

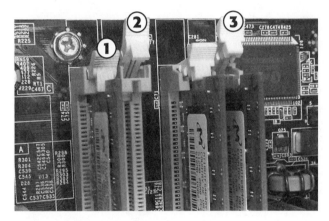

1. Installed module
   (locking lever closed)
2. Empty slot
   (locking lever open)
3. Module being installed
   (locking lever open)

Figure 2-5   Installing memory modules.

To learn more about memory types and slots, see Chapter 5, "RAM."

Expansion Slots

Motherboards use **expansion slots** to provide support for additional I/O devices and high-speed video/graphics cards. The most common expansion slots on recent systems include peripheral component interconnect (PCI) and PCI-Express (also known as PCIe). Some systems also feature communications network riser (CNR) slots for specific purposes.

PCI Slots

The **PCI** slot (originally developed in 1992) can be used for many types of add-on cards, including network, video, audio, I/O, and storage host adapters for SCSI, PATA, and SATA drives. There are several types of PCI slots, but the one found in desktop computers is the 32-bit slot running at 33MHz (see Figure 2-6 in the next section). PCI slots are also available in 66MHz versions and in 64-bit versions.

NOTE   Early PCI cards used 5V DC power, but virtually all 32-bit PCI cards in use for a number of years use 3.3V DC power.

PCI-X Slots

PCI-X is a faster version of 64-bit PCI, running at speeds of 133MHz. PCI-X slots also support PCI cards. In fact, the PCI-X slot uses the same connectors as 64-bit PCI slot (refer to Figure 2-6). A PCI-X bus supports two PCI-X slots, but if you install a PCI-X card into a PCI-X slot on the same bus as a PCI card, the PCI-X card runs at the same speed as the PCI card. PCI-X slots are typically used in servers and workstations.

PCI-X 2.0 (introduced in 2008) also supports 266MHz and 533MHz speeds; however, like PCI, both types of PCI-X are being replaced by PCIe. Figure 2.6 compares 32-bit and 64-bit PCI and PCI-X slots and card connectors to each other.

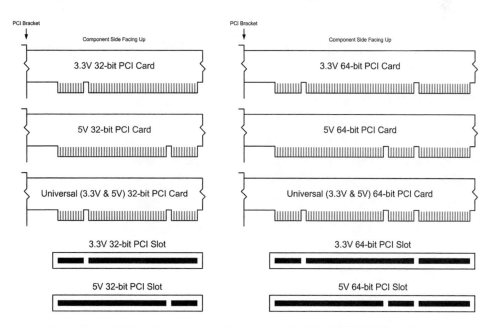

Figure 2-6   32-bit PCI cards and slots (left) compared to 64-bit PCI/PCI-X cards and slots (right). Image courtesy of Wikimedia Commons (see http://en.wikipedia.org/wiki/File:PCI_Keying.png for details).

AGP

The **AGP** slot was introduced as a dedicated slot for high-speed video (3D graphics display) in 1996. Since 2005, the PCIe (PCI Express) x16 slot (described in the next section) has replaced it in most new systems. There have been several versions of the AGP slot, reflecting changes in the AGP standard, as shown in Figure 2-7. All types of AGP slots can temporarily "borrow" system memory when creating 3D textures.

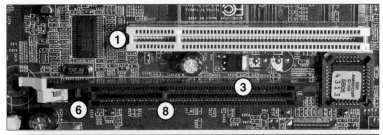
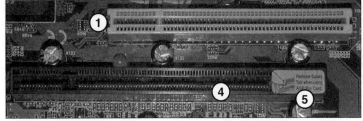

1. PCI slots
2. AGP 1x/2x (3.3v) slot
3. AGP 4x/8x (1.5v) slot
4. AGP Pro/Universal slot
5. AGP Pro slot cover
6. AGP 4x/8x retaining latch
7. AGP 1x/2x key
8. AGP 4x/8x key

Figure 2-7 PCI slots compared to an AGP 1x/2x slot (top), an AGP 4x/8x slot (middle), and an AGP Pro/Universal slot (bottom).

The AGP 1x/2x and AGP 4x/8x slots have their keys in different positions. This prevents you from installing the wrong type of AGP card into the slot. AGP 1x/2x cards use 3.3V, whereas most AGP 4x cards use 1.5V. AGP 8x cards use 0.8 or 1.5V. The AGP Pro/Universal slot is longer than a normal AGP slot to support the greater electrical requirements of AGP Pro cards (which are used in technical workstations). The protective cover over a part of the slot is intended to prevent normal

AGP cards from being inserted into the wrong part of the slot. The slot is referred to as a *universal* slot because it supports both 3.3V and 1.5V AGP cards.

> **CAUTION**   An AGP Pro slot cover might be removed after a system has been in service for awhile, even if an AGP Pro card isn't inserted in a computer. If you see an AGP Pro slot without a cover and you're preparing to install an AGP card, cover the extension with a sticker to prevent damaging a standard AGP card by inserting it improperly.

PCIe (PCI Express) Slots

PCI Express (often abbreviated as **PCIe** or **PCIE**) began to replace both PCI and AGP slots in new system designs starting in 2005. PCIe slots are available in four types:

- x1
- x4
- x8
- x16

The most common versions include the x1, x4, and x16 designs, as shown in Figure 2-8.

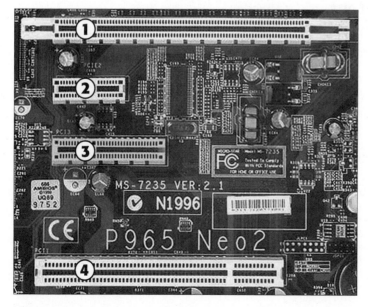

1. PCI Express x16 slot
2. PCI Express x1 slot
3. PCI Express x4 slot
4. PCI slot (32-bit, 33MHz)

Figure 2-8   PCI Express slots compared to a PCI slot.

PCI Express x1 and x4 slots are designed to replace the PCI slot, and x8 and x16 are designed to replace the AGP and PCI-X slots. Table 2-2 compares the performance of PCI, AGP, PCI-X, and PCIe.

Table 2-2 Technical Information About Expansion Slot Types

Slot Type	Performance	Suggested Uses
PCI 32-bit, 33MHz	133MBps	Video, network, mass storage (PATA, SATA, SCSI), sound card
PCI 32-bit, 66MHz	266MBps	Network, mass storage (workstation and server)
PCI 64-bit, 33MHz	266MBps	Network, mass storage (workstation and server)
PCI 64-bit, 66MHz	533MBps	Network, mass storage (workstation and server)
PCI-X 66MHz	533MBps	Network, mass storage (workstation and server)
PCI-X 133MHz	1,066MBps	Network, mass storage (workstation and server)
PCI-X 2.0 266MHz	2,133MBps	Network, mass storage (workstation and server)
PCI-X 2.0 533MHz	4,266MBps	Network, mass storage (workstation and server)
AGP 1x	266MBps	Video
AGP 2x	533MBps	Video
AGP 4x	1,066MBps	Video
AGP 8x	2,133MBps	Video
PCIe x1 v1	500MBps*	Network, I/O
PCIe x2 v1	1,000MBps*	Network
PCIe x8 v1	4,000MBps*	SLI video secondary card on older systems
PCIe x16 v1	8,000MBps*	Video (including SLI, CrossFire, and CrossFire X primary and secondary cards)
PCIe x1 v2	1,000MBps*	Network, I/O
PCIe x2 v2	2,000MBps*	Network
PCIe x8 v2	8,000MBps*	SLI video secondary card
PCIe x16 v2	16,000MBps*	Video (including SLI, CrossFire, and CrossFire X primary and secondary cards)

Bidirectional data rates (full duplex simultaneous send/receive); unidirectional data rates are one-half of values listed. All versions of PCIe, including forthcoming v3, use the same connectors.

SLI is the NVIDIA method for using two or more graphics processing units (GPUs) to render 3D game graphics.

CrossFire (including CrossFire X) is the AMD (formerly ATI) method for using two or more graphics cards to render 3D game graphics.

NOTE   Mini-PCI and Mini-PCIe are reduced-size versions of the PCI and PCIe standards. They are used in notebook and laptop computers. To learn more, see Chapter 9, "Laptop and Notebook Computers."

CNR and AMR Slots

Some motherboards have one of two specialized expansion slots in addition to the standard PCI, PCI Express, or AGP slots. The audio modem riser (**AMR**) slot enables motherboard designers to place analog modem and audio connectors and the codec chip used to translate between analog and digital signals on a small riser card. AMR slots are frequently found on older systems with chipsets that integrate software modems and audio functions.

The AMR was replaced by the communications network riser (**CNR**) slot, a longer design that can support up to six-channel audio, S/PDIF digital audio, and home networking functions. Some vendors have used the CNR slot to implement high-quality integrated audio. Few AMR riser cards were ever sold, but some motherboard vendors have bundled CNR riser cards with their motherboards to provide six-channel audio output and other features.

Figure 2-9 compares the AMR, PCI, and CNR slots. Figure 2-10 illustrates the AMR and CNR riser cards.

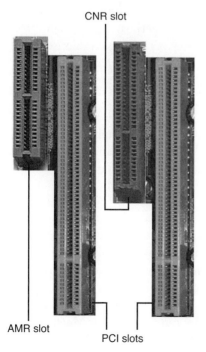

CNR slot

AMR slot

PCI slots

Figure 2-9   An AMR slot and a PCI slot (left) compared to a CNR slot and PCI slot (right).

Figure 2-10   An AMR riser card used for soft modem support (left) and a CNR riser card used for six-channel (5.1) analog and digital audio support (right).

The AMR or CNR slot, when present, is usually located on the edge of the motherboard. The AMR slot was often found on Pentium III or AMD Athlon-based systems, whereas the CNR slot was used by some Pentium 4–based systems. Current systems integrate network and audio features directly into the motherboard and its port cluster, making both types of slots obsolete.

NOTE   AMR and CNR riser cards were generally provided by motherboard makers because they are customized to the design of particular motherboards. Although some parts suppliers have sold AMR and CNR cards separately, it's best to get the riser card from the same vendor as the motherboard to ensure proper hardware compatibility and driver support.

To learn more about PCI, PCIe, and AGP slots when used for graphics cards, see Chapter 7, "Video Displays and Video Cards." To learn more about installing adapter cards, see Chapter 8, "Customized PCs and Multimedia Devices."

Chipset Components

Although the CPU gets most of the attention from casual PC users when evaluating a system, the chipset is just as important. The **chipset** determines what CPUs a system can use, what integrated ports the system can provide without the use of third-party products, and the number and types of expansion slots a motherboard can feature. If the chipset includes the memory controller, it is also responsible for determining what type and speeds of RAM a system can use. As Scott Mueller points out in Chapter 4 of *Upgrading and Repairing PCs*, "The chipset is the motherboard." So, what exactly is a chipset and what does it do?

Most chipsets include two components:

- **Northbridge**—Also known as the memory controller hub (MCH) or, on Intel systems with chipset integrated graphics, the graphics memory controller hub (GMCH)

- **Southbridge**—Also known as the I/O controller hub (ICH)

The northbridge chip connects to the CPU and other high-speed components such as memory, PCIe or AGP graphics (either via expansion slots or integrated into the chipset), and other high-speed components.

The southbridge chip connects to lower-speed components, such as mass storage interfaces, PCI expansion slots, USB ports, and the CMOS.

Unlike the CPU, which is removable and upgradable, the chipset's components are surface-mounted to the motherboard. The only way to change the chipset is to replace the motherboard. To protect the chipset's components from damaging heat, chipsets are frequently covered by heat sinks.

Figure 2-11 illustrates the location of the CPU, northbridge, and southbridge chips on a typical motherboard and the components they communicate with.

1. AMD CPU with integrated memory controller
2. Northbridge
3. Southbridge

Figure 2-11 An AMD Phenom II X6 processor has a built-in memory controller, so the north-bridge chip (hidden under a passive heat sink) controls PCIe expansion slots. Slower devices, such as PCI expansion slots, PATA, SATA, and floppy drive adapters, and ports on header cables and the port cluster, are controlled by the southbridge (also hidden under a passive heat sink).

The system BIOS is responsible for configuring the ports and features controlled by the chipset, and the CMOS chip on the motherboard stores the settings. The CMOS battery provides power to maintain the contents of the CMOS chip. To learn more about the system BIOS and CMOS, see Chapter 3, "BIOS."

Jumpers and Jumper Blocks

A **jumper** is a set of two or more pins, and a **jumper block** is a small plastic block with a metal insert. When the jumper block is fitted across two pins, a connection is made. A jumper and jumper block are used for PATA drive configurations and, on older motherboards, for CPU and memory settings.

On current systems, jumpers and jumper blocks are used for maintaining and clearing CMOS memory (see Figure 2-12). And on systems with integrated video, jumpers are often used to select whether HDMI or DVI will be used for digital video connections to an LCD display.

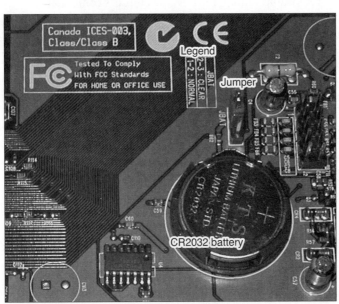

Figure 2-12   A typical CMOS battery (CR2032) with the CMOS jumper pins (JBAT) configured for normal operation.

Fan Connectors

Almost all motherboards have a **CPU fan connector** and several **system fan connectors** (used for fans connected to the case). Both types of fan connectors have a monitor connection to provide fan speed information to the PC health or system monitor feature built in to the system BIOS. Some motherboards also have a connector to monitor the speed of the fan built in the power supply.

The CPU fan differs from the system fan connectors and has a fourth pin used for speed control. Figure 2-13 shows a typical CPU fan connector and system fan connector before and after connecting the fan leads.

Figure 2-13   CPU (left) and system fan (right) connectors.

Audio Connectors

Typical motherboards feature one or more audio connectors designed for different purposes:

- **Front-panel audio**—Microphone and headphones; found on almost all motherboards.

- **Music CD playback from CD and DVD drives**—This feature is rarely needed because Windows Media Player and other media player programs can play music through the PATA or SATA interface.

- **SPDIF header**—Designed to support an optional SPDIF bracket for digital audio playback; the bracket is provided by the motherboard vendor but is not always bundled with compatible motherboards.

Figure 2-14 illustrates these connectors on a typical motherboard.

Front-panel audio   Connects to SPDIF port

Connects to CD or DVD drive for audio playback

Figure 2-14   Front-panel audio, music CD, and SPDIF bracket headers on a typical motherboard.

> **NOTE**   Front-panel audio cables often have two sets of connectors: one for HD au-
> dio and one for the older AC97 audio standard. Use the connector that corresponds
> to the audio version supported by your motherboard.

Front-Panel Connectors

ATX, BTX, and ITX-family motherboards include several **front-panel connectors**
for the power switch, power light, drive activity lights, reset button, and case speaker
(if present). These connectors are grouped together on or near the front edge of the
motherboard (see Figure 2-15).

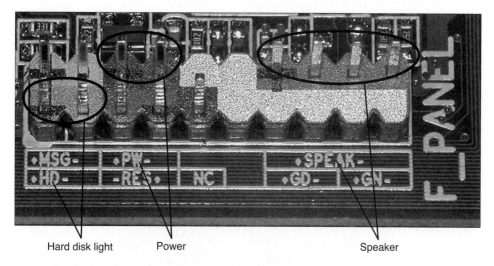

Hard disk light   Power   Speaker

Figure 2-15   A typical two-row front-panel connector.

Because front-panel leads are small and are difficult to install, some motherboard vendors provide a quick-connect extender for easier installation: Connect the leads to the extender, and then connect the extender to the front-panel headers. See Figure 2-16 for a typical example.

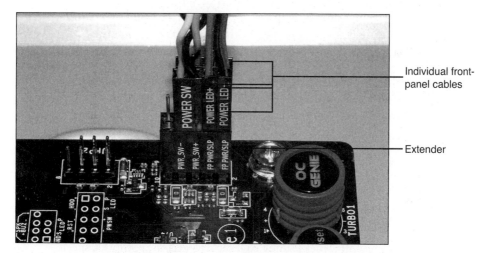

Individual front-panel cables

Extender

Figure 2-16   Individual front-panel cables connected via an extender to the motherboard.

Installing Motherboards

The current A+ Certification exam competencies do not list installing mother-boards as an objective. However, if you are called upon to build or upgrade a system, chances are you will need to understand the process.

What keeps a motherboard from sliding around inside the case? If you look at an unmounted motherboard from the top, you can see that motherboards have several holes around the edges and several holes toward the middle of the mother-board. Most ATX-family (as well as ITX and BTX) motherboards are held in place by screws that are fastened to brass spacers threaded into holes in the case or a removable motherboard tray. Holes intended for use with screws are metal-rimmed or metal-reinforced. Holes that are designed for use with plastic spacers are not reinforced.

NOTE Before you start working with motherboards or other static-sensitive parts such as CPUs and memory, see the section "Computer Safety" in Chapter 18, "Operational Procedures and Communication Methods," for ESD and other precautions you should follow.

Step-by-Step Motherboard Removal

Removing the motherboard is an important task for the computer technician. For safety's sake, you should also remove the motherboard before you install a CPU upgrade.

To remove ATX-family, BTX-family, or mini-ITX motherboards from standard cases, follow these steps:

Step 1.   Turn off the power switch, and disconnect the AC power cable from the power supply.

Step 2.   Disconnect all cables (including data and power leads) connected to add-on cards after labeling them for easy reconnection.

Step 3.   Disconnect all ribbon cables attached to built-in ports on the mother-board (I/O, storage, and so on) after labeling them for easy reconnection.

Step 4.   Disconnect all cables leading to internal speakers, key locks, speed switches, and other front-panel cables. Most recent systems use clearly marked cables, as shown in Figure 2-17, but if the cables are not marked, mark them before you disconnect them so that you can easily reconnect them later.

Figure 2-17 Front-panel cables attached to a typical motherboard. The cables control system power to the motherboard, case speaker, drive and power lights, and so on.

TIP You can purchase premade labels for common types of cables, but if these are not available, you can use a label maker or blank address labels to custom-make your own labels.

Step 5.   Remove all add-on cards and place them on an antistatic mat or in (not on top of) antistatic bags.

Step 6.   Disconnect header cables from front- or rear-mounted ports and remove them from the system (see Figure 2-18).

Step 7.   Disconnect the power-supply leads from the motherboard. If the new motherboard uses different power supply connections than the old motherboard, replace the power supply. See Chapter 4 for details about power supply connections.

Step 8.   If possible, remove the heat sink and the processor before you remove the motherboard, and place them on an antistatic mat. Removing these items before you remove the motherboard helps prevent excessive flexing of the motherboard and makes it easier to slip the motherboard out of the case. However, skip this step if removing the heat sink requires a lot of downward pressure and if the motherboard is not well supported around the heat sink/processor area or the heat sink is attached to a metal plate on the bottom of the motherboard, as is common with many high-performance third-party heat sinks.

Expansion slot bracket

USB header cable connected to motherboard

Figure 2-18 A typical dual-USB 2.0 port header cable that uses an expansion slot bracket.

Step 9.   Remove the motherboard mounting screws (refer to Figure 2-1 for typical screw locations) and store for reuse; verify that all screws have been removed.

CAUTION   Easy does it with the screwdriver! Whether you're removing screws or putting them back in, skip the electric model and do it the old-fashioned way to avoid damaging the motherboard. If your motherboard is held in place with hex screws, use a hex driver instead of a screwdriver to be even more careful.

Step 10.   Remove the motherboard out of the case and place it on an antistatic mat. Remove the I/O shield (the metal plate on the rear of the system that has cutouts for the built-in ports; see Figure 2-19) and store it with the old motherboard.

Preparing the Motherboard for Installation

Before you install the new motherboard into the computer, perform the following steps:

Step 1.   Check the manual supplied with the new motherboard to determine correct sizes of memory supported, processor types supported, and configuration information.

Step 2.   Install the wanted amount of memory. See Chapter 5 for details.

Step 3.   Install the CPU and heat sink as described later in this chapter.

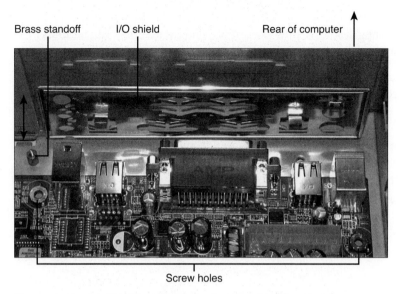

Brass standoff   I/O shield   Rear of computer

Screw holes

Figure 2-19 An ATX I/O shield and motherboard during installation.

Step-by-Step Motherboard Installation

After you prepare the motherboard for installation, follow these steps to install it:

Step 1.   Determine which mounting holes should be used for brass spacers. You might find it useful to hold the old motherboard over the new motherboard. Matching the motherboards helps you determine whether the new motherboard will fit correctly in the system.

Step 2.   Install or remove brass spacers as needed to accommodate the mounting holes in the motherboard.

Step 3.   Place the I/O shield into the opening at the back of the case. The I/O shield is marked to help you determine the port types on the rear of the motherboard. If the port cutouts on some I/O shields are not completely removed, remove them before you install the shield.

Step 4.   Determine which holes in the motherboard have brass stand-off spacers beneath them, and secure the motherboard using the screws removed from the old motherboard (refer to Figure 2-19).

Step 5.   Connect front-panel wires to the speaker, reset switch, drive activity light, and power light connectors on the motherboard.

Step 6.   Connect the ribbon cables from the drives to the motherboard's PATA and floppy disk drive interfaces (if present). Match the ribbon cable's colored side to pin 1 on the interfaces.

Step 7.   Connect cables from the SATA drives to the SATA ports on the motherboard. Use SATA port 1 for the first SATA drive, and so on.

Step 8.   Connect the power supply connectors to the motherboard.

Step 9.   Install the add-on cards you removed from the old motherboard; make sure your existing cards don't duplicate any features found on the new motherboard (such as sound, SATA host adapters, and so on). If they do, and you want to continue to use the card, you must disable the corresponding feature on the motherboard.

Step 10.   Connect header cables that use expansion card slot brackets into empty slots, and connect the header cables to the appropriate ports on the motherboard.

Step 11.   Connect any cables used by front-mounted ports, such as USB, serial, or IEEE-1394 ports, to the motherboard and case.

Step 12.   Connect power supply leads to drives and add-on cards as needed.

Troubleshooting Motherboards

When you're troubleshooting a computer, there is no shortage of places to look for problems. However, because the motherboard is the home for the most essential system resources, it's often the source of many problems. If you see the following problems, consider the motherboard as a likely place to look for the cause.

Unexpected Shutdowns

Typical causes for unexpected shutdowns include

- **Dead short caused by loose screws, slot covers, or cards**—Shut down system and secure all metal components.

- **Power supply overheating**—Check power supply fan and clean it if possible; replace power supply with higher wattage–rated unit if problem persists. See "Overheating" in Chapter 4 for details.

Continuous Reboots (Power Supply and BSOD Problems)

Continuous reboots can be caused by problems with the power supply or by a Windows configuration setting:

- **Power Good voltage is too high or too low**—When the Power Good line to the motherboard carries too high or too low a voltage, the processor resets, shutting down the system and rebooting it. Test the power supply voltage levels; replace the power supply if Power Good tests out of specifications. See "Testing Power Supplies and Other Devices with a Multimeter" in Chapter 4 for details.

- **Windows configuration setting for dealing with STOP error (Blue Screen of Death, or BSOD)**—If Windows is configured to reboot when a STOP error occurs, the system will continuously reboot until the error is resolved. To leave a STOP error message onscreen until you decide to restart the system, clear the Automatically Restart check box in the System Failure setting in the Startup and Recovery section of Advanced System Properties.

STOP errors cause the system to halt or reboot. A STOP error can have many causes, including motherboard, CPU, or memory problems; device problems; overclocking the processor or RAM; and others.

To determine the cause of a STOP error, note the name of the error (for example, STOP 0x0000007F [UNEXPECTED_KERNEL_MODE_TRAP]) and look it up at the Microsoft support website: http://support.microsoft.com.

NOTE STOP errors are often referred to with a shortened version of the error code or by name. For example, the short version of a 0x0000007F error is 0x7F.

BIOS Time and Settings Resets

Problems with BIOS time and settings resets are typically caused by a problem with either the CMOS battery on the motherboard or the CMOS chip itself.

If date and time settings or other BIOS settings reset to system defaults, replace the CMOS battery and reset the BIOS settings to correct values. A CMOS battery (usually a CR2032 on recent systems) will work properly for about 3 years before it needs to be replaced.

If replacing the battery does not solve the problem, the CMOS chip on the motherboard might be damaged. This is a surface-mounted chip that cannot be replaced, so the motherboard itself must be replaced.

System Lockups

System lockups are typically caused by the corruption of memory contents. Following these steps:

Step 1.   Shut down the system, remove and reinstall memory, and remove dust from the modules and the sockets. If the problem persists, memory might be overheating.

Step 2.   Check the specifications for memory; the memory installed might not be the correct type for the motherboard and processor. If memory is incorrect for CPU or motherboard, replace it with correct-specification memory.

Step 3.   If memory has been overclocked, reset the memory to factory specifications by using the Auto or by SPD options in the system BIOS setup. See Chapters 3 and 8 for details.

Step 4.   Add additional system cooling. See Chapter 4 for details.

POST Code Beeps at Startup

POST code beeps at startup are caused by a variety of fatal errors that can relate to CPU, memory, or motherboard problems. Consult the documentation for your system's BIOS chip to interpret the meaning of a particular beep code. Replace the defective component. See Chapter 3 for more information.

Blank Screen on Bootup

A blank screen on bootup can be caused by a variety of incorrect storage and video configurations or cabling problems, some of which can be caused by motherboard issues:

- On systems with PATA drives, reversing the data cable to the drive will prevent the system from receiving a response from the drive at startup, and the system boot process won't get far enough to display anything onscreen. See Chapter 12 for details.

- A cable plugged in to an inactive port on a system will also cause a blank screen. For example, many (but not all) systems deactivate onboard video when you install a video card. If onboard video offers DVI and HDMI ports, typically only one can be selected (usually with motherboard jumpers).

Smoke or Burning Smells

Smoke or burning smells inside the system usually indicate a failure of a capacitor or of the power supply. The capacitors are cylindrical components near the CPU socket on the motherboard or inside the power supply. If capacitors fail or other components burn up, replace the component.

System Will Not Start

If the computer will not start, check the following:

- Incorrect front panel wiring connections to the motherboard
- Loose or missing power leads from power supply
- Loose or missing memory modules
- Loose BIOS chips
- Incorrect connection of EIDE/PATA cables to onboard host adapter
- Dead short in system
- Incorrect positioning of a standoff
- Loose screws or slot covers

The following sections describe each of these possible problems.

Incorrect Front Panel Wiring Connections to the Motherboard

The power switch is wired to the motherboard, which in turn signals the power supply to start. If the power lead is plugged in to the wrong pins on the mother-board, or has been disconnected from the motherboard, the system will not start and you will not see an error message.

Check the markings on the front panel connectors, the motherboard, or the motherboard/system manual to determine the correct pinouts and installation (refer to Figure 2-15).

Loose or Missing Power Leads from Power Supply

Make sure both the ATX and ATX12V power leads from the power supply are connected firmly to the motherboard. For details, see Chapter 4.

Loose or Missing Memory Modules

If the motherboard cannot recognize any system memory, it will not start properly. You might see a memory error message or hear beep codes depending on the BIOS used by the system.

Make sure memory modules are properly locked into place and that there is no corrosion on the memory contacts on the motherboard or on the memory modules. To remove corrosion from memory module contacts, remove the memory modules from the motherboard and gently wipe off the contacts to remove any built-up film or corrosion. An Artgum eraser (but not the conventional rubber or highly abrasive ink eraser) can be used for stubborn cases. Be sure to rub in a direction away from the memory chips to avoid damage. Reinsert the modules and lock them into place.

Loose BIOS Chips

Socketed motherboard chips that don't have retaining mechanisms, such as BIOS chips, can cause system failures if the chips work loose from their sockets. The motherboard BIOS chip (see Figure 2-20) is responsible for displaying boot errors, and if it is not properly mounted in its socket, the system cannot start and no error messages will be produced. (Many recent systems have surface-mounted BIOS chips.)

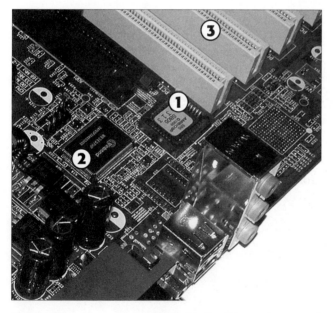

1. System BIOS chip
2. LPC I/O chip (for comparison)
3. PCI slots (for comparison)

Figure 2-20   If a socketed BIOS chip like this one becomes loose, the system cannot boot.

The cycle of heating (during operation) and cooling (after the power is shut down) can lead to **chip creep**, in which socketed chips gradually loosen in the sockets. To cure chip creep, push the chips back into their sockets. Use even force to press a square BIOS chip into place. On older systems that use rectangular BIOS chips, alternately push on each end of the chip until the chip is securely mounted.

NOTE   Check your system or motherboard documentation to determine the location of the BIOS chip.

Dead Short (Short Circuit) in System

A **dead short** (short circuit) in your system will prevent a computer from showing any signs of life when you turn it on. Some of the main causes for dead shorts that involve motherboards include

- Incorrect positioning of a standoff
- Loose screws or slot covers (discussed earlier in this chapter)

Brass standoffs should be lined up with the mounting holes in the motherboard (refer to Figure 2-1 for typical locations). Some motherboards have two types of holes: plain holes that are not intended for use with brass standoffs (they might be used for heat sink mounting or for plastic standoffs) and reinforced holes used for brass standoffs. Figure 2-21 compares these hole types.

Plain hole (not used for motherboard installation)

Metal-reinforced hole designed to ground the motherboard when mounted with brass standoffs

Figure 2-21   Mounting holes compared to other holes on a typical motherboard.

If a brass standoff is under a part of the motherboard not meant for mounting, such as under a plain hole or under the solder connections, the standoff could cause a dead short that prevents the system from starting.

Processors and CPUs

220-801

Objective:
220-801: 1.6

To do well on A+ Certification exams, you must understand the major types of processors available for recent systems, their technologies, how to install them, and how to troubleshoot them.

Overview of Processor Differences

Although Intel and AMD processors share two common architectures, x86 (used for 32-bit processors and for 64-bit processors running in 32-bit mode) and x64 (an extension of x86 that enables larger files, larger memory sizes, and more complex programs), these processor families differ in many ways from each other, including

- Different processor sockets.

- Differences in multicore processor designs. (Two or more processor cores help run multiple programs and programs with multiple execution threads more efficiently.)

- Cache sizes.

Intel Processors

Intel has used many processor sockets over the years, but the 220-801 exam specifically cites the following recent and current socket designs:

- LGA 775

- LGA 1155

- LGA 1156

- LGA 1366

NOTE   To learn more about the technologies and features in the following sections, see the section "CPU Technologies."

Land Grid Array

All these sockets use the **land grid array (LGA)** design. The LGA design uses spring-loaded lands in the processor socket that connect to bumps on the backside of the processor. To hold the processor in place, a hinged clamping mechanism is used; before the processor is installed, the mechanism holds a plastic protection plate in place (Figure 2-22).

Figure 2-22   An LGA-1155 socket is covered by a protective plate before processor installation.

The heat sink snaps into mounting holes offset from the four corners of the processor socket. An LGA 1155 socket is shown in Figure 2-23, and the same socket after the processor is installed is shown in Figure 2-24.

CPR retention frame

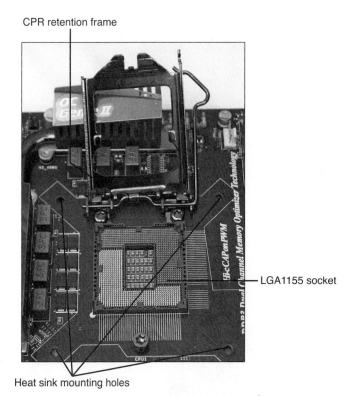

LGA1155 socket

Heat sink mounting holes

Figure 2-23   An LGA-1155 socket prepared for processor installation.

Figure 2-24   An LGA-1155 socket after a Core i5 processor is installed.

LGA 775

LGA 775 has been used by the following processors: late-model Pentium 4, all Pentium D, late-model Celeron Desktop processors, all Core 2 Duo, all Core 2 Quad, and all Core 2 Extreme. Table 2-3 compares the technologies supported by these processors.

Table 2-3 LGA 775 Processor Technologies and Features

Processor Family	# of Cores	Intel 64 (x64)	L2 Cache	HT Tech	Intel VT-x	Bus Speed (FSB)
Pentium 4 and P4 EE	1	Some	1MB–2MB	Varies	Varies	533MHz–1066MHz
Pentium D	2	Yes	2MB–4MB	No	Varies	533MHz–800MHz
Celeron D	1	Varies	256KB–512KB	No	No	533MHz–800MHz
Celeron Desktop	1	Yes	512KB–1MB	No	Varies	800MHz
Pentium Desktop	2	Yes	1MB–2MB	No	Varies	800MHz–1066MHz
Pentium Desktop EE	2	Yes	2MB–4MB	Yes	Yes	800MHz–1066MHz
Core 2 Duo	2	Yes	2MB–6MB	No	Varies	800MHz–1333MHz
Core 2 Quad	4	Yes	4MB–12MB	No	Varies	1066MHz–1333MHz
Core 2 Extreme	2,4	Yes	4MB–12MB	No	Yes	1066MHz–1600MHz

EE – Extreme Edition – Very high-performance processor

FSB – Front Side Bus

VT-x – Virtualization

HT Tech – Hyperthreading

Intel 64 – 64-bit processor

Pentium D – Essentially two Pentium 4 cores in a single processor assembly; cores communicate via memory controller hub (northbridge)

Processors using LGA 775 range in clock speed from as low as 2.30GHz (Celeron Desktop) to as high as 3.73GHz (Pentium 4 EE, Pentium Desktop EE).

NOTE   Several different chipsets have been used with LGA 775 processors; different chipsets support different processors. To determine a particular system compatibility with a particular processor, check the motherboard or system documentation.

LGA 1366

LGA 1366 was used by the Core i7 9xx series Extreme Edition CPUs for desktops and by Xeon processors used for workstations and servers. LGA 1366 uses a new interconnect method called quick path interconnect (QPI) to connect to the I/O controller hub (northbridge); the memory controller is built in to the CPU and supports triple-channel DDR3 memory. Table 2-4 compares the technologies supported by the Core i7 and Extreme Edition CPUs for desktops.

Table 2-4   LGA 1366 Desktop Processor Technologies and Features

Processor Family	# of Cores	Intel 64 (x64)	Smart Cache	Turbo Boost	HT Tech	Intel VT-x	Bus Speed
Core i7 990X, 980X EP, 980, 970	6	Yes	12MB	Yes	Yes	Yes	6.4GTps
Core i7 9xx EP, 9xx	4	Yes	8MB	Yes	Yes	Yes	6.4GTps

EP – Extreme Processor – Very high-performance processor

GT – Gigatransfers

Processors using LGA 1366 range in clock speed from as low as 2.66GHz (Core i7 –920) to as high as 3.46GHz (Core i7 Extreme-990X). Turbo Boost maximum Turbo frequency ranges from as low as 2.93GHz (920) to 3.73GHz (990X).

LGA 1156

LGA 1156 was used by the first-generation Core i3 and Core i5 processors and by Core i7 CPUs that did not use LGA 1366. (These processors are currently listed on the Intel ARK website as "previous-generation" Core i3, i5, and i7 processors.) LGA 1156, like LGA 1366, is designed to connect to a memory controller built in to the CPU. LGA 1156-compatible CPUs support dual-channel DDR3 memory. Some processors that use LGA 1156 also include CPU-integrated video.

Table 2-5 compares the technologies supported by these processors.

Table 2-5 LGA 1156 Processor Technologies and Features

Processor Family	# of Cores	Intel 64 (x64)	Smart Cache	Turbo Boost	HT Tech	Intel VT-x	Bus Speed
Core i7 8xx	4	Yes	8MB	Yes	Yes	Yes	2.5GTps
Core i5 7xx, 6xx	2,4	Yes	4MB–8MB	Yes	Yes	Yes	2.5GTps
Core i3 5xx	2	Yes	4MB	No	Yes	Yes	2.5GTps
Celeron G1xxx	2	Yes	2MB	No	No	No	2.5GTps
Pentium G6xxx	2	Yes	3MB	No	No	Yes	2.5GTps

7xx – 4-core version of Core i5
6xx – 2-core version of Core i5

Processors using LGA 1156 range in clock speed from as low as 2.26GHz (Celeron G1101) to as high as 3.06GHz (Core i7-880). Turbo Boost maximum Turbo frequency ranges from 3.20GHz (Core i5-750) to 3.86GHz (Core i5-680).

LGA 1155

LGA 1155 is used by the second-generation or Sandy Bridge architecture Core i3, Core i5, and Core i7 CPUs. Compared to the first-generation processors, these processors feature better L1 and L2 caches, CPU integrated video, two load and store operations per CPU cycle, and better performance for advanced mathematical operations. Table 2-6 compares the technologies used by these processors.

Table 2-6 LGA 1155 Processor Technologies and Features

Processor Family	# of Cores	Intel 64 (x64)	Smart Cache	Turbo Boost 2.0	HT Tech	Intel VT-x	Bus Speed
Core i7 2xxxK	4	Yes	8MB	Yes	Yes	Yes	5GTps
Core i5 2xxx	2,4	Yes	3MB–6MB	Yes	No	Yes	5GTps
Core i3 21xx	2	Yes	3MB	No	Yes	Yes	5GTps
Pentium Desktop 350	2	Yes	3MB	No	Yes	Yes	5GTps
Pentium Desktop G6xx, G8xx	2	Yes	3MB	No	No	Yes	5GTps
Celeron G4xx	1	Yes	1MB–1.5MB	No	Varies	Yes	5GTps
Celeron G5xx	2	Yes	2MB	No	No	Yes	5GTps

Processors using LGA 1155 range in clock speed from as low as 1.60GHz (Celeron G440) to as high as 3.40GHz (various Core i5 and i7 models). Turbo Boost maximum Turbo frequency ranges from 3.10GHz (Core i5-2300) to 3.90GHz (Core i7-2700K).

AMD Processors

AMD has used many processor sockets over the years, but the 220-801 exam specifically cites the following recent and current socket designs:

- Socket 940
- Socket AM2
- Socket AM2+
- Socket AM3
- Socket AM3+
- Socket F
- Socket FM1

All these sockets, except for Socket F, use the pin grid array (PGA) design. All the AMD processors on the 220-801 exam have integrated memory controllers.

> **NOTE**   Socket F, which was used starting in 2006 by some AMD Opteron server and workstation processors, uses an LGA design similar in function to those used by Intel processors. Its replacements, Socket C32 and G34, also use LGA designs.

PGA Sockets

The **pin grid array (PGA)** design uses pins on the backside of the CPU to connect to pins in the processor socket. To hold the CPU in place, a zero insertion force (ZIF) socket mechanism is used. Open the arm and insert the processor; then close the arm to clamp the CPU pins in place.

The heat sink clips to mounting lugs on two sides of the processor socket. All PGA sockets listed at the beginning of this section work in the same way.

Socket AM3 is shown in Figure 2-25 before installing a processor, and Figure 2-26 shows the same socket after an AMD Phenom II X6 processor has been installed.

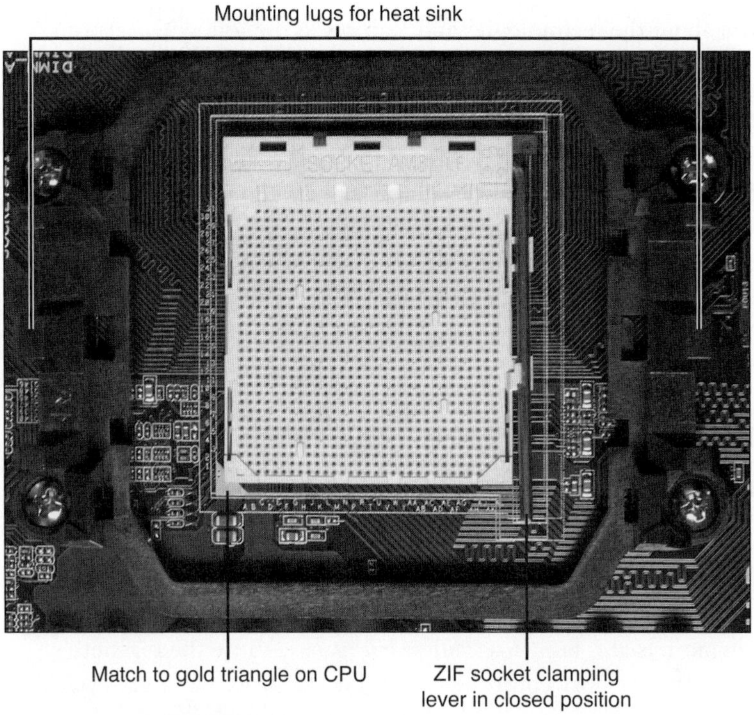
Mounting lugs for heat sink
SOCKET AM3
Match to gold triangle on CPU
ZIF socket clamping lever in closed position

Figure 2-25 Socket AM3 before processor installation.

SOCKET AM3
AMD Phenom™ II
AMD
DIFFUSED IN GERMANY
MADE IN MALAYSIA

Figure 2-26 Socket AM3 after an AMD Phenom II X6 processor has been installed.

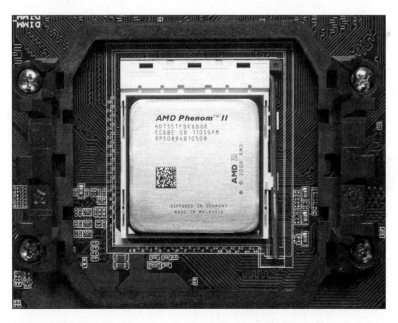

> **NOTE**   To learn more about the technologies and features in the following sections, see the section "CPU Technologies."

Socket 940

Socket 940 was used by the first-generation Athlon 64 FX (FX-51) and by early Opteron workstation and server processors. Unlike later AMD designs for desktop processors, processors using Socket 940 must use registered memory. See Table 2-7 for the technologies and features supported by AMD desktop processors using Socket 940.

Table 2-7   Socket 940 Desktop Processor Technologies and Features

Processor Family	# of Cores	AMD 64 (x64)	L2 Cache Size	Memory Supported	AMD-V	HyperTransport speed
Athlon 64 FX-51, 53	1	Yes	1MB	Registered DDR dual-channel	No	1GHz

> **NOTE**   Registered memory is also known as *buffered memory* because the register between the DRAM and the memory controller in the CPU provides a single-cycle buffer during read and write operations. This makes registered memory slower but more reliable.

Socket AM2

Socket AM2 replaced older Sockets 754, 939, and 940. All processors that use Socket AM2 support dual-channel DDR2 memory. See Table 2-8 for the technologies and features supported by AMD desktop processors using Socket AM2.

Table 2-8   Socket AM2 Desktop Processor Technologies and Features

Processor Family	# of Cores	AMD 64 (x64)	L2 Cache Size	L3 Cache	AMD-V	HyperTransport Speed
Athlon 64 3500+– 3800+	1	Yes	512KB	No	Yes	1GHz
Athlon 64 3000+– 4000+	1	Yes	512KB	No	Yes	1GHz
Sempron 3000+– 3800+	1	Yes	128KB, 256KB	No	No	800MHz
Athlon X2 4450B–5600B, 3250e–5050e, BE-2xxx	2	Yes	1MB	No	Yes	1GHz

Processor Family	# of Cores	AMD 64 (x64)	L2 Cache Size	L3 Cache	AMD-V	HyperTransport Speed
Sempron X2 2100–2300	2	Yes	512KB	No	No	800MHz
Athlon 64 X2 3600+–6000+	2	Yes	512KB–2MB	No	Yes	1GHz
Athlon 64 FX 60, FX 70–74	2	Yes	2MB	No	Yes	1GHz

Desktop processors using Socket AM2 range in clock speed from as low as 1.60GHz (Sempron 3000+) to as high as 3.0GHz (Athlon 64 FX 70).

Socket AM2+

Socket AM2+ is an enhanced version of Socket AM2 that supports Socket AM2 processors as well as the Phenom and lower-cost Athlon processors based on the Phenom design. Socket AM2+ runs at faster speeds than Socket AM2 and also supports processors with L3 cache. All processors that use Socket AM2+ support dual-channel DDR2 memory. See Table 2-9 for the technologies and features supported by AMD desktop processors using Socket AM2+.

Table 2-9   Socket AM2+ Desktop Processor Technologies and Features

Processor Family	# of Cores	AMD 64 (x64)	L2 Cache Size	L3 Cache Size	AMD-V	HyperTransport Speed
Athlon X2	2	Yes	1MB	2MB	Yes	1.8GHz
Phenom X3	3	Yes	1.5MB	2MB	Yes	1.6GHz–1.8GHz
Phenom X4	4	Yes	2MB	2MB	Yes	1.6GHz–2.0GHz

Desktop processors using Socket AM2+ range in speed from as low as 1.80GHz (Phenom X3) to as high as 2.80GHz (Athlon X2).

Socket AM3

Socket AM3 supports processors with dual-channel DDR3 or DDR2 memory controllers onboard, including the Phenom II as well as lower-cost processors based on the Phenom II's architecture. See Table 2-10 for the technologies and features supported by AMD desktop processors using Socket AM3.

Table 2-10   Socket AM3 Desktop Processor Technologies and Features

Processor Family	# of Cores	AMD 64 (x64)	L2 Cache Size	L3 Cache Size	RAM Type	Turbo CORE	AMD-V	HyperTransport Speed
Phenom II X6	6	Yes	3MB	6MB	DDR3	Yes	Yes	8GBps*
Phenom II X4	4	Yes	2MB	6MB	DDR3	Yes	Yes	8GBps*
Phenom II X4	4	Yes	1.5MB	4MB–6MB (most models)	DDR3	No	Yes	8GBps*
Athlon II X4	4	Yes	2MB	None	DDR2, DDR3	No	Yes	8GBps*
Phenom II X3	3	Yes	1.5MB	6MB	DDR3	No	Yes	8GBps*
Athlon II X3	3	Yes	1.5MB	None	DDR2, DDR3	No	Yes	8GBps*
Phenom II X2	2	Yes	1MB	6MB	DDR3	No	Yes	8GBps*
Athlon II X2	2	Yes	1MB–2MB	None	DDR2, DDR3	No	Yes	8GBps*
Athlon II 1xxu	1	Yes	1MB	None	DDR2	No	Yes	8GBps*
Sempron 1xx	1	Yes	1MB	None	DDR2	No	Yes	8GBps*

*16GBps in HyperTransport 3.0 mode

Desktop processors using Socket AM3 range in speed from as low as 1.8GHz (Athlon II 1xxu) to as high as 3.7GHz (Phenom II X4).

Socket AM3+

Socket AM3+ supports processors with up to eight cores, such as the FX 8xxx series. Like Socket AM3, it supports processors with dual-channel DDR3 memory controllers onboard. See Table 2-11 for the technologies and features supported by AMD desktop processors using Socket AM3+.

Table 2-11   Socket AM3+ Desktop Processor Technologies and Features

Processor Family	# of Cores	AMD 64 (x64)	L2 Cache Size	L3 Cache Size	Turbo CORE	AMD-V	HyperTransport Speed
FX 8xxx	8	Yes	8MB	8MB	Yes	Yes	8GBps*
FX 6xxx	6	Yes	6MB	8MB	Yes	Yes	8GBps*
FX 4xxx	4	Yes	4MB	8MB	No	Yes	8GBps*

*16GBps in HyperTransport 3.0 mode

Desktop processors using Socket AM3+ range in speed from as low as 3.1GHz (FX 8100) to as high as 4.2GHz (FX 4170). Turbo CORE speeds range from 3.7GHz (FX 8100) to as high as 4.3GHz (FX 4170).

Socket FM1

Socket FM1 supports AMD's first processors with integrated on-chip video, the A-series and E-series APUs (Advanced Processing Units), as well as the 6x1 editions of the Athlon II X4 processor. Processors using Socket FM1 support dual-channel DDR3 memory (Athlon II X4 also supports dual-channel DDR2 memory). See Table 2-12 for the technologies and features supported by AMD desktop processors using Socket FM1.

Table 2-12 Socket FM1 Desktop Processor Technologies and Features

Processor Family	# of Cores	AMD 64 (x64)	L2 Cache Size	L3 Cache Size	Turbo CORE	AMD-V	Radeon Cores on Die	HyperTransport Speed
A8-38xx	4	Yes	4MB	None	Yes	Yes	400	8GBps*
A6-36xx	4	Yes	4MB	None	Yes	Yes	320	8GBps*
A6-35xx	3	Yes	3MB	None	Yes	Yes	320	8GBps*
A4-34xx	2	Yes	1MB	None	Yes	Yes	160	8GBps*
A4-33xx	2	Yes	1MB	None	Yes	Yes	160	8GBps*
Athlon II X4 6x1	4	Yes	4MB	None	No	Yes	N/A	8GBps*

16GBps in HyperTransport 3.0 mode

Desktop processors using Socket FM1 range in speed from as low as 2.1GHz (A4-3500) to as high as 3.0GHz (A8-3870K).

CPU Technologies

> **220-801**
>
> **Objective:**
> **220-801: 1.6**

Processor technologies in the following sections might be used by AMD only, by Intel only, or by both vendors. These technologies are used to help distinguish different processors from each other in terms of performance or features.

NOTE To learn more about a particular processor's support for x64 operation, hardware virtualization, and other features, look up the processor specifications at the manufacturers' website: http://ark.intel.com (Intel processors) or www.amd.com (AMD processors).

Hyperthreading (HT Technology)

Hyperthreading (HT Technology) is a technology developed by Intel for processing two execution threads within a single processor core. Essentially, when HT Technology is enabled in the system BIOS and the processor is running a multithreaded application, the processor is emulating two physical processors. The Pentium 4 was the first desktop processor to support HT Technology, which Intel first developed for its Xeon workstation and server processor family.

Pentium 4 processors with processor numbers all support HT Technology, as do older models with 800MHz FSB and a clock speed of 3.06GHz or higher. HT Technology is also incorporated in a number of more recent processors to further improve the execution of multithreaded applications.

Multicore

Two or more physical processors in a system enable it to perform much faster when multitasking or running multithreaded applications. However, systems with multiple processors are expensive to produce, and some operating systems cannot work with multiple processors. **Multicore** processors, which combine two or more processor cores into a single physical processor, provide virtually all the benefits of multiple physical processors and are lower in cost and work with any operating system that supports traditional single-core processors.

Cache

Cache memory improves system performance by enabling the processor to reuse recently retrieved memory locations without needing to fetch them from main memory. Processors from AMD and Intel feature at least two levels of cache:

- **Level 1 (L1) cache** is built in to the processor core. L1 cache is relatively small (8KB–128KB). When the processor needs to access memory, it checks the contents of L1 cache first.

- **Level 2 (L2) cache** is also built in to the processor die. If the processor does not find the wanted memory locations in L1 cache, it checks L2 cache next.

- **Level 3 (L3) cache** is found on some high-performance processors from Intel (such as the Core i7 series) and on several high-performance and mid-level processors from AMD. L3 is also built in to the processor die. On systems with L3 cache, the processor checks L3 cache after checking L1 and L2 caches.

If cache memory does not contain the needed information, the processor retrieves the needed information from the main memory and stores copies of that information in its cache memory (L1 and L2, or L1, L2, and L3). Processors with larger L2 caches (or L2 and L3 caches) perform most tasks quicker than processors that have smaller L2 caches for two reasons. Cache memory is faster than main memory, and the processor checks cache memory for needed information before checking main memory.

Bus Speeds

Different components of the motherboard, such as the CPU, memory, chipset, expansion slots, storage interfaces, and I/O ports, connect with each other at different speeds. The term **bus speeds** refers to the speeds at which different buses in the motherboard connect to different components.

Some of these speeds, such as the speed of I/O ports and expansion slots (USB, FireWire, parallel, serial, SATA, and PATA ports; PCI, AGP, and PCIe slots), are established by the design of the port or by the capabilities of the devices connected to them. However, depending on the motherboard, you might be able to fine-tune the bus speeds used by the processor, the chipset interconnect, and memory. These adjustments, where available, are typically performed through BIOS settings in menus such as Memory, Overclocking, AI Tweaker, and others.

Figure 2-27 is the Advanced dialog from an overclockable system with an AMD Phenom II X6 processor. The top portion of the dialog indicates the current CPU speed, HyperTransport chipset interconnect speed (HT Link), and that these speeds can be adjusted.

Figure 2-28 illustrates the speed adjustment (AI Tweaker) dialog on the same system. To change CPU speed, HT Link speed, or other adjustments, change the Auto setting and enter the wanted values. On this system and others, you can select a CPU overclocking value, and other settings will be adjusted automatically as needed.

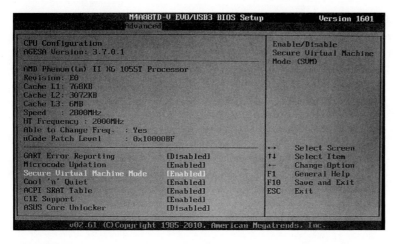

Figure 2-27   CPU and chipset speed information on a system that allows speed adjustment.

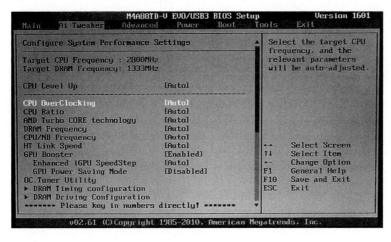

Figure 2-28   Preparing to overclock a system.

Overclocking

Overclocking refers to the practice of running a processor or other components, such as memory or the video card's graphics processing unit (GPU), at speeds higher than normal. Overclocking methods used for processors include increasing the clock multiplier or running the front side bus (FSB) at speeds faster than normal. These changes are performed by altering the normal settings in the system BIOS setup for the processor's configuration.

Most processors feature locked clock multipliers. That is, the clock multiplier frequency cannot be changed. In such cases, the only way to overclock the processor is to increase the front side bus (FSB) speed, which is the speed at which the processor communicates with system memory. Increasing the FSB speed can lead to greater system instability than changing the clock multipliers.

Some processors from Intel and AMD feature unlocked clock multipliers (Intel refers to its as Extreme Edition or Extreme Processor, or uses the K suffix at the end of the model number, whereas AMD uses the term Black Edition or uses the K suffix) so that the user can choose the best method for overclocking the system. Overclocked processors and other components run hotter than normal, so techniques such as using additional cooling fans, replacing standard active heat sinks with models that feature greater cooling, and adjusting processor voltages are often used to help maintain system stability at faster speeds.

Intel's Core i7, Core i5, and AMD's Phenom II and A-series support automatic overclocking according to processor load. Intel refers to this feature as Turbo Boost, whereas AMD's term is Turbo CORE.

CAUTION   Overclocking is not recommended for mission-critical systems. However, many gaming-oriented systems have the heavy-duty cooling and extensive BIOS adjustments needed to make overclocking a success.

32-bit Versus 64-bit Architecture

Processors developed before the AMD Athlon 64 were designed only for 32-bit operating systems and applications. 32-bit software cannot access more than 4GB of RAM (32-bit Windows programs can use only 3.25GB of RAM), which makes working with large data files difficult because only a portion of a file larger than the maximum memory size can be loaded into memory at one time.

The Athlon 64 was the first desktop processor to support 64-bit extensions to the 32-bit **x86** architecture. These 64-bit extensions, commonly known as **x64**, enable processors to use more than 4GB of RAM and run 64-bit operating systems but maintain full compatibility with 32-bit operating systems and applications.

Virtualization Support

Most current AMD and Intel processors support **hardware-assisted virtualization**. Virtualization technology enables a host program (known as a hypervisor) or a host operating system to support one or more guest operating systems running at the same time in windows on the host's desktop. Hardware-assisted virtualization enables virtualized operating systems and applications to run faster and use fewer system resources.

Some of the best-known virtualization programs include Microsoft's Virtual PC 2007 and 2004, Windows Virtual PC, and Hyper-V. Major third-party virtualization programs include VMware (www.vmware.com) and DOSBox (www.dosbox.com).

To learn more about using virtualization in Microsoft Windows, see "Client-Side Virtualization" in Chapter 14, "Using and Managing Windows."

Integrated GPU

Intel's Core i3, i5, and i7 CPUs and AMD's A-series advanced processing units (APUs) are the first processors to have **integrated GPU**s. By integrating the GPU into the processor, faster video processing, easier access to memory, and lower-cost systems result.

Intel's integrated GPUs are based on its HD3000 chipset integrated graphics processor, whereas AMD's is based on its RADEON 6000-series GPUs. Note that Intel's second-generation Sandy Bridge CPUs offer faster video decoding than the first generation.

Use the integrated GPU for non-3D video output (web surfing, office automation, and HTPC video playback), but for 3D gaming, a system still needs a video card with the best discrete GPU that fits in the system budget.

CPU Cooling

220-801

Objective:
220-801: 1.6

A CPU is one of the most expensive components found in any computer, so keeping it cool is important. The basic requirements for proper CPU cooling include the use of an appropriate active heat sink (which includes a fan) and application of an appropriate thermal material (grease, paste, or a pre-applied thermal or phase-change compound). Advanced systems might use liquid cooling instead.

Passive and Active Heat Sinks

All processors require a **heat sink**. A heat sink is a finned metal device that radiates heat away from the processor. In almost all cases, an **active heat sink** (a heat sink with a fan) is required for adequate cooling, unless the system case (chassis) is specially designed to move air directly over the processor, and a **passive heat sink**.

Although aluminum has been the most common material used for heat sinks, copper has better thermal transfer properties, and many designs mix copper and aluminum components. Traditional active heat sinks include a cooling fan that rests on top of the heat sink and pulls air past the heat sink in a vertical direction (see Figure 2-29). However, many aftermarket heat sinks use other designs (see Figure 2-30).

Figure 2-29   Stock (original equipment) active heat sinks made for AMD (left) and Intel (right) processors.

Before installing a heat sink bundled with a processor, remove the protective cover over the pre-applied thermal material (also known as phase-change material) on the heat sink. When the heat sink is installed on the processor, this material helps ensure good contact between the CPU and the heat sink.

If you need to remove and reapply a heat sink, be sure to remove all residue from both the processor and heat sink and apply new thermal paste or other thermal transfer material to the top of the CPU.

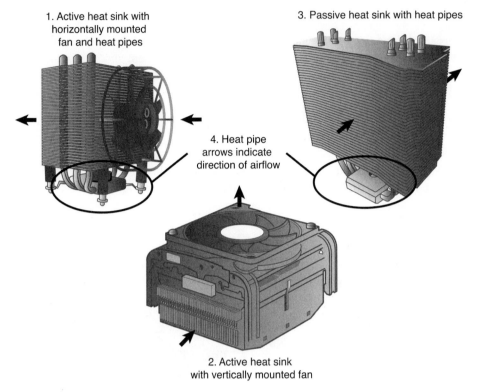

1. Active heat sink with horizontally mounted fan and heat pipes

3. Passive heat sink with heat pipes

4. Heat pipe arrows indicate direction of airflow

2. Active heat sink with vertically mounted fan

Figure 2-30   Typical third-party active and passive heat sinks. The passive heat sink has more fins than the active heat sinks do to help promote better cooling.

Liquid Cooling Systems

Liquid cooling systems for processors, motherboard chipsets, and GPUs are now available. Some are integrated into a custom case, whereas others can be retrofitted into an existing system that has openings for cooling fans.

Liquid cooling systems attach a liquid cooling unit instead of an active heat sink to the processor and other supported components. A pump moves the liquid (which might be water or a special solution, depending on the cooling system) through the computer to a heat exchanger, which uses a fan to cool the warm liquid before it is sent back to the processor. Liquid cooling systems are designed primarily for high-performance systems, especially overclocked systems. It's essential that only approved cooling liquids and hoses be used in these systems (check with cooling system vendors for details); unauthorized types of liquids or hoses could leak and corrode system components.

Figure 2-31 illustrates a typical liquid cooling system for cooling the processor.

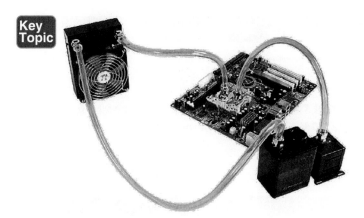

Figure 2-31   A typical liquid cooling system.

Exam Preparation Tasks

Review All the Key Topics

Review the most important topics in the chapter, noted with the Key Topic icon in the outer margin of the page. Table 2-13 lists a reference of these key topics and the page numbers on which each is found.

Table 2-13 Key Topics for Chapter 2

Key Topic Element	Description	Page Number
Text	Motherboards and their components	30
Text	ATX and microATX	31
Text	ITX	32
Figure 2-2	ATX, microATX, FlexATX, and Mini-ITX motherboards	33
Figure 2-3	Typical port clusters on ATX motherboards	34
Text	PCI slots	36
Text	PCI-X slots	37
Text	AGP	38
Text	PCIe (PCI Express) slots	39
List	Northbridge and southbridge	43
Figure 2-12	CMOS battery and CMOS jumper pins	44
Figure 2-13	CPU and system fan connectors	45
Text	Front-panel connectors	46
Text	Continuous reboots	53
Text	BIOS time and settings resets	53
List	System will not start	55
List	Intel processor sockets	58
List	AMD processor sockets	64
Figure 2-29	Stock active heat sinks for AMD and Intel CPUs	75
Figure 2-31	Liquid cooling system	77

Complete the Tables and Lists from Memory

Print a copy of Appendix A, "Memory Tables" (found on the CD), or at least the section for this chapter, and complete the tables and lists from memory. Appendix B, "Memory Tables Answer Key," also on the CD, includes completed tables and lists to check your work.

Define Key Terms

Define the following key terms from this chapter, and check your answers in the glossary.

active heat sink, AGP (Accelerated Graphics Port), AMR (Audio Modem Riser), ATX (Advanced Technology Integrated), bus speeds, chip creep, chipset, CNR, continuous reboots, CPU (Central Processing Unit), CPU fan connector, dead short, expansion slots, FlexATX, form factor, front-panel connectors, hardware-assisted virtualization, heat sink, Hyperthreading (HT Technology), integrated GPU, integrated I/O ports, jumper , jumper block, Land grid array (LGA), Level 1 (L1) cache, Level 2 (L2) cache, Level 3 (L3) cache, LGA1155, LGA1156, LGA1366, LGA775, Mini-ITX, motherboard, Multicore, overclocking, PCI (Peripheral component Interconnect), PCI Express (PCIe), PCI-X, Pin grid array (PGA), Socket 940, Socket AM2, Socket AM2+, Socket AM3, Socket AM3+, Socket FM1, system fan connectors, system lockups, x64, x86, passive heat sink, liquid cooling

Complete Hands-On Lab

Complete the hands-on labs, and then see the answers and explanations at the end of the chapter.

Lab 2-1: Determine Available USB Ports, Locations, and Types

Scenario: You are a technician on a service call. A client wants to know whether all the available USB ports on the motherboard are accessible.

Equipment needed: System or motherboard documentation and tools to open the case (if needed).

Procedure: Open the system and look for unused USB ports. Use the system or motherboard documentation to determine whether there are any unused USB port headers. To convert a port header into a working USB port, connect a header cable to it.

Lab 2-2: Determine Smallest Form Factor Suitable for a New PC

Scenario: You are a technician tasked with sourcing a new PC. The user's requirements include one PCIe x16 video card, 4GB of RAM, a 1TB hard disk, four USB 2.0 or faster ports, and quiet operation.

Procedure: Check vendors selling mini-ITX and microATX/FlexATX motherboards to determine whether you can find a suitable system. Design at least one system build using each motherboard if possible. Specify brand and model numbers of major components.

Answer Review Questions

Answer these review questions, and then see the answers and explanations at the end of the chapter.

1. Which of the following are considered expansion slots? (Choose all that apply.)

    a. PCI

    b. FireWire

    c. AGP

    d. USB

2. Which of the following expansion slots provides the fastest performance for 3D video and graphics?

    a. AGP 8x

    b. PCI-X 2.0

    c. PCI

    d. PCIe x16

3. Which of the following motherboards would you select if you need the largest number of expansion slots?

    a. ATX

    b. microATX

    c. Mini-ITX

    d. FlexATX

4. Which of the following ports is not found in a port cluster?

   a. SATA port

   b. Network port

   c. USB port

   d. PS/2 mouse and keyboard

5. You must specify a multicore processor for a client's system. The client prefers at least six cores. Which of the following product families will meet this requirement? (Choose all that apply.)

   a. Core i3

   b. Core 2 Extreme

   c. Phenom II

   d. Core i7 9xx

6. On a recent system, which of the following is typically configured with a jumper block on the motherboard?

   a. PATA master/slave

   b. CMOS memory

   c. SATA speed

   d. PnP BIOS

7. Which of the following best describes hyperthreading?

   a. Overclocking your CPU.

   b. Processing two execution threads simultaneously.

   c. Having more than one processor.

   d. None of these options is correct.

8. If you remove the processor from the motherboard, what device should you remove first?

   a. Power supply

   b. RAM chip

   c. Heat sink

   d. Thermal compound

9. You are installing a new motherboard. Which of the following headers should you use for the CPU fan?

   a. Three-pin fan

   b. USB

   c. Front-panel header

   d. Four-pin fan

10. Your client's PC needs an upgraded CPU. The current socket is an LGA 1155. Which of the following CPUs are most likely to be compatible?

   a. AMD A8 series

   b. Intel Core i7 2700K

   c. Intel Core i7 990X

   d. Intel Core 2 Extreme

11. You are installing a new CPU and bundled heat sink. Which of the following steps should you follow to ensure proper cooling?

   a. Remove protective tape from top of CPU.

   b. Apply thermal paste to heat sink.

   c. Apply thermal paste to top of CPU.

   d. Remove protective tape from bottom of heat sink.

12. The system cannot retain correct date and time information. Which of the following should you replace first?

   a. Video card

   b. RAM

   c. CMOS battery

   d. Motherboard

Answers to Hands-On Lab

Lab 2-1: Determine Available USB Ports, Locations, and Types

Answer: Answers will vary according to the system. Check your work against system or motherboard documentation.

Lab 2-2: Determine Smallest Form Factor Suitable for a New PC

Answer: Answers will vary according to the needs of the system and available components. Check vendor specifications carefully and ensure support for Windows 7.

Answers and Explanations to Review Questions

1. **A, C.** PCI and AGP are expansion slots. The others are connections for external devices.

2. **D.** PCIe x16 has replaced AGP (which in turn replaced PCI) for 3D video and graphics. PCI-X 2.0 is used for mass storage and high-speed network adapters on workstations and servers.

3. **A.** ATX motherboards typically have seven expansion slots, compared to four or fewer for the other form factors listed.

4. **A.** The eSATA port, not the SATA port, is found (along with the others listed) in typical port clusters.

5. **C, D.** The AMD Phenom II X6 has six cores, as does the Intel Core i7 9xx processor.

6. **B.** A motherboard jumper is used to retain or clear CMOS memory on most systems. PATA master/slave jumpering is performed on each drive connected to a PATA port. Some SATA drives can be configured for slower speeds with a jumper block on the drive.

7. **B.** A hyperthreaded CPU processes two execution threads at the same time. Programs that monitor processor activity, such as Windows Task Manager, display a separate icon for the two virtual cores in a hyperthreaded CPU when hyperthreading is enabled in the system BIOS.

8. **C.** In most cases, you should remove the heat sink first. The exception is for some third-party heat sinks that require the motherboard be removed first.

9. **D.** The four-pin fan header uses the fourth pin for speed control, whereas the three-pin fan header provides power and speed monitoring only.

10. **B.** The Intel Core i7 2700K is the only one of the processors listed that can fit into LGA 1155.

11. **D.** Heat sinks supplied with boxed processors have pre-applied thermal material. Remove the tape before installing the heat sink.

12. **C.** A bad CMOS battery will prevent the system from retaining date and time information. Replace the motherboard only if replacing the battery doesn't solve the problem with date and time or other CMOS settings.

This chapter covers the following subjects:

- **Understanding BIOS, CMOS, and Firmware**—This section explains the motherboard's firmware, known as the BIOS. It also describes the relationship between the CMOS and the BIOS.

- **Configuring the System BIOS**—This section demonstrates how to access the BIOS and modify settings, for example, RAM, processor, and video settings.

- **Power-on self-test (POST) and Error Reporting**—This section describes the POST and audible and visible errors that the POST reports.

- **BIOS Updates**—In this section you learn how to upgrade the BIOS through a process known as flashing.

This chapter covers **CompTIA A+ 220-801 objective 1.1** and **CompTIA A+ 220-802 objective 4.2**.

CHAPTER 3

BIOS

The **basic input/output system (BIOS)** is an essential component of the motherboard. This boot firmware, also known as System BIOS, is the first code run by a computer when it is booted. It prepares the machine by testing it during bootup and paves the way for the operating system to start. It tests and initializes components such as the processor, RAM, video card, magnetic disks, and optical disks. If any errors occur, the BIOS reports them as part of the testing stage, known as the **power-on self test (POST)**. The BIOS resides on a ROM chip and stores a setup program that you can access when the computer first boots up. From this program, a user can change settings in the BIOS and upgrade the BIOS as well. In this chapter, you find out about how the BIOS, **CMOS**, and batteries on the motherboard interact and learn how to configure and upgrade the BIOS.

Foundation Topics

Understanding BIOS, CMOS, and Firmware

220-801

Objective:
220-801: 1.1

You know what the CPU does—it does the "thinking" for the computer. But how does the CPU "know" what kinds of drives are connected to the computer? What tells the CPU when the memory is ready to be read or written to? What determines how the USB ports are set or whether an SATA port emulates an IDE port or supports advanced SATA-only features? The answer to all these questions is the BIOS.

The BIOS is an example of firmware (software on a chip). Next to the CPU, the BIOS chip is the most important chip found on the motherboard. Figure 3-1 illustrates the location of the BIOS chip on some typical systems.

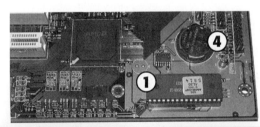

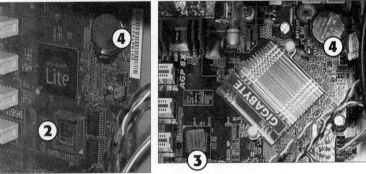

1. DIP-Type socketed BIOS chip
2. PLCC-type socketed BIOS chip
3. Surface-mounted BIOS chip
4. CR2032 CMOS batteries

Figure 3-1 BIOS chips and CMOS batteries on typical motherboards.

The BIOS is a complex piece of firmware ("software on a chip") that provides support for the following devices and features of your system:

- Selection and configuration of storage devices connected to the motherboard's host adapters, such as hard drives, USB drives, floppy drives, and optical (CD, DVD, and BD) drives

- Configuration of onboard memory (RAM)

- Configuration of built-in ports, such as SATA, eSATA, PATA, and floppy disk storage devices; USB and IEEE-1394 ports; and legacy ports (serial, parallel, and PS/2 mouse) if present

- Configuration of integrated (built in to the motherboard chipset) audio, network, and graphics features when present

- Configuration of AGP, PCI, and PCIe slots

- Selection and configuration of special motherboard features, such as memory error correction, antivirus protection, and fast memory access

- Support for different CPU types, speeds, and special features, including virtualization

- Power management

- Intrusion detection

- Security features such as passwords and drive encryption (TPM)

- Hardware monitoring (processor temperature, voltage levels, and fan performance)

- Direct access to the Web or other services without booting the computer

Without the BIOS, your computer would be a collection of metal and plastic parts that couldn't interact with one another or do much of anything but gather dust.

The BIOS also performs two other important tasks:

- It runs the power-on self test (POST) when the system is started.

- It establishes a list of locations that can be used by an operating system to boot the computer (hard disk, optical drive, USB drive, floppy drive, and network) and turns over control of the system by using the Bootstrap loader after completing its startup tasks.

The BIOS doesn't do its job alone. It works with two other important components:

- CMOS memory
- Motherboard battery (also called the CMOS battery; refer to Figures 3-1 and 3-2)

In the following sections, you learn more about how these components work together to control system startup and onboard hardware.

> **NOTE**   For much more information about BIOS functions, beep codes, and upgrades, see the BIOS chapter in the 20th edition of Scott Mueller's *Upgrading and Repairing PCs*.

Standard settings are configured by the motherboard or system vendor but can be overridden by the user to enable the system to work with different types of hardware or to provide higher performance. CMOS memory, also referred to as nonvolatile memory, is used to store BIOS settings. CMOS memory should not be confused with system memory (RAM); CMOS memory is built in to the motherboard and cannot be removed by the user.

The contents of CMOS memory are retained as long as a constant flow of DC current from a battery on the motherboard is provided. Some typical CMOS batteries are shown in Figure 3-2.

Figure 3-2   The CR2032 lithium watch battery (center) is the most common battery used to maintain CMOS settings in recent systems, but other batteries, such as the Dallas Semiconductor DS12887A clock/battery chip (left) and the AA-size 3.6 volt (V) Eternacell (right), have also been used in older systems.

When the battery starts to fail, the clock starts to lose time. Complete battery failure causes the loss of all CMOS configuration information (such as drive types, settings for onboard ports, CPU and memory speeds, and much more). When this takes place, the CMOS information must be reentered each time the system is started until you install a new battery and reenter all CMOS configuration information by using the CMOS configuration program.

Because the battery that maintains settings can fail at any time, and viruses and power surges can also affect the CMOS configuration, you should record important information before it is lost.

TIP   To document BIOS settings for easy reference, use a digital camera set for macro (closeup) mode and turn off the flash.

Configuring the System BIOS

220-801

Objective:
220-801: 1.1

The system BIOS has default settings provided by the system or motherboard maker, but as a system is built up with storage devices, memory modules, adapter cards, and other components, it is usually necessary to alter the standard settings.

To perform this task, the system assembler must use the BIOS setup program to make changes and save them to the CMOS. Originally, the BIOS setup program was run from a bootable floppy disk, but for many years virtually all system BIOS chips have included the setup program.

Accessing the BIOS Setup Program

On most systems built since the late 1980s, the BIOS configuration program is stored in the BIOS chip itself. Just press the key or key combination displayed onscreen (or described in the manual) to get started.

Although these keystrokes vary from system to system, the most popular keys on current systems include the escape (Esc) key, the Delete (Del) key, the F1 key, the F2 key, the F10 key, and various combinations of Ctrl+Alt+ another specified key.

Most recent systems display the key(s) necessary to start the BIOS setup program at startup, as shown in Figure 3-3. However, if you don't know which key to press to start your computer's BIOS setup program, check the system or motherboard manual for the correct key(s).

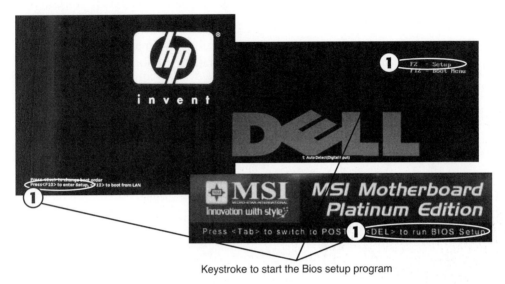

Keystroke to start the Bios setup program

Figure 3-3   The splash screens used by many recent systems display the keystrokes needed to start the BIOS setup program.

NOTE   Because the settings you make in the BIOS setup program are stored in the nonvolatile CMOS, the settings are often called CMOS settings or BIOS settings.

The following sections review the typical setup process, using systems running Intel Sandy Bridge Core i5 and AMD Phenom II X6 processors.

CAUTION   BIOS programs vary widely, but the screens used in the following sections are representative of the options available on typical recent systems; your system might have similar options but place the settings on different screens than those shown here. Laptop and corporate desktop systems generally offer fewer options than those shown here.

Be sure to consult the manual that came with your computer or motherboard before toying with the settings you find here. Fiddling with the settings can improve performance, but it can also wreak havoc on an otherwise healthy PC if you don't know what you're doing. Be warned!

UEFI and Traditional BIOS

Many recent computers now use a new type of firmware called the Unified Extensible Firmware Initiative (UEFI) to display a mouse-driven GUI menu of additional options when you start the computer. UEFI menus can include options for surfing the web, backing up your hard disk, or launching games without the need to boot your operating system, as well as access to the BIOS setup program. Figures 3-4 and 3-5 illustrate two examples of options included in UEFI firmware.

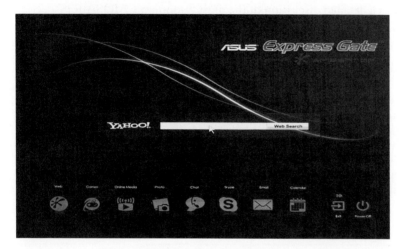

Figure 3-4   UEFI firmware offering web and media access without booting the OS.

Figure 3-5   UEFI firmware that includes BIOS settings (main menu shown).

On a system that uses UEFI firmware, you might start the BIOS setup program by selecting Settings or Setup from the UEFI menu, or you might use a keystroke to start the setup when prompted. In either case, UEFI BIOS offers similar settings to those used by a traditional BIOS along with additional options (refer to Figures 3-4 and 3-5).

BIOS Settings Overview

Table 3-1 provides a detailed discussion of the most important CMOS/BIOS settings. Use this table as a quick reference to the settings you need to make or verify in any system. Examples of these and other settings are provided in the following sections.

Table 3-1   Major CMOS/BIOS Settings

Option	Settings	Notes
Boot Sequence	Hard disk, optical (CD/DVD, Blu-ray), USB, floppy, network ROM; order as wanted	To boot from bootable Windows or diagnostic CDs or DVDs, place the CD or DVD (optical) drive before the hard drive in the boot sequence. To boot from a bootable USB device, place the USB device before the hard drive in the boot sequence. You can enable or disable additional boot devices on some systems.
Memory Configuration	By SPD or Auto (default); Manual settings (Frequency, CAS Latency [CL], Fast R-2-R turnaround, and so on) also available	Provides stable operation using the settings stored in memory by the vendor. Use manual settings for overclocking (running memory at faster than normal speeds; see Chapter 8, "Customized PCs and Multimedia Devices," for details) or to enable memory of different speeds to be used safely by selecting slower settings.
CPU Clock and Frequency	Automatically detected on most recent systems	Faster or higher settings overclock the system but could cause instability (see Chapter 8 for details). Some systems default to low values if the system doesn't start properly.
Hardware Monitor	Enable display for all fans plugged in to the motherboard	Also known as PC Health on some systems; can be monitored from within Windows with vendor-supplied or third-party utilities.
Onboard Audio, Modem, or Network	Enable or disable	Enable if you don't use add-on cards for any of these functions; disable each setting before installing a replacement card. Some systems include two network adapters.
PS/2 Mouse	Varies with mouse type	Disable if you use USB mouse; some systems use a motherboard jumper.

Option	Settings	Notes
USB Legacy	Enable if USB keyboard is used	Enables USB keyboard to work outside Windows.
Serial Ports	Disable unused ports; use default settings for port you use	Avoid setting two serial ports to use the same IRQ.
Parallel Port	Disable unused port; use EPP/ECP mode with default IRQ/DMA if parallel port or device is connected	Compatible with almost any recent parallel printer or device; be sure to use an IEEE-1284-compatible printer cable.
USB Function	Enable	If motherboard supports USB 2.0 (Hi-Speed USB) ports, be sure to enable USB 2.0 function and load USB 2.0 drivers in Windows.
USB 3.0 Function	Enable	USB 3.0 ports also support USB 2.0 and USB 1.1 devices. Disable if USB 3.0 drivers are not available for operating system.
Keyboard	NumLock, auto-repeat rate/delay	Leave at defaults (NumLock On) unless keyboard has problems.
Plug-and-Play OS	Enable for all except some Linux distributions, Windows NT, MS-DOS	When enabled, Windows configures devices.
Primary VGA BIOS	Varies	Select the primary graphics card type (PCIe or AGP) unless you have PCIe or AGP and PCI graphics (video) cards installed that won't work unless PCI is set as primary.
Shadowing	Varies	Enable shadowing for video BIOS; leave other shadowing disabled.
Quiet Boot	Varies	Disable to display system configuration information at startup.
Boot-Time Diagnostic Screen	Varies	Enable to display system configuration information at startup.
Virtualization	Varies	Enable to run hardware-based virtualization programs, such as Windows Virtual PC, so that you can run multiple operating systems, each in its own window.
Power Management (Menu)	Enable unless you have problems with devices	Enable CPU fan settings to receive warnings of CPU fan failure.

Table 3-1 Continued

Option	Settings	Notes
S1 or S3 standby	Enable S3	Use S1 (which saves minimal power) only if you use devices that do not properly wake up from S3 standby.
AC Pwr Loss Restart	Enable restart or Full on	Prevents the system from staying down if a power failure takes place.
Wake on LAN (WOL)	Enable if you use WOL-compatible network card or modem	WOL-compatible cards use a small cable between the card and the motherboard. Some integrated network ports also support WOL.
User/Power-On Password	Blocks system from starting if password is not known	Enable if physical security settings are needed, but be sure to record the password in a secure place.
Setup Password	Blocks access to setup if password is not known	Both passwords can be cleared on both systems if CMOS RAM is cleared.
Write-Protect Boot Sector	Varies	Enable for normal use, but disable when installing drives or using a multiboot system. Helps prevent accidental formatting but might not stop third-party disk prep software from working.
Boot Virus Detection (Antivirus Boot Sector)	Enable	Stops true infections but allows multiboot configuration.
Floppy Drive	Usually 3.5-inch 1.44MB	Set to actual drive type/capacity; some systems default to other sizes. Disable if no drive is present.
PATA (IDE), SATA Drives	Varies	Auto-detects drive type and settings at startup time. Select CD/DVD for CD/DVD/Blu-ray drive; select None if drive is not present or to disable an installed drive.
SATA Drive configuration	IDE, AHCI, RAID	IDE setting emulates PATA drives. To take advantage of hot-swapping and native command queuing (NCQ) to improve performance, select AHCI. Use RAID if the drive will be used as part of a RAID array.

Automatic Configuration of BIOS/CMOS Settings

As you can see from Table 3-1, there are many options to select when configuring the BIOS. Many BIOS versions enable you to automatically configure your system with a choice of these options from the main menu:

- BIOS defaults (also referred to as Original/Fail-Safe on some systems)
- Setup defaults (also referred to as Optimal on some systems)
- Turbo

These options primarily deal with performance configuration settings in the BIOS, such as memory timings, memory cache, and the like. The settings used by each BIOS setup option are customized by the motherboard or system manufacturer.

Use BIOS defaults to troubleshoot the system because these settings are conservative in memory timings and other options. Normally, the setup defaults provide better performance. Turbo, if present, speeds the memory refresh rate used by the system. As you view the setup screens in this chapter, you'll note these options are listed.

CAUTION   If you use automatic setup after you make manual changes, all your manual changes will be overridden. Use one of these settings first (try Turbo or Setup Defaults), and then make any other changes you want.

With many recent systems, you can select Optimal or Setup defaults, save your changes and exit, and the system will work acceptably. However, to configure drive settings, USB settings, or to enable or disable ports, you also need to work with individual BIOS settings, such as the ones shown in the following sections.

TIP   On typical systems, you set numerical settings, such as date and time, by scrolling through allowable values with keys such as + and − or page up/page down. However, to select settings with a limited range of options, such as enable/disable or choices from a menu, press the Enter or right-arrow key on the keyboard, and choose the option you want from the available choices.

Main Menu

When you start the BIOS configuration program for your system, you might see a menu similar to the CMOS Setup Utility menu shown in Figure 3-6. (Some systems with UEFI might use a graphical version such as the one shown in Figure 3.5.) From this menu, you can go to any menu, select default settings, save changes, or exit the CMOS setup menu.

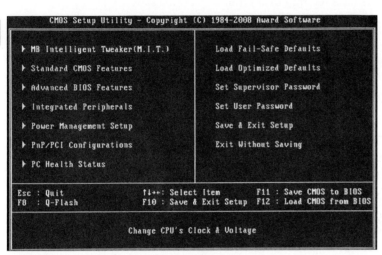

Figure 3-6 A typical CMOS Setup Utility main menu.

TIP If you need to quickly find a particular BIOS setting and don't have the manual for the system or the motherboard, visit the system or motherboard vendor's website and download the manual. In most cases, especially with a motherboard-specific manual, the BIOS screens are illustrated. Most vendors provide the manuals in Adobe Reader (PDF) format.

Standard Features/Settings

The Standard Features/Settings menu (see Figure 3-7) is typically used to configure the system's date and time as well as drives connected to SATA, PATA (ATA/IDE), and floppy drive interfaces on the motherboard.

NOTE Some BIOS setup programs open to this menu and provide access to other menus with a top-level menu bar.

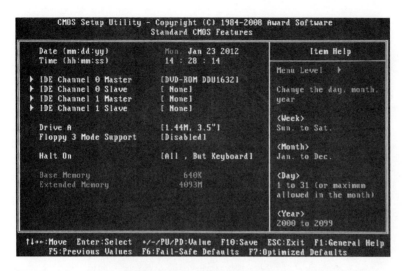

Figure 3-7   A typical CMOS Standard Features/Settings menu.

PATA and SATA BIOS Configuration

Most recent systems automatically detect the drive connected to each PATA and SATA host adapter, as shown earlier in Figure 3-7. However, some systems might use manual entry of the correct settings instead. These are usually listed on the drive's faceplate or in the instruction manual. See Chapter 12, "Storage Devices," for details.

CAUTION   Although some users recommend that you configure the settings for hard drives to user-defined, which will list the exact settings for each hard drive, this can cause a major problem if your BIOS settings are lost due to a virus, battery failure, or other causes. Unless you are trying to shave a few seconds off boot time by preventing the BIOS from detecting each drive, I highly recommend you let your computer do the work by using the Auto feature. If you use manual configuration, be sure to choose LBA mode as the drive access type. Using Large or CHS limits the available capacity of the hard disk.

Floppy Drive BIOS Configuration

On systems that have an onboard floppy drive, the floppy drive type must be selected manually if a different type of floppy drive is installed, or if the floppy drive is not present (see Figure 3-8). If you use a USB floppy drive, select Disabled on this dialog.

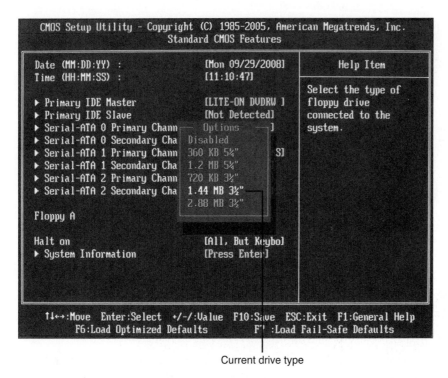

Current drive type

Figure 3-8   Viewing available floppy disk drive types.

TIP   If your system supports an internal floppy drive but you don't use the drive, you might be able to disable the floppy controller within the BIOS setup. In such cases, you will no longer need to select Disabled from the menu shown in Figure 3-8.

System Information

Some systems display system information such as processor type, clock speed, cache memory size, installed memory (RAM), and BIOS information from within the BIOS (see Figure 3-9). Use this information to help determine whether a system needs a processor, memory, or BIOS update.

Boot Settings and Boot Sequence

Many computers include settings that control how the system boots and the sequence in which drives are checked for bootable operating system files. Depending on the system, these settings might be part of an Advanced Settings menu or might be in separate menus, such as the Boot Settings menu shown in Figure 3-10 and the Boot Sequence menu shown in Figure 3-11.

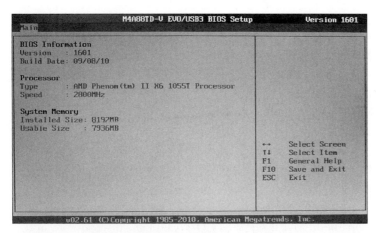

Figure 3-9 Viewing system information.

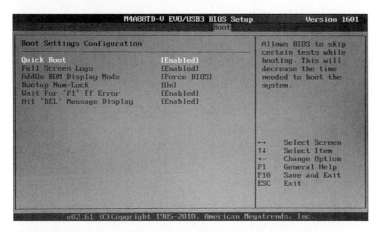

Figure 3-10 Typical boot settings options on a recent system.

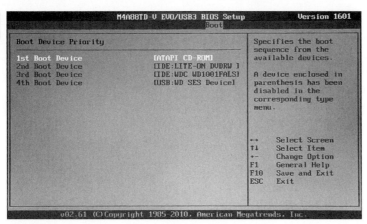

Figure 3-11 A typical Boot Sequence submenu configured to permit booting from a CD/DVD before the hard disk.

Enabling Quick Boot skips memory and drive tests to enable faster startup. Enabling Boot Up Num-Lock turns on the keyboard's NumLock option. Enabling Boot Sector Protection (not shown) provides some protection against boot sector computer viruses.

The Boot Sequence submenu shown in Figure 3-11 is used to adjust the order in which drives are checked for bootable media. For faster booting, set the hard disk with system files as the first boot device. However, if you want to have the option to boot from an optical (CD/DVD/Blu-ray), USB flash or hard disk drive, or floppy drive for diagnostics or operating system installations, put those drives before the SATA or PATA hard disk.

NOTE   Even when the first boot drive is set up as CD/DVD, some discs will prompt the user to press a key to boot from the CD/DVD drive when a bootable disk is found. Otherwise, the system checks the next available device for boot files.

Integrated Ports and Peripherals

Typical desktop systems are loaded with onboard ports and features, and the menus shown in Figures 3-12, 3-13, and 3-14 are typical of the BIOS menus used to enable, disable, and configure storage, audio, network, and USB ports.

SATA and PATA/IDE Configuration

Use the SATA configuration options (such as those shown in Figure 3-12) to enable or disable SATA and eSATA ports and to configure SATA host adapters to run in compatible (emulating PATA), native (AHCI), or RAID modes. AHCI supports Native Command Queuing (NCQ) for faster performance and permits hot-swapping of eSATA drives.

Use the PATA configuration menu (see Figure 3-13) to enable or disable PATA/IDE host adapters and to enable or disable bus-mastering. Bus-mastering should be enabled because disabling it causes drive access to be slow. When bus-mastering (the default on most systems) is enabled, the operating system must load chipset-specific drivers to permit this option to work. Some systems (but not the one shown in Figure 3-13) have two or more PATA host adapters and support RAID functions with PATA drives.

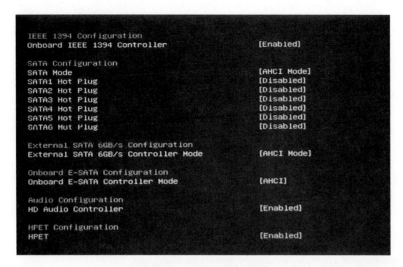

Figure 3-12   A UEFI configuration dialog for SATA, eSATA, IEEE-1394, and HD audio.

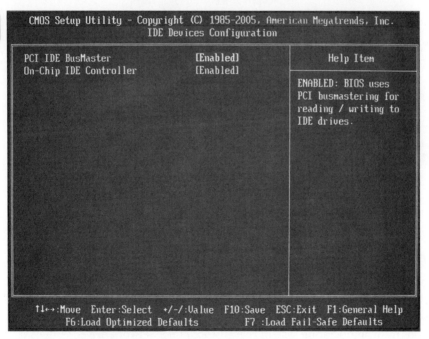

Figure 3-13   Typical PATA configuration menu.

To learn more about RAID configuration, see "Creating an ATA or SATA RAID Array," in Chapter 12.

> **TIP** To ensure that the PATA/IDE bus-mastering feature works properly, install the most up-to-date drivers available for the motherboard. Check the motherboard or system vendor's website for the latest drivers for the version of Windows or other operating system in use.

USB Host Adapters

Most systems have separate settings for the USB controller and USB 2.0 controller, or for USB (2.0) and USB 3.0 (a.k.a. SuperSpeed) controllers (on systems that have USB 3.0 ports). If you don't enable USB 2.0 or USB 3.0 in your system BIOS, all your system's USB ports will run at the next lower speed. Figure 3-14 shows how to enable or disable an onboard USB controller.

Figure 3-14 Configuring a USB controller.

IEEE-1394, Audio, Ethernet Ports

The Onboard Devices submenu, shown in Figure 3-15, is used to enable or disable ports such as IEEE-1394 (FireWire), audio, and Ethernet LAN ports (this system has two). The onboard LAN option ROM is disabled on this system. Enable it if you want to boot from an operating system that is stored on a network drive.

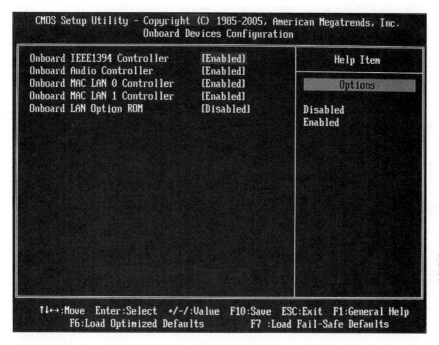

Figure 3-15 A typical Onboard Devices submenu.

I/O Devices

Most systems that include legacy ports such as floppy, serial (COM), and parallel port (LPT) use a separate BIOS settings menu for configuration, as in the I/O Devices submenu in Figure 3-16. Some systems might also have a setting for the PS/2 mouse port on this or another CMOS/BIOS menu.

The COM (serial) port is disabled on this system because there are no devices connected to it. (Most devices that formerly used COM ports, such as modems, pointing devices, and printers, now use USB ports; similarly, most mice that formerly used PS/2 ports now use USB ports.) The parallel (LPT) port is enabled because it is used by a printer.

NOTE You should disable ports that are not used to make it easier for the system to assign other ports, such as the ones in the Onboard Devices menu, their own hardware resources.

To learn more about ECP, EPP, IRQ, and DMA settings for parallel ports, see Chapter 6, "I/O and Input Ports and Devices."

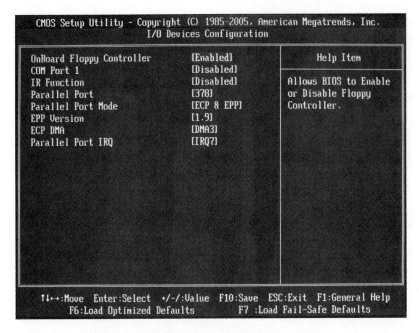

Figure 3-16   A typical I/O Devices submenu.

Power Management

Although Windows includes power management features, the BIOS controls how any given system responds to standby or power-out conditions. Figure 3-17 illustrates a typical power management menu.

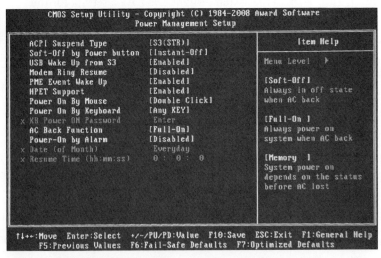

Figure 3-17   Typical power management configuration menu.

ACPI is the power management function used in modern systems, replacing the older APM standard; it should be enabled. Most systems offer two ACPI standby states: S1/POS (power on standby) and S3/STR (suspend to RAM). Use S3/STR whenever possible because it uses much less power when the system is idle than S1/POS.

You can also configure your system power button, specify how to restart your system if AC power is lost and specify how to wake up a system from standby, sleep, or hibernation modes. Some systems display these settings in the same dialog as power management, whereas others use a separate dialog or submenu.

PnP/PCI Configurations

The PnP/PCI Configuration dialog shown in Figure 3-18 is used to specify which graphics adapter is primary (PCI Express versus PCI or, on older systems, AGP versus PCI), the IRQ settings to use for PCI slots, and the settings for the PCI latency timer.

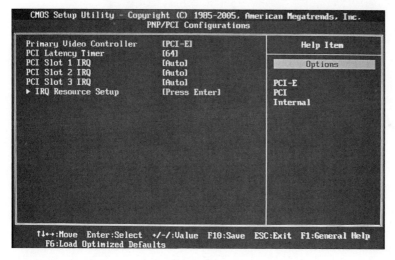

Figure 3-18 Configuring PnP/PCI settings.

Generally, the default settings do not need to be changed. However, if you need to make a PCI graphics adapter card—rather than a PCI Express or AGP card—the primary graphics adapter, be sure to select the correct video card type.

Hardware Monitor

As hot as a small room containing a PC can get, it's a whole lot hotter inside the PC itself. Excessive heat is the enemy of system stability and shortens the life of your hardware. Adding fans can help, but if they fail, you have problems. See Chapter 4, "Power Supplies and System Cooling," for more information.

The Hardware Monitor BIOS dialog (sometimes referred to as PC Health) is a common feature in most recent systems. It helps you make sure that your computer's temperature and voltage conditions are at safe levels for your computer (see Figure 3-19), and it sometimes also includes the Chassis Intrusion feature. Use this dialog to assure that cooling fans on the CPU and installed in the system are working correctly. Windows-based hardware monitoring programs can also be used to display this information during normal system operation.

```
                    M4A88TD-V EVO/USB3 BIOS Setup        Version 1601
                              Power

  Hardware Monitor                              CPU Temperature

  CPU Temperature            [43°C/109°F]
  MB Temperature             [30°C/86°F]

  CPU Fan Speed              [3970RPM]
  Chassis Fan Speed          [2800RPM]
  Power Fan Speed            [1083RPM]

  VCORE  Voltage             [ 1.416V]
  3.3V  Voltage              [ 3.252V]
  5V  Voltage                [ 5.040V]
  12V  Voltage               [12.230V]      ←→      Select Screen
                                            ↑↓      Select Item
  CPU Q-Fan Function         [Disabled]     +-      Change Option
  Chassis Q-Fan Function     [Disabled]     F1      General Help
                                            F10     Save and Exit
                                            ESC     Exit


          v02.61 (C)Copyright 1985-2010, American Megatrends, Inc.
```

Figure 3-19   A typical Hardware Monitor screen.

Processor and Memory Configuration

Some desktop and laptop systems made for gaming and customization enable you to adjust processor speed, memory timings, voltages, and other settings from within the BIOS to improve performance. This process is known as overclocking and is covered in Chapter 8.

Virtualization Support

Virtualization is the capability to run multiple operating systems on a single computer at the same time. Although virtualization does not require processor support, virtualization programs such as Windows Virtual PC and recent versions of VMware Workstation provide much better performance on systems that have hardware-assisted virtualization support enabled.

For a system to support hardware-assisted virtualization, it must include a CPU that supports virtualization and virtualization must be enabled in the system BIOS.

NOTE Intel processors that include VT-x technology support hardware-assisted virtualization. AMD processors that include AMD-V technology support hardware-assisted virtualization. To determine whether a computer running Windows can support hardware-assisted virtualization, download and run havdetectiontool.exe, available from the Microsoft Download Center at www.microsoft.com.

Intel-based systems with VT support might have two entries for virtualization, as shown in Figure 3-20. Intel Virtualization Tech (also known as VT or VT-x) must be enabled for hardware-assisted virtualization to be supported. Intel VT with Directed I/O (VT-D Tech) can also be enabled to help improve I/O performance, although processors that support VT-x vary in their levels of VT-D support.

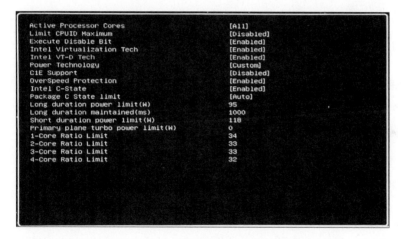

Figure 3-20 Intel VT and VT-D have been enabled on this system.

AMD-based systems that support hardware-assisted virtualization feature a single BIOS setting that might be labeled Virtualization, Secure Virtual Machine Mode, or SVM (see Figure 3-21).

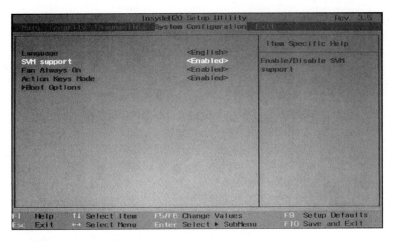

Figure 3-21   AMD-V has been enabled on this system.

Security Features

Security features of various types are scattered around the typical system BIOS dialogs. Features and their locations vary by system and might include

- **BIOS password**—BIOS Settings Password or Security dialogs

- **Power-on password**—Configured through the Security dialog

- **Chassis intrusion**—Various locations

- **Boot sector protection**—Advanced BIOS Features dialog

- **LoJack for Laptops**—Embedded in firmware; not managed with BIOS dialogs

- **TPM (trusted program module)**—Security dialog

Use the BIOS password to provide access to BIOS setup dialogs only for those with the password. The power-on password option prevents anyone without the password from starting the system. Note that these options can be defeated by opening the system and clearing the CMOS memory.

The Chassis Intrusion option, when enabled, displays a warning on startup that the system has been opened.

Boot sector protection, found primarily on older systems, protects the default hard disk's boot sector from being changed by viruses or other unwanted programs. Depending on the implementation, this option might need to be disabled before an operating system installation or upgrade.

A TPM module is used by the Windows Vista and Windows 7 Ultimate BitLocker full-disk encryption feature to protect the contents of the system hard disk (Vista) or any specified drive (7). Although many corporate laptops include a built-in TPM module, desktop computers and servers might include a connection for an optional TPM. For more information about using BitLocker, see Chapter 14, "Using and Managing Windows."

LoJack for Laptops is a popular security feature embedded in the laptop BIOSes of a number of systems and can be added to other systems. It consists of two components: a BIOS-resident component and the Computrace Agent, which is activated by LoJack when a computer is reported as stolen. To learn more about LoJack for Laptops, see www.absolute.com/en/lojackforlaptops/home.aspx.

Exiting the BIOS and Saving/Discarding Changes

When you exit the BIOS setup program, you can elect to save configuration changes or discard them. Choose the option to save changes (see Figure 3-22a) if you made changes you want to keep. Choose the option to discard changes (see Figure 3-22b) if you were "just looking" and did not intend to make any changes. When you exit the BIOS setup program with either option, the system restarts.

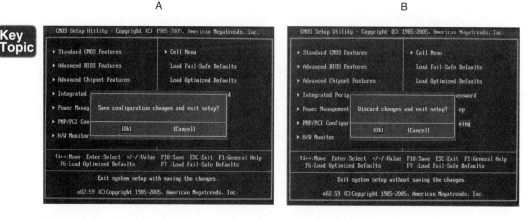

Figure 3-22   Typical exit dialogs: saving changes (a) and discarding changes (b).

Power-On Self Test (POST) and Error Reporting

220-802

Objective:
220-802: 4.2

Every time you turn on a PC, the BIOS performs one of its most important jobs: the POST. The POST portion of the BIOS enables the BIOS to find and report errors in the computer's hardware.

The POST checks the following parts of the computer:

- The CPU and the POST ROM portion of the BIOS
- The system timer
- Video display (graphics) card
- Memory
- The keyboard
- The disk drives

In a properly working system, the POST detects no errors. However, if the POST detects a serious or fatal error, it stops the boot process. During the POST process, the BIOS uses any one of several methods to report problems:

- Beep codes
- POST error messages (displayed on the monitor)
- POST (hex) error codes

The next sections describe each method in detail.

> **NOTE** A *fatal error* is an error that is so serious that the computer cannot continue the boot process. A fatal error includes a problem with the CPU, the POST ROM, the system timer, or memory. The *serious error* that beep codes report is a problem with your video display card or circuit.

Beep Codes

Beep codes are used by most BIOS versions to indicate either a fatal error or a serious error. Beep codes vary by the BIOS maker. Although some vendors create their own BIOS chips and firmware, most major brands of computers and virtually all "clones" use a BIOS made by one of the "Big Three" BIOS vendors: American Megatrends (AMI), Phoenix Technologies, and Award Software (now owned by Phoenix Technologies).

As you might expect, the beep codes and philosophies used by these three companies vary a great deal. AMI, for example, uses beep codes for more than 10 fatal errors. It also uses eight beeps to indicate a defective or missing video card. Phoenix uses beep codes for both defects and normal procedures (but has no beep code for a video problem), and the Award BIOS has only a single beep code (one long, two short), indicating a problem with video.

Because beep codes do not report all possible problems during the startup process, you can't rely exclusively on beep codes to help you detect and solve system problems. Also, beep codes can be heard only on systems with built-in speakers.

The most common beep codes you're likely to encounter are listed in Table 3-2.

Table 3-2   Common System Errors and Their Beep Codes

Problem	Phoenix BIOS	Award BIOS	AMI BIOS	IBM BIOS
Memory	Beep sequences: 1-3-4-1 1-3-4-3 1-4-1-1	Beeping (other than 2 long, 1 short)	1 or 3 or 11 beeps 1 long, 3 short beeps	(None)
Video	(None)	2 long, 1 short beep	8 beeps 1 long, 8 short beeps	1 long, 3 short beeps, or 1 beep
Processor or motherboard	Beep sequence: 1-2-2-3	High-frequency beeps Repeating high-low beeps	5 beeps or 9 beeps	1 long, 1 short beep

For additional beep codes, see the following resources:

- **AMI BIOS**—www.ami.com/support/bios.cfm
- **Phoenix BIOS**—www.phoenix.com/
- **IBM, Dell, Acer, other brands**—www.bioscentral.com; http://wimsbios.com

NOTE   Don't mix up your boops and beeps! Many systems play a single short boop (usually a bit different in tone than a beep) when the system boots successfully. This is normal.

POST Error Messages

Most BIOS versions do an excellent job of displaying POST error messages indicating what the problem with the system is. These messages can indicate problems with memory, keyboards, hard disk drives, and other components. For example, if the CMOS memory used to store system setup information is corrupt (possibly because of a battery failure or because the CMOS memory has been cleared), systems display a message such as the following:

- System CMOS Checksum Bad - Run Setup—Phoenix BIOS
- CMOS Checksum Invalid—AMI BIOS
- CMOS Checksum Error - Defaults Loaded—Award BIOS

Some systems document these messages in their manuals, or you can go to the BIOS vendors' websites or the third-party sites listed earlier in this chapter for more information.

NOTE   Keep in mind that the system almost always stops after the first error, so if a system has more than one serious or fatal error, the first problem might stop the boot process before the video card has been initialized to display error messages.

POST Hex Codes

There are beep codes and text messages to tell you that there's a problem with your computer, but there's also a third way your PC can let you know it needs help: by transmitting hexadecimal codes to an I/O port address (usually 80h) that indicate the progress of testing and booting. The hexadecimal codes output by the BIOS change rapidly during a normal startup process as different milestones in the boot process are reached. These codes provide vital clues about what has gone wrong when your system won't boot and you don't have a beep code or onscreen message to help you. It would be handy if systems included some way to view these codes, but most do not. (A few systems include a four-LED header cable that displays boot progress, but this is only a partial solution for a system that won't start properly.)

To monitor these codes, you need a POST card such as the one shown in Figure 3-23, available from a variety of vendors, including Elston Systems (www.elstonsystems.com), Sintech (www.sintech.cn), Ultra-X (www.ultra-x.com), and many others. The POST card shown in Figure 3-23 plugs into PCI slots, but other versions are available for use in PCIe slots, laptop mini-PCI and mini-PCIe slots, the long-obsolete ISA slot, and LPT (printer) ports.

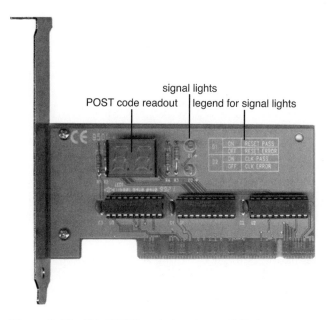

Figure 3-23   This POST card plugs in to a PCI slot.

The simplest ones have a two-digit LED area that displays the hex codes, whereas more complicated (and expensive) models display the code's meaning, and some also perform additional built-in tests.

The same hex code has different meanings to different BIOS versions. For example, POST code 31h means "display (video) memory read/write test" on an AMI BIOS, but it means "test base and extended memory" on the Award BIOS, and it is not used on Phoenix BIOS. As with other types of error messages, check your manual, the BIOS manufacturer's website, or one of the third-party resources earlier in this chapter for the meaning of any given code.

> **TIP**   The worst time to learn how to interpret a POST card is when your system is
> sick. On the other hand, the best way to learn to use a POST card is to plug it into a
> healthy system and watch the codes change during a normal system startup. Typically,
> the codes change quickly until the final code (often FF) is reached and the system
> starts. On a defective system, the codes will pause or stop when a defective item on
> the system is tested. The cards don't need to be left in systems routinely.

BIOS Updates

220-801

Objective:
220-801: 1.1

The BIOS chip can be regarded as the "glue" that binds the hardware to the operating system. If the BIOS doesn't recognize the operating system or the hardware it
communicates with, you're sure to have problems.

Because the BIOS chip bridges hardware to the operating system, you need to
update the BIOS whenever your current BIOS version is unable to properly support

- New hardware, such as large SATA and PATA/IDE hard drives and different
  types of removable-storage drives

- New CPU models

- Memory modules with different capacities or timings

- New operating systems and features (such as virtualization or power
  management)

- New BIOS options

BIOS updates can also be used to solve problems with power management or other
hardware-related issues.

A computer that is more than 1 year old or that is a candidate for a new processor
might need a BIOS update. In the 1980s into the early 1990s, a BIOS update
required a physical chip swap and, sometimes, reprogramming the chip with a device
called an electrically erasable programmable read-only memory (EEPROM) burner.
If the replacement or reprogrammed BIOS chip was installed incorrectly into the
socket, it could be destroyed.

Fortunately, since the mid-1990s, a BIOS update can now be performed with software. The Flash BIOS chips in use on practically every recent system contain a special type of memory that can be changed through a software download from the system or motherboard maker.

Although Flash BIOS updates are easier to perform than the older replace-the-chip style, you still need to be careful. An incomplete or incorrect BIOS update will prevent your system from being accessed. No BIOS, no boot! Regardless of the method, for maximum safety, follow these initial steps:

Step 1.   Back up important data.

Step 2.   Record the current BIOS configuration, especially hard disk settings as discussed earlier in this chapter.

CAUTION   BIOS configuration information might need to be reentered after a BIOS update, especially if you must install a different chip.

Flash BIOS Update

So, you've decided you need a Flash BIOS update. Where do you get it? Don't ask the BIOS manufacturers (Phoenix, AMI, and Award/Phoenix). They don't sell BIOS updates because their basic products are modified by motherboard and system vendors. Following are the general steps to locate a Flash BIOS update and install it:

Step 1.   For major brands of computers, go to the vendor's website and look for "downloads" or "tech support" links. The BIOS updates are listed by system model and by version; avoid beta (prerelease) versions.

TIP   If your system is a generic system (that is, it came with a mainboard or motherboard manual and other component manuals rather than a full system manual), you need to contact the motherboard maker.

To determine the motherboard's make and model, you can download and run Belarc Advisor (free for personal use) from www.belarc.com/free_download.html.

See the following websites for additional help:

- Wim's BIOS page (www.wimsbios.com)

- eSupport (www.biosagentplus.com)

- American Megatrend's BIOS Support page (www.ami.com/support/bios.cfm)

You can also buy replacement flash BIOS code from www.eSupport.com if you cannot get updated BIOS code from your system or motherboard vendor.

Step 2.   Locate the correct BIOS update for your system or motherboard. For generic motherboards, Wim's BIOS page also has links to the motherboard vendors' websites.

Step 3.   Determine the installation media needed to install the BIOS image. Many recent systems use a Windows-based installer, but some use a bootable CD, whereas older systems use a bootable floppy disk. Some systems with UEFI firmware can install a BIOS update from floppy or CD media from within a UEFI menu.

Step 4.   Be sure to download all files needed to install the BIOS image. In most cases, a download contains the appropriate loader program and the BIOS image, but for some motherboards, you might also need to download a separate loader program. If the website has instructions posted, print or save them for reference.

For installation from bootable media, see Steps 5 and 6.

Step 5.   If you need to create bootable media, follow the vendor's instructions to create the media and place the loader and BIOS image files on the media.

Step 6.   To install from bootable media, make sure the drive is the first item in the BIOS boot sequence. Insert or connect your media, and restart the system. If prompted, press a key to start the upgrade process. Some upgrades run automatically, others require you to choose the image from a menu, and still others require the actual filename of the BIOS. The BIOS update might also prompt you to save your current BIOS image. Choose this option if possible so that you have a copy of your current BIOS in case there's a problem. After the process starts, it takes approximately 3 minutes to rewrite the contents of the BIOS chip with the updated information.

For installation from Windows, see Step 5a and Step 6a.

Step 5a.   Close all Windows programs before starting the update process.

Step 6a.   Navigate to the folder containing the BIOS update, and double-click it to start the update process. Follow the prompts onscreen to complete the process. It takes approximately 3 minutes to rewrite the contents of the BIOS chip with the updated information.

CAUTION   While performing a Flash upgrade, make sure you don't turn off the power to your PC and that you keep children or pets away from the computer to prevent an accidental shutdown. (Read: Your four-year-old decides to unplug the computer.) Wait for a message indicating the BIOS update has been completed before you even *think* about touching the computer. If the power goes out during the Flash update, the BIOS chip could be rendered useless.

Step 7.   Remove the media and restart the system to use your new BIOS features. Reconfigure the BIOS settings if necessary.

TIP   Some motherboards have a jumper on the motherboard that can be set to write-protect the Flash BIOS. Take a quick look at your documentation before you start the process, and disable this jumper first. Then, reenable the write-protect jumper after you finish the upgrade.

Recovering from a Failed BIOS Update

If the primary system BIOS is damaged, keep in mind that some motherboard vendors offer dual BIOS chips on some products. You can switch to the secondary BIOS if the primary BIOS stops working.

If you use the wrong Flash BIOS file to update your BIOS, or if the update process doesn't finish, your system can't start. You might need to contact the system or motherboard maker for service or purchase a replacement BIOS chip.

Some BIOSes contain a "mini-BIOS" that can be reinstalled from a reserved part of the chip. Systems with this feature have a jumper on the motherboard called the **Flash recovery jumper.**

To use this feature, download the correct Flash BIOS, make the floppy disk, and take it to the computer with the defective BIOS. Set the jumper to Recovery, insert the floppy disk, and rerun the setup process. Listen for beeps and watch for the drive light to run during this process because the video won't work. Turn off the computer, reset the jumper to Normal, and restart the computer.

If the update can't be installed, your motherboard might have a jumper that write-protects the Flash BIOS. Check the manual to see whether your system has this feature. To update a BIOS on a system with a write-protected jumper, you must follow these steps:

Step 1. Disable the write protection.

Step 2. Perform the update.

Step 3. Reenable the write-protection to keep unauthorized people from changing the BIOS.

BIOS Chip Replacement

On motherboards whose BIOS programs can't be upgraded with software, you might be able to purchase a replacement BIOS from vendors such as eSupport.com or Badflash.com. Before you order a BIOS chip replacement, consider the following:

- BIOS chip upgrades cost approximately $30–$40 each.

- Although the BIOS will be updated, the rest of the system might still be out of date. If your system is more than 2 years old and is not fast enough for your needs, you might be better off buying a replacement motherboard or system.

- Your BIOS chip must be socketed; if it is surface mounted, it cannot be replaced.

- A replacement BIOS enables you to improve system operation without reinstalling Windows.

If you decide to update the BIOS chip, first verify whether the vendor has the correct BIOS chip replacement. The replacement needs to

- Plug in to your current motherboard; as you saw in Figure 3-1, some BIOS chips are square, whereas others are rectangular.

- Support your motherboard/chipset.

- Provide the features you need (such as support for larger hard disks, particular processor speeds, and so on).

It might be a different brand of BIOS than your current BIOS. If so, make sure that you have recorded your hard drive information. You will need to reenter this and other manually configured options into the new BIOS chip's setup program.

How does the BIOS vendor know what your system uses? The vendor will identify the BIOS chip you need by the motherboard ID information displayed at bootup. eSupport.com offers a free download utility to display this information for you. To replace the chip, follow these steps:

Step 1.   Locate the BIOS chip on your motherboard after you open the case to perform the upgrade. It sometimes has a sticker listing the BIOS maker and model number. If not, go to Step 2.

Step 2.   The BIOS chips might be in a DIP-type package (rectangular with legs on two sides) or in a PLCC (Plastic Leaded Chip Carrier; square with connectors on four sides). Refer to Figure 3-1. The vendor typically supplies a chip extraction tool to perform the removal.

Step 3.   Use the chip extraction tool to remove the BIOS chip. Don't try to remove the chip all at once; gently loosen each connected side until the chip can be lifted free.

Step 4.   Remove the existing BIOS chip carefully, and put it on antistatic material in case you need to reuse it in that system.

Step 5.   Align thc new BIOS chip with the socket. Note that a DIP-type BIOS can be installed backward (which will destroy the chip when power is turned on), so be sure to align the dimpled end of the chip with the cut-out end of the socket. PLCC BIOS chips have one corner cut out.

Step 6.   Adjust the legs on a new DIP-type BIOS chip so that it fits into the sockets, and press it down until the legs on both sides are inserted fully. Press the PLCC BIOS chip into the socket.

Step 7.   Double-check the alignment and leg positions on the BIOS chip before you start the system; if the chip is aligned with the wrong end of the socket, you'll destroy it when the power comes on.

Step 8.   Turn on the system, and use the new BIOS's keystroke(s) to start the setup program to reenter any information. You might get a "CMOS" error at startup, which is normal with a new BIOS chip. After you reenter the BIOS data from your printout and save the changes, the system will run without error messages.

NOTE   A CMOS Checksum error is normal after you replace the BIOS chip or update the BIOS. However, after you run the BIOS setup program and save the settings, this error should go away. If you continue to see this error, test the motherboard battery. If the battery checks out okay, contact the motherboard or system vendor for help.

Exam Preparation Tasks

Review All the Key Topics

Review the most important topics in the chapter, noted with the Key Topic icon in the outer margin of the page. Table 3-3 lists a reference to these key topics and the page numbers on which each is found.

Table 3-3   Key Topics for Chapter 3

Key Topic Element	Description	Page Number
Figure 3-1	BIOS chip and CMOS battery on a typical motherboard	86
Figure 3-2	The CR2032 lithium battery	88
Text	Common keystrokes used to access BIOS Setup	89
Table 3-1	Major CMOS/BIOS Settings	92
Figure 3-6	A typical CMOS Setup main menu	96
Figure 3-11	A typical Boot Sequence submenu configured to permit booting from a CD/DVD before the hard disk	99
Figure 3-13	Typical PATA configuration menu	101
Figure 3-17	Typical power management configuration menu	104
Figure 3-19	A typical hardware monitor screen	106
Figure 3-22	Typical exit dialogs: (a) saving changes and (b) discarding changes	109
Table 3-2	Common system errors and their beep codes	111
Text	Flash BIOS update	115
Text	BIOS chip replacement	118

Complete the Tables and Lists from Memory

Print a copy of Appendix A, "Memory Tables" (found on the CD), or at least the section for this chapter, and complete the tables and lists from memory. Appendix B, "Memory Tables Answer Key," also on the CD, includes completed tables and lists to check your work.

Define Key Terms

Define the following key terms from this chapter, and check your answers in the glossary.

BIOS, POST, CMOS

Complete Hands-On Labs

Complete the hands-on labs, and then see the answers and explanations at the end of the chapter.

Lab 3-1: Disable Onboard Audio

Scenario: You are a technician working at a PC repair bench. You need to install a sound card into a system that has onboard audio. Before you can do this, you need to turn off the onboard audio feature in the system BIOS.

Step 1. Review the BIOS screens listed earlier in this chapter. From Figure 3-6, which menu selection would you choose?

Step 2. Review the BIOS screens (Figures 3-7 through 3-22). Which figure has the correct menu option for disabling onboard audio?

Step 3. What is the menu called?

Step 4. What is the option called?

Step 5. What is the current setting?

Step 6. What is the setting you need to select?

Step 7. What key do you press to exit setup and save changes?

Lab 3-2: Check Fan and Voltage Levels

Scenario: You are a technician working at a PC repair bench. Your client reports that the computer is overheating. You need to check the performance of fans connected to the motherboard and the voltage levels on the motherboard.

Step 1. Review the CMOS (BIOS) setup screens listed earlier in this chapter. From Figure 3-6, which menu selection would you choose?

Step 2. Review the CMOS (BIOS) setup screens (Figures 3-7 through 3-22). Which figure displays fan speeds and voltage levels?

Step 3. What is the dialog called?

Step 4.   What is the CPU fan speed?

Step 5.   What is the CPU voltage called?

Step 6.   What is the voltage for the CPU?

Step 7.   What key do you press to exit setup without saving changes?

Answer Review Questions

Answer these review questions, and then see the answers and explanations at the end of the chapter.

1. What is the CMOS memory used for?

   a. Keeping the time.

   b. Storing BIOS settings.

   c. Booting the computer.

   d. None of these options is correct.

2. What happens when the CMOS battery fails?

   a. All the CMOS configuration information is lost.

   b. The computer won't boot.

   c. The computer is destroyed.

   d. The motherboard is dead.

3. If your system does not display the correct key to press to enter the BIOS setup program on startup, which of the following actions might work?

   a. Press the **F2** key.

   b. Run compmgmt.msc in Windows.

   c. Press the **F8** key.

   d. Press **Ctrl+Alt+Del**.

4. Which BIOS settings will allow you to automatically configure your system? (Choose all that apply.)

   a. BIOS defaults

   b. Setup defaults

   c. Turbo

   d. Function

5. Which of the following can be used if you are working with a UEFI-based system to configure or view BIOS settings? (Choose all that apply.)

    a. Touch screen

    b. The Enter key

    c. The + key

    d. The mouse

6. Of the following system information, which can be viewed in the BIOS? (Choose all that apply.)

    a. Installed memory (RAM)

    b. BIOS information

    c. Number of expansion slots

    d. Processor speed

    e. Video card memory size

    f. Feature settings

7. Which features can typically be found in the advanced BIOS settings? (Choose two.)

    a. Enable quick boot

    b. Change the clock

    c. View information

    d. Enable boot sector protection

8. In recent systems, what common feature is used to help prevent excessive heat from damaging your computer?

    a. Task Manager

    b. System Monitor

    c. Hardware Monitor

    d. Drive Lock

9. Which of the following security features are included in many of the currently used BIOS programs?

    a. BIOS password

    b. Power on password

    c. Chassis intrusion

    d. Boot sector protection

    e. All these options are correct.

10. Which option would you use if you are in the BIOS of your computer and you want to exit without making any changes? (Choose all that apply.)

    a. Save Configuration.

    b. Discard Changes.

    c. Press the ESC key.

    d. Press F8 to return to the desktop.

11. When you start your computer, it performs an important test. What is this test known as?

    a. CPU Processing

    b. POST

    c. A CMOS test

    d. Hard drive test

12. What are BIOS beep codes used for? (Choose two.)

    a. A fatal error

    b. A system message

    c. A serious error

    d. A warning message

13. If you are installing a larger memory module that is listed as compatible and it is not detected at full capacity, which of the following is most likely to solve the problem?

    a. Update the BIOS.

    b. Contact the manufacturer of the module.

    c. Set memory timings manually.

    d. Run Windows Update.

14. What is the process called when upgrading the BIOS?

    a. Putting a new BIOS chip on the motherboard

    b. Removing the CMOS battery

    c. Flashing the BIOS

    d. Windows Update

Answers to Hands-On Labs

Lab 3-1: Disable Onboard Audio

Answers:

Step 1.	Integrated Peripherals (also known as Onboard Devices)
Step 2.	Figure 3-15
Step 3.	Onboard Devices Configuration
Step 4.	Onboard Audio Controller
Step 5.	Enabled
Step 6.	Disabled
Step 7.	F10

Lab 3-2: Check Fan and Voltage Levels

Answers:

Step 1.	PC Health Status (also known as Hardware Monitor)
Step 2.	Figure 3-19
Step 3.	Power or Hardware Monitor
Step 4.	3970RPM
Step 5.	VCORE
Step 6.	1.416V
Step 7.	ESC

Answers and Explanations to Review Questions

1. **B.** CMOS memory, also referred to as nonvolatile memory, is used to store BIOS settings and should not be confused with system memory (RAM). CMOS stands for complimentary metal-oxide semiconductor.

2. **A.** If the CMOS battery fails, it will lose all information, such as time/date, CPU information, and drive types.

3. **A.** Most motherboards use either a function key, the Delete key, or a combination of keys to enter the BIOS setup program. Which key you use depends on the manufacture of the motherboard. F2 is a common key when entering the BIOS, as are F1, F10, and Delete. The F8 key is not used to start the BIOS setup program; it is used by the Windows Advanced Options Boot menu when accessing options such as Safe Mode. A few systems also use F8 to select which drive to boot from. Compmgmt.msc starts the Computer Management Console (used for managing services, drives, and other Windows features).

4. **A, B, C.** Many BIOS versions enable you to automatically configure your system with a choice of these options from the main menu.

5. **B, C, D.** Although touch screens cannot be used to access the BIOS, a mouse and the keyboard can be used in most UEFI firmware setup screens to make changes. If the mouse is not supported, use the keyboard.

6. **A, B, D.** The type and speed of the processor, amount of RAM, and the details of the BIOS program can all be viewed from within the BIOS setup. The number of expansion slots can be determined by a physical examination of the computer or by using a hardware testing program such as SiSoftware Sandra. Feature settings refer to the ability to configure various features of the operating system.

7. **A, D.** When accessing the BIOS advanced settings, some of the features available are quick boot, which will skip memory and drive test to enable faster startups, and also protection against boot sector viruses.

8. **C.** The Hardware Monitor screen (sometimes referred to as PC Health) is a common feature in most recent systems. It helps you make sure that your computer's temperature and voltage conditions are at safe levels for your computer, and it sometimes also includes the Chassis Intrusion feature.

9. **E.** Security features of various types are scattered around the typical system BIOS dialogs. All the features listed can be used to secure your computer systems from hackers or unauthorized personnel.

10. **B, C.** When you are in the BIOS and are not planning on making any changes, be sure to choose Discard Changes to prevent accidental changes to BIOS settings.

11. **B.** Every time you start from power-down (aka cold boot), your computer goes through a test known as POST or power-on self test. If the BIOS finds any errors with the system, it notifies you by error messages known as beep codes.

12. **A, C.** Beep codes are used by most BIOS versions to indicate either a fatal error or a serious error. A fatal error is an error that is so serious that the computer cannot continue the boot process. A fatal error includes a problem with the CPU, the POST ROM, the system timer, or memory. Serious error beep codes report a problem with your video display card or circuit. Although systems can boot without video, you do not want to boot without video because you can't see what the system is doing.

13. **A.** Sometimes the BIOS does not support newer technologies. When making changes to the systems, such as adding a faster CPU, a larger memory module, or a larger SATA or PATA drive, you might need to update the BIOS. The module manufacturer typically uses the most recent support information to determine whether a module will work in a particular system. Setting memory timings manually is typically done for overclocking and will not affect the system's capability to use larger modules. Windows Update checks for updates to Windows, not to the BIOS.

14. **C.** When it is time for a BIOS update, go to the system or motherboard manufacturer's website to see whether a new update has been released. Flashing the BIOS is the act of erasing all the BIOS's current contents and writing a new BIOS to the BIOS chip. You can do this by booting off of a special floppy disk, from CD-ROM, and from within Windows. This process in now much easier than it used to be, but to be safe you should still back up your BIOS settings before performing this task.

This chapter covers the following subjects:

- **Power Supplies**—This section describes the device that transforms AC power from the wall outlet into DC power that your computer can use. It also describes the various form factors and voltage levels, and how to protect your power supply.

- **Troubleshooting Power Problems**—This section demonstrates how to troubleshoot complete failure and intermittent power supply problems that you might encounter.

- **Avoiding Power Supply Hazards**—This section has guidelines for avoiding shock and fire hazards when working with power supplies.

- **Power Protection Types**—In this section you learn about devices that can protect your computer from over and under voltage issues. These include surge protectors, uninterruptible power supplies, and line conditioners.

- **System Cooling**—This last section describes the various ways to cool your system, including fans and liquid cooling, and demonstrates how to monitor the system temperature.

This chapter covers **CompTIA A+ 220-801 objectives 1.8 and 5.2** and **CompTIA A+ 220-802 objective 4.2**.

CHAPTER 4

Power Supplies and System Cooling

Clean, well-planned power is imperative, from the AC outlet to the electrical protection equipment to the power supply. Many of the issues that you see concerning power are due to lack of protection or improper planning, and as such you will see several questions on the A+ exams regarding this subject.

In this chapter we delve into how power is conveyed to the computer, which power supply to select depending on your configuration and needs, how to install and troubleshoot power supplies, and how to cool the system.

Foundation Topics

Power Supplies

220-801

Objective:
220-801: 1.8

Power issues are largely ignored by most computer users, but a properly working power supply is the foundation to correct operation of the system. When the power supply stops working, the computer stops working, and when a power supply stops functioning properly—even slightly—all sorts of computer problems can take place. From unexpected system reboots to data corruption, from unrecognized bus-powered USB devices to system overheating, a bad power supply is bad news. The power supply is vital to the health of the computer. So, if your computer is acting "sick," you should test the power supply to see if it's the cause. To keep the power supply working properly, use surge suppression and battery backup (UPS) units.

The **power supply** is really misnamed: It is actually a power converter that changes high-voltage alternating current (**AC**) to low-voltage direct current (**DC**). There are lots of wire coils, capacitors, and other components inside the power supply that do the work, and during the conversion process, a great deal of heat is produced. Most power supplies include one or two fans to dissipate the heat created by the operation of the power supply; however, a few power supplies designed for silent operation use passive heat sink technology instead of fans. On power supplies that include fans, fans also help to cool the rest of the computer. Figure 4-1 shows a typical desktop computer's power supply.

Power Supply Ratings

Power supply capacity is rated in watts, and the more watts a power supply provides, the more devices it can safely power.

You can use the label attached to the power supply, shown in Figure 4-2, to determine its wattage rating and see important safety reminders.

Figure 4-1 A typical ATX power supply.

NOTE The power supply shown in Figure 4-2 is a so-called "split rail" design with two separate 12V outputs (+12V$_1$ and +12V$_2$). This type of design is frequently used today to provide separate 12V power sources for processors (which reduce 12V power to the power level needed) and other devices such as PCI Express video cards, fans, and drives). Add the values together to get the total 12V output in amps (34A).

Typically, power supplies in recent tower-case (upright case) machines use 400-watt or larger power supplies, reflecting the greater number of drives and cards that can be installed in these computers. Power supplies used in slimline desktop computers have typical ratings of around 220–300 watts,. The power supply rating is found on the top or side of the power supply, along with safety rating information and amperage levels produced by the power supply's different DC outputs.

How can you tell whether a power supply meets minimum safety standards? Look for the appropriate safety certification mark for your country or locale. For example, in the U.S. and Canada, the backward UR logo is used to indicate the power supply has the UL and UL Canada safety certifications as a component (the familiar circled UL logo is used for finished products only).

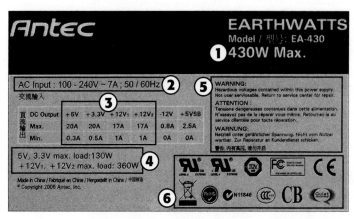

1. Power supply rating
2. AC input voltage levels
3. DC output levels by type
4. +3.3V, +5V, and +12V maximum load
5. Hazard warnings
6. Product certifications

Figure 4-2   A typical power supply label.

CAUTION   Power supplies that do not bear the UL or other certification marks should not be used, as their safety is unknown. For a visual guide to electrical and other safety certification marks in use around the world, visit the Standard Certification Marks page at www.technick.net/public/code/cp_dpage.php?aiocp_dp=guide_safetymarks.

Use the following methods to determine the wattage rating needed for a replacement power supply:

- Whip out your calculator and add up the wattage ratings for everything connected to your computer that uses the power supply, including the motherboard, processor, memory, cards, drives, and bus-powered USB devices. If the total wattage used exceeds 70% of the wattage rating of your power supply, you should upgrade to a larger power supply. Check the vendor spec sheets for wattage ratings.

- If you have amperage ratings instead of wattage ratings, multiply the amperage by the volts to determine wattage and then start adding. If a device uses two or three different voltage levels, be sure to carry out this calculation for each voltage level, and add up the figures to determine the wattage requirement for the device.

- Use an interactive power supply sizing tool such as the calculators provided by eXtreme Outervision (www.extreme.outervision.com) or PC Power and Cooling (www.pcpower.com).

Table 4-1 provides calculations for typical compact desktop and performance desktop systems.

Table 4-1   Calculating Power Supply Requirements

MicroATX System with Integrated Video		Full-Size ATX System with SLI (Dual Graphics Cards)	
Components	**Wattage**	**Components**	**Wattage**
AMD A8 3800 (4 core with in-core graphics and L2 cache)	65	Intel Core i7-3960X Extreme Edition (6 cores with L3 cache)	130
microATX motherboard	60	ATX motherboard	100
4GB RAM	60	8GB RAM	120
Rewritable DVD drive	30	Rewritable Blu-ray drive	30
SATA hard disk	20	SATA hard disk	20
Two case fans	6	Three case fans	9
CPU fan	3	CPU fan	3
Integrated graphics (in CPU)	—	High-end SLI video cards (2)	210 (105×2)
Estimated wattage	244	Estimated wattage	622
Minimum power supply size recommended (80% efficiency assumed)	350	Minimum power supply size recommended (80% efficiency assumed)	750

NOTE   The 80 PLUS certification standard is an industry standard for evaluating power supply efficiency. 80 PLUS certified power supplies achieve 80% efficiency at up to 100% of rated load. The use of power supplies with 80 PLUS certification is assumed in Table 4-1. Higher standards (80 PLUS Bronze, Silver, Gold, and Platinum) achieve up to 89% efficiency at 100% of rated load on 115V power and up to 91% on 230V power. For more information, see the Ecova Plug Load Solutions website at http://www.plugloadsolutions.com/. For non-80 PLUS power supplies, assume 70% efficiency.

Multivoltage Power Supplies

Most power supplies are designed to handle two different voltage ranges:

- 110–120V/60Hz
- 220–240V/50Hz

Standard North American power is now 115–120V/60Hz-cycle AC (the previous standard was 110V). The power used in European and Asian countries is typically 230–240V/50Hz AC (previously 220V). Power supplies typically have a slider switch with two markings: 115 (for North American 110–120V/60HzAC) and 230 (for European and Asian 220–240V/50Hz AC). Figure 4-3 shows a slider switch set for correct North American voltage. If a power supply is set to the wrong input voltage, the system will not work. Setting a power supply for 230V with 110–120V current is harmless; however, feeding 220–240V into a power supply set for 115V will destroy the power supply, and possibly other onboard hardware.

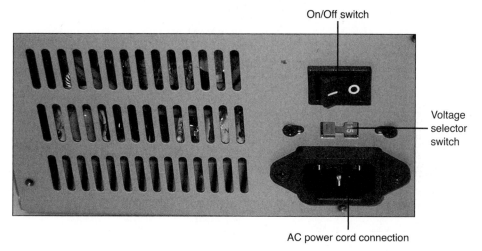

Figure 4-3   A typical power supply's sliding voltage switch set for correct North American voltage (115V). Slide it to 230V for use in Europe and Asia.

NOTE   Note that some power supplies for desktop and notebook computers can automatically determine the correct voltage level and cycle rate. These are referred to as *autoswitching power supplies* and lack the voltage/cycle selection switch shown in Figure 4-3.

The on/off switch shown in Figure 4-3 controls the flow of current into the power supply. It is not the system power switch, which is located on the front of most recent systems and is connected to the motherboard. When you press the system power switch, the motherboard signals the power supply to provide power.

> **CAUTION**   Unless the power supply is disconnected from AC current or is turned off, a small amount of power can still be flowing through the system, even when it is not running. Do not install or remove components or perform other types of service to the inside of a PC unless you disconnect the AC power cord or turn off the power supply. Wait a few seconds afterward to ensure that the power is completely off. Some desktop motherboards have indicator lights that turn off when the power has completely drained from the system.

Power Supply Form Factors and Connectors

When you shop for a power supply, you also need to make sure it can connect to your motherboard. There are two major types of power connectors on motherboards:

- 20-pin, used by older motherboards in the ATX family

- 24-pin, used by recent ATX/BTX motherboards requiring the ATX12V 2.2 power supply standard

Some high-wattage power supplies with 20-pin connectors might also include a 20-pin to 24-pin adapter. Some 24-pin power supplies include a 24-pin to 20-pin connector.

Some motherboards use power supplies that feature several additional connectors to supply added power, as follows (see Figure 4-4):

- The four-wire square ATX12V connector provides additional 12V power to the motherboard; this connector is sometimes referred to as a "P4" or "Pentium 4" connector.

- Many recent high-end power supplies use the eight-wire EPS12V connector (see Figure 4-6) instead of the ATX12V power connector. Often, the EPS12V lead is split into two four-wire square connectors to be compatible with motherboards that use either ATX12V or EPS12V power leads.

- Some older motherboards use a six-wire AUX connector to provide additional power.

Figure 4-5 lists the pinouts for the 20-pin and 24-pin ATX power supply connectors shown in Figure 4-4.

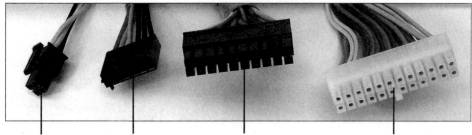

ATX12V secondary   AUX secondary   ATX primary (20-pin)   ATX12V 2.2 primary (24-pin)

Figure 4-4   20-pin ATX and 24-pin ATX power connectors compared to four-pin ATX12V and six-wire AUX power connectors.

ATX 20-pin power connector (top view)

11	+3.3v	Orange		Orange	+3.3v	1
12	-12v	Blue		Orange	+3.3v	2
13	Ground	Black		Black	Ground	3
14	PS-On	Green		Red	+5v	4
15	Ground	Black		Black	Ground	5
16	Ground	Black		Red	+5v	6
17	Ground	Black		Black	Ground	7
18	-5v	White		Gray	Power Good	8
19	+5v	Red		Purple	+5v Standby	9
20	+5v	Red		Yellow	+12v	10

ATX version 2.2 24-pin power connector (top view)

13	+3.3v	Orange		Orange	+3.3v	1
14	-12v	Blue		Orange	+3.3v	2
15	Ground	Black		Black	Ground	3
16	PS-On	Green		Red	+5v	4
17	Ground	Black		Black	Ground	5
18	Ground	Black		Red	+5v	6
19	Ground	Black		Black	Ground	7
20	NC	White		Gray	Power Good	8
21	+5v	Red		Purple	+5v Standby	9
22	+5v	Red		Yellow	+12v	10
23	+5v	Red		Yellow	+12v	11
24	Ground	Black		Orange	+3.3v	12

Figure 4-5   Pinout for standard ATX 20-pin and 24-pin power connectors.

The power supply also powers various peripherals, such as the following:

- PATA hard disks, CD and DVD optical drives, and case fans that do not plug into the motherboard use a four-pin Molex power connector.

- 3.5-inch floppy drives use a four-pin Berg power connector.

- Serial ATA (SATA) hard disks use an L-shaped 15-pin thinline power connector.

- High-performance PCI Express x16 video cards that require additional 12V power use a PCI Express six-pin or eight-pin power cable.

Figure 4-6 illustrates these power connectors.

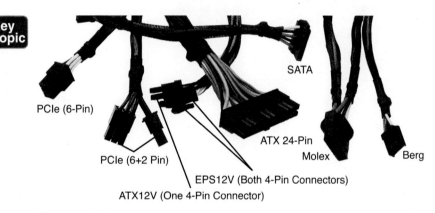

Figure 4-6   Power supply connectors for peripherals and modern motherboards.

If your power supply doesn't have enough connectors, you can add Y-splitters to divide one power lead into two, but these can short out and can also reduce your power supply's efficiency. You can also convert a standard Molex connector into an SATA or floppy drive power connector with the appropriate adapter.

Some power supplies (see Figure 4-7) use modular connections so that you can customize the power supply connections needed for your hardware.

CAUTION   Many recent and older Dell desktop computers use proprietary versions of the 20-pin or 24-pin ATX power supply connectors. Dell's versions use a different pinout that routes voltages to different wires than in standard power supplies. Consequently, if you plug a standard power supply into a Dell PC that uses the proprietary version or use a regular motherboard as an upgrade for a model that has the proprietary power supply, stand by for smoke and fire! To determine whether a particular Dell computer model requires a proprietary power supply, check the PC Power and Cooling PSU recommendation for your Dell system at www.pcpower.com/Dell.html.

Figure 4-7   A modular power supply includes cables you can attach to customize support for your system's needs.

If your wattage calculations or your tests (covered later in this chapter) agree that it's time to replace the power supply, make sure the replacement meets the following criteria:

- Have the same power supply connectors and the same pinout as the original.

- Have the same form factor (shape, size, and switch location)

- Have the same or higher wattage rating; a higher wattage rating is highly desirable

- Support any special features required by your CPU, video card, and mother-board, such as SLI support (support for PCI Express connectors to power dual high-performance PCI Express x16 video cards), high levels of +12V power (ATX12V v2.2 4-pin or EPS12V 8-pin power connectors), and so on

TIP   To ensure form factor connector compatibility, consider removing the old power supply and taking it with you if you plan to buy a replacement at retail. If you are buying a replacement online, measure the dimensions of your existing power supply to ensure that a new one will fit properly in the system.

Removing and Replacing the Power Supply

Installing a new power supply is one of the easier repairs to make. You don't need to fiddle with driver CDs or Windows Update to get the new one working. But, you do need to be fairly handy with a screwdriver or nut driver.

Typical power supplies are held in place by several screws that attach the power supply to the rear panel of the computer. The power supply also is supported by a shelf inside the case, and screws can secure the power supply to that shelf. To remove a power supply, follow these steps:

Step 1.   Power down the computer. If the power supply has an on/off switch, turn it off as well.

Step 2.   Disconnect the AC power cord from the computer.

Step 3.   Open the case to expose the power supply, which might be as simple as removing the cover on a desktop unit or as involved as removing both side panels, front bezel, and case lid on a tower PC. Consult the documentation that came with your computer to determine how to expose the power supply for removal.

Step 4.   Disconnect the existing power supply from the motherboard (see Figure 4-8). The catch securing the power supply connector must be released to permit the connector to be removed.

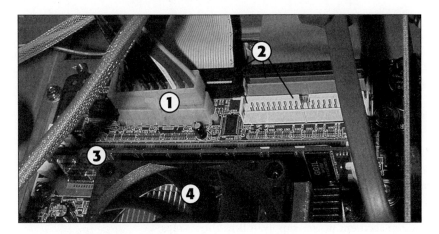

1. Catch securing power supply connector
2. PATA/IDE drive connectors
3. Memory module
4. Active heat sink for processor

Figure 4-8   Disconnecting the power supply from the motherboard.

Step 5.   Disconnect all other power supply leads to the motherboard (fan monitors, ATX12V, EPS12V, AUX).

Step 6.   Disconnect the power supply from all drives and add-on cards.

Step 7.   Disconnect the power supply from all fans.

Step 8.   Remove the power supply screws from the rear of the computer case (see Figure 4-9).

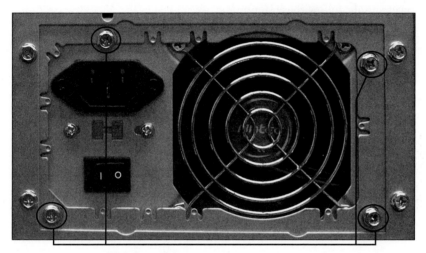

Mounting screws

Figure 4-9   Removing the mounting screws from a typical power supply.

Step 9.   Remove any screws holding the power supply in place inside the case. (Your PC might not use these additional screws.)

Step 10. Lift or slide the power supply out of the case.

Before installing the replacement power supply, compare it to the original, making sure the form factor, motherboard power connectors, and switch position match the original. If the new power supply has a fan on top (as well as the typical rear-mounted fan), make sure the fan faces the inside of the case.

To install the replacement power supply, follow these steps:

Step 1.   Lift or slide the power supply into the case.

Step 2.   Attach the power supply to the shelf with screws (if required).

Step 3.   Slide the power supply to the rear of the computer case; line up the holes in the unit carefully with the holes in the outside of the case.

Step 4.   Connect the power supply to all fans, drives, add-on cards, and motherboard.

Step 5.   Check the voltage setting on the power supply. Change it to the correct voltage for your location if necessary.

Step 6.   Connect the AC power cord to the new power supply.

Step 7.   Turn on the computer.

Step 8.   Start the system normally to verify correct operation, and then run the normal shutdown procedure for the operating system. If necessary, turn off the system with the front power switch only.

Step 9.   Close the case and secure it.

Troubleshooting Power Supplies

Problems with power supplies can cause a variety of symptoms, including

- Overheating
- Spontaneous rebooting
- Intermittent device failure (particularly of bus-powered USB devices)
- Loud noises

What can cause these symptoms, and how can you solve the problems behind the symptoms?

Overloaded Power Supplies—Symptoms and Solutions

What happens if you connect devices that require more wattage than a power supply can provide? This is a big problem called an *overload*. An overloaded power supply has three major symptoms:

- Overheating
- Spontaneous rebooting (cold boot with memory test) due to incorrect voltage on the Power Good line running from the power supply to the motherboard

- Intermittent failures of USB bus-powered devices (mice, keyboard, USB flash drives, portable USB hard disks) because these devices draw power from the system's power supply via the USB port

Here's a good rule of thumb: If your system starts spontaneously rebooting and you don't see a blue screen (STOP) error, replace the power supply as soon as possible. However, power supply overheating can have multiple causes; follow the steps listed in the section "Overheating," later in this chapter, before replacing an overheated power supply.

To determine whether Power Good or other motherboard voltage levels are within limits, perform the measurements listed in the section "Testing Power Supplies and Other Devices with a Multimeter," later in this chapter.

Loud Noises from the Power Supply

Computers usually run quietly, but if you hear loud noises coming from the power supply, it's a sure sign of problems. A whirring, rattling, or thumping noise while the system is on usually indicates a fan failure. If a fan built in to a component such as a heat sink or power supply is failing, replace the component immediately.

> **CAUTION**   Should you try to replace a standard power supply fan? No. Because the power supply is a sealed unit, you would need to remove the cover from most power supplies to gain access to the fan. The capacitors inside a power supply retain potentially *lethal* electrical charges. Instead, scrap the power supply and replace it with a higher-rated unit. Refer to the section "Removing and Replacing the Power Supply," earlier in the chapter.

A power supply that makes a loud bang, followed by a system crash, has had an onboard capacitor blow up. The easiest way to diagnose this is to smell the power supply after turning it off and disconnecting it from AC power. If you can smell a burnt odor with a chemical overtone to it coming from the power supply's outside vent, your power supply has died. This odor can linger for weeks. Sadly, when a power supply blows up like this, it can also destroy the motherboard, bus-powered USB devices connected to the computer, and other components.

Finding Solutions to a "Dead" System

A dead system that gives no signs of life when turned on can be caused by the following:

- Defects in AC power to the system

- Power supply failure or misconfiguration

- Temporary short circuits in internal or external components

- Power supply or other component failure

With four suspects, it's time to play detective. Use the procedure outlined next to find the actual cause of a dead system. If one of the test procedures in the following list corrects the problem, the item that was changed is the cause of the problem. Power supplies have a built-in safety feature that shuts down the unit immediately in case of short circuit.

The following steps are designed to determine whether the power problem is caused by a short circuit or another problem:

Step 1. Smell the power supply's outside vent. If you can detect a burnt odor, the power supply has failed (see previous section).

Step 2. Check the AC power to the system; a loose or disconnected power cord, a disconnected surge protector, a surge protector that has been turned off, or a dead AC wall socket will prevent a system from receiving power. If the wall socket has no power, reset the circuit breaker in the electrical service box for the location.

Step 3. Check the AC voltage switch on the power supply; it should be set to 115V for North America. Turn off the power, reset the switch, and restart the system if the switch was set to 230V. Note that many desktop computer power supplies no longer require a switch selection because they are autoranging.

CAUTION If your area uses 230V and the power supply is set to 115V, you need a new power supply and possibly other components, because they've been damaged or destroyed by 100% overvoltage.

Step 4. If the system uses a PS/2 mouse or keyboard, check the connectors; a loose keyboard connector could cause a short circuit.

Step 5.   Turn off the system, disconnect power, and open the system. Verify that the power leads are properly connected to the motherboard. Connect loose power leads, reconnect power, and restart the computer.

Step 6.   Check for loose screws or other components such as loose slot covers, modem speakers, or other metal items that can cause a short circuit. Correct them and retest.

Step 7.   Remove all expansion cards and disconnect power to all drives; restart the system and use a multimeter to test power to the motherboard per Table 4-3.

Step 8.   If the power tests within accepted limits with all peripherals disconnected, reinstall one card at a time and check the power. If the power tests within accepted limits, reattach one drive at a time and check the power.

Step 9.   If a defective card or drive has a dead short, reattaching the defective card or drive should stop the system immediately upon power-up. Replace the card or drive and retest.

Step 10.   Check the Power Good line at the power supply motherboard connector with a multimeter.

It's a long list, but chances are you will track down the offending component before you reach the end of it.

Overheating

Got an overheated power supply? Not sure? If you touch the power supply case and it's too hot to touch, it's overheated. Overheated power supplies can cause system failure and possible component damage, due to any of the following causes:

- Overloading
- Fan failure
- Inadequate airflow outside the system
- Inadequate airflow inside the system
- Dirt and dust

Use the following sections to figure out the possible effects of these problems in any given situation.

Overloading

An overloaded power supply is caused by connecting devices that draw more power (in watts) than the power supply is designed to handle. As you add more card-based devices to expansion slots, use more bus-powered USB and IEEE-1394 drives and devices, and install more internal drives in a system, the odds of having an overloaded power supply increase.

If a power supply fails or overheats, check the causes listed in the following sections before determining whether you should replace the power supply. If you determine that you should replace the power supply, purchase a unit that has a higher wattage rating.

Fan Failure

The fan(s) inside the power supply cool it and are partly responsible for cooling the rest of the computer. If they fail, the power supply and the entire computer are at risk of damage. Fans also might stop turning as a symptom of other power problems.

A fan that stops immediately after the power comes on usually indicates incorrect input voltage or a short circuit. If you turn off the system and turn it back on again under these conditions, the fan will stop each time.

To determine whether a fan has failed, listen to the unit; it should make less noise if the fan has failed. You can also see the fan blades spinning rapidly on a power supply fan that is working correctly. If the blades aren't turning or are turning very slowly, the fan has failed or is too clogged with dust to operate correctly.

To determine whether case fans have failed, look at them through the front or rear of the system, or, if they are connected to the motherboard, use the system monitoring feature in the system BIOS to check fan speed. Figure 4-10 illustrates a typical example.

NOTE   If a fan has failed because of a short circuit or incorrect input voltage, you will not see any picture onscreen because the system cannot operate.

If the system starts normally but the fan stops turning later, this indicates a true fan failure instead of a power problem.

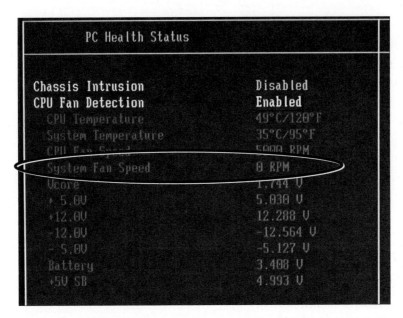

Figure 4-10   The system fan (case fan) has either failed or was never connected to the mother-board power/monitor header.

Inadequate Airflow Outside the System

The power supply's capability to cool the system depends in part on free airflow space outside the system. If the computer is kept in a confined area (such as a closet or security cabinet) without adequate ventilation, power supply failures due to over-heating are likely.

Even systems in ordinary office environments can have airflow problems; make sure that several inches of free air space exist behind the fan outputs for any computer.

Inadequate Airflow Inside the System

As you have seen in previous chapters, the interior of the typical computer is a messy place. Wide ribbon cables used for some types of drives, drive power cables, and expansion cards create small air dams that block airflow between the heat sources—such as the motherboard, CPU, drives, and memory modules—and the fans in the power supply. Figure 4-11 illustrates a typical system with a lot of cable clutter that can interfere with airflow.

Figure 4-11   A cluttered system with plenty of unsecured cables to block airflow.

You can do the following to improve airflow inside the computer:

- Use cable ties to secure excess ribbon cable and power connectors out of the way of the fans and the power supply.

- Replace any missing slot covers.

- Make sure that auxiliary case fans, chipset fans, and CPU fans are working correctly.

- Use SATA drives in place of PATA drives. SATA drives use narrow data cables.

Figure 4-12 illustrates a different system that uses cable management (cable ties, bundling cables between the drive bays and outer case wall, and routing behind the motherboard) to improve airflow.

For more information about cooling issues, see the section "System Cooling," later in this chapter for details.

Figure 4-12   A system with good airflow due to intelligent cable management.

Dirt and Dust

Most power supplies, except for a few of the early ATX power supplies, use a cooling technique called *negative pressure*; in other words, the power supply fan works like a weak vacuum cleaner, pulling air through vents in the case, past the components, and out through the fan. Vacuum cleaners are used to remove dust, dirt, cat hairs, and so on from living rooms and offices, and even the power supply's weak impression of a vacuum cleaner works the same way.

When you open a system for any kind of maintenance, look for the following:

- Dirt, dust, hair, and gunk clogging the case vents

- A thin layer of dust on the motherboard and expansion slots

- Dirt and dust on the power supply vent and fans

Yuck! You never know what you'll find inside a PC that hasn't been cleaned out for a year or two. So how can you get rid of the dust and gunk? You can use either a vacuum cleaner specially designed for computer use or compressed air to remove dirt and dust from inside the system. If you use compressed air, be sure to spread newspapers around the system to catch the dirt and dust. If possible, remove the computer from the computer room so the dust is not spread to other equipment.

Fans Turn But System Doesn't Start

Fans connected directly to the power supply will run as soon as the system is turned on, but if the system doesn't start up, this could indicate a variety of problems. Check the following:

- Make sure the main ATX and 12V ATX or EPS power leads are securely connected to the appropriate sockets.

- Make sure the CPU and memory modules are securely installed in the appropriate sockets.

Testing Power Supplies and Other Devices with a Multimeter

How can you find out that a defective power supply is really defective? How can you make sure that a cable has the right pinouts? Use a multimeter. A **multimeter** is one of the most flexible diagnostic tools around. It is covered in this chapter because of its usefulness in testing power supplies, but it also can be used to test coaxial, serial, and parallel cables, as well as fuses, resistors, and batteries.

Multimeters are designed to perform many different types of electrical tests, including the following:

- DC voltage and polarity

- AC voltage and polarity

- Resistance (Ohms)

- Diodes

- Continuity

- Amperage

All multimeters are equipped with red and black test leads. When used for voltage tests, the red is attached to the power source to be measured and the black is attached to ground.

Multimeters use two different readout styles: digital and analog. Digital multimeters are usually *autoranging*, which means they automatically adjust to the correct range for the test selected and the voltage present. Analog multimeters, or non–autoranging digital meters, must be set manually to the correct range and can be damaged more easily by overvoltage. Figure 4-13 compares typical analog and digital multimeters.

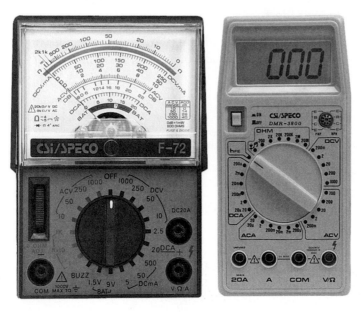

Figure 4-13   Typical analog (left) and digital (right) multimeters. Photos courtesy of Colacino Electric Supply, Newark, NJ.

Multimeters are designed to perform tests in two ways: in series and in parallel. Most tests are performed in parallel mode, in which the multimeter is not part of the circuit but runs parallel to it. On the other hand, amperage tests require that the multimeter be part of the circuit, so these tests are performed in series mode. Many low-cost multimeters do not include the ammeter feature for testing amperage (current), but you might be able to add it as an option.

Figure 4-14 shows a typical parallel mode test (DC voltage for a motherboard CMOS battery) and the current (amperage) test, which is a serial-mode test.

Table 4-2 summarizes the tests you can perform with a multimeter.

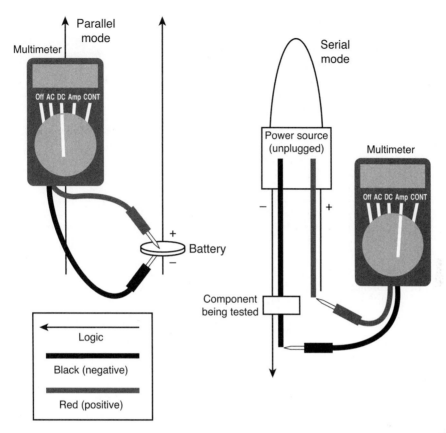

Figure 4-14 A parallel-mode (DC current) test setup (left) and an amperage (current) serial-mode test setup (right).

Table 4-2 Using a Multimeter

Test to Perform	Multimeter Setting	Probe Positions	Procedure
AC voltage (wall outlet)	AC	Red to hot, black to ground.	Read voltage from meter; should be near 115V in North America.
DC voltage (power supply outputs to motherboard, drives, batteries)	DC	Red to hot, black to ground.	Read voltage from meter; compare to default values.

Table 4-2 Continued

Test to Perform	Multimeter Setting	Probe Positions	Procedure
Continuity (cables, fuses)	CONT	Red to lead at one end of cable; black to corresponding lead at other end.	No CONT signal indicates bad cable or bad fuse.
		For a straight-through cable, check the same pin at each end. For other types of cables, consult a cable pinout to select the correct leads.	Double-check leads and retest to be sure.
Resistance (Ohms)	Ohms	Connect one lead to each end of resistor.	Check reading; compare to rating for resistor.
			A fuse should have no resistance.
Amperage (Ammeter)	Ammeter	Red probe to positive lead of circuit (power disconnected!); black lead to negative lead running through component to be tested.	Check reading; compare to rating for component tested.

You can use a multimeter to find out whether a power supply is properly converting AC power to DC power. Here's how: Measure the DC power going from the power supply to the motherboard. A power supply that does not meet the measurement standards listed in Table 4-3 should be replaced.

If the system monitor functions in the system BIOS do not display voltage levels (refer to Figure 4-10 for an example of a system that does display voltage levels in the BIOS), you can take the voltage measurements directly from the power supply connection to the motherboard. Both 20-pin and 24-pin P1 (ATX) power connectors are designed to be back-probed as shown in Figure 4-15; you can run the red probe through the top of the power connector to take a reading (the black probe uses the power supply enclosure or metal case frame for ground). Some motherboards bring these same voltage levels to a more convenient location on the motherboard for testing.

Table 4-3 Acceptable Voltage Levels

Rated DC Volts	Acceptable Range
+5.0	+4.8–5.2
-5.0	-4.8–5.2
-12.0	-11.4–12.6
+12.0	+11.4–12.6
+3.3	+3.14–3.5
Power Good	+3.0–6.0

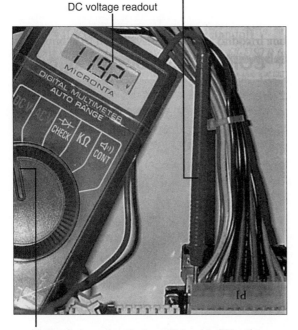

Red probe from multimeter back-probing +12V line

DC voltage readout

Multimeter's mode selector switch set to DV voltage

Figure 4-15   Testing the +12V line on an ATX power supply. The voltage level indicated (+11.92V) is well within limits.

If a power supply fails any of these measurements, replace it and retest the new unit.

Avoiding Power Supply Hazards

220-801

Objective:
220-801: 5.2

To avoid shock and fire hazards when working with power supplies, follow these important guidelines:

- **Never disassemble a power supply or push metal tools through the openings in the case**—Long after you shut off the system, the capacitors inside the power supply retain potentially fatal voltage levels. If you want to see the interior of a power supply safely, check the websites of leading power supply vendors such as PC Power and Cooling.

- **If you are replacing the power supply in a Dell desktop computer, determine whether the computer uses a standard ATX or Dell proprietary ATX power supply**—Many Dell computers built from September 1998 to the present use a nonstandard version of the ATX power supply with a different pinout for the power connector. Install a standard power supply on a system built to use a Dell proprietary model, or upgrade from a Dell motherboard that uses the Dell proprietary ATX design to a standard motherboard, and you can literally cause a power supply and system fire!

> **NOTE** The proprietary Dell version of the 20-pin ATX (P1) connector has no 3.3V (orange) lines, and its Power Good (gray wire) line is pin 5, not pin 8 as with a standard ATX power supply. The 3.3V (orange) wires are routed to the 6-pin Dell proprietary auxiliary connector. The proprietary Dell version of the 24-pin ATX (P1) connector also uses pin 5 for Power Good and provides 3.3V power (blue/white) through pins 11, 12, and 23, rather than through 1, 2, 12, and 13 as with a standard 24-pin ATX power supply. Make sure you buy a power supply made specifically for your Dell model.

- **Always use a properly wired and grounded outlet for your computer and its peripherals**—You can use a plug-in wiring tester to quickly determine whether a three-prong outlet is properly wired; signal lights on the tester indicate the outlet's status (see Figure 4-16).

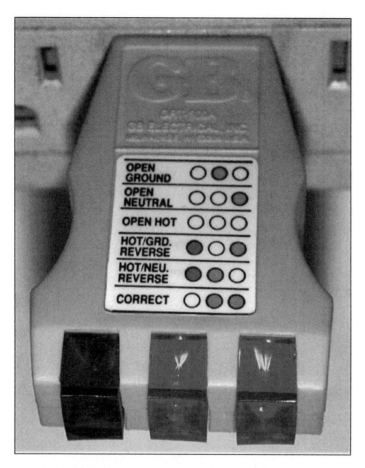

Figure 4-16 An outlet tester like this one can find wiring problems quickly. This outlet is wired correctly.

Power Protection Types

220-801

Objective:
220-801: 5.2

Question. How well can a power supply work if it has poor-quality AC power to work with?

Answer. Not very well. Because computers and many popular computer peripherals run on DC power that has been converted from AC power, it's essential to make sure that proper levels of AC power flow to the computer and its peripherals. There are four problems you might run into:

- Overvoltages (spikes and surges)

- Undervoltages (brownouts)

- Power failure (blackouts)

- Noisy power (interference)

Extremely high levels of transient or sustained overvoltages can damage the power supply of the computer and peripherals, and voltage that is significantly lower than required will cause the computer and peripherals to shut down. Shutdowns happen immediately when all power fails. A fourth problem with power is interference; "noisy" electrical power can cause subtle damage, and all four types of problems put the most valuable property of any computer, the data stored on the computer, at risk. Protect your computer's power supply and other components with appropriate devices:

- Surge suppressors, which are also referred to as surge protectors

- Battery backup systems, which are also referred to as uninterruptible power supply (UPS) or standby power supply (SPS) systems

- Power conditioning devices

Surge Suppressors

Stop that surge! While properly designed **surge suppressors** can prevent power surges (chronic overvoltage) and spikes (brief extremely high voltage) from damaging your computer, low-cost ones are often useless because they lack sufficient components to absorb dangerous surges. Surge suppressors range in price from under $10 to close to $100 per unit.

Both spikes and surges are overvoltages: voltage levels higher than the normal voltage levels that come out of the wall socket. *Spikes* are momentary overvoltages, whereas surges last longer. Both can damage or destroy equipment and can come through data lines (such as RJ-11 phone or RJ-45 network cables) as well as through power lines. In other words, if you think of your PC as a house, spikes and surges can come in through the back door or the garage as well as through the front door. Better "lock" (protect) all the doors. Many vendors sell data-line surge suppressors.

How can you tell the real surge suppressors from the phonies? Check for a TVSS (transient voltage surge suppressor) rating on the unit. Multi-outlet power strips do not have a TVSS rating.

Beyond the TVSS rating, look for the following features to be useful in preventing power problems:

- A low TVSS let-through voltage level (400V AC or less). This might seem high compared to the 115V standard, but power supplies have been tested to handle up to 800V AC themselves without damage.

- A covered-equipment warranty that includes lightning strikes (one of the biggest causes of surges and spikes).

- A high Joule rating. Joules measure electrical energy, and surge suppressors with higher Joule ratings can dissipate greater levels of surges or spikes.

- Fusing that prevents fatal surges from getting through.

- Protection for data cables such as telephone/fax (RJ-11), network (RJ-45), or coaxial (RG6).

- EMI/RFI noise filtration (a form of line conditioning).

- Site fault wiring indicator (no ground, reversed polarity warnings).

- Fast response time to surges. If the surge suppressor doesn't clamp fast enough, the surge can get through.

- Protection against surges on hot, neutral, and ground lines.

If you use surge protectors with these features, you will minimize power problems. The site-fault wiring indicator will alert you to wiring problems that can negate grounding and can cause serious damage in ordinary use.

A surge suppressor that meets the UL 1449 or ANSI/IEEE C62.41 Category A (formerly IEEE 587 Category A) standards provides protection for your equipment. You might need to check with the vendor to determine whether a particular unit meets one of these standards.

NOTE   To learn more about UL 1449 and the other UL standards it incorporates, see http://ulstandardsinfonet.ul.com/scopes/scopes.asp?fn=1449.html.

CAUTION   High-quality surge protectors require grounding. If you plug them into an ungrounded electrical outlet, they don't work properly. The two- to three-prong adapter you use to enable grounded equipment to plug into an ungrounded outlet is designed to be attached to a ground such as a metal water pipe (that's what the metal loop on the adapter is for). If you can't ground the adapter, don't use a computer or other electronic device with it. If you do, sooner or later you'll be sorry.

Battery Backup Units (UPS and SPS)

A UPS is another name for a **battery backup** unit. A UPS provides emergency power when a power failure strikes (a blackout) or when power falls below minimum levels (a brownout).

There are two different types of UPS systems: true UPS and SPS systems. A true UPS runs your computer from its battery at all times, isolating the computer and monitor from AC power. There is no switchover time with a true UPS when AC power fails because the battery is already running the computer. A true UPS inherently provides power conditioning (preventing spikes, surges, and brownouts from reaching the computer) because the computer receives only battery power, not the AC power coming from the wall outlet. True UPS units are sometimes referred to as line-interactive battery backup units because the battery backup unit interacts with the AC line, rather than the AC line going directly to the computer and other components.

An SPS is also referred to as a UPS, but its design is quite different. Its battery is used only when AC power fails. A momentary gap in power (about 1ms or less) occurs between the loss of AC power and the start of standby battery power; however, this switchover time is far faster than is required to avoid system shutdown because computers can coast for several milliseconds before shutting down. SPS-type battery backup units are far less expensive than true UPSs but work just as well as true UPSs when properly equipped with power-conditioning features.

NOTE In the rest of this section, the term *UPS* refers to both true UPS or SPS units except as noted, because most backup units on the market technically are SPS but are called UPS units by their vendors. Make sure you understand the differences between these units for the exam.

Battery backup units can be distinguished from each other by differences in the following:

- **Runtimes**—The amount of time a computer will keep running on power from the UPS. A longer runtime unit uses a bigger battery and usually costs more than a unit with a shorter runtime. Fifteen minutes is a minimum recommendation for a UPS for an individual workstation; much larger systems are recommended for servers that might need to complete a lengthy shutdown procedure.

- **Network support**—Battery backup units made for use on networks are shipped with software that broadcasts a message to users about a server shutdown so that users can save open files and close open applications and then shuts down the server automatically before the battery runs down.

- **Automatic shutdown**—Some low-cost UPS units lack this feature, but it is essential for servers or other unattended units. The automatic shutdown feature requires an available USB (or RS-232 serial) port and appropriate software from the UPS maker. If you change operating systems, you need to update the software for your UPS to be supported by the new operating system.

- **Surge suppression features**—Virtually all UPS units today have integrated surge suppression, but the efficiency of integrated surge suppression can vary as much as separate units. Check for UL-1449 and ANSI/IEEE C62.41 Category A ratings to find reliable surge suppression in UPS units.

Figure 4-17 illustrates the rear of a typical UPS unit.

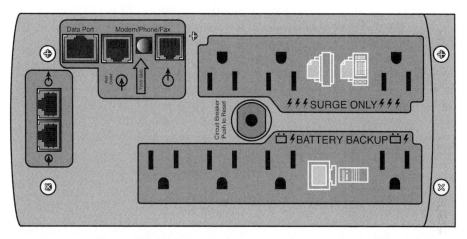

Figure 4-17   A typical UPS with integrated surge suppression for printers and other AC powered devices, 10/100/1000 Ethernet (including VoIP), and conventional telephony devices.

NOTE   Always plug a UPS directly into a wall outlet, not into a power strip or surge suppressor.

Buying the Correct-Sized Battery Backup System

Battery backups can't run forever. But then, they're not supposed to. This section describes how you can make sure you get enough time to save your files and shut down your computer. UPS units are rated in VA (volt-amps), and their manufacturers have interactive buying guides you can use online or download to help you select a model with adequate capacity. If you use a UPS with an inadequate VA rating for your equipment, your runtime will be substantially shorter than it should be.

Here's how to do the math: You can calculate the correct VA rating for your equipment by adding up the wattage ratings of your computer and monitor and multiplying the result by 1.4. If your equipment is rated in amperage (amps), multiply the amp rating by 120 (volts) to get the VA rating.

For example, my computer has a 450W power supply, which would require a 630VA-rated UPS (450×1.4) and a 17-inch monitor that is rated in amps, not watts. The monitor draws 0.9A, which would require a 108VA-rated UPS (0.9×120). Add the VA ratings together, and my computer needs a 750VA-rated battery backup unit or larger. Specifying a UPS with a VA rating at least twice what is required by the equipment attached to the UPS (for example, a 1500VA or higher rating, based on a minimum requirement of 750VA) will greatly improve the runtime of the battery.

In this example, a typical 750VA battery backup unit would provide about 5 minutes of runtime when used with my equipment. However, if I used a 1500VA battery backup, I could increase my runtime to more than 15 minutes because my equipment would use only about half the rated capacity of the UPS unit.

If you need a more precise calculation, for example, if you will also power an additional monitor or other external device, use the interactive sizing guides provided by battery backup vendors, such as American Power Conversion (www.apc.com).

CAUTION   You should not attach laser printers to the battery-backup outlets on a UPS because their high current draw will cause the runtime of the battery to be very short. If the UPS has some outlets that provide surge protection only, you can use those outlets for a laser printer. In most cases, only the computer and monitor need to be attached to the UPS. However, inkjet printers, external modems, and external USB or FireWire hard disks have low current draw and can be attached to the UPS with little reduction in runtime.

Power-Conditioning Devices

Although power supplies are designed to work with voltages that do not exactly meet the 115V or 230V standards, power that is substantially higher or lower than what the computer is designed for can damage the system. Electrical noise on the power line, even with power at the correct voltage, also causes problems because it disrupts the correct sinewave alternating-current pattern the computer, monitor, and other devices are designed to use.

Better-quality surge protectors often provide power filtration to handle electromagnetic interference (EMI)/radio frequency interference (RFI) noise problems from laser printers and other devices that generate a lot of electrical interference.

However, to deal with voltage that is too high or too low, you need a true power conditioner.

Power-conditioning units take substandard or overstandard power levels and adjust them to the correct range needed by your equipment. Some units also include high-quality surge protection features.

To determine whether you need a power-conditioning unit, you can contact your local electric utility company to see whether it loans or rents power-monitoring devices. Alternatively, you can rent them from power consultants. These units track power level and quality over a set period of time (such as overnight or longer) and provide reports to help you see the overall quality of power on a given line.

Moving surge- and interference-causing devices such as microwaves, vacuum cleaners, refrigerators, freezers, and furnaces to circuits away from the computer circuits helps minimize power problems. However, in older buildings, or during times of peak demand, power conditioning might still be necessary. A true (line-interactive) UPS provides built-in power conditioning by its very nature (see the previous discussion).

System Cooling

220-802

Objective:
220-802: 4.2

Today's computers often run much hotter than systems of a few years ago, so it's important to understand how to keep the hottest-running components running cooler. The following sections discuss the components that are most in need of cooling and how to cool them (processor cooling is discussed in Chapter 2, "Motherboards and Processors").

Northbridge and Southbridge Chips and Voltage Regulators

Motherboards use a one-chip or two-chip chipset (also referred to as northbridge and southbridge chips) to route data to and from the processor. The northbridge or Memory Controller Hub (MCH) chip, because it carries high-speed data such as memory and video to and from the processor, becomes hot during operation, and, if the component overheats and is damaged, the entire motherboard must be replaced. For this reason, most motherboards feature some type of cooler for the northbridge chip.

Although the southbridge or I/O Controller Hub (ICH) chip carries lower-speed traffic, such as hard disk, audio, and network traffic, it can also become overheated. As a result, most recent motherboards also feature cooling for the southbridge chip. Some chipsets combine both functions into a single chip, which also requires cooling.

Three methods have been used for cooling the motherboard chipset. Passive heat sinks attached directly to the chipset chips are inexpensive but do not provide sufficient cooling for high-performance systems. Active heat sinks provide better cooling than passive heat sinks, but low-quality sleeve-bearing fans often used in these coolers can cause premature fan failure and lead to overheating. The latest trend in chipset and motherboard cooling uses heat pipes, which draw heat away from the chipset or other high-temperature components, such as the voltage regulator for CPU power, and dissipates it through high-performance, very large passive heat sinks located away from the chipset itself. While you can add other types of coolers to chipset chips, heat pipes are factory-installed.

Figure 4-18 illustrates passive and active heat sinks for northbridge and southbridge chips.

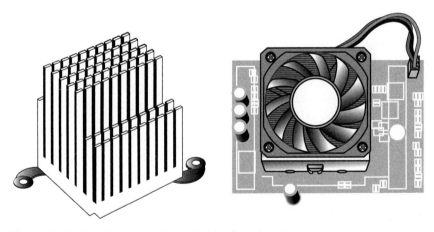

Figure 4-18   Passive and active heat sinks for chipsets.

Figure 4-19 illustrates a motherboard that uses heat pipes for component cooling.

Figure 4-19   Motherboard with heat pipe cooling. Heat is transferred from components under heat sink (A) via heat pipe (B) to be dissipated by radiator at rear of motherboard (C).

Video Card Cooling

Another major heat source in modern systems is the video card's graphics processing unit (GPU) chip, which renders the desktop, graphics, and everything else you see on your computer screen. With the exception of a few low-end video cards, almost all video cards use active heat sinks to blow hot air away from the GPU.

However, the memory chips on a video card can also become very hot. To cool both the GPU and video memory, most recent midrange and high-end video card designs use a fan shroud to cool both components. Fan shrouds often require enough space to prevent the expansion slot next to the video card from being used.

Figure 4-20 illustrates a typical video card with a two-slot fan shroud.

Case Fans

Most ATX chassis have provisions for at least two case fans: one at the front of the system and one at the rear of the system. Case fans can be powered by the motherboard or by using a Y-splitter connected to a four-pin Molex power connector. Case fans at the front of the system should draw air into the system, while case fans at the rear of the system should draw air out of the system.

Figure 4-20   The EVGA GeForce GTX 580 is a high-performance PCI Express x16 video card that requires a two-slot fan shroud. Image courtesy of EVGA Corporation.

Figure 4-21 shows a typical rear case fan. You can plug fans like this into the three-prong chassis fan connection found on many recent motherboards or into the 4-pin Molex drive power connector used by hard drives. If the motherboard power connector is used, the PC Health or hardware monitor function found in many recent system BIOS setup programs can monitor fan speed (refer to Figure 4-10).

NOTE   Some case fans that can be powered by a Molex power connector include a special power cable that permits the fan speed to be monitored by the motherboard, even though the motherboard is not used to power the fan.

Case fans are available in various sizes up to 200mm (80, 92, and 120mm are the most common sizes). Measure the opening at the rear of the case to determine which fan size to purchase. Some systems, such as the one shown earlier in Figure 4-11, might feature two rear fans or a rear fan and a top fan.

Thermal Compound

When passive or active heat sinks are installed on a processor, northbridge or south-bridge chip, GPU or other component, **thermal compound** (also known as thermal transfer material, thermal grease, or phase change material) must be used to provide the best possible thermal transfer between the component and the heat sink.

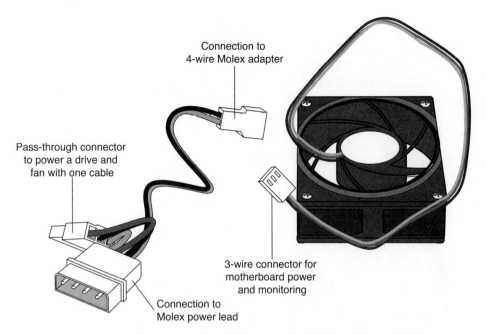

Connection to
4-wire Molex adapter

Pass-through connector
to power a drive and
fan with one cable

3-wire connector for
motherboard power
and monitoring

Connection to
Molex power lead

Figure 4-21   A case fan that can be plugged into the motherboard or into a Molex power connector.

Heat sinks supplied with boxed processors might use a preapplied phase-change material on the heat sink, whereas OEM processors with third-party heat sinks usually require the installer to use a paste or thick liquid thermal grease or silver-based compound. Coolers for northbridge or southbridge chips might use thermal grease or a phase-change pad.

If the thermal material is preapplied to the heat sink, make sure you remove the protective tape before you install the heat sink. If a third-party heat sink is used, or if the original heat sink is removed and reinstalled, carefully remove any existing thermal transfer material from the heat sink and processor die surface. Then, apply new thermal transfer material to the processor die before you reinstall the heat sink on the processor. Figure 4-22 illustrates the application of thermal compound to a northbridge chip before attaching a heat sink.

Figure 4-22   Applying thermal grease to the northbridge chip.

Exam Preparation Tasks

Review All the Key Topics

Review the most important topics in the chapter, noted with the key topics icon in the outer margin of the page. Table 4-4 lists a reference of these key topics and the page numbers on which each is found.

Table 4-4 Key Topics for Chapter 4

Key Topic Element	Description	Page Number
Text	Power supply converts AC to DC	130
Text	A typical ATX power supply	130
Figure 4-1	Power supply ratings	131
List	Determining the wattage rating needed for a replacement power supply	132
List	Voltage ranges supported by power supplies	133
Figure 4-4	20-pin, 24-pin, and ATX12V and AUX connectors	136
Figure 4-5	Power supply pinouts	136
Figure 4-6	Power supply connectors for peripheral and modern motherboards	137
List	Steps for removing the power supply	139
List	Symptoms of an overloaded power supply	141
Text	Fan failure indicators	142
List	Causes for a "dead" system	143
List	Diagnosing power supply problems	143
List	Causes of overheating	144
Text	Multimeter test procedures	150
Table 4-3	Acceptable voltage levels	153
List	Power supply hazards	154
Text	Surge suppressors	156
Text	Battery backup units	158
Text	Power conditioning units	161
Text	Cooling motherboard chipsets	162

Complete the Tables and Lists from Memory

Print a copy of Appendix A, "Memory Tables," (found on the CD), or at least the section for this chapter, and complete the tables and lists from memory. Appendix B, "Memory Tables Answer Key," also on the CD, includes completed tables and lists to check your work.

Define Key Terms

Define the following key terms from this chapter, and check your answers in the glossary.

power supply, AC, DC, multimeter, surge suppressor, battery backup, thermal compound

Complete Hands-On Lab

Complete the hands-on labs, and then see the answers and explanations at the end of the chapter.

Lab 4-1: Check Power Supply Voltages

Scenario: You are a technician working at a PC repair bench. You need to determine whether the power supply is supplying correct voltage to the motherboard without opening the system.

Procedure: Start the system, open the BIOS setup program, and open the dialog that displays power levels (System Health, PC Health, System Monitor are typical names). Check the voltage levels listed against those listed in Table 4-3.

> **NOTE** If the system does not display voltage levels in the system BIOS, use a multimeter and the information in Figure 4-5, Table 4-2, and Table 4-3 to check voltage levels.

Lab 4-2: Check for Airflow Problems Inside the System

Scenario: You are a technician working at a PC repair bench. You need to determine whether the cable layout inside the system may be causing overheating.

Procedure: Use the procedure for Lab 4-1 to check system temperature after running the system for about a half-hour. Record the current temperature. Shut down the system, unplug it from AC power, and open the system. Compare the interior of the system to Figures 4-11 and 4-12. If the system resembles Figure 4-11, the system needs better cable organization.

Answer Review Questions

Answer these review questions and then see the answers and explanations at the end of the chapter.

1. Which of the following would you use to keep the power supply working properly? (Choose two.)

   a. Surge protector

   b. Extra power supply

   c. UPS units

   d. Multimeter

2. Power supplies are rated using which of the following units?

   a. Amps

   b. Volts

   c. Watts

   d. Output

3. Newer tower-case computers' power supplies typically have which of the following power output ratings?

   a. 300 watts

   b. 400 watts

   c. 250 watts

   d. 500 watts or higher

4. Most power supplies in use today are designed to handle which two voltage ranges? (Choose two.)

   a. 115

   b. 300

   c. 230

   d. 450

5. Which of the following are causes of power supply overheating?

    a. Overloading the power supply.

    b. Fan failure.

    c. Dirt or dust.

    d. All of these options are correct.

6. How many pins are used for the main power connection by recent ATX/BTX motherboards with ATX12V 2.2 power supplies?

    a. 24

    b. 48

    c. 32

    d. 16

7. What is the four-pin square power connector on the motherboard used for?

    a. Extra power to PCIe slots

    b. 5-volt power for fans

    c. 12-volt power for processors

    d. 12-volt power for fans

8. What is the six-pin power lead on the power supply used for?

    a. Extra power to PCIe x16 cards

    b. Extra power for PCI cards

    c. Power for case fans

    d. Power supply diagnostics

9. Which of the following steps would you use to remove a power supply?

    a. Shut down the computer. If the power supply has an on/off switch, turn it off as well.

    b. Disconnect the AC power cord from the computer.

    c. Disconnect power connections from the motherboard, hard drives, and optical drives.

    d. All of these options are correct.

10. To avoid power supply hazards you must never do which of the following? (Choose two.)

    a. Disassemble the power supply.

    b. Put metal tools through the openings.

    c. Switch the voltage to 220.

    d. Put a smaller power supply in the computer.

11. Which device provides emergency power to a computer in case of a complete power failure?

    a. UTP

    b. UPS

    c. Power strip

    d. Surge protector

12. What is the minimum time recommendation for a UPS to supply power for an individual workstation?

    a. 30 minutes

    b. 45 minutes

    c. 1 hour

    d. 15 minutes

13. Which of the following correctly describe an SPS? (Choose all that apply.)

    a. The battery on an SPS is only used when the AC power fails.

    b. An SPS is on all the time.

    c. A momentary gap in power occurs between loss of AC power and when the SPS comes online.

    d. An SPS is far less expensive than a UPS.

14. When a system is dead and gives no signs of life when you turn on the computer, which of the following might be the cause? (Choose all that apply.)

    a. Defects in AC power to the system

    b. Power supply failure or misconfiguration

    c. Temporary short circuits in internal or external components

    d. Power button or other component failure

15. Processors and other components use a finned metal device to help with cooling. What is this device called? (Choose two.)

    a. Passive heat sink

    b. Thermal compound

    c. Active heat sink

    d. Chassis heat sink

16. What is the purpose of thermal compound?

    a. Provides the best possible thermal transfer between a component and its heat sink

    b. Provides the best possible thermal transfer between a component's heat sink and its fan

    c. To negate the effects of thermal contraction and expansion in adapter cards

    d. Provides the best possible thermal transfer between the northbridge and its fan

Answers to Hands-On Lab

Lab 4-1: Check Power Supply Voltages

Answer: If the voltage levels are within limits, the power supply is healthy. If any of the voltage levels are out of range, the power supply should be replaced with a power supply of the same or higher wattage rating.

Lab 4-2: Check for Airflow Problems Inside the System

Answer: Use cable ties and reroute long cables between the drive bays at the back wall of the system or along the edge of the motherboard to reduce snarls and improve airflow. After reassembling the system, reconnecting it to AC power, and booting the system to the BIOS setup program, recheck system temperature after running the system for a half-hour. If the temperature is lower, you have improved airflow inside the system. Even if the system temperature remains the same, you have made it easier to work inside the system in the future.

Answers and Explanations to Review Questions

1. **A, C.** To keep your power supply up and running and to help prevent damage from power surges, you should use a surge protector. The UPS will supply power for a short period of time to the computer system in case of total power outage.

2. **C.** Power supplies are rated in watts, and the more watts a power supply provides, the more devices it can safely power.

3. **D.** Most newer tower computers have 500 watt or larger power supplies in them because of the greater number of drives and expansion cards that are available now.

4. **A, C.** Standard North American power is 115 volts, and power in most parts of Europe and Asia is 230 volts. Some power supplies have a slider on the back to switch between the two voltages.

5. **D.** All of the listed reasons can cause damage to the power supply as well as overheating your computer.

6. **A.** Most of the newer power supplies in use today have 24 pins. Older motherboards have a 20-pin connection.

7. **C.** This connector is the ATX12V connector, which provides 12V power dedicated to the processor (a voltage regulator on the motherboard reduces 12V to the actual power required by the processor).

8. **A.** The six-pin (or 6+2 pin) power supply lead provides additional power needed by high-performance PCIe x16 cards, such as those used for SLI or for CrossFire X multi-GPU installations.

9. **D.** All of the listed answers are correct. You must disconnect from the wall first; then once inside the computer unhook the connection to the motherboard, drives, and other devices.

10. **A, B.** The capacitors inside the power supply retain potentially fatal voltage levels. To prevent shock you should not disassemble power supplies or stick in a metal object such as a screwdriver.

11. **B.** A UPS (uninterruptible power supply) will keep a standard desktop up and running in case of a complete power outage.

12. **D.** UPSs are designed to supply power to a computer long enough for you to complete a formal shutdown.

13. **A, C, D.** When an SPS is used there is a momentary gap, usually about 1ms or less, between when the power goes off and when the SPS starts supplying power. SPSs are also less expensive and are not used at all times.

14. **A, B, C, D.** When turning on a system that shows no signs of life you must consider all of these as potential problems.

15. **A, C.** All processors require a heat sink. A heat sink is a finned metal device that radiates heat away from the processor. An active heat sink (a heat sink with a fan) is required for adequate processor cooling on current systems. Some older systems used a specially designed duct to direct airflow over a processor with a passive heat sink (a heat sink without a fan). Most motherboards' northbridges use passive heat sinks or heat pipes.

16. **A.** Thermal compound (also known as thermal transfer material, thermal grease, or phase change material) provides for the best possible thermal transfer between a component (for example a CPU) and its heat sink. This prevents CPU damage. The fan and adapter cards should not have thermal compound applied to them.

This chapter covers the following subjects:

- **RAM Basics**—This section talks about what RAM does, how it works, and how it relates to the rest of the computer system.

- **Memory Modules**—In this section you learn about the various types of RAM available, including SDRAM, DDR, and Rambus. Their architecture, capacity, and speed are also described. This section also discusses the operational characteristics and features of memory modules, and types of memory such as ECC, registered, and unbuffered.

- **Installing Memory Modules**—This section demonstrates how to install DIMMs properly within a motherboard's memory slots.

- **Troubleshooting Memory**—This section covers some issues you might encounter with RAM due to incompatible memory speeds and types. Due to the possibility of memory overheating, this section also describes some measures you can take to keep your memory modules clean and protected.

This chapter covers portions of **CompTIA A+ 220-801 objective 1.3** and **CompTIA A+ 220-802 objective 4.2**.

CHAPTER 5

RAM

When it's time for the CPU to process something, **RAM (random access memory)** is the workspace it uses. RAM is one of two types of memory found in your computer; the other type of memory is ROM (read-only memory). What's the difference? RAM's contents can be changed at any time, while ROM's contents require special procedures to change. Think of RAM as a blank sheet of paper and a pencil: You can write on it, erase what you've done, and keep making changes. On the other hand, ROM is like a newspaper. If you want to change what's printed on the newspaper, you must recycle it so it can be reprocessed back into newsprint and sent through the newspaper's printing presses again. This chapter focuses on the types, installation, and troubleshooting of RAM.

Foundation Topics

RAM Basics

220-801

Objective:
220-801: 1.3

RAM is used for programs and data, and by the operating system for disk caching (using RAM to hold recently accessed disk sectors). Thus, installing more RAM improves transfers between the CPU and both RAM and disk drives. If your computer runs short of RAM, Windows can also use the hard disk as *virtual memory*, a slow substitute for RAM. This virtual memory, or **paging file** in Windows 7/ Vista/XP is a file on the hard disk used to hold part of the contents of memory if the installed RAM on the system isn't large enough for the tasks currently being performed.

Although the hard disk can substitute for RAM in a pinch, don't confuse RAM with magnetic storage devices such as hard disks. Although the contents of RAM and magnetic storage can be changed freely, RAM loses its contents as soon as you shut down the computer, while magnetic storage can hold data for years. Although RAM's contents are temporary, RAM is much faster than magnetic storage: RAM speed is measured in nanoseconds (billionths of a second), while magnetic storage is measured in milliseconds (thousandths of a second).

Even though every computer ever made is shipped with RAM, you will probably need to add more RAM to a computer as time passes. Ever-increasing amounts of RAM are needed as operating systems and applications get more powerful and add more features. Because RAM is one of the most popular upgrades to add to any system during its lifespan, you need to understand how RAM works, what types of RAM exist, and how to add it to provide the biggest performance boost to the systems you maintain.

When you must specify memory for a given system, there are several variables you need to know:

- **Memory module type (240-pin DIMM, 184-pin DIMM, 168-pin DIMM, and so on)**—The module type your system can use has a great deal to do with the memory upgrade options you have with any given system. Although a few systems can use more than one memory module type, in most cases if you want to change to a faster type of memory module, such as from 184-pin DIMM (used by DDR SDRAM) to 240-pin DIMM (such as DDR2 or DDR3 SDRAM), you need to upgrade the motherboard first.

- **Memory chip type used on the module (SDRAM, DDR SDRAM, RDRAM, and so on)**—Today, a particular memory module type uses only one type of memory. However, older memory module types such as 72-pin SIMMs and early 168-pin DIMMs were available with different types of memory chips. You need to specify the right memory chip type in such cases to avoid conflicts with onboard memory and provide stable performance.

- **Memory module speed (60ns, PC-133, PC800, PC2700, PC2-6400, PC3-10600, and so on)**—There are three ways to specify the speed of a memory module: the actual speed in ns (nanoseconds) of the chips on the module (60ns), the clock speed of the data bus (PC-133 is 133 MHz; PC800 is 800 MHz), or the throughput (in MBps) of the memory (for example, PC2700 is 2,700 MBps or 2.7 GBps DDR; PC2-2 6400 is 6,400 MBps or 6.4 GBps; PC3-10600 is 10,667 MBps or 10.6 GBps). The throughput method is used by current memory types.

- **Error checking (parity, non-parity, ECC)**—Most systems don't perform parity checking (to verify the contents of memory) or correct errors, but some motherboards and systems support these functions. Although parity-checked memory mainly slows down the system, ECC memory can detect memory errors as well as correct them. If a system is performing critical work (high-level mathematics or financial functions, departmental or enterprise-level server tasks), ECC support in the motherboard and ECC memory are worthwhile options to specify. Some systems also support registered or nonregistered modules. Registered modules are more reliable but are slower because they include a chip that boosts the memory signal.

- **Allowable module sizes and combinations**—Some motherboards insist you use the same speeds and sometimes the same sizes of memory in each memory socket, while others are more flexible. To find out which is true about a particular system, check the motherboard or system documentation before you install memory or add more memory.

- **The number of modules needed per bank of memory**—Systems address memory in banks, and the number of modules per bank varies with the processor and the memory module type installed. If you need more than one module per bank, and only one module is installed, the system will ignore it. Systems that require multiple modules per bank require that modules be the same size and speed.

- **Whether the system requires or supports dual-channel memory (two identical memory modules instead of one at a time) or triple-channel memory (three identical memory modules)**—Dual-channel memory and triple-channel memory are accessed in an interleaved manner to improve memory latency (the time required between memory accesses). As a result, systems running dual-channel memory offer faster memory performance than systems running single-channel memory. Intel's Core i7 processor is the first processor to use triple-channel memory (which runs even faster than dual-channel memory), although it can also use dual-channel memory if only two identical modules are installed.

- **The total number of modules that can be installed**—The number of sockets on the motherboard determines the number of modules that can be installed. Very small-footprint systems (such as those that use microATX, flexATX, or Mini-ITX motherboards) often support only one or two modules, but systems that use full-size ATX motherboards often support three or more modules, especially those designed for dual-channel or triple-channel memory.

When it comes to memory, compatibility is important. The memory module type must fit the motherboard; speed must be compatible, and the module storage size/combination must match your computer system as well. To find out exactly what type of memory modules are compatible with your motherboard, visit a memory manufacturer's website and check within their database. Be sure to have the model number of the motherboard, or the model of the computer handy.

Memory Modules

220-801

Objective:
220-801: 1.3

While today's systems use memory modules built from a combination of chips, rather than individual chips plugged into the motherboard as with early PC systems, it's still necessary to understand the different types of memory chips that have been and are used to build memory modules.

DRAM

Virtually all memory modules use some type of *dynamic* RAM, or **DRAM** chips. DRAM requires frequent recharges of memory to retain its contents. Early types of

DRAM, including variations such as fast-page mode (FPM) and extended data-out (EDO), were speed rated by access time, measured in nanoseconds (ns; smaller is faster). Typical speeds for regular DRAM chips were 100ns or slower; FPM memory, used primarily in 30-pin and 72-pin SIMM modules, ran at speeds of 70ns, 80ns, and 100ns. EDO DRAM, which was used primarily in 72-pin SIMM modules and a few 168-pin DIMM modules, typically ran at 60ns.

While these types of DRAM are long obsolete, other types of DRAM, including SDRAM, DDR SDRAM, DDR2 SDRAM, and DDR3 SDRAM are used in more recent systems.

SRAM

Static random-access memory (SRAM) is RAM that does not need to be periodically refreshed. Memory refreshing is common to other types of RAM and is basically the act of reading information from a specific area of memory and immediately rewriting that information back to the same area without modifying it. Due to SRAM's architecture, it does not require this refresh. You will find SRAM being used as cache memory for CPUs, as buffers on the motherboard or within hard drives, and as temporary storage for LCD screens. Normally, SRAM is soldered directly to a printed circuit board (PCB) or integrated directly to a chip. This means that you probably won't be replacing SRAM. SRAM is faster than, and is usually found in smaller quantities than its distant cousin DRAM.

SDRAM

Synchronous DRAM (SDRAM) was the first type of memory to run in sync with the processor bus (the connection between the processor, or CPU, and other components on the motherboard). Most 168-pin DIMM modules use SDRAM memory. To determine whether a DIMM module contains SDRAM memory, check its speed markings. SDRAM memory is rated by bus speed (PC66 equals 66 MHz bus speed; PC100 equals 100 MHz bus speed; PC133 equals 133 MHz bus speed).

Depending on the specific module and motherboard chipset combination, PC133 modules can sometimes be used on systems that are designed for PC100 modules.

DDR SDRAM

The second generation of systems running synchronous DRAM use double data rate SDRAM (DDR SDRAM). **DDR SDRAM** performs two transfers per clock cycle, instead of one as with regular SDRAM. 184-pin DIMM memory modules use DDR SDRAM chips.

While DDR SDRAM is sometimes rated in MHz, it is more often rated by throughput (MBps). Common speeds for DDR SDRAM include PC1600 (200 MHz/1600 MBps), PC2100 (266 MHz/2100 MBps), PC2700 (333 MHz/2700 MBps), and PC3200 (400 MHz/3200 MBps), but other speeds are available from some vendors.

DDR2 SDRAM

Double double data rate SDRAM (DDR2 SDRAM) is the successor to DDR SDRAM. DDR2 SDRAM runs its external data bus at twice the speed of DDR SDRAM, enabling faster performance. However, DDR2 SDRAM memory has greater latency than DDR SDRAM memory. Latency is a measure of how long it takes to receive information from memory; the higher the number, the greater the latency. Typical latency values for mainstream DDR2 memory are CL=5 and CL=6, compared to CL=2.5 and CL=3 for DDR memory. 240-pin memory modules use DDR2 SDRAM.

DDR2 SDRAM memory might be referred to by the effective memory speed of the memory chips on the module (the memory clock speed x4 or the I/O bus clock speed x2), for example, DDR2-533 (133 MHz memory clock x4 or 266 MHz I/O bus clock x2)=533 MHz) or by module throughput (DDR2-533 is used in PC2-4200 modules, which have a throughput of more than 4200 MBps). PC2- indicates the module uses DDR2 memory, while PC- indicates the module uses DDR memory.

Other common speeds for DDR2 SDRAM modules include PC2-3200 (DDR2-400; 3200 MBps throughput); PC2-5300 (DDR2-667); PC2-6400 (DDR2-800).

DDR3 SDRAM

Double data rate 3 SDRAM (DDR3 SDRAM) is the latest generation of SDRAM. Compared to DDR2, DDR3 runs at lower voltages, has twice the internal banks, and most versions run at faster speeds than DDR2. As with DDR2 versus DDR, DDR3 has greater latency than DDR2. Typical latency values for mainstream DDR3 memory are CL7, compared to CL5 or CL6 for DDR2. Although DDR3 modules use 240 pins, their layout and keying are different than DDR2, and they cannot be interchanged.

DDR3 SDRAM memory might be referred to by the effective memory speed of the memory chips on the module (the memory clock speed x4 or the I/O bus clock speed x2), for example, DDR3-1333 (333 MHz memory clock x4 or 666 MHz I/O bus clock x2)=1333 MHz) or by module throughput (DDR3-1333 is used in PC3-10600 modules, which have a throughput of more than 10,600 MBps or 10.6 GBps). PC3- indicates the module uses DDR3 memory.

Other common speeds for DDR3 SDRAM modules include PC3-8500 (DDR3-1066; 8500 MBps throughput); PC3-12800 (DDR3-1600); PC3-17000 (DDR3-2133).

Rambus

Rambus Direct RAM (RDRAM) memory was used by early Pentium 4-based chipsets from Intel, including the i820, i840, and E7205 Granite Bay workstation chipset, but has not been used by more recent systems. RDRAM modules are known as RIMMs and were produced in 16-bit and 32-bit versions.

16-bit RIMMs use a 184-pin connector, while 32-bit RIMMs use a 232-pin connector. 32-bit motherboards that use RIMMs must use pairs of 16-bit modules. Empty RIMM sockets must be occupied by a continuity module (resembles a RIMM but without memory; also known as a CRIMM).

Common Rambus 16-bit module speeds include PC600 (1200 MBps bandwidth); PC700 (1420 MBps bandwidth); PC800 (1600 MBps bandwidth); PC1066 (also known as RIMM 2100; 2133 MBps bandwidth); and PC1200 (also called RIMM 2400; 2400 MBps bandwidth).

32-bit (dual-channel) RIMM modules use the RIMM *xxxx* identifier, listing the throughput in MBps as part of the name, for example, RIMM 3200 (3200 MBps bandwidth); RIMM 4200 (4200 MBps bandwidth); RIMM 4800 (4800 MBps bandwidth); and RIMM 6400 (6400 MBps bandwidth).

Table 5-1 shows a comparison of the types of RAM you need to know for the exam.

Table 5-1   RAM Comparisons

RAM Type	Pins	Common Type and Speed	Defining Characteristic
DRAM	30 and 72	33 or 66 MHz	Obsolete.
SDRAM	168	PC133 = 133 MHz	This original version of SDRAM is now obsolete and has given way to DDR, DDR2, and DDR3 memory.
DDR SDRAM	184	PC3200 = 400 MHz/3200 MBps	Double the transfers per clock cycle compared to regular SDRAM.
DDR2 SDRAM	240	DDR2-800 (PC2-6400) = 800 MHz/6400 MBps	External data bus speed (I/O bus clock) is 2x faster than DDR SDRAM.

Table 5-1 Continued

RAM Type	Pins	Common Type and Speed	Defining Characteristic
DDR3 SDRAM	240 (the keying on DDR3 is offset to one side compared to DDR2)	DDR3-1333 (PC3-10600) =1333MHz/10,600 MBps	External data bus speed (I/O bus clock) is 2x faster than DDR2 SDRAM (4x faster than DDR SDRAM).
Rambus (RDRAM)	184 and 232	PC800 = 1600 MBps	Not used in new computers, but you still might see existing systems using Rambus memory modules.

Operational Characteristics

Memory modules can be classified in various ways, including

- The amount of memory (in bits) found on the module

- The differences between parity and non-parity memory

- The differences between ECC and non-ECC memory

- The differences between registered and unbuffered memory

- The differences between single-sided and double-sided memory

The following sections deal with these operational characteristics.

Comparison of Memory Modules

All systems built since the early 1990s have used some form of memory module, and most of these systems have used standard versions of these modules. These modules come in these major types:

- **Single Inline Memory Module (SIMM)**—Has a single row of 30 or 72 edge connectors on the bottom of the module. Single refers to both sides of the module having the same pinout.

- **Single Inline Pin Package (SIPP)**—A short-lived variation on the 30-pin SIMM, which substituted pins for the edge connector used by SIMM modules.

- **Dual Inline Memory Module (DIMM)**—These are available in 168-pin, 184-pin, and 240-pin versions. Dual refers to each side of the module having a different pinout.

- **Small Outline DIMM (SODIMM)**—A compact version of the standard DIMM module, available in various pinouts for use in notebook computers and laser/LED printers. To learn more about SODIMM modules, see Chapter 9, "Laptop and Notebook Computers."

- **Rambus RDRAM Module**—A memory module using Direct Rambus memory (RDRAM) chips. Kingston Technology has copyrighted the name RIMM for its Rambus RDRAM modules, but Rambus RDRAM modules are often referred to as RIMMs, regardless of their actual manufacturer.

- **Small Outline Rambus Module**—A compact version of the standard Rambus module for use in notebook computers.

NOTE   To see a comparison of DDR, DDR2, and DDR3 keying, see http://www.intel.com/support/motherboards/desktop/sb/CS-012038.htm.

Figure 5-1 illustrates SIMM, SIPP, and DIMM modules used in desktop computers.

Memory Module Width

Memory modules are classified in a variety of ways, including size, speed, memory type, and width in bits. A byte is the basic building block used to determine storage and RAM capacity, and eight bits make a byte. Memory module widths (in bits) have become wider as the memory bus sizes of processors have increased.

Memory must be added in banks, and a bank of memory refers to a memory module, or modules, whose width in bits adds up to the width of the memory bus and is identical in other characteristics, such as size and speed. Most of today's computers have a default memory bus-width of 64 bits. A bank will by default be inhabited by one DIMM. If you are using dual-channel memory, the bank will be composed of two 64-bit DIMMs. More on dual-channel technology later in this chapter.

Parity and Non-Parity Memory

Two methods have been used to protect the reliability of memory:

- Parity checking
- ECC (error-correcting code)

Both of these methods depend upon the presence of an additional memory chip over the chips required for the data bus of the module. For example, a module that uses eight chips for data would use a ninth chip to support parity or ECC.

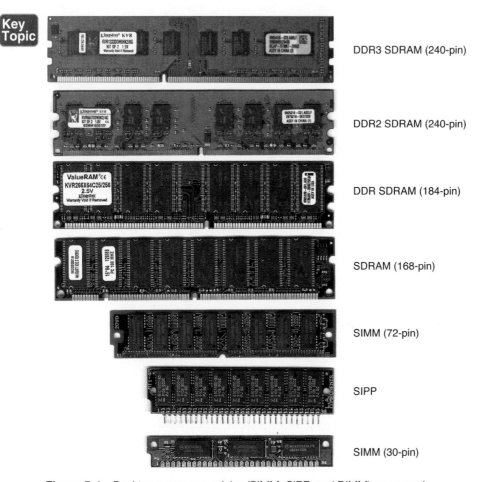

Key Topic

DDR3 SDRAM (240-pin)

DDR2 SDRAM (240-pin)

DDR SDRAM (184-pin)

SDRAM (168-pin)

SIMM (72-pin)

SIPP

SIMM (30-pin)

Figure 5-1 Desktop memory modules (SIMM, SIPP, and DIMM) compared.

Parity checking, which goes back to the original IBM PC, works like this: Whenever memory is accessed, each data bit has a value of 0 or 1. When these values are added to the value in the parity bit, the resulting checksum should be an odd number. This is called *odd parity*. A memory problem typically causes the data bit values plus the parity bit value to total an even number. This triggers a parity error, and your system halts with a parity error message. Note that parity checking requires parity-enabled memory and support in the motherboard. On modules that support parity-checking, there's a parity bit for each group of eight bits.

The method used to fix this type of error varies with the system. On museum-piece systems that use individual memory chips, you must open the system, push all memory chips back into place, and test the memory thoroughly if you have no spares (using memory testing software), or replace the memory if you have spare memory chips. If the computer uses memory modules, replace one module at a time, test the memory (or at least run the computer for awhile) to determine whether the problem has gone away. If the problem recurs, replace the original module, swap out the second module and repeat.

TIP Some systems' error message tells you the logical location of the error so you can take the system documentation and determine which module or modules to replace.

NOTE Parity checking has always cost more because of the extra chips involved and the additional features required in the motherboard and chipset, and it fell out of fashion for PCs starting in the mid-1990s. Systems that lack parity checking freeze up when a memory problem occurs and do not display any message onscreen.

Because parity checking "protects" you from bad memory by shutting down the computer (which can cause you to lose data), vendors created a better way to use the parity bits to solve memory errors using a method called ECC.

ECC and Non-ECC Memory

For critical applications, network servers have long used a special type of memory called **error-correcting code (ECC)**. This memory enables the system to correct single-bit errors and notify you of larger errors.

Although most desktops do not support ECC, some workstations and most servers do offer ECC support. On systems that offer ECC support, ECC support might be enabled or disabled through the system BIOS, or it might be a standard feature. The parity bit in parity memory is used by the ECC feature to determine when the content of memory is corrupt and to fix single-bit errors. Unlike parity checking, which only warns you of memory errors, ECC memory actually corrects errors.

ECC is recommended for maximum data safety, although parity and ECC do provide a small slowdown in performance in return for the extra safety. ECC memory modules use the same types of memory chips used by standard modules, but they use more chips and might have a different internal design to allow ECC operation. ECC modules, like parity-checked modules, have an extra bit for each group of eight data bits.

To determine whether a system supports parity-checked or ECC memory, check the system BIOS memory configuration (typically on the Advanced or Chipset screens). Systems that support parity or ECC memory can use non-parity checked memory if parity checking and ECC are disabled. Another name for ECC is EDAC (Error Detection and Correction).

Registered and Unbuffered Memory

Most types of desktop memory modules use unbuffered memory. However, many servers and some desktop or workstation computers use a type of memory module called *registered memory*. Registered memory modules contain a register chip that enables the system to remain stable with large amounts of memory installed. The register chip acts as a buffer, which slightly slows down memory access.

Registered memory modules can be built with or without ECC support. However, most registered memory modules are used by servers and include ECC support. Figure 5-2 compares a standard (unbuffered) memory module with a registered memory module that also supports ECC.

Parity chips for ECC error correction

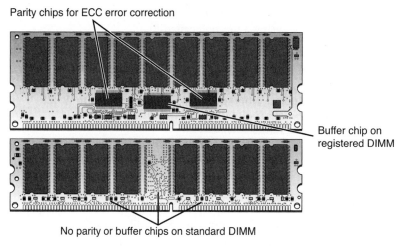

Buffer chip on
registered DIMM

No parity or buffer chips on standard DIMM

Figure 5-2   A registered module with ECC (top) compared to a standard unbuffered module (bottom).

Single-Sided and Double-Sided Memory

A double-sided SIMM acts like two conventional SIMMs in one, and can be recognized by having data chips on both sides of the module. Some systems work with both double-sided and single-sided SIMM memory modules, while others restrict the number of double-sided modules you can use or won't let you use them at all.

Read the manual for the system or motherboard to determine whether you can use double-sided SIMMs.

On modern systems that use DIMMs, the term "double-sided" refers to a module that contains two memory banks. On systems that restrict the number of banks that can be installed, you can install more single-sided DIMMs than double-sided DIMMs. To determine whether a particular system (motherboard) has this type of restriction, see its documentation.

Installing Memory Modules

> **220-801**
>
> **Objective:**
> **220-801: 1.3**

Memory modules are the memory "sticks" installed into the slots of a motherboard. Installing DIMMs and Rambus RDRAM memory modules is fairly easy, and can be a fun initial task for people who have never worked on a computer before. However, precautions must be taken not to damage the memory module or the motherboard. Before working with any memory modules, turn the computer off, and unplug it from the AC outlet. Be sure to employ electrostatic discharge (ESD) protection in the form of an antistatic strap and antistatic mat. Use an antistatic bag to hold the memory modules while you are not working with them. Before actually handling any components, touch an unpainted portion of the case chassis in a further effort to ground yourself. Try not to touch any of the chips, connectors, or circuitry of the memory module; instead hold them from the sides.

DIMM and Rambus RDRAM module sockets have an improved keying mechanism and a better locking mechanism compared to SIMMs.

To install the DIMM or Rambus RDRAM module, follow these steps:

Step 1. Line up the modules' connectors with the socket. Both DIMMs and Rambus modules have connections with different widths, preventing the module from being inserted backwards.

Step 2. Verify that the locking tabs on the socket are swiveled to the outside (open) position.

Step 3. After verifying that the module is lined up correctly with the socket, push the module straight down into the socket until the swivel locks on each end of the socket snap into place at the top corners of the module (see

Figure 5-3). A fair amount of force is required to engage the locks. Do not touch the gold-plated connectors on the bottom of the module; this can cause corrosion or ESD.

For clarity, the memory module installation pictured in Figure 5-3 was photographed with the motherboard out of the case. However, the tangle of cables around and over the DIMM sockets in Figure 5-4 provides a much more realistic view of the challenges you face when you install memory in a working system.

Locking clips not engaged

Locking clips engaged; module locked in place

Figure 5-3   A DIMM partly inserted (top) and fully inserted (bottom). The memory module must be pressed firmly into place before the locking tabs will engage.

When you install memory on a motherboard inside a working system, use the following tips to help your upgrade go smoothly and the module to work properly:

- If the system is a tower system, consider placing the system on its side to make the upgrade easier. Doing this also helps to prevent tipping the system over by accident when you push on the memory to lock it into the socket.

- Move the locking mechanisms on the DIMM sockets to the open position before you try to insert the module. In Figure 5-4, the locks on the empty socket are in the closed position. Figure 5-3 shows open and closed locks for comparison.

- Move power and drive cables away from the memory sockets so you can access the sockets. Disconnect drive cables if necessary.

- Use a flashlight to shine light into the interior of the system so you can see the memory sockets and locking mechanisms clearly; this enables you to determine the proper orientation of the module and to make sure the sockets' locking mechanisms are open.

- Use a flashlight to double-check your memory installation to make sure the module is completely inserted into the slot and locked into place.

- Replace any cables you moved or disconnected during the process before you close the case and restart the system.

TIP Note the positions of any cables before you remove them to perform an internal upgrade. I like to use self-stick colored dots on a drive and its matching data and power cables. You can purchase sheets of colored dots at most office-supply and discount stores.

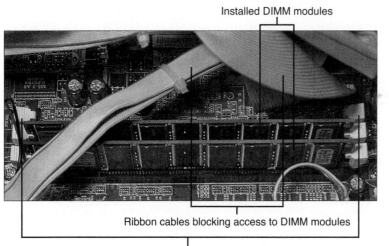

Installed DIMM modules

Ribbon cables blocking access to DIMM modules

Locking mechanism on empty DIMM socket in closed position;
must be opened before another module can be installed

Figure 5-4   DDR DIMM sockets in a typical system are often surrounded and covered up by drive and power cables, making it difficult to properly install additional memory.

Troubleshooting Memory

220-802

Objective:
220-802: 4.2

Because all information you create with a computer starts out in RAM, keeping RAM working properly is important. This section describes troubleshooting problems that might affect memory.

Verifying RAM Compatibility

Because of the wide range of speeds, latencies (CL ratings), and other performance factors, it's easier than ever before to install a memory module that fits into a system but is not compatible with the system. Incompatible memory modules can cause system lockups or crashes or corrupted data.

To determine whether a particular module will work in a particular system or motherboard, check the module for brand and model number markings, and then use a lookup or system analysis tool provided by the memory module vendor to determine which modules are recommended for a particular system or motherboard. Most memory vendors provide these tools on their websites. If the module is not recommended for the system or motherboard, don't install it.

Overclocking Can Lead to System Instability

If you run the processor or memory at speeds faster than those recommended, a process called *overclocking*, you could cause components to overheat and the system to crash. If your system crashes after overclocking, return the settings to standard values and restart the system. If the system is now stable, don't overclock it until you can add adequate cooling to the system. Overclocking is not recommended for business uses or for beginners.

CAUTION   Overclocking generates excess heat, which alone can cause damage to components. To make matters worse, one of the favorite ways that overclockers have to improve system stability is to slightly increase the voltage going to the processor core (Vcore) or to the memory modules, which further increases heat.

Don't even think about overclocking unless you study overclocking-oriented websites such as www.overclockers.com or publications such as MaximumPC (www.maximumpc.com). A careful perusal of these and other resources will tell you that successful overclocking requires a lot of time, a fair amount of cash, a lot of tolerance for damaged components, frequent rebooting, crashes, voided warranties, and so on.

> **NOTE**   Some motherboards come with a basic type of overclocking that only increases CPU frequency by 10% maximum. An example of this is Intel's TurboBoost technology. While this type of technology is relatively safe, it should still be approached with caution.

Use Caution When Mismatching RAM Speeds

Motherboards are designed to use particular speeds of memory modules, and all memory modules installed in a computer should meet or exceed the memory speed required by the system. Depending on the system, memory might be rated in nanoseconds (ns), by the bus speed of the CPU (such as PC-133), or by their throughput (such as DDR2-6400).

Newer systems are generally more tolerant of differences in memory timing. Some systems can access each module at its maximum speed, whereas others might slow down automatically to adjust to the slower access time. Some older systems might crash if additional memory is a different speed than the memory originally installed. Adjusting BIOS settings for memory timing might improve reliability in such cases.

Memory speeds can be determined from the memory chips themselves on SIMMs or from the markings on DIMMs or Rambus RDRAM modules (see Figure 5-5).

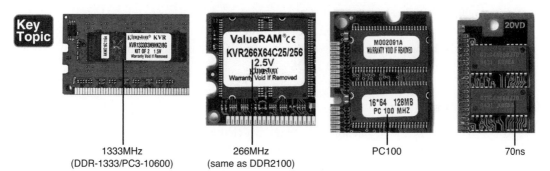

1333MHz
(DDR-1333/PC3-10600)   266MHz
(same as DDR2100)   PC100   70ns

Figure 5-5   Memory-speed markings on a DDR3 DIMM module (left), a DDR DIMM module, a standard SDRAM DIMM module (center), and a 72-pin SIMM (right).

As you can see from Figure 5-5, newer DIMM modules often have more informative markings than old modules. If you need to read the memory speed directly from the chips on the module, use these rules of thumb:

- Generally, the speed (in nanoseconds) is the last two numbers (often following a dash or alphanumerics) on the memory module: xxxxx - 15 (15ns) yyyyyyyy - 60 (60ns).

- Some memory chips use an abbreviated marking: xxxxx - 7 (70ns) yyyyy - 10 (100ns).

To verify speeds, you can use a standalone RAM tester, a small device that has connectors for different types of memory and a readout indicating actual speed, size, and other information.

For more information about testing RAM with both diagnostics software and hardware testing devices, see "Other Methods for RAM Testing," later in this chapter.

"Parity Error - System Halted" Message

Parity errors halt your system and require you to restart your computer. To use parity checking, you must be using parity-checked RAM (x9, x36, or x72 module types), and your computer must support parity checking and have this feature enabled. Parity errors can result from

- Mixing parity and non-parity RAM on parity-checked systems

- Mixing slow and fast RAM in the same bank or on the same motherboard

- Loose or corroded chip and module connectors

- Memory module/chip failure

If you enable parity checking in the BIOS setup and don't have parity modules, you'll have immediate errors. You can use parity memory along with non-parity memory by disabling parity checking in the system BIOS. Refer to Chapter 3, "BIOS," for more information about BIOS.

RAM-Sizing Errors at Bootup

Most systems test memory, and some alert you to a change in the memory size detected compared to the BIOS value. This is normal if you have just added memory. In such cases, enter the system BIOS setup program, exit and save changes, and restart the computer. However, a memory size error that occurs later indicates a memory problem. To determine which module is affected, follow these steps:

Step 1.   Note the memory count reached onscreen when the memory error is detected.

Step 2. Check the motherboard documentation to see which modules must be installed first.

Step 3. Change one module at a time, starting with the one you think is defective, until the error goes away.

Step 4. Disable cache RAM in the BIOS setup when testing memory.

A memory-sizing error that won't go away after all memory is changed might indicate a defective motherboard or defective cache memory.

Determining Whether Cache RAM Is the Source of a Memory Problem

Because cache RAM holds a copy of the information in main memory, errors in cache RAM can appear to be errors in system RAM. Use the following procedure to determine whether cache RAM is the cause of a memory problem:

Step 1. Disable L2 cache first.

Step 2. If the memory problem goes away, determine where L2 cache is located (processor or motherboard). If the motherboard uses removable cache chips or a cache module (some very old systems used cache chips or modules), replace the cache memory. If the motherboard uses nonremovable cache chips, replace the motherboard. If L2 cache is built into the processor, replace the processor.

Step 3. If the system runs normally, the replacement is successful. If the problem persists after replacing the component containing cache RAM, return the original component(s) to the system.

Step 4. Disable L1 cache.

Step 5. If the system runs normally, replace the CPU and retest.

Step 6. If the system runs normally after replacement, the CPU's L1 cache is faulty.

NOTE If the processor includes both L2 and L3 cache, disable both in Step 1. Check the system BIOS for an option such as CPU Internal cache. Some memory testing programs can be configured to bypass cache memory when testing main memory. See the documentation or help system for your memory testing program for details.

Other Methods for RAM Testing

Many utility programs, including CheckIt, AMIDiag, RAMExam, and others feature powerful memory-testing programs that can run continuously and use many more testing options than the fast POST test performed by the computer at startup. Many of these programs are run from optical media, so they bypass the normal operating system.

Here are a few more memory testing programs available online:

- **GoldMemory:** http://www.goldmemory.cz/

- **MemTest86:** http://www.memtest86.com/

- **PC-Diagnosys:** http://www.windsortech.com/pcdiags.html

- **Windows Memory Diagnostic:** http://oca.microsoft.com/en/windiag.asp

These can help diagnose whether a memory module needs to be replaced. But in general, trust in your senses; look at and listen to the computer to help diagnose any RAM issues that might occur.

If you install or replace a large number of memory modules, a dedicated RAM tester provides the most accurate and complete method for finding RAM problems. RAM testers can be used to do the following:

- Determine memory type, size, and true speed.

- Separate good RAM from bad RAM when all RAM is removed from a system.

- Heat test and stress test RAM independently of the motherboard or operating system.

Preventative Maintenance for Memory

The contents of memory are sensitive to overheating. To avoid overheated memory modules, perform the following tasks as needed:

- Keep the surfaces of the modules clean. You can use compressed air or a data-rated vacuum cleaner to remove dust.

- Make sure you are using the recommended voltage level for the memory installed if your system's BIOS setup permits voltage adjustments.

- Install additional case fans over or behind the location of memory modules to pull hot air out of the system.

- Keep air intake vents in the front of the system clean.

- Replace any defective cooling fans.

To learn more about system cooling issues, see Chapter 4, "Power Supplies and System Cooling." To learn more about BIOS configuration issues, see Chapter 3.

Exam Preparation Tasks

Review All the Key Topics

Review the most important topics in the chapter, noted with the key topics icon in the outer margin of the page. Table 5-2 lists a reference of these key topics and the page numbers on which each is found.

Table 5-2   Key Topics for Chapter 5

Key Topic Element	Description	Page Number
Table 5-1	RAM comparisons	183
Figure 5-1	Desktop memory modules (SIMM, SIPP, and DIMM) compared	186
Figure 5-3	A DIMM partly inserted (top) and fully inserted (bottom)	190
Figure 5-5	Memory-speed markings	193

Complete the Tables and Lists from Memory

Print a copy of Appendix A, "Memory Tables" (found on the CD), or at least the section for this chapter, and complete the tables and lists from memory. Appendix B, "Memory Tables Answer Key," also on the CD, includes completed tables and lists to check your work.

Define Key Terms

Define the following key terms from this chapter, and check your answers in the glossary.

RAM, paging file (virtual memory), SRAM, DRAM, SDRAM, DDR SDRAM, DDR2 SDRAM, DDR3 SDRAM, Rambus, DIMM, SODIMM, SIMM, Rambus RDRAM Module, Small Outline Rambus Module, ECC

Complete Hands-On Labs

Complete the hands-on labs, and then see the answers and explanations at the end of the chapter.

Lab 5-1: Select and Install the Correct RAM

Scenario: You are a technician working at a PC repair bench. You are required to install two sticks of DDR3 RAM into the first channel of the dual channel memory slots in a motherboard. When completed, this should form a "bank" of memory.

Procedure: Select the proper RAM memory modules from the figure and "place" them within the proper memory slots on the motherboard by checking off the correct RAM modules and memory slots in Figures 5-6 and 5-7.

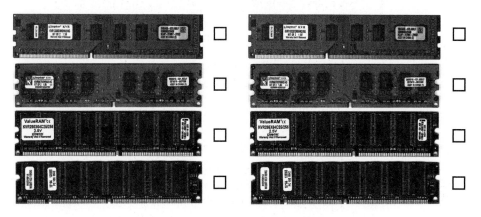

Figure 5-6   Lab 5-1.

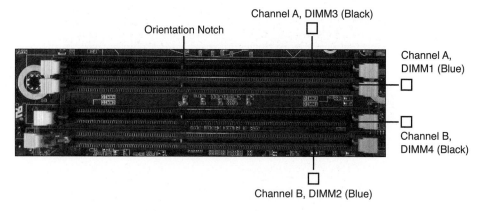

Figure 5-7   Lab 5-1.

Answer Review Questions

Answer these review questions and then see the answers and explanations at the end of the chapter.

1. Which of the following loses its contents when you shut down the computer?
   a. Hard disk drive
   b. USB flash drive
   c. RAM
   d. ROM

2. Which type of memory chip is much bulkier and more expensive than DRAM?
   a. SDRAM
   b. SRAM
   c. DRAM
   d. DDR

3. What type of RAM must be installed in pairs?
   a. DDR
   b. SDRAM
   c. DDR2
   d. Rambus

4. Which type of memory was the first to run in sync with the memory bus?
   a. DDR2
   b. SDRAM
   c. SRAM
   d. Rambus

5. What two methods are used to protect the reliability of memory. (Select the two best answers.)
   a. Parity checking
   b. System checking
   c. ECC (error-correcting code)
   d. Smart checking

6. Most types of desktop memory modules use which kind of memory?

   a. Unbuffered memory

   b. No memory

   c. SIMM module

   d. Stable memory

7. Critical applications and network servers have a special type of memory. What is it called?

   a. ECC memory

   b. Unbuffered memory

   c. Static memory

   d. Desktop memory

8. To correctly install a DIMM or Rambus module, what should you do? (Choose all that apply.)

   a. Line up the module connectors with the socket.

   b. Verify that the locking tabs on the socket are swiveled to the outside (open) position.

   c. Verify that the module is lined up correctly with the socket. Then, push the module straight down until the locks on each end of the socket snap into place at the top corners of the module.

   d. None of these options is correct.

9. Which of the following is the name for running the processor or memory at speeds faster than what is recommended?

   a. CPU tweaking

   b. Overclocking

   c. Memory leak

   d. CPU duplicating

10. Which of the following type of RAM can transmit 6,400 MBps?

   a. DDR3-800

   b. DDR3-1066

   c. DDR3-1333

   d. DDR3-1600

11. Which of the following are utilities used to check memory? (Choose all that apply.)

   a. CheckIT

   b. AMIDiag

   c. Windows Memory Diagnostic Tool

   d. All of these options are correct.

12. To prevent overheating memory modules, which of the following tasks should you perform? (Choose all that apply.)

   a. Keep the surfaces of the modules clean. You can use compressed air or a data-rated vacuum cleaner to remove dust.

   b. Make sure you are using the recommended voltage level for the memory installed if your system's BIOS setup permits voltage adjustments.

   c. Install additional case fans over or behind the location of memory modules to pull hot air out of the system.

   d. All these options are correct.

13. Which of the following statements is correct when comparing DDR3 memory to DDR2 memory?

   a. DDR3 has the same pinouts as DDR2.

   b. DDR3 and DDR2 both use 240-pin connectors.

   c. DDR3 uses higher voltages than DDR2.

   d. All these options are correct.

14. You are required to install a DDR2 memory module that can transfer 6,400 MBps. Which kind of DDR2 memory module should you select?

   a. PC2-5300

   b. PC2-6400

   c. PC3-6400

   d. DDR2-667

15. How much data can DDR3-1333 transfer per second?

   a. 6,400 MBps

   b. 8,533 MBps

   c. 10,667 MBps

   d. 12,800 MBps

Answers to Hands-On Labs

Lab 5-1: Select and Install the Correct RAM

Answer: The first set of RAM (DDR3) should have been selected. Note that DDR3's center notch is to the left of the older DDR2 and DDR center notch. The memory modules should have been installed to the DIMM1 (blue) slot of Channel A and the DIMM2 (blue) slot of Channel B, collectively forming the first Bank of RAM. (See Figures 5-8 and 5-9.)

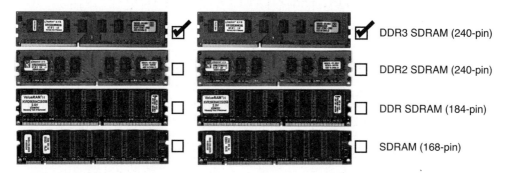

Figure 5-8 Lab 5-1 solution.

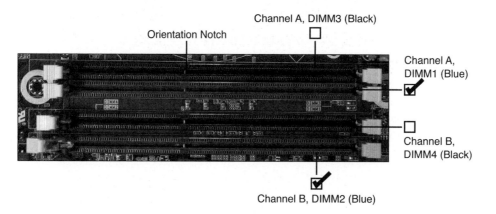

Figure 5-8 Lab 5-1 solution.

The memory notch should be aligned with the slot's corresponding notch, and then placed in the slot and pressed down until the ears lock into place. When installing RAM, try not to touch the chips or connectors. Handle the RAM from the sides and press down on the RAM with your thumbs after it has been placed in the slot.

Answers and Explanations to Review Questions

1. **C.** Random access memory (RAM) loses its contents when the computer shuts down. Hard disk drives, USB flash drives, and read-only memory (ROM) are designed to retain their contents even if they are not receiving power.

2. **B.** SRAM or Static RAM is bulkier and more expensive than DRAM. It does not require electricity as often as DRAM.

3. **D.** Rambus memory that uses 32-bit RIMMs must use pairs, and unused sockets must be occupied by a continuity module.

4. **B.** SDRAM was the first memory type that was in sync with the motherboard's memory bus.

5. **A, C.** Parity memory and ECC have an additional memory chip added for parity.

6. **A.** Unbuffered memory is used in most desktop computers sold in the market. This kind of memory is also used in some servers and workstations.

7. **A.** ECC memory enables the system to correct single-bit errors and notify you of larger errors.

8. **A, B, C.** To correctly insert the memory modules, you should follow all the steps listed. You might also have to use a fair amount of pressure to securely lock these modules in place.

9. **B.** Overclocking is the process in which you can set the speeds of the CPU or memory to run at a faster rate than normal. It can lead to overheating and system crashes.

10. **A.** DDR3-800 can transmit 6,400 MBps. DDR3-1066 transmits 8,533 MBps. DDR3-1333 transmits 10,667 MBps. DDR3-1600 transmits 12,800 MBps.

11. **D.** CheckIT, AMIDiag, and the Windows Memory Diagnostic Tool can all be used to test memory.

12. **D.** All of these can be done to help prevent any memory issues, such as overheating.

13. **B.** DDR3 and DDR2 both use 240-pin connectors is the only correct answer. While DDR3 and DDR2 both use 240-pin connectors, the connectors use different pinouts and are keyed differently to avoid installing DDR3 in a DDR2 slot or vice-versa. DDR3 uses lower voltage than DDR2. DDR3 memory uses 1.5V DC power, compared to 1.8V DC for DDR2.

14. B. The correct answer is PC2-6400. This is a type of DDR2 memory module that can transfer 6,400 MBps. It is based on the DDR2-800 standard. PC2-5300 can only transfer 5,333 MBps; that is known as the DDR2-667 standard. PC3-6400 does transfer 6,400 MBps, but it is a DDR3 standard known as DDR3-800. DDR3 modules cannot be installed into DDR2 memory slots. DDR2-667 once again is a DDR2 standard that specifies 5,333 MBps data transfer.

15. C. DDR3-1333 is the DDR3 standard that allows for up to 10,667 MBps data transfer rates. DDR3-800 can transfer 6,400 MBps. DDR3-1066 can transfer 8,533 MBps. DDR3-1600 can transfer 12,800 MBps.

This chapter covers the following subjects:

- **Introduction to I/O Ports**—This section describes the types of I/O ports used to send information to and from the processor and memory.
- **USB**—This section describes the characteristics of USB 1.1, 2.0, and 3.0 ports and cables and how to troubleshoot this technology.
- **IEEE-1394 (FireWire)**—This section describes the characteristics of IEEE 1394a and 1394b ports and cables and how to troubleshoot this technology.
- **SCSI**—This section describes the characteristics of SCSI ports and cables and how to troubleshoot this technology.
- **COM (Serial)**—This section describes the characteristics of serial ports and cables and how to troubleshoot this technology.
- **LPT (Parallel)**—This section describes the characteristics of parallel ports and cables and how to troubleshoot this technology.
- **PS/2 Mouse and Keyboard**—This section describes the characteristics of PS/2 mouse and keyboard ports.
- **Audio**—This section describes the characteristics of analog and digital audio cables and ports.
- **Mouse**—This section describes the characteristics of mice and how to configure and troubleshoot them.
- **Keyboard**—This section describes the characteristics of keyboards and how to configure and troubleshoot them.
- **Bar Code Reader**—This section describes the characteristics of bar code readers.
- **Touch Screen**—This section describes the characteristics of touch screens and how to configure and troubleshoot them.
- **KVM Switch**—This section describes the characteristics of KVM switches.

This chapter covers portions of **CompTIA A+ 220-801 objectives 1.7, 1.11, 1.12** and **CompTIA A+ 220-802 objective 4.2.**

CHAPTER 6

I/O and Input Ports and Devices

Input/output (I/O) devices enable you to control the computer and display information in a variety of ways. A plethora of ports connect these devices to the computer; for example, the well-known USB port. To fully understand how to install, configure, and troubleshoot input and output devices, you must know the ports like the back of your hand. In this chapter you learn about USB, FireWire, serial, parallel, SCSI, audio, and PS/2 keyboard and mouse ports; the goal is to make you proficient with the various interfaces you will see in the IT field.

Foundation Topics

Introduction to I/O Ports

> **220-801**
>
> **Objectives:**
> **220-801: 1.7,**
> **1.11**

I/O ports send information to and from the processor and memory. Although the most important I/O port on recent systems is the USB port, you might also encounter other ports, including FireWire and legacy ports such as serial and parallel. The following sections explain the major features of each port type covered by the A+ Certification exams.

NOTE eSATA ports are discussed in Chapter 12, "Storage Devices."

NOTE Legacy ports, such as serial, parallel, and PS/2 mouse ports, use hardware resources known as interrupt request (IRQ), direct memory access (DMA), and I/O port addresses. Depending on the port, the resources might be adjustable or might be fixed in place. Although newer types of ports, such as USB and FireWire, also use these resources as well as a fourth one, memory address, current system designs enable Windows to map the resources needed for a port to any unused location. Thus, conflicts between ports are extremely rare on systems built in the past decade.

USB

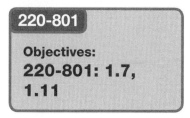

220-801

Objectives:
220-801: 1.7,
1.11

Universal Serial Bus (USB) ports have largely replaced PS/2 (mini-DIN) mouse and keyboard, serial (COM), and parallel (LPT) ports on recent systems. Most recent desktop systems have at least six USB ports, and many systems support as many as ten or more front- and rear-mounted USB ports. Figure 6-1 shows the rear panel of a typical ATX system, including USB and other port types discussed in this chapter.

Figure 6-1 A high-performance ATX motherboard's I/O ports, complete with legacy PS/2 mouse/keyboard combo port, six USB 2.0, two USB 3.0, one IEEE 1394, two Ethernet, two eSATA, and audio ports.

The following sections describe USB port types and how to add more USB ports.

USB Port Types, Speeds, and Technical Details

There are three standards for USB ports:

- USB 1.1
- USB 2.0 (also called **Hi-Speed USB**)
- USB 3.0 (also called **SuperSpeed USB**)

USB 1.1 and 2.0 standards use the same cable and connector types, which are shown in Figure 6-2.

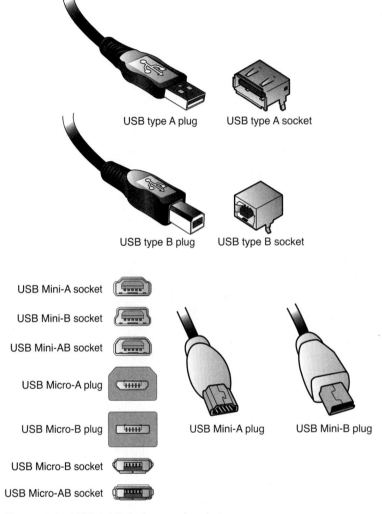

Figure 6-2   USB 1.1/2.0 plugs and sockets.

USB 1.1/2.0 cables use two different types of connectors: Series A (also called Type A) and Series B (also called Type B). Series A connectors are used on USB root hubs (the USB ports in the computer) and USB external hubs to support USB devices. Series B connectors are used for devices that employ a removable USB cable, such as a USB printer or a generic (external) hub. Generally, you need a Series A–to–Series B cable to attach most devices to a USB root or external hub. Cables that are Series A–to–Series A or Series B–to–Series B are used to extend standard cables and can cause problems if the combined length of the cables exceeds recommended distances. Adapters are available to convert Series B cables into Mini-B cables, which support the Mini-B port design used on many recent USB devices.

TIP I don't recommend using extension cables or cables that are longer than 6 feet (especially with USB 1.1 ports or with any type of hub-powered device); I've seen some devices stop working when longer-than-normal cables were used. If you need a longer cable run, use a self-powered hub between the PC and the device. The self-powered hub provides the power needed for any USB device and keeps the signal at full strength.

USB 3.0 Standard-A connectors are similar to USB 1.1/2.0 Series A connectors but have additional contacts. They are compatible with any USB cable. However, USB 3.0 Series B connectors are available in two forms: Standard-B and Micro-B. Micro-B was originally intended for mobile devices but is often used by both portable and desktop USB 3.0 hard disk drives. USB 3.0 Type B and Micro Type B cables can be used only with USB 3.0 devices. USB 3.0 designs also include Micro-AB and Micro-A, but these are not in common use. Figure 6-3 illustrates USB 3.0 Standard-B and Micro-B cables and receptacles.

Figure 6-3 USB 3.0 Standard-B (left) and Micro-B (right) cables and receptacles.

USB 1.1 ports run at a top speed (full-speed USB) of 12 megabits per second (Mbps); low-speed USB devices, such as a mouse or a keyboard, run at 1.5Mbps; and USB 2.0 (Hi-Speed USB) ports run at a top speed of 480Mbps. USB 2.0 ports are backward compatible with USB 1.1 devices and speeds and manage multiple USB

1.1 devices better than a USB 1.1 port does. USB 3.0 ports run at a maximum speed of 5Gbps and are backward compatible with USB 1.1 and USB 2.0 devices and speeds.

USB packaging and device markings frequently use the official logos shown in Figure 6-4 to distinguish the three versions of USB in common use. The industry uses the term Hi-Speed USB for USB 2.0 and SuperSpeed USB for USB 3.0.

Figure 6-4   The USB logo (left) is used for USB 1.1–compatible devices, the Hi-Speed USB logo (center) is used for USB 2.0–compatible devices, and the SuperSpeed USB logo (right) is used for USB 3.0–compatible devices. Devices bearing these logos have been certified by the USB Implementers Forum, Inc. (USB-IF). Images courtesy of USB-IF.

With any version of USB, a single USB port on an add-on card or motherboard is designed to handle up to 127 devices through the use of multiport hubs and daisy-chaining hubs. Starting with Windows 98, USB devices are Plug and Play (PnP) devices that are hot swappable (can be connected and disconnected without turning off the system).

The maximum length for a cable attached to 12Mbps or 480Mbps USB devices is 5 meters, whereas the maximum length for low-speed (1.5Mbps) devices, such as mice and keyboards, is 3 meters. USB 3.0 does not have a specified maximum cable length, but cables no longer than 3 meters are recommended for best performance.

A **root hub** supports two USB ports. If a third-party USB 3.0 root hub is present, it will be listed separately from USB 1.1/2.0 root hubs. Root hubs are connected to host controllers, but the relationship between the number of root hubs and host controllers listed in Windows Device Manager differs depending upon the USB version in use. Table 6-1 lays out the rules.

Table 6-1   Host Controllers and USB Root Hubs in Windows Device Manager

	USB 1.1	USB 2.0	USB 3.0
Number of host controllers listed in Device Manager	One for each root hub	One	One

If an external USB hub is attached to the computer, a generic hub also will be listed in the Windows Device Manager. On systems that support hardware virtualization, a separate category for USB Virtualization is also listed. See Figure 6-5 for examples.

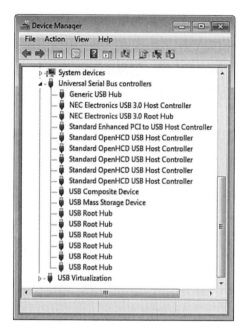

Figure 6-5   The USB section of the Windows 7 Device Manager on a system with USB 2.0 and USB 3.0 ports.

Adding USB Ports

Need more USB ports? You can add USB ports with any of the following methods:

- Motherboard connectors for USB header cables
- Hubs
- Add-on cards

Some motherboards have USB header cable connectors, which enable you to make additional USB ports available on the rear or front of the computer. Some motherboard vendors include these **header cables** with the motherboard, whereas others require you to purchase them separately. Most recent cases also include front-mounted USB ports, which can also be connected to the motherboard. Because of vendor-specific differences in how motherboards implement header cables, the header cable might use separate connectors for each signal instead of the more common single connector for all signals.

USB **generic hubs** enable you to connect multiple devices to the same USB port and to increase the distance between the device and the USB port. There are two types of generic hubs:

- Bus-powered
- Self-powered

Bus-powered hubs might be built in to other devices, such as monitors and keyboards, or can be standalone devices. A **bus-powered hub** distributes both USB signals and power via the USB bus to other devices. Different USB devices use different amounts of power, and some devices require more power than others. A bus-powered hub provides no more than 100 milliamps (mA) of power to each device connected to it. Thus, some devices fail when connected to a bus-powered hub.

A **self-powered hub**, on the other hand, has its own power source; it plugs in to an AC wall outlet. A self-powered hub designed for USB 1.1 or USB 2.0 devices provides up to 500mA of power to each device connected to it, whereas a self-powered hub designed for USB 3.0 devices provides up to 900mA of power to each device. Note that USB hubs are backward compatible to previous USB versions. A self-powered hub supports a wider range of USB devices than a bus-powered hub does, and I recommend using it instead of a bus-powered hub whenever possible.

Add-on cards can be used to provide additional USB ports as an alternative to hubs. One advantage of an add-on card is its capability to provide support for more recent USB standards. For example, you can add a USB 3.0 card to a system that has only USB 1.1/2.0 ports to permit use of USB 3.0 hard disks at full performance. Add-on cards for USB 1.1 or USB 2.0 ports connect to PCI slots on desktop computers and CardBus or ExpressCard slots on laptop computers, whereas USB 3.0 cards connect to PCIe x1 or wider slots on desktop computers and ExpressCard slots on laptop computers.

Figure 6-6 illustrates a typical USB 3.0 card, a USB 2.0 self-powered hub, and a USB 2.0 port header cable.

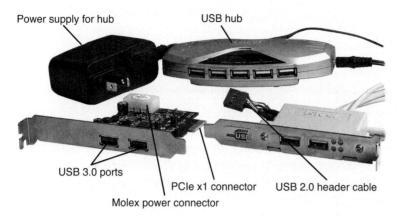

Figure 6-6   USB 2.0 and 3.0 hardware.

Troubleshooting USB Ports and Devices

USB ports are the most common type of I/O port used on current systems. Use the following sections to solve problems with USB ports.

■ **USB port not enabled in system BIOS**—USB ports can be disabled in the system BIOS. To re-enable USB ports, follow these steps:

Step 1. Start the system.

Step 2. Open the BIOS setup program.

Step 3. Locate the correct menu for the USB ports (might be Advanced Chipset, Peripherals, or others, depending on the system).

Step 4. Enable USB ports.

Step 5. Save the changes.

Step 6. Exit setup and reboot.

Step 7. Windows installs drivers (or prompts for driver files) for USB ports if they are not already installed.

■ **USB port not properly designed on early systems**—Some of the early USB ports do not conform to current USB 1.1, 2.0, or 3.0 standards and do not work with some or all USB peripherals, even using a supported version of Windows. Disable these ports and replace them with an add-on card containing USB ports.

- **Drivers for device not properly installed**—Windows XP, Windows Vista, and Windows 7 contain drivers for USB mass storage and input devices, but other types of USB devices, such as printers, scanners, all-in-one units, digital cameras, webcams, and network adapters, require manufacturer-specific drivers that must be installed first. See the documentation for the device for details.

- **Not enough power for the device (1)**—If a device that uses more power than a bus-powered generic hub can provide is connected to a bus-powered generic hub, the device will fail. In some cases, you might see a warning displayed in the Windows system tray (see Figure 6-7). By opening Device Manager and viewing the properties for the hub, you can verify the power provided per port and compare that value to the power required by the device.

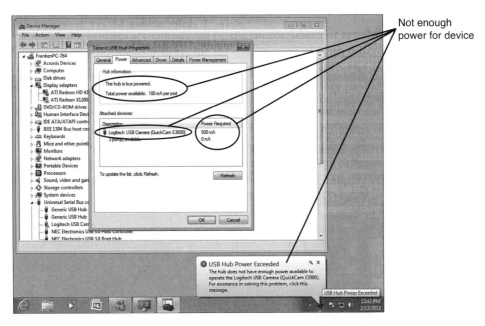

Figure 6-7 The Power tab in the Generic USB Hub Properties sheet in Windows 7 indicates the webcam requires more power than the (bus-powered) hub can provide. In some cases, a pop-up warning (lower right) is displayed on the Windows desktop.

- **Not enough power for the device (2)**—Portable hard disks that connect to USB ports might not receive enough power from a root hub or self-powered USB hub to be recognized or to operate properly. Although these drives are designed to use only 500mA of power, some drives require more power to spin up, and some USB ports cannot provide additional power to start the drive. To solve this problem, use a y-cable to connect the drive to two USB ports; the second connector on the cable provides additional power.

- **Not enough power for the device (3)**—Self-powered 7-port hubs need to use a power supply providing 3.5A or more to enable all ports to supply 500mA of power. 7 port hubs equipped with lower amperage power supplies will not provide full power, although the hub's properties sheet might not indicate the problem.

- **Not enough power for a USB 3.0 card or device**—Most USB 3.0 add-on cards include a four-pin Molex power connector. If you don't connect power to the card, the card might not be recognized or might not provide adequate power to bus-powered devices such as portable hard disks. USB 3.0 ports provide up to 900mA of power.

- **USB controller displays a black exclamation point on a yellow field (!) in Windows Device Manager**—The USB PCI to USB controller (which runs the USB ports in the computer) might require a unique IRQ and I/O port address range on some older systems running Windows XP unless IRQ sharing has been enabled in the system BIOS. Select nonconflicting IRQ and I/O port address ranges in the Properties sheet (Resources tab) for the USB controller, and restart the system if necessary. See http://support.microsoft.com/kb/133240 for more information.

- **Too many full-speed (12Mbps) USB devices attached to a single USB 1.1 port**—If the speed of existing devices drops after attaching a new device to the same USB hub, connect the new device to another USB port. If your system has USB 1.1 ports only, use a new hub connected to a separate USB port if needed to separate full-speed from low-speed USB devices. If your system has both USB 1.1 and USB 2.0 ports, attach a USB 2.0–compatible hub to a USB 2.0 port and attach all low-speed USB 1.1 devices to it. As an alternative, use a generic USB 2.0 (or 3.0) hub that has multiple transaction translators (TTs); multiple TTs enable a hub to better support mixtures of low-speed and high-speed devices. To determine whether a generic hub has multiple TTs, check the Advanced tab of the hub's properties sheet in Device Manager.

- **USB 2.0 devices do not operate at maximum speed**—Some systems can be configured to run USB ports in USB 1.1 or USB 2.0 modes. If USB ports are configured to run in USB 1.1 mode only, USB 2.0 devices will run slowly, and a few might not work at all. Make sure USB ports are configured to run in USB 2.0 mode.

IEEE-1394 (FireWire)

220-801

Objectives:
220-801: 1.7,
1.11

IEEE 1394 is a family of high-speed, bidirectional, serial transmission ports that can connect PCs to each other, digital devices to PCs, or digital devices to each other.

The most common version of IEEE 1394 is known as **IEEE 1394a,** and is also known as **FireWire 400.** Sony's version is known as **i.LINK.** IEEE 1394a has a maximum speed of 400Mbps and can be implemented either as a built-in port on the motherboard (refer to Figure 6-1) or as part of an add-on card (see Figure 6-8). **FireWire 800 (IEEE 1394b)** runs at up to 800Mbps but is more often used on systems running Mac OS X than those running Windows.

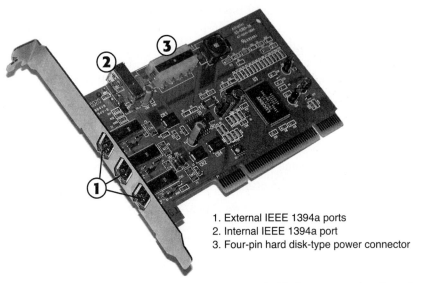

1. External IEEE 1394a ports
2. Internal IEEE 1394a port
3. Four-pin hard disk-type power connector

Figure 6-8   A typical IEEE 1394a host adapter card with three external and one internal ports.

IEEE 1394 Ports and Cables

Standard IEEE 1394a ports and cables use a 6-pin interface (four pins for data, two for power), but some digital camcorders and all i.LINK ports use the alternative

4-pin interface, which supplies data and signals but no power to the device. Six-wire to four-wire cables enable these devices to communicate with each other.

A faster version of the IEEE 1394 standard, IEEE 1394b (also known as FireWire 800), runs at 800Mbps. IEEE 1394b ports use a 9-pin interface. There are two versions of the IEEE 1394b port: The Beta port and cable are used only for 1394b-to-1394b connections, whereas the Bilingual cable and port are used for 1394b-to-1394a or 1394b-to-1394b connections. Beta cables and ports have a wide notch at the top of the cable and port, whereas Bilingual cables and ports have a narrow notch at the 1394b end and use either the 4-pin or 6-pin 1394a connection at the other end of the cable. All four cable types are shown in Figure 6-9.

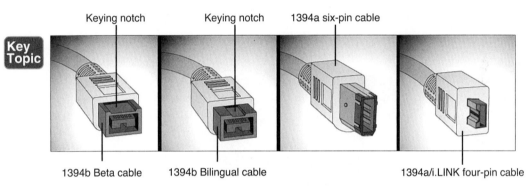

Figure 6-9   1394b and 1394a cable connectors compared.

IEEE 1394–Compatible Devices

IEEE 1394–compatible devices include internal and external hard drives, digital camcorders (also referred to as DV camcorders), web cameras, MP3 players (such as older models of Apple's iPod), and high-performance scanners and printers, as well as hubs, repeaters, and SCSI to IEEE 1394 converters. IEEE 1394 ports support hot-swapping, enabling you to add or remove a device from an IEEE 1394 port without shutting down the system. 1394 ports can also be used for networking with Windows XP (but not Vista or 7).

Up to 16 IEEE 1394 devices can be connected to a single IEEE 1394 port through daisy-chaining. Most external IEEE 1394 devices have two ports to enable daisy-chaining.

IEEE 1394 cards can use PCI or PCI Express buses. (Versions for laptops use ExpressCard or CardBus designs.)

Installing an IEEE 1394 Card

To install and configure an IEEE 1394 card, follow this procedure:

Step 1.   Turn off the computer and remove the case cover.

Step 2.   Locate an available PCI or PCI Express expansion slot.

Step 3.   Remove the slot cover and insert the card into the slot. Secure the card in the slot.

Step 4.   Some IEEE 1394 cards are powered by the expansion slot, whereas others require a 4-pin connector for power. Connect a power lead if the card requires it; you can use a Y-splitter to free up a power lead if necessary (see Figure 6-10).

Figure 6-10   A typical IEEE 1394a card after installation. This card requires a four-wire power cable and also includes an internal port.

Step 5.   Close the system, reattach AC power, restart it, and provide the driver media if requested by the system.

Troubleshooting IEEE 1394 Ports and Devices

The following sections discuss the most common problems and solutions that apply to IEEE 1394 ports and devices.

So, you put the card in the system, turned it on, and Windows ignored it? If an IEEE 1394 card can't be detected after it is physically installed in the system, check the following. (Be sure to turn off the system if you need to open it up again!)

■ **The card's position in the slot**—If the card is not properly seated in the expansion slot, reseat it.

- **Power lead on cards that require an external power source**—Some IEEE 1394 cards require additional power from a Molex power connector. If the power connector isn't connected to the card, the card will not work when the system is turned on. Connect the power to the card and restart the system.

CAUTION   If you need to use a power splitter or extender to reach the card, make sure it's connected to the power supply.

If a known-working 1394 device is not detected when you connect it to an integrated 1394 port, check the following.

- **Port not enabled in system BIOS**—If the 1394 ports built in to the system don't work, chances are they're not enabled in the system BIOS. Restart the computer, enter the BIOS setup program, and enable them. Save the changes and exit.

- **Header cable not properly connected to motherboard**—If a 1394 port on the computer's front panel or card bracket doesn't work, but you have enabled the integrated 1394 controller in the system BIOS, check the header cable connection to the motherboard. If the header cable uses a separate connection for each wire, it is essential to route each cable wire to the correct connection, or you might damage the port, the motherboard, or any device connected to the port.

If a known-working 1394 device that is bus powered is not detected or does not operate properly when connected to either a card-based or integrated port, check the following:

- Six-pin 1394a port on device connected to four-pin port on computer— Four-pin 1394a ports don't provide power.

SCSI

220-801

Objectives:
220-801: 1.11

A Small Computer Systems Interface (**SCSI**) is a flexible interface because it can accommodate many devices in addition to hard disk drives. Currently, SCSI interfaces, either on the motherboard or as add-on cards, are found primarily in servers and are used for mass storage (hard disk and tape backup), although you might encounter workstations or older PCs that use SCSI interfaces for devices such as

- High-performance and high-capacity hard drives

- Image scanners

- Removable-media drives such as Iomega Zip and Jaz

- High-performance laser printers

- Optical drives

- Tape backups

So-called Narrow SCSI host adapters (which use an 8-bit data channel) can accommodate up to seven devices of different varieties on a single connector. Wide SCSI host adapters use a 16-bit data channel and accommodate up to 15 devices on a single connector.

Multiple Device Support with SCSI Host Adapters

All true SCSI host adapters are designed to support multiple devices, although some low-cost SCSI host adapters made especially for scanners and Zip drives might not support multiple devices (also known as **daisy-chaining**). These SCSI features permit daisy-chaining:

- External SCSI peripherals have two SCSI ports, enabling daisy-chaining of multiple devices.

- Both internal and external SCSI peripherals enable the user to choose a unique device ID number for each device to distinguish one peripheral from another in the daisy chain (see Figure 6-11).

Multiple device support enables the different types of devices listed previously to work on a single SCSI host adapter. To determine which device IDs are in use, you can

- Physically examine each SCSI device's device ID settings.

- Scan the SCSI bus with a utility program made to detect SCSI IDs or with the BIOS routines built in to some SCSI host adapters.

- View the properties for each SCSI device in the Windows Device Manager.

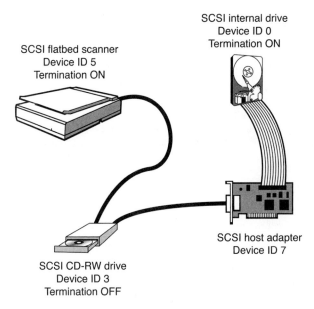

SCSI internal drive
Device ID 0
Termination ON

SCSI flatbed scanner
Device ID 5
Termination ON

SCSI host adapter
Device ID 7

SCSI CD-RW drive
Device ID 3
Termination OFF

Figure 6-11   When a SCSI host adapter card with internal and external connectors is used, the SCSI daisy chain can extend through the card. The devices on each end of the chain are terminated, and each device (including the host adapter) has a unique device ID number.

Jumper Block and DIP Switch Settings for Device IDs

Each SCSI device must have a unique **device ID** to distinguish itself from other SCSI devices connected to the same SCSI channel. Narrow SCSI (25-pin or 50-pin data cable) devices use a set of three jumpers or DIP switches to set the device ID. Wide SCSI (68-pin data cable) devices use a set of four jumpers or DIP switches to set the device ID.

The device ID is set in binary (base 2) values in order from bit 0 (least significant bit or LSB) to the most significant bit or MSB. Table 6-2 lists the settings for narrow SCSI devices (IDs 0–7); Table 6-3 lists the settings for wide SCSI devices (IDs 0–15). In the following tables, 1 means jumper block on or DIP switch set to ON; 0 means jumper block off or DIP switch set to OFF.

Device ID 7 is usually reserved for use by the SCSI host adapter.

Tables 6-2 and 6-3 assume that the jumper blocks or DIP switches place bit 0 at the left. If the device places bit 0 at the right, reverse the order in the preceding list when setting the configuration.

TIP The jumper blocks or DIP switches used to configure the device ID might be part of a larger array of jumper blocks or DIP switches used to set all drive features. Check the documentation for the drive to determine which jumper blocks or DIP switches to use.

Table 6-2 Narrow SCSI LSB-to-MSB Device ID Settings

Device ID	Bit 0 (LSB)	Bit 1	Bit 2 (MSB)
0	0	0	0
1	1	0	0
2	0	1	0
3	1	1	0
4	0	0	1
5	1	0	1
6	0	1	1
7	1	1	1

Table 6-3 Wide SCSI LSB-to-MSB Device ID Settings

Device ID	Bit 0 (LSB)	Bit 1	Bit 2	Bit 3 (MSB)
0	0	0	0	0
1	1	0	0	0
2	0	1	0	0
3	1	1	0	0
4	0	0	1	0
5	1	0	1	0
6	0	1	1	0
7	1	1	1	0
8	0	0	0	1
9	1	0	0	1
10	0	1	0	1
11	1	1	0	1
12	0	0	1	1
13	1	0	1	1
14	0	1	1	1
15	1	1	1	1

SCSI Standards

SCSI actually is the family name for a wide range of standards, which differ from each other in the speed of devices, number of devices, and other technical details. The major SCSI standards are listed in Table 6-4.

Table 6-4 Popular SCSI Standards

Popular Name	Speed	Number of Devices	Data Bus	Signal Type
Fast	10MBps	7	8-bit	SE[1]
Fast-Wide	10MBps	15	16-bit	SE
Ultra	20MBps	7	8-bit	SE
Ultra-Wide	20MBps	15	16-bit	SE
Ultra2	40MBps	7	8-bit	LVD[2]
Ultra2Wide	80MBps	15	16-bit	LVD
Ultra 160	160MBps	15	16-bit	LVD
Ultra 320	320MBps	15	16-bit	LVD

[1]Single-ended
[2]Low-voltage differential

8-bit versions of SCSI use a 50-pin cable or a 25-pin cable; wide (16-bit) versions use a 68-pin cable.

SCSI host adapters are generally backward compatible, enabling older and newer SCSI standards to be mixed on the same host adapter. However, mixing slower and faster devices can cause the faster devices to slow down unless you use a host adapter with dual buses that can run at different speeds.

SCSI Cables

Just as no single SCSI standard exists, no single SCSI cabling standard exists. In addition to the 50-pin versus 68-pin difference between standard and wide devices, differences also appear in the Narrow SCSI external cables. Figure 6-12 compares internal SCSI cables for wide and narrow applications, and Figure 6-13 compares various types of external SCSI cables and ports.

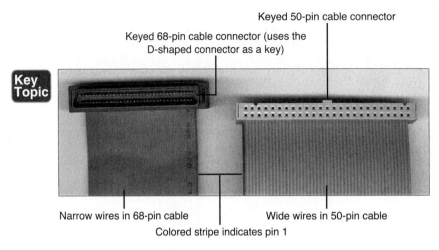

Figure 6-12   A wide (68-pin) SCSI ribbon cable (left) compared to a narrow (50-pin) SCSI ribbon cable (right).

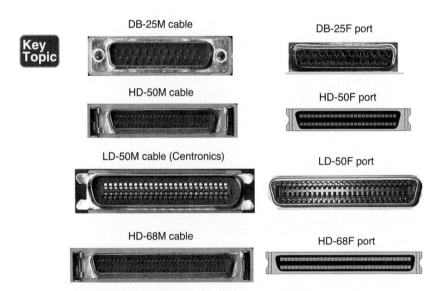

Figure 6-13   Wide (68-pin) and narrow (50-pin, 25-pin) SCSI cable connectors (left) and the corresponding SCSI port connectors (right).

Three different types of Narrow SCSI external connectors are available:

- **50-pin Centronics**—Similar to, but wider than, the 36-pin Centronics port used for parallel printers. Also called LD50.

- **50-pin high-density connector (HD50)**—The Wide SCSI 68-pin connector (HD68) uses the same design but with 34 pins per row instead of 25 pins per row.

- **25-pin DB-25F**—Physically, but not electronically, similar to the DB-25F parallel printer port.

Most recent external 8-bit (narrow) SCSI devices use the HD50 connector, whereas older models use the LD50 (Centronics) connector. However, a few low-cost SCSI devices, such as the Iomega Zip-100 drive and some SCSI scanners, use only the 25-pin connector, which lacks much of the grounding found on the 50-pin cable. Some SCSI devices provide two different types of SCSI connectors. Consequently, you need to determine what cable connectors are used by any external SCSI devices you want to connect together.

SCSI Signaling Types

In Table 6-3 (previously shown), SE stands for single-ended, a SCSI signaling type that runs at speeds of up to 20MBps only. SE signaling enables relatively inexpensive SCSI devices and host adapters to be developed but reduces the length of cables and the top speed possible.

Ultra2, Ultra2Wide, Ultra 160, and Ultra 320 devices all use a signaling standard called low-voltage differential (LVD), which enables longer cable runs and faster, more reliable operation than the single-ended (SE) standard allows. Some LVD devices can also be used on the same bus with SE devices, but these multimode, or LVD/SE devices, will be forced to slow down to the SE maximum of 20MBps when mixed with SE devices on the same bus. Some advanced SCSI host adapters feature both an SE and an LVD bus to enable the same adapter to control both types of devices at the correct speeds.

Daisy-Chaining SCSI Devices

When you create a SCSI daisy-chain, you must keep all these factors in mind:

- Each device must have a unique SCSI device ID (refer to Table 6-2 and Table 6-3).

- Each end of the daisy-chain must be terminated. Some devices have an integral switch or jumper block for **termination** (see Figures 6-14 and 16-15), whereas some external devices require that you attach a terminator (which resembles the end of a SCSI cable) to the unused SCSI connector.

- When daisy-chaining external devices, double-check the cable connector type and purchase appropriate cables. You will often need SCSI cables that have different connectors at each end because of the different connector types used (see Figure 6-15).

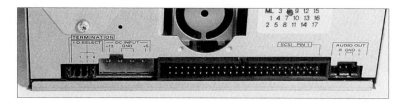

Figure 6-14   A SCSI-based internal CD-R drive with (left to right) well-marked jumpers for termination and device ID, power connector, data cable pin 1, and CD-audio cable.

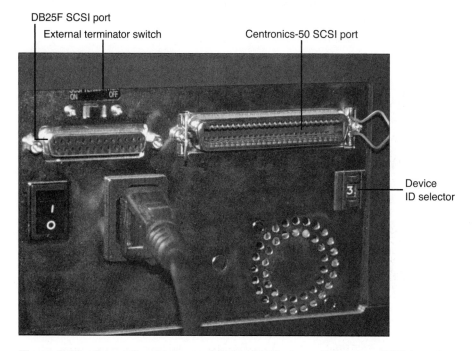

Figure 6-15   External termination and device ID selector switches on a SCSI-based scanner. This scanner has both DB25-F and Centronics-50 (also called LD50-F) SCSI ports.

SCSI Host Adapter Card Installation

Follow these steps to install a PnP SCSI host adapter card:

Step 1.   Shut down the system and disconnect the system from AC power.

Step 2.   Open the system and locate an unused slot that matches the card's connection type.

Step 3.   Remove the card bracket and slide the card into the slot.

Step 4.   Close the system, reconnect AC power, and turn on the system.

Step 5.   After the card is detected by the system, you might be prompted for installation software. Insert the appropriate media and follow the prompt to complete the installation.

Step 6.   Use Windows Device Manager to view the card's configuration.

SCSI Daisy-Chain Maximum Length

The maximum length of a SCSI daisy chain depends on the speed of the devices used and the type of signaling in use. SE cables have a maximum length of 3 meters with any number of devices when used with Narrow 20Mbps or slower host adapters, but only 1.5 meters when used with more than four devices on Ultra/Wide or Ultra SCSI 20Mbps or faster host adapters.

Low-voltage differential (LVD) SCSI signaling (supported on Ultra2 SCSI and faster versions) supports cabling length of 12 meters with any number of devices.

Figure 6-16 shows the standard markings used to identify SE, LVD, and LVD-SE SCSI devices. LVD-SE devices can be used with either SE or LVD devices on the same daisy chain.

Figure 6-16   SE, LVD, and LVD-SE SCSI device markings.

SCSI Termination Methods

Both ends of a SCSI daisy chain need to be terminated for proper operation. Although SCSI host adapters are designed to provide automatic termination, you must terminate other types of devices manually.

Low-speed external SCSI devices, such as scanners and Zip drives, often feature internal termination, which is configured with a switch on the unit. Some internal SCSI devices use a jumper block or DIP switch to configure termination; others use a terminating resistor pack.

Terminators are connected to the unused port on an external SCSI device or inline with the ribbon cable on an internal SCSI device if built-in termination is not available or is not used. There are two types of external termination: passive and active. Passive terminators use no power. Passive terminators are not recommended if more than two SE devices are on a SCSI daisy chain and are not recommended with LVD or LVD-SE devices. Active terminators use an external power source to provide a voltage regulator for better termination. They can be used with LVD, LVD-SE, and SE-based SCSI daisy chains.

TIP Make sure you know the connector type, speed, and termination type appropriate for your SCSI device before you order a terminator. Ask the vendor for help if you aren't sure what you need. There are many varieties to choose from.

Troubleshooting SCSI Devices

On systems that use SCSI hardware, you will find this information useful; however, this information is not required for the 2012 CompTIA A+ Certification exams.

SCSI problems can usually be traced to incorrect device ID, termination, or cabling.

External SCSI Device Isn't Available

External SCSI devices might not be available for any of the following reasons:

- Device not powered on when the system was turned on

- Incorrect termination

- Excess cable length or excessive daisy-chain length

If an external SCSI device isn't turned on a few seconds before the system is turned on, it might not initialize properly. If an external SCSI device is not turned on and the system has booted, it might be possible to use the Device Manager to activate the device by following this procedure:

Step 1. Turn on the device.

Step 2. Open Windows Device Manager.

Step 3. Scan for hardware changes and wait for the system to recheck all connected devices.

Step 4. If the SCSI device now appears in Device Manager, you should be able to use it normally.

Step 5. If the device doesn't appear, restart the system.

SCSI is a daisy-chained interface; both ends of the daisy chain must be terminated. Make sure that the terminator switch or external terminator is located at the end of the external daisy chain. (The external terminator is plugged in to the SCSI port not used by the SCSI cable attached to the device.) If a new device has been added to the end of the daisy chain, you must disable termination of the old device and add termination to the new device.

Check the overall length of the daisy chain if some external devices are unavailable, and use the shortest cable lengths possible to avoid exceeding standards.

External or Internal SCSI Device Isn't Available

If a new external or internal SCSI device is not available, two common reasons include duplicate device ID numbers or failure to install drivers for the device.

If multiple SCSI devices have the same device ID number, the devices will interfere with each other. To solve this problem, power down all SCSI devices and the system, and make sure each device has a unique device ID number before restarting.

Both the SCSI host adapter card and the SCSI devices attached to the card need operating system–compatible drivers to operate. If the drivers are not loaded, use the Device Manager's Properties sheet for each device to install a new driver.

If you need to install multiple SCSI devices, you should install one device and its device drivers before installing another device.

COM (Serial)

220-801

Objectives:
220-801: 1.7, 1.11

220-802

220-802: 4.2

The **serial port**, also known as an **RS-232** or **COM** (communication) port, historically has rivaled the parallel port in versatility (see Figure 6-17). Serial ports have been used to connect the following:

- External analog (dial-up) modems
- Mouse or pointing devices such as trackballs or touchpads
- Plotters
- Label printers

- Dot-matrix or laser printers

- PDA docking stations

- Digital cameras

- PC-to-PC connections used by file transfer programs such as LapLink

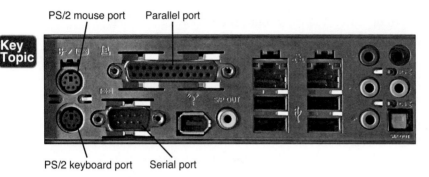

Figure 6-17   A typical ATX motherboard with legacy ports including serial, parallel, and PS/2 mouse and keyboard ports.

However, you are likely to encounter these uses primarily with older systems. On current systems, the roles once played by serial devices and ports are now fulfilled by USB devices and ports.

NOTE   The DB-9 is actually a DE-9 connector but is colloquially known as DB-9 and will most likely be referred to as such on the exam. The smaller the D-sub connector, the higher the letter.

How do serial ports compare in speed with parallel ports? Serial ports transmit data 1 bit at a time (parallel ports send and receive data 8 bits at a time), and their maximum speeds are far slower than parallel ports. However, serial cables can carry data reliably at far greater distances than parallel cables. Serial ports, unlike parallel ports, have no provision for daisy-chaining; only one device can be connected to a serial port.

Serial ports come in two forms: DB-9M (male) and DB-25M (male). Either type can be adapted to the other connector type with a low-cost adapter (see Figure 6-18). The difference is possible because serial communications need only a few wires. Unlike parallel printers, which use a standard cable, each type of serial device uses a specially wired cable. DB-9M connectors are used on all but the oldest systems.

Figure 6-18 A typical DB-25F to DB-9M serial port converter. The DB-25F connector (lower left) connects to a 25-pin serial port and converts its signals for use by devices attaching to the DB-9M port at the other end (upper right).

Serial Port Pinouts

At a minimum, a serial cable must use at least three wires, plus ground:

- Transmit data wire

- Receive data wire

- Signal wire

Tables 6-5 and 6-6 can be used to determine the correct pinout for any specified serial cable configuration. Unlike parallel devices, which all use the same standard cable wiring, serial devices use differently wired cables. A modem cable, for example, will be wired much differently than a serial printer cable. And different serial printers might each use a unique pinout.

Table 6-5 9-Pin Serial Port Pinout

Use	Pin	Direction
Carrier Detect	1	In
Receive Data	2	In
Transmit Data	3	Out
Data Terminal Ready	4	Out
Signal Ground	5	—
Data Set Ready	6	In
Request to Send	7	Out
Clear to Send	8	In
Ring Indicator	9	In

Table 6-6   25-Pin Serial Port Pinout

Use	Pin	Direction
Transmit Data	2	Out
Receive Data	3	In
Request to Send	4	Out
Clear to Send	5	In
Data Set Ready	6	In
Signal Ground	7	—
Received Line Signal Indicator	8	In
+ Transmit Current Loop Data	9	Out
– Transmit Current Loop Data	11	Out
+ Receive Current Loop Data	18	In
Data Terminal Ready	20	Out
Ring Indicator	22	In
– Receive Current Loop Return	25	In

The major difference between the 9-pin serial interface and the 25-pin serial interface is the 25-pin port's support for current loop data, a type of serial communications primarily used for data collection in industrial uses.

When a 9-pin to 25-pin serial port adapter is used, the pinouts are as listed in Table 6-7. Serial ports assume that one end of the connection transmits and the other end receives.

Table 6-7   9-Pin to 25-Pin Serial Port Converter/Serial Modem Pinout

Use	Pin # (9-Pin)	Pin # (25-Pin)
Carrier Detect (CD)	1	8
Receive Data (RD)	2	3
Transmit Data (TD)	3	2
Data Terminal Ready (DTR)	4	20
Signal Ground (SG)	5	7
Data Set Ready (DSR)	6	6
Request to Send (RTS)	7	4
Clear to Send (CTS)	8	5
Ring Indicator (RI)	9	22

Types of Serial Cables

Unlike parallel cables, serial cables can be constructed in many different ways. In fact, cables for serial devices are usually specified by device type rather than port type because different devices use different pinouts. Some of the most common examples of serial cables include null-modem (data transfer) cable and modem cable.

A **null-modem** cable enables two computers to communicate directly with each other by crossing the receive and transmit wires (meaning that two computers can send and receive data, much like a computer network, though much slower). The best known of these programs is LapLink. Although these programs support serial cable transfers, parallel port transfers are much faster, and USB transfers are much faster than parallel (Windows Vista and 7 use a proprietary USB-to-USB cable for Easy Windows Transfer file transfer); these methods for direct connection are recommended for most versions of Windows.

A modem cable is used to connect an external modem to a serial port. Some modems include a built-in cable, but others require you to use a DB-9F to DB-25M cable from the 9-pin connector on the serial port to the 25-pin port on the modem. This cable typically uses the same pinout shown in Table 6-7. Serial printers (used primarily on older ASCII terminals) require custom-built cables.

Standard IRQ and I/O Port Addresses

On older systems, you might need to know this information to help resolve conflicts; however, it is not necessary for the 2012 CompTIA A+ Certification exams.

Serial ports require two hardware resources: IRQ and I/O port address. Table 6-8 lists the standard IRQ and I/O port addresses used for COM ports 1–4. Some systems and add-on cards enable alternative IRQs to be used, either through jumper blocks (older cards) or via software/Device Manager configuration (newer cards). Use Windows Device Manager to see settings for COM ports in your system.

Serial ports never require a DMA channel (and thus can't have DMA conflicts with other devices). However, there's another way to stumble when working with serial ports: IRQ conflicts. IRQ 4 is shared by default between COM 1 and COM 3; IRQ 3 is shared by default between COM 2 and COM 4. However, with serial ports that use the same IRQ, sharing does *not* mean that both serial ports can be used at the same time. If a device on COM 1 and a device on COM 3 that share the same IRQ are used at the same time, both devices stop working and they might shut down the system.

Table 6-8   Standard Settings for COM (Serial) Ports 1–4

COM Port #	IRQ	I/O Port Address
1	4	3F8-3FFh
2	3	2F8-2FFh
3	4	3E8-3EFh
4	3	2E8-2EFh

How to Configure or Disable Serial Ports

Depending on the location of the serial port, there are several ways to configure the port settings to select different IRQ and I/O port addresses for a serial port, or to disable the serial port. These include

- BIOS setup program for built-in ports
- PnP mode for use with Windows

To adjust the configuration of a serial port built into the system's motherboard, follow these steps:

Step 1.   Start the BIOS setup program.

Step 2.   Go to the peripherals configuration screen.

Step 3.   Select the serial port you want to adjust.

Step 4.   To change the port's configuration, choose the IRQ and I/O port address you want to use or select Disabled to prevent the system from detecting and using the serial port (see Figure 6-19). If you don't use serial ports, select Disabled.

Step 5.   Save changes and exit; the system reboots.

Serial ports on PCI or PCI Express cards are configured by the PnP BIOS. In some cases, you can use the Windows Device Manager to change the port configuration (see Chapter 15, "Troubleshooting and Maintaining Windows," for details).

Serial Port Software Configuration

Unlike parallel ports, serial ports have many different configuration options, making a successful setup more challenging. Through software settings at the computer end, and by hardware or software settings at the device end, serial devices can use

- A wide variety of transmission speeds, from as low as 300bps to as high as 115,200bps or faster
- Different word lengths (7 bit or 8 bit)

Serial port I/O port address/IRQ

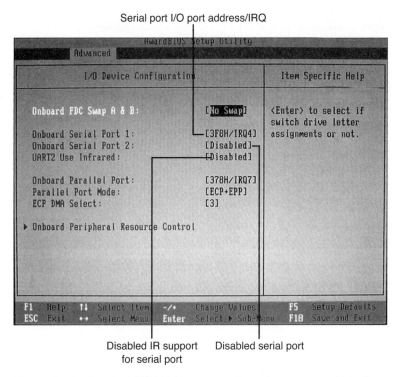

Disabled IR support   Disabled serial port
for serial port

Figure 6-19 A typical BIOS I/O device configuration screen with the first serial port enabled, the second port disabled, and IR (infrared) support disabled.

- Different methods of flow control (XON/XOFF or DTR/DSR)
- Different methods of ensuring reliable data transmission (even parity, odd parity, no parity, 1-bit or 2-bit parity length)

Although simple devices such as a mouse or a label printer don't require that these settings be made manually (the software drivers do it), serial printers used with PCs running terminal-emulation software, PCs communicating with mainframe computers, serial pen plotters, serial printers, and PCs using modems often do require that these options be set correctly. Both ends of a serial connection must have these configurations set to identical values, or the communications between your computer and the other device will fail.

Figure 6-20 illustrates how Windows XP configures the port speed, flow control, and hardware settings for a serial port connected to an external modem.

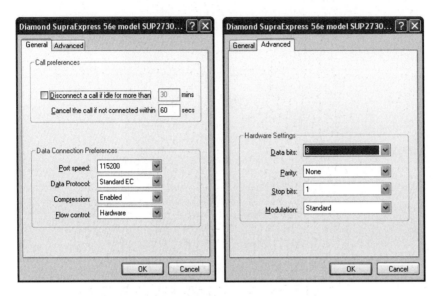

Figure 6-20   General (left) and Advanced (right) dialog boxes used in Windows XP to configure a serial port connected to an external modem.

Adding Additional Serial Ports

You can add additional serial ports to a system with any of the following:

- PCI-based serial or multi-I/O card

- PCI Express–based serial or multi-I/O card

- USB-to-serial-port adapter

Troubleshooting Serial Ports and Devices

Use the following sections to help diagnose problems with serial ports.

COM 4 I/O Port Conflicts

Some video cards use an I/O port range that conflicts with the default I/O port range used by COM 4 (2E8-2EF). To prevent conflicts, you need to choose one of the following solutions:

- Change the I/O port address used by COM 4.

- Disable COM 4.

- Change the video card's I/O port address range to a nonconflicting option with Windows Device Manager.

Check the documentation for your system, serial port, multi-I/O card, or video card to determine which of these methods to use.

Can't Connect Serial Devices to Port Because of Mismatched Connectors

Some older systems might use a 25-pin serial port (the original design used by the IBM PC) instead of the now-standard 9-pin connector. Occasionally, some serial devices using one type of connector must be connected to serial ports that use the other type of connector. Use the appropriate 9-pin to 25-pin adapter to allow a 9-pin port to use a 25-pin device, or vice versa.

Serial Cabling and Port Problems

Damaged or incorrectly wired serial cables can cause several problems with any serial device. To avoid cabling problems, verify whether you are using the correct serial cable with any given device. For serial port external modems, purchase a modem cable; for serial printers, buy a cable made especially for that printer, and so forth.

Damaged cables will cause device problems. If an external serial device will not work at all or produces garbage input or output, first check the communications parameters for the port and the devices. If these are correct, replace the cable with a cable that you know to be working and retry the device. Damaged ports will cause problems with any cable.

If the serial port is connected to the motherboard or add-on card with a header cable, make sure the header cable is properly connected to the motherboard or add-on card.

Serial Configuration Problems

The serial port or modem connected to a serial port must be configured correctly to communicate properly with devices such as serial printers or remote computers. If gibberish output from a printer or gibberish screen displays during a remote communications session occurs, make sure the baud rate, parity, and word length are set correctly. For more information about these settings, refer to the section "Serial Port Software Configuration," earlier in this chapter.

Testing Serial Ports

To determine whether a serial port is damaged, first make sure there are no IRQ conflicts (use the Windows Device Manager as described in Chapter 15) and that the header cable (if any) is properly attached to the motherboard. Then, use a diagnostic program, such as AMIDIAG, CheckIt, or others, and attach the appropriate loopback plug to the port. If the port cannot pass a loopback test, the port is damaged, and you should replace it. For more information about using loopback plugs, see the following section.

LPT (Parallel)

220-801

Objectives:
**220-801: 1.7,
1.11**

220-802

220-802: 4.2

The **parallel port**, also known as the Line Printer (**LPT**) port, was originally designed for use with parallel printers. However, don't let the name "LPT port" fool you. Historically, the parallel port has been among the most versatile of I/O ports in the system because it was also used by a variety of devices, including tape backups, external CD-ROM and optical drives, scanners, and removable-media drives such as Zip drives. Although newer devices in these categories are now designed to use USB or IEEE 1394 ports, the parallel port is an important external I/O device for older systems and devices.

CAUTION   Devices other than printers that plug in to the parallel (LPT) port have two connectors: one for the cable that runs from the device to the parallel port, and another for the cable that runs from the device to the printer. Although it's theoretically possible to create a long daisy chain of devices ending with a printer, in practice you should have no more than one device plus a printer plugged in to a parallel port. If you use more than one device, you could have problems getting the devices (not to mention the printer) to work reliably.

The parallel (LPT) port is unusual because it uses two completely different connector types:

- Since the first IBM PC in 1981, all IBM and compatible computers with parallel ports have used the DB-25F port, as shown in Figure 6-21, with pins 1–13 on the top and pins 14–25 on the bottom. This is also referred to as the type IEEE-1284-A connector. (IEEE 1284 is an international standard for parallel port connectors, cabling, and signaling.)

- The port used by parallel printers of all types, however, is the same Centronics 36-pin port used since the days of the Apple II and other early microcomputers of the late 1970s, as shown in Figure 6-21. This port is also referred to as the IEEE-1284-B port. It is an edge connector with 36 connectors, 18 per side.

Printer port

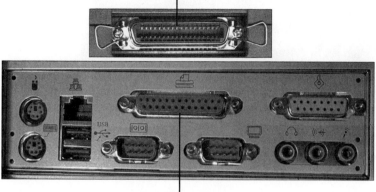

Parallel port on computer

Figure 6-21 Parallel devices use the Centronics port (top) for printers and some other types of parallel devices, whereas the DB-25F port (bottom) is used for the computer's parallel port. Some external devices also use a DB-25F port.

NOTE Some Hewlett-Packard LaserJet printers also use a miniature version of the Centronics connector known as the IEEE-1284-C, which is also a 36-pin edge connector. The 1284-C connector doesn't use wire clips.

Accordingly, a parallel printer cable also has different connectors at each end, as shown in Figure 6-22.

Parallel cables have the pinout described in Table 6-9.

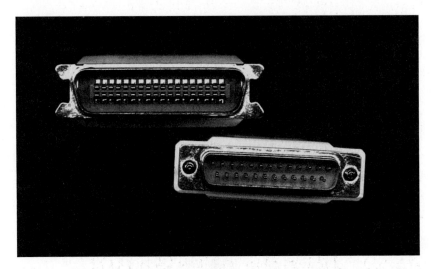

Figure 6-22   The ends of a typical IBM-style parallel cable. The Centronics 36-pin connector (upper left) connects to the printer; the DB-25M connector (lower right) connects to the computer's DB-25F parallel port.

Table 6-9   Parallel Port Pinout (DB-25F Connector)

Pin #	Description	I/O	Pin #	Description	I/O
1	–Strobe	Out	8	+Data bit 6	Out
2	+Data bit 0	Out	9	+Data bit 7	Out
3	+Data bit 1	Out	10	–Acknowledge	In
4	+Data bit 2	Out	11	+Busy	In
5	+Data bit 3	Out	12	+Paper End	In
6	+Data bit 4	Out	13	+Select	In
7	+Data bit 5	Out	14	–Auto Feed	Out
15	–Error	I	21	–Ground (Data bit 3 Return)	In
16	–Initialize Printer	Out	22	–Ground (Data bit 4 Return)	In
17	–Select Input	Out	23	–Ground (Data bit 5 Return)	In
18	–Ground (Data bit 0 Return)	In	24	–Ground (Data bit 6 Return)	In
19	–Ground (Data bit 1 Return)	In	25	–Ground (Data bit 7 Return)	In
20	–Ground (Data bit 2 Return)	In			

NOTE   The parallel designation for the LPT port comes from its use of eight data lines (pins 2–9) and that the port has provisions for printer status messages (pins 10–12).

Parallel Port Configuration

The configuration of the LPT port consists of the following:

- Selecting the port's operating mode
- Selecting the IRQ, I/O port address, and DMA channel (for certain modes)

The LPT port can be configured for a variety of operating modes. The options available for a particular port depend on the capabilities of the system. Most systems you're likely to work with should offer all these modes.

These modes differ in several ways, including port performance, whether the port is configured for output only or for bidirectional (input/output) operation, and the types of hardware resources such as IRQ, DMA, and I/O port addresses used.

The standard mode of the LPT port is the configuration first used on PCs, and it is the only mode available on very old systems. On some systems, this is also known as compatible mode. Although configuration for this mode typically includes both the IRQ and I/O port address, only the I/O port address is actually used for printing. If the parallel port is used in standard/compatible mode, IRQ 7 can be used for another device. The standard mode is the slowest mode (150 kilobytes per second [KBps] output/50KBps input), but it is the most suitable mode for very old printers. In this mode, eight lines are used for output, but only four lines are used for input. The port can send or receive, but only in one direction at a time.

Standard mode works with any parallel cable.

The next mode available on most systems is the PS/2 or bidirectional mode. This mode was pioneered by the old IBM PS/2 computers and is the simplest mode available on some computer models.

Bidirectional mode is more suitable for use with devices other than printers because eight lines are used for both input and output, and it uses only I/O port addresses. This mode is no faster than the compatible mode for printing but accepts incoming data at a faster rate than the compatible mode; the port sends and transmits data at 150KBps.

The bidirectional mode requires a bidirectional printer cable or IEEE-1284 printer cable.

There are also IEEE-1284 high-speed bidirectional modes. Three modes that are fully bidirectional (can send and receive data 8 bits at a time) and are also much faster than the original PS/2-style bidirectional port include

- **EPP (Enhanced Parallel Port)**—Uses both an IRQ and an I/O port address. This is the mode supported by most high-speed printers and drives attached to the parallel port.

- **ECP (Enhanced Capabilities Port)**—Designed for daisy-chaining different devices (such as printers and scanners) to a single port. It uses an IRQ, an I/O port address, and a DMA channel, making it the most resource hungry of all the different parallel port modes.

- **EPP/ECP**—Many recent systems support a combined EPP/ECP mode, making it possible to run devices preferring either mode on a single port.

These modes, which transmit data at up to 2 megabytes per second (MBps) and receive data at 500KBps, have all been incorporated into the IEEE-1284 parallel port standard. All these require an IEEE-1284–compliant parallel cable. These modes are suitable for use with

- High-speed laser and inkjet printers

- External tape-backup drives, optical drives, and Zip drives

- Scanners

- Data-transfer programs such as Direct Cable Connection (old Windows versions), Direct Parallel Connection (Windows XP), LapLink, Interlink, and others

Types of Parallel Cables

There are three major types of parallel cables:

- **Printer**—Uses the DB-25M connector on one end and the Centronics connector on the other.

- **Switchbox/Device**—Most use the DB-25M connector on both ends.

- **Data transfer**—Uses the DB-25M connector at both ends and crosses the transmit and receive wires at one end (meaning that two computers can send and receive data, much like a computer network, though much slower). These cables are much thinner than switchbox cables.

Any cable identified as IEEE 1284-compliant can be used with any parallel port mode and has these features:

- IEEE-1284 cables feature several types of shielding in both the cable and at the printer end of the cable. This shielding is designed to minimize interference from outside sources. Normal cables have minimal shielding.

- IEEE-1284 cables use a twisted-wire pair construction internally, running 18 wire pairs to the printer. The wire pairs help minimize crosstalk (interference between different wires in the cable). Standard (compatible) cables don't use as many wire pairs, and bidirectional cables use less shielding. As a result, IEEE-1284 cables are both a good deal thicker and more expensive than ordinary or bidirectional printer cables.

Standard and Optional Parallel Port Settings

This information can be useful in solving configuration problems on older systems; however, it is not required for the 2012 CompTIA A+ Certification exams.

Parallel ports can be configured as LPT1, LPT2, and LPT3. When a single parallel port is found in the system, regardless of its configuration, it is always designated as LPT1. The configurations for LPT2 and LPT3, shown in Table 6-10, apply when you have a computer with more than one parallel port.

If one of the ports is an ECP or EPP/ECP port, DMA 3 is normally used on most systems along with the IRQ and I/O port address ranges listed here. Some computers default to DMA 1 for an ECP or EPP/ECP parallel port, but DMA 1 will conflict with most sound cards running in Sound Blaster emulation mode.

PCI or PCI Express-based multi-I/O cards can place the parallel port at any available IRQ. PCI parallel port or multi-I/O (parallel and serial ports and possibly others on the same card) cards can share IRQs with other PCI cards. However, parallel ports built in to the motherboard cannot share IRQs when used in EPP, ECP, or EPP/ECP mode. (These modes use an IRQ.)

Table 6-10 Typical Parallel Port Hardware Configuration Settings

LPT Port #	IRQ	I/O Port Address Range
LPT1	7	378-37Fh or 3BC-38Fh
LPT2	5	278-27Fh or 378-37Fh
LPT3	5	278-27Fh

How to Configure or Disable Parallel Ports

Depending on the location of the parallel port, there are a couple of ways to configure the port settings. These include

- BIOS setup program for built-in ports
- PnP mode for use with Windows

Follow these steps to adjust the configuration of a parallel port built in to the system's motherboard:

Step 1.   Start the computer and open the BIOS setup program.

Step 2.   Go to the I/O device or peripheral configuration screen (see Figure 6-23).

Step 3.   Select the mode, IRQ, I/O port address, and DMA channel if required. If you aren't using parallel-port printers or devices, select Disable.

Step 4.   Save changes and exit; the system reboots.

PCI-based parallel ports are configured by the PnP BIOS. In some cases, you can adjust the settings used by a PnP parallel port or a motherboard-based parallel port with Windows Device Manager.

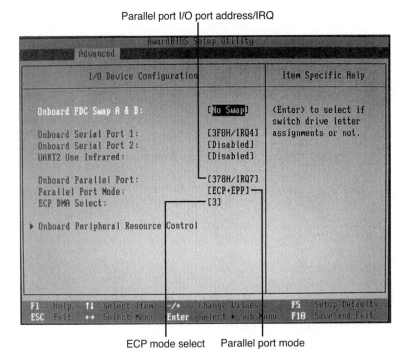

Figure 6-23   A typical BIOS I/O device configuration screen with the parallel port configured for EPP/ECP mode with default settings.

Adding Parallel Ports

Although you can daisy-chain a printer and another parallel-port device to a single parallel port, you can't connect two printers to the same port unless you use a switchbox. If you want to have two parallel printers that can be used at the same time, or if you want to provide different parallel-port devices with their own ports, you need to add a parallel port. What are your options?

You can add additional parallel ports to a system with any of the following:

- PCI-based parallel or multi-I/O card

- PCI Express-based parallel or multi-I/O card

- USB-to-parallel-port adapter

TIP   A USB-to-parallel port adapter has a USB Type A connection at one end and a Centronics connection at the other end. This adapter enables you to connect a parallel printer to your USB port so that you can use the parallel port for other devices. However, this type of adapter isn't designed to support other types of parallel-port devices. If you want to connect a parallel port drive or scanner, you must use a real parallel port.

Troubleshooting Parallel (LPT) Ports, Devices, and Switchboxes

If you cannot use devices connected to parallel ports (such as printers), check the following:

- **Parallel port mode not compatible with devices attached to the parallel port**—Make sure you use a mode compatible with all devices. (EPP/ECP is a good choice for most recent parallel devices.)

- **Incorrect order of devices when daisy-chaining multiple devices**—The printer is always at the end of the daisy chain. For other devices, consult the vendor's documentation.

- **Cabling problems, including inadequate cabling for the parallel port mode selected, cabling too long for reliable printing, damage to port or cable, and incorrect cabling of parallel port header cable on multi-I/O cards**—Use an IEEE 1284-compatible cable for all parallel printers and avoid cables longer than 10 feet. Damaged ports or cables can cause gibberish printing. (Verify the correct printer driver is used, though, because an incorrect driver can also cause gibberish printing.)

- **Switchbox problems**—To avoid damage to IEEE 1284–compliant ports, use only electronically switched switchboxes (not mechanical switchboxes) and use IEEE 1284–compliant cables to ensure status messages (out of toner, and so on) are received properly by the PCs sharing the port.

Testing Parallel and Serial Ports

To determine whether a parallel or serial port is damaged, first make sure there are no IRQ conflicts and that the header cable (if any) is properly attached to the motherboard. Then, use a diagnostic program such as AMIDIAG, CheckIt, or others and attach the appropriate loopback plug to the port. If the port cannot pass a loopback test, the port is damaged, and you should replace it. Figure 6-24 illustrates the use of loopback plugs to test parallel and serial ports.

TIP   Parallel and serial port loopback plugs resemble the connectors at the ends of parallel or serial cables but they don't have cables, and internally they're very different. Each loopback plug routes the transmit pins to the receive pins in the connector. The testing software used with the loopback plug sends data and compares the sent data to the data received. If the data doesn't match, the port is defective. Different programs used for loopback testing use different pin combinations for testing, so make sure you get the loopback plugs that are made especially for the testing software you use. You can purchase them in a bundle with the software, or you can purchase them separately.

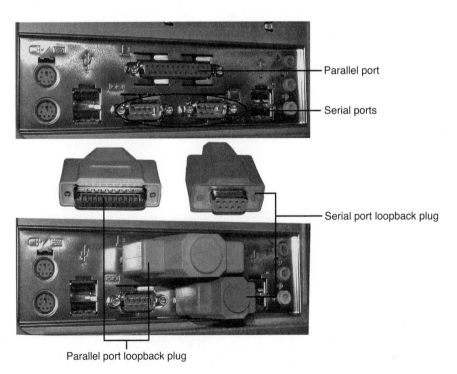

Parallel port

Serial ports

Serial port loopback plug

Parallel port loopback plug

Figure 6-24   An ATX motherboard's serial and parallel ports before and after loopback plugs (middle) are installed for testing.

PS/2 Mouse and Keyboard

220-801

Objective:
220-801: 1.11

PS/2 ports (also referred to as Mini-DIN ports) are used by PS/2 keyboards, mice, and pointing devices. Most desktop systems, and many older laptop and portable systems, include PS/2 ports.

In a typical ATX port cluster, the bottom **PS/2 port** is used for keyboards and the top PS/2 port is used for mice and pointing devices. On systems and devices that use the standard PC99 color coding for ports, PS/2 keyboard ports (and cables) are purple and PS/2 mouse ports (and cables) are green. Refer to Figure 6-17 for the location of these ports. Some recent systems have a single combo mouse/keyboard port marked with both purple and green. Refer to Figure 6-1 for an example.

To install the keyboard or mouse, turn off the power and insert the connector end of the cable into the appropriate connector. No special drivers are required unless the keyboard has special keys, has a programmable feature, or is a wireless model that uses a receiver. To remove the keyboard or mouse, turn off the power before removing the connector end of the keyboard cable from the keyboard connector.

Audio

220-801

Objective:
220-801: 1.11

Motherboards with built-in audio always have analog jacks and some have digital ports as well.

Analog Audio Mini-Jacks

The 1/8-inch (3.5mm) **audio mini-jack** is used by sound cards and motherboard-integrated sound for speakers, microphone, and line-in jacks, as shown in Figure 6-1.

To avoid confusion, most recent systems and sound cards use the PC99 color coding listed as follows:

- **Pink**—Microphone in
- **Light blue**—Line in
- **Lime green**—Stereo/headphone out
- **Brown**—Left-to-right speaker
- **Orange**—Subwoofer

SPDIF Digital Audio

Many systems include both analog audio (delivered through 1/8-inch audio mini-jacks) and digital audio. Sony/Philips Digital Interconnect Format (**SPDIF**) ports output digital audio signals to amplifiers, such as those used in home theater systems, and come in two forms: optical and coaxial. Sound cards might incorporate SPDIF ports into the card or into drive bay or external extension modules.

Optical SPDIF uses a fiber-optic cable, whereas coaxial SPDIF uses a shielded cable with an RCA connector. The cables are shown in Figure 6-25. To see SPDIF ports, refer to Figure 6-1.

TIP By default, systems with both analog and digital output use analog output. To enable digital output, use the Sounds and Audio Devices dialog in Windows Control Panel or the proprietary mixer provided with some sound cards or onboard audio devices.

To learn how to install sound cards and USB-based audio devices, and how to troubleshoot integrated or add-on audio devices, see "Sound Cards," in Chapter 8, "Customized PCs and Multimedia Devices."

Figure 6-25   SPDIF optical (top) and coaxial (bottom) cables.

Mouse

220-801

Objective:
220-801: 1.12

Next to the keyboard, the mouse is the most important device used to send commands to the computer. For Windows users who don't perform data entry, the mouse is even more important than the keyboard. Mouse alternatives, such as touch-screens, trackballs, or touchpads, are considered mouse devices because they install and are configured the same way. Currently, mice and pointing devices use USB ports, but some systems use the PS/2 mouse port or the serial (COM) port for mice or compatible pointing devices.

USB mice are part of the human interface device (**HID**) device category, and Windows installs HID drivers after the mouse is connected.

Some mice sold at retail work with either the USB port or the PS/2 port and include a PS/2 adapter (see Figure 6-26); some older mice worked with either the PS/2 or serial port. Adapters cannot be used successfully unless the mouse (or keyboard) is designed to use an adapter. A mouse designed to use an adapter is sometimes called a hybrid mouse.

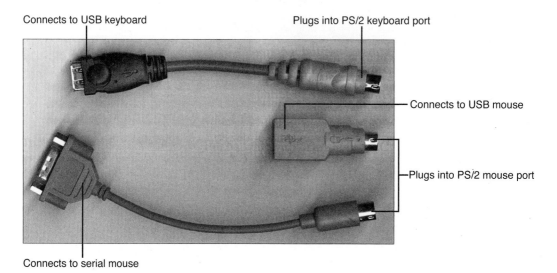

Figure 6-26 A USB keyboard–to–PS/2 keyboard port adapter (top) compared to a USB mouse–to–PS/2 mouse port adapter (middle) and serial mouse–to–PS/2 mouse port adapter (bottom).

Mouse Hardware Resource Use

A PS/2 mouse uses IRQ 12; if IRQ 12 is not available, the device using that IRQ must be moved to another IRQ to enable IRQ 12 to be used by the mouse. A serial mouse uses the IRQ and I/O port address of the serial port to which it is connected.

To install a USB mouse or other pointing device (such as a touchpad), plug it in to any USB port. Install any software drivers required. Unlike keyboards, mouse devices require software drivers. Windows includes support for standard mice from Microsoft and other vendors. However, if you are installing a mouse that includes zooming, tilt-wheel, or additional buttons, you might need to install the drivers provided with the mouse or updated versions provided by the vendor to ensure full support for additional features.

> **NOTE** Touch tablets can be used as mouse alternatives, but their primary purpose is to provide precision pointer control for creating digital art with programs such as Adobe Photoshop, Adobe Illustrator, and other programs.
>
> Touch tablets connect via the USB port and include a stylus. Some might also include a mouse that uses the touch tablet surface.
>
> In most cases, touch tablets are supported by built-in Windows drivers, but you might need to download a driver to gain full benefit from the tablet.

Troubleshooting Mice and Pointing Devices

Although Windows supports keyboard shortcuts for some operations, a mouse is required for maximum utility. Use this section to prepare for troubleshooting questions on the A+ Certification exams and day-to-day mouse problems.

Table 6-11 shows you how to use the Mouse Properties sheet for Windows XP, Vista, and 7 to solve common pointing device problems. All Properties sheet tabs except Hardware are shown in Figure 6-27.

Table 6-11   Using the Pointing Device Properties Sheet

Problem	Properties Sheet Tab to Use	Solution
I need to set up a mouse for a left-handed user.	Buttons	Select the Switch Primary and Secondary Buttons box.
Double-click doesn't work consistently.	Buttons	Use the Double-Click Speed slider and test box to adjust speed.
Items are dragged around the screen after I click on them, even if I don't hold down the primary mouse button.	Buttons	Clear the ClickLock option box; if the ClickLock option isn't selected, the primary mouse button is probably broken and you should replace the mouse.
I need different (larger, animated, high-contrast) mouse pointers.	Pointers	Select the wanted mouse scheme from the menu; install the mouse software provided by the mouse vendor to provide additional schemes.
The pointer moves too fast or too slow.	Pointer Options	Adjust the Motion slider to the wanted speed.
The pointer is hard to move over short distances or hard to stop.	Pointer Options	Enable the Enhance Pointer Precision option.
I'm tired of moving the pointer to the dialog box to click OK.	Pointer Options	Enable the Snap To option.

Table 6-11   Continued

Problem	Properties Sheet Tab to Use	Solution
The pointer disappears when moved quickly (especially on LCD displays).	Pointer Options	Enable the Pointer Trails option, and select the wanted length of the trail.
The mouse pointer disappears or only appears on parts of the screen.	Pointer Options	Enable the Show Location of Pointer When I Press the CTRL Key option.
The pointer covers up typed text.	Pointer Options	Enable the Hide Pointer While Typing option.
The pointer is hard to find on a cluttered screen.	Pointer Options	Enable the Show Location of Pointer When I Press the CTRL Key option.
The scroll wheel motion is too fast (or too slow).	Wheel	Select the number of lines to scroll with each click of the wheel, or select one screen at a time. Mice with both vertical and horizontal scrolling have separate adjustments.
On a system with more than one pointing device, I'm not sure which pointing devices are active.	Hardware	Look at the listing of the current device(s) to determine which are active. Use the shortcuts to Troubleshooter and Properties if necessary.

Mouse Pointer Won't Move

If the mouse pointer won't move when the mouse is moved, check the following:

- **The mouse software driver**—Use the Mouse icon in the Control Panel to verify whether the correct mouse driver has been selected under Windows. Using the wrong mouse driver can cause the mouse pointer to freeze.

- **The mouse connection to the system**—If a PS/2 mouse isn't plugged in tightly, the system must be shut down, the mouse reconnected to the PS/2 mouse port, and the system restarted to enable the mouse to work. USB mouse devices can be hot-swapped at any time. If a serial mouse is used on the system and it is not detected during Windows startup, Windows normally displays a message instructing you to plug in the mouse.

Figure 6-27 The Mouse Properties sheet for a wheel mouse used on a system running Windows 7.

- **Hardware conflicts**—Serial and PS/2 mouse devices must have exclusive access to the IRQ used by the port to which the mouse is connected. If you use another device that uses the same IRQ, the mouse pointer will freeze onscreen and the system can lock up. Use the Windows Device Manager to verify that there are no IRQ conflicts between the port used by the mouse and other devices. If necessary, use the PnP configuration in the system BIOS setup to select IRQ 12 (used for PS/2 mouse devices) as excluded or as an ISA IRQ.

- **Make sure the port used by the mouse is enabled in the system BIOS**—If the PS/2 mouse port is disabled, a PS/2 mouse won't work. If the USB ports are disabled, a USB mouse won't work. Recent systems with four or more USB ports sometimes provide an option for enabling only some of the USB ports. Check the system BIOS and make any changes needed. (See Chapter 4, "Power Supplies and System Cooling," for details.)

- **Make sure the mouse can work with a port adapter**—Many mouse devices sold at retail can be used with either a serial port or PS/2 port, or with either a USB port or PS/2 mouse port. The mouse has one port type built in and uses an adapter supplied with the mouse to attach to the other port type with which it is compatible. These mouse devices also contain special circuitry to enable them to work with either port type. Don't mix up the adapters used by different brands and models of mouse devices; mismatches might not work. Mouse devices bundled with systems typically don't have the extra circuitry needed to work with an adapter; they're built to attach to one port type only. Mouse devices that can work with adapters are sometimes referred to as hybrid mouse devices.

Jerky Mouse Pointer Movement

The most common causes of jerky mouse pointer movement include

- **Dirt or dust on the mouse or trackball rollers that are used to transmit movement signals to the computer**—Applies to mechanical mice.

- **Low battery power**—Applies to wireless mice.

- **Unsuitable mousing surface**—Applies to wired and wireless mice with optical sensors.

- **Interference from other wireless devices**—Applies to wireless mice.

- **Obstructions between mouse and receiver**—Applies to wireless mice.

- **Unsuitable mousing surface (no detail)**—Applies to nonlaser optical mice.

- **Interference from other wireless mice**—Applies to 27Hz wireless mice but not to 2.4GHz or Bluetooth mice. Use a different frequency.

- **Speed of the mouse pointer is too fast or too slow for user**—Use the Pointer Options tab on the Mouse properties sheet to adjust pointer speed.

User Can't Double-Click Icons

Damaged mouse buttons can prevent a user from double-clicking icons in Windows. Turn off the system if necessary, substitute an identical mouse, and restart the system to see whether the mouse is the problem. If changing mouse devices doesn't solve the problem, use the Mouse icon in the Windows Control Panel to adjust the double-click speed to the user's preference.

Maintaining Mice and Pointing Devices

Three types of motion sensors have been used in mouse devices: mechanical, optical, and laser.

Most mice with mechanical sensors use a ball and roller design. The motion of the mouse ball against a mouse pad, desk, or tabletop can pick up dust and dirt that can cause erratic mouse-pointer movement. The ball and the rollers should be cleaned periodically. Clean the mouse with a specially designed mouse cleaning kit, or use a nonabrasive damp cloth to remove gunk from the rollers and the ball.

To remove the mouse ball for access to the rollers, follow these steps:

Step 1.   Turn over the mouse; an access cover on the bottom of the mouse holds the ball in place.

Step 2.   Follow the arrows on the access cover as a guide to turn or slide the cover to one side; lift the plate out of the way to release the ball.

Step 3.   Move the rollers until you see dirt or grit; wipe them clean and clean the ball.

Step 4.   Remove loose dust and gunk from the mouse.

Step 5.   After you finish the cleaning process, replace the ball and access panel.

Optical mice and laser mice do not require disassembly. To keep an optical mouse in proper working order, wipe dust and dirt away from the LED light and sensor camera lens. To keep a laser mouse working properly, wipe dust and dirt away from the laser.

For wireless mice, be sure to check batteries periodically for leakage, and replace batteries when the cursor action becomes erratic. For mice that use rechargeable batteries, be sure to use approved types and charge the batteries as recommended by the battery vendor.

To maintain trackballs, remove the trackball and clean the rollers to keep the trackball working properly.

To maintain touchpads, periodically wipe the surface with a dampened cloth to remove skin oils that can prevent proper sensing of finger movements.

Keyboard

220-801

Objective:
220-801: 1.12

The keyboard remains the primary method used to send commands to the computer and enter data. You can even use it to maneuver around the Windows desktop if your mouse or another pointing device stops working.

Keyboards can be connected through dedicated keyboard connectors or through the USB port. Extremely old systems use the 5-pin DIN connector, whereas some recent systems use the smaller 6-pin mini-DIN connector—also called the PS/2 keyboard connector (refer to Figure 6-17).

Most recent systems use the **104-key keyboard** layout, which includes Windows keys on each side of the space bar and a right-click key next to the right Ctrl key. Otherwise, the 104-key keyboard's layout is the same as the older 101-key keyboard.

The keyboard can be plugged and unplugged as wanted without shutting down the system. Some USB keyboards include an adapter that enables them to connect to PS/2 keyboard ports (refer to Figure 6-26). USB keyboards are part of the human interface device (HID) device category, and Windows installs HID drivers after the keyboard is connected.

Troubleshooting Keyboards

Keyboard problems usually result from a few simple causes:

- A damaged keyboard cable
- Dirt, dust, or gunk in the keyboard

To determine whether a keyboard has failed, plug it into another system. A defective keyboard will not work in any system. However, if every keyboard plugged in to a keyboard port fails to work, the keyboard port is defective. Use a USB keyboard or replace the motherboard. If a USB keyboard doesn't work, shut down the system, reattach a PS/2 keyboard, and check the USB Legacy mode setting in the system BIOS.

If the normal keys on the keyboard work but multimedia or other special keys do not work, reinstall the drivers made for that keyboard.

If a wireless keyboard stops working, check its batteries. If you replace the batteries, follow the procedure for reconnecting to the receiver.

Maintaining Keyboards

Keyboards can become unresponsive or erratic due to dust, dirt, and debris under the keytops, and the keytops can become dirty and sticky. Here's how (and how not) to clean them:

Step 1. Don't use sprays to clean a keyboard; use a cloth dampened with an anti-static surface cleaner to wipe off grime while the system is turned off.

Step 2. Use compressed air or a data-grade vacuum cleaner to remove dirt and dust under the keys, or remove the keys if possible for cleaning with compressed air or a data-grade vacuum cleaner.

TIP If you're not certain whether the keytops can be removed, check with the keyboard vendor.

To remove the keytops from the keyboard, I recommend you use a chip puller, a U-shaped tool included with many computer toolkits. Grasp two sides of the keytop with the chip puller, and lift it from the keyboard. If you don't have a chip puller, use a pair of flat-bladed screwdrivers to carefully lift the keytop from opposite sides at once.

Bar Code Reader

220-801

Objective:
220-801: 1.12

Bar code readers are used in a variety of point-of-sale retail, library, industrial, medical, and other environments to track inventory.

Bar code readers use one of the following technologies:

- Pen-based readers use a pen-shaped device that includes a light source and photo diode in the tip. The point of the pen is dragged across the bar code to read the varying thicknesses and positions of the bars in the bar code and translate them into a digitized code that is transmitted to the POS or inventory system.

- Laser scanners are commonly used in grocery and mass-market stores. They use a horizontal-mounted or vertical-mounted prism or mirror and laser beam protected by a transparent glass cover to read bar codes.

- CCD or CMOS readers use a hand-held gun-shaped device to hold an array of light sensors mounted in a row. The reader emits light that is reflected off the bar code and is detected by the light sensors.

- Camera-based readers contain many rows of CCD sensors that generate an image of the sensor that is processed to decode the barcode information.

Wired bar code readers typically interface through the USB port, PS/2 keyboard port, or the serial (COM, RS-232) port. Bar code readers that plug in to the PS/2 keyboard port use a device known as a keyboard wedge to enable a keyboard and bar code reader to be plugged in to the keyboard port at the same time. Serial interface bar code readers use a software program to convert serial data into keystrokes or to perform dynamic data exchange (DDE) to applications. USB-based bar code readers emulate either the PS/2 or serial interface, depending on the software used to interface the reader.

See the documentation for the reader to determine whether you install the driver before or after connecting the reader. If the reader plugs in to a PS/2 keyboard or serial port, you must shut down the computer before connecting the reader. If the reader plugs in to a USB port, you can connect the reader while the system is running.

NOTE   Some bar code readers use Bluetooth to make a wireless connection between the reader and the computer or other data-acquisition device. In such cases, you need a Bluetooth receiver in your PC. To learn more about Bluetooth, see Chapter 16, "Networking."

Touch Screen

220-801

Objective:
220-801: 1.12

Touch screen (or touchscreen) monitors enable the user to transfer data into the computer by pressing onscreen icons. Touch screen monitors are popular in public-access and point-of-sale installations and are also included in all-in-one PCs.

Touch screen monitors use CRT or LCD technology and also incorporate one of the following surface treatments to make the monitor touch-sensitive:

- **Four-wire resistive technology**—Uses a glass panel coated with multiple layers that conduct and resist electricity. A flexible polyester cover sheet fits over the glass panel and is separated from the panel with insulating separator dots. The outer side of the cover has a durable coating; the inner side has a conductive coating. When the cover is pressed, an electrical signal is generated and is sent through the interface to the computer. The lowest-cost touchscreen technology, this type of screen is designed for public use.

- **Five-wire resistive technology**—A more sensitive and more accurate version of four-wire resistive technology suitable for use by trained personnel (offices, point-of-sale, and so on).

- **Surface wave**—Uses horizontal and vertical piezoelectric transducers to create ultrasonic waves. Touching the screen overlay disrupts the waves, and the coordinates of the touch determine what signal is sent to the computer. It's a durable surface that can compensate for surface damage and dirt and is suitable for self-service applications such as banking or information kiosks.

- **Touch-on-tube**—Combines surface wave technology with direct touch contact to the CRT; no overlay is necessary. LCDs use an overlay with a simple air gap between the overlay and the panel surface. Suitable for self-service applications.

- **Scanning infrared**—A light grid created by infrared (IR) signals is used to sense touches. Works with plasma as well as other types of displays.

Touch screens are available in freestanding versions similar to normal desktop CRT and LCD displays as well as in kiosk and built-in designs.

> **NOTE**   Some Windows 7 systems using an all-in-one design use LCD-based touch screens. With the release of Windows 8 and its enhanced touch screen support, you are likely to see many more touch screen–enabled systems in home and office environments in late 2012 and beyond.

Touch Screen Interfacing to the Computer

Like ordinary LCD and CRT monitors, touch screens use standard VGA analog or DVI digital interfaces to the video card. However, the touch signals are transmitted to the computer through a separate interface known as the touch screen controller. Touch screen controllers can use either of the following interfaces:

- **Serial (RS-232)**—Some touch screen monitors have an internal serial controller; others use an external serial controller. The internal serial controller might use a standard 9-pin serial cable or a special PS/2–to–9-pin serial cable to connect the controller to a serial (COM) port on the computer, depending on the monitor model. The external serial controller uses a controller with a built-in serial cable.

- **USB**—A touch screen monitor with an internal USB interface uses a standard USB cable to connect to a USB port on the computer.

Installing a Touch Screen

To install a touch screen monitor, follow these steps:

Step 1. Shut down the computer and disconnect it from AC power.

Step 2. Connect the monitor to the appropriate video port on your computer.

Step 3. Connect the serial or USB cable to the touch screen and to the appropriate port on the computer.

Step 4. Reconnect the computer to AC power and restart it.

Step 5. Install the serial or USB driver for the touch screen interface.

Troubleshooting a Touch Screen

Touch screens can malfunction for several reasons, including

- Display problems common to any monitor (loss of signal, incorrect colors, and so on).

- Software problems, such as corrupted or incorrectly configured drivers or applications.

- Video alignment problems. (You touch the screen but the wrong menu item or action takes place or the cursor moves in the opposite direction of your finger or stylus.)

- Hardware problems caused by the touch screen itself, the controller, cabling, or power.

To troubleshoot hardware or software problems, use the diagnostic programs supplied with the touch screen to verify whether the hardware is working. If the hardware is working correctly, the driver software used to interface the operating system and the touch screen must be checked. See the documentation for the touch screen monitor for details.

To solve problems caused by misalignment, realign the video using the utilities provided with the touch screen.

To troubleshoot hardware problems, use the diagnostic features provided with the touch screen controller to determine whether it is working correctly. The controller might use LEDs or onscreen messages to indicate problems. Next, use utilities provided by the touch screen vendor to determine whether the controller is transmitting touch data.

If constant touch data is being sent by the controller when you aren't touching the screen, the controller might be defective, the monitor bezel might be touching the screen, or the touch screen or cable has a short. If no touch data is being sent by the controller when you touch the screen, check the controller, cable, power supply, or controller setup.

KVM Switch

A keyboard-video-mouse (KVM) switch enables a single keyboard, display, and mouse to support two or more computers. **KVM switch**es are popular in server rooms and are also useful in tech support environments.

The simplest KVM switch is a box with input connectors for USB or PS/2 mouse and keyboard and VGA or other display and two or more sets of cables leading to the corresponding I/O ports and video ports on the computers that will be hosted. Some KVM switches also support audio. With this type of KVM switch, a special key combination or a push button on the switch is used to switch between computers.

KVM switches for server rooms and data centers are known as local remote KVM and typically use CAT5 or higher-quality cables to run to special interface devices on each server.

Exam Preparation Tasks

Review All the Key Topics

Review the most important topics in the chapter, noted with the Key Topic icon in the outer margin of the page. Table 6-12 lists a reference of these key topics and the page numbers on which each is found.

Table 6-12   Key Topics for Chapter 6

Key Topic Element	Description	Page Number
Figure 6-1	ATX motherboard I/O ports	209
Text	USB port standards	209
Figure 6-2	USB 1.1/2.0 plugs and sockets	210
Figure 6-3	USB 3.0 plugs and sockets	211
Text	USB generic hub types bus versus self-powered	214
List	Not enough power for (USB) device	216
Text	IEEE 1394a, b performance	218
Figure 6-8	IEEE 1394a card	218
Figure 6-9	IEEE 1394a, b connectors	219
Text	Multiple Device Support with SCSI Host Adapters	222
Table 6-4	SCSI standards	225
Figure 6-12	SCSI ribbon cables	226
Figure 6-13	SCSI external cables	226
Figure 6-17	Motherboard with legacy ports	232
Table 6-5	9-pin serial port pinout	233
Text	How to configure or disable serial ports	236
Figure 6-21	Parallel ports	241
Text	IEEE-1284 modes	244
Text	PS/2 mouse and keyboard ports	249
List	Audio jack color coding	250
Figure 6-25	SPDIF audio cables	251
Text	KVM switch	263

Complete the Tables and Lists from Memory

Print a copy of Appendix A, "Memory Tables" (found on the CD), or at least the section for this chapter, and complete the tables and lists from memory. Appendix B, "Memory Tables Answer Key," also on the CD, includes completed tables and lists to check your work.

Define Key Terms

Define the following key terms from this chapter, and check your answers in the glossary.

I/O port, Universal Serial Bus (USB), Hi-Speed USB, SuperSpeed USB, root hub, header cable, generic hub, bus-powered hub, self-powered hub, IEEE 1394, FireWire 400, FireWire 800, i.LINK, SCSI, daisy-chaining, device ID, termination, serial port, RS-232, COM, null-modem, parallel port, LPT, PS/2 port, audio mini-jack, SPDIF, HID, 104-key keyboard, KVM switch

Complete Hands-On Lab

Complete the hands-on lab, and then see the answers and explanations at the end of the chapter.

Lab 6-1: Check USB Device Power Usage

Scenario: You are a technician on a service call. A client has reported problems with a USB device plugged in to a keyboard. (Some keyboards can act as USB hubs.) Your task: Determine whether a USB device can be plugged in to a bus-powered hub (such as a keyboard) or if it must be connected to a root hub or a self-powered hub.

Equipment needed: Two or more USB devices, such as a USB mouse or keyboard, a USB thumb drive, a USB hard disk, or a USB webcam or scanner.

Procedure: Connect the USB devices to root hubs (built-in USB ports on the computer). Open Device Manager to check USB device power usage.

Answer Review Questions

Answer these review questions, and then see the answers and explanations at the end of the chapter.

1. Which of the following are popular standards for USB ports? (Choose two.)

   a. USB 1.2

   b. USB 3.0

   c. USB 2.1

   d. USB 2.0

2. You need to connect a USB 3.0 hard disk to the motherboard, but the port cluster has no USB 3.0 ports. Which of the following options should you choose to add the needed port? (Choose one.)

   a. Cable header to motherboard

   b. PCIe card with USB 3.0 ports

   c. PCI card with USB 3.0 ports

   d. USB 3.0 to USB 2.0 converter

3. Which port is known as IEEE 1394?

   a. USB

   b. Parallel port

   c. FireWire

   d. PS/2

4. An IEEE 1394b bilingual port supports which of the following? (Choose all that apply.)

   a. IEEE 1394a

   b. i.LINK

   c. IEEE 1284

   d. IEEE 1394b

5. When daisy-chaining SCSI devices, what must each device have? (Choose two.)

   a. Each device must have a unique SCSI device ID.

   b. Each device must have a separate bus.

   c. Each end of the daisy chain must be terminated.

   d. Each device requires its own adapter.

6. A serial port can hook up devices such as external modems and label printers. What is this port usually called?

   a. SCSI port

   b. COM port

   c. PS/2 port

   d. Parallel port

7. If you need to connect a printer and a scanner to a parallel port, which of the following should you select in port setup?

   a. PS/2 mode

   b. LPT mode

   c. ECP mode

   d. Compatible mode

8. A PS/2 port marked in green and purple means you can use which of the following devices?

   a. Mouse only

   b. Keyboard only

   c. Touchpad only

   d. Mouse and keyboard

9. If you need to connect audio sources using RCA jacks to audio jacks on the computer, you need an adapter from RCA to which of the following sizes?

   a. 6mm

   b. 1/8 inch

   c. 1/4 inch

   d. 1 inch

10. A PS/2 mouse plugged in to a computer has stopped working. It isn't feasible to shut down the computer at this time. Which of the following procedures is most likely to enable the user to keep working as usual?

   a. Disconnect the PS/2 mouse, and plug in another PS/2 mouse.

   b. Connect a USB mouse.

   c. Use a game controller.

   d. Use touch screen interface.

11. If you need to connect a bar code reader to a computer that does not have a serial port or a USB port, which of the following do you also need to install?

    a. Mouse emulator

    b. Keyboard wedge

    c. Bar code interface card

    d. Keyboard emulator

12. You need to select a keyboard that can be hot-swapped as needed for use on a computer. Which of the following interfaces should you use?

    a. 1/8 inch mini-jack

    b. PS/2 connector

    c. USB connector

    d. PS/3 connector

13. Which of the following can cause problems with keyboards? (Choose all that apply.)

    a. A damaged keyboard connector on the computer.

    b. A damaged keyboard cable.

    c. Dirt, dust, or gunk in the keyboard.

    d. None of these apply.

14. Which of the following would you check first when troubleshooting multiple USB devices that are not recognized by Windows?

    a. Disable the device in Windows.

    b. Reinstall the driver.

    c. Enable USB ports in the BIOS.

    d. Flash the BIOS.

15. You have been informed by a user that his mouse is not working correctly. Which of the following questions should you ask before asking the user to unplug and reconnect the mouse?

    a. What is the type of mouse (ball, optical, or laser)?

    b. Are you using a mouse pad?

    c. Is the mouse connector round or flat?

    d. What brand is the mouse?

Answers to Hands-On Lab

Lab 6-1: Check USB Device Power Usage

Answer: Any device that uses 100mA or less can be plugged in to a bus-powered hub. Any device that uses more than 100mA must be plugged in to a root hub or a self-powered hub.

Answers and Explanations to Review Questions

1. **B, D.** USB 2.0 is the established USB standard found on almost any PC, whereas USB 3.0 is a high-performance version now available on most of the latest PCs.

2. **B.** You cannot use a cable header if the motherboard has no provision for USB 3.0 ports. PCI is too slow to support USB 3.0 performance. USB 3.0 devices can plug in to USB 2.0 ports without a converter but perform only at USB 2.0 levels.

3. **C.** Another term for the IEEE 1394 and FireWire ports is i.LINK (used by Sony to refer to a four-pin implementation of IEEE 1394a).

4. **A, B, D.** A bilingual port can connect to either IEEE 1394b or 1394a and i.LINK devices by using the appropriate cable.

5. **A, C.** The SCSI device ID is used to identify the different devices on the SCSI bus. Terminating each end of the bus prevents signal problems.

6. **B.** Another name for the serial port is the COM (short for communications) port.

7. **C.** ECP mode enables printers and devices such as scanners to operate in daisy-chain mode on a parallel port.

8. **D.** Green is the PC99 color standard for PS/2 mice, and purple is the PC99 color standard for PS/2 keyboards. A port marked with both colors can work with either device, or with both if a Y-adapter cable is used.

9. **B.** The 1/8-inch audio mini-jack is used by sound cards and motherboard-integrated sound for speakers, microphone, and line-in jacks. Also, to avoid confusion, most recent systems have color-coded jacks.

10. **B.** You can hot-connect a USB mouse, but PS/2 mice can be safely connected and disconnected only if the system is shut down and disconnected from AC power. A game controller does not emulate a mouse, and there is no indication this system has a touchscreen.

11. B. To connect a bar code reader to a computer via the keyboard port, you must also connect a keyboard wedge.

12. C. A USB keyboard can be hot-swapped (assuming the system is configured to use a USB keyboard in the system BIOS). The 1/8-inch jack is used for audio, PS/2 keyboards cannot be hot-swapped, and there is no PS/3 connector.

13. A, B, C. These are mostly simple causes that can occur. You also want to make sure that you never plug a PS/2 keyboard in while the power is on. It could destroy the motherboard.

14. C. When more than one USB device is not recognized by Windows, one possible reason is that the USB ports have not been enabled in the BIOS program. Disabling the device in Windows only makes Windows ignore the device regardless of what you do in the BIOS, thus making the problem worse. Reinstalling the driver could be a possible solution if only one USB device is malfunctioning or is not recognized properly by Windows. Flashing the BIOS isn't necessary in a scenario like this and is definitely not the first thing to check.

15. C. A flat mouse connector is a USB connector, meaning that the mouse can be hot-swapped safely. The other questions would apply to further trouble-shooting.

This chapter covers the following subjects:

- **Video Card Types**—In this section you learn about the different types of video cards including PCI, AGP, and PCIe, and the various methods of cooling video cards.

- **Display Types**—This section describes CRTs, LCDs, and data projectors.

- **Installing a Video Card**—Learn the ins and outs of video card installation, from the BIOS, to physical installation and driver setup.

- **Video Connector Types**—This section talks about VGA, DVI, HDMI, and all the other video connections you need to know for the exam. This section also briefly demonstrates how to install a video monitor.

- **Video Display Settings**—This section demonstrates how to configure resolution and the refresh settings.

- **Troubleshooting Displays and Video Cards**—Due to the many possible video issues you might encounter, this section demonstrates how to troubleshoot with OSD and the advanced display properties. This section also describes how to keep the display clean and maintain good airflow.

This chapter covers a portion of the **CompTIA A+ 220-801 objectives 1.4, 1.7, 1.10, and 1.11** and **CompTIA A+ 220-802 objective 4.4**.

CHAPTER 7

Video Displays and Video Cards

The monitor and video card work together as the display subsystem to provide real-time notification of the computer's activities to the user. Because you might spend all day (and sometimes all night) gazing into the display, keeping it working to full efficiency is important. This chapter helps you prepare for the A+ Certification exams by enhancing your understanding of the major types of video cards and displays and showing you how to install, configure, and troubleshoot them.

Foundation Topics

Video Card Types

220-801

Objective:
220-801: 1.11

The **video card** (also known as the graphics card or graphics accelerator card) is an add-on card (or circuit on the motherboard of portable computers and some desktop computers) that creates the image you see on the monitor. No video card means no picture.

NOTE The terms *video card* and *graphics card* are often used interchangeably in the IT field.

Currently, video cards use the following bus types:

- PCI Express (PCIe)
- PCI
- AGP

Many low-cost desktop systems use integrated video instead of a video card, although many recent desktops also include a PCI Express (PCIe) slot. For more information about these expansion slot standards, see the section "Expansion Slots," in Chapter 2, "Motherboards and Processors."

In the mid 1990s, the most common type of expansion slot used for video cards was PCI. Although PCI was the leading general-purpose expansion slot type, the advent of the Pentium II CPU led to the development of the Accelerated Graphics Port (AGP) expansion slot, which is dedicated solely to high-speed video.

AGP slots have largely been replaced in recent systems by PCI Express x16 slots. Most computers and motherboards have a single PCIe x16 slot. However, many recent high-performance systems feature two PCI Express x16 slots that support either the NVIDIA-developed SLI or the ATI-developed CrossFire technologies for rendering 3D scenes on one video card with two (or more) graphics processing units

(GPUs), or two video cards that work in unison; a GPU is the graphics processing chip on a video card. To see a typical motherboard that supports NVIDIA's SLI, refer to Figure 2-1 in Chapter 2.

Video Card Cooling

All video cards contain a component called the graphics processing unit (GPU). The GPU is used to render information on its way to the display, and especially when performing 3D rendering, it can become very hot. Memory chips on the video card can also become very hot. Consequently both the GPU and memory require cooling.

Cooling can be provided through passive heat sinks or through cooling fans and fan shrouds as shown in Figures 7-1 and 7-2. Passive heat sinks, such as the one in Figure 7-1, are found on older video cards and typically cover only the GPU, but newer ones provide cooling for both the GPU and memory as might be seen with newer "quiet" operation video cards used in home theater PCs (HTPCs) and other media-based PCs. Video cards with passive heat sinks are good choices for these types of computers because these PCs need to run as quietly as possible. These computers often run Windows 7 Home Premium or Ultimate, Windows Vista Home Premium or Ultimate, or Windows XP Media Center Edition.

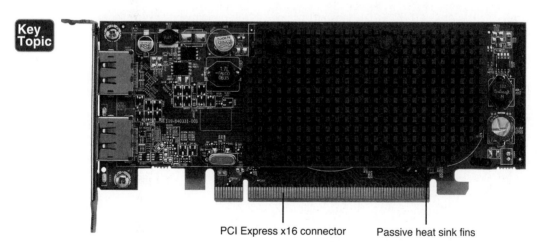

Key Topic

PCI Express x16 connector   Passive heat sink fins

Figure 7-1   This AMD FireMV 2260 video card for technical workstations uses a passive heat sink to cool the GPU and memory. Photo courtesy of AMD.

NOTE   Some video cards use a variation of passive heat sinks known as cooling pipes. Cooling pipes use pipes to route heat from the GPU and memory to a radiator-type passive cooler on the card. A cooling pipe cooler provides better cooling than a standard passive heat sink, but requires extra space around the video card.

The video card shown in Figure 7-2 uses a fan and a fan shroud to cool the GPU and memory. Some low-performance video cards that use a fan for cooling the GPU don't use a fan shroud, relying on case fans to cool video card memory.

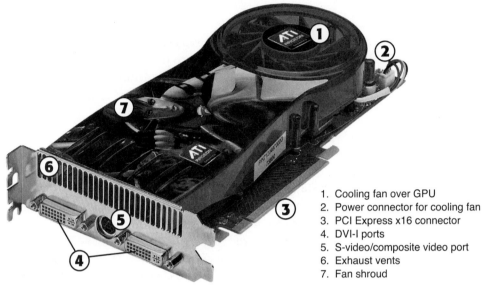

1. Cooling fan over GPU
2. Power connector for cooling fan
3. PCI Express x16 connector
4. DVI-I ports
5. S-video/composite video port
6. Exhaust vents
7. Fan shroud

Figure 7-2   This AMD ATI HD3870 video card includes a high-performance fan cooler and shroud over the GPU and memory to dissipate heat. Photo courtesy of AMD.

Display Types

220-801

Objective:
220-801: 1.10

There are six major types of displays you need to understand for the A+ Certification exams:

- CRT monitors
- LCD monitors
- LED monitors
- Plasma

- Data projectors

- OLED

The following sections help you understand the common and unique features of each.

CRT Monitor

Cathode ray tube (CRT) displays are now fading in popularity but are still in widespread use on older systems. CRTs use a picture tube that is similar to the picture tube in a tube-based TV set. The narrow end of the tube contains an electron gun that projects three electron beams (red, blue, green) toward the wide end, which is coated with phosphors that glow when they are hit by the electron beams. Just before the phosphor coating, a metal plate called a shadow mask is used to divide the image created by the electron guns into red, green, and blue pixels or stripes that form the image. Shadow masks use one of three technologies:

- A phosphor triad (a group of three phosphors—red, green, and blue). The distance between each triad is called the dot pitch.

- An aperture grill, which uses vertical red, green, and blue phosphor strips. The distance between each group is called the stripe pitch.

- A slotted mask, which uses small blocks of red, green, and blue phosphor strips. The distance between each horizontal group is also called stripe pitch.

If you look closely at a CRT display, you can see the individual triads or strips. However, from normal viewing distances, they blend into a clear picture. Figure 7-3 shows the design of a typical CRT monitor.

Generally, the smaller the dot or stripe pitch, the clearer and sharper the onscreen image will be. Typical standards for CRT monitors call for a dot pitch of .28 millimeters (mm) or smaller. Generally, low-cost monitors have poorer picture quality than higher-cost monitors of the same size because of wider dot pitch, low refresh rates at their highest resolutions, and poor focus at their highest resolutions.

Typical CRT displays range in size from 15 inches (diagonal measure) to 19 inches, and feature support for a wide range of resolutions. CRTs are analog display devices that can display an unlimited range of colors, and use the 15-pin VGA connector. To learn more about VGA connectors, see the section "VGA," later in this chapter.

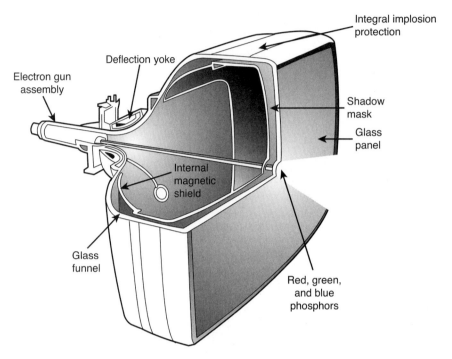

Figure 7-3   A cutaway of a typical CRT display.

LCD Monitor

LCD displays use liquid crystal cells to polarize light passing through the display to create the image shown on the monitor. In color LCD displays, liquid crystal cells are grouped into three cells for each pixel: one each for red, green, and blue light. LCD displays use a cold cathode fluorescent lamp (CCFL) as the lighting source. The CCFL develops ultraviolet light by discharging mercury into the lamp. The lamp's inner fluorescent coating then allows for the emitting of visible light, which is sent to the actual display panel.

All LCD displays use active matrix technology, which uses a transistor to control each cell, as the basic technology. Variations in how quickly a display can refresh, how wide the viewing angle, and how bright the display help distinguish different brands and models from each other.

An LCD monitor is a digital design, but many models, particularly low-end models and older designs, use the same VGA analog interface as CRTs. In such cases, the monitor must include an analog-digital converter to change the analog signal received by the VGA cable into a digital signal. High-end LCD displays and most recent midrange models also support digital signals and use DVI-D ports. To learn more about active-matrix displays, see "LCD Screen Technologies," in Chapter 9, "Laptops and Notebook Computers." To learn more about DVI-D connectors, see the section "DVI," later in this chapter.

Compared to CRT monitors, LCDs are much lighter, require much less power, emit less heat, and use much less desk space.

An LCD display has only one native resolution; it must scale lower resolutions to fit the panel or, depending on the options configured in the video card driver, might use only a portion of the display when a lower resolution is selected. When a lower resolution is scaled, the display is less sharp than when the native resolution is used.

LCD displays are found in both standard (4:3 or 1.33:1) and widescreen (16:9 or 16:10) aspect ratios, and range in size from 14 inches (diagonal measure) to 24 inches or larger.

LED Monitor

LED monitors utilize light-emitting diodes to display images. LED display technology is used in computer monitors, televisions, billboards, and storefront signs. LED monitors can use two different kinds of technologies: conventional discrete LEDs and surface-mounted device (SMD) technology. SMD is more common for LED monitors; it uses red, green, and blue diodes mounted as individual triads as opposed to discrete LED technology, which clusters these triads together into pixels.

LED monitors are essentially LCD monitors with a different backlight. Whereas LCD monitors use CCFL as the illumination source, LED monitors use light-emitting diodes, which release photons; this process is known as electroluminescence. These are commonly known as LED-backlit LCD displays.

> **NOTE**   In general, concepts referring to LCD in this chapter also pertain to LED.

Plasma

Plasma displays are rarely found in computer monitors but are often found in televisions. Nowadays, computers can use many types of televisions as their display, including plasma, as long as the computer has the correct type of video port. Plasma displays use small cells that contain electrically charged ionized gases; effectively, these are fluorescent lamps. Plasma screens are known for brightness and low-luminance black level in comparison to LCD screens. This makes the plasma screen a higher energy consumer than LCD. It also prompted the LCD community to release LED-backlit LCD displays that were mentioned previously.

Data Projector

Data projectors can be used in place of a primary display or can be used as a clone of the primary display to permit computer information and graphics to be displayed on a projection screen or a wall.

Data projectors use one of the following technologies:

- Liquid crystal display (LCD)
- Digital light processing (DLP)

LCD projectors use separate LCD panels for red, green, and blue light, and combine the separate images into a single RGB image for projection, using dichroic mirrors. A dichroic mirror reflects light in some wavelengths, while permitting light in other wavelengths to pass through. In Figure 7-4, red and blue dichroic mirrors are used to split the image into red, blue, and green wavelengths. After passing through the appropriate LCD, a dichroic combiner cube recombines the separate red, green, and blue images into a single RGB image for projection.

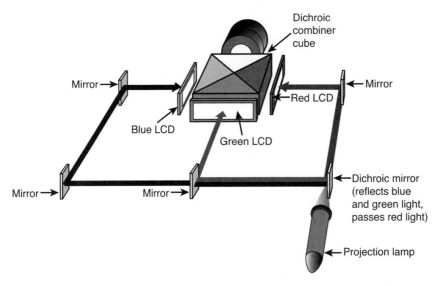

Figure 7-4   How a typical three-LCD data projector works.

LCD projectors use a relatively hot projection lamp, so LCD projectors include cooling fans that run both during projector operation and after the projector is turned off to cool down the lamp.

DLP projectors use a spinning wheel with red, green, and blue sections to add color data to light being reflected from an array of tiny mirrors known as a digital micro-mirror device (DMD). Each mirror corresponds to a pixel, and the mirrors reflect light toward or away from the projector optics. The spinning wheel might use only three segments (RGB), four segments (RGB+clear), or six segments (RGB+RGB). More segments help improve picture quality. Figure 7-5 illustrates how a DLP projector works.

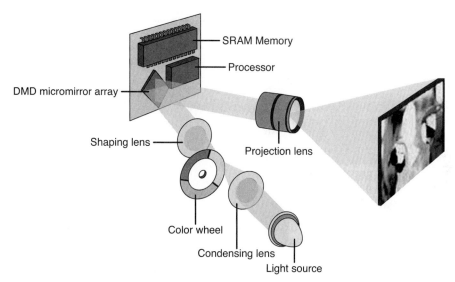

Figure 7-5   How a typical DLP projector works.

OLED

OLED stands for organic light emitting diodes. **OLED** displays use organic semi-conductor material usually in the form of polymers. Organic colored molecules are held in place between electrodes. A conductive layer made up of plastic molecules allows the organic colored molecules to emit light. The main advantage of OLED over LED is expected to be cost; OLEDs can be "printed" onto just about any substrate using simple printing processes. However, as of the writing of this book, manufacturing processes have not realized this cost reduction. OLED is still an emerging technology and as such is expensive and will not be seen often in the workplace.

Installing a Video Card

> **220-801**
>
> Objectives:
> **220-801: 1.4,
> 1.7, and 1.11**

The installation process for a video card includes three phases:

Step 1.   Configuring the BIOS for the video card being installed

Step 2.   Physically installing the video card

Step 3.   Installing drivers for the video card

BIOS Configuration

The BIOS settings involving the video card might include some or all of the following, depending upon the video card type:

- **AGP speed settings**—Found in systems with an AGP slot. Most systems automatically detect the type of AGP card installed (2x, 4x, or 8x) and configure speed settings accordingly. However, you can override the settings if necessary.

  For example, enable AGP Fast Write to improve graphics performance, but disable it if the system crashes.

- **Primary VGA BIOS (also known as Primary Graphics Adapter)**—Set this to AGP or AGP->PCI if you use an AGP video card; PCIE or PCIE->PCI if you use a PCI Express video card. Use PCI, PCI->PCIE, or PCI->AGP if you use a PCI video card. For onboard video, see the manufacturer's recommendation (onboard video can use PCI, AGP, or PCI Express buses built into the motherboard).

- **Graphics aperture size**—Found in systems with an AGP slot. Use the default size, which is typically the same as the amount of memory on the AGP card.

Adjust these settings as needed.

Video Card Physical and Driver Installation

Although all video cards created since the beginning of the 1990s are based on VGA, virtually every one uses a unique chipset that requires special software drivers to control acceleration features (faster onscreen video), color depth, and resolution. So, whenever you change video cards, you must change video driver software as well. Otherwise, Windows will drop into a low-resolution, ugly 16-color mode and give you an error message because the driver doesn't match the video cardHere's how to replace a video card (or upgrade from integrated video to a video card) and install the drivers in Windows 7/Vista/XP:

Step 1.   Go into Device Manager and delete the listing for the current video card.

Step 2.   Shut down the system and unplug it.

Step 3.   Turn off the monitor.

Step 4.   Disconnect the data cable attached to the video card.

Step 5.   Open the case and remove the old video card. Remove the screw holding the card bracket in place and release the card-retention mechanism that holds an AGP or PCI Express video card in place (see Figure 7-6).

Card-retention mechanism is
open; card can be removed.

Figure 7-6   Releasing the card-retention mechanism before removing an AGP video card.

NOTE   Card-retention mechanisms vary widely from motherboard to motherboard. In addition to the design shown in Figure 7-6, some use a lever that can be pushed to one side to release the lock, while others use a knob that is pulled out to release the lock.

Step 6.   Insert the new video card. Lock the card into position with the card retention mechanism (if you are installing an AGP or PCI Express card) and with the screw for the card bracket.

Step 7.   Reattach the data cable from the monitor to the new video card. If you are connecting a monitor with a VGA cable to a video card that uses only DVI-I ports (refer to Figure 7-2 earlier in the chapter), attach an adapter between the DVI-I port and the VGA connector (see Figure 7-7).

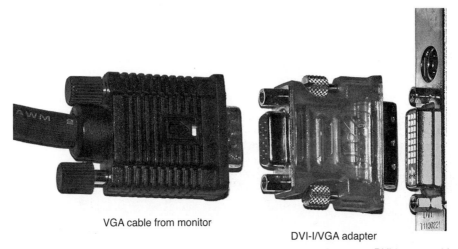

VGA cable from monitor

DVI-I/VGA adapter

DVI-I port on video card

Figure 7-7   Using a DVI-I/VGA adapter.

Step 8.   Turn on the monitor.

Step 9.   Turn on the computer and press F8 to display the startup menu.

Step 10.   Select Enable VGA Mode from the startup menu.

Step 11.   Provide video drivers as requested; you might need to run an installer program for the drivers.

Step 12.   If the monitor is not detected as a Plug and Play monitor but as a Default monitor, install a driver for the monitor. A driver disc might have been packed with the monitor, or you might need to download a driver from the monitor vendor's website. If you do not install a driver for a monitor identified as a Default monitor, you will not be able to choose from the full range of resolutions and refresh rates the monitor actually supports.

To learn more about connector types used by monitors and video cards, see the following section "Video Connector Types."

Video Connector Types

When selecting a monitor or projector for use with a particular video card or integrated video port, it's helpful to understand the physical and feature differences between different video connector types, such as VGA, DVI, HDMI, DisplayPort Component/RGB, S-video, and composite.

VGA

VGA is an analog display standard. By varying the levels of red, green, or blue per dot (pixel) onscreen, a VGA port and monitor can display an unlimited number of colors. Practical color limits (if you call more than 16 million colors limiting) are based on the video card's memory and the desired screen resolution.

All VGA cards made for use with standard analog monitors use a DB-15F 15-pin female connector, which plugs into the DB-15M connector used by the VGA cable from the monitor. Figure 7-8 compares these connectors.

DB15M VGA cable   DB15F VGA port

Key Topic

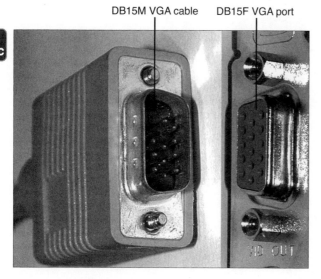

Figure 7-8   DB15M (cable) and DB15F (port) connectors used for VGA video signals.

SVGA may refer to 800×600 VGA resolution or to any VGA display setting that uses more than 16 colors or a higher resolution than 640×480.

DVI

The **DVI** port is the current standard for digital LCD monitors. The DVI port commonly comes in two forms: DVI-D supports only digital signals and is found on digital LCD displays. Most of these displays also support analog video signals through separate VGA ports. However, video cards with DVI ports use the DVI-I version, which provides both digital and analog output and supports the use of a VGA/DVI-I adapter for use with analog displays (refer to Figure 7-7). Figure 7-9 illustrates a DVI-D cable and DVI-I port.

DVI-D video cable supports digital signals only

DVI-I video port supports analog and digital signals

Figure 7-9   DVI-I video port and DVI-D video cable.

HDMI

Video cards and systems with integrated video that are designed for home theater use support a unique type of digital video standard known as **High-Definition Multimedia Interface (HDMI)**. HDMI has the capability to support digital audio as well as video through a single cable. HDMI ports are found on most late-model HDTVs as well as home theater hardware such as amplifiers and DVD players.

The most recent HDMI standard, version 1.3b, supports up to 1080p HDTV, 24-bit or greater color depths, and various types of uncompressed and compressed digital audio. However, all versions of HDMI use the cable shown in Figure 7-10 and the port shown in Figure 7-11.

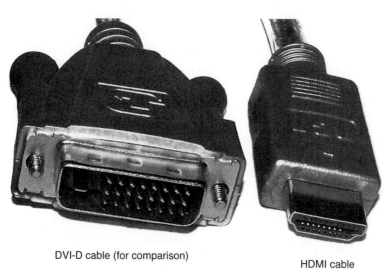

DVI-D cable (for comparison)

HDMI cable

Figure 7-10   HDMI cable (right) compared to DVI-D cable (left).

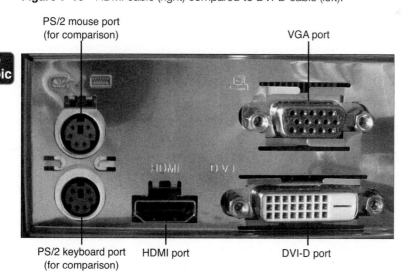

PS/2 mouse port
(for comparison)

VGA port

Key
Topic

PS/2 keyboard port   HDMI port
(for comparison)

DVI-D port

Figure 7-11   HDMI, DVI-D, and VGA ports on the rear of a typical PC built for use with Windows Media Center and home theater integration.

Systems and video cards with integrated HDMI ports might also feature DVI-I or VGA ports, as in Figure 7-11.

A converter cable with a DVI connector on one end and an HDMI connector on the other end can be used to interface a PC with an HDTV if the PC doesn't have an HDMI port.

The most common HDMI port is Type A, which has 19 pins. It is used to achieve high definition resolutions such as 1920 x 1080 (known as 1080p or 1080i). Type B ports have 29 pins and can perform at even higher resolutions such as 3840 x 2400 (WQUXGA). HDMI cables perform their best if they adhere to the latest standard. For example, as of the writing of this book, you should look for a cable that conforms to version 1.3 or higher. The HDMI 1.3 specification also defines a miniHDMI connector (Type C). It is smaller than the Type A plug but has the same 19-pin configuration. The HDMI 1.4 specification defines a microHDMI connector (Type D), which again uses the same 19-pin configuration but in a connector the size of a micro-USB plug.

DisplayPort

DisplayPort was designed by the Video Electronics Standards Association (VESA) as a royalty-free interface to replace DVI and VGA. It offers similar performance to HDMI but is not expected to compete with the HDMI standard.

DisplayPort utilizes packet transmission similar to Ethernet and USB. Each packet transmitted has the clock embedded as opposed to DVI and HDMI, which utilize a separate clocking signal.

The DisplayPort connector looks similar to a USB connector; however, it has teeth that will stop it from being inserted into a USB port (aside from the slight difference in size). DisplayPort connectors are not compatible with USB, DVI, or HDMI; however, the DisplayPort technology is capable of sending HDMI and DVI signals with the use of an adapter. DisplayPort offers a maximum transmission distance of 3 meters over passive cable, and 33 meters over active cable. There are 20 pins in a DisplayPort connector, with pins 19 and 20 being used for 3.3V, 500 mA power on active cables.

Version 1.0 and 1.1 had a maximum data transfer rate of 8.64 Gbps. Version 1.2 improves this to 17.28 Gbps. It can be encrypted with the 128-bit Advanced Encryption Standard (AES) algorithm, and the 56-bit High-bandwidth Digital Content Protection (HDCP) protocol for DRM purposes. Common resolutions include 1280 x 720 and 1920 x 1080, all the way up to 3840 x 2160.

Component/RGB

Some data projectors and virtually all HDTVs support a high-resolution type of analog video known as component video. Component video uses separate RCA cables and ports to carry red, green, and blue signals (**RGB**), and can support up to 720p HDTV resolutions.

S-Video

S-video divides a video signal into separate luma and chroma signals, providing a better signal for use with standard TVs, projectors, DVD players, and VCRs than a composite signal. The so-called "TV-out" port on the back of many video cards is actually an S-video port (see Figure 7-12).

Composite

The lowest-quality video signal supported by PCs is composite video, which uses a single RCA cable and port to transmit a video signal. Video cards sold in Europe usually use a composite signal for their TV-out signal.

Composite video can be used by standard definition TVs (SDTVs) and VCRs. If you need to connect a PC with an S-video port to a TV or VCR that has a composite port, you can use an S-video to composite video adapter.

Figure 7-12 compares component, S-video, and composite video cables and ports to each other. Note that composite video cables are often bundled with stereo audio cables but can also be purchased separately.

Installing a Monitor

To install a monitor in Windows, follow this procedure:

Step 1.   Determine whether the monitor is using a cable compatible with your video card. If you can change the cable, do so if necessary. In the case of an LCD display, you will have better picture quality if you use DVI rather than VGA interfacing.

Step 2.   If the system is currently running, open the Advanced dialog and choose a resolution and refresh rate supported by both the current monitor and the new monitor, and then shut down the system.

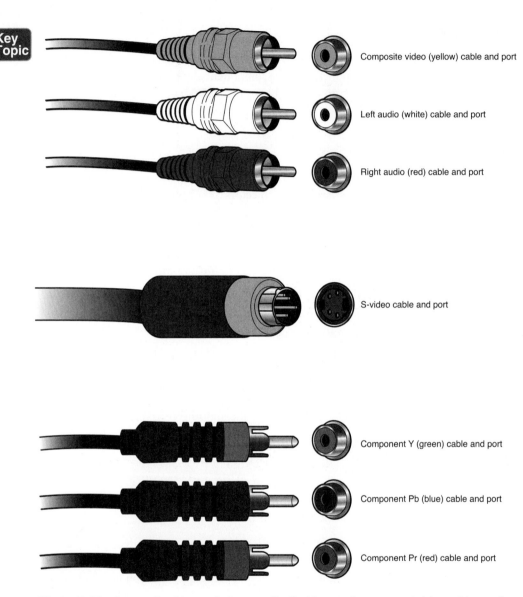

Composite video (yellow) cable and port

Left audio (white) cable and port

Right audio (red) cable and port

S-video cable and port

Component Y (green) cable and port

Component Pb (blue) cable and port

Component Pr (red) cable and port

Figure 7-12 Composite video and stereo audio, S-video, and component video cables and ports compared.

Step 3.   Connect the cable between the monitor and the video card. Fasten the thumbscrews to hold the VGA or DVI cable in place (see Figure 7-13).

Figure 7-13   Fastening the video cable into place.

Step 4.   Plug in the monitor to an AC outlet, turn it on, and restart the computer.

Step 5.   Open the appropriate display settings window for your operating system (see Figures 7-14 through 7-16 in the next section).

Step 6.   If your monitor is listed as Plug and Play or by brand and model, adjust the resolution. If not, install a new driver for the monitor before continuing. The monitor driver might be provided on a CD, or you might need to download it.

Step 7.   If you are installing a CRT display, open the Advanced dialog and choose an appropriate flicker-free refresh rate.

Video Display Settings

> **220-801**
>
> **Objective:**
> **220-801: 1.10**

Once a display is connected to your computer, it might need to be properly configured. The following sections discuss display settings issues you might encounter in A+ Certification exams.

Resolution

Display **resolution** is described as the amount of pixels (picture elements) on a screen. It is measured horizontally by vertically (HxV). The word "resolution" is somewhat of a misnomer and will also be referred to as pixel dimensions. Table 7-1 shows some of the typical resolutions used in Windows. The more commonly used resolutions are in bold.

Table 7-1 List of Resolutions Used in Windows

Resolution Type	Full Name	Pixel Dimensions	Aspect Ratio
VGA*	Video Graphics Array	640×480	4:3 (1.333)
SVGA*	Super Video Graphics Array	800×600	4:3 (1.333)
XGA	eXtended Graphics Array	1024×768	4:3 (1.333)
WXGA	Widescreen eXtended Graphics Array	1280×800	16:10 (1.6:1)
WXGA (HD)	Widescreen eXtended Graphics Array (High Definition)	1366×768	16:9 (1.78:1)
SXGA	Super eXtended Graphics Array	1280×1024	5:4 (1.25)
WSXGA+	Widescreen Super eXtended Graphics Array Plus	1680×1050	16:10 (1.6:1)
WSXGA+ (HD)	Widescreen Super eXtended Graphics Array Plus (High-Definition)	1680×945	16:9 (1.78:1)
WUXGA	Widescreen Ultra eXtended Graphics Array	1920×1200	8:5 (1.6)
1080P and 1080i	Full High Definition	1920×1080	16:9 (1.778)

VGA and SVGA modes are usually only seen if you attempt to boot the system into Safe Mode or another advanced boot mode, or if the driver has failed.

To modify screen resolution do the following:

- **In Windows 7**—Right-click the desktop and select Screen Resolution. Use the vertical slider to select the desired pixel dimensions (see Figure 7-14).

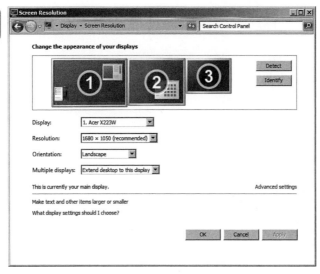

Figure 7-14   The Screen Resolution window in Windows 7 controls display resolution, can detect monitors, and offers multiple monitor support.

- **In Windows Vista**—Right-click the desktop and select Personalize. Then click the Display Settings link. Toward the bottom left of the window is a box called Resolution, which has a slider that enables you to configure the pixel dimensions (see Figure 7-15).

- **In Windows XP**—Right-click the desktop and select Properties. Then click the Settings tab within the Display Properties window. Toward the bottom left of the window is a box called Screen Resolution, which has a slider that enables you to configure the pixel dimensions. This dialog is also used to select color quality and to enable multiple displays on a system that supports two or more monitors (see Figure 7-16).

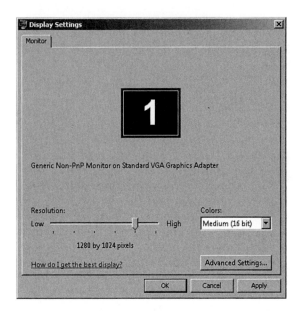

Figure 7-15   The Display Settings dialog box in Windows Vista controls display resolution and Advanced Settings.

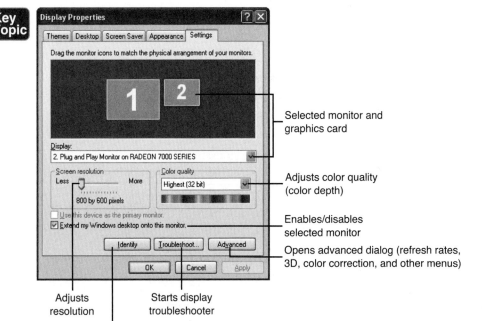

Figure 7-16   The Settings tab in Windows XP controls display resolution, multiple monitor support, color quality (color depth), and provides access to advanced settings.

Unless you need to select a lower resolution for specific purposes, you should select an LCD monitor's native resolution (see the instruction manual or specification sheet for this information). For a CRT, choose a resolution that is comfortable to view and enables the monitor to run in a flicker-free refresh rate, ideally 75Hz or higher.

Color Quality (Color Depth)

Color quality (also known as color depth or bit depth) is a term used to describe the number of bits that represent color. For example, 1-bit color is known as monochrome, those old screens with a black background and one color for the text, as in the classic movie *War Games*. But what is 1-bit? 1-bit in the binary numbering system means a binary number with one digit; this can be a zero or a one, a total of two values: usually black and white. This is defined in scientific notation as 2^1, (2 to the 1st power, which is 2). Another example would be 4-bit color, used by the ancient but awesome Commodore 64. In a 4-bit color system you can have 16 colors total. In this case $2^4 = 16$.

Now that you know the basics, take a look at Table 7-2, which shows the different color depths used in Windows.

Table 7-2 List of Color Depths Used in Windows

Color Depth	Number of Colors	Calculation
8-bit	256	2^8
16-bit	65,536	2^{16}
24-bit	16,777,216	2^{24}
32-bit	4,294,967,296	2^{32}

8-bit color is used in VGA mode, which is uncommon for normal use. But you might see it if you boot into Safe Mode, or other advanced modes that disable the video driver. 16-bit is usually enough for the average user who works with basic applications; however, many computers are configured by default to 24-bit or 32-bit (also known as 3 bytes and 4 bytes, respectively). Most users will not need 32-bit color depth; in fact, it uses up video resources. If the user works on only basic applications, consider scaling them down to 24-bit or 16-bit to increase system performance. However, gamers, graphics artists, and other designers probably will want 32-bit color depth.

NOTE Typically, only video cards or onboard video circuits that lack 3D support list 24-bit color as the best color quality option; systems and onboard video with 3D support list 32-bit color instead of 24-bit color as the best color quality option.

To modify color quality, do the following:

- **In Windows 7**—Right-click the desktop, select Screen Resolution, and click Advanced Settings. Click List All Modes (adapter tag) and select the pixel dimensions, color quality, and refresh rate desired.

- **In Windows Vista**—Right-click the desktop and select Personalize. Then click the Display Settings link. A drop-down menu for color quality is located on the bottom right.

- **In Windows XP**—Right-click the desktop and select Properties. Then click the Settings tab within the Display Properties window. A drop-down menu for color quality is located on the bottom right.

Refresh Rates

The vertical **refresh rate** refers to how quickly the monitor redraws the screen and is measured in hertz (Hz), or times per second. Typical vertical refresh rates for CRT monitors vary from 56Hz to 85Hz or higher, with refresh rates of 75Hz causing less flicker onscreen.

TIP Flicker-free (75Hz or higher) refresh rates are better for users running CRTs, producing less eyestrain and more comfort during long computing sessions. Note that LCD monitors never flicker, so the Windows default refresh rate of 60Hz works well with any LCD display.

The vertical refresh in Windows 7 can be adjusted by accessing the Screen Resolution window, clicking Advanced Settings and then clicking the List All Modes button within the Adapter tab, or from the Monitor tab. It can be configured in Windows Vista and XP through the Advanced portion of the Display Properties sheet within the Adapter tab or the Monitor tab. These two options are illustrated in Figure 7-17.

A   B

Figure 7-17   Selecting the vertical refresh rate from the Monitor dialog (a) and from the Adapter dialog (b).

NOTE   If your monitor is listed as Default monitor rather than Plug and Play monitor or as a specific monitor model, you will not be able to choose flicker-free refresh rates. Install a driver provided by the vendor.

CAUTION   Selecting a refresh rate that exceeds the monitor's specifications can damage the monitor or cause the monitor to display a blank screen or a "signal out of range" error. If you select a refresh rate that exceeds the monitor's specifications, press the ESC (Escape) key on the keyboard to return to the previous setting.

Troubleshooting Displays and Video Cards

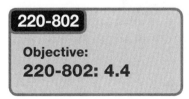

220-802

Objective:
220-802: 4.4

Some problems with the display subsystem are caused by the video card, while others are caused by the monitor or projector, and still others might involve the

Windows driver. Use the following sections to determine the causes and find solutions for common problems.

Troubleshooting Picture Quality Problems with OSD

Picture quality problems of all types, ranging from barrel or pincushion distortion and color fringing on CRT monitors to picture size and centering, contrast and brightness on both CRT and LCD monitors, can be fixed by using onscreen picture controls, also known as the OSD. The OSD is controlled with push buttons on the front of both CRT and LCD displays, and provide a greater number of adjustments than older types of digital display controls.

Typical picture adjustments available on virtually all monitors include

- Horizontal picture size

- Horizontal picture centering

- Vertical picture size

- Vertical picture centering

- Contrast

- Brightness

CRT displays also offer settings for removing picture distortion, color balance, color temperature, **degaussing** (removes color fringing in a CRT display caused by the magnetic fields in the monitor), and options for the language and position of the onscreen display (OSD).

Figure 7-18 shows typical examples of OSDs for CRT and LCD monitors.

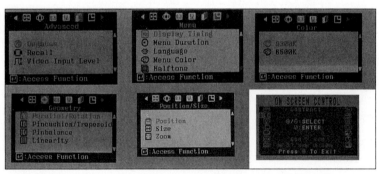

Figure 7-18 Typical OSD adjustments for CRT and LCD monitors. A portion of an LCD monitor's OSD is shown in the inset at lower right; the other images are from a typical CRT's OSD.

Figure 7-19 shows examples of barrel (outward curving image sides), pincushion (inward curving image sides), parallelogram, and trapezoidal distortions that can take place on CRT displays when different resolution settings or image-size adjustments are made. OSDs can adjust these picture geometry errors away as well.

NOTE   Typically, when you make an adjustment to picture size, centering, or geometry, a CRT display will "remember" the settings and use them again. However, if you change to a different refresh rate, you must reset these options so they can be stored for that refresh rate as well.

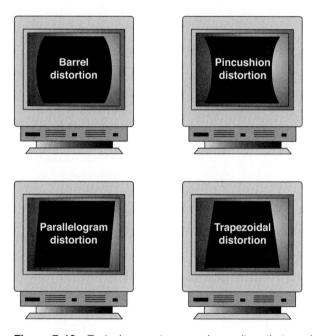

Figure 7-19   Typical geometry errors in monitors that can be corrected with digital or OSD controls available on most monitors.

Using Advanced Display Properties for Troubleshooting

The Advanced Display properties sheet offers a variety of ways to solve various types of display problems as shown in Table 7-3.

Table 7-3 Advanced Adjustments for Display Quality and Features

Adjustment Needed	Tab	Menu Item or Button	Notes
Icons and text too small	General	DPI setting	Custom lets you select the setting you want.
Need to update video card driver	Adapter	Properties	Click Driver tab to update driver.
Need to adjust vertical refresh rate to eliminate flicker	Adapter or Monitor (varies by Windows version)	(Screen) refresh rate	Use 75Hz or higher refresh rate (up to limits of monitor) to reduce or eliminate flicker.
Graphics or mouse pointer problems	Troubleshoot (Windows XP/Vista/7) or Performance (other Windows versions)	Hardware Acceleration	Drag to left to reduce acceleration; download and install new mouse and display drivers as soon as possible.
Colors don't match between screen and printer	Color Management	Add (color profile)	Get color profiles from printer or graphics software vendors.
3D game performance too low	OpenGL or Direct3D	Adjust settings for performance	If not available on your system, download the latest driver from your 3D video card vendor.
3D game image quality too low	OpenGL or Direct3D	Adjust settings for quality	If not available on your system, download the latest driver from your 3D video card vendor.
Color balance, brightness, and contrast need adjusting	Color	Adjust options as needed	Many 3D games are very dark; use Full Screen 3D option (if available) to adjust display for 3D gaming only.

Troubleshooting Video Hardware

Table 7-4 lists suggestions for troubleshooting other video hardware issues.

Table 7-4 Troubleshooting Monitors, Projectors, and Video Cards

Symptom	Problem	Solution
Color fringes around text and graphics on monitor screen.	Magnetic distortion is affecting image quality.	Use degaussing option (use degauss button, turn monitor off and on, or check OSD menu on some monitors).
Colors flicker onscreen.	Loose video cable.	Turn off monitor and system; tighten cable and restart.
Picture changes size.	Power supply not supplying consistent voltage.	Repair or replace monitors.
Picture occasionally displays wavy lines.	Interference caused by poorly shielded devices in the area.	Look for source of interference (such as microwave oven); move interference away from computer.
Picture quality garbled while changing video mode in Windows.	Wrong resolution or refresh rate selected.	Press Esc key to cancel change; check video card and monitor documentation for resolutions and refresh rates supported by both; select from these.
Can't select desired color depth at a given resolution.	Video card does not have enough memory onboard for desired color depth/resolution combination.	Upgrade video card memory, reduce color depth or resolution, or replace video card.
	Incorrect video card driver might be in use.	Double-check video card driver selected; replace with correct video driver if necessary.
Can't select resolution or refresh rate desired.	Wrong monitor might be selected.	Double-check monitor type; replace with correct monitor driver if necessary.
No picture when replacing built-in video with a replacement video card.	Old and new video circuits have a conflict.	Move new video card to a different slot; check for a motherboard setting to disable onboard video; try a different video card model.
LCD or DLP projector won't display image.	The projector has not been recognized by the system.	Shut down the computer and projector. Wait 30 seconds, then turn on the projector first. After the projector is turned on, turn on the computer. In some cases, you might need to select the computer as the video source.

Table 7-4 Continued

Symptom	Problem	Solution
	The monitor is running at a different resolution than the projector.	Use the Display properties sheet to set the primary display (computer display) to the same resolution as the projector. Enable the Clone Display or Mirror option (see the computer or video card documentation for details).
	The refresh rate for the projector is set too high.	Adjust the refresh rate to 60Hz using the Adapter or Monitor setting in the Advanced Display properties.
LCD projector won't display some colors.	One of the LCD panels might have failed or cable might be loose.	Try the projector with a different system. If the problem persists, replace the video cable. If the problem persists, the projector needs to be repaired or replaced.
LCD or DLP projector projected image is dim.	Projector might be set for bulb-saver (low power mode) or bulb might need replacing.	If the projector has a bulb-saver (low-power) setting, turn off the setting. If not, replace the bulb.
LCD projector has colored dots on the image.	Clean the LCD panels inside the projector.	Contact the vendor for service.
LCD or DLP projector image is not square.	The projector is tilted in relation to the screen.	Adjust the screen position; use the keystone correction feature in the projector menu.

Preventative Maintenance for Displays

The display is one of the most expensive components used by a PC, and a video card can be the biggest single expense inside a computer, so keeping them in good working order makes sense. Here's how:

- Do not block ventilation holes in CRT and LCD displays. Blocked ventilation holes can lead to overheating and component failure.

- Use antistatic cleaners made for electronics to clean screens and other surfaces.

- Do not spray cleaners directly onto screens or enclosures; an electrical short could result if the cleaner drips inside the unit. Instead, spray the cleaner on a lint-free cloth, and use the cloth to clean the screen or enclosure.

- Use thumbscrews to hold VGA and DVI cables in place on displays, projectors, and video cards. Loose cables can cause poor-quality images and can lead to broken pins if the cable is snagged and pulled out of place. Broken pins could also cause poor-quality picture or loss of picture altogether.

- When a system is opened for upgrades or service, check the condition of the cooling features of the video card. Remove hair, dust, or dirt in or on the heat sink, cooling fan, fan shroud, or heat pipe radiator. Make sure airflow around and behind the video card is not obstructed by cables, dirt, dust, or other components.

- Allow plenty of clearance around the video card slot. Don't use the slot next to the video card if the card would limit airflow to the video card's cooling features.

Exam Preparation Tasks

Review All the Key Topics

Review the most important topics in the chapter, noted with the key topics icon in the outer margin of the page. Table 7-5 lists a reference of these key topics and the page numbers on which each is found.

Table 7-5   Key Topics for Chapter 7

Key Topic Element	Description	Page Number
Figure 7-1	Video card designed to cool the GPU and memory.	275
Figure 7-2	Video card designed to dissipate heat.	276
Figure 7-8	DB15M (cable) and DB15F (port) connectors used for VGA video signals.	285
Figure 7-9	DVI-I video port and DVI-D video cable.	286
Figure 7-11	HDMI, DVI-D, and VGA ports.	287
Figure 7-12	Composite video and stereo audio, S-video, and component video cables and ports compared.	290
Figure 7-14	The Screen Resolution window in Windows 7.	293
Figure 7-16	The Settings tab in Windows XP.	294
Figure 7-17	Selecting the vertical refresh rate from the monitor dialog (a) and from the adapter dialog (b).	297
Figure 7-18	Typical OSD adjustments for CRT and LCD monitors.	298
Table 7-4	Troubleshooting monitors, projectors, and video cards.	301

Complete the Tables and Lists from Memory

Print a copy of Appendix A, "Memory Tables" (found on the CD), or at least the section for this chapter, and complete the tables and lists from memory. Appendix B, "Memory Tables Answer Key," also on the CD, includes completed tables and lists to check your work.

Define Key Terms

Define the following key terms from this chapter, and check your answers in the glossary.

video card, CRT, LCD, VGA, SVGA, DVI, HDMI, DisplayPort, RGB, S-Video, resolution, refresh rate, degaussing, LED, OLED, plasma

Complete Hands-On Labs

Complete the hands-on labs, and then see the answers and explanations at the end of the chapter.

Lab 7-1: Select the Appropriate Video Connectors

Scenario: You are required to connect three different types of video cables to the appropriate ports.

Procedure: Within Figure 7-20 write the name of each of the following ports in the corresponding box (not all boxes are used to answer this).

- HDMI

- DVI

- VGA

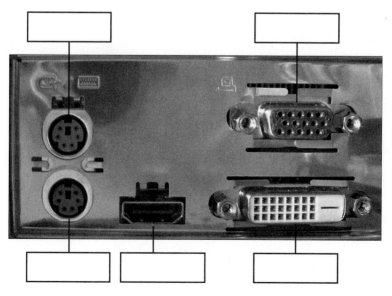

Figure 7-20   Lab 7-1.

Answer Review Questions

Answer these review questions and then see the answers and explanations at the end of the chapter.

1. Which of the following bus types are used for video cards? (Choose all that apply.)

   a. PCI

   b. AGP

   c. DMI

   d. PCI Express

2. Which of the following are used to keep the video card cool? (Choose all that apply.)

   a. Passive heat sinks

   b. Thermal glue

   c. Cooling fans

   d. Shrouds

3. When installing a new video card, there are three phases. What are they? Select the best three answers.

   a. Configuring the BIOS for the video card being installed.

   b. Physically installing the video card.

   c. Making sure the video card is in the protective antistatic bag.

   d. Installing drivers for the video card.

4. You install a new video card in your system, but are not getting all the features. What would you need to do to correct the problem?

   a. Reboot the computer.

   b. Install the device driver.

   c. Take the card out and put it back in.

   d. Call a technician.

5. What are three major types of display devices in use in today's industry? (Choose all that apply.)

   a. CRT monitors

   b. LCD monitors

   c. Data projectors

   d. USB monitors

6. Identify three types of video connectors.

   a. VGA type

   b. DVI type

   c. HDMI type

   d. USB type

7. If you are installing a new LCD monitor, what current standard port will you need for digital signals?

   a. LCD monitor

   b. AGP slot

   c. A DVI port on the video card

   d. A VGA video port

8. What two tabs can you utilize to configure the vertical refresh in Windows 7?

   a. Adapter tab

   b. Troubleshoot tab

   c. Monitor tab

   d. Color Management tab

9. When installing a new monitor, what should you do first? (Choose the best answer.)

   a. Determine what type of cable is compatible with your video card.

   b. Go to the advanced dialog screen and choose a resolution.

   c. Connect the cable to the video card.

   d. None of these options is correct.

10. If the colors are flickering on your monitor, what is most likely the problem?

    a. Refresh rate too slow.

    b. Refresh rate too fast.

    c. Loose video cable.

    d. The monitor is bad.

11. If your monitor has low contrast and brightness, what might you do to correct the problem?

    a. Change the refresh rate.

    b. Reinstall the monitor.

    c. Check the connection.

    d. Use the OSD buttons on the front of the monitor.

12. Which of the following steps should you take when maintaining monitors? (Choose all that apply.)

    a. Do not block ventilation holes in CRT and LCD displays.

    b. Use antistatic cleaners made for electronics to clean screens and other surfaces.

    c. Do not spray cleaners directly onto screens or enclosures.

    d. Use thumbscrews to hold VGA and DVI cables in place on displays, projectors, and video cards.

    e. When a system is opened for upgrades or service, check the condition of the cooling features of the video card. Remove hair, dust, or dirt in or on the heat sink, cooling fan, fan shroud, or heat pipe radiator. Make sure airflow around and behind the video card is not obstructed by cables, dirt, dust, or other components.

    f. Allow plenty of clearance around the video card slot. Don't use the slot next to the video card if the card would limit airflow to the video card's cooling features.

13. Where would you go to set your display resolution in Windows XP?

    a. My Computer

    b. Display Properties

    c. Screen Saver tab

    d. Appearance tab

14. What is the difference between LCD monitors and LED monitors?

    a. LCD monitors use organic material.

    b. LED monitors use electrically charged ionized gas.

    c. LCD monitors project images on a screen or wall.

    d. LED monitors use light emitting diodes instead of CCFLs.

15. Which of the following video types uses a packet transmission scheme similar to Ethernet?

    a. HDMI

    b. DisplayPort

    c. VGA

    d. DVI

Answers to Hands-On Labs

Lab 7-1: Select the Appropriate Video Connectors

Answer: Figure 7-21 shows the answers as well as the other ports not covered in the question.

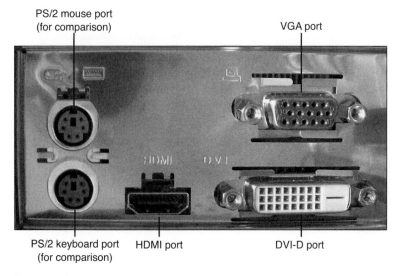

Figure 7-21   Lab 7-1 solution.

Answers and Explanations to Review Questions

1. **A, B, D.** Currently, video cards use the following bus types: PCI, AGP, and the newer PCI Express.

2. **A, C, D.** Cooling can be provided through passive heat sinks or through cooling fans and fan shrouds. Passive heat sinks on older video cards typically cover only the graphics processing unit (GPU), but newer ones provide cooling for both the GPU and memory. Video cards with passive heat sinks are good choices for home theater PCs, such as those running Windows Media Center, because these PCs need to run as quietly as possible. The material used to transfer heat between heat sinks and cooling fans is known as thermal paste or phase-change material, not thermal glue.

3. **A, B, D.** With the addition of the plug and play BIOS, most of the time you will be able to skip the BIOS configuration. But some cards might not be recognized and you must configure the BIOS manually.

4. **B.** Without the device driver installed, you will not be able to use all the features that come with it. Most of the time you get an install disc when you purchase a new card.

5. **A, B, C.** The three main types of display devices in use today are LCD monitors (the most common), CRT monitors, and data projectors.

6. **A, B, C.** VGA, DVI, and HDMI are the three main types of connectors you will be dealing with. You can also use S-Video for a connection.

7. **C.** The DVI port is the current standard for digital LCD monitors. The DVI port comes in two forms: DVI-D supports only digital signals and is found on digital LCD displays. DVI-I provides both digital and analog output and supports the use of a VGA/DVI-I adapter for use with analog displays.

8. **A, C.** The vertical refresh in Windows 7 can be adjusted by accessing the Screen Resolution window, and then clicking the Advanced Settings link. From there, use the Adapter or Monitor tabs. The Troubleshoot tab is used to have Windows 7 guide you through the troubleshooting process of your display driver and settings. The color management tab is where you would associate color profiles to your monitors.

9. **A.** The three steps listed are all ways to install a monitor; however, if you have a monitor that your video card does not support, you must either get another cable or a new video card that supports the cable you have.

10. **C.** Most of the time if you see the colors flickering on the monitor, you can turn off the monitor and the system, tighten the cable, and restart the computer.

11. **D.** When installing a new monitor it might not accept the current settings, so using the buttons on the front of the monitor, you can adjust your picture size.

12. **A, B, C, D, E, F.** It is recommended that you use all of the solutions listed to help prevent problems with your monitor as well as with your video card.

13. **B.** Right-clicking on the desktop and selecting Properties opens the Display Properties window. Select the Settings tab to modify the display resolution.

14. **D.** LED monitors use light-emitting diodes instead of cold cathode fluorescent lamps (CCFLs) such as LCDs use. It is OLEDs that use organic materials. Plasma displays use electrically charged ionized gas. And data projectors will project images on a screen or wall.

15. **B.** DisplayPort uses a packet transmission scheme similar to Ethernet or USB. It is the first of the listed answers to rely on this kind of transmission of video data. This allows the clock to be embedded in each packet instead of being transmitted as a separate clock signal as in VGA, HDMI, and DVI.

This chapter covers the following subjects:

- **Customized PC Configurations**—The CompTIA A+ Certification exam objectives list eight different customized PC configurations you might need to build or to create by upgrading an existing system. In this section you learn why the recommendations are important and the types of products you can use.

- **Evaluating Onboard Components**—Learn how to discover what's "under the hood" of existing systems that might be candidates for customized PC configurations.

- **Installing and Configuring Multimedia Devices**—Many of the customized PC configurations discussed earlier in this chapter might require you to install or replace existing multimedia hardware. In this section, you'll learn how to do it.

This chapter covers the **CompTIA A+ 220-801 objective 1.9 and portions of objectives 1.4 and 1.12.**

CHAPTER 8

Customized PCs and Multimedia Devices

For this chapter, it is highly recommended that you download as many of the configuration programs as you can and use them on a variety of desktop and laptop systems. Try to learn as much as you can about a system without opening it. You should also obtain and install multimedia cards and practice working with the audio mixing features in Windows.

Foundation Topics

Customized PC Configurations

220-801

Objective:
220-801: 1.9

Part of your responsibilities as a PC technician might be to evaluate and select appropriate components for a **custom system configuration** to better meet the needs or specifications of your client or customer. You might need to custom-build a system or upgrade a system to meet those requirements.

The CompTIA A+ Certification exam objectives provide guidelines for eight different configurations for graphics, A/V editing, virtualization, gaming, home theater, thick and thin clients, and home servers. In the following sections, we discuss the specific requirements of each type of system and guidelines for building or upgrading a system to meet them.

Graphic/CAD/CAM Design Workstation

A workstation optimized for graphics or **CAD/CAM** design needs the maximum performance available at the time of purchase. Because of the heavy demands that 3D CAD rendering or RAW photo editing place on the workstation, there is no place for cost-cutting when equipping this system. Don't be surprised if the total cost of a new workstation optimized for these tasks rivals that of a server. Table 8-1 lists the major features needed for this type of computer and the additional information you need to understand why.

Table 8-1 Graphic/CAD/CAM Design Workstation Features

Features	Benefits	Recommendations	Notes
Powerful processor	Fast rendering of 3D or 2D graphics	3.0GHz or faster, six cores or more, large cache (8MB or more total cache), 64-bit support	Fastest multicore CPUs available from Intel or AMD.
		Intel Core i7 Extreme Edition, Core i7 "Ivy Bridge" or "Sandy Bridge"	
		AMD Phenom II X6 (six-core), "Zambezi" FX-8150 (eight-core)	

Features	Benefits	Recommendations	Notes
High-end video	Faster rendering of 3D or 2D graphics on applications that support GPU acceleration (AutoCAD, Photoshop CS5, and others)	PCIe CAD/CAM or 3D cards with 2GB or more RAM optimized for OpenGL 4.x, DirectX 11, support for two or more displays AMD FirePro V-series (CAD, CAM, CGI) AMD Radeon 78xx, 79xx (Photoshop) NVIDIA Quadro (CAD, CAM, CGI) NVIDIA GeForce GTX 6xx, GTS 5xx (Photoshop)	Fastest GPUs available from AMD or NVIDIA. More GPU RAM provides faster performance when rendering large 3D objects. FirePro and Quadro cards use drivers optimized for CAD/CAM/CGI.
Maximum RAM	Reduces swapping to disk during editing or rendering	8GB or more DDR2 or DDR3 Use matched memory modules running in dual-channel or triple-channel configurations	System should be running 64-bit version of Windows (preferably Vista or 7).
ATX motherboard	Room for two PCIe x16 slots, two or more PCIe x1 or x4 slots, and a PCI slot for maximum flexibility in configuration (see Figure 8-1)	Support for two PCIe x16 slots, 8-16GB of DDR3 RAM, PCIe x1 or x4 slots Various vendors	Motherboard should include USB 3.0 and SATA 6Gbps for fastest interfacing with external and internal storage.
ATX full tower chassis	Adequate space for two or more internal hard disks, DVD and/or BD (Blu-ray) drives, high-end cooling	Choose chassis with easy access to drive bays, large fan options (120mm or larger) for cooling All-metal chassis provides better cooling	Power supply of 750 watts (82% efficiency) or greater recommended.

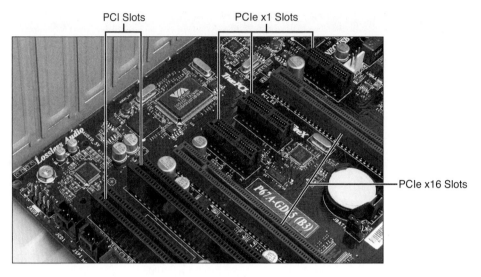

Figure 8-1   This motherboard features two PCIe x16 slots, three PCIe x1 slots, and two PCI slots.

Audio/Video Editing Workstation

An audio/video editing workstation has many component features in common with the CAD/CAM/graphics workstation detailed in the previous section. In fact, the recommendations in Table 8-2 for hard disks and displays are suitable for either type of workstation, and the CPU suggestions in Table 8-1 are also suitable for this type of workstation. Table 8-2 lists the major features needed for this type of computer and why they're important.

Table 8-2   Audio/Video Editing Workstation Features

Features	Benefits	Recommendations	Notes
Specialized audio card	Higher sampling rates and higher signal-to-noise ratios for better audio quality	24-bit, 192kHz or better audio performance; upgradable Op-amp sockets; PCI or PCIe interface	PCIe interface is preferred because it is faster than PCI.
		Sound Blaster X-Fi Titanium HD	Upgradable op-amp sockets allow customization of audio characteristics.
		ASUS Xonar family	
		M-Audio Audiophile 192	

Features	Benefits	Recommendations	Notes
Specialized video card	Faster performance when rendering video	PCIe 3D cards with 2GB or more RAM optimized for OpenGL 4.x, DirectX 11, support for two or more displays	Fastest GPUs on market.
		AMD Radeon 78xx, 79xx	HDMI, DisplayPort, or DVI.
		NVIDIA GeForce GTX 6xx, GTS 5xx	
Large, fast hard drive	Faster disk writes during saves, faster retrieval of source material during media editing and creation	Maximum performance: SSD SATA 6Gbps large enough for Windows and applications (128-512GB) and separate data drive	
		Good performance: 2TB or larger hard disk, 32MB or larger cache, 7200RPM or faster, SATA 6Gbps internal or USB 3.0 external	
		Seagate Barracuda XT (Internal)	
		Seagate Backup Plus Desktop Drive (External)	
		WD Caviar Black (Internal)	
		WD My Book Essential (External)	
Dual displays	Editing software menus and playback can be on separate screens	24-inch or larger from many vendors	HDMI or DisplayPort interfaces recommended; DVI acceptable; avoid VGA-only displays.
	Can render and edit while using secondary display for other applications		

Figure 8-2 shows a typical system with two NVIDIA PCIe x16 video cards configured for SLI.

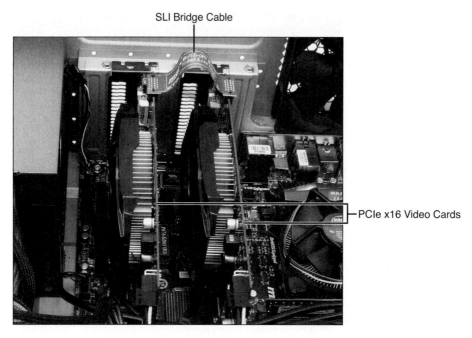

Figure 8-2   A typical system with two NVIDIA PCIe x16 video cards configured for SLI.

Virtualization Workstation

A **virtualization** workstation is intended to be a host for two or more operating systems running at the same time in separate virtual machines (VMs). To ensure adequate resources for each VM, this configuration (see Table 8-3) emphasizes RAM and CPU components.

Table 8-3   Virtualization Workstation Features

Features	Benefits	Recommendations	Notes
Maximum RAM	By increasing RAM well above the recommended level for a system running a single operating system, you help ensure sufficient RAM for each VM in use.	8-16GB RAM (64-bit system) Two, three, or four 4GB modules from major vendors (on 64-bit systems)	Systems running 32-bit versions of Windows cannot use more than 4GB of RAM.

Features	Benefits	Recommendations	Notes
Maximum CPU cores	Multiple VMs use more execution threads than a single operating system, so a multicore CPU helps VMs perform better.	2.8GHz or faster, six cores or more, large cache (8MB or more total cache), 64-bit support Intel Core i7 Extreme Edition, Core i7 "Ivy Bridge" or "Sandy Bridge" AMD Phenom II X6 (six-core), "Zambezi" FX-8150 (eight-core)	Fastest and most powerful Intel or AMD CPU. System needs support for hardware-assisted virtualization in processor and BIOS for best performance (see Figure 8-3).

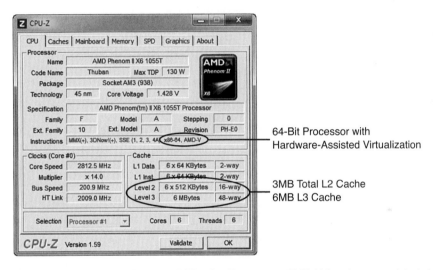

Figure 8-3   The AMD Phenom II X6 1055T supports AMD-V (hardware-assisted virtualization) and has a large amount of L2 and L3 cache as reported by CPU-Z.

Gaming PC

A gaming PC's components are selected with just one objective in mind: provide the user with the computing firepower needed to defeat opponents as quickly as possible. The configuration covered in Table 8-4 is similar to others previously detailed but adds high-end cooling because these systems are frequently overclocked to enhance performance (at a cost in extra heat output).

Table 8-4   Gaming PC Features

Features	Benefits	Recommendations	Notes
Powerful processor	High performance for maximum frame rates, 3D rendering, and audio performance on games where CPU performance is most significant factor	3.0GHz or faster, six cores or more, large cache (8MB or more total cache), 64-bit support Intel Core i7 Extreme Edition, Core i7 "Ivy Bridge" or "Sandy Bridge" AMD Phenom II X6 (six-core) or "Zambezi" FX-8150 (eight-core)	Although multicore CPUs are also the fastest CPUs available from Intel and AMD, many games are not yet optimized for multicore processors.
High-end video/ Specialized GPU	High performance for maximum frame rates in 3D rendering where GPU performance is most significant factor	PCIe 3D cards with 2GB or more RAM optimized for OpenGL 4.x, DirectX 11, support for two or more displays with SLI (NVIDIA) or CrossFire X (AMD) multi-GPU support (see Figure 8-4) AMD Radeon 79xx, 78xx NVIDIA GeForce GTX 6xx, GTS 5xx	Fastest available GPUs available from AMD and NVIDIA.
Better sound card	5.1 or 7.1 surround audio for realistic, high-performance 3D audio rendering.	24-bit, 96kHz or better audio performance; PCI or PCIe interface; hardware acceleration Sound Blaster X-Fi Extreme Gamer Sound Blaster Recon3D series Sound Blaster Fatal1ty series ASUS Xonar DG Azuntech X-Fi Forte	PCIe sound cards provide faster performance than PCI sound cards. Connect to 5.1 or 7.1 surround audio speakers or headsets for 3D audio effects.
High-end cooling	Overclocking is common to reach highest system speeds; overclocked systems can overheat if OEM cooling is not supplemented or replaced by more powerful cooling solutions.	Heat-pipe-based CPU cooler for fan or liquid cooling; heat sinks on RAM; dual-slot video card with high-performance cooler; all optional fan bays on chassis equipped with fans. See www.FrostyTech.com for reviews of numerous heat-pipe CPU cooling products. See www.frozencpu.com for numerous cooling products for CPUs (liquid and heat-pipe), GPUs, and RAM modules.	Be sure to verify compatibility with CPU, clearance around CPU socket, and power requirements for a particular system.

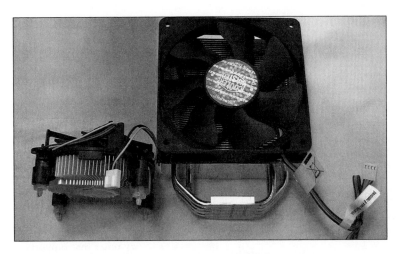

Figure 8-4 A standard Intel active heat sink for a Core i5 CPU (left) compared to a high-performance heat-pipe active heat sink designed to support overclocking (right).

 Key Topic

Home Theater PC

Increasing numbers of users are using Windows Media Center to create PCs designed to be an integral part of a home theater system. The components in this section (see Table 8-5) emphasize compatibility with common home theater audio and video requirements that fit into the low-profile HTPC chassis designed to complement the rest of the home theater equipment.

Table 8-5 Home Theater PC Features

Features	Benefits	Recommendations	Notes
Surround sound audio	5.1 or 7.1 audio sound from home theater speaker system.	For older home theater amps: coax or optical SPDIF audio output. For home theater amps with HDMI: Verify that onboard or card-based audio can output to HDMI.	Adjust sound mixer settings in Windows to output to SPDIF or HDMI digital audio.
HDMI output	Connect digital A/V output to home theater and HDTV with a single cable.	Look for multiple HDMI ports on an HDTV to make connecting to multiple sources easier.	HDMI version 1.4 supports Ethernet as well as A/V.

Table 8-5   Continued

Features	Benefits	Recommendations	Notes
HTPC compact form factor	Integrated A/V components on a mini-ITX or MicroATX motherboard form factor enable a small system in a horizontal chassis.	Mini-ITX and MicroATX motherboards and chassis from many vendors. See www.htpc-reviews.com for specialized reviews and product recommendations.	Most HTPC motherboards use integrated video; AMD Fusion and Intel Sandy Bridge processors include video output integrated into the CPU.
TV tuner	Watch digital broadcast (ATSC) and unencrypted digital cable TV (ClearQAM).	PCI, PCIe, or USB 3.0 or 2.0 (3.0 recommended) with support for digital TV. Major vendors: www.Hauppauge.com www.avermedia-usa.com www.diamondmm.com www.silicondust.com	For connection to encrypted cable TV, choose a TV tuner that supports CableCard.

Standard Thick Client

Unlike the system configurations discussed earlier in this chapter, almost any computer you can purchase at a retail store qualifies as a **standard thick client**. The requirements are simple, as you can see from Table 8-6.

Table 8-6   Standard Thick Client Features

Features	Benefits	Implementation	Notes
Desktop applications	Perform a broad range of office procedures (word processing, spreadsheets, presentations, database, email, and calendaring)	Current versions of Microsoft Office including PowerPoint and Access Current version of OpenOffice or Corel WordPerfect Office	
Meets recommended requirements for using Windows	See Chapter 13 for details	Desktop or laptop computers running Windows 7 or Vista Home Premium or better	Some older systems might require memory upgrades to meet recommended requirements for Windows.

Thin Client

A **thin client** is the most basic type of system configuration. A netbook, laptop, or desktop are all suitable thin clients, as Table 8-7 indicates.

Table 8-7 Thin Client Features

Features	Benefits	Implementation	Notes
Basic applications	Perform basic office procedures (web browsing, word processing, spreadsheets)	Current version of Internet Explorer or Mozilla Firefox or Google Chrome or other web browser Current versions of Microsoft Office Word and Excel or OpenOffice or WordPerfect Office	
Meets minimum requirements for using Windows	Runs Windows at basic performance levels	Netbooks, laptops, desktops running Windows 7 Home Basic, Windows Vista Home Basic, or better editions (see Chapter 13 for details)	Some older systems might require memory upgrades to meet minimum requirements for Windows.

Home Server PC

A **home server PC** configuration is designed to permit resource sharing, media streaming, and high-speed data retrieval from online or local storage, as detailed in Table 8-8.

Table 8-8 Home Server PC Features

Features	Benefits	Implementation	Notes
Media streaming	Enables media playback on connected systems even if normal file sharing is not enabled	Configured through Network and Sharing Center (Vista, 7) Also supported on Windows Home Server	Install latest available version of Windows Media Player on Windows XP to permit access to streamed media.
File sharing	Enables file read or read/write access across the network	Configured through Share with or Sharing tab on folders; must enable File and Printer sharing through Network and Sharing Center (Vista, 7) or Network settings (XP) Also supported on Windows Home Server	With Windows 7, use HomeGroup for easiest configuration if all computers or network have Windows 7.

Table 8-8   Continued

Features	Benefits	Implementation	Notes
Print sharing	Enables printing from any computer on the network	Configured through Sharing tab on printer properties sheet; must enable File and Printer sharing through Network and Sharing Center (Vista, 7) or Network settings (XP) Also supported on Windows Home Server	With Windows 7, use HomeGroup for easiest configuration if all computers or network have Windows 7.
Gigabit NIC	Data transfer between computers or computer and router up to 10x faster than with Fast Ethernet NIC	Integrated into many recent systems or available as low-cost add-on card for PCIe x1 or ExpressCard slots	Router or switch in network must support Gigabit Ethernet.
RAID Array	Faster boot times (RAID 0), protection against failure of one drive (RAID 1), or both (RAID 10)	Use two or four drives with same capacity and configure using BIOS RAID Manager	Install latest storage drivers for motherboard chipset.

Evaluating Onboard Components

220-801

Objective:
220-801: 1.9

From Tables 8-1 to 8-8, you can see that a PC can be customized in many different ways during initial build and setup. However, if you need to upgrade an existing system to optimize it for a particular task, it's important to know what components are already installed. The following methods, Windows features, and third-party utilities can help you find out what's "under the hood" of an existing system.

General System Information

- **BIOS setup**—Some systems display information about installed hardware during startup, and you can also find out information such as RAID level, integrated ports, and other information by starting the BIOS setup program and moving through the screens. Be sure to discard changes when exiting.

- **System Information**—A built-in Windows utility (MSInfo32.exe) that reports processor type and speed, BIOS version and date, operating system information, memory size, components (including multimedia), and software environment. Report can be saved, printed, and searched. Use Run or Instant Desktop Search to start program.

- **Device Manager**—A built-in Windows utility that reports installed hard disk drives, USB ports, video cards, and other information. Available from System properties.

- **Belarc System Advisor**—A free (for personal use) ActiveX utility that displays hardware, software, and Windows security update information, including motherboard information. Available from www.belarc.com. See Figure 8-5 for a portion of a typical report.

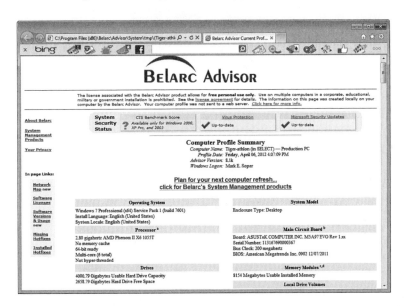

Figure 8-5   The hardware portion of the Belarc System Advisor report on the author's system provides details about the CPU, motherboard, and operating system.

- **SiSoftware Sandra**—Displays extensive information about system hardware including expansion slots, memory, processor details, and much more. Available evaluation and commercial editions from www.sisoftware.net (see Figure 8-6).

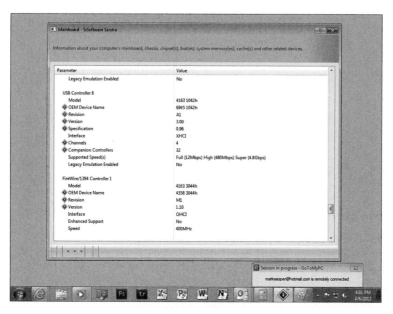

Figure 8-6 A portion of the SiSoftware Sandra Lite report on the mainboard (motherboard) displays detailed information about the SuperSpeed USB (USB 3.0) and FireWire 400 (IEEE 1394a) controllers onboard.

> **NOTE** For the most accurate information about a system, use more than one reporting program. For example, the Belarc System Advisor example report shown in Figure 8-5 incorrectly reports the CPU as having no cache, while the CPU-Z report on the same processor in Figure 8-3 accurately reports the presence of L1, L2, and L3 cache and its layout.

Processor Information and Hardware-Assisted Virtualization Readiness

AMD, Intel, Microsoft, and third-party vendors provide various tools to help determine details about a processor, including whether a system supports hardware assisted virtualization:

- **AMD Virtualization Technology and Microsoft Hyper-V System Compatibility Check Utility**—Available from http://support.amd.com

- **CPU-Z**—Available from http://www.cpuid.com/

- **Intel Processor Identification Utility**—Available from www.intel.com

- **Microsoft Windows Hardware-Assisted Virtualization Detection Tool**—Available from the Download Center at www.microsoft.com

- Gibson Research Corporations SecurAble—Available from www.grc.com

TIP Find direct links to these programs and a useful discussion at http://www.vikitech.com/8208/check-if-processor-supports-virtualization.

Installing and Configuring Multimedia Devices

220-801

Objectives:
**220-801: 1.4,
1.12**

Multimedia devices are frequently required or recommended as part of a customized computer build. The most common multimedia devices include digital cameras, microphones, webcams, camcorders, sound cards (including MIDI enabled devices), speakers, and video capture cards. See the following sections for details.

Webcams

A **webcam** is a simple digital camera capable of taking video or still images for transmission over the Internet. Unlike digital cameras (next section), webcams don't include storage capabilities.

Virtually all webcams plug into a USB port. Webcams are generally used in live chat situations, such as with AOL Instant Messenger or other IM clients. They offer resolutions ranging from sub-VGA to full 1080p HD. Some offer autofocus and zoom features for better image clarity, and most have built-in microphones.

Installing and Configuring a Webcam

Before connecting the webcam, you typically need to install driver and configuration software. Obtain the most up-to-date drivers from the vendor's website.

After the webcam is installed, use its setup menu to adjust white balance, exposure, gain, and other options (see Figure 8.7). If you plan to use the webcam's microphone, disable other microphones in your computer's audio mixer application.

Before using the webcam for IM or phone calls, make sure the application is configured to use the webcam.

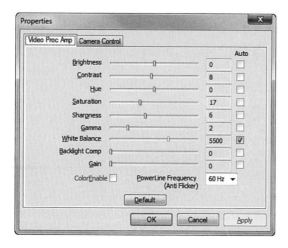

Figure 8.7 A typical webcam properties sheet being used to configure the camera's video processor.

Digital Cameras

Digital cameras have almost completely replaced film cameras for both amateur and professional photography. They use CMOS or CCD image sensors to record images onto internal or card-based flash memory form factors such as Compact Flash, SD, Memory Stick, xD-Picture Card, and Smart Media. Digital cameras transfer images to computers for emailing, printing, or storage via either flash memory card readers or direct USB port connections.

Installing a Digital Camera

To connect a digital camera to your PC, follow these steps:

Step 1. Connect the USB cable provided with the camera to the camera's USB port and the computer's USB port.

Step 2. Turn on the camera.

Step 3. If the camera is not recognized after a few seconds, select the picture playback option on the camera. If the camera is still not recognized, install drivers for the camera.

Some digital cameras are assigned a drive letter (see Figure 8.8), while others show up as an **imaging device** in My Computer/Computer.

Figure 8.8   This digital camera was assigned drive letter H: and can be browsed with Windows Explorer or can be treated as an imaging device.

If the camera is assigned a drive letter, you can drag and drop photos from the camera to other storage locations just as you would with any other disk drive. If the camera is detected as an imaging device, you can use utilities included in the operating system, utilities included with your camera, or add-on programs such as Windows Live Photo Gallery to transfer pictures to your computer.

NOTE   If you are configuring a computer to work with RAW photos, you should add the appropriate RAW codec (coder-decoder) program to the computer so image thumbnails are visible in Windows Explorer. RAW codecs are available from the camera vendor, from Microsoft, or from third-party vendors. The Microsoft Camera Codec Pack for 32-bit and 64-bit versions of Windows Vista and Windows 7 is available from the Microsoft Download Center. Commercial codecs for use with Windows XP, Vista, and 7 are available from fastpicturereviewer.com, Ardfry.com, and others.

Sound Cards

Sound cards are used to record and play back analog audio, and most can also play back digital audio sources as well. When recording analog audio sources such as CDs, line in or microphone in, sound cards digitize the audio at varying sample rates and store files in either uncompressed forms such as WAV or compressed forms such as WMA or MP3.

Most recent sound cards support 5.1 or 7.1 surround audio, and many sound cards also support digital stereo or surround audio playback standards via SPDIF ports. In recent years, sound cards have become less popular due to the popularity of onboard audio, but high-end sound cards are preferred by users who create audio recordings because higher sampling levels and better signal to noise ratios are available. Figure 8-9 illustrates a typical sound card for PCI slots. Sound cards are also available for PCIe x1 expansion slots.

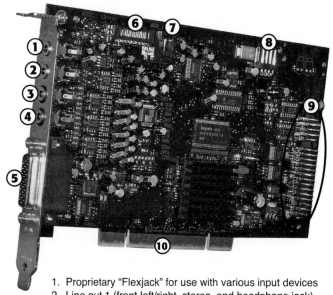

1. Proprietary "Flexjack" for use with various input devices
2. Line out 1 (front left/right, stereo, and headphone jack)
3. Line out 2 (rear and side speakers in home theater systems)
4. Line out 3 (center, subwoofer, and side speakers in home theater systems)
5. Proprietary connector to external I/O breakout box
6. Proprietary connector
7. Aux-In from internal analog audio (CD/DVD drives, TV tuners)
8. Power connector for internal I/O breakout box
9. Data connector for internal I/O breakout box
10. 32-bit PCI slot connector

Figure 8-9 Typical input and output jacks on a typical sound card (the Creative Labs X-Fi Xtreme Gamer).

Table 8-9 lists the standard color-codings for audio jacks and cable connectors established by the **PC99 system design guide**. This color scheme is followed by almost all audio hardware vendors.

Table 8-9   PC99 Audio Jacks and Cables Color Standards

Connector Usage	Color
Mono microphone in	Pink
Stereo Line-in	Light blue
Stereo (headset) output	Lime green
Rear speaker output	Black
Side speaker output	Silver
Center speaker or subwoofer output	Orange
Game port or connection for MIDI cables	Gold*

Omitted from most recent systems; use USB devices for these purposes.

Installing a Sound Card

Before installing a sound card, be sure to disable onboard audio with the system BIOS setup program.

To install a sound card, follow these steps:

Step 1.   Shut down the computer and disconnect it from AC power.

Step 2.   Open the case to gain access to the PC's expansion slots.

Step 3.   Select an empty PCI or PCIe expansion slot as needed for the form factor of sound card to be installed.

Step 4.   Remove the corresponding bracket from the back of the case.

Step 5.   Insert the card into the slot.

Step 6.   Secure the card bracket into place, using the screw or locking mechanism you removed or released in Step 4.

Step 7.   Close the system.

Step 8.   Reconnect AC power and restart the system.

Step 9.   Install the drivers provided with the sound card, or updated versions provided by the vendor.

Step 10.   Connect speakers, microphone, line-in and line-out cables as needed to support your audio or home theater subsystem.

Step 11.   Uninstall any proprietary mixer or configuration utilities provided for use by the integrated sound hardware.

Step 12.   If not already installed in Step 9, install the mixer and configuration utilities provided with the new sound card.

Step 13.   Open the Sound and Audio Devices/Sound icon in Control Panel and configure volume and speaker settings to match your configuration.

> **NOTE**   You can also add surround audio with a USB-based audio device. This is a good solution for laptops and for systems with limited or no expansion slots.

Configuring a Sound Card with Windows

To configure a sound card or onboard audio with Windows:

Step 1.   Open Control Panel

Step 2.   Open the Sound applet.

Step 3.   Select playback devices and adjust settings with the Playback tab.

Step 4.   Select Recording devices and adjust settings with the Recording tab.

Step 5.   To specify sounds to play during Windows events (startup, shutdown, errors, program events), use the Sounds tab.

Step 6.   Click Apply, then OK, to accept changes.

If the sound card or onboard audio includes proprietary management or configuration programs, run them from the Start menu.

Installing a MIDI Enabled Device

Although sounds cards and onboard audio can play MIDI files, **MIDI** interfacing must be available if you need to connect a MIDI enabled device to a PC (a MIDI port is a five-pin DIN port). Some older sound cards had provision for a MIDI port adapter to be connected via the sound card's joystick port. Newer sound cards use breakout boxes for MIDI ports, or you can attach a self-contained MIDI port via the USB port.

After assuring that a MIDI port is available on a system, you can install a MIDI enabled device. When connecting a MIDI enabled device:

- Connect MIDI Out on the device to MIDI In on your PC's MIDI interface.
- Connect MIDI Out on your PC's MIDI interface to MIDI In on the device.

Microphone

Microphones plug into the 1/8-inch (3.5mm) mini-jack microphone jack on a sound card or integrated motherboard audio. The most common microphones used on PCs include those built in to headsets (see Figure 8-10) or those that use a stand.

Microphone volume is controlled by the Windows Sounds and Audio Devices/ Sound applet's mixer control. Open the Recording tab to adjust volume, to mute or unmute the microphone, or to adjust microphone boost.

Figure 8-10   A typical PC stereo headset with microphone.

> **NOTE**   The microphone jack is monaural, whereas the line-in jack supports stereo. Be sure to use the line-in jack to record from a stereo audio source.

Installing and Configuring a Microphone

To install a microphone on a PC with a sound card or integrated audio, follow this procedure:

Step 1.   Connect the microphone into the microphone jack, which is marked with a pink ring or a microphone icon.

Step 2. Audio hardware that supports AC'97 version 2.3 audio or HD Audio standards might pop up a dialog that asks you to confirm the device you have plugged into the microphone jack. Select Microphone from the list of devices.

Step 3. If the microphone has an on-off switch, make sure the microphone is turned on.

To verify that the microphone is working in Windows XP:

Step 1. Open the Sounds and Audio Devices icon in Control Panel.

Step 2. Click Test Hardware.

Step 3. Click Next.

Step 4. If prompted by Windows Firewall, unblock the test program (you might see more than one prompt).

Step 5. Speak into the microphone when prompted to test your microphone and then click Next.

Step 6. Speak into the microphone when prompted to test your speakers and then click Next.

Step 7. Click Finish.

If you do not hear any output from the microphone, open the Audio tab, click the Volume button in the Sound Recording section of the dialog, and make sure the Microphone volume control is not muted. Adjust the volume level as desired.

To verify that the microphone is working in Windows Vista/7:

Step 1. Open the Sounds icon in Control Panel.

Step 2. Click the Recording tab.

Step 3. Make sure the microphone you installed is enabled and selected as the default device.

Step 4. Click Configure.

Step 5. From the Speech Recognition menu that opens, click Set Up Microphone.

Step 6. Select the microphone type and click Next.

Step 7. Adjust the microphone position and click Next.

Step 8. Read the onscreen text when prompted and click Next when finished.

Step 9. Click Finish. Close the Speech Recognition dialog to return to the Sounds dialog.

> **TIP** If the volume displayed in Step 8 is too low or too high, click Properties from the Sounds dialog. Click the Levels tab, adjust Microphone boost to the midpoint (10.0db), and retry Steps 4-9. If the volume is still too low or too high, adjust the volume on the Levels tab.

Video Capture and TV Tuner Cards

As the name suggests, **video capture** cards are used to capture live video from various sources, including analog camcorders, VCRs, analog or digital output from DV camcorders, broadcast TV, and cable TV. Most recent cards with video capture capabilities are actually multipurpose cards that include other functions. These include video (graphics) cards with VIVO (video-in/video-out) S-video or composite video ports, TV tuner cards and USB devices. Video can be stored in a variety of formats, including MPEG, AVI, and others for use in video productions.

Installing a Video Capture Card

The process of installing a video capture card includes the following steps.

Step 1. Shut down the computer and disconnect it from AC power.

Step 2. Open the case to gain access to the PC's expansion slots.

Step 3. Determine the type of slot needed for the sound card. Some use PCI slots, while others use PCI Express x1 slots.

Step 4. Locate an empty PCI or PCI Express expansion slot as needed.

Step 5. Remove the corresponding bracket from the back of the case.

Step 6. Slide the card into the slot.

Step 7. Fasten the card bracket into place, using the screw or locking mechanism you removed or released in Step 5.

Step 8. Close the system.

Step 9. Reconnect AC power and restart the system.

Step 10. Install the drivers provided with the video capture card, or updated versions provided by the vendor.

Step 11. Connect the cables needed for video sources, such as composite or S-video (to capture video from VCRs, TV-out ports, or analog camcorders), RG-6 coaxial (to capture video from TV sources such as antennas or cable TV), or HDMI (to capture digital video from digital camcorders or HDTV).

Step 12. Set up the video capture software to work with the video source(s) you are using.

NOTE If you use a USB-based video capture or TV tuner device, start with Step 10, add step 10a (connect the device to a USB 2.0 or USB 3.0 port) and continue with Step 11.

Configuring a TV Tuner Card

The process of installing a **TV tuner** card is the same as that of installing a video capture card. However, after the card is installed, it must be configured to pick up TV signals. The software with a TV tuner card might include TV viewing and recording software, or you might configure Windows Media Center (included in some editions of Windows XP, Vista, and 7) to perform this task.

During the configuration process, you will typically:

- Specify your location.

- Select the source of the TV signals you want to watch: broadcast TV or cable TV.

- If broadcast TV, select the channels to watch (a signal strength utility is typically available to help determine which channels are strong enough to watch).

- If cable TV, select the cable TV provider and channel package.

- Remove unavailable or unwanted channels if necessary.

- Subscribe to the television program guide offered (if available).

- Select the screen layout (4:3 or 16:9).

- Set up recordings of individual episodes or entire series (optional).

Exam Preparation Tasks

Review All the Key Topics

Review the most important topics in the chapter, noted with the key topics icon in the outer margin of the page. Table 8-10 lists a reference of these key topics and the page numbers on which each is found.

Table 8-10   Key Topics for Chapter 8

Key Topic Element	Description	Page Number
Text	Graphic/CAD/CAM Design Workstation	314
Text	Audio/Video Editing Workstation	316
Text	Virtualization Workstation	318
Text	Gaming PC	319
Text	Home Theater PC	321
Text	Standard Thick Client	322
Text	Thin Client	323
Text	Home Server PC	323
List	Processor Information and Hardware-Assisted Virtualization Readiness	326
Text	Installing and Configuring a Webcam	327
Text	Installing a Digital Camera	328
Text	Configuring a Sound Card with Windows	332
List	Connecting a MIDI enabled device	332
Text	Installing and Configuring a Microphone	333
Text	Installing a Video Capture Card	335
Text	Configuring a TV Tuner Card	336

Complete the Tables and Lists from Memory

Print a copy of Appendix A, "Memory Tables" (found on the CD), or at least the section for this chapter, and complete the tables and lists from memory. Appendix B, "Memory Tables Answer Key," also on the CD, includes completed tables and lists to check your work.

Define Key Terms

Define the following key terms from this chapter, and check your answers in the glossary.

> **custom system configuration, CAD/CAM, virtualization, standard thick client, thin client, home server PC, System Information, Device Manager, Belarc System Advisor, SiSoftware Sandra, CPU-Z, webcam, digital camera, imaging device, sound card, PC99 system design guide, MIDI, AC'97 version 2.3 audio, HD Audio, video capture, TV tuner**

Complete Hands-On Labs

Complete the hands-on labs, and then see the answers and explanations at the end of the chapter.

Lab 8-1: Evaluate a Computer's Suitability for Various Tasks

Scenario: You are a technician working at a PC setup bench. The system you are evaluating meets the current requirements for running Windows XP, Vista, or 7. Evaluate the following specific requirements based on the computer configurations listed in Tables 8-1 through 8-8. Use as many of the methods discussed in this chapter as feasible.

What processor and speed is installed? _____

How determined

__ Startup display   __ Visual inspection   __ Looked up system specifications

__ Software (specify program _____)

__ Other (specify method _____)

What video card (GPU, model, RAM size) is installed? _____

How determined

__ Startup display   __ Visual inspection   __ Looked up system specifications

__ Software (specify program _____)

__ Other (specify method _____)

What sound card or integrated audio is installed? _____

How determined

__ Startup display   __ Visual inspection   __ Looked up system specifications

__ Software (specify program _____)

__ Other (specify method _____)

What expansion slots (types, how many) are available in this system?

__ PCI (# _____) __ PCIe x1 (#____) __ PCIe x16 (#____)

How determined

__ Startup display   __ Visual inspection   __ Looked up system specifications

__ Software (specify program _____)

__ Other (specify method _____)

What hard disk (brand, model, size) is installed? _____

How determined

__ Startup display   __ Visual inspection   __ Looked up system specifications

__ Software (specify program _____)

__ Other (specify method _____)

Is the system compatible with hardware-assisted virtualization?

__ Yes __ No

How determined

__ Startup display   __ Visual inspection   __ Looked up system specifications

__ Software (specify program _____)

__ Other (specify method _____)

Does the system include high-end cooling, such as additional fans, heat-pipe based CPU coolers, or water cooling?

__ Yes __ No

Specify (types, brands and models if available)

Number of case fans _____

Enhanced heat sink _____

Does the system have HDMI output?

__ Yes __ No

How determined

__ Startup display __ Visual inspection __ Looked up system specifications

__ Software (specify program _____)

__ Other (specify method _____)

Does the system have a TV tuner?

__ Yes __ No

What form factor? __ USB   __ PCIe   __ PCI   __ ExpressCard

How determined

__ Startup display __ Visual inspection __ Looked up system specifications

__ Software (specify program _____)

__ Other (specify method _____)

Is the system configured for File and Printer Sharing?

__ Yes __ No

How determined

__ Startup display __ Visual inspection __ Looked up system specifications

__ Software (specify program _____)

__ Other (specify method _____)

What speed NIC is (are) installed in the system?

__ 100Mbps wired (Fast Ethernet) __ 1000Mbps wired (Gigabit Ethernet)

__ 802.11g wireless __ 802.11n wireless

What form factor(s)? __ USB   __ PCIe   __ PCI   __ ExpressCard

How determined

__ Startup display __ Visual inspection __ Looked up system specifications

__ Software (specify program _____)

__ Other (specify method _____)

Is a RAID array installed in the system?

__ Yes __ No

What type?

__ RAID 0 __ RAID 1 __ RAID 10 __ Other (specify _____)

How determined

__ Startup display __ Visual inspection __ Looked up system specifications

__ Software (specify program _____)

__ Other (specify method _____)

Answer Review Questions

Answer these review questions and then see the answers and explanations at the end of the chapter.

1. You need to set up an existing computer for use with virtualization software. For best performance, which of the following should you determine first?

   a. Memory size

   b. Processor compatibility with hardware assisted virtualization

   c. Windows version

   d. Free disk space

2. You want to use an existing system for a home theater, but it lacks a TV tuner. Which of the following methods is the best way to add this capability?

   a. Replace motherboard with a model that includes an integrated TV tuner.

   b. Install new video card with a model that has an integrated TV tuner.

   c. Use an existing USB port or expansion slot to add a TV tuner.

   d. Replace the computer.

3. You have connected a digital camera to a system with its included USB cable and the camera is not detected. Which of the following should you check first?

   a. USB port

   b. Camera on/off switch

   c. Battery charge in camera

   d. USB cable

4. You are connecting a headset that is not color-coded to a computer. Which of the following audio jack colors is used for stereo speakers or a headset?

   a. Black

   b. Pink

   c. Light blue

   d. Lime green

5. A client is attempting to listen to music but keeps hearing background noise. Which of the following should be muted?

   a. Line in

   b. System sounds in Windows

   c. MIDI In

   d. Microphone in

6. Your client has installed a webcam for video chatting. The webcam's video output is working, but the audio is not being transmitted to the remote computer. The computer was previously configured for a headset microphone, but the user prefers to use the webcam's built-in microphone. What needs to be done?

   a. Replace the webcam—it is defective.

   b. Switch the default audio playback source to webcam.

   c. Configure the system for closed captioning.

   d. Change the microphone configuration in the video chat software.

7. Your client has transferred pictures from a digital camera set for RAW mode to a computer. The pictures can be viewed and edited, but Windows Explorer displays them as icons. What should be done to display the images as thumbnails for easier management?

   a. Upgrade to Windows 7.

   b. Install a video codec.

   c. Set the camera to shoot JPEG photos.

   d. Install the Microsoft Camera Codec Pack.

Answers to Hands-On Labs

Lab 8-1: Evaluate a Computer's Suitability for Various Tasks

Answer: Varies with hardware inspected. You can use physical inspection, system configuration programs, and BIOS setup. If you use system configuration programs, check the results you obtain by using a second program or by using the system BIOS setup program.

Answers and Explanations to Review Questions

1. **B.** A processor with hardware assisted virtualization is the first factor to consider when selecting a computer as a virtualization workstation.

2. **C.** You can add a TV tuner via a USB 2.0 or faster port or by adding a card.

3. **B.** The camera must be turned on before pictures can be transferred.

4. **D.** Lime green is the color of the stereo audio out jack. It is also used for headphones and headsets.

5. **D.** The microphone should be muted.

6. **D.** Assuming the headset microphone is still connected, the chat program uses the system default unless you specify a different source, such as the webcam's microphone.

7. **D.** Installing the Microsoft Camera Codec Pack or any RAW codec that supports the digital camera's RAW file format will enable Windows Explorer to display thumbnail versions of the RAW photos.

This chapter covers the following subjects:

- **Laptop Expansion Options**—Discover options such as ExpressCard, PC Card, CardBus, memory, and card readers.

- **Best Practices for Laptop Disassembly**—Learn how to keep laptop components organized and prevent damage during disassembly.

- **Hardware Device Replacement**—Learn how to remove and replace hard drives, memory, batteries, Wi-Fi radio cards, screen assemblies, processors, and more.

- **Laptop Displays**—Learn about common display resolutions, technologies, and components.

- **Laptop Features**—How to control laptops with special function keys, use projectors and external displays, use docking stations and port replicators, and maintain physical security.

- **Troubleshooting Laptop Problems**—Learn how to solve display, power, keyboard, and network problems.

This chapter covers **CompTIA A+ 220-801 objectives 3.1, 3.2, and 3.3** and **CompTIA A+ 220-802 objective 4.8**.

CHAPTER 9

Laptop and Notebook Computers

Laptops were originally designed for niche markets, but today they are used in businesses almost as much as regular PCs are. Laptops (also known as netbooks, notebooks, or portable computers) have integrated displays, keyboards, and pointing devices, which makes them easy to transport and easy to use in confined spaces.

Although laptops have many of the same components as desktop computers, they differ in two significant ways:

- How they are expanded
- How internal components are upgraded, replaced, or serviced

For the A+ exams, you must know the unique components of a laptop, how to safely remove and reinstall laptop hardware, the ports built in to a typical laptop, and how to troubleshoot laptops.

Foundation Topics

Laptop Expansion Options

220-801

Objective:
220-801: 3.1

Current laptop computers typically include the following user-installable expansion options:

- An ExpressCard/34 or /54 slot

- Upgradable SODIMM memory

- USB ports suitable for use with USB flash memory or hard drive drives

- A Flash memory card reader slot

Older laptop computers use the PCMCIA (PC Card or CardBus slot) and typically lack a flash memory card reader. Learn more about these options in the following sections.

PCMCIA (PC Card, CardBus)

PC Cards (originally referred to as Personal Computer Memory Card International Association [PCMCIA] cards) provide a range of options for laptops with PC Card slots.

Most older laptops have at least one Type II PC Card slot, as shown in Figure 9-1. Many have two.

PC Cards can be hot-swapped; the card can be shut down, removed, and replaced with another without shutting down the system. Cards must be "stopped" before being removed, or the system can become unstable and the cards or system can be damaged.

The Personal Computer Memory Card International Association gave PC Cards their original name of PCMCIA cards and developed standards for these cards. There are three types of PC Card slots, each designed for particular types of devices (see Table 9-1).

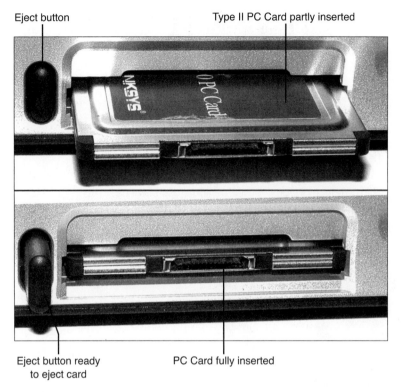

Eject button   Type II PC Card partly inserted

Eject button ready   PC Card fully inserted
to eject card

Figure 9-1   A typical notebook with a Type II PC Card partly installed (top) and completely installed (bottom). Note the positions of the ejection button.

Table 9-1   PC Card Type Comparison

PC Card Type	Thickness	Typical Uses	Notes
Type I	3.3mm	Memory	Obsolete
Type II	5.5mm	I/O ports, wired or wireless networking, modems, external drive interfaces, hard drives	Older I/O port cards used dongles for I/O ports.
Type III	10.5mm	Hard drives, combo I/O ports	Type III slot also supports two Type II devices.

All three types use a two-row connector with 68-pins total.

Most systems with **PC Card** slots feature two stacked Type II slots that can handle
all types of cards: a single Type III card, two Type II cards, or two Type I cards at a
time. Figure 9-2 compares the thicknesses of these cards, and Figure 9-3 illustrates a
Type II PC Card with a dongle.

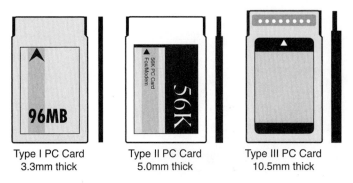

Type I PC Card
3.3mm thick

Type II PC Card
5.0mm thick

Type III PC Card
10.5mm thick

Figure 9-2   Typical Type I, Type II, and Type III PC cards and cross-sections.

Dongle connects to rear of card

Signal lights for Ethernet
connection status

Socket for Category
5 UTP cable

Figure 9-3   A typical Type II PC Card 10/100 Ethernet card with the dongle used to attach the card to standard Category 5 UTP cable. Photo courtesy Linksys.

> **NOTE**   If you lose or damage the dongle, your PC Card is useless until you replace it.

Almost all laptops with PC Card slots support **CardBus**. CardBus slots are compatible with both 16-bit PC Cards and 32-bit CardBus cards, but CardBus cards can't be used in ordinary PC Card slots.

To verify whether a laptop has CardBus support, open Windows Device Manager and the category marked PCMCIA Adapters. If a CardBus controller is listed, the portable supports CardBus. If it's not listed, you can use only 16-bit PC Cards in that system.

NOTE CardBus cards have a gold edge on the connector but ordinary PC Cards do not.

Another variation on standard PC Card slots is Zoomed Video (ZV) support. Laptops that support ZV can use PCMCIA cards with a high-speed video connector for processes such as teleconferencing or dual-display support. As with CardBus, use ZV-compatible cards only in compatible systems. However, ZV is not supported by all CardBus slots. To determine whether a system with CardBus slots also supports ZV, check with the vendor.

Type I and Type II PC Card cards aren't thick enough to use standard RJ11 telephone (for modem), SCSI, RJ45 UTP network cables, or video cables unless a pop-out connector or a dongle is used.

Some Type II PC Cards use a pop-out connector for telephone or network cables; others require the use of a device called a dongle—a proprietary extension to the PCMCIA card that enables standard cables to be connected to the card. Type III PC Cards are thick enough to provide standard connections but don't fit into some systems.

NOTE Combo PC Cards contain multiple functions and connections on a single card. The most common combination includes a modem plus Ethernet network interfacing or USB plus IEEE-1394a ports.

To insert a PC Card or CardBus card, just push it into the slot until it stops. Then, attach any cables or dongles needed for operation.

To remove a PC Card or CardBus card, follow these steps:

Step 1. Look for an ejector button next to the PC Card slot; on some systems, the button is folded into the unit for storage. Unfold the button.

Step 2. Remove any cables or dongles from the card.

Step 3. Click the Safely Remove Hardware or Eject icon in the Windows taskbar, and select the card you want to remove from the list of cards.

Step 4. Stop and wait for the system to acknowledge the card can be removed.

Step 5.   Click OK to close the message.

Step 6.   Push in the ejector button to eject the PC Card (refer to Figure 9-1). Pull the PC Card the rest of the way out of the slot, and store it in its original case or an antistatic bag.

ExpressCard

Recent laptops have replaced PC Card slots with ExpressCard slots. The ExpressCard standard was developed by the same organization that developed the PCMCIA (PC Card) standard, but **ExpressCard** provides a much faster interface than a PC Card or CardBus and is compatible with PCI Express and USB standards. An ExpressCard is up to 2.5 times faster than a CardBus card and uses a 26-contact connector.

ExpressCard slots and devices support one of two variations:

- ExpressCard/34 is 34mm wide.

- ExpressCard/54 is 54mm wide; ExpressCard/54 slots can use either ExpressCard/54 or ExpressCard/34 devices and are sometimes referred to as Universal slots.

Both types of ExpressCard modules are 75mm long and 5mm high. Figure 9-4 compares typical ExpressCard modules to a CardBus module.

NOTE   Some vendors supply ExpressCard/34 cards with removable adapters that permit cards to be inserted more securely into ExpressCard/54 slots.

ExpressCard can use one of two methods to communicate with the system chipset: PCI Express or USB. These methods provide much faster performance than with CardBus, which connects to the system chipset via the CardBus controller and the PCI bus.

NOTE   For more information about PCMCIA, CardBus, and ExpressCard slots and devices, see the official website of the USB Implementers Forum at www.usb.org. USB Implementers Forum took over responsibility for these standards when PCMCIA was dissolved in March 2009.

To insert an ExpressCard, just push it into the slot until it stops. Then, attach any cables or dongles needed for operation.

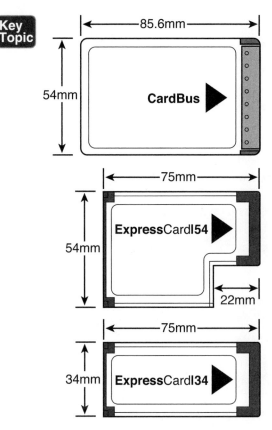

Figure 9-4 A CardBus 32-bit PC Card compared to ExpressCard/34 and ExpressCard/54 cards.

To remove an ExpressCard, follow these steps:

Step 1. Remove any cables or dongles from the card.

Step 2. Click the Safely Remove Hardware and Eject Media icon in the Windows taskbar, and select the card you want to remove from the list of cards.

Step 3. Stop and wait for the system to acknowledge the card can be removed.

Step 4. Click OK to close the message.

Step 5. Push in the card to release it. Pull the ExpressCard the rest of the way out of the slot, and store it in its original case or an antistatic bag.

> **NOTE** Some systems with ExpressCard slots use the slot to store a media remote control. If a media remote control is stored in the ExpressCard slot, go directly to Step 5 to remove it.

Memory

Generally, laptops have two connectors for additional memory, typically using small outline DIMMs (SODIMMs), which are reduced-size versions of DIMM modules. Figure 9-5 compares a typical DDR2 **SODIMM** with a DDR2 DIMM.

Figure 9-5   Comparison of a DIMM (above) and SODIMM (below).

> **TIP** The best memory upgrade for a portable system is to add the largest-capacity memory modules that can be installed in the system. Use matched sets on systems that support dual-channel or triple-channel memory to improve performance.

Connecting USB Drives to Your Laptop

Laptops, like desktops, typically include several USB ports. Most models now include USB 3.0 as well as USB 2.0. Keep in mind that some laptops don't provide as much power on their USB ports as typical desktops. If necessary, use a Y-cable to pull USB power from two ports if a bus-powered USB drive doesn't work when connected to a laptop.

Flash Memory Cards

Most recent laptops include a single-slot flash memory card reader that is compatible with the most common memory card standards, such as SD, SDHC, Sony Memory Stick/Pro, and Olympus/Fujifilm xD-Picture Card.

If you use Compact Flash or other memory card types with a laptop, you will need to connect a memory card reader to a USB port.

Best Practices for Laptop Disassembly

220-802

Objective:
220-802: 4.8

Whether you need to disassemble a laptop to upgrade internal hardware or to replace a defective component, there are several best practices you should use to make the reassembly process as easy as possible:

- **Refer to manufacturer documentation**—Documentation helps you properly identify screw types, screw lengths, number of screws (some laptops have more than 100), cable and component locations, and other information needed. Most vendors offer this information online.

- **Use appropriate hand tools for case disassembly and component removal**— Using recommended tool types and sizes helps prevent problems such as damaging screw heads by using too large a Phillips-head screwdriver. Repair documentation typically lists the recommended tools for each procedure.

- **Document and label cable and screw locations**—Laptops typically use a mixture of screw lengths and sometimes screw types. Mix them up, and you could damage components or not secure them properly.

- **Organize parts**—Consider using a multiple-compartment parts tray available at hardware stores for parts sorting and storage.

> **NOTE**   The Laptop Repair Help website (www.laptoprepair101.com) provides many useful resources, including links to major vendors' laptop service manuals, illustrated step-by-step procedures for the removal of many components, and links to parts sources.

Hardware Device Replacement

220-801

Objective:
220-801: 3.1

Because a laptop integrates its display, keyboard, and network hardware, and uses specialized or proprietary components for hard drive, optical drive, system board, CPU, and other components, replacing these devices involves much different procedures than on a desktop computer. Some of the general differences include

- **Component sources**—Replacement components such as display, keyboard, network card, and system board must generally be purchased from the original manufacturer. Other components, such as optical drives and hard drives, memory, and the CPU can be purchased from third-party sources but differ greatly from their desktop counterparts.

- **Power sources**—A laptop is powered by an internal battery and an AC adapter that also charges the battery. As with other laptop components, the original vendor is the most typical source for replacements, although some third-party vendors sell so-called "universal" replacement AC adapters.

- **Components unique to laptops**—Laptops include several components typically not included on desktop computers, including integrated wireless networking implemented via an antenna in the display connecting to a mini-PCIe or mini-PCI card, a keyboard with an integrated touchpad or pointing stick, and integrated speakers.

These differences, along with the extensive use of plastics and the use of tiny screws, make servicing a laptop a major challenge, even if you are experienced with servicing a desktop computer.

CAUTION   Laptops contain proprietary parts. If you break an internal drive or an integrated keyboard, you can't run to your favorite electronics superstore for a replacement. You have been warned.

Removing and Replacing the Battery

Before performing any replacement of internal components, the system must be removed from all power sources. Follow this procedure:

Step 1.   Turn off the computer.

Step 2.   Disconnect the AC adapter or line cord from the computer.

Step 3.   Open the battery compartment in the unit; it might be secured by a sliding lock or by screws.

Step 4.   If the battery is under a removable cover, remove the battery compartment cover.

Step 5.   Open the lock that holds the battery in place.

Step 6.   Slide out or lift out the battery (see Figure 9-6). If the battery is a flat assembly, it might be held in place by a clip; push the clip to one side to release the battery.

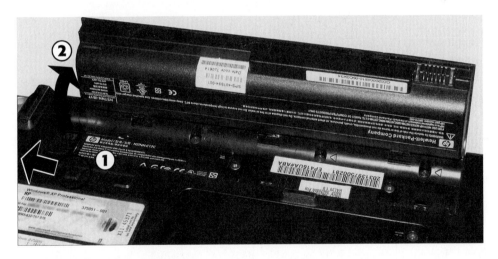

1. Releasing the battery catch
2. Rotating the battery up and out of the battery compartment

Figure 9-6   Removing a battery from a typical laptop computer.

Step 7.   Examine the battery contacts inside the computer for dirt or corrosion, and clean dirty contacts with a soft cloth.

To replace the battery, follow these steps:

Step 1. Line up the replacement battery with the contacts inside the battery compartment. Make sure you insert the battery so that the positive and negative terminals are in the right directions.

Step 2. Slide in or clip the battery into place.

Step 3. Replace any cover over the battery compartment.

Step 4. If the battery must be charged before use, plug in the line cord or AC adapter to both the computer and wall outlet. Check the computer's manual for the proper charge time for a new battery.

CAUTION Take precautions against ESD when you change the battery. Discharge any static electricity in your body by touching a metal object before you open the battery compartment, and don't touch the contacts on the battery or the contacts in the battery compartment with your hands.

If you need to purchase a replacement battery for a laptop, consider a larger-capacity battery. Relative battery capacity is measured in cells. For example, a nine-cell battery will have a longer run time than a six-cell battery. Keep in mind that larger-capacity batteries are bulkier.

Replacing a Laptop Keyboard or Pointing Device

If a laptop keyboard or its **pointing device** (**touchpad** or **pointing stick**) fails, you must replace the unit. Laptops with touchpads have separate keyboards and touchpads, whereas laptops with pointing sticks integrate the pointing stick with the keyboard. Some laptops have both types of pointing devices.

NOTE Touchpads are generally located in the palm rest (which extends below the keyboard), while pointing sticks, such as the IBM/Lenovo TrackPoint and Toshiba AccuPoint, are located in the middle of the keyboard (the buttons are located in the palm rest).

To replace a keyboard, including keyboards with pointing sticks, follow this basic procedure:

Step 1. Position the laptop so the bottom of the unit faces upward.

Step 2. Remove the screws that hold the keyboard in place.

Step 3. Turn over the laptop.

Step 4. Open the screen so that the keyboard is visible.

Step 5. If necessary, remove the bezel that holds the keyboard in place.

Step 6. Lift up the keyboard to expose the keyboard cable.

Step 7. Remove any hold-down devices used to hold the keyboard cable in place.

Step 8. Disconnect the keyboard cable from the system board (see Figure 9-7).

Figure 9-7 Removing the keyboard cable.

Step 9. Remove the keyboard.

To install the replacement, reverse these steps.

> **NOTE** On some laptops, you must remove the display assembly first before you can remove the keyboard.

If you need to replace the touchpad, you must partially disassemble the portable computer. Details vary from unit to unit (check with your vendor for details), but the basic procedure is described here. To remove the touchpad, follow these steps:

Step 1. Check service documents to determine whether the touchpad is a separate component or is built in to the top cover. If the touchpad is built in to the top cover, remove the top cover.

Step 2.   If the touchpad is a separate component, remove components that block access to the screws that hold the touchpad in place. These might include the hard drive, WLAN cover, optical drive, keyboard, keyboard cover, display assembly, and top cover.

Step 3.   Place the system so the bottom of the system faces up.

Step 4.   Disconnect the cable from the pointing devices to the motherboard.

Step 5.   Remove the clips or screws holding the touchpad in place.

Step 6.   Remove the touchpad assembly.

To replace the touchpad, reverse these steps.

Replacing Speakers

To remove speakers, follow this basic procedure:

Step 1.   After removing power from the laptop, remove components that block access to the speakers. These might include the hard drive, WLAN cover, optical drive, keyboard, keyboard cover, display assembly, and top cover.

Step 2.   If necessary, turn the laptop over.

Step 3.   Disconnect the Num Lock cable or other cables as directed.

Step 4.   Remove the screws holding the speakers in place.

Step 5.   Lift out the speakers.

To replace the speakers, reverse these steps.

Replacing a Laptop Hard Drive

Laptop computers use 2.5-inch hard drives. (Larger 3.5-inch drives are used in desktop drive enclosures or in desktop computers.)

Although a few laptop computers require you to remove the keyboard to access the hard driver, most laptops feature hard drives that can be accessed from the bottom of the system. Follow this procedure to remove and replace a hard drive accessible from the bottom:

Step 1.   After disconnecting power sources, turn over the laptop so that the bottom of the laptop faces upward.

Step 2.   Loosen or remove the screw or screws used to hold the drive cover in place.

Step 3.   Slide the cover away from the retaining lug or clips and remove it. On some systems, the drive might be mounted to the cover (see Figure 9-8a), whereas on other systems, the drive is mounted to the chassis (see Figure 9-8b).

Step 4.   If the drive is fastened to the chassis, shown in Figure 9-8b, remove the screws holding the drive to the chassis.

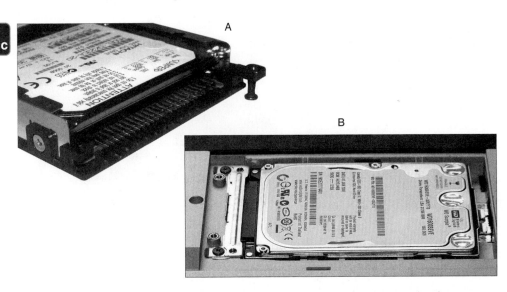

Figure 9-8   A laptop hard drive that fastens to the cover (a) compared to one that fastens to a separate frame inside the chassis (b).

Step 5.   Slide the drive away from the retaining screw holes, and lift it out of the chassis.

Step 6.   Remove the screws fastening the drive to the drive cover or frame (see Figure 9-9).

Step 7.   Remove the drive from the drive cover or frame.

Step 8.   Insert the new hard drive into the drive cover or frame.

Reverse these steps to install the new hard drive. Older systems use a 44-pin portable version of the PATA interface, whereas newer systems use the SATA interface.

After the system is restarted, enter the BIOS setup program to verify that the new hard drive has been properly recognized by the system.

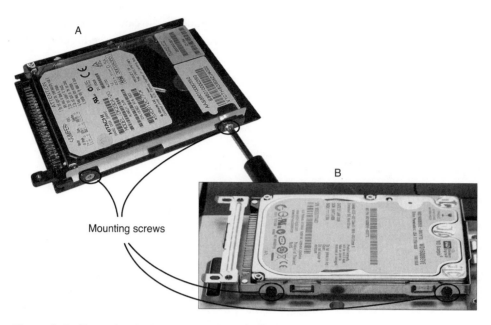

Figure 9-9   Removing the hard drive mounting screws from the cover (a) or the frame (b).

Performing a Memory Upgrade

You need to know the following information before you can select the right memory upgrade for a laptop:

- **Form factor**—Recent laptops use DDR2 or DDR3 SODIMMs, whereas older laptops might use DDR SODIMMs or proprietary modules.

- **Memory speed**—If you plan to add a module, make sure it is the same speed as the existing module. If you plan to replace the modules, buy a matched set of modules in the fastest speed supported by the system.

- **Memory timing**—The most common way to refer to memory timing is by its column address strobe (CAS) value. If you install memory modules that use different CAS values, the laptop could become unstable and crash or lock up.

To determine the correct memory to use for a memory upgrade, use one of the following methods:

- **Use the interactive memory upgrade tools available from major third-party memory vendors' websites**—These tools list the memory modules suitable for particular laptops, and some use an ActiveX web control to detect the currently installed memory.

- **Check the vendor's memory specifications**—You can determine part numbers using this method, but this method is best if memory must be purchased from the laptop vendor rather than from a memory vendor.

Follow these steps to perform a typical memory upgrade:

Step 1. After disconnecting all power sources, remove the cover over the memory upgrade socket on the bottom of the system.

Step 2. Remove any screws or hold-down devices.

Step 3. Remove the old memory module(s) if necessary. To remove a memory module, pull back the clips on both sides and swing the memory up and out.

Step 4. Insert the new memory upgrade, making sure the contacts (on the back side or edge of the module) make a firm connection with the connector.

Step 5. Push the top of the module down until the latches lock into place (see Figure 9-10).

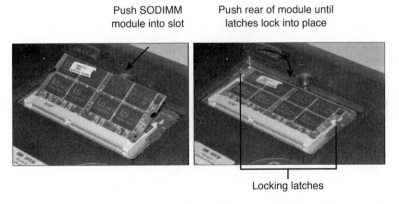

Figure 9-10   Installing an SODIMM module on a typical portable computer.

Step 6. If the memory socket uses screws to secure the memory in place, install them.

Step 7. Close the cover and secure it to complete the upgrade.

Step 8. Test the upgrade by starting the system and running a memory diagnostic tool (Windows Vista and 7 include memory testing software, or you can download a memory testing program).

Replacing an Optical Drive

Some laptops feature modular optical drives designed for swapping. However, if the optical drive is not designed for swapping, follow this procedure to remove it:

Step 1. After disconnecting all power sources, turn the laptop over so that the bottom faces upward.

Step 2. Locate the latch that holds the drive in place, or locate the mounting screw that holds the drive in place and unscrew it. It might be located inside the access panel for another component, such as the mini-PCI board or memory modules.

Step 3. Slide open the latch or remove the mounting screw.

Step 4. Slide the drive out of the system. See Figure 9-11 for a typical example.

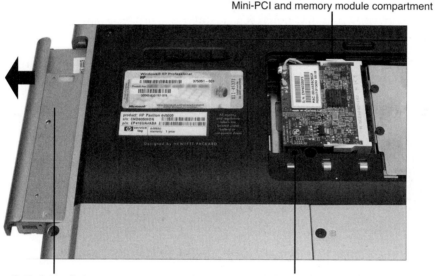

Mini-PCI and memory module compartment

Optical drive being removed from system

Hole for drive retaining bolt

Figure 9-11 Removing an optical drive from a typical laptop.

To reinstall the drive, reverse the preceding steps. If a range of drives are available for a laptop, you can use this method to upgrade to a better drive.

Removing a Wireless Card (Mini-PCI or Mini-PCIe)

Laptops with Wi-Fi support typically use a mini-PCI or mini-PCIe card to provide wireless network support.

There are three major types of **mini-PCI** cards:

- Type I
- Type II
- Type III

Type I and Type II cards use a 100-pin stacking connector that plugs directly into the system board. Type II cards, unlike Type I cards, have network or modem connectors built in to the card. Type III, which uses an edge connector, has become the most popular of the three formats. Like Type I, Type III mini-PCI cards do not incorporate RJ11 (modem) or RJ45 (Ethernet network) connectors; Type I and Type III mini-PCI cards use modem and network connectors built in to the system.

Mini-PCI cards are used to configure different models of a particular portable computer with different features and are not available at retail. Because mini-PCI cards can be replaced, this enables you to replace a failed or outdated network/modem component without replacing the entire motherboard. Figure 9-12 shows a typical Type III mini-PCI modem card and connector compared to a typical Type II PC Card.

Protective plastic covering over components

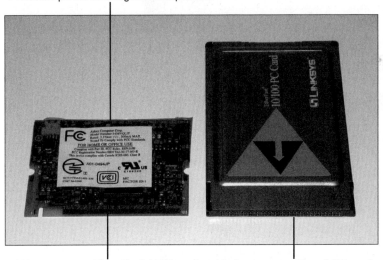

Edge connector (Type III mini-PCI card)   68-pin connector (Type II PC card)

Figure 9-12 A typical mini-PCI Type III modem (left) compared to a typical PC Card Type II network adapter (right).

NOTE   Some mini-PCI cards that include wireless Ethernet (Wi-Fi) radios have the antenna leads soldered to the card. If these cards become damaged, a factory-trained technician should replace them.

In many recent laptop models, mini-PCI has been replaced by mini-PCI Express (also known as **Mini-PCIe**). Mini-PCIe cards are much smaller than mini-PCI cards and use a two-part, double-sided, 52-pin edge connector. Mini-PCIe supports PCIe, USB, SMBus, GPS, SIM card, and Wi-Fi connections and runs on 1.5V and 3.3V DC power.

Figure 9-13 compares a mini-PCI Type III card similar to the one shown in Figure 9-12 with a mini-PCIe card.

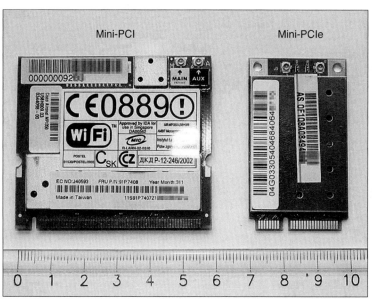

Figure 9-13   A typical mini-PCI Type III modem (left) compared to a typical Mini-PCIe card (right). Image source: Wikimedia Commons.

To remove a mini-PCI or mini-PCIe card, follow this basic procedure:

Step 1.   Verify the location of the card. Some laptops have the card under the keyboard, whereas others have the card located under a removable cover on the bottom of the computer.

Step 2.   After disconnecting all power sources, place the computer appropriately for access to the card.

Step 3a. If the card is located under the keyboard, remove the keyboard bezel and remove the keyboard.

Step 3b. If the card is located under an access panel, remove the screws holding the access panel in place.

Step 4. Disconnect any wires connected to the adapter. They might be screwed into place or snapped into place. Note their positions.

Step 5. Push the card out of the connector and remove it from the system.

To reinstall the card or replace it with a different card, reverse these steps.

Replacing the Screen

Screen replacement on laptops can be complex, especially if you need to replace the LCD display panel or the backlight, or if the screen assembly includes the Wi-Fi antenna, as on most recent models. LCD display panels built in to portable computers are customized for each model of portable computer and require the disassembly of the computer for removal and replacement. You can get replacements from either the vendor or an authorized repair parts depot. Many vendors require that you be an authorized technician before you remove or replace LCD display panels in portable computers. However, the process of replacing the entire LCD display assembly is simpler and might be possible for you to perform in the field.

> **CAUTION** Should you do your own LCD display panel replacement? Vendors are of two minds about this. Some vendors provide online documentation that guides you through the entire process of reducing an intact portable into a pile of parts and rebuilding it. However, this information is primarily intended for professional computer service staff.

The details of the process for removing an LCD display assembly from a portable computer vary by model, but they follow this basic outline:

Step 1. After removing power from the system, if the system has an integrated Wi-Fi (wireless Ethernet adapter), disconnect the antenna leads attached to the adapter (usually a mini-PCIe or mini-PCI card).

Step 2. Remove the keyboard frame and keyboard.

Step 3. Disconnect the FPC cable from the system board (also known as the display cable); this cable transmits power and data to the LCD display assembly.

Step 4. If the system has integrated Wi-Fi, remove the antenna leads from the clips in the top cover.

Step 5. Rotate the display assembly to a 90-degree angle to the base unit.

Step 6. Remove the screws that secure the display assembly.

Step 7. Pull the display assembly free from the base unit.

Step 8. Be sure to save all screws, ground springs, and other hardware that you removed during the disassembly process.

NOTE   If you need to replace the inverter, the backlight, or the webcam, further disassembly is necessary.

Many vendors offer replacement LCD display assemblies that can be installed by following the previous steps in reverse order. Although you can also purchase components of the assembly, such as the LCD display panel or backlight, this type of repair is difficult and time-consuming, and should be performed at a repair depot.

Although you can't get a panel with a different resolution, you might be able to swap a glossy LCD panel optimized for video playback for a low-reflectivity matte panel that's preferred by some for working with documents.

Replacing the Fan, Heat Sink, and CPU

Before replacing the CPU in a laptop, you must determine which models are supported by the laptop. A BIOS update might enable additional CPUs to be used successfully.

The CPU cannot be replaced without removing the fan and heat sink module. If the fan is separate from the heat sink, follow this procedure:

Step 1. After removing power from the system (including the battery), remove other components as directed. These might include the hard drive, WLAN cover, optical drive, keyboard, keyboard cover, display assembly, and top cover.

Step 2. Depending on the specific unit, you might need to turn over the system.

Step 3. Remove the screws holding the fan in place.

Step 4. Disconnect the fan's power lead from the motherboard.

Step 5. Lift the fan out of the system. Retain it for reuse.

Laptop heat sinks are typically one-piece or two-piece units that pull heat away from the chipset and the processor. Some units incorporate the fan. To remove the heat sink (see Figure 9-14), follow these steps:

Step 1.   Remove the screws holding the heat sink in place.

Step 2.   If the heat sink incorporates a fan, disconnect the fan power lead from the motherboard.

Step 3.   Lift up on the heat sink to remove it. (Move it from side to side if necessary to loosen the thermal material.) Retain it for reuse.

Step 4.   If some components that use a heat sink are located on the reverse side of the motherboard, turn over the motherboard and repeat steps 1–3. For example, the system shown in Figure 9-14 has a separate heat sink for the graphics chipset (a) and the CPU (b).

A   B

Figure 9-14   Heat sinks for the graphics chipset (a) and CPU (b) on a typical laptop computer.

To remove the CPU, follow these steps:

Step 1.   Loosen the processor locking screw. Note the markings on the CPU and the socket. The CPU must be aligned in the same position when installed.

Step 2.   Remove the CPU from the socket. Retain it for possible reuse. See Figure 9-15.

A   B

Figure 9-15   A typical laptop processor (a) and its socket (b).

If you are using a factory CPU assembly, use the new CPU and heat sink in the reassembly process. Before doing so, be sure to remove the old thermal material from the fan and other motherboard components that use the heat sink. The new heat sink includes thermal material (thermal pads and/or paste). Use 70% or higher isopropyl alcohol for cleaning these components.

> **NOTE**   Laptop processors use different sockets than desktop processors. They are not interchangeable.

If you are reinstalling the same processor and heat sink, or if you are using a heat sink and processor from a vendor other than your laptop vendor, you typically need to supply your own thermal material. Be sure to clean old thermal material from the fan, processor, heat sink, and other motherboard components before applying new material.

Install the processor first, followed by the heat sink, fan (if not built in to the heat sink), and the remainder of the components you removed.

Laptop Displays

220-801

Objective:
220-801: 3.2

Laptop displays typically include an LCD, LED, plasma, or OLED display; a backlight, an inverter, and one or more Wi-Fi antennas. The following sections provide the information you need about these components for the A+ Certification exams.

LCD Displays

Until recently, almost all laptops used active-matrix liquid crystal displays (LCDs). Active-matrix refers to screens that use a transistor for every dot seen onscreen: for example, a 1,280 × 800 active-matrix LCD screen has 1,024,000 transistors. Although active-matrix displays are much faster and brighter than older LCD technologies such as passive-matrix and DSTN, all standard LCD displays include a fluorescent backlight and are often referred to as LCD-CCFL (cold cathode fluorescent) displays. As with any fluorescent light source, the backlight contains poisonous mercury, so it must be recycled properly. Fluorescent backlights often produce uneven screen brightness and make precise color control difficult.

LCD displays on laptops typically have vertical refresh rates of approximately 60Hz, which is much slower than the 120 or 240Hz refresh rates on mid-range and high-end LCD-based HDTVs. Lower refresh rates tend not to handle fast action as well as higher refresh rates.

LED Displays

Many recent laptops have replaced LCDs with fluorescent backlighting with LED-backlit displays. These displays are based on LCD technology but replace the CCFL backlight with an array of LEDs. LEDs produce even screen brightness, more accurate and vivid color, better blacks, and higher contrast ratios, and use about half the power of LCD-CCFL displays. LED-backlit displays are sometimes referred to as LCD-LED displays.

To determine whether a particular laptop uses an LCD-CCFL or an LCD-LED display, read the specifications carefully.

OLED Displays

Organic LED (OLED) displays use a layer of organic compounds between two electrodes to emit light. OLED displays have been developed in two forms, passive matrix (PMOLED) and active matrix (AMOLED), which supports larger sizes and higher resolutions.

OLED displays do not need a separate backlight but are currently very expensive to produce in the sizes needed for laptop displays. Although a few prototype laptops using OLED displays have been built, OLED displays are currently being used in digital cameras and mobile phones.

Plasma Displays

Although plasma displays are popular for HDTVs, they have not been used in laptops for many years. (And those displays were monochrome.) The high-power consumption and internal design of modern full-color plasma displays make them unsuitable for use in laptops.

Display Resolutions and Viewing Quality Considerations

Screen resolutions are identified in one of two ways: either by the number of horizontal and vertical pixels or by the display standard. Common display standards and pixel resolutions used by recent laptop and portable computers are listed in Table 9-2.

Table 9-2 Common Laptop Screen Resolution Standards

Standard	Also Known As	Horizontal Resolution	Vertical Resolution	Aspect Ratio
XGA	Extended Graphics Array	1024	768	1.33:1
WXGA*	Wide XGA	1280	800	1.6:1
WXGA+	Wide XGA+	1440	900	1.6:1
SXGA+	Super Extended Graphics Array Plus	1400	1050	1.33:1
UXGA	Ultra Extended Graphics Array	1600	1200	1.33:1
WUXGA	Wide Ultra Extended Graphics Array	1920	1200	1.6:1

Resolutions such as 1360 × 768 or 1366 × 768 are also identified as WXGA.

Aspect ratios larger than 1.33:1 are widescreen.

When comparing laptops, consider the following factors that affect screen quality:

- **LCD design**—As mentioned earlier, LCD-LED displays offer better picture quality than LCD-CCFL displays. However, there are three types of LCD-CCFL displays: in plane switching (IPS), vertical alignment (VA), and twisted nematic (TN), in order of quality (best to worst).

- **Contrast ratio**—The difference in brightness between the lightest and darkest portions of the display. When looking at two otherwise-similar displays, the one with the higher contrast ratio is preferred.

- **Viewing angles**—The angle at which an LCD display provides acceptable viewing quality. For example, if a display provides acceptable viewing quality at an angle of 80° from either side of a straight-on (0°) view, it has a viewing angle of 160° (80° × 2). A narrower viewing angle is preferred for privacy (because it's more difficult for onlookers to view the screen), but a wider viewing angle is preferred when multiple users need to see the display.

- **Recommended (native) and scaled resolutions**—LCD displays have only one native resolution (also known as recommended resolution) and might scale (zoom) the display to achieve lower resolutions or use only the actual pixels needed for the lower resolution. This might be necessary when running in a cloned mode when an external display or projector is used, or if a particular resolution is required for creating screen shots or for other technical reasons. When a scaled resolution is selected, the screen usually appears slightly less sharp than when the native resolution is selected.

Nonnative resolutions are selected through the Screen Resolution dialog in Windows 7 (see Figure 9-16), which is also used to detect additional displays and change orientation. Windows XP uses the Display properties Settings tab (refer to Figure 9-19); Windows Vista's Display Settings section of the Personalize menu is almost identical to Windows 7's Screen Resolution dialog.

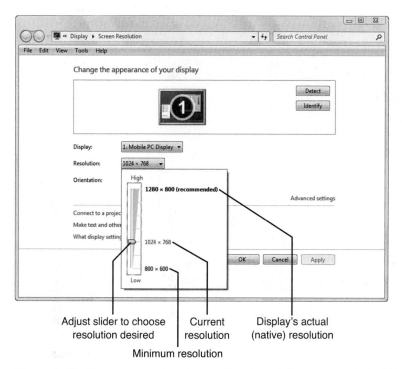

Figure 9-16 Recommended and currently set resolutions on a typical widescreen laptop running Windows 7.

NOTE   When only the actual pixels needed for the lower resolution are used instead of scaling the resolution, a black border is displayed around the pixels in use. This effect is called windowboxing.

Inverter and Backlight Components

A normal laptop display is easy to read because of two components: the inverter and the backlight. If either fails, the laptop display becomes so dim that it is almost impossible to use.

The **inverter** (see Figure 9-17) is a power converter, changing low-voltage DC power into higher-voltage AC power needed to power a CCFL backlight. If the inverter fails, there is no power to run the backlight. Inverter failure is the most common cause of LCD display failure. However, inverter replacement is relatively inexpensive, and inverters can be purchased for do-it-yourself (DIY) replacement.

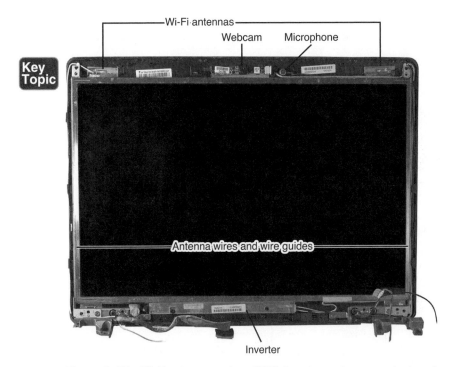

Figure 9-17   Wi-Fi antennas, wires, CCFL inverter, webcam, and microphone in a typical LCD-CCFL display.

A **CCFL backlight** failure is far less common than an inverter failure. If the CCFL backlight fails, a complete disassembly of the display down to individual component level is required. If a CCFL backlight failure occurs, swapping the screen assembly for a known-working replacement often makes more sense than attempting a repair unless you are experienced with screen disassembly.

Because both inverter and backlight failures cause dim displays, keep in mind that an off-color or unevenly lit display indicates a backlight failure, whereas a display that is dim overall is more likely an inverter failure.

When servicing the inverter on a typical laptop, follow this general procedure:

Step 1.   After removing power from the system (including the battery), follow the procedure to remove the screen assembly.

Step 2.   Follow the procedure to remove the display panel from the screen assembly.

Step 3.   Disconnect the wires from the inverter.

Step 4.   Remove any screws or clips used to secure the inverter.

Step 5.   Remove the inverter.

To replace the inverter, reverse this process.

Wi-Fi Antenna Components

Although the mini-PCI or mini-PCIe card that contains the Wi-Fi radio is located in the base of the laptop, the antennas are usually part of the screen assembly (refer to Figure 9-17). If a laptop screen is damaged, the Wi-Fi antennas might also be damaged.

When servicing the antennas on a typical laptop, follow this general procedure:

Step 1.   After removing power from the system (including the battery), turn over the unit and open the cover over the Wi-Fi radio card.

Step 2.   Disconnect the wires from the Wi-Fi radio card.

Step 3.   Follow the procedure to remove the screen assembly.

Step 4.   Follow the procedure to remove the display panel from the screen assembly.

Step 5.   Remove the antennas and wires. When reassembling the screen assembly, be sure to replace the wires into the guides located on either side of the display.

Laptop Features

220-801

Objective:
220-801: 3.3

Because laptop computers incorporate multimedia and networking components, they include special function keys on the keyboard and special controls for displays, wireless, volume, screen brightness, Bluetooth networking, and (in some cases) keyboard backlighting.

Laptops also have special provisions for expansion, such as docking stations and port replicators, and provision for physical security through locking mechanisms.

Learn more in the following sections.

Special Laptop Function Keys

To save space, laptops use keyboards with fewer keys than desktop computers have. However, laptop computers also need to control screen displays and other options not needed on desktop computers.

To enable reduced-size keyboards to perform all the functions needed, laptop and portable keyboards use Fn keys. While the **Fn key** is held down, pressing any key with an additional Fn function performs the Fn function; when the Fn key is released, the key reverts to its normal operation. Fn functions are usually printed below or beside the normal key legend and sometimes in a contrasting color (usually blue).

Typical Fn+key features include

- Adjust screen brightness and/or contrast
- Connect to external display
- Enable/disable Bluetooth
- Enable/disable Wi-Fi
- Enable/disable backlit keyboard
- Turn on/turn off embedded keypad

Figure 9-18 shows a typical portable keyboard with the Fn key and some Fn functions highlighted.

Press and hold the Fn key...

...and press any of these keys to perform special tasks, such as adjusting screen brightness or audio volume.

Figure 9-18 A typical laptop keyboard's Fn keys.

> **NOTE** There is no standard for Fn key assignments, and available Fn keys on a given laptop depend upon the exact hardware installed.
>
> In addition to Fn keys, some laptops include front-mounted controls for adjusting system volume or enabling/disabling Wi-Fi or Bluetooth. Others include touch-sensitive controls above the keyboard for enabling/disabling Wi-Fi, adjusting audio volume, or muting audio.

Working with Dual Displays

Windows XP, Windows Vista, and Windows 7 support DualView with virtually all recent laptop display hardware. **DualView** enables a secondary display that is plugged in to a laptop's external video ports, such as TV-out, S-video, VGA, DVI, or HDMI, to be used to extend the desktop; it can also be used to mirror the desktop if wanted.

Extending the Desktop

To enable Extended Desktop in Windows XP or Vista, follow these steps:

Step 1. Before turning on the computer, plug in the appropriate video cable to the video port.

Step 2. Turn on the external monitor, TV, or projector.

Step 3. Turn on the computer.

Step 4. If the computer does not automatically extend the desktop, right-click an empty area on the desktop and select **Properties** (XP) or **Personalize** (Vista), or open **Control Panel** and open the Display properties icon.

Step 5. Open the **Settings** tab on the Display properties icon (see Figure 9-19a) in Windows XP; in Windows Vista, click **Display Settings**.

Step 6. To enable the secondary display, click it, and select **Extend My Windows Desktop onto This Monitor**.

Step 7. Adjust the screen resolution as needed for the second display (see Figure 9-19b). To determine usable resolutions, check the documentation for the display.

Step 8. Click **Apply** and then **OK** to use the settings.

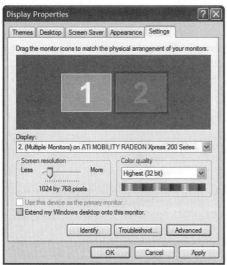
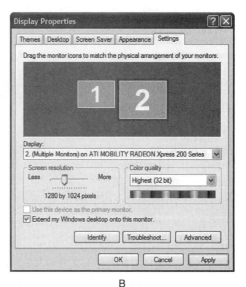

A   B

Figure 9-19 The settings dialog before (a) and after (b) enabling a secondary display as an extended desktop with Windows XP or Vista.

To enable extended desktop in Windows 7, follow these steps:

Step 1. Before turning on the computer, plug in the appropriate video cable to the video port.

Step 2. Turn on the external monitor, TV, or projector.

Step 3. Turn on the computer.

Step 4. Right-click an empty area on the desktop, and select **Screen Resolution**.

Step 5.   To enable the secondary display, click **Detect** (see Figure 9-20).

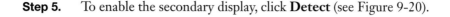

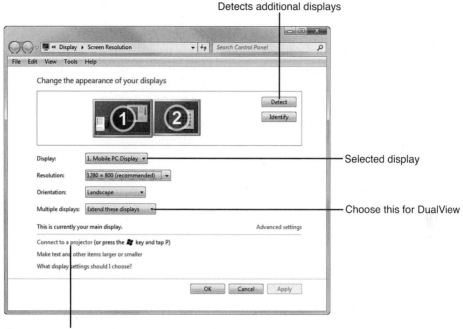

Detects additional displays

Selected display

Choose this for DualView

Click to connect to a projector

Figure 9-20   The Windows 7 Screen Resolution dialog after enabling a secondary display as an extended desktop.

Step 6.   Open the Multiple Displays menu, and select whether to **Extend These Displays** (Dual View) or **Duplicate These Displays** (display cloning).

Step 7.   Click **Apply**.

Step 8.   Select the second display and adjust the screen resolution as needed (refer to Figure 9-16). To determine usable resolutions, check the documentation for the display.

Step 9.   Click **Apply** and then **OK** to use the settings.

Cloning the Laptop Display to a Secondary Display or Projector

If you need to display the same information on an external display or projector, such as for a presentation, follow this procedure for Windows XP:

Step 1.   Check the native resolution of the secondary display or projector. Most projectors offer resolutions such as SVGA (800 × 600), XGA (1024 × 768), WXGA (1280 × 800), and so on.

Step 2.   Adjust the resolution of the laptop's internal display to match the native resolution of secondary display or projector's resolution, or choose a resolution for the internal display that is also supported by the external display.

Step 3.   Do not extend the desktop to the secondary display. Instead, locate the Fn key combination on the keyboard that toggles the display into clone mode. Typically, you must press this key combination several times to move through different display combinations until the displays are cloned. Wait a few moments after you press the key combination to allow the display mode to change before continuing.

NOTE   Some laptops use a proprietary display-management program to clone the displays. Access it by right-clicking an empty portion of the desktop and selecting it from the menu.

With Windows Vista Business/Ultimate/Enterprise:

Step 1.   Right-click the desktop and select **Personalization**.

Step 2.   Click Connect to a Projector or Other External Device.

Step 3.   The Windows Mobility Center opens (see Figure 9-21).

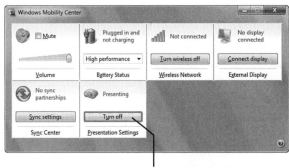

Toggles presentation settings On/Off

Figure 9-21   Using Windows Mobility Center.

Step 4.   Click **Presentation Settings** to turn on the projector and clone your desktop to the projector.

NOTE   To adjust Presentation Settings (which also turns off notifications), click the Projector icon and make changes as wanted.

Mobility Center also provides options for turning off wireless connections, and Presentation Settings also turns off notifications and prevents the computer from going to sleep or turning off the display. Some vendors offer additional Windows Mobility Center options customized to their hardware.

With Windows 7 Professional/Ultimate/Enterprise, you can run Windows Mobility Center by searching for Mobility Center with Instant Desktop Search or by running it from Control Panel. However, you can also connect to a projector and choose from a variety of display options by using this method:

Step 1. Right-click the desktop and select **Screen Resolution**.

Step 2. Click **Connect to a Projector**.

Step 3. Select the settings you want from the pop-up menu (see Figure 9-22).

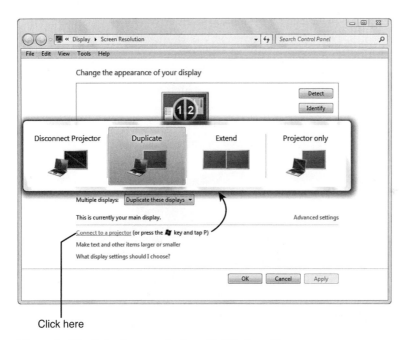

Click here

Figure 9-22   Selecting a projector with Windows 7.

Step 4. When you are finished, repeat Steps 1–3 to reset the display to your normal configuration.

Working with Port Replicators and Docking Stations

A docking station expands the capability of a portable computer by adding features such as

- One or more expansion slots

- Additional I/O ports, such as serial, parallel, ExpressCard or PC Card, display output (VGA, DVI, HDMI, component video), SPDIF digital audio, eSATA, or USB ports.

- Additional drive bays

- Power connection for the laptop

- Connectors for a standard keyboard and mouse

Most docking stations are produced by portable computer vendors and connect to the computer through a proprietary expansion bus on the rear or bottom of the computer. The user can leave desktop-type peripherals connected to the docking station and can access them by connecting the portable computer to the docking station. Figure 9-23 illustrates the HP QuickDock, which provides additional USB ports, audio ports, and component video ports as well as one-touch power and charging capabilities to supported HP and Compaq laptop computers. See Figure 9-24 for the proprietary expansion bus used by the QuickDock.

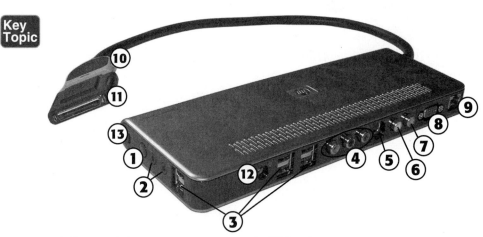

1. Power switch
2. Audio minijacks
3. USB ports (6)
4. Component video ports for HDTV
5. S-video port
6. Composite video port
7. SPDIF coaxial digital audio port
8. VGA port
9. 10/100 Ethernet port
10. Connector to laptop
11. Connector adapter
12. Power connector
13. Security lock port

Figure 9-23   The HP QuickDock docking station supports several series of HP and Compaq laptop computers.

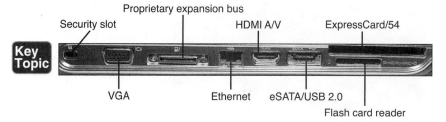

Security slot
Proprietary expansion bus
HDMI A/V
ExpressCard/54

Key Topic

VGA
Ethernet
eSATA/USB 2.0
Flash card reader

Figure 9-24 A laptop security slot and other ports on a typical HP laptop.

NOTE Some older thin and light portable computers are designed to use a modular media slice for optical and removable-media drives. This unit connects to the bottom of the computer and can be left in place at all times, or it can be removed when it's not needed.

A port replicator usually connects to the same proprietary expansion bus that can be used by a docking station; however, many portable computers that do not have docking stations support optional port replicators.

Port replicators enable a portable computer user fast, easy connection to a full-sized keyboard, regular mouse or pointing device, desktop monitor, modem, and printer without needing to attach or remove multiple cables. Because portable cable connectors can wear out, using a port replicator extends the life of the system and makes desktop use faster and easier.

Port replicators normally are built by the same company that makes the portable computer, but some third-party vendors produce both dedicated models (designed to attach to the proprietary expansion bus of a given model) and universal versions, which attach through USB ports and can be freely moved among different brands and models of portable computers.

NOTE Software drivers must be installed before connecting universal port replicators. Standard port replicators might include drivers, or the drivers might already be installed by the laptop vendor.

Physically Securing a Laptop Computer

The laptop security slot shown in Figure 9-24 is designed to work with the laptop cable lock shown in Figure 9-25. Laptop locks use a combination or keyed lock and are designed to lock the laptop (or other secured device) to a fixed location such as a table.

Figure 9-25 A combination laptop security lock.

To prevent data theft from occurring, you should also use the password-lock function in Windows to require a password whenever the keyboard is locked using the Windows+L keys and some type of full-disk encryption such as Windows Vista and 7's BitLocker or a third-party solution such as TrueCrypt or PGPDisk (among others).

Troubleshooting Laptop Problems

220-802

Objective:
220-802: 4.8

In addition to the same problems that desktop computers face, laptop computers can have a number of unique problems. Use the symptoms list in the following sections to determine the most likely causes and suggested solutions.

Troubleshooting Display Problems

This section covers troubleshooting the following display problems:

- No display
- Cannot display to external monitor or projector

- Dim display

- Flickering display

- Ghost cursor

No Display

No display can be caused by the failure of the LCD inverter or backlight, a damaged cable leading to or from an LCD inverter, the failure of the onboard display circuit, or by toggling the laptop to use an external display only with an Fn key.

First, try toggling the laptop to use the internal display. If this doesn't help, connect it to a monitor or projector. If the external display works, the problem might be with the cable to the LCD inverter or the LCD inverter (easy to replace) or the LCD-CCFL backlight (difficult to replace). If the external display doesn't work, the motherboard needs to be repaired or replaced.

Cannot Display to External Monitor or Projector

If the laptop cannot display on an external monitor or projector, the most likely cause is that the display has not been connected or detected.

Verify display has been connected; then use appropriate Fn key combination, Windows Display Properties, Windows Mobility Center, or Connect to a Projector to connect to the projector or monitor.

Dim Display

The most likely cause of a dim display is the failure of the LCD inverter. If the screen flashes for a moment and then becomes dim at startup, the LCD inverter is almost always the cause. Replace it.

Flickering Display

A flickering display is almost always caused by a dying LCD-CCFL backlight. You can replace it, but it's easier to swap the complete screen assembly for a remanufactured unit. It is often cost-effective to replace the laptop or use it strictly with an external display.

Ghost Cursor

A ghost cursor is usually caused by mouse movement too fast for screen refresh rate. To make the mouse pointer easier to see, adjust the mouse properties to slow down mouse acceleration, use a larger mouse pointer, or enable visibility options (pointer trails, or press the Ctrl key to display mouse location).

Power Problems

This section covers troubleshooting the following power problems:

- No power
- Battery not charging or not holding a charge

No Power

If the laptop cannot run when plugged in to an AC outlet, verify that the battery is not the problem. Remove it. If the laptop cannot run without the battery while plugged in to an AC outlet, check the following:

- Make sure the laptop is plugged in to a working AC outlet. Check the outlet with an outlet tester. Use a voltmeter or a multimeter set to AC voltage to determine whether the output is within acceptable limits.

- Make sure the AC power cord running from the AC outlet to the external AC adapter "power brick" is plugged in completely to the outlet and the adapter. If the power cord or plug is damaged, replace the cord.

- To determine whether the adapter is outputting the correct DC voltage, use a voltmeter or multimeter set to DC voltage to test the voltage coming from the adapter and compare it to the nominal output values marked on the adapter. As Figure 9-26 illustrates, it might be necessary to use a bent paperclip to enable an accurate voltage reading. A value of +/– 5% is acceptable.

Battery Not Charging or Not Holding a Charge

If the system works when plugged in to AC power, but not on battery power, check the following:

- Make sure the battery is installed properly.
- Wipe off any corrosion or dirt on the battery and laptop battery contacts.
- Determine whether the battery can hold a charge. Make sure the battery is properly installed and the AC adapter has proper DC voltage output levels. Leave the system plugged in for the recommended amount of time needed to charge the battery; then try to run the system on battery power. If the battery cannot run the system, or the system runs out of battery power in less than 1 hour, replace the battery. If replacing the battery does not solve the problem, the laptop needs to be serviced or replaced.

- If the battery is hot after being charged or has a warped exterior, it might have an internal short. Replace it.

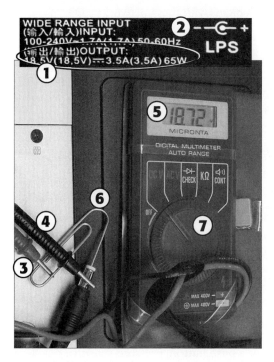

1. Nominal output voltage
2. AC adapter tip polarity
3. Positive (red) lead from multimeter
4. Negative (black) lead from multimeter
5. Measured DC voltage output
6. Bent paperclip inserted into adapter tip
7. Multimeter mode selector

Figure 9-26   Checking the output voltage from a laptop's AC adapter.

Keyboard Problems

Sticking keys usually indicate a problem with the keyboard. It is not always necessary to replace the entire keyboard. Several online vendors offer individual key replacements. If more than one or two keys are sticking, it may be most cost-effective to replace the entire keyboard.

> **NOTE**   Some laptop models might use two or more key styles. Use the illustrations available on some sites to determine exactly which key style you need.

If the embedded number pad is turned on when you want to use the keyboard in its normal mode, it's most likely that you accidentally pressed the Fn-key combination to switch to NumLock mode. Toggle the NumLock feature off. If the problem persists, check the keyboard connection inside the laptop. If the keyboard connection is OK, replace the keyboard.

Network Problems

Both Wi-Fi (wireless Ethernet) and Bluetooth are common in recent laptops. Use the following sections to help diagnose problems with these networks.

No Wi-Fi Connectivity

Most laptops have a push button, pressure-sensitive touch button, or Fn-key combination to enable or disable Wi-Fi networking. If there is no connection, press the button or Fn-key combination to enable the connection. Most laptops display an indicator light when the connection is enabled.

If the connection fails, check the Wi-Fi connection dialog in the notification area. You might need to reconnect manually. If there is no Wi-Fi connection dialog, open the Device Manager and check the Network Adapters category. If the Wi-Fi adapter is not listed, rescan for hardware changes.

If the Wi-Fi adapter cannot be located, shut down the system, disconnect it from all power sources, and open the access panel to the Wi-Fi card. If the card is loose, reconnect it and retry the connection after restoring power and restarting the computer.

No Bluetooth Connectivity

Most laptops with built-in Bluetooth have a push button, pressure-sensitive touch button, or Fn-key combination to enable or disable Bluetooth networking. Here's how to diagnose problems with Bluetooth:

Step 1.   If there is no connection, press the button or Fn-key combination to enable the connection. Most laptops display an indicator light when the connection is enabled.

Step 2.   If the connection fails, verify that a Bluetooth adapter is installed and enabled. If the Bluetooth adapter is accessible from the outside of the unit, you can physically verify proper connection. Also check Windows Device Manager. If Device Manager does not list the adapter, restart the computer and verify that the Bluetooth adapter is enabled in system BIOS setup.

Step 3.   If the Bluetooth adapter is installed, use the Bluetooth configuration utility provided by the computer vendor (or device vendor, in the case of a USB Bluetooth adapter) to set up the adapter to connect to other devices.

Step 4.   If the adapter is already set up to connect to other devices, check the Bluetooth settings on those devices.

Exam Preparation Tasks

Review All the Key Topics

Review the most important topics in the chapter, noted with the Key Topic icon in the outer margin of the page. Table 9-3 lists a reference of these key topics and the page numbers on which each is found.

Table 9-3 Key Topics for Chapter 9

Key Topic Element	Description	Page Number
List	Laptop expansion options	346
List	Removing a CardBus or PC Card	349
Figure 9-4	ExpressCard versus CardBus	351
List	Removing an ExpressCard	351
Figure 9-5	DIMM and SODIMM comparison	352
List	Best practices for laptop disassembly	353
List	Replacing a keyboard	356
List	Replacing a laptop hard drive	358
Figure 9-8	Hard drives for laptops	359
List	Laptop memory information	360
List	Upgrading laptop memory	361
Figure 9-13	Mini-PCI and mini-PCIe cards	364
Figure 9-15	Laptop CPU and socket	368
Figure 9-17	Laptop screen assembly components	372
Figure 9-18	Fn keys on a typical laptop	375
Figure 9-19	Extending the desktop to a secondary display	376
Figure 9-23	QuickDock docking station	380
Figure 9-24	Laptop ports and QuickDock proprietary bus	381
Figure 9-25	Laptop security lock	382

Complete the Tables and Lists from Memory

Print a copy of Appendix A, "Memory Tables" (found on the CD), or at least the section for this chapter, and complete the tables and lists from memory. Appendix B, "Memory Tables Answer Key," also on the CD, includes completed tables and lists to check your work.

Define Key Terms

Define the following key terms from this chapter, and check your answers in the glossary.

CardBus, CCFL backlight, docking station, DualView, ExpressCard, Fn key, inverter, PC Card, pointing device, pointing stick, port replicator, SODIMM, touchpad, WXGA, XGA

Complete Hands-On Lab

Complete the hands-on labs, and then see the answers and explanations at the end of the chapter.

Lab 9-1: Locate Laptop Hard Drive and Memory

Scenario: You are a technician working at a PC repair bench. You need to install more memory and a larger hard drive.

Prepare system for upgrade: Select the correct order for these steps: Remove battery. Turn over computer. Disconnect AC power. Turn off computer. Enter the steps into Table 9-4.

Table 9-4 Preparing a Laptop for Upgrading

Procedure	Task
Step 1	
Step 2	
Step 3	
Step 4	

Select Components

You will be installing a laptop hard disk and a DDR3 SODIMM module. Examine Figures 9-27 through 9-30. Enter the correct answers into Table 9-5 and Table 9-6.

Figure 9-27   Name the component.

Figure 9-28   Name the component.

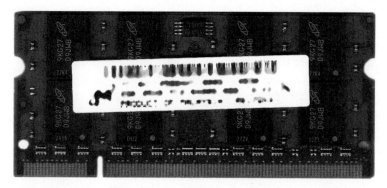

Figure 9-29   Name the component.

Figure 9-30   Name the component

Complete Table 9-5 by entering the correct figure numbers.

Table 9-5   Components for Laptop Upgrade

Component	Figure Number
Laptop hard disk	
DDR3 SODIMM	

Leftover Parts

After you complete Table 9-5, two components are left. Enter the component name and the figure numbers for those into Table 9-6.

Table 9-6 Leftover Components

Component Name	Figure Number

Answer Review Questions

Answer these review questions, and then see the answers and explanations at the end of the chapter.

1. What is the special key on laptops that is used along with other keys to enable special functions?

   a. The F keys

   b. Fn key

   c. NumLock key

   d. Delete key

2. What type of laptop memory is installed in all newer model laptops?

   a. DIMM

   b. SIMM

   c. SDRAM

   d. SODIMM

3. What is the size of a typical laptop hard drive?

   a. 3.5 in.

   b. 2.5 in.

   c. 5.5 in.

   d. 4.5 in.

4. Which of the following expansion options requires a proprietary connection on the laptop?

   a. A docking station

   b. A laptop case

   c. A smart card

   d. None of these options is correct.

5. A late-model laptop's integrated Wi-Fi adapter typically uses which of the following connection types?

    a. PCI

    b. AGP card

    c. Mini-PCIe

    d. CardBus

6. If a laptop with built-in Wi-Fi can't connect, which of the following should you check first?

    a. Device Manager

    b. Wi-Fi cable

    c. Wi-Fi button

    d. Ethernet cable

7. If a laptop LCD display is dim, failure of which of the following components are the most likely cause?

    a. Backlight

    b. VGA port

    c. ExpressCard bus

    d. Inverter

8. If you need to replace a hard drive in a typical laptop, which of the following is typically NOT necessary?

    a. Remove the heat sink.

    b. Disconnect the AC power.

    c. Remove the access panel over the hard drive.

    d. Remove the battery.

9. You need to replace memory in a laptop that uses DDR3 memory. Which of the following is necessary to know? (Choose all that apply.)

    a. DIMM or SODIMM

    b. Memory speed

    c. Memory timing

    d. Brand of memory

10. If you need to install an expansion card to provide USB 3.0 ports in a laptop, which of the following card types is the most likely choice?

   a. SODIMM

   b. ExpressCard

   c. Mini-PCIe

   d. CardBus

11. You need to evaluate damage in a laptop with a cracked screen; the base of the laptop is not damaged. In addition to the LCD panel, which other components might be damaged? (Choose all that apply.)

   a. Hard drive

   b. Wi-Fi antenna

   c. Wi-Fi radio

   d. Webcam

12. You need to replace a laptop's processor. You have a desktop processor with a similar model number. Can you use it as a replacement?

   a. Yes, they are interchangeable.

   b. Yes, if you install an adapter.

   c. No, the sockets are different.

   d. Yes, if you change the heat sink.

13. Which of the following are ways to troubleshoot power problems on a laptop?

   a. Use a multimeter.

   b. Turn off the computer.

   c. Make sure the laptop is unplugged.

   d. None of these options is correct.

14. You need to clone a display from a laptop running at 1280 × 800 resolution to a projector running at 1024 × 768. Which of the following is correct?

   a. You can't clone the display because resolutions don't match.

   b. Change the laptop display resolution to 1024 × 768.

   c. Use S-video output between the laptop and projector.

   d. Use composite video output between the laptop and projector.

Answers to Hands-On Lab

Lab 9-1: Locate Laptop Hard Drive and Memory

Answer

Prepare system for upgrade: Select the correct order for these steps: Remove battery. Turn over computer. Disconnect AC power. Turn off computer. Enter the steps into Table 9-4.

Table 9-4   Preparing a Laptop for Upgrading

Procedure	Task
Step 1	Turn off computer.
Step 2	Disconnect AC power.
Step 3	Turn over computer.
Step 4	Remove battery.

Table 9-5   Components for Laptop Upgrade

Component	Figure Number
Laptop hard disk	Figure 9-28
DDR3 SODIMM	Figure 9-30

Table 9-6   Leftover Components

Component Name	Figure Number
SATA hard disk	Figure 9-27
DDR2 SODIMM	Figure 9-29

Answers and Explanations to Review Questions

1. **B.** The Fn key is used along with other keys to perform special functions such as adjusting screen brightness, switching between displays, and so on.

2. **D.** Small outline DIMMs are used on virtually all laptops in use.

3. **B.** 2.5-inch hard drives are used in virtually all laptops. These drives can also be adapted to desktop computers' larger 3.5-inch bays.

4. **A.** A docking station requires a proprietary bus connector.

5. **C.** Mini-PCIe is used for most late-model laptops' Wi-Fi radio. PCI and AGP are desktop expansion slots, and CardBus is an expansion slot used by older laptops.

6. **C.** Although A and B should also be checked if problems persist, the most likely cause of a failure to connect is the Wi-Fi being turned off by an external button or switch.

7. **D.** An inverter failure is the most likely cause, followed by the backlight.

8. **A.** The heat sink is used to prevent the CPU and chipset from overheating, not the hard drive. The other steps are necessary.

9. **B, C.** You must know the correct memory speeds and timings recommended for the laptop (as well as size, which is not listed here). The memory used in any laptop using DDR3 RAM is always in SODIMM form factor. The brand is not a requirement either.

10. **B.** ExpressCard, because it can connect to the high-speed PCI Express bus, is the best choice. SODIMM is a memory module form factor, not an expansion slot standard. Mini-PCIe is used for integrated features such as Wi-Fi. CardBus is an obsolete 32-bit laptop card standard that cannot run fast enough to support USB 3.0.

11. **B, D.** Both of these items (when present) are located in the screen assembly and might be damaged if the screen is cracked. The hard drive and Wi-Fi radio are located in the base.

12. **C.** Laptop and desktop processors are not interchangeable. Laptop processors use different sockets than desktop processors, are optimized for low-power mobile use (and thus need much smaller heat sinks than desktop processors), and often have different feature sets than similarly named desktop processors.

13. **A.** When troubleshooting power problems, use a multimeter to check to see whether the outlet is working properly. Make sure the multimeter is set for DC power.

14. **B.** Both devices must be set to the same resolution to enable cloning. S-video and composite output are designed for TV-out (standard definition) and have much lower resolution than either display resolution listed here.

This chapter covers the following subjects:

- **Mobile Device Hardware**—In this section you learn about the basic hardware used by mobile devices, the differences and similarities of laptops and tablet computers, and how to upgrade and replace memory cards and batteries.

- **Mobile Operating Systems**—This section delves into the differences between open-source and closed-source operating systems such as Android and iOS. It also gets into where to find applications for both OSes and how to adjust the displays on both systems. Finally, GPS and how it relates to mobile devices is briefly covered.

- **Mobile Network Connectivity**—This section talks about all the different network connectivity you will encounter with mobile devices including Cellular, Wi-Fi, and Bluetooth. It also demonstrates how to connect email accounts.

- **Mobile Synchronization**—Here you learn how to connect and synchronize iOS and Android-based devices' files and settings.

- **Mobile Security**—In this last section you discover how to secure a mobile device through passcodes, antivirus software, and operating system updates. We also discuss applications for backing up data, remote wiping of data, and locator applications. Finally we cover soft and hard resets.

This chapter covers **CompTIA A+ 220-802 objectives 3.1 through 3.5**.

CHAPTER 10

Mobile Devices

More and more people are switching from desktops and laptops to smaller light-weight mobile devices such as tablets and smartphones. You find them everywhere: on the train, in coffee shops, in meetings; perhaps you are reading this from a mobile device right now.

This chapter assumes a basic knowledge of how to operate these devices and moves ahead to the hardware and software that are propelling the devices into the main-stream. Afterward, we cover how to leverage the power of networking systems to connect to everything and synchronize information between one mobile device to another, and out to desktop computers. Finally, we discuss how to secure these devices so that we can prevent the compromise of important information.

Foundation Topics

Mobile Device Hardware

220-802

Objective:
220-802: 3.4

Mobile devices use different hardware than PCs and laptops. But remember that they are still computers, though small ones; they contain a CPU, RAM, storage device, color display, external ports, and so on. This section talks about the basic hardware components of mobile devices and discusses the hardware differences between tablets and laptops.

Examples of Mobile Device Hardware

A common device as of the writing of this book is the Apple iPad2. It is known as a tablet computer and is manufactured by Foxconn, which also constructs the iPhone, Kindle, Playstation 3, and Xbox 360. This device uses an extremely small 1GHz dual-core CPU known as the Apple A5, a processor based off the ARM Cortex-A9.

Advanced RISC Machine (ARM) is a 32-bit reduced instruction set computing architecture designed for simplicity and low-power applications. ARM processors were originally designed for microcomputers but now find their home in 90% of all RISC-based processing devices such as tablets, smartphones, PDAs, music players, hand-held gaming consoles, calculators, routers, and the list goes on. Low power and the ability to scale down the frequency of the CPU make it an excellent choice for devices such as the iPad2. The iPad2 has 512MB of DDR2 RAM, similar (but smaller) than the DDR2 modules you might install in a PC. For storage, a tablet such as this one uses flash memory, usually in 16GB increments.

The display is a capacitive touch screen; when you "tap" the touch interface, a distortion in its electrostatic field results, which can be measured as a change in capacitance (the amount of electric energy stored for a given electric potential). The distortion that is created is located and sent to the touch screen controller for processing. iPad2 displays are known as **multitouch touch screens**. This means that they can sense the presence of two or more contact points. This technology is used to spread or pinch photos and documents, rotate items, and to open specific applications.

The battery used by the iPad2 is a lithium-ion polymer battery, a common battery in mobile devices. This battery evolved from the lithium-ion batteries common in laptops. The beauty of this type of battery is that the manufacturer can make it into just about any shape, which is instrumental in the thin tablet and smartphone devices of today. It is 90 kilojoules and provides 25 watt-hours, about enough time to use for 10 working hours before having to be recharged. The iPad and iPad2 are charged via AC outlet or USB, both of which require a proprietary cable; the port on the tablet is not a typical Micro-USB port.

NOTE   Newer versions of tablets are constantly being released. In fact, while this book was being edited, Apple released a newer version of the iPad to succeed the iPad2, which they simply call "iPad." However, it is similar to the iPad2 previously described. You'll hear IT technicians refer to the device as an iPad2, or simply an iPad, both of which are acceptable.

Similar tablets (but with different software) include the Motorola Xoom, Samsung Galaxy, and Asus Transformer. These often are less proprietary than an Apple device; for example, they might use Micro-USB ports for charging and synchronization of data. You might also see different names for the touch interface of a device. For example, the company HTC developed a user interface called TouchFLO for its smartphones, which allowed the user to drag the screen up, left, or right. This has been replaced by HTC Sense, which is a multitouch-enabled touch screen similar to the Apple multitouch technology. As of 2012, most new smartphones and tablets feature multitouch touch screens.

Differences Between Tablets and Laptops

It's important to realize some of the differences between tablets and laptops. One of the big distinctions is the lack of field serviceable parts in tablets and other mobile devices. Another variation is the fact that tablets and other similar devices are usually not upgradable. Some mobile devices, such as smartphones, can have upgraded memory cards and/or batteries, but that's about it, and these are usually not serviceable in the field because it is difficult to protect yourself from ESD when working on these devices. (But that doesn't mean it isn't done.) Many organizations recommend you bring the device back to the lab for upgrades or parts swaps. Other devices such as the iPad2 are not user-serviceable whatsoever, and any attempt at doing so will void the warranty. Many organizations utilize the warranties that are built-into these products if repair, upgrade, or replacement is necessary, instead of trying to do any work in-house.

If you think about it, a laptop (or notebook) is really just a smaller, portable version of a desktop computer. Like the desktop computer, it contains a similar processor, similar volatile DDR RAM, and a hard drive that could possibly be solid-state, but regardless will most likely be plugged into an SATA port. It also has a keyboard, and a touchpad that is similar to a mouse. All this hardware is designed to make the best use of operating systems (such as Windows) that you would normally find on a desktop computer. Tablets on the other hand use ARM-based processors and use nonvolatile flash memory that is hard wired to the system instead of a magnetic or solid-state hard drive. So, as you can imagine, the tablet has a loss of performance when compared to a laptop. In addition, the tablet utilizes an onscreen keyboard and doesn't require any type of mouse due to the touch screen capability. All this hardware is designed to run mobile device software such as Android or iOS.

Tablet and Laptop Similarities

Although there are many differences, there are also a few similarities between laptops and tablets. For example, some laptops can be purchased with touch screen displays that work in the same manner as with a tablet. Also, the laptop uses a lithium-ion battery, and the tablet uses a lithium-ion polymer battery, smaller and customizable, but similar in their recharging techniques. Plus, you can add on devices such as keyboards to your tablet. Both devices make use of various wireless communications such as WLAN, Bluetooth, and GSM.

Upgrading and Replacing the Memory Card and the Battery in a Smartphone

Upgrading the memory card in a smartphone is fairly simple. The most difficult parts are keeping yourself grounded and not damaging the tiny memory cards during installation. Memory cards that have been damaged during installation by ESD or otherwise can cause intermittent issues when accessing data, or it could cause the memory to fail altogether. Let's show how to *upgrade a memory card* now. In the process you see how easy it is to swap out a battery if need be.

Step 1.   Find a space to work and prepare antistatic measures. Ready an antistatic mat. Place the device on the mat. Wear an antistatic strap and connect the alligator clip of the strap and the mat to a ground source. If you have a computer case chassis handy, use that, just be sure that the computer is not plugged in. Touch the chassis of the computer case before you begin working.

Step 2.   Pry open the case of the smartphone. Most phones have a plastic back plate that needs to be pried off. You can use a plastic or wooden shim for this. (One time I used chopsticks with an angled end, and they worked quite admirably.) Once the back plate is removed you should see the inside of the phone and the battery as shown in Figure 10-1.

Battery
Notch

Battery

Back Plate

Figure 10-1   Opened smartphone showing back plate, exposed battery, and battery notch.

Step 3.   Now remove the battery. Use your shim to pry it out by inserting the shim in the notch and underneath the battery. You could also use your finger in most cases. (Some phones don't have a back plate and instead the battery is removed by moving a latch.) Once the battery is removed you see something similar to Figure 10-2. Note the memory card and memory card latch.

Step 4.   Now remove the memory card. First, press down on the latch, this disconnects the memory card, and the top end should pop up allowing you to remove it. If for some reason you are not able to employ antistatic measures, use plastic tweezers to remove the memory card. Place the memory card face down on an antistatic bag, or in a memory card case. Note in Figure 10-3 that the contacts on the microSD memory card are face up. This helps to prevent damage to the card.

Figure 10-2   Smartphone with battery removed, exposed memory card.

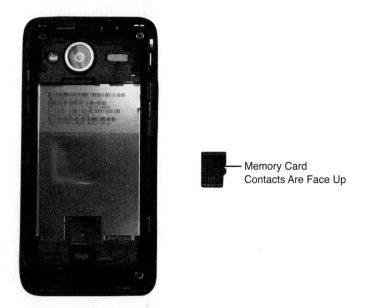

Figure 10-3   Smartphone with memory card removed, contacts are face up.

Step 5. Upgrade the memory card. Insert the microSD memory card of your choice in the memory slot with the contacts facing down. Press down on the memory card until it snaps into place. Remember, when handling the memory card, never touch the contacts, and make sure you are grounded!

Step 6. Upgrade the battery at this time if you wish. Sometimes devices need a replacement battery, and in some cases the manufacturer releases more efficient and longer lasting batteries that are available for upgrade. Insert the battery with the contacts facing down, the logo facing you, and the arrow pointing toward the bottom of the device.

Step 7. Replace the back plate. This usually snaps on. Start at one corner and gently snap it into place. Then move around the perimeter of the device snapping one portion of the back plate at a time. Continue until the entire back plate is firmly attached.

Step 8. Boot the device and test it. Make sure that applications function. Make sure the phone recognizes the new memory. Try connecting the phone to the computer and copying data via USB from the computer to the phone's new memory card. Then disconnect the phone and see whether it can access that data. Reboot the phone several times to make sure it works properly. Store the old memory card in a safe place. It should be stored in a memory card holder, or antistatic bag, and left in a cool, dry location. You never know if you might need to downgrade at some point. Recycle the battery (if you upgraded it) or store it in the same fashion as the memory card.

Hardware Wrap-Up

Remember that whether it's tablets, smartphones, e-readers, ultra-mobile PCs (UMPCs), rugged hand-held computers, or whatever small footprint mobile computing device you work with; you won't often be repairing these. Usually they will be under warranty, and if they need to be repaired, they will have to be taken to an authorized service center. So for the A+ exams you should understand the following:

- The types of hardware in mobile devices
- The differences (and similarities) of laptops and tablets
- How to replace memory cards and batteries in a smartphone

If you by chance obtain a position with an authorized service center, you will most likely acquire special training on how to open these devices, and how to replace printed circuit boards, displays, and batteries. Those are the three items serviced the most often when it comes to mobile devices.

Mobile Hardware Wrap-Up

A final word for this section: New and updated mobile devices are constantly being released. The competition is fierce, so you need to keep up to date with the latest and greatest. But as far as hardware goes, the concepts covered in this section will most likely remain essentially the same. Sure, they will be faster and improved, but it's safe to say that the hardware will adhere to the same basic principles for a while to come.

Mobile Operating Systems

> **220-802**
>
> **Objective:**
> **220-802: 3.1**

Mobile devices also use different software than PCs and laptops. The two main operating systems in use today are Android and iOS, one open-sourced and the other vendor specific. This section compares those two OSes and talks about how to download applications, how to modify and calibrate the display within the OS, and how to use GPS.

Android Versus iOS

Currently, mobile device software comes in one of two forms: open-source, which is effectively free to download and modify, and closed-source, otherwise known as vendor specific, which cannot be modified without express permission and licensing. Let's discuss each of these now.

Open-Source: Android

Android is an example of open-source software. It is a Linux-based operating system used mostly on smartphones and tablet computers and is developed by the Open Handset Alliance, a group directed by Google. Google releases the Android OS code as open-source, allowing developers to modify it and freely create applications for it. Google also commissioned the Android Open-Source Project (AOSP); their mission is to maintain and further develop Android. You know you are dealing with the Android open-source OS and related apps when you see the stylized robot, usually in green. An example of Android running on a smartphone can be seen in Figure 10-4.

Figure 10-4   Android OS Home screen on a smartphone.

Android OS versions are dubbed with cute names such as Cupcake, Gingerbread, and the two latest: Honeycomb (version 3) and Ice Cream Sandwich (version 4).

To find out the version you are currently running, start at the Home screen; this is the main screen that boots up by default. Tap the Menu button, and then tap Settings. Scroll to the bottom and tap the About Phone (or just About) option. Then tap Software Information or similar option. This displays the version of Android. Figure 10-5 shows a smartphone using version 2.3.3 (Gingerbread).

Let's say a company wanted to create a custom version of the Android OS for a hand-held computer that they were developing. According to the license, they would be able to do this and customize the OS to their specific hardware. Some companies opt to use Android for this purpose, whereas others use Windows CE or Windows Mobile (for a fee), both designed for hand-held computer.

Figure 10-5   Smartphone using Version 2.3.3 of Android.

Closed-Source: iOS

Apple's iOS is an example of closed-source software. Previously known as the iPhone Operating System, it is now simply referred to as iOS, since it is used on iPhones and iPads as well. It is based off of Mac OS X (used on Mac desktops and laptops) and is effectively Unix-based. Figure 10-6 shows the Home screen of an iPad2.

To find out the version of iOS you are running go to the Home screen and tap Settings. Tap General and then tap About. You will see the Version number. For example, Figure 10-7 shows an iPad2 running Version 5.0 (9A334). The build numbers is 9A334; this was the public release of version 5.0.

Unlike Android, iOS is not open-source, and is not available for download to developers. Only Apple hardware uses this operating system; this is known as being *vendor-specific*. However, if developers want to create an application for iOS they can download the iOS SDK (software development kit). Apple license fees are required when a developer is ready to go live with the application.

Figure 10-6   iPad2 Home screen.

Figure 10-7   iPad2 using Version 5.0 of iOS.

Where and How to Get Applications

Mobile devices are nothing without applications. To this end, both Android and iOS have application sources where you can download free and/or small-fee applications.

Android users download applications from the Android Market (also accessible through Google Play). This can be done directly from the mobile device. Or, if a mobile device is connected via USB to a computer, the user can browse apps on the Google Play website while working on the computer and download directly from the site to the phone, passing through the computer.

iOS users download applications from the App Store. This was originally an update to the iTunes store, but on newer iOS mobile devices it is now a separate icon on the Home screen. Apps can also be downloaded from a Mac, or from a PC through the iTunes application.

Regardless of the OS, a user searches for the name of the application he or she wants, downloads it, starts the installation process, agrees to a license, and then finally uses the app.

Some applications don't work unless a person hacks the OS and gains superuser privileges. In the Android world this is known as "rooting" the phone or other mobile device. In the iOS world it is jailbreaking. This could be a breach of the user license agreement. It can also be dangerous. These types of hacks often require a person to back up all data on the mobile device, wipe it out completely, and install a special application that may or may not be trustworthy. Many phones are rendered useless or are compromised when attempting this procedure. Applications that have anything to do with rooting or jailbreaking should generally be avoided.

Adjusting the Display

The displayof a mobile device might need to be configured, oriented, and calibrated properly for efficient usage. Today's mobile devices are usually pretty good out-of-the-box, but a user might need to lock rotation, or could possibly cause the touch screen to behave improperly by misconfiguring it, or by installing applications that modify the display's functionality. Let's discuss display rotation (otherwise known as orientation) and calibration now.

Mobile device displays rotate by default if the user rotates the device, allowing the screen to be viewed vertically or horizontally. This helps when looking at pictures, movies, or viewing websites. But in some cases, a user might want to lock the rotation of the device so that it stays as either vertical or horizontal, without moving. On an Android device this can be done by accessing Settings, tapping Display, and then deselecting the Auto-rotate screen. On an iOS device (version 4 or 5) this can be done by double-tapping the Home button (which brings up the multitasking bar on the bottom), then swiping the bar all the way to the right. Finally, a circular arrow is shown to the far left, tap this, and rotation will be locked. Some iPads (such as the iPad2) also have a side switch that can be configured to enable/disable rotation lock; this feature can be turned on in **Settings > General > Use side switch to: Lock Rotation**.

Screen orientation is a pretty simple concept to understand and use. But it can be more complicated when it comes to applications. For example, Apple mobile devices use the **Accelerometer**: a combination of hardware and software that measure velocity; they detect rotation, shaking of the device, and so on. The accelerometer enables a mobile device to automatically adjust from portrait (vertical) to landscape (horizontal) mode. It's actually three accelerometers, one for each axis X (left to right), Y (up and down), and Z (back to front). These are manipulated by developers for special applications (such as a compass app) and games so that the program recognizes particular movements of the device and translates to various functions in-game or within the application. Newer Apple devices include a **gyroscope**, which adds the measurements of pitch, roll, and yaw, just like in the concept of flight dynamics. For example, imagine your tablet computer is a model airplane and you are holding it flat in front of you. To change pitch, you would raise or lower the nose of the airplane. To initiate roll, you would turn the airplane right or left so the wings move, but the fuselage of the plane rotates but otherwise doesn't move. To start a yaw, you would rotate the airplane left or right while keeping it flat. Now apply this to a tablet computer, as is illustrated in Figure 10-8. You won't need a pilot's license to use an iPad, but this additional measurement of movement has a great impact on the development of newer applications and especially games. Of course, if the accelerometers or gyroscope of the mobile device fail, and a reset of the device doesn't fix the problem, it will have to be repaired at an authorized service center.

Android devices have a **screen calibration** utility called G-Sensor calibration. It is found in **Settings > Display**. To make sure that the three axes are calibrated properly, this program is run while the mobile device is laid on a flat surface. You can tell whether the surface is level by the horizontal and vertical leveling bubbles on the display. Then press the Calibrate button to reset the G-Sensor as shown in Figure 10-9.

Other mobile devices' calibration programs show a crosshair or similar image in the center of the screen. You need to tap with a stylus as close to the center of the display as possible. If a stylus is not available, use the pointed end of a pen cap.

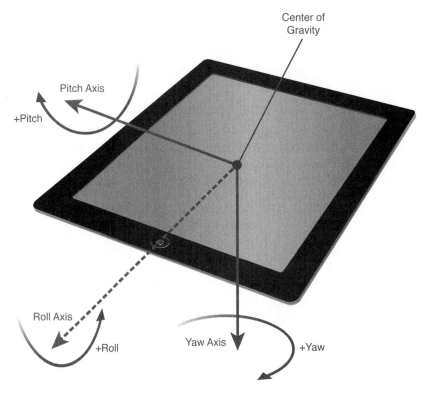

Figure 10-8   Examples of iPad2 gyroscopic pitch, roll, and yaw.

Figure 10-9   G-Sensor calibration on a typical smartphone.

A reset can also fix problems with calibration (as well as other types of problems). There are two types of resets: soft and hard. A soft reset is usually performed simply by powering the device off and then powering it back on again. This can fix temporary problems quickly and easily. It is similar to rebooting a PC. However, more advanced problems require a hard reset. Warning! A hard reset removes all data and applications and returns the device to its original factory state. Do not perform a hard reset without backing up the contents of the memory card in the mobile device, and any additional settings you require. More information on resets can be found in the section "Mobile Security" later in this chapter.

Today's Apple devices do not offer a calibration utility. Sometimes, issues that appear to be calibration problems are actually something else with an easy fix. For example, cheaper screen protectors can bubble and otherwise cause problems when tapping on the screen. Removing the protector and installing a new one properly can fix this problem. When installing a screen protector, use a long flat surface to squeeze all the bubbles out; shims can be purchased for just this purpose. Use a decent screen protector such as Ghost Armor or something similar. Good quality screen protectors not only protect the display, but they also reduce glare, smudging, and fingerprints, without reducing sensitivity. Dirty screens can also be a culprit when a user is having difficulty tapping on icons or smaller items. Clean the display with a lint-free cloth. If the screen is very dirty, mix 50% isopropyl alcohol and 50% water, apply conservatively to the cloth, then clean the display with the cloth. Make sure all traces of liquid are removed when you are done. If none of these steps work, the device will need to be brought in to an authorized service center for repair.

GPS and Geotracking

The **Global Positioning System (GPS)**, developed by the United States Department of Defense is a worldwide system of satellites that provide location information for anything with a GPS receiver. Any mobile device with a GPS receiver can use this system to identify its location and utilize mapping programs and any other applications that rely on GPS. Some mobile devices do not have a GPS receiver, and instead use Location Services or something with a similar name that uses crowd-sourced Wi-Fi locations to determine the approximate location of the device. This is common in mobile devices that do not have a GSM module. So essentially, if a mobile device cannot be used to make phone calls, it also can't be used with GPS-enabled applications.

To enable/disable GPS on an Android-based device go to **Settings > Location**, and select **Use GPS satellites**. To enable/disable GPS on an Apple device such as an iPad, go to **Settings > Location Services**.

Geotracking is the practice of tracking and recording the location of a mobile device over time. This location tracking is done by Apple and Google as well as other organizations and governments. Privacy issues aside, this practice *is* being done, so if a user doesn't want her location known, simply disable the GPS setting.

Mobile OS Wrap-Up

A last word about mobile operating systems. For the exam, be sure to know the difference between open-source and closed source. Understand the basics of how to navigate around the Android and the iOS operating systems, and know where to get applications for both OSes. Get to know the different screen orientation and calibration options for both platforms. Finally, know how to enable GPS.

Mobile Network Connectivity

220-802

Objective:
220-802: 3.2

Mobile devices use all kinds of network connectivity, most of it wireless. From cellular GSM connections to Wi-Fi and Bluetooth, a mobile device can create connections to computers and networks, download email, and work with headsets and remote printers. Let's begin with connecting to wireless networks.

GSM Cellular Connectivity

Cellular phones use the Global System for Mobile Communications (GSM) to make voice calls, and GSM or the general packet radio service (GPRS) to send data at 2G speeds through the cellular network. Extensions of these standards, 3GPP and EDGE are used to attain 3G speeds. 4G speeds can be attained only if a mobile device complies with the International Mobile Telecommunications Advanced (IMT-Advanced) requirements, has a 4G antenna, and is in range of a 4G transmitter, which as of the writing of this book, are only common in urban areas.

Most devices cannot shut off the cellular antenna by itself. However, every device manufactured now is required to have an "airplane mode," which turns off any wireless antenna in the device including GSM, Wi-Fi, GPS, and Bluetooth. On a typical Android device this can be done by going to **Settings > Wireless & Networks >** and check marking **Airplane Mode** as shown in Figure 10-10. Note the airplane icon in the upper portion of the figure. You will find that some airlines don't consider this to be acceptable and will still ask you to turn off your device, either for the duration of the flight or at least during takeoff and landing. On Android devices you can also access Airplane Mode by pressing and holding the power button.

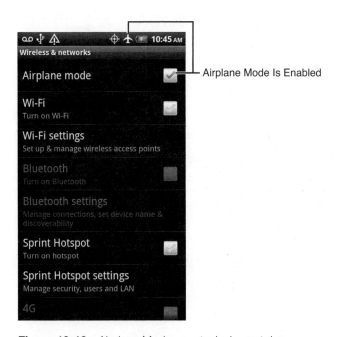

Figure 10-10   Airplane Mode on a typical smartphone.

To enable airplane mode on an Apple tablet, go to **Settings > Airplane Mode** as shown in Figure 10-11. Again, note the icon of an airplane at the top left of the figure.

Figure 10-11   Airplane Mode on a typical Apple tablet.

Wi-Fi Network Connectivity

Using a cellular connection can be slow when transmitting data. That's why all mobile devices are equipped with an embedded wireless antenna to connect to wireless LANs. This WLAN antenna (often referred to as a Wi-Fi antenna) usually allows access to 802.11b, g, and n networks, and possibly wireless 802.11a networks. The wireless configuration works similarly to a wireless connection on a PC or laptop. See Chapter 16, "Networking," for a detailed description of connecting to wireless networks.

In general, the mobile device must first search for wireless networks. On a typical Android smartphone this is done by

Step 1.   Go to **Settings > Wireless & Networks > Wi-Fi Settings**.

Step 2.   From there, most devices usually scan for wireless networks automatically, or you could tap **Add Wi-Fi Network** to add one manually.

Step 3.   If adding a network manually, enter the SSID of the wireless access point as shown in Figure 10-12.

Step 4.   Enter the passcode for the network. If the code is correct, then the wireless adapter in the mobile device gets an IP address allowing it to communicate with the network. If a wireless network uses WPA2, and the mobile device isn't compatible, you should search for an update to the operating system to make it WPA2 compliant.

Figure 10-12   Android OS prompting for the user to enter an SSID.

Accessing wireless networks on an iPad or similar device is done by

Step 1.   Go to **Settings > Wi-Fi**.

Step 2.   The device usually scans for networks automatically. To connect to a network manually, tap **Other**.

Step 3.   If adding a network manually, type the SSID of the network in the Name field.

Step 4.   Type the passcode for the network. If adding the network manually, you can select the type of security, for example WPA2, as shown in Figure 10-13.

Figure 10-13   iOS prompting for the user to enter an SSID for a WPA2-secured network.

Almost all types of devices display the universal wireless icon when connected to a wireless network as shown in Figure 10-14. This icon not only lets you know when you are connected, but how strong the connection is. The more curved lines you see, the better the connection.

Figure 10-14   Universal wireless symbol.

Many mobile devices can also perform **Wi-Fi tethering**. This is when the mobile device shares its Internet connection with other Wi-Fi capable devices. For example, if one user had a smartphone that was able to access the Internet through 3G or GPRS networks, then it could be configured to become a portable Wi-Fi hotspot for other mobile devices that are Wi-Fi capable but have no cellular or GPRS option.

A lot of devices can also be configured for **Internet pass-through** as well. This means that the phone or other device connects to a PC via USB and accesses the Internet using the PC's Internet connection.

Wi-Fi Troubleshooting

When troubleshooting mobile device wireless connections, always make sure of the following basic wireless troubleshooting methods:

- The device is within range of the wireless network.

- The correct SSID was entered (if manually connecting).

- The device supports the encryption protocol of the wireless network.

- Wi-Fi tethering or Internet pass-through is not conflicting with the wireless connection.

If you still have trouble, here are a few more methods that can help to connect, or reconnect to a wireless network:

- Power cycle the mobile device.

- Power cycle Wi-Fi.

- Remove or "forget" the particular wireless network and then attempt to connect to it again.

- Access the advanced settings and check whether there is a proxy configuration, whether a static IP is used, or whether there is a Wi-Fi sleep policy. Any of these could possibly cause a conflict. You might also try renewing the lease of an IP address, if the device is obtaining one from a DHCP server (which it most likely will be). Some devices also have an option for "best Wi-Fi performance," which uses more power but might help when connecting to distant WAPs. Advanced settings can be found on an Android device by going to Settings > Wireless and Networks > Wi-Fi Settings; then tap the Menu button and select Advanced. This is shown in Figure 10-15. On an Apple iPad advanced settings can be located at Settings > Wi-Fi, and then tap on the arrow of an individual wireless network. This is shown in Figure 10-16.

Figure 10-15 Advanced wireless settings in Android.

Figure 10-16 Advanced wireless settings in iOS.

One of the previous methods usually works when troubleshooting a wireless connection, but if all else fails, a hard reset brings the device back to factory settings. (Always back up all data and settings before performing a hard reset.) And if the mobile device still can't connect to any of several known good wireless networks, bring the device to an authorized service center.

Bluetooth Configuration

Bluetooth is a wireless standard for transmitting data over short distances. It is commonly implemented in the form of a headset or printer connection by mobile users, and is also used to create wireless personal area networks between multiple Bluetooth-enabled mobile devices.

By default, Bluetooth is usually disabled on Android devices but is enabled on devices such as iPads. To connect a Bluetooth device to a mobile device, Bluetooth first needs to be enabled; then the Bluetooth device needs to be synchronized to the mobile device. This is known as pairing or linking. It sometimes requires a PIN code. Once synchronized the device needs to be connected. Finally, the Bluetooth connection should be tested. Let's show the steps involved in connecting a Bluetooth headset to a typical Android-based device and to an iPad. Before you begin, make sure the Bluetooth headset is charged.

Steps to Configure a Bluetooth Headset on an Android-Based Device

Step 1. Go to **Settings > Wireless & Networks >** and check the box for **Bluetooth**. This enables Bluetooth on the mobile device.

Step 2. Tap **Bluetooth Settings**. This displays the Bluetooth Setting screen.

Step 3. Prepare the headset. This varies from headset to headset. For example, on a typical Motorola Bluetooth headset, you press and hold the button while opening the microphone. If necessary keep holding the button while completing the next step.

Step 4. Tap **Scan for Devices** on the Android device. Keep holding the button on the headset until the Android device finds it.

Step 5. On the Android device, under the Bluetooth device tap **Pair with This Device**. Most Android devices pair the Bluetooth headset to the mobile device, and then complete the connection automatically, allowing full use of the device.

Step 6. Enter a PIN code if necessary. Many devices come with a default pin of 0000.

When finished, the screen on the Android device looks similar to Figure 10-17. Note the Bluetooth icon at the top of the screen. This icon tells you whether Bluetooth is running on the device. It will remain even if you disconnect the Bluetooth device. For this headset device we would test it simply by making a phone call. To disconnect it, simply tap the device on the screen and tap OK. It will remain paired but nonfunctional until a connection is made again.

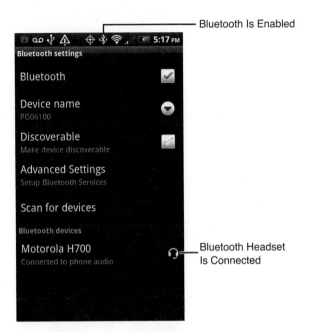

Figure 10-17 Bluetooth Settings screen on an Android smartphone showing the Motorola H700 headset connected.

Mobile devices can also connect to other Bluetooth-enabled devices (forming a PAN), or to a computer equipped with a Bluetooth dongle. To do this, you must set the mobile device to discoverable (which generally lasts for only 2 minutes). In the same fashion that the headset was discovered by the mobile device in the previous procedure, so can a mobile device be discovered by a computer or other mobile device. When connecting a mobile device to another mobile device or PC, it can be identified by its name. For example, the mobile device in Figure 10-17 is listed as PG06100. You can modify this name if you want. It is authenticated by a PIN code chosen at the PC or other mobile device. We would test these types of connections by sending data or through communications.

Steps to Configure a Bluetooth Headset on an iOS-Based Device

For this exercise we refer to an iPad2.

Step 1. Go to **Settings > General >** and tap **Bluetooth**. This displays the Bluetooth screen.

Step 2. Tap **Bluetooth** to enable it (if it isn't enabled already). This automatically starts searching for devices and will continue to do so.

Step 3. Prepare the headset. This varies from headset to headset. For example, on a typical Motorola Bluetooth headset, you press and hold the button while opening the mic. Keep holding the button. The iPad2 automatically recognizes the device and lists it as discoverable.

Step 4. Tap the device name, and it should automatically connect as shown in Figure 10-18.

Step 5. Enter a PIN code if necessary.

To remove the device, click on it, and on the next screen click Forget.

Figure 10-18   A connected Bluetooth headset on an iPad2.

Note that Bluetooth devices can only be connected to one mobile device at a time. If you need to switch the Bluetooth device from one mobile device to another, be sure to disconnect it or "forget" it from the current connection before making a new one.

Troubleshooting Bluetooth Connections

If you have trouble pairing a Bluetooth device, and connecting or reconnecting to Bluetooth devices or PANs, try some of the following methods:

- Make sure the phone or other mobile device is Bluetooth-capable.
- Verify that your devices are fully charged, especially Bluetooth headsets.

- Check whether you are within range. For example, Class 2 Bluetooth devices have a range of 10 meters.

- Try restarting the mobile device and attempt to reconnect.

- Try using a known good Bluetooth device with the mobile device to make sure the mobile device's Bluetooth is functional.

- Remove or "forget" the particular Bluetooth device; then turn off Bluetooth in general, restart the mobile device, and attempt to reconnect.

Email Configurations

Although there are many other types of communication available to mobile users, email still accounts for huge percentage. It's important to know how to configure a mobile device for web-based email services such as Gmail, Yahoo, and so on. It is also necessary to know how to configure POP3, IMAP, and connections to Microsoft Exchange Servers.

Web-Based Email for Mobile Devices

Mobile devices can access web-based email through a browser, the way a user would on a PC, but this is not necessary nowadays due to the "app." For example, Android devices come with a Gmail application built in, allowing a user to access Gmail directly without having to use the browser. Apple iOS devices allow connectivity to Gmail, Yahoo, and a host of other email providers as well.

Connecting to these services is simple, and works similarly to using a desktop or laptop computer. Choose the type of provider you use, enter a username (the email address) and password (on Apple devices an Apple ID is also required), and the user will have access to web-based email.

When troubleshooting issues with email, make sure that the username and password are typed correctly. Using onscreen keyboards often leads to mistyped passwords. Also make sure that the mobile device is currently connected to the Internet.

POP3, IMAP, and Exchange

If you need to connect your mobile device to a specific organization's email system, it gets a little more complicated. You must know the server that you want to connect to, the port you need to use, and whether security is being employed.

The following is a step-by-step process of how to connect a typical Android smartphone to a POP3 account.

Step 1. Go to Home and tap the **Menu** button. Then select **All Apps**.

Step 2. Scroll down until you see the Mail app, and tap it (this might also be listed as E-mail).

Step 3. Select whether you want a POP3, IMAP, or Exchange. (For this step-by-step we select POP3.)

Step 4. Type the email address and the password of the account and tap **Next**.

Step 5. Configure the incoming settings. Change the username if desired to something different than the email address, and then type the POP server name. By default, it takes the domain name portion of the email address, which is usually correct. If security is being used, select SSL or TLS. This information should be supplied by the network administrator. Type the port number—for POP3, this is 110 by default. If port numbers are different, they will be supplied to you by the network administrator. Then tap **Next**.

Step 6. Configure the outgoing settings. Type the SMTP server. Organizations often use the same server name as the POP3 server. However, small office and home users might have to use their ISP's SMTP server. If security is being used, select SSL or TLS. Type the port number. For SMTP this is 25. Then tap **Next**.

Step 7. Configure account options. From here you can tell the mobile device how often to check for mail and whether to notify you when it arrives. Tap **Next**. At this point, new email should start downloading.

Step 8. Finally, you can give the account an easier name for you to remember it by. Tap **Done**.

Now let's show a step-by-step process on how to connect an iPad2 to a POP3 account.

Step 1. Go to Home and tap the **Settings** button.

Step 2. Tap **Mail, Contacts, Calendars**.

Step 3. Tap **Add Account**.

Step 4. Tap **Other** at the bottom of the list.

Step 5. Tap **Add Mail Account**.

Step 6. Type the name, email address, and password (and an optional description) and tap **Next**.

Step 7.   Tap **Pop**. Then under Incoming Mail Server, type the POP3 server name and the username. Under Outgoing Mail Server, type the SMTP server. Then tap **Save**.

Step 8.   The system verifies the address and password. If successful, the process is finished. If not, check that everything was typed correctly and that the correct parameters, such as the type of server and security, have been configured.

Now, if you instead have to connect an IMAP account, you must type the IMAP server (for downloading mail), which uses port 143 by default, and the outgoing SMTP server (for receiving mail). If you connect to a Microsoft Exchange mail server, that server name often takes care of both downloading and uploading email. You might need to know the domain that the Exchange server is a member of. Secure email sessions require the use of SSL or TLS on port 443. Check with the network administrator to find out which protocol to use. POP3 also has a secure derivative known as APOP, a challenge/response protocol that uses a hashing function to prevent replay attacks during an email session. This protocol can be chosen from the Android platform and is also used by Mozilla Thunderbird, Windows Live Mail, and Apple Mail.

Configuring email accounts for other devices, such as the BlackBerry, works similarly to other smartphones; however, you also have the option to connect to a BlackBerry Enterprise Server, which is similar to Microsoft Exchange. These Black-Berry servers are the core of "pushed" email, which BlackBerry pioneered for users to get their email immediately when it reaches the mail server.

Troubleshooting Email Connections

If you have trouble connecting an email account, try some of the following methods:

- Make sure the mobile device has Internet access. If connecting through the cellular network, make sure there is a decent reception.

- Verify that the username, password, and server names are typed correctly. Remember that the username is often the email address itself.

- Check the port numbers. By default POP3 is 110, SMTP is 25, and IMAP is 143. However, network administrators might decide to use nondefault port numbers!

- Double-check whether security is required in the form of SSL or TLS. For nonstandard port numbers and security configurations, check with your network administrator.

Mobile Network Connectivity Wrap-Up

A last word about network connectivity. There is virtually endless information when it comes to mobile device networking. For the CompTIA A+ exams remember that mobile devices can connect to the Internet via cellular networks, Wi-Fi, and through a desktop computer. Understand how to troubleshoot wireless Internet connections. Know how to connect a Bluetooth device to a mobile device and how to troubleshoot problematic connections. Finally, understand the various email configurations on a phone including POP3, IMAP, Exchange, and web-based systems such as Gmail.

Mobile Synchronization

> **220-802**
>
> **Objective:**
> **220-802: 3.5**

Now that we have talked about the different OSes of mobile devices, and how to configure network connectivity, let's move on to the subject of how to synchronize the contents of the mobile devices with PCs. **Synchronization** is the matching up of files, email, and other types of data between one computer and another. We use synchronization to bring files in line with each other and to force devices to coordinate their data. When dealing with synchronization, a mobile device can connect to a PC via USB (the most common), other serial connections (much less common), Wi-Fi, and Bluetooth. Let's show how to synchronize an Android device and an iPad to a PC via USB now.

Synchronizing an Android Device to a PC

First of all, if you connect just about any Android-based mobile device to a PC via USB, Windows will most likely recognize it, and you will have a few options display on the Android screen as shown in Figure 10-19.

Figure 10-19   PC connection options on Android.

The first option is Charge Only. Aside from charging the Android device by connecting it to an AC outlet, a PC's USB port can charge it (though it will probably take longer). This first option is the default, so if you need to only charge a device, you won't have to change this setting. We'll skip the second option for now and come back to it later. The third option is Disk Drive. If you want to display the contents of the mobile device's memory card within Windows, select this. Then, the device shows up as a removable disk in Windows Explorer. From there, data can be copied back and forth between the PC and the mobile device as you usually would within Windows. Older Android devices required you to tap "mount" to have the phone show as a removable disk. Also note USB tethering on the list. This enables you to share the mobile device's cellular network with the PC. The last item on the list is Internet Pass-through, which we mentioned previously. It enables you to use the PC's Internet connection on the mobile device.

Now, none of these so far allow you to synchronize information from the mobile device to the PC. Only the second option, HTC Sync, allows this synchronization, but with a caveat: The PC must have the appropriate synchronization software installed. Keep in mind that this software (and connection name) will be different depending on the manufacturer of the device. In this example we are showing an HTC Evo smartphone.

Most synchronization software requires the PC to have Windows XP or higher, 1GB of RAM or more, USB 2.0 ports minimum, and 300MB of free space on the hard drive. Syncing software is freely downloadable from the manufacturer's website. Figure 10-20 shows an example of HTCSync software with the HTC Evo connected via USB and set to HTCSync.

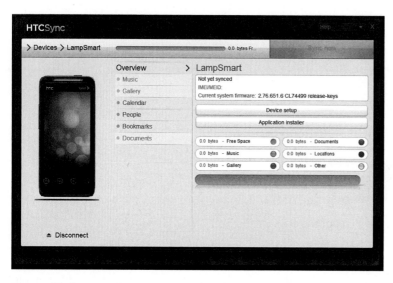

Figure 10-20   HTCSync software on a PC.

In the figure, you can see that we can synchronize music, pictures, the calendar, bookmarks, and more. This synchronization can be initiated from the mobile device or from the program on the PC. Documents, music, pictures, and video are synchronized by default to the Windows Libraries of the same names.

If you are using the mobile device's built-in contacts and email programs, the information within those programs is transferred to the PC's corresponding programs; for example, the Calendar and Contacts will be synchronized with Microsoft Outlook. However, for this mobile device, Gmail or Exchange contacts information will not be synchronized, nor will any other third-party data besides data that originates from, or is destined for, a Microsoft application.

However, not everyone uses synchronization software. Some people exclusively use Gmail on the Android platform. Google automatically synchronizes mail, contacts, and the Calendar, so that you can view the information on the mobile device or on the PC (when connected to the Gmail website). However, because the data is stored on a Google server, security can be compromised. If you choose to do this, you should use an extremely strong password, change it every month or so, and use a secure browser when connecting to Gmail from your PC. The same people who use Gmail will usually transfer data by simply mounting the mobile device as a disk drive in Windows. This effectively renders the synchronization software unnecessary for those people.

Synchronization software also allows a person to rename the device (I just renamed mine to "LampSmart") and install programs to the mobile device from the PC. You can also quickly see how much space you have available.

Third-party tools (such as Mark/Space) are available if a person wants to synchronize an Android device with a PC or Mac via Bluetooth or Wi-Fi. Standard Microsoft ActiveSync is not used to synchronize data between Android and Windows. However, Exchange ActiveSync can be used to synchronize email, contacts, and calendars between an Android 2.0 mobile device and higher with an Exchange Server.

Synchronizing an iPad2 to a PC

Before we get into synchronizing, let's talk about charging. The best way to charge an iPad is by plugging the AC adapter into an outlet. If the iPad is connected to a desktop computer via USB and is turned on it will not charge. However, if it is connected by USB and it is sleeping or off, it will slowly charge. If the computer is not equipped with a high-power USB port, this could take a long time. Regardless, Apple recommends plugging these devices into the AC outlet to charge.

If you plug in an iPad to a PC via USB, Windows should automatically recognize it and install the driver for it. At that point you can move files between the PC and the iPad's memory card. The iPad will show up in Windows Explorer as Apple iPad directly inside Computer.

To synchronize data such as contacts, calendars, and so on, PC users need to use iTunes for Windows. From iTunes a user would select Sync Contacts or Sync Calendars for example. This information can be synchronized to Microsoft Outlook 2003 or higher, Windows Address Book (in Windows XP), and Windows Contacts (in Windows 7/Vista). Mac users benefit from the simplicity of synchronization across all Apple products. They can use iTunes, or can use the iCloud to store, back up, and synchronize information across all Apple devices. This can be done by USB, or via Wi-Fi if the various Apple devices are on the same wireless network. Items can also be synced from the iPad itself by going to **Settings > Mail, Contacts, Calendars**. Then scrolling down and selecting Sync as shown in Figure 10-21.

Figure 10-21   Apple iPad2 synchronization example.

Synchronizing Other Devices

The two operating systems the CompTIA objectives are concerned with are Android and iOS. However, these are not the only players on the field! Let's mention a few other devices.

First of all, the BlackBerry deserves some mention. For the longest time, this was the standard device a businessperson would use. It has lost some momentum, but you still see plenty of them in the field. BlackBerry offers what they call Desktop Software. Separate versions for PC and Mac are available at this link: http://us.blackberry.com/apps-software/desktop/.

The software works similarly to other synchronization software for Android or iOS.

And let's not forget about Microsoft mobile operating systems. Windows CE and Windows Mobile are commonly found in the transportation, medical, and surveying fields, as well as other niche markets that require rugged, waterproof devices. These devices synchronize to the PC by way of Microsoft ActiveSync (for Windows XP or earlier) and the Windows Mobile Device Center (Windows Vista or newer). The Windows Mobile Device Center is available at this link: http://www.microsoft.com/download/en/details.aspx?id=14.

These programs can synchronize data between the mobile device and the PC via USB or Bluetooth connections. Microsoft does not allow synchronization over Wi-Fi as it is deemed a security issue.

Mobile Sync Wrap-Up

Synchronization is of utmost importance. Most professionals deal with more than one electronic device. Your average person has a computer and at least one mobile device, possibly two, and some throw in a laptop for good measure! These devices need to have their files, contacts, calendars, and email synchronized to do business efficiently. Whether that data is synchronized by a program on a desktop computer or by a server in the cloud, the user needs it to be available in as close to real-time as possible. Understand how to synchronize data from Android and iOS devices to a PC.

Mobile Security

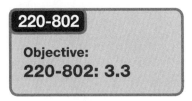

Mobile devices need to be secured just like any other computing devices, but due to their transportable nature, some security techniques are a bit different. It's important to prepare for the possibility of a stolen, lost, damaged, or compromised device. The methods listed in the following sections help you to recover from any of these problems, and also aid you in preventing them from happening.

Protecting Against Stolen or Lost Devices

Because mobile devices are expensive and could contain confidential data, they become a target for thieves. Add to that the facts that they are small and easy to conceal, makes them easier to steal. But there are some things we can do to protect our data and attempt to get the mobile device back.

The first thing a user should do when receiving a mobile device is to set a *passcode*, which is a set of numbers. This one of several types of **screen locks**. These lock the device making it inaccessible to everyone except experienced hackers. The screen lock can be a pattern that is drawn on the display, a PIN (passcode), or a password. A very strong password is usually the strongest form of screen lock.

This can be accessed on an Android device by going to **Settings > Security**. This screen on a typical Android smartphone is shown in Figure 10-22.

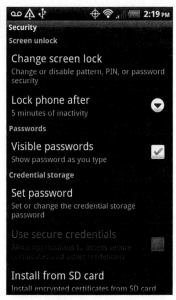

Figure 10-22   Android Security screen.

You can also select how long the phone waits after inactivity to lock. Generally this is set to 3 or 5 minutes or so, but in a confidential environment you might set this to "immediate."

The next option on the Security screen is Visible Passwords. If check marked, this shows the current letter of the password being typed by the user. This type of setting is vulnerable to shoulder surfers (people looking over your shoulder to find out your password) and should be deselected. When deselected, only asterisks (*) are shown when the user types a password.

There is also a Credential Storage option. By default, secure credentials are dropped after a session is over. (an exception to this rule is a Gmail or other similar login). But, if Use Secure Credentials is check marked, and a user accesses a website or application that requires a secure certificate, the credentials are stored on the device. A user can set a password here so that only he or she can view or clear credentials, or install credentials from a memory card. The use of secure credentials is usually only configured if a user needs access to confidential company information on the Internet.

Passcode locking can be accessed on an iPad device by going to **Settings > General > and tapping Passcode Lock.** This displays the Passcode Lock screen. Tap Turn Passcode On to set a passcode as shown in Figure 10-23. Be sure that the Auto-Lock on the previous screen is set to an amount of minutes. If it is set to "never" then the device will never sleep, negating the security of the passcode, and using valuable battery power. The default setting is 2 minutes. Also note in Figure 10-23 that Simple Passcode is enabled. This allows four-digit numeric passcodes only. As this is probably not going to be secure enough for an organization, you should turn off the Simple Passcode option; that will allow alphanumeric passwords to be entered.

Figure 10-23   iPad2 passcode lock screen.

Aside from the default timeout, devices can also be locked by pressing the power button quickly. If configured, the passcode must be supplied whenever a mobile device comes out of a sleep or lock state and whenever it is first booted.

If a person fails to enter the correct passcode after a certain amount of attempts, the device will lock temporarily and the person will have to wait a certain amount of time before attempting the passcode again. For example, by default on the Android this is five attempts; if they all fail the user has to wait 30 seconds. If the person fails to enter the correct passcode again, the timeout will increase on most devices. After a certain amount of attempts, the device will either need to be connected to the computer it was last synced to, or will have to be restored to factory condition with a hard reset (which will wipe the data). Some devices (such as the iPhone) have a setting where the device will be erased after a certain amount of incorrect password attempts (10 in the case of the iPhone). There are also third-party apps available for download for most mobile devices that will wipe the data after *x* amount of attempts. Some apps configure the device to automatically take a picture after three failed attempts and email the picture to the owner.

There's an app for virtually everything. For example, let's say the device was lost or stolen. If the user had previously installed a locator application such as Where's my Droid, Lookout Mobile Security, or Find iPhone, and the GPS/Location Services was enabled on the device, then the user would be able to track where the device is.

Now, even if you track your mobile device and find it, it might be too late. A hacker can get past passcodes and other screen locks. It's just a matter of time before the hacker has access to the data. So, an organization with confidential information should consider a remote wipe program. As long as the mobile device still has access to the Internet, the remote wipe program can be initiated from a desktop computer, which deletes all the contents of the remote mobile device. Examples of software that can accomplish this include Google Sync, Google Apps Device Policy, Apple's Data Protection, and third-party apps such as Mobile Defense. In some cases, such as Apple's Data Protection, the command that starts the remote wipe must be issued from an Exchange server or Mobile Device Management server. Of course, you should have a backup plan in place as well so that data on the mobile device is backed up to a secure location at regular intervals. This way, if the data needs to be wiped, you are secure in the fact that most of the data can be recovered. The type of remote wipe program, backup program, and policies regarding how these are implemented vary from one organization to the next. Be sure to read up on your organization's policies to see exactly what is allowed from a mobile security standpoint.

Protecting Against Compromised or Damaged Devices

Theft and loss aren't the only risks a mobile device faces. We should protect against the chance that a mobile device is physically (or logically) damaged, or if the device's security is compromised.

First, many organizations implement backup and remote backup policies. iOS devices can be backed up to a PC via USB connection and by using iTunes. Also, they can be backed up remotely to the iCloud. Although there are other third-party apps for remote backup (such as iDrive and Mozy), many iOS users use iTunes or the iCloud. Information can even be restored to new iOS devices. Android (as of the writing of this book) doesn't allow a complete backup without rooting the phone (which we don't recommend). However, almost all the data and settings can be backed up in a collection of ways.

First, the Android Cloud backup can be used to back up email, contacts, and other information. However, if you are using Gmail, email, contacts, and calendars are backed up (and synchronized) to Google servers. If a mobile device is lost, the information can be quickly accessed from a desktop computer or other mobile device. Unlike Apple, Android applications can be backed up, if they are not copy protected, with an app such as Astro. Android settings can be backed up and restored from **Settings > Privacy**. If you choose not to use the Android cloud to back up files, or the synchronization program that came with the device, plenty of third-party apps (such as iDrive, Mozy, HandyBackup, and so on) can be used to back up via USB to a PC, or to back up to the cloud.

One way to protect mobile devices from compromise is to patch or update the operating system. By default, you are notified automatically about available updates on Android and iOS-based devices. However, you should know where to go to manually update these devices as well. For Android go to **Settings > System Updates > HTC Software Update**. From here tap **Check Now**. If you have a connection to the Internet, you receive any information concerning system updates; an example is shown in Figure 10-24.

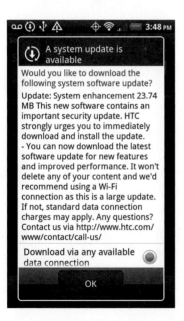

Figure 10-24   Android system update is available.

As you can see in Figure 10-24, the system update has an important new security feature that should be installed right away (which I will do when I finish writing this sentence!). Security updates are a large percentage of system updates because there

are a lot of attackers around the world that want to compromise the Android operating system. Updates for iOS can be located at **Settings > General > Software
Update**. As shown in Figure 10-25, this iOS needs to be updated from 5.0 to 5.1 and
should be done as soon as possible to patch up any security flaws, and make the best
use of the system.

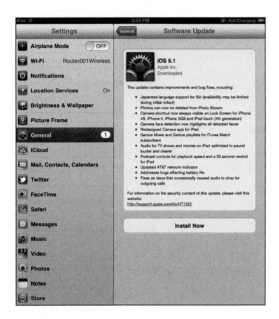

Figure 10-25   iOS system update is available.

Just like there is antivirus software for PCs, there is also AV software for mobile
devices. These are third-party applications that need to be paid for, downloaded,
and installed to the mobile device. Some common examples for Android include
McAfee's Virusscan Mobile, AVG, Lookout, Dr. Web, and NetQin.

iOS works a bit differently. iOS is a tightly controlled operating system. One of the
benefits of being a closed-source OS is that it can be more difficult to write viruses
for it, making it somewhat more difficult to compromise. But there is no OS that
can't be compromised. For the longest time there was no antivirus software for iOS.
That is until 2011 when a type of jailbreaking software called jailbreakme used a
simple PDF to move insecure code to the root of the device causing a jailbreak.

> **NOTE**   iOS **jailbreaking** is the process of removing the limitations that
> Apple imposes on its devices that run iOS. This enables users to gain root
> access to the system and allows the download of previously unavailable
> applications and software not authorized by Apple.

Jailbreakme is used to gain root level access and take control of the device without the user's consent. Finally, Apple consented to the first antivirus software for iOS, Intego's VirusBarrier, a paid download through the App Store.

Any AV software for Android or iOS should be checked regularly for updates. The mobile AV market is still somewhat new, so you have to be ready for errors, and possibly having to reinstall the AV application.

When it comes to large organizations that have many mobile devices, a **Mobile Device Management (MDM)** suite should be used. McAfee (and many other companies from AirWatch to LANDesk Mobility Manager to Sybase) have Mobile Device Management software suites that can take care of pushing updates and configuring many mobile devices from a central location. Decent quality MDM software will secure, monitor, manage, and support multiple different mobile devices across the enterprise.

Turning Off Applications and Resets

Applications can get in the way of your mobile device performing properly. Sometimes, they can't be stopped in the conventional way, and a reset is necessary. Resets might also be necessary if the device locks up, if the device has been compromised, or if hardware stops working properly. Let's talk about how to turn off apps and how to initiate resets.

Turning Off Apps

Applications opened on a mobile device continue to run in the background unless they are specifically turned off within the app or within the OS.

To turn off apps (or services) that are running on an Android-based system go to **Settings > Applications > Running Services**. That will display all the currently running services and applications as shown in Figure 10-26.

You will see several apps and services running, including the droid VNC server, Calendar, and a GPS program. To see all of the services and apps you would need to scroll down. Just like with PCs, mobile device apps use RAM. The bottom of the figure shows that 194MB of RAM is currently being used, and 139MB of RAM is free. The more RAM used by the mobile device, the worse it will perform: It will slow it down and eat up battery power. So, to close an app, simply tap it and tap Stop. You also can stop services or processes in this manner (for example, HTC DM in the figure), but this might require a Force Stop. If you are not absolutely sure what the service is, do not initiate a Force Stop.

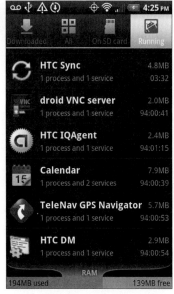

Figure 10-26   Running services on Android.

To force quit an app on an iOS-based device press and hold the Sleep/Wake button for a few seconds until a red slider appears. Then press and hold the home button until the app quits.

Third-party apps can close down all the apps in one shot if you need to save time. These include Task Manager, TasKiller, and AppControl.

If an application is causing the device to lock up and you can't stop the app, a soft reset or a hard reset is necessary.

Soft Resets

A soft reset is done by simply powering off the phone and powering it back on. This resets the drivers and the OS. So, soft resets are similar to shutting down a PC and powering it back up. Some technicians also call this a power cycle. The soft reset can help when certain applications are not functioning properly, or if network connectivity is failing. If a smartphone is still locked up when it is restarted, try pulling the battery, replacing it, and restarting the phone again. In fact, for BlackBerry devices, soft resets require a battery pull.

iOS-based devices can do a variety of more advanced software resets such as Reset All Settings, Erase All Content, Reset Networking Settings, and so on. This is available by tapping **Settings > General > Reset**.

Hard Resets

Hard resets should only be initiated when things have gone terribly wrong—for example, if hardware or software has been compromised, or has failed, and a soft reset does not fix the problem. You want to make sure that all data is backed up before performing a hard reset, as the hard reset will reset the phone to the original factory condition.

CAUTION   All data will be wiped when a hard reset is initiated on an Android device!

Hard resets vary from one device to the next. For example, most Android-based systems such as the HTC smartphone mentioned previously use the following steps:

Step 1.   Turn off the power. If the device is locked (frozen), pull the battery out and reinsert it.

Step 2.   Hold the Volume Down button and press and release the Power button.

Step 3.   This displays a menu that allows for Fastbook, Recovery, Clear Storage, and Simlock. Select Clear Storage by pressing the Volume Down button.

Step 4.   Press and release the Power button.

Step 5.   Confirm by pressing Volume Up for Yes or Volume Down for No.

At this point, the device will be reset and you will have to restore data from backup.

Hardware resets on iOS-based devices do not delete data. They instead stop all apps, and reset the OS and drivers. This can be accomplished by

Step 1.   Make sure that the device has at least 20% battery life remaining. (This process could take some time and you don't want the battery to discharge completely in the middle of it.)

Step 2.   Press the Sleep/Wake and Home buttons simultaneously for 10 seconds or until the Apple logo appears. (Ignore the red slider.)

Step 3.   Once the logo has appeared the hard reset has been initiated. It may take several minutes to complete.

To fully reset an iOS-based device such as the iPad2 to factory condition, you need to go to **Settings > General > Reset > Erase all Content and Settings**. Then initiate a hard reset.

Security Wrap-Up

For the CompTIA A+ exams, be sure to know how to set passcodes on Android and iOS devices. Understand the ways that devices can be backed up and wiped remotely. Know how to locate a lost or stolen device with a locator app. Finally, understand the basics of mobile device antivirus software and know how to perform OS updates.

Exam Preparation Tasks

Review All the Key Topics

Review the most important topics in the chapter, noted with the key topics icon in the outer margin of the page. Table 10-1 lists a reference of these key topics and the page numbers on which each is found.

Table 10-1 Key Topics for Chapter 10

Key Topic Element	Description	Page Number
Step-by-step	Upgrade a memory card	400
Figure 10-5	Smartphone using Version 2.3.3 of Android	406
Figure 10-7	iPad2 using Version 5.0 of iOS	407
Figure 10-9	G-Sensor calibration on a typical smartphone	410
Figure 10-11	Airplane Mode on a typical Apple tablet	413
Step-by-step	Android Wi-Fi connectivity	414
Step-by-step	iPad Wi-Fi connectivity	415
Bulleted list	Wi-Fi troubleshooting	416
Figure 10-15	Advanced wireless settings in Android	417
Figure 10-16	Advanced wireless settings in iOS	417
Step-by-step	Steps to configure a Bluetooth headset on an Android device	418
Step-by-step	Steps to configure a Bluetooth headset on an iOS device	420
Bulleted list	Troubleshooting Bluetooth connections	420
Step-by-step	Android POP3 account	422
Step-by-step	iPad2 POP3 account	422
Bulleted list	Troubleshooting email connections	423
Figure 10-19	PC connections options on Android	425
Figure 10-21	Apple iPad2 synchronization example	428
Figure 10-22	Android security screen	430
Figure 10-23	iPad2 passcode lock screen	431
Figure 10-26	Running services on Android	436

Define Key Terms

Define the following key terms from this chapter, and check your answers in the glossary.

Advanced RISC Machine (ARM), multitouch touch screens, screen calibration, Global Positioning System (GPS), geotracking, Wi-Fi tethering, Internet pass-through, synchronization, jailbreaking, Mobile Device Management (MDM), accelerometer, gyroscope, screen locks

Complete Hands-On Labs

Complete the hands-on labs, and then see the answers and explanations at the end of the chapter.

Lab 10-1: Troubleshoot a Mobile Wi-Fi Connection

Scenario: A customer is having trouble with a phone's Wi-Fi connection. Troubleshoot the problem. List five things that you can check and try while troubleshooting.

_____

_____

_____

_____

_____

Lab 10-2: Secure a Mobile Device

Scenario: A customer wants you to secure his Motorola tablet computer. Name five ways that you could do this:

_____

_____

_____

_____

_____

Answer Review Questions

Answer these review questions and then see the answers and explanations at the end of the chapter.

1. What type of CPU do mobile devices use?

   a. ARM

   b. Core i7

   c. Phenom II

   d. Pentium

2. What kind of display would an iPad2 use?

   a. CRT

   b. Tap screen

   c. Multitouch

   d. Singletouch

3. What type of port do Android mobile devices use for charging?

   a. Mini-USB

   b. Micro-USB

   c. Proprietary

   d. PAN

4. What are a couple of differences between a tablet computer and a laptop? (Select the two best answers.)

   a. Tablets have little or no field serviceable parts.

   b. Tablets are upgradable.

   c. Laptops don't use touch screens.

   d. Tablets use integrated flash memory as the hard drive.

   e. Tablets use RAM.

5. What are two common operating systems used by mobile devices? (Select the two best answers.)

   a. Blueberry OS

   b. iOS

   c. Android OS

   d. Google OS

6. Which OS is considered to be closed-source?

   a. Android OS

   b. iOS

   c. Bluetooth

   d. Linux

7. A user wants to stop his tablet from shifting horizontally when he turns it. Which of the following should you enable?

   a. Accelerometer

   b. Gyroscope

   c. Lock Rotation

   d. Screen Calibration

8. You are required to install a locator application on a mobile device. What is this application dependent on? (Select the two best answers.)

   a. Location Services

   b. Bluetooth

   c. GPS

   d. GSM

9. When configuring a Wi-Fi connection, what step occurs after successfully entering the SSID?

   a. Enter a passcode for the network.

   b. Select POP3.

   c. Check whether the device is within range of the WAP.

   d. Scan for networks.

10. Which of the following allows other mobile devices to share your mobile device's Internet connection?

   a. Internet pass-through

   b. Wi-Fi tethering

   c. Locator application

   d. IMAP

11. Where might you find applications for mobile devices? (Select the three best answers.)

    a. App store

    b. Windows Media Player

    c. Market

    d. Google Play

12. Which technology would you use if you wanted to connect a headset to your mobile phone?

    a. GSM

    b. Wi-Fi

    c. Bluetooth

    d. Exchange

13. What would a user need to synchronize contacts from an iPad to a PC?

    a. Android Synchronization Application

    b. iTunes

    c. Google Play

    d. ActiveSync

14. Your organization is concerned about a scenario where a mobile device with confidential data is stolen. What should you recommend first? (Select the best answer.)

    a. Remote wipe program

    b. Remote backup application

    c. Passcode locks

    d. Locator application

15. You are concerned with the possibility of jailbreaks on your organization's iPhones, and viruses on the Android-based devices. What should you implement?

    a. Firewall

    b. AV software

    c. Mobile Device Management

    d. Device reset

Answers to Hands-On Labs

Lab 10-1: Troubleshoot a Mobile Wi-Fi Connection

Answers: If a customer is having trouble with a phone's Wi-Fi connection make sure of the following:

- The device is within range.

- The correct SSID was entered (if manually connecting).

- The device supports the encryption protocol of the wireless network.

- Wi-Fi tethering or Internet pass-through is not conflicting with the wireless connection.

If you still have trouble, here are a few more methods that can help to connect or reconnect to a wireless network:

- Power cycle the mobile device.

- Power cycle Wi-Fi.

- Remove or "forget" the particular wireless network and then attempt to connect to it again.

- Check advanced settings.

Lab 10-2: Secure a Mobile Device

Answers: If a customer wants you to secure his Motorola tablet computer you should try the following:

- Enable a passcode.

- Install AV software.

- Patch the OS.

- Back up the system; consider automated remote backup.

- Consider remote wipe and locator apps.

Answers and Explanations to Review Questions

1. **A.** Most commonly, mobile devices use ARM (Advanced RISC Machine) CPUs. Core i7, Phenom II, and the older Pentium are used by desktop and laptop computers.

2. **C.** iPad2 devices and many other devices use multitouch screens, which allow more than one contact point. Cathode ray tube (CRT) is an older technology monitor used by desktop computers. You would "tap" the screen, but it is known as a touch screen. Singletouch screens are an older technology, you won't see much of that in the field.

3. **B.** Most Android mobile devices use a Micro-USB port for charging (or similar port that is backward compatible to Micro-USB). It can be plugged into a PC or into an AC outlet. Mini-USB is the older port used by mobile devices. Apple devices use a proprietary port for charging. A PAN is a personal area network, often inhabited by Bluetooth devices.

4. **A, D.** Unlike laptops, tablets are not field serviceable, and they use integrated flash memory instead of an SATA magnetic or SSD hard drive. Tablets are for the most part not upgradable. Some laptops do come with touch screens. Both tablets and laptops use RAM.

5. **B, C.** Two common OSes used by mobile devices are iOS, used by Apple devices, and Android OS, used by many different companies. *Black*Berry OS is the OS used on BlackBerry devices. Android is effectively controlled by Google. There is a Google Chrome OS designed to work with web applications, which is also open-source.

6. **B.** The Apple iOS is a closed-source vendor-specific operating system. Android is a type of Linux, which are both open-source. Bluetooth is a wireless standard, not an OS.

7. **C.** You should enable Lock Rotation on Apple devices. On Android devices you should disable Auto-rotate. The Accelerometer is a term used by Apple to describe the hardware/software that controls the three axes of movement. The Gyroscope is another term used by Apple to describe the device that measures the additional three movements (pitch, roll, and yaw) of newer Apple devices. Screen calibration is used to reset the device that measures the three axes.

8. **A, C.** The locator application will be dependent on enabled GPS or Location Services. Bluetooth deals with the communication of wireless devices over short distances. GSM is used to make phone calls over cellular networks.

9. **A.** After you enter the SSID (if it's correct) you would enter the passcode for the network. POP3 has to do with configuring an email account. If you have already entered the SSID, you should be within range of the wireless access point (WAP). Scanning for networks is the first thing you do when setting up a Wi-Fi connection.

10. **B.** Wi-Fi tethering allows a mobile device to share its Internet connection with other Wi-Fi capable devices. Internet pass-through is when the mobile device connects to a PC to share the PC's Internet connection. Locator applications are used to find lost or stolen mobile devices through GPS. IMAP is another email protocol similar to POP3.

11. **A, C, D.** When it comes to applications, Apple uses the App Store (which can also be accessed through iTunes). Android devices use the Android Market and Google Play. Windows Media Player is used to play audio and video files within Windows.

12. **C.** The Bluetooth standard is used to connect a headset and other similar devices over short range to a mobile device. GSM is used to make voice calls over cellular networks. Wi-Fi is used to connect mobile devices to the Internet. Exchange is a Microsoft email server; some mobile devices have the ability to connect to email accounts stored on an Exchange server.

13. **B.** PC users need iTunes to synchronize contacts and other data from an iPad to a PC. There are many Android sync programs, but they do not work on Apple devices. Google Play is a place to get applications and other items. ActiveSync is the older Microsoft sync program used to synchronize Windows CE and Mobile to PCs.

14. **A.** The remote wipe application is the most important one listed. This will prevent a thief from accessing the data on the device. Afterward, you might recommend a backup program (in case the data needs to be wiped), as well as passcode locks and a locator application.

15. **B.** You should implement antivirus (AV) software. This can protect against viruses and other malware as well as jailbreaks on Apple devices. As of the writing of this book, firewalls for mobile devices are not common, but that could change in the future. Mobile Device Management (MDM) is software that runs at a central computer enabling a user to configure and monitor multiple mobile devices. Device resets are used to restart the mobile device, or to reset it to factory condition depending on the type of reset, and the manufacturer of the device.

This chapter covers the following subjects:

- **Laser Printers**—This section describes the basics of laser printers and the seven-step laser printing process.

- **Inkjet Printers**—This section describes the major features of inkjet printers, how ink cartridges work, and why calibration might be necessary.

- **Thermal Printers**—This section explains the differences in direct thermal printing, thermal transfer printing, and dye-sublimation printing.

- **Impact Printers**—This section describes the operation of dot-matrix impact printers and printheads.

- **Printer Installation and Configuration**—This section demonstrates how to install printers properly, upgrade RAM and firmware, select ports, configure Windows options, and use the Print Spooler service.

- **Printer Maintenance**—Discusses how the major types of printers are maintained and when to perform those operations.

- **Printer Troubleshooting**—How to solve print quality problems, work with print queues, fix paper feed problems, and translate error codes.

This chapter covers the **CompTIA A+ 220-801 Domain 4.0 (objectives 4.1, 4.2, and 4.3)** and **CompTIA A+ 220-802 objective 4.9**.

CHAPTER 11

Printers

Printers, whether standalone devices or multifunction devices that also incorporate copy, scan, and fax features, are important output devices, second only to video displays. They output hard-copy versions of files stored on the computer, such as documents, spreadsheets, and web pages. Printers can connect to a computer's USB or parallel port, or they can connect directly to the network. This chapter focuses on laser, inkjet, thermal, and impact printers.

Generally, Windows Vista and Windows 7 behave the same as Windows XP when it comes to printers. So whenever Windows is mentioned in this chapter, the information applies to Windows XP, Vista, and 7 unless otherwise stated.

Foundation Topics

Laser Printers

220-801

Objective:
220-801: 4.1

A **laser printer** is a page printer that stores the entire contents of the page to be printed in its memory before printing it. By contrast, inkjet, thermal, and impact printers print the page as a series of narrow bands.

The major components of a laser printer include

- **Imaging drum**—Applies the page image to the transfer belt or roller; frequently combined with the toner supply in a toner cartridge

- **Fuser assembly**—Fuses the page image to the paper

- **Transfer belt or transfer roller**—Transfers the page image from the drum to the page

- **Pickup rollers**—Picks up paper

- **Paper separation pad**—Enables pickup rollers to pick up only one sheet of paper at a time

- **Duplexing assembly (optional)**—An assembly that switches paper from the front to the back side so that the printer can print on both sides of the paper

Here's a closer look at how these and other components work together to make printing possible.

Toner Cartridges

Most monochrome laser printers use **toner cartridges** that combine the imaging drum and the developer along with a supply of black toner. This provides you with an efficient and easy way to replace the laser printer items with the greatest potential to wear out.

Depending on the model, a new toner cartridge might also require that you change a wiper used to remove excess toner during the fusing cycle. This is normally packaged with the toner cartridge.

NOTE   Recycled toner cartridges are controversial in some circles, but many firms have used new and rebuilt toner cartridges for years without problems. Major manufacturers, such as Apple, HP, and Canon, place a postage-paid return label in cartridge boxes to encourage you to recycle your toner cartridges.

Reputable toner cartridge rebuilders can save you as much as 30% off the price of a new toner cartridge.

When you install the toner cartridge, be sure to follow the directions for cleaning areas near the toner cartridge. Depending on the make and model of the laser printer, this can involve cleaning the mirror that reflects the laser beam, cleaning up stray toner, or cleaning the charging corona wire or conditioning rollers inside the printer. If you need to clean the charging corona wire (also called the *primary corona wire* on some models), the laser printer will contain a special tool for this purpose. The printer instruction manual will show you how to clean the item.

Keep the cartridge closed; it is sensitive to light, and leaving it out of the printer in room light can damage the enclosed imaging drum's surface.

CAUTION   When you change a toner cartridge, take care to avoid getting toner on your face, hands, or clothing. It can leave a messy residue that's hard to clean.

The Laser Printing (EP) Process

A laser printer is an example of a page printer. A page printer does not start printing until the entire page is received. At that point, the page is transferred to the print mechanism, which pulls the paper through the printer as the page is transferred from the printer to the paper.

TIP   To master this section, make sure you

- Memorize the seven steps involved in laser printer imaging.

- Master the details of each step and their sequence.

- Be prepared to answer troubleshooting questions based on these steps.

Key Topic

The laser printing process often is referred to as the **electrophotographic (EP) process.**

Before the seven-step laser printing process can take place, the following events must occur:

- Laser printers are page-based; they must receive the entire page before they can start printing.

- After the page has been received, the printer pulls a sheet of paper into the printer with its feed rollers.

After the paper has been fed into the print mechanism, a series of seven steps takes place, which results in a printed page: processing, conditioning, exposing (also known as writing), developing, transferring, fusing, and cleaning.

The following steps describe this process in more detail. Steps 1–7 are identified in Figure 11-1.

TIP   Compared to discussions of the EP process in earlier versions of the CompTIA A+ Certification exam, the exam now recognizes the role of processing in laser printing, and has renamed some of the steps and changed the starting and ending point of the process. Use the new terms and sequence listed in this chapter as you prepare for the examination.

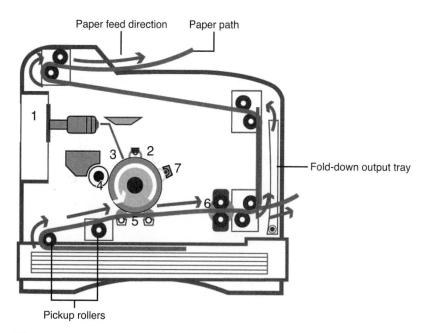

Figure 11-1   A conceptual drawing of a typical laser print process.

Step 1: Processing

The printer's raster image processing engine receives the page, font, text, and graphics data from the printer driver, creates a page image, and stores it in memory. Depending on the amount of information on the page compared to the amount of memory in the printer, the printer might need to compress the page image to store it. If there is not enough memory to store the page image, a memory error is triggered.

Step 2: Conditioning

The cylinder-shaped imaging drum receives an electrostatic charge of –600Vdc (DC voltage) from a conditioning roller. (Older printers used a primary corona wire.) The smooth surface of the drum retains this charge uniformly over its entire surface. The drum is photosensitive and will retain this charge only while kept in darkness.

Step 3: Exposing

A moving mirror moves the laser beam across the surface of the drum. As it moves, the laser beam temporarily records the image of the page to be printed on the surface of the drum by reducing the voltage of the charge applied by the charger corona to –100Vdc. Instead of using a laser beam, an LED printer activates its LED array to record the image on the page.

Step 4: Developing

The drum has toner applied to it from the developer; because the toner is electrostatic and is also at –600Vdc, the toner stays on only the portions of the drum that have been reduced in voltage to create the image. It is not attracted to the rest of the drum because both the toner and the drum are at the same voltage, and like charges repel each other. This "like charges repel" phenomenon is similar to two like poles of magnets that repel each other.

Step 5: Transferring

While the sheet is being fed into the printer, it receives an electrostatic charge of +600Vdc from a corona wire or roller; this enables it to attract toner from the drum, which is negatively charged (see Step 3). As the drum's surface moves close to the charged paper, the toner adhering to the drum is attracted to the electrostatically charged paper to create the printed page.

As the paper continues to move through the printer, its charge is canceled by a static eliminator strip, so the paper itself isn't attracted to the drum.

Step 6: Fusing

The printed sheet of paper is pulled through fuser rollers, using high temperatures (approximately 350°F) to heat the toner and press it into the paper. The printed image is slightly raised above the surface of the paper.

The paper is ejected into the paper tray, and the drum must be prepared for another page.

Step 7: Cleaning

To prepare the drum for a new page, the image of the preceding page placed on the drum by the laser or LED array (see Step 3) is removed by a discharge lamp. Toner that is not adhering to the surface of the drum is scraped from the drum's surface for reuse.

Color Laser Printing Differences

Color laser printers differ from monochrome laser printers in two important ways: They include four different colors of toner (cyan, magenta, yellow, and black), and the imaging drum is separate from the toner. Thus, instead of waste toner being reused as in a monochrome laser printer that has a toner cartridge with an integrated imaging drum, waste toner in a color printer is sent to a separate waste toner container.

Color laser printers use the same basic process as monochrome lasers, but some use a transfer belt instead of an imaging drum. The use of a transfer belt enables all four colors (cyan, magenta, yellow, and black) to be placed on the paper at the same time, enabling color print speeds comparable to monochrome print speeds. When a transfer belt is used, the conditioning and transferring processes are performed on the transfer belt. See Figure 11-2.

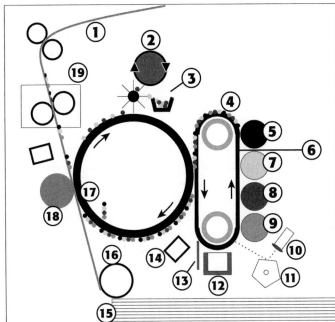

1. Paper path
2. Cleaning unit
3. Waste toner
4. Toner particles
5. Black toner
6. OPC belt
7. Yellow toner
8. Magenta toner
9. Cyan toner
10. Laser
11. Laser mirror
12. Charger
13. Cleaning blade
14. Erase lamp
15. Paper in paper tray
16. Paper pickup
17. Imaging drum
18. Transfer roller
19. Fusing rollers

Figure 11-2 The printing process in a typical color laser that uses a transfer belt.

Inkjet Printers

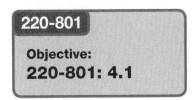

220-801

Objective:
220-801: 4.1

Inkjet printers represent the most popular type of printer in small-office/home-office (SOHO) use today and are also popular in large offices. Their print quality can rival laser printers, and virtually all inkjet printers in use today can print both color and black text and photographs.

From a tightly spaced group of nozzles, **inkjet printers** spray controlled dots of ink onto the paper to form characters and graphics. On a typical 5,760 × 1,440 dots per inch (dpi) printer, the number of nozzles can be as high as 180 for black ink and more than 50 per color (cyan, magenta, and yellow). The tiny ink droplet size and high nozzle density enables inkjet printers to perform the seemingly impossible at resolutions as high as 1,200dpi or higher: fully formed characters from what is actually a high-resolution, non-impact, dot-matrix technology.

Inkjet printers are character/line printers. They print one line at a time of single characters or graphics up to the limit of the printhead matrix. Inkjet printers are functionally fully formed character printers because their inkjet matrix of small droplets forming the image is so carefully controlled that individual dots are not visible.

Larger characters are created by printing a portion of the characters across the page, advancing the page to allow the printhead to print another portion of the characters, and so on until the entire line of characters is printed. Thus, an inkjet printer is both a character and a line printer because it must connect lines of printing to build large characters. Some inkjet printers require realignment after each ink cartridge/printhead change to make sure that vertical lines formed by multiple printhead passes stay straight (this may be automatic or require the user to start the process); with other models, alignment can be performed on demand through a utility provided as part of the printer driver when print quality declines due to misalignment.

The essential components in the inkjet printing process include ink cartridges, print heads, roller, feeder, duplexing assembly, carriage, and belt. Figure 11-3 shows how many of these components look in a typical printer.

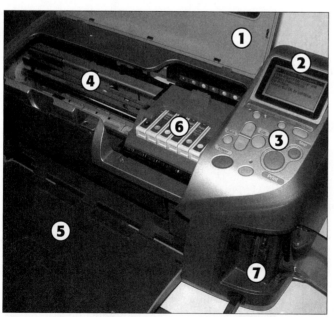

1. Dust cover
2. LCD instruction panel
3. Control panel
4. Printhead drive belt
5. Output tray
6. Ink cartridges
7. Flash memory card reader

Figure 11-3   A typical inkjet printer with its cover open.

Ink Cartridges

Inkjet printers use ink cartridges filled with liquid ink for printing. Some older inkjet printers use a large tank of black ink and a second tank with separate compartments for each color (typically cyan, magenta, and yellow; some models feature light versions of some of these colors for better photo-printing quality). However, almost all inkjet printers produced for a number of years use a separate cartridge for each color. This improves print economy for the user because only one color at a time needs to be replaced. With a multicolor cartridge, the entire cartridge needs to be replaced, even when only one of the colors runs out.

NOTE   Inkjet printers are sometimes referred to as CMYK devices because of the four ink colors used on most models: **c**yan, **m**agenta, **y**ellow, and blac**k**.

Depending on the printer, the printhead might be incorporated into the ink tank; be a separate, user-replaceable item; or be built in to the printer.

Some inkjet printers feature an extra-wide (more nozzles) printhead or a dual printhead for speedy black printing. Some models enable the user to replace either the ink cartridge only or an assembly composed of the printhead and a replaceable ink cartridge.

An inkjet printer is only as good as its printhead and ink cartridges. Clogged or damaged printheads or ink cartridges render the printer useless. If an inkjet printer fails after its warranty expires, you should check service costs carefully before repairing the unit. Failed inkjet printers are often "throwaway" models and can be replaced, rather than repaired, even during the warranty period.

CAUTION   Inkjet printers should never be turned off with the power switch on a surge suppressor; doing so prevents the printer from self-capping its ink cartridges, which is a major cause of service calls and printer failures. Cleaning the printhead, with the printer's own cleaning feature, a cleaning utility built in to the printer driver, or with a moistened cleaning sheet, will restore most printers to service.

Always use the printer's own power switch, which enables the printer to protect the ink cartridges and perform other periodic tasks (such as self-cleaning) properly.

Two major methods are used by inkjet printers to create the ink dots that make up the page. Most inkjet printers heat the ink to boiling, creating a tiny bubble of ink that is allowed to escape through the printhead onto the paper. This is the origin of the name BubbleJet for the Canon line of inkjet printers. Printers using this method feature either ink cartridges that include the printhead or printheads with removable ink cartridge inserts. In case of a severely clogged printhead, you can simply replace the ink cartridge if the ink cartridge incorporates the printhead.

Another popular method uses a piezo-electric crystal to distribute the ink through the printhead. This method makes achieving high resolutions easier; the Epson printers using this method were the first to achieve 5,760 × 1,440dpi resolutions. This method also provides a longer printhead life because the ink is not heated and cooled. However, the printheads are built in to the printer, making cleaning a severely clogged printhead more difficult. Both types of inkjet printers are sometimes referred to as drop-on-demand printers.

During the inkjet print process

1. The paper or media in a feed tray is pulled into position by a roller mechanism.

2. The printhead is suspended on a carriage over the paper and is moved across the paper by a belt. As the printhead moves across the paper, it places black and color ink droplets as directed by the printer driver.

3. At the end of the line, the paper or media is advanced and the printhead either reverses direction and continues to print (often referred to as Hi-Speed mode) or returns to the left margin before printing continues.

4. After the page is completed, the media is ejected.

Calibrating the Printer

Inkjet printers and multifunction units might require or recommend some type of **calibration**, most typically printhead alignment. This process involves printing one or more sheets of paper and selecting the print setting that produces straight lines.

NOTE With some printers and multifunction units, it might be necessary to realign the printhead each time after changing ink cartridges. However, with others, it might be an optional utility that you can run on an as-needed basis.

Thermal Printers

220-801

Objective:
220-801: 4.1

Thermal printers use heat transfer to create text and graphics on the paper. Thermal printers are used in point-of-sale and retail environments as well as for some types of portable printing.

Thermal printers are available using three different technologies:

- **Thermal transfer**
- **Direct thermal**
- **Dye sublimation**

Thermal printers can use a dot-matrix print mechanism or a dye-sublimation technology to transfer images. Some thermal printers use heat-sensitive paper, whereas others use a wax, resin, or dye ribbon to create the image. Let's start by discussing the thermal printer ribbon.

Thermal Print Processes

Although thermal transfer, direct thermal printing, and dye-sublimation all involve heating the elements in a printhead to a particular temperature to transfer the image, there are some differences in operation. The basic process of thermal printing works like this:

1. The printhead has a matrix of dots that can be heated in various combinations to create text and graphics.

2. The printhead transfers text and graphics directly to heat-sensitive thermal paper in direct thermal printing or to a ribbon that melts onto the paper in thermal transfer printing.

3. If a multicolor ribbon is used on a thermal transfer or dye-sublimation printer, each ribbon is moved past the printhead to print the appropriate color. In the case of dye-sublimation printers, the paper is moved back into position to enable the next color to be printed.

4. After all colors have been printed, the paper is ejected.

Figure 11-4 compares direct thermal and thermal transfer printing technologies.

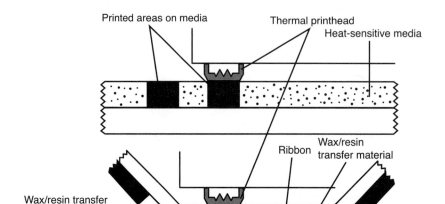

Figure 11-4   Direct thermal (top) and thermal transfer (bottom) printing technologies.

Thermal Printer Ribbons

Thermal transfer printers use wax or resin-based ribbons, which are often bundled with paper made especially for the printer. Dye-sublimation (dye-sub) printers use dye-based film ribbon technology to print continuous-tone photographs. Examples of consumer-grade dye-sublimation printers include Kodak printer docks and Canon's Selphy CP series; these printers print 4 × 6-inch photos. Many vendors also sell larger-format, dye-sublimation printers for use in photo labs and professional photography studios.

Figure 11-5 illustrates a typical dye-sublimation ribbon for a Canon Selphy CP printer.

Thermal transfer printers used in point-of-sale or retail environments typically use non-impact, dot-matrix printheads.

Thermal Printer Paper

Direct thermal printers use heat-sensitized paper, whereas thermal transfer printers might use either standard copy paper or glossy photo paper, depending on their intended use.

Figure 11-5 A dye-sublimation ribbon for a 4 × 6-inch photo printer (Canon Selphy CP).

If the printer uses direct thermal printing, heat-sensitive paper with characteristics matching the printer's design specifications must be used. For portable printers using direct thermal printing, such as the Brother (formerly Pentax) PocketJet series, the usual source for such paper is the printer vendor or its authorized resellers. If the direct thermal printer is used for bar codes or point-of-sale transactions, you can get suitable paper or label stock from bar code or POS equipment suppliers and resellers.

If the printer uses thermal transfer and is not designed for photo printing, most smooth paper and label stocks are satisfactory, including both natural and synthetic materials. However, dye-sublimation photo printers must use special media kits that include both a ribbon and suitable photo paper stocks.

Impact Printers

> **220-801**
>
> **Objective:**
> **220-801: 4.1**

Impact printers are so named because they use a mechanical printhead that presses against an inked ribbon to print characters and graphics. Impact printers are the oldest printer technology and are primarily used today in industrial and point-of-sale applications.

Dot-matrix printers, the most common form of impact printers, are so named because they create the appearance of fully formed characters from dots placed on the page.

Impact Dot Matrix Print Process

Impact dot-matrix printers have the following parts moving in coordination with each other during the printing process:

Step 1.   The paper is moved past the printhead vertically by pull or push tractors or by a platen.

Step 2.   The printhead moves across the paper horizontally, propelled along the printhead carriage by a drive belt, printing as it moves from left to right. Bidirectional printing prints in both directions but is often disabled for high-quality printing because it can be difficult to align the printing precisely.

Step 3.   As the printhead moves, the pins in the printhead are moving in and out against an inked ribbon as the printhead travels across the paper to form the text or create graphics.

Step 4.   The ribbon is also moving to reduce wear during the printing process.

Steps 1–4 are repeated for each line until the page is printed. Figure 11-6 illustrates a typical impact dot-matrix printer.

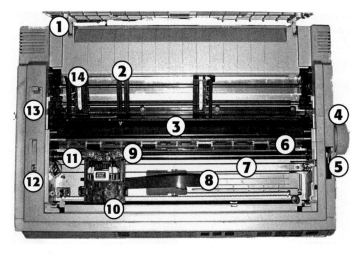

1. Rear cover (top cover removed, not shown)
2. Paper supports for tractor-feed paper path
3. Platen for using single sheets of paper
4. Manual paper advance knob
5. Paper bail lifter
6. Paper bail
7. Timing/drive belt
8. Printhead signal control cable
9. Printhead with heat sink
10. Ribbon holder
11. Printhead support rod
12. Head gap adjustment
13. Tractor/friction-feed selector lever
14. Tractor feed

Figure 11-6   Components of a typical impact dot-matrix printer. The model pictured is a wide-carriage version, but its features are typical of models using either standard or wide-carriage paper.

Impact Dot-Matrix Printheads

The most common types of printheads include 9-pin, 18-pin (two columns of nine pins), and 24-pin (which produces Near Letter Quality or NLQ quality printing when used in best quality mode).

Figure 11-7 shows actual print samples from a typical 9-pin printer's draft mode, a typical 24-pin printer's draft mode, and the Near Letter Quality (NLQ) mode of the same 24-pin printer.

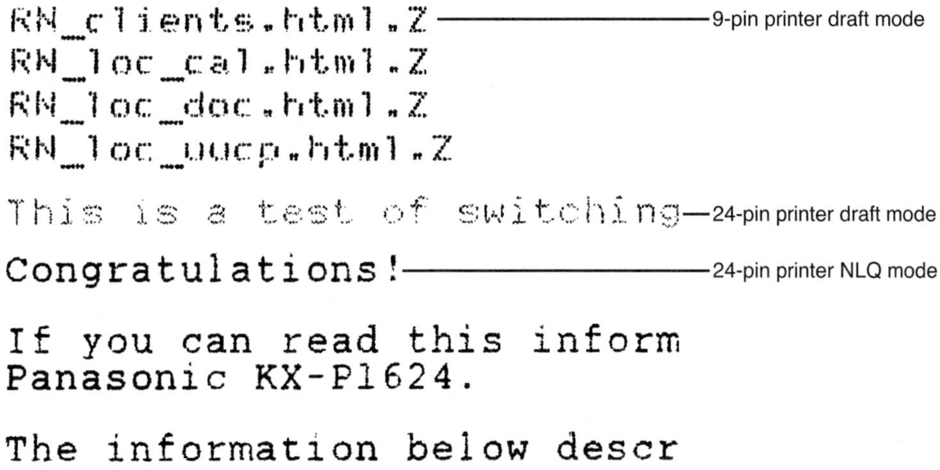

```
RN_clients.html.Z ——————————————— 9-pin printer draft mode
RN_loc_cal.html.Z
RN_loc_doc.html.Z
RN_loc_uucp.html.Z

This is a test of switching — 24-pin printer draft mode

Congratulations! ———————————— 24-pin printer NLQ mode

If you can read this inform
Panasonic KX-P1624.

The information below descr
```

Figure 11-7 Actual print samples illustrating the differences in 24-pin and 9-pin impact dot-matrix printers.

> **NOTE** The print samples shown in Figure 11-7 are taken from printers that use 8.5 × 11-inch or wider paper sizes. The printhead design and print quality vary greatly on printers that use smaller paper sizes in point-of-sale applications.

Impact Printer Ribbons

Printer ribbons for impact printers use various types of cartridge designs. Some span the entire width of the paper, and others snap over the printhead. Figure 11-8 compares various types of ribbons for impact printers.

Figure 11-8 Some typical ribbons for impact dot-matrix printers.

Impact Printer Paper and Media

Impact printers use plain uncoated paper or labels in various widths and sizes. Impact printers designed for point-of-sale receipt printing might use roll paper or larger sizes of paper. When larger sizes of paper are used, these printers typically use a tractor-feed mechanism to pull or push the paper past the printhead. Paper used with tractor-fed printers has fixed or removable sprocket holes on both sides of the paper.

Printer Installation and Configuration

> **220-801**
>
> **Objective:**
> **220-801: 4.2**

Printer drivers are used to control and configure printers and the print features of multifunction devices. Printer drivers might be supplied by Microsoft on the Windows distribution media or by the printer vendor. Generally, printer drivers provided by the printer vendor offer more configuration options and utilities for cleaning and maintenance than the drivers provided by Microsoft. Driver features might vary by Windows version, even if a single driver file supports more than one Windows version.

NOTE It's a good idea to check for updated versions of printer or multifunction device drivers before installing the device and periodically thereafter. Updated drivers might include bug fixes or enhanced features. Also, if a system is upgraded to a newer version of Windows or another operating system, you will need new drivers. You can use Windows Update to locate drivers or download them directly from the printer vendor.

Installing a Printer

Device drivers for printers can be installed in one of the following ways:

- Using the Add Printer option in the Printers and Faxes folder in Control Panel

- Using the Add Printer option in the Devices and Printers folder in Control Panel (Windows 7)

- Installing from a vendor-supplied driver disc

- Installing from a vendor-supplied downloadable file

Using the Add Printer Wizard (Windows Vista and XP)

The Add Printer option is suitable if Windows includes a suitable driver and the enhanced features that might be provided by a vendor-supplied driver are not necessary. To install a printer using the Add Printer Wizard, follow these steps:

Step 1. Open the **Printers** (Vista) or **Printer and Faxes** (XP) folder. You can use the **Control Panel** or a shortcut located on the **Start** button such as **Settings**, **Printer**, or **Printer and Faxes**.

Step 2. Click the **Add a Printer** link in the Printer Tasks pane to open the Add Printer Wizard.

Step 3. Choose whether the new printer is connected through a local port or through a network—Windows XP/Vista automatically detects a Plug-and-Play (PnP) printer by default (assuming the printer is turned on and connected to your computer).

Step 4. Select the port (for local printers) or network share, wireless or Bluetooth network (for network, wireless, or Bluetooth printers). If the printer is a network printer, specify whether you want to send MS-DOS print jobs to the printer.

Step 5. Select the brand and model of your printer.

If you have an installation disk or CD-ROM provided by the vendor, click **Have Disk** and browse to the installation disk or CD-ROM for the printer (see Figure 11-9). Windows Vista also offers Windows Update for a driver source.

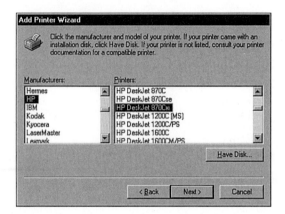

Figure 11-9   Selecting a printer by brand and model (Windows XP); if the printer isn't listed, or if you have a driver disk, click **Have Disk**.

Step 6.   Specify whether the printer will be the default printer (if you are installing an additional printer).

Step 7.   Specify whether you want to share the printer if prompted.

Step 8.   You can opt out of printing a test page; however, printing a test page is recommended to help make sure your new printer is working properly.

Step 9.   Vista and XP display the printer selections. With Windows XP only, you can click the **Back** button to make changes. Windows Vista does not let you go back at this point.

Step 10.   Click **Finish** to install the driver.

After you click Finish, the printer will be installed into the Printers folder and will be available to all Windows applications.

Using the Add Printer Wizard (Windows 7)

You can use the Add Printer option if Windows includes a suitable driver and the enhanced features that might be provided by a vendor-supplied driver are not necessary. To install a printer using the Add Printer Wizard in Windows 7, follow these steps:

Step 1.   Open the **Devices and Printers** folder. You can use the Control Panel or a shortcut located on the Start button.

Step 2.   Click the **Add a Printer** link in the menu.

Continue with Steps 3–10 from the instructions for Windows XP and Vista described in the preceding section.

Installing a Printer with a Vendor-Supplied Driver

Whether you use a vendor-supplied install disc or a downloaded file, the installation process is quite different from the Add Printer method:

Step 1. Insert the install disc into the computer's CD or DVD drive. After a few moments, the install program might start automatically. If it doesn't, open My Computer or Computer, navigate to the CD or DVD drive, and double-click the setup program's icon. If the driver file was downloaded, navigate to the folder containing the downloaded install program. Double-click the .exe file to start the installation program.

Step 2. Connect your device to the USB or FireWire port, but do not turn it on. (If the device uses a non-PnP port, you must connect it while the system is turned off.)

Step 3. The install program starts. If prompted, select your device.

Step 4. When prompted, turn on your device. When the install program detects your device, it will complete the installation process.

Step 5. You might be prompted to restart your computer after the installation process is over. If that happens, remove the install disc and restart your system.

Installing RAM

Laser and solid ink printers use memory modules to hold more page information, to reduce or eliminate the need to compress page information when printing, or to enable higher-resolution printing with complex pages.

Most recent printers with upgradeable memory use the DIMM memory module form factor, but printers do not use the same types of DIMMs as desktop or laptop computers. To order additional memory, you can

- Contact the printer vendor.

- Contact a third-party memory vendor that offers compatible memory.

To install a DIMM or SODIMM-based memory module, follow this basic procedure:

Step 1. Consult the printer's service manual to determine how to upgrade printer memory properly.

Step 2. Shut down the printer, and disconnect it from AC power.

Step 3.   Disconnect interface cables (USB, Ethernet, parallel, and so on) from the printer.

Step 4.   Open the door covering the upgrade socket.

Step 5.   Remove the memory module from its antistatic packaging. Don't touch the memory chips or connectors on the module.

Step 6.   Line up the module with the socket, and make sure the label and contact side of the module faces toward you.

Step 7.   Insert the module into the socket at a slight angle and lower it into place until the retaining clips on each side of the socket click (see Figure 11-10).

Step 8.   Close the door over the upgrade socket.

Step 9.   Reconnect power and data cables, and restart the printer.

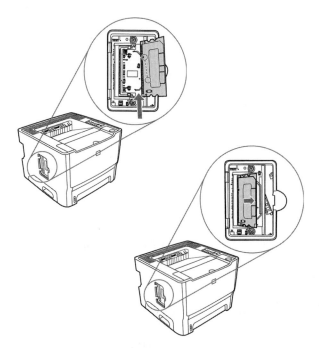

Figure 11-10   Inserting a DIMM into a printer and locking it into place.

TIP   After installing memory, make sure the printer properties sheet accurately reflects the installed amount of RAM.

Upgrading Firmware

Firmware (software on a chip) is used to change the personality of a printer or to add features. You can use firmware updates to add Postscript compatibility to a printer that supports PCL, to add support for Bluetooth or other interface types, or to fix various bugs and problems.

You can perform firmware updates for printers in a variety of ways, including

- Update via the USB cable.

- Update via connection of a flash memory card or USB flash memory drive.

- Install a personality DIMM.

- Update flash memory via sending the upgrade file via FTP to a networked printer. (This method also works if a directly attached printer is connected via the USB port and is shared on the network.)

- Update flash memory via sending the file via the parallel port to a directly attached printer.

The exact method you should use depends on the printer. Consult the support website for the printer to determine whether a firmware update is available, what its benefits are, and how to install it.

Printer Interface Types

Interface types used by printers include the following:

- **USB**—Used by most inkjet, solid ink, dye-sublimation, thermal, and laser printers, either when connected directly to a PC or connected to a network via a print server. Also used by most multifunction (all-in-one) units.

- **Parallel**—Used by legacy impact printers as well as older inkjet and laser printers. Also used by some legacy all-in-one units.

- **RS-232 (serial)**—Used by legacy impact and laser printers.

- **SCSI**—Used by high-end Postscript laser printers.

- **Bluetooth**—Used by some recent inkjet and laser printers.

- **Infrared**—Used by some legacy inkjet, impact, and laser printers.

- **Ethernet**—Used by inkjet and laser printers that are network-ready.

- **IEEE 802.11 (wireless Ethernet)**—Used by inkjet and laser printers that are wireless network-ready.

- **FireWire (IEEE 1394)**—Used by some recent high-end inkjet printers used by graphic designers.

Many printers include more than one interface.

If you need to connect a printer using a different interface than its normal interface, you can sometimes use an adapter or print server device.

Adding Bluetooth Support

To add support for the Bluetooth short-range wireless network to a printer with a USB port, connect a Bluetooth printer adapter. Note that the best results are usually obtained when the adapter is made especially for your printer.

Adding Ethernet Support

To add support for Ethernet local area networking to a printer that does not have a built-in Ethernet port, connect it to an Ethernet print server. Print servers are available in versions that support USB or parallel printers, and they enable the printer to be accessed via the print server's IP address. Figure 11-11 illustrates a typical Ethernet print server for USB printers.

Figure 11-11   Front and rear views of an Ethernet print server that supports USB printers.

NOTE   Some laser printers can be upgraded with an internal Ethernet print server card.

When a printer includes its own Ethernet port, it is assigned an IP address on a TCP/IP network; similarly, a print server is also assigned an IP address on a TCP/IP network. To configure a printer for network use, you might need to install a network printer driver instead of the normal printer driver; you also need to specify whether the printer has a manually assigned IP address or receives an IP address from a DHCP server on the network. To learn more about TCP/IP, see Chapter 16, "Networking."

Adding 802.11 Wireless Ethernet (Wi-Fi) Support

To add support for 802.11 Wireless Ethernet local area networking to a printer, connect it to a Wireless Ethernet (Wi-Fi) print server. Print servers are available in versions that support USB or parallel printers, and enable the printer to be accessed via the print server's IP address.

> **NOTE** Most Wireless Ethernet print servers also include Ethernet support.

Adding Infrared Support

To add support for infrared (IrDA) printing to a printer, connect it to an IrDA adapter. These are available for either USB printers or parallel printers.

Printer Sharing in Windows

Printers can be shared on a network using the following methods:

- Printers with built-in Ethernet or Wi-Fi networking can be connected directly to a network.

- Printers can be connected to Ethernet or Wi-Fi print sharing devices.

- Printers directly connected to a computer on a network can be shared with other network user.

Printer sharing in Windows XP requires the computer with the shared printer to install File and Printer Sharing. This can be installed automatically by running the Home Networking Wizard and specifying this option or manually by enabling File and Printer Sharing for Microsoft Networks in the properties sheet for your network adapter. All computers on the network must be part of the same workgroup to use a shared printer.

Printer sharing in Windows Vista and Windows 7 is enabled through the Network and Sharing Center. All computers on a Windows Vista network, or a network with a mixture of Windows 7, Vista, and XP (any two or all three), must be part of the same workgroup.

> **TIP** With Windows XP SP2, you might need to open the Windows Firewall and set File and Printer Sharing as an exception (a program allowed access by the firewall).

If you have only Windows 7 on a network specified as a Home network, you can also set up a homegroup to permit all computers in the homegroup to access a shared printer.

Configuring Options and Device Settings

Users can change printer options before printing a document. However, if the printer will be used in the same way most of the time, it can be useful to configure the device with the most commonly used settings.

Printer options are configured through the printer's properties sheet. You can access printer properties sheets by doing one of the following:

- Right-click the printer's icon in the Printers, Printers and Faxes, or Devices and Printers folder in Control Panel and select **Printer Properties**. Use this method to set defaults that will be used for all print jobs.

- Open the Print dialog in an application and click the **Properties** button. Use this method to change settings for the current print job.

If the printer uses a Microsoft-supplied printer driver, the properties sheet will have some or all of the following tabs:

- **General**—Features the Print Test Page button, which prints a test page of graphics and text, listing the driver files, and the Printing Preferences button, which opens the Printer Preferences menu.

- **Sharing**—Enables or disables printer sharing over the network. In Windows XP this is available only if File and Print Sharing is enabled on the system. To enable Printer Sharing in Windows 7/Vista go to **Start**, **Control Panel**, **Network and Sharing Center**, click the down arrow for Printer Sharing, and select the radio button labeled **Turn on Printer Sharing**.

NOTE   The Sharing tab also features the Additional Drivers button. When configured by the local user, this permits remote users to connect to the printer with other versions of Windows. If this feature is not configured, users running other versions of Windows must download and install the appropriate driver for their version of Windows before they can connect to a remote printer.

- **Ports**—Lists and configures printer ports and paths to network printers.
- **Advanced**—Schedules the availability of the printer, selects spooling methods, printer priority, print defaults (quality, paper type, orientation, and so forth), printer driver, print processor, and separator page.

- **Security**—Enables you to select which users can print and manage print jobs and documents; available only if user-level sharing is enabled, such as if the printer is connected to a computer that is part of a network being managed by a Windows server or if Windows XP's Simple File Sharing feature is disabled.

- **Device Settings**—Selects the default paper tray, font substitutions, page protection, font cartridges, and printer memory.

- **Color Management**—Selects the default color profile.

- **About/Version Information**—Lists the driver version and/or driver files used by the printer.

The selections made on these tabs are automatically saved as the defaults when you click OK and close the dialog.

TIP   Some laser printers report the amount of memory installed to the operating system so that the properties sheet reflects this information. However, you should not assume that all laser printers do so. Be sure to verify that the memory size shown in the printer properties sheet is accurate. If not, change it to match the installed memory size.

To determine the installed memory size, use the printer's own print test option.

The **Printer Preferences** button on the General tab opens the preferences menu for the printer. The preferences menu can vary a great deal from printer to printer, but typically includes options such as these:

- **Inkjet printers**—Paper type, paper size, paper layout, print mode, utilities (head cleaning, alignment, ink levels), and watermarking

- **Laser printers**—Layout, page order, resolution, font substitutions, printer features, pages per sheet, and watermarking

As you can see in Figures 11-12 and 11-13, these options can appear in various menus, depending on the printer and the operating system in use.

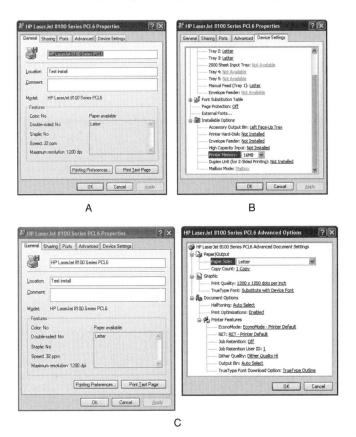

Figure 11-12   Windows XP General (a), Device Settings (b), and Advanced Print Properties (c) properties sheets for a typical departmental laser printer.

NOTE   In Windows 7, select **Printing Preferences** from the right-click menu to go directly to the multitabbed printing preferences menu, such as the one in Figure 11-13. To go to more general settings, such as the ones shown in Figure 11-12, select **Printer Properties**. If you select Properties (not Printer Properties or Printing Preferences) from the right-click menu in Devices and Printers for a printer or multifunction device, you see a two-tabbed interface: General lists basic device information, and Hardware lists the device functions.

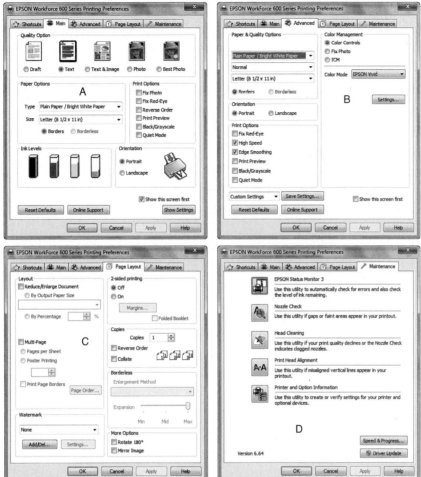

Figure 11-13 Windows 7 Main (a), Advanced (b), Page Layout (c), and Maintenance (d) preference sheets for a typical ink jet multifunction device using a vendor-supplied driver.

To save changes to default settings, click **Apply** and then **OK**. Some printers offer the option to save settings under different names, so you can retrieve a particular setting before printing a particular type of document, such as a photo on glossy paper or a web page on plain paper.

TIP Before configuring options and settings on a printer, consult with the user to find out how the printer will be used.

Printing a Test Page

If you use the Add Printer Wizard to install a printer, you are prompted to print a test page at the end of the installation process. You can also print a test page by clicking the **Print Test Page** button from the General tab of Printer properties. A typical Windows test page resembles the one in Figure 11-14.

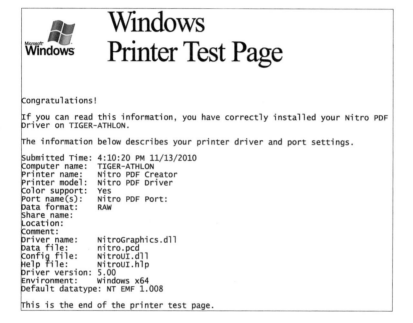

Figure 11-14   A Windows 7 test print page.

Note in particular whether the Windows logo looks correct: On a color printer, the upper-left quadrant is red, the upper-right quadrant is green, the lower-left quadrant is blue, and the lower-right quadrant is yellow. All quadrants feature shading. If you see streaks, lines, or other print quality problems in either the logo or text printing, or if the printer doesn't print, you need to troubleshoot your printer to solve the problem. See the "Printer Troubleshooting" section in this chapter.

With most laser printers, you can also print a self-test page by pressing a button or combination of buttons on the printer. The self-test page lists the firmware revision used by the printer, the number of pages printed, and the amount of installed memory.

Working with the Print Spooler

The **print spooler** service receives print jobs and releases them to the printer in the order received. After a print job is received, it is placed in a print queue until the printer is ready to receive it.

The print spooler service should be configured to start automatically. (As of Windows XP Service Pack 2, this is the default setting.) To verify that the spooler is properly configured, follow this procedure:

Step 1. Right-click **Computer/My Computer** and select **Manage**. (This opens the Computer Management Console.)

Step 2. Double-click **Services and Applications** in the right pane.

Step 3. Double-click **Services** in the right pane.

Step 4. Scroll down to Print Spooler to make sure the spooler status is listed as Started and the startup type is listed as Automatic (see Figure 11-15).

Step 5. To make changes in the Print Spooler settings, double-click the **Print Spooler** listing. This opens the Print Spooler properties sheet. Make the wanted changes, click **Apply**, and then click **OK**.

> **NOTE** Some inkjet printers use their own print spooler or other printer utility service. These services should also be configured to start automatically. Check the printer's documentation to determine the name of the service.

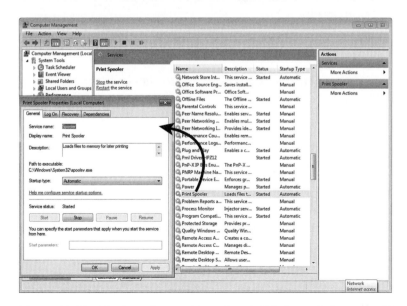

Figure 11-15 Viewing print spooler settings in Windows 7's Computer Management console.

To learn how to handle a backed up or stalled print queue, see the "Backed Up Print Queue" section later in this chapter.

Printer Maintenance

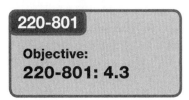

To achieve and retain maximum print quality, laser, inkjet, thermal, and impact printers must be maintained periodically as described in the following sections.

Laser Printer Maintenance

The major elements in laser printer maintenance include replacing toner, applying a maintenance kit, calibration (color lasers only), and cleaning.

Replacing Toner Cartridges

If the laser printer's toner cartridge also includes the imaging drum, replacing the toner cartridge also replaces the imaging drum. Because the imaging drum's surface can become damaged, leaving marks on print output, changing the toner cartridge is helpful in improving print quality.

Installing Maintenance Kits

Many HP and other laser printers feature components that should be replaced at periodic intervals. These components often include fuser assemblies, air filters, transfer rollers, pickup rollers, other types of rollers, and separation pads. These components wear out over time and can usually be purchased as a maintenance kit as well as separately.

A printer that uses a maintenance kit displays a message or an error code with a meaning such as Perform Printer Maintenance or Perform User Maintenance when the printer reaches the recommended page count for maintenance kit replacement. Depending on the printer model and whether it is used for color or monochrome printing, the recommended page count could be as few as 50,000 pages or as much as 300,000 pages or more.

NOTE   Sources for maintenance kits can also provide useful installation instructions. Sources for HP and Lexmark printers include PrinterTechs.com, Inc. (www.printertechs.com/maintenance-kits.php) and Depot International (www.depot-america.com) among others.

Resetting Paper Counts

After a fuser assembly or full maintenance kit is installed in a laser printer, the page count must be reset; otherwise, you will not know when to perform recommended maintenance again. Typically, the page count is reset by pressing a specified combination of buttons on the printer's control panel.

NOTE   If the printer is under service contract or being charged on a per-page (or click) basis, it is not recommended to reset the paper count after servicing. However, most laser printers print the page count when you perform a self-test.

Calibration

Color laser printers should be calibrated if image quality declines. The calibration process on a color laser printer adjusts image density settings to make up for changes caused by environmental differences or aging print cartridges.

Some color laser printers perform automatic calibration, but you can also force the printer to perform calibration on an as-needed basis. See the instruction manual for your printer for details.

Cleaning

Because laser printers use fine-grain powdered toner, keeping the inside of a laser printer clean is an important step in periodic maintenance. If you want to use a vacuum cleaner to pick up loose toner, be sure to use a vacuum cleaner designed to pick up toner because toner particles are so small they can pass through conventional bags and filters. If you prefer to use a damp cloth, be sure to turn off the laser printer and disconnect it from power first.

To keep the paper path and rollers clean, use cleaning sheets made for laser printers, as follows:

Step 1.   Insert the sheet into the manual feed tray on the laser printer.

Step 2.   Create a short document with Notepad, WordPad, or some other text editor, and print it on the sheet.

As the sheet passes through the printer, it cleans the rollers. If a specialized cleaning sheet is not available, you can also use transparency film designed for laser printers. Some laser printers use a special software program to print a cleaning pattern onto plain paper.

CAUTION   Never use transparency media not designed for laser printers in a laser printer. Copier or inkjet media isn't designed to handle the high heat of a laser printer and can melt or warp and possibly damage the printer.

Inkjet Printer Maintenance

Ink cartridge replacement, calibration, nozzle check, and head cleaning are the major elements in maintaining an inkjet printer.

Replacing Ink Cartridges

Some printers run automatic nozzle cleaning or calibration routines when you change ink cartridges. If the ink cartridge includes a printhead, whenever you change the ink cartridge, you also change the printhead. Consequently, replacing ink cartridges is the single best maintenance item you can perform on an inkjet printer.

Calibration

Inkjet printers might require or recommend some type of calibration, most typically printhead alignment. This process involves printing one or more sheets of paper and selecting the print setting that produces straight lines. Some printers perform this step automatically, whereas others might require user intervention to determine the best setting.

Some inkjet printers can use two printing methods: unidirectional, in which the printer prints only when the print head is moving from left to right; and bidirectional, in which the printer prints when the print head is moving in either direction (left to right or right to left). If the printhead is misaligned, bidirectional printing (sometimes referred to as high-speed printing) will have much poorer print quality than unidirectional printing.

Be sure to align the printhead as needed, using the calibration or alignment utility provided in the printer driver (see Figure 11-16a), to permit successful use of bidirectional printing.

To enable bidirectional printing, select this option (when it's offered) in the Print Preferences menu (see Figure 11-16b).

A   B

Figure 11-16   Aligning the printhead (a) helps produce better-quality, high-speed (bidirectional) printing (b).

NOTE   With some printers, you might need to realign the printhead each time after changing ink cartridges. However, with others, it might be an optional utility that you can run on an as-needed basis.

Nozzle Check and Head Cleaning

Periodically, especially if a printer has not been used for awhile or has been used only for monochrome printing, it's a good idea to use the nozzle check routine to verify that all the printheads' nozzles are working correctly.

The **nozzle check** routine prints a pattern that uses all the nozzles in all the printheads and displays the pattern's correct appearance. Compare the printout to the on-screen display, and if you see gaps or missing colors, activate the head-cleaning routine. Repeat these steps until the nozzle check printout matches the screen display.

Depending on the printer, these options might be located in the printer preferences' Maintenance tab, a Toolbox dialog, or other places, such as the printer's onboard menu. See your printer's documentation for details.

CAUTION   If you use a Windows-provided printer driver, these options might not be available. Install a driver from your printer vendor.

Thermal Printer Maintenance

The elements of thermal printer maintenance include replacing paper or ribbons as needed; cleaning the heating element as directed; and removing debris from the heating element, rollers, or other components as needed.

Thermal Printer Paper and Ribbons

Direct thermal printers use heat-sensitized paper, whereas thermal transfer printers might use either standard copy paper or glossy photo paper, depending on their intended use.

If the printer uses direct thermal printing, heat-sensitive paper with characteristics matching the printer's design specifications must be used. For portable printers using direct thermal printing, such as the Brother (formerly Pentax) PocketJet series, the usual source for such paper is the printer vendor or its authorized resellers. If the direct thermal printer is used for bar codes or point-of-sale transactions, you can get suitable paper or label stock from bar code or POS equipment suppliers and resellers.

Thermal transfer ribbons are available in three categories: wax (for paper; smooth paper produces the best results), wax/resin (synthetics), and resin (glossy hard films such as polyester). Choose the appropriate ribbon type for the material you will be printing on.

Dye-sublimation photo printers in the consumer space use special media kits that include both a ribbon and suitable photo paper stocks. Larger format dye-sublimation printers can vary.

Cleaning Heating Elements

Because the heating element in a thermal printer is the equivalent to the printhead in impact or inkjet printers, it must be kept clean to provide maximum print quality. Many vendors recommend cleaning the printhead after each roll of thermal transfer ribbon.

Some thermal transfer ribbons for POS and warehouse printers include special cleaning materials at the beginning of the roll. Some thermal printer vendors also supply special cleaning film you can use to remove dust, debris, and coating residue from printheads.

You can also use isopropyl alcohol to clean printheads. It is available in wipes, pens, pads, and swabs from various vendors. The ribbon must be removed before using isopropyl alcohol. When isopropyl alcohol is used in cleaning, you must wait until the printer dries out before reinstalling the ribbon.

Removing Debris

Debris from torn paper, solid ink flakes, and label coatings can build up on rollers and other components as well as the printhead. Use isopropyl alcohol wipes or other cleaning materials as recommended by the printer supplies to clean up debris for better print quality and longer print life.

Impact Printer Maintenance

The keys to successful maintenance of an impact printer include replacing the ribbon, replacing the printhead, and replacing the paper.

Replacing the Ribbon

When the ribbon is worn, the quality of printing goes down. But what you might not realize is that the ribbon on an impact dot-matrix printer also lubricates the pins in the printhead and protects the printhead from impact damage.

In addition to replacing the ribbon when print quality is no longer acceptable, be sure to immediately discard a ribbon that develops cuts or snags because these can snag a printhead pin and break or bend the pin.

Replacing the Printhead

If you replace ribbons when needed, you minimize the chances of needing to replace the printhead. However, if a printhead suffers damage to one or more pins, you must replace it. Damaged pins might snag the ribbon, and if a pin breaks, it will leave a gap in the characters output by the printer.

Instead of purchasing a new printhead, consider having the old printhead reconditioned or rebuilt.

TIP If you need a replacement quickly, some vendors offer advance exchange programs, which enable you to obtain a remanufactured or refurbished printhead on a cross-shipped basis rather than waiting until they receive your old printhead.

Replacing Paper

When you replace paper, be sure to check continuous-feed (tractor-fed) paper for problems with torn sprocket holes, separated tear-offs, and damaged sheets. Tear off any problem pages and use only good paper from the stack in your printer.

Be sure tractor feeders are properly adjusted, and if the printer can be run as either a push tractor (enables zero-tear paper feed) or a pull tractor, ensure the printer is properly configured for the feed type.

Check the head gap carefully: be sure to adjust it if you need to run multipart forms, thick labels, or envelopes. An incorrect head gap can lead to ribbon and printhead damage.

Printer Troubleshooting

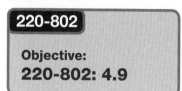

For businesses and individuals who rely on printers, keeping a printer properly maintained helps avoid problems. However, if a printer's print quality is reduced or the printer can't print, check the symptoms and solutions listed here for help.

Streaks and Smudges

Streaks and smudges can have many causes, depending on the type of printer in use.

Laser Printer

Randomized streaks in printed output, such as uneven printing or blank spots, are usually caused by low toner. As a temporary workaround, remove the toner cartridge and gently shake it to redistribute the toner. Install a new toner cartridge as quickly as possible.

Long vertical streaks that repeat on each page are usually caused by damage to the imaging drum. Replace the drum or toner cartridge if it includes the drum.

Inkjet Printer

Smudged print output from an inkjet printer can be caused by dirty printheads or paper rollers, incorrect head gap settings, and incorrect resolution and media settings.

If you see smudges only when printing on heavy paper stock, card stock, labels, or envelopes, check the head gap setting; use the default setting for paper up to 24 lb. rating; and use the wider gap for labels, card stock, and envelopes.

Clean the printhead. If the cleaning process doesn't result in acceptable results, remove the printhead (if possible) and clean it. If the printhead is built in to the printer or if the paper-feed rollers or platen have ink smudges, use a cleaning sheet to clean the paper-feed rollers, platen, and printhead.

Check the Printer Properties setting in the operating system to ensure that the correct resolution and paper options are set for the paper in use. Horizontal streaks in inkjet output are usually caused by trying to print on glossy photo paper using plain paper setting.

Unlike laser output—which can be handled as soon as the page is ejected—inkjet output, particularly from older printers, printed to old paper stocks made for older printers, or output on transparencies or glossy photo paper, often requires time to dry. For best results, use paper specially designed for inkjet printers. Paper should be stored in a cool, dry environment; damp paper also will result in smudged printing.

Thermal Printers

Streaky output in thermal transfer printers can have several causes, including media and print head problems.

If the coating on the media is poor quality, replace the media. If preprinted ink on the media is sticking to the printhead, replace the media with media printed using heat-resistant ink.

If the heating element is dirty, clean the heating element.

Smeared output (primarily when printing bar codes) can be caused by incorrect print head energy settings, too high a print speed, and using a 90-degree or 270-degree orientation.

With direct thermal printers, check for improperly stored paper or an incorrect setting in the printer driver. If the printer can be used in either direct or thermal transfer modes, an incorrect driver setting can cause print quality problems of various types.

Impact Printers

Streaky output in dot-matrix impact printers is usually caused by a dried-out ribbon. If the ribbon has an auxiliary ink reservoir, activate it. Otherwise, replace the ribbon.

Faded Prints

Faded prints also have many possible causes, depending on the printer.

Laser Printers

If the printing is even, the printer might be set for Economode or a similar mode that uses less toner. Adjust the printer properties to use normal print modes for final drafts.

For a color laser printer, also check the toner levels or the operation of the toner belt.

Inkjet Printers

The print nozzles might be clogged or some colors may be out of ink. Clean the nozzles, and use the nozzle check utility to verify proper operation. Replace any cartridges that are out of ink.

Thermal Printers

A faded image can result from installing a thermal transfer ribbon backward. Remove, verify proper loading, and reinstall.

If the ribbon is installed correctly, the ribbon might not be compatible with the media. Check the media settings in the printer configuration to verify.

Impact Printers

If the print is evenly faded, the ribbon is dried out. Replace the ribbon to achieve better print quality and protect the printhead. If the print appears more faded on the top of each line than on the bottom, the head gap is set too wide for the paper type in use. Adjust the head gap to the correct width to improve printing and protect the printhead from damage.

Ghost Images

Laser printers that display a ghost image of part or all the previous page on a new printout might have problems with the toner cartridge, imaging drum wiper blade, or fusing unit. To determine the cause of the ghosting, measure the distance between the top of the page and the ghost image and consult the service manual for the printer.

Toner Not Fused to Paper

If the printed output from a laser printer can be wiped or blown off the paper after the printout emerges from the laser printer, the fuser needs to be repaired or replaced. The fuser is supposed to heat the paper to fuse the toner to the paper; if it fails, the toner won't stick to the paper.

Creased Paper

Creased paper is usually caused by incorrect adjustment of the paper guides for feeding pages. If the paper guide is not set to the actual paper width, the paper might move horizontally during the feed process and become creased.

Paper Not Feeding

With an inkjet, laser, or impact printer running single-sheet paper, check the paper's positioning in the paper tray. Remove the paper, fan it, and replace it. If the problem continues, check for paper jams. If there are no paper jams, the pickup rollers might be worn out.

With a printer that uses continuous-feed paper (impact or thermal), check the tension of the feeder rollers or the position and operation of the tractor-feed mechanism.

Paper Jam

Paper jams have a variety of causes, depending on the printer type. Use the following sections to solve paper jams.

Paper Path Issues

The more turns the paper must pass through during the printing process, the greater the chances of paper jams. Curved paper paths are typical of some inkjet and many laser printers as well as dot-matrix printers using push tractors: The paper is pulled from the front of the printer, pulled through and around a series of rollers inside the printer during the print process, and then ejected through the front or top of the printer onto a paper tray. Because the cross-section of this paper path resembles a *C*, this is sometimes referred to as a *C-shaped paper path*.

Some printers, especially those with bottom-mounted paper trays, have more complex paper paths that resemble an *S*.

A straight-through paper path is a typical option on laser printers with a curved paper path. Printers with this feature have a rear paper output tray that can be lowered for use, which overrides the normal top paper output tray. Some also have a front paper tray. Use both front and rear trays for a true straight-through path; this is recommended for printing on envelopes, labels, or card stock. Inkjet printers with input paper trays at the rear of the printer and an output tray at the front also use this method or a variation in which the paper path resembles a flattened *V*.

Paper Loading, Paper Type, and Media Thickness Issues

Paper jams can be caused by incorrect paper-loading procedures, overloading the input tray, or using paper or card stock that is thicker than the recommended types for the printer. If the printer jams, open the exit cover or front cover or remove the paper tray(s) as needed to clear the jam.

Media Caught Inside the Printer

If paper or other media comes apart or tears inside the printer, you must remove all debris to avoid additional paper jams. Don't try to use creased paper because it increases the likelihood of a paper jam. However, if paper jams continue to happen, check the paper feed or paper tray operation.

Avoid using paper with damaged edges or damp paper; this can cause paper jams and lead to poor-quality printing.

TIP   When you insert a stack of sheet paper into any type of printer, be sure to fan the pages before you insert the paper into the tray to prevent sticking.

No Connectivity

A loose printer or network cable can cause a loss of connectivity, as can a router or switch failure. If the shared printer is connected to a computer, determine whether the computer can connect to the network. If not, the problem is network-related. If it can, the problem is related to the printer, printer port, or printer cable.

If the printer has an integrated network connection or connects to a print sharing device on the network, check the network settings on the printer or device.

Garbled Characters on Paper

Garbled characters or gibberish printing can occur for several reasons. Check the printer driver first: If the printer driver files are corrupted or the incorrect printer driver has been selected for a printer, gibberish printing is a likely result.

If you can use a printer in an emulation mode or change it to use a different printer language with a personality module or DIMM, be sure you have correctly configured the printer and the printer driver or installed a new printer driver.

A parallel printer cable that fails can also cause this type of problem.

Vertical Lines on a Page

Black marks on a laser-printed page are usually caused by debris stuck to the imaging drum, surface damage to the imaging drum, or dirty components in the printer (fuser, paper rollers, charging rollers, and so on). To determine which component is the cause, compare the distance between marks on the paper with the circumference of each component. The printer's manual will provide this information. Replace the imaging drum (part of the toner cartridge on many printer models) if the drum is at fault. Clean other components if they're at fault, and retest.

Vertical lines on a page printer with an inkjet printer are usually caused by ink on a feed roller. Clean the feed rollers, and if the problem persists, there might be a problem with a leaky ink cartridge.

Vertical lines in thermal printer output can be caused by a dirty heating element or by the failure of part of the heating element. Angled streaks can be caused by a creased ribbon. To solve this problem, adjust the ribbon feed mechanism.

Vertical lines on impact printer output usually indicate dirt on the paper. Replace the paper.

Backed Up Print Queue

The Windows print spooler switches to offline mode if the printer goes offline, is turned off, or has stopped for some other reason (such as a paper jam or loss of connection to the network). Print jobs are sent to the **print queue,** but the queue fills up until the print jobs are dealt with. After the printer goes online, you can release the print jobs. You can also kill all print jobs or kill selected print jobs.

To access the print queue, open the Printer icon in the notification area, or go to Printers, Printers and Faxes, or Devices and Printers and open the printer icon.

Releasing a Print Queue

To release print jobs stored in the queue in offline mode after the printer is available, use one of these methods:

Step 1.   Open the print queue.

Step 2.   Open the Printer menu.

Step 3.   Click **Use Printer Offline** (it's a toggle) and the print jobs will go to the printer.

Clearing Select Print Jobs or All Print Jobs in a Queue

You might need to clear a print queue for a variety of reasons:

- The wrong options are selected for the installed paper.
- Gibberish printing occurs because of a problem with the printer driver, cable, or port.
- You decide not to print the queued documents.

You can clear selected print jobs or all print jobs in a queue. To discard a print job in the print queue, follow these steps:

Step 1.   Open the print queue.

Step 2.   Right-click the print job you want to discard.

Step 3.   Select **Cancel Print** and the print job will be discarded.

To discard all print jobs in the queue, follow these steps:

Step 1.   Open the print queue.

Step 2.   Right-click **Printer**.

Step 3.   Click **Cancel All Documents** (varies by Windows version) to discard all print jobs.

Low Memory Errors

If you send a page to a laser printer that requires more memory than the laser printer contains, the laser printer tries to print the page but stops after the printer's memory is full. The printer displays an error message or blinks error status lights, at which point you must manually eject the page. Only a portion of the page is printed.

If the page requires an amount of memory close to the maximum in the laser printer, most laser printers have techniques for compressing the data going to the printer. Although this technique means that more pages can be printed successfully, compressing the data can slow down the print process.

You can use three options if the pages you need to print require too much memory:

- Reduce the resolution of the print job. Most laser printers today have a standard resolution of 600dpi or 1,200dpi. Reducing the graphics resolution to the next lower figure (from 1,200 to 600dpi or from 600dpi to 300dpi) will reduce the memory requirement for printing the page by a factor of four. The option, when present, could be located on various tabs of the printer's properties sheet. See Figure 11-17 for a typical example.

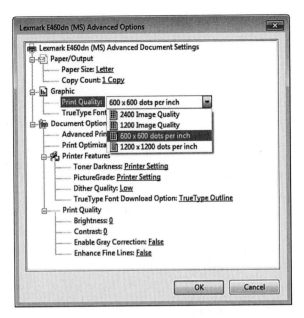

Figure 11-17 The Layout – Advanced – Graphics – Print Quality dialog in Windows 7 for a Lexmark laser printer enables you to adjust the graphics resolution; text quality is not affected by this option.

- Eliminate or reduce the size of graphics on the page.

- Convert color photos to black-and-white photos before placing in a desktop publishing document or printing them directly from the file. This can actually enhance the output quality from a monochrome laser printer as well as reduce the memory requirement for pages with photos.

These options are temporary workarounds that might be unsatisfactory for permanent use. The best solution to out-of-memory problems with a printer, as with the computer, is to add more RAM. To learn more about memory upgrades for laser and LED printers, see the section "Installing RAM," earlier in this chapter.

NOTE If you reduce the graphics resolution, text resolution stays the same, so a document that is not designed for reproduction or mass distribution will still have acceptable quality. However, graphics resolutions of 600 dots per inch (dpi) or less produce poor-quality photo output.

Access Denied

If you get an Access Denied message when trying to print to a network printer, make sure your account has been granted access to the printer or to the computer hosting the networked printer.

Printer Won't Print

If the printer produces a blank page immediately after the toner cartridge has been changed, remove the toner cartridge, and make sure the tape that holds the toner in place has been removed; without toner, the printer can't print.

If the printer produces a blank page after printing thousands of pages, the toner probably is exhausted. Replace the toner cartridge.

If you send a print job to a printer that has specified hours of activity, the print job will not be released to the printer until the printer is ready for it.

If you set up a printer manually and the wrong printer port is specified, the printer won't print.

Color Output in Wrong Print Colors

If a color printer produces output in the wrong colors, the most likely cause on an color inkjet printer is a clogged printhead. On a color laser, check for low color toner or an empty color toner cartridge.

If the print colors are close but not exactly what is wanted on a color photograph or a document with colored graphics or text, you need to set up color management on the printer and the display(s) used to edit the document.

Unable to Install Printer

To install a printer, you need administrator (elevated) access. If you are installing a printer in Windows Vista or Windows 7, provide the administrator password when prompted by User Account Control.

Error Codes

HP LaserJet printers use the following error codes to describe printing problems:

- **13 or 13.xx**—Paper jam. (Replace .xx with specific numeric values that indicate exactly where the paper jam has occurred.)

- **20**—Insufficient memory; press Go or Continue to print a partial page.

- **40**—Bad transmission to EIO interface card.

- **41.xx**—Various printer errors involving media or other problems. (Replace .xx with a value indicating the specific error.)

- **49.xx**—Firmware error.

- **50.4**—Line voltage.

- **50.x**—Fuser error.

- **51.x**—Beam detect (.1) or laser error (.2).

- **52.x**—Scanner speed errors; startup error (.1); rotation error (.2).

- **53.xy.zz**—DIMM memory error in specified module (x = DIMM type; y = location; and zz = error number).

- **54.1**—Sealing tape not removed from the toner cartridge.

- **54.4**—Line voltage error.

- **55.xx**—Internal communications error; can be caused by formatter, firmware DIMM, engine controller board, or fuser problems.

- **56.x**—Error in paper input or accessory (.1) or output bin (.2) connection.

- **57.x**—Printer fan (.4), duplex fan (.7), or main motor (older printer models in LaserJet 4, 5 series) failure.

- **58.2**—Environmental thermistor (TH3) failure.

- **59.x**—Main motor error (.0), startup error (.1), or rotation error (.2).

- **62.x**—Printer memory error in internal memory (.0) or DIMM slots (.1–.4).

- **64**—Scan buffer error.

- **66.xx.yy**—External paper-handling device error.

- **68**—NVRAM or permanent storage error.

- **69.x**—Temporary printing error.

- **79**—Printer detected error (can be caused by memory, firmware, EIO, and formatter).

- **8x.yyyy**—EIO device or slot error.

A good resource for both numerical- and text-based error codes for HP LaserJet printers is the HP LaserJet Error Codes page at PrinterTechs.com: www.printertechs.com/tech/error-codes/error-codes-index.php. Lexmark error codes are available at www.all-laser.com/aerrorlex/.

Exam Preparation Tasks

Review All the Key Topics

Review the most important topics in the chapter, noted with the Key Topic icon in the outer margin of the page. Table 11-1 lists a reference of these key topics and the page numbers on which each is found.

Table 11-1   Key Topics for Chapter 11

Key Topic Element	Description	Page Number
List	Major components of a laser printer	450
List	EP process (preliminaries and steps 1–7)	452
Figure 11-2	Color laser printing process	455
Text	Inkjet print technology	455
Text	Essential inkjet printer components	456
Figure 11-3	Inkjet printer	456
List	Inkjet print process	458
List	Thermal printer technologies	459
List	Thermal print processes	459
List	Impact dot-matrix print process	462
List	Printer sharing in Windows	471
Figure 11-13	Windows 7 printer preference sheets	475
Text	Nozzle check and head cleaning	481
List	Error codes	492

Define Key Terms

Define the following key terms from this chapter, and check your answers in the glossary.

calibration, direct thermal, dye sublimation, impact printer, inkjet printer, laser printer, nozzle check, print queue, print spooler, printer preferences, printer properties, thermal transfer

Complete the Hands-On Lab

Complete the hands-on labs, and then see the answers and explanations at the end of the chapter.

Lab 11-1: Solve Inkjet Printing Problems

Scenario: You are a technician adding an inkjet printer to a workstation. During the test print, there are gaps in the Windows logo, and vertical lines on the page are not straight. Users are also complaining about needing to reorder multiple-page prints.

Refer to Figure 11-16 to answer the following questions:

Question 1: Which option should you select to see if the printhead needs cleaning?

Question 2: Which option calibrates the printhead to improve vertical line printing?

Question 3: Which option would you select so that a multipage document prints so that the first page is on the top of the stack?

Answer Review Questions

Answer these review questions, and then see the answers and explanations at the end of the chapter.

1. You notice vertical lines on the printout from a laser printer that uses a toner cartridge with an integrated imaging drum. Which is the most likely solution to this problem?

   a. Clean the mirror.

   b. Replace the toner cartridge.

   c. Remove ink from the feed rollers.

   d. Remove the toner cartridge, shake it, and reinstall it.

2. Which of the following steps is listed in the incorrect order in the EP print process?

   a. Step 5. Transferring

   b. Step 1. Cleaning

   c. Step 3. Exposing

   d. Step 4. Developing

3. A color laser printer with a transfer belt will _____. (Choose all that apply.)

   a. Print color pages as quickly as monochrome pages.

   b. Print color pages faster than monochrome pages.

   c. Use a waste toner container.

   d. None of the above are correct.

4. If an inkjet printer has clogged printheads, which of the following should you do first?

   a. Print a test page.

   b. Clean the printheads.

   c. Run Nozzle Check.

   d. Recalibrate the printer.

5. A thermal printer can create an image in which of the following ways? (Choose all that apply.)

   a. Using a laser to heat the paper

   b. Heating the paper with a special printhead

   c. Heating a wax or resin-based ribbon with a special printhead

   d. Using the bubble-jet process

6. A client with an impact printer is seeing gaps in the printed output. Which of these is the most likely cause?

   a. Incorrect setting of paper type

   b. Broken pin in printhead

   c. Clogged printhead nozzle

   d. Laser failure

7. You want a printer on the network to have its own IP address. Which of the following methods of connecting the printer can provide this? (Choose all that apply.)

   a. A print server

   b. A printer NIC card

   c. A Bluetooth adapter

   d. A USB port

8. You want to use the most up-to-date drivers to install a printer. Which of the following is most likely to provide these drivers?

  a. Windows Update

  b. The vendor's website

  c. The installation disc packed with the printer

  d. The driver list on the Windows CD or DVD

9. Where would you find the setting for the print spooler on a Windows operating system?

  a. Computer Management

  b. The Printers folder

  c. In Server Properties

  d. Device Manager

10. When preparing to upgrade a printer's memory, you notice that the printer uses a DIMM memory module. Can you use the same type of memory for a laptop or desktop?

  a. Yes, they use the same memory.

  b. Yes, you can also use printer memory in a desktop.

  c. No, they do not use the same type of memory.

  d. Yes, but the printer will run more slowly.

11. Which of the following are considered troubleshooting tools and techniques for printers? (Choose all that apply.)

  a. Increase memory.

  b. Print a test page.

  c. Identify symptoms.

  d. Review device error codes.

12. A laser printer maintenance kit should be installed under which of the following circumstances? (Choose all that apply.)

  a. When a Perform Maintenance message is displayed

  b. After every third toner cartridge replacement

  c. When the fuser stops working

  d. After 100,000 pages

13. An inkjet printer has gone offline because it is out of cyan ink. Which of the following would enable you to keep printing?

   a. Replace the cyan ink cartridge.

   b. Adjust the print spooler to print all documents in black.

   c. Redirect the print spooler to send all print jobs to another printer.

   d. All the above.

14. You are trying to print a complex page on an HP LaserJet printer. A 20 error appears. Which of the following happens when you press Go on the printer?

   a. A partial page prints.

   b. You must remove a paper jam before you can print.

   c. You see directions for replacing the toner cartridge.

   d. The full page prints after a delay.

Answers to Hands-On Lab

Lab 11-1: Solve Inkjet Printing Problems

Answers:

Question 1: Nozzle check

Question 2: Print head alignment

Question 3: Reverse order

Answers and Explanations to Review Questions

1. **B.** The toner cartridge's drum surface has been damaged. It must be replaced. A and D are used to handle other problems. C applies to inkjet printers.

2. **B.** Cleaning takes place in Step 7, not Step 1. It is the last step because it takes place after the page has been printed.

3. **A, C.** A transfer belt enables all four colors to be printed in a single pass. Color laser printers use a waste toner container that must be periodically emptied. A color laser printer that doesn't use a transfer belt prints each color separately, so it is slower (not faster) when printing color pages rather than monochrome.

4. **B.** Whether the printer has built-in or removable printheads, cleaning the heads is always the first choice. The Nozzle Check routine helps determine whether the heads are clean. Recalibration is used to ensure straight lines are being created and to provide high-quality bidirectional printing.

5. **B, C.** Thermal printers use a special printhead (not a laser) to heat the paper or the ribbon. Bubble-jet is a term used by Canon to describe its inkjet printing process.

6. **B.** A broken pin in the printhead causes a gap in printed output on impact dot-matrix printers. The other problems are associated with inkjet (A, C) or laser (D—but this problem would cause no printing at all).

7. **A, B.** To add support for Ethernet local area networking to a printer that does not have built-in networking capability, connect it to an Ethernet print server. Print servers are available in versions that support USB or parallel printers and enable the printer to be accessed via the print server's IP address. Some printers also support the installation of an optional printer NIC card.

8. **B.** You should go to the vendor's website to download the most up-to-date drivers. After a printer is installed, you might be able to use Windows Update to find updated drivers. The driver disc might not have updated drivers. The printer list on the Windows CD or DVD will not list updated drivers either.

9. **A.** You can find the print spool settings in Computer Management. You select Services and Applications, Services and then scroll down to the print spooler, right-click it, and go to Properties.

10. **C.** Most recent printers with upgradeable memory use the DIMM memory module form factor, but printers do not use the same types of DIMMs as desktop or laptop computers.

11. **B, C, D.** By printing or scanning a test page you might be able to discern what is causing the problem with the device. Identifying symptoms, such as slow printing, can help you speed up the time that it takes to troubleshoot. If your device has an LCD display, it probably displays error codes that can save you some time. Blinking lights on some models are also used to display error codes.

12. **A, C.** Some laser printers display a message indicating that maintenance needs to be performed. If the maintenance kit includes a fuser assembly, you can install the kit and replace other components as well as the fuser. A typical printer can use many toner cartridges before a maintenance kit is necessary, and the page count varies by printer model.

13. **A.** Most late-model inkjet printers stop printing if one of the ink cartridges is empty. You cannot change the ink color used by documents in the print spooler, nor can you direct output from one printer to another after the document is in the print queue.

14. **A.** An Error 20 is a memory error, indicating the page being printed needs more RAM than the printer has. A partial page is printed when you press Go. A paper jam displays a different error.

This chapter covers the following subjects:

- **Drive Interface Types**—How internal and external drives connect to the system.

- **Hard Disk Drives**—Hard drives are the most common and most important storage devices. You learn about SATA, PATA (IDE), jumpering, installation, creating arrays of redundant disks, and optimizing performance.

- **SSD and Flash Drives**—This section discusses SSD drives and flash media, such as USB thumb drives, memory cards, and card readers, and how to use and optimize them.

- **RAID**—The major features and benefits of RAID arrays, differences between 0, 1, 5, and 10, and how to install and configure a RAID array.

- **Optical Drives**—This section describes the various types of CD, DVD, and Blu-ray drives and media; media capacities; how to record to CD, DVD, and Blu-ray; and any possible installation issues you might encounter.

- **Floppy Drives**—Standard end users might not use these anymore, but technicians do, for several reasons. You learn what a PC technician needs to know about floppy drives, including types, hardware configuration, installation, BIOS configuration, and care of floppy drives.

- **Tape Drives**—This section covers the major types of tape drives, interfaces, and native and compressed capacity.

- **Troubleshooting Hard Drives, SSDs, and RAID Arrays**—In this section, you learn how to identify and fix problems related to SATA, eSATA, and PATA drives and RAID arrays.

> This chapter covers **CompTIA A+ 220-801 objectives 1.5** and **1.7** and **CompTIA A+ 220-802 objective 4.3**.

CHAPTER 12

Storage Devices

Modern desktop computers feature a variety of storage devices, from the venerable floppy disk drive to its replacement, USB flash memory drives. Other typical storage devices include magnetic and SSD hard drives; Blu-ray, CD, and DVD optical drives and media; removable storage using tape cartridges or flash memory cards; and external storage devices of various types. The following sections teach you what you need to know about each item.

Foundation Topics

Drive Interface Types

220-801

Objectives:
220-801: 1.5, 1.7

Drive interfaces can be divided into two categories: external and internal. The CompTIA A+ Certification exam classifies network interfaces in the external drive interfaces category, but they are discussed separately here.

External and Internal Drive Interfaces

Network interfaces such as Fast Ethernet and Gigabit Ethernet are used for hard disk drives being used for shared storage on a network. Some drives equipped with these ports can also be connected via a USB port or might have interchangeable connectors to permit connectivity via a USB or FireWire port. External drive interfaces, such as eSATA and FireWire (IEEE 1394), are used primarily by hard disk drives. USB 2.0 and USB 3.0 interfaces can be used by hard disk drives as well as optical drives, flash memory card readers, and flash memory thumb drives.

Internal drive interfaces such as SATA and PATA are used by hard disk drives, RAID arrays, optical drives, and tape backups. An SATA port can be converted into an eSATA port by a low-cost header cable.

SCSI can be used by hard disk drives, RAID arrays, tape backups, and other devices for both internal and external devices.

The floppy interface, when present, is currently used only by floppy drives, although low-capacity tape backup drives have also used it in the past. Many motherboards now omit floppy interfaces.

Table 12-1 provides an overview of these interfaces.

Table 12-1 Drive Interface Overview

Interface	Location	Interface Speeds	Drive Types Supported
eSATA	External	1.5Gbps 3Gbps 6Gbps	Hard disk drives
IEEE 1394a (FireWire 400)	External	400Mbps	Hard disk drives, optical drives, tape backups
IEEE 1394b (FireWire 800)	External	800Mbps	Hard disk drives, optical drives, tape backups
Fast Ethernet	External (Network)	100Mbps	Hard disk drives for network access
Gigabit Ethernet	External (Network)	1000Mbps	Hard disk drives for network access
USB 2.0	External	480Mbps	Hard disk drives, flash memory, card readers, floppy drives, optical drives
USB 3.0	External	5Gbps	Hard disk drives, SSD, flash memory, card readers, floppy drives, optical drives
SATA1*	Internal	1.5Gbps	Hard disk drives, optical (DVD, BD media) drives, RAID arrays, SSD Can be converted to eSATA via header cable
SATA2*	Internal	3.0Gbps	Hard drives, optical (DVD, BD media) drives, RAID arrays, SSD Can be converted to eSATA via header cable
SATA3*	Internal	6.0Gbps	Hard drives, RAID arrays, SSD Backward compatible with SATA1, SATA2
PATA (IDE)#	Internal	100MBps 133MBps	Hard disk drives, optical (CD, DVD) drives, RAID arrays Two drives per interface
SCSI	Internal and External	Up to 40MBps (narrow) Up to 320MBps (wide)	Up to 7 (narrow) or 15 (wide) per interface; see Table 6-4, Chapter 6, for details
Floppy	Internal	Up to 1Mbps	Up to two drives per interface

*Objective 1.7 in 220-801 exam uses these terms, but the SATA1 is more properly referred to as SATA 1.5Gbps; SATA2 as SATA 3.0Gbps, and SATA3 as SATA 6.0Gbps.

Objective 1.7 in 220-801 exam uses this terms, but PATA is the current term for this interface.

To see a typical implementation of eSATA, USB 2.0, and USB 3.0 ports, refer to Figure 6-1 (Chapter 6, "I/O and Input Ports and Devices"). Figure 12-1 illustrates SATA, PATA, and floppy drive interfaces on a typical motherboard.

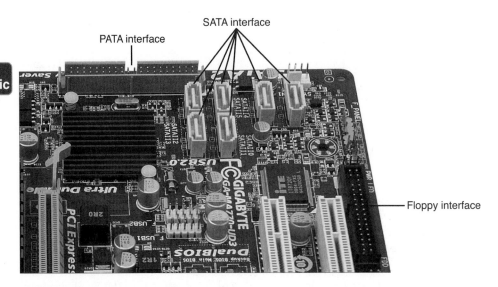

Figure 12-1 A typical late-model motherboard with one PATA interface, one floppy interface, and six SATA interfaces.

TIP Objective 1.7 of the 220-801 exam lists the IDE (PATA) and SATA speeds in Table 12-1. Be sure to memorize these.

PATA and SATA Performance Characteristics

A series of standards for PATA and SATA drives are referred to as the **ATA** specifications (AT Attachment). Table 12-2 provides an overview of the differences in the various ATA specifications.

Table 12-2 ATA Specifications and Features

ATA Specification	Major Features
ATA-1 (original)	Standardized master/slave jumpers
	IDE Identify command for automatic configuration and detection of parameters
	PIO mode 0 (3.33MBps, 16-bit interface)
	PIO mode 1 (5.22MBps, 16-bit interface)
	PIO mode 3 (8.33MBps, 16-bit interface)
	CHS (standard cylinder head sector) and LBA (logical block addressing, sector-translated) parameters
ATA-2	PIO mode 3 (11.11MBps, 32-bit interface)
	PIO mode 4 (16.67MBps, 32-bit interface)
	Power management
	CHS/LBA translation for drives up to 8.4GB
	Primary and secondary IDE channels
	IDE block mode
ATA-3	S.M.A.R.T. self-diagnostics feature for use with monitoring software
	Password protection
	Improved reliability of PIO mode 4
ATA-4	UDMA 33 (33MBps)
	ATAPI support
	80-wire/40-pin cable
	BIOS support for LBA increased to 136.9GB (28-bit LBA)
ATA-5	UDMA 66 (66MBps)
	Required use of 80-wire/40-pin cable with UDMA 66
ATA-6	UDMA 100 (100MBps)
	Increased capacity of LBA to 144 petabytes (PB; 1PB = 1 quadrillion bytes) (48-bit LBA)
ATA-7	UDMA 133 (133MBps)
	Serial ATA (SATA) 1.5Gbps
ATA-8	Hybrid solid-state/mechanical and solid-state drives; SATA 3Gbps (SATA Revision 2.0); SATA 6Gbps (SATA Revision 3.0)

PATA Cabling, Configuration, and Setup

Although **PATA** hard disks have largely been replaced by SATA drives in new computers, many computers you are likely to encounter in repair work use this interface for hard disks, and many computers continue to use PATA for optical drives.

PATA drive configuration is accomplished in three ways: cabling, jumper block configuration, and BIOS settings.

PATA Cables

PATA cables are available in two versions: 40-wire and 80-wire. Both have 40 connectors, but the 80-wire versions has a ground wire for each data or signal wire, and can thus support the highest speeds available. 80-wire PATA cables are recommended for all PATA devices. See Figure 12-2.

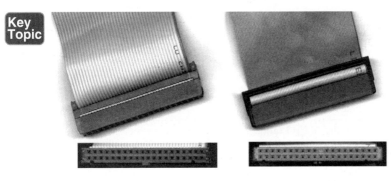

40-wire PATA data cable   80-wire PATA data cable

Figure 12-2   40-wire and 80-wire PATA data cables. 80-wire cables are required by modern PATA hard disks and recommended for other types of PATA devices.

The blue connector on an 80-wire PATA cable is connected to the motherboard PATA interface. The black connector on the other end of the cable is used for the primary drive. The gray connector between the blue and black connectors is used for the secondary drive. To enable the cable to determine drive assignments, the jumper blocks on the drive must be set correctly.

NOTE   The colors listed for 80-wire PATA cable connectors might vary with some cables, such as the custom-colored cables supplied with some motherboards. In those cases, keep in mind that the distance between the primary and secondary drive connectors is much shorter than the distance between the secondary drive connector and the motherboard connector.

PATA Jumper Block Configuration

The cables you use for PATA drives help determine how the jumper blocks are configured. Most PATA drives have jumper blocks located by the power and data connectors, but a few drives have jumper blocks on the bottom of the drive. Manufacturers often use labels on their drives to indicate jumper block settings.

With 40-wire cables, the selection of primary and secondary drives is made with jumper blocks: The drive you want to use as primary is jumpered as Master, and the drive you want to use as secondary is jumpered as Slave.

TIP   Depending on the drive, you might use the Master position when a single drive is installed, or remove the jumper (or park it across two pins horizontally) for a single-drive installation. (This is typical with Western Digital hard disks.)

With 80-wire cables, the jumpers on the drives are both set to Cable Select (CS). See Figure 12-3 for examples of CS and other jumper block settings.

NOTE   Some old drives include a jumper that reduces the reported capacity of the hard disk, whereas others include a jumper that adjusts the hard disk interface's speed.

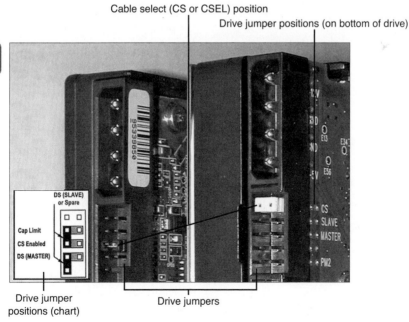

Figure 12-3   Two typical PATA drives configured for cable select. Some drives, such as the one on the left, require the user to consult a chart on the drive's top plate or in the system documentation for correct settings, whereas the drive on the right has the jumper settings marked on the drive's circuit board.

PATA BIOS Configuration

After the drives have been properly configured, the system BIOS can detect and recognize their capacity, performance, and other features. Use Auto to ensure correct configuration for new drives.

However, if a drive has been previously used in a different computer and contains data you need to access, it might be necessary to manually configure the drive's BIOS settings. Before removing the drive from the old computer, view the BIOS settings for the drive and record them.

CAUTION Make the following changes only if the drive's contents cannot be accessed using the normal Auto drive setting.

Settings you might need to change include

Drive Type—User Defined enables you to select values for the drive's geometry.

Cylinders, Heads, Sectors—Use the values supplied in the old system's BIOS setup. These are also known collectively as the drive's geometry.

Write Precompensation—Use the value supplied (if any) in the old system's BIOS setup.

Drive access mode—Use CHS for old hard disks less than 512MB. Use Large for drives more than 512MB if the normal setting, LBA, does not enable you to access the drive's contents.

Figure 12-4 illustrates custom settings (highlighted) used for access to a 40GB hard disk.

SATA Configuration and Cabling

SATA hard drives have completely replaced PATA hard disks in new computers, and most new computers also include SATA optical drives. Figure 12-5 compares the power and data connectors used by typical SATA and PATA hard drives.

```
         AMIBIOS NEW SETUP UTILITY - VERSION 3.31a
┌────────────────────────────────────┬──────────────────────┐
│      Primary IDE Master            │    [ Setup Help ]    │
│                                    │                      │
│   Type                     User    │   Select <Auto> for a│
│   Cylinders                19680   │   hard disk > 512 MB │
│   Heads                    16      │   under DOS and Windows,│
│   Write Precompensation    0       │   Select <Disabled> under│
│   Sectors                  255     │   Nerware and UNIX.  │
│     Maximum Capacity       41111 Mb│                      │
│   LBA Mode                 On      │                      │
│   Block Mode               On      │                      │
│   Fast Programmed I/O Modes 4      │                      │
│   32 Bit Transfer Mode     On      │                      │
│                                    │                      │
│                                    │                      │
│                                    │                      │
├────────────────────────────────────┴──────────────────────┤
│ F1:Help      ↑↓:Select Item    +/-:Change Values   F7:Setup Defaults│
│ Esc:Previous Menu          Enter:Select ▶Sub-Menu  F6:Hi-Performance│
└────────────────────────────────────────────────────────────┘
```

Figure 12-4   Viewing an older hard disk's User Defined drive type settings.

Figure 12-5   The power and data cable connectors on SATA and PATA hard drives.

Unlike with a PATA drive, an SATA drive has a one-to-one connection to the corresponding SATA interface on the motherboard. Drive jumpers on SATA drives are used for the following purposes:

- Reduce drive interface speed from the default to the next lower speed (from 6.0Gbps to 3.0Gbps or from 3.0Gbps to 1.5Gbps).

- Enable spread spectrum clocking.

See the specific drive's documentation for details.

SATA 1.5Gbps and 3.0Gbps drives and interfaces use the same cabling. However, SATA 6.0Gbps drives and interfaces use an improved version for greater reliability. Cables made for SATA 6.0Gbps are typically marked as such and can also be used with slower SATA drives and interfaces. All SATA data cables use an L-shaped seven-pin connector, and all SATA power cables use a larger L-shaped 15-pin connector.

SATA data cables are available with straight-through connectors on both ends or with a right-angle connector on one end for easier connection to SATA drives. Some cables, either straight-through or right-angle, include a metal clip to help lock the drive into place.

eSATA cable headers convert standard SATA headers into eSATA ports available from the rear of the system.

See Figure 12-6 for examples of these cables.

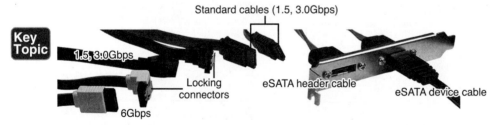

Figure 12-6 SATA and eSATA data cables.

SCSI IDs

Because a single SCSI interface can support up to 7 (narrow SCSI) or 15 (wide SCSI) devices, the SCSI specification includes a device-numbering scheme known as the SCSI device ID to identify the different devices connected to a SCSI interface on the motherboard or on a host adapter card. The SCSI device ID can be implemented with jumper blocks or with a selector switch, and ranges from 0–7 for narrow SCSI, and from 0–15 for wide SCSI. See "SCSI," in Chapter 6 for details.

Hot-Swappable Drive Interfaces

USB 2.0, USB 3.0, and FireWire (IEEE 1394a and 1394b) interfaces all support hot-swapping of hard disks or other drive types. When the drive is connected, the drive is automatically identified by Windows and made available.

To eject a USB or FireWire drive safely, open the Safely Remove Hardware dialog available from the notification area in Windows and follow the prompts to select and eject the drive.

Windows optimizes flash memory cards and USB flash memory drives for quick removal. To safely remove a flash memory card from a card reader, close any Explorer window displaying the card's contents or navigate to a different folder. Check the status light to make sure the card is not being accessed, and then remove the card.

NOTE   Some USB flash memory drives include their own management software. In such cases, use the Eject feature provided with the drive instead of Safely Remove Hardware.

The SATA and eSATA drive interfaces are also designed to support hot-swapping but must be configured for **AHCI** mode (also known as native mode) in the system BIOS. If the interface is configured for IDE mode (also known as emulation mode), the drive connected to it cannot be hot-swapped and will also lose access to advanced SATA and eSATA features such as native command queuing (NCQ). Refer to Figure 3-12 (in Chapter 3, "BIOS") for an example.

CAUTION   If internal SATA hard disks are configured to support hot-swapping (configured as AHCI devices in the system BIOS), they also show up in the Safely Remove Hardware list. Do not select these drives for removal.

Hard Disk Drives

> **220-801**
>
> **Objectives:**
> **220-801: 1.5, 1.7**

Hard disk drives are the most important storage device used by a personal computer. Hard disk drives store the operating system (Windows, Linux, or others) and load it into the computer's memory (RAM) at startup. Hard disk drives also store applications, system configuration files used by applications and the operating system, and data files created by the user.

Traditional hard disk drives use one or more double-sided platters formed from rigid materials such as aluminum or glass. These platters are coated with a durable magnetic surface divided into sectors. Each sector contains 512 bytes of storage along with information about where the sector is located on the disk medium. Sectors are organized in concentric circles from the edge of the media inward toward the middle of the platter. These concentric circles are called tracks.

Hard disk drives, unlike floppy drives, are found in almost every PC, with the exception of netbook and Ultrabook portable computers, which typically use SSDs. Internal hard disk drives for desktop computers use the same 3.5-inch form factor as floppy drives but are installed into internal drive bays. Their capacities range up to 3TB, but most desktop drives in recent systems have capacities ranging from 500GB to 2TB. The most common interface type used for both internal hard disks and for external hard disks is SATA.

External drives typically use SATA hard disks with a bridge controller for use with USB 2.0, USB 3.0, or FireWire ports. Some external drives can also connect to eSATA ports. External drives that use 3.5-inch desktop hard disks require AC power, but most external drives that use 2.5-inch or smaller mobile hard disks can be bus-powered, receiving power from the USB or FireWire port on the host computer.

Performance Factors for SATA and PATA Hard Disks

As you learned earlier in this chapter, SATA hard disks are available in three standards: 1.5Gbps, 3.0Gbps, and 6.0Gbps. However, different drives that support the same interface standard might provide different levels of performance. Several factors influence the performance of a given hard disk drive. In addition to the interface type, factors such as spin rate and internal buffer (cache) size have large impacts on how well a particular drive performs in both benchmarks and real-world situations.

Spin Rate

The speed at which hard disk media turns, its spin rate, is measured in revolutions per minute (**RPM**). Low-performance or "green" hard disks typically spin at 5,400RPM. Mid-performance drives spin at 7,200RPM. High-performance desktop drives spin at 10,000RPM. Drives designed for use in enterprise computing, such as servers, spin at rates up to 15,000RPM.

TIP   Although some hard disks may run at different speeds, the speed measurement method (RPMs) and the specific RPM speeds in this section are a focus of Objective 1.7 on the 220-801 exam.

Buffer Size

In addition to spin rate, the size of the hard disk drive's internal buffer or cache memory also has an impact on performance, particularly in data-read mode. Just as with processor cache memory, which often enables the CPU to read cache memory instead of slower main memory to reused previously read information, hard disks with larger buffers can reread recently transferred information more quickly from cache than from the drive's magnetic storage.

Typical buffer sizes in late-model drives range from 8MB up to 64MB, with larger buffer sizes providing slightly better performance.

Hybrid Drive

Windows 7 is the first version of Windows to support so-called hybrid drives, which combine a standard SATA hard disk with up to 8GB of single-level cell (SLC) memory, the same type of memory used in SSDs. SLC memory, just as in SSD disk drives, provides much faster data access than purely mechanical hard disk drives. Consequently, when information needed by the CPU is available in the hybrid drive's SLC memory, it is read from that memory, and this boosts performance. Seagate is the first vendor to supply hybrid drives (Momentus XT), whereas other vendors have turned a combination of a standard SATA hard disk with a PCIe x4 card containing SLC memory into a hybrid drive (OCZ RevoDrive Hybrid PCIe SSD).

Internal Hard Disk Drive Installation

The most common types of internal drives you will install are PATA and SATA hard disks. The following sections provide step-by-step installation instructions for these types of drives. You can also use these instructions for other types of PATA and SATA drives, such as optical, tape, or removable-media drives as noted.

Following are common steps for SATA and PATA drives:

Step 1.   Shut down the system and disconnect it from AC power.

Step 2.   Open the system and check for an unused 3.5-inch drive bay or an unused 5.25-inch drive bay. The 3.5-inch drive bay is used for hard disks and some tape, floppy, and removable-media drives. The 5.25-inch drive bay is used for optical drives and can be used for other types of drives as well.

Step 3a.   For 3.5-inch drives, install the drive into a 3.5-inch drive bay. If a 3.5-inch drive bay is not available but a 5.25-inch drive bay is, attach the appropriate adapter kit and rails as needed, as shown in Figure 12-7. Continue with Step 4.

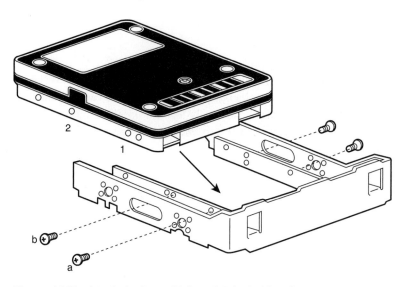

Figure 12-7   A typical adapter kit for a 3.5-inch drive. Screw a attaches the frame at hole #1; screw b attaches the frame at hole #2, with corresponding attachments on the opposite side of the drive and frame. Drive rails used by some cases can be attached to the adapter kit.

Step 3b.   For 5.25-inch drives or drives adapted to 5.25-inch, if the 5.25-inch drive bays on the system use rails to hold drives in position, attach the appropriate rails. Continue with Step 4.

Step 3c.   For 2.5-inch drives (such as hybrid or SSDs), attach a 2.5-inch to 3.5-inch adapter kit to the drive and install it in a 3.5-inch drive bay. Continue with Step 4.

SATA-Specific Installation Steps

To install an SATA drive, continue with these steps:

Step 4.   Install the drive into the appropriate drive bay using screws supplied by the drive vendor. Depending on the chassis layout and the drive type being installed, you might need to remove a cover from the drive bay or remove the drive bay itself. See Figure 12-8.

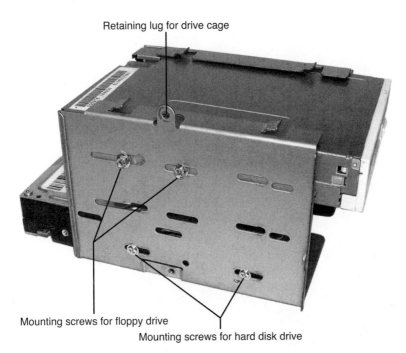

Retaining lug for drive cage

Mounting screws for floppy drive

Mounting screws for hard disk drive

Figure 12-8   A removable drive cage with the attachment screws for the floppy disk drive and hard drive. The opposite side of each drive is also secured with screws (not shown).

Step 5.   Connect the SATA cable to the drive; it is keyed so that it can be connected in only one direction.

Step 6.   Connect the SATA power lead; if the computer's power supply doesn't have an SATA edge connector, use the adapter provided with the drive or purchased separately to convert a standard Molex connector to the edge connector type used by SATA. See Figure 12-9.

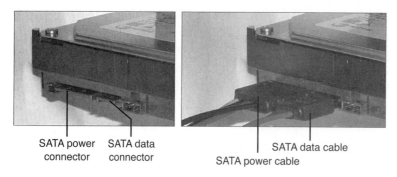

SATA power   SATA data   SATA data cable
connector   connector
                          SATA power cable

Figure 12-9   A typical SATA hard disk before (left) and after (right) installing power and data cables.

Step 7.   Connect the SATA data cable to the connector on the motherboard or host adapter card. See Figure 12-10.

1. Match keyed data cable to header.   2. Push cable into header.

Figure 12-10   Connecting an SATA cable to the SATA header on the motherboard.

Step 8.   Reconnect the system to AC power and turn it on.

Step 9.   Start the BIOS configuration program (if the SATA host adapter is built in to the motherboard). Enable the SATA host adapter (if necessary), configure SATA settings, save changes, and restart your system. Install drivers if your new SATA drive is not recognized by Windows.

Figure 12-9 shows a typical SATA drive before and after attaching power and data cables.

> **NOTE** If you need to install an SATA hard disk in a system that lacks an SATA host adapter, or you need to install an SATA RAID array in a system that lacks RAID support, you need to install an SATA or SATA RAID host adapter card into a PCI or PCIe (preferred) expansion slot. This type of card has an onboard BIOS (firmware) used to set up and configure the drive(s) attached to it.

PATA-Specific Installation Steps

To install a PATA drive, continue with these steps (after Steps 1–3 mentioned earlier):

Step 4.   Jumper the drive according to the cable type used: 40-wire cables use **master** and **slave**; 80-wire cables use **cable select** or master and slave. (Use master/slave jumpers only if cable select does not work.) Use only 80-wire cables for hard disks. Other types of drives can use 40-wire or 80-wire cables, but 80-wire cables are preferred.

Step 5.   Install the drive into the appropriate drive bay using screws supplied by the drive vendor. Depending on the chassis layout and the drive type being installed, you might need to remove a cover from the drive bay or remove the drive bay itself. Refer to Figure 12-8.

Step 6.   Connect the appropriate connector to the drive, making sure to match the colored marking on the edge of the cable to the end of the drive connector with pin 1. Pin 1 might be marked with a square solder hole on the bottom of the drive or with a label. If no markings are visible, pin 1 is usually nearest the drive's power connector. Disconnect the cable from the host adapter or other PATA drive if necessary to create sufficient slack. See Figure 12-11.

Step 7.   Attach the power connector to the drive; most PATA drives use the Molex power connector originally used on 5.25-inch floppy disk drives. Use a Y-splitter to create two power connectors from one if necessary. See Figure 12-11.

Step 8.   Connect the data cable to the other PATA drive.

ATA/IDE data connector on drive

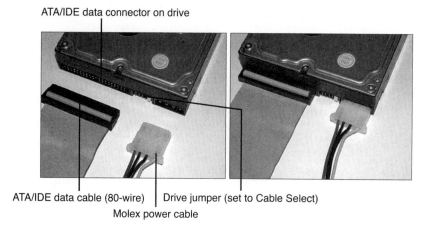

ATA/IDE data cable (80-wire)   Drive jumper (set to Cable Select)
              Molex power cable

Figure 12-11   Attaching power and data cables to a typical PATA drive.

Step 9.   Configure the jumper on the other PATA drive on the same cable if
               necessary. With 80-wire cables, both drives can be jumpered as cable
               select, with the drive at the far end of the cable being treated as Master,
               and the middle drive as Slave. With 40-wire cables, only Master and Slave
               jumper positions are used with most brands. See the drive markings or
               documentation for details.

Step 10.   Connect the data cable to the PATA header on the motherboard (if it is
               not already connected). See Figure 12-12.

1. Line up cable key with
   cutout in connector.   2. Push cable evenly into connector.

Figure 12-12   Connecting the PATA cable to the motherboard.

NOTE Move the jumper simply by grasping it with a pair of tweezers or small needle-nose pliers and gently pulling straight back. It's always best to change jumper settings before inserting the drive into the PC because they can be especially difficult to reach after the drive is installed.

Step 11. Verify correct data and power connections to all installed drives and host adapters.

Step 12. Reconnect AC power to the system, and start the BIOS configuration program.

Refer to Figure 12-11 to see a typical PATA drive before and after power and data cables are attached.

Figure 12-12 shows a PATA cable being connected to the motherboard's PATA header.

eSATA Drives

eSATA is an extension of SATA standards, enabling SATA-based external drives to be connected to desktop and laptop PCs via modified SATA ports.

eSATA host adapters plug in to PCI Express (PCIe) x1 or x4 slots. An SATA port can be converted to an eSATA port by connecting a header cable that mounts in an empty expansion slot. Single-port and dual-port cables are available (refer to Figure 12-6). eSATA cables (refer to Figure 12-6) are heavier than SATA cables, and use a different keying system.

NOTE If you want to adapt SATA ports on the motherboard to use eSATA ports with a header cable, you should configure the computer's SATA ports to run in AHCI mode. This enables hot-swapping and supports advanced SATA features for better performance.

Figure 12-13 illustrates an external hard disk with USB 2.0, eSATA, and dual IEEE-1394a (FireWire 400) ports.

Some laptops have combo eSATA/USB 2.0 ports. This type of port can connect to either type of device. Laptops with USB 3.0 drives can use third-party adapters to enable USB 3.0 ports to be connected to eSATA drives.

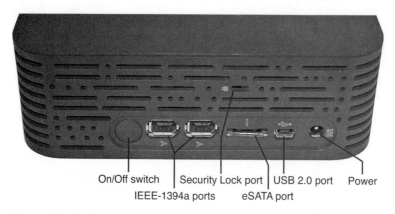

On/Off switch | Security Lock port | USB 2.0 port   Power
          IEEE-1394a ports   eSATA port

Figure 12-13   A multi-interface external hard disk with IEEE-1394a, eSATA, and USB 2.0 ports.

SSD and Flash Drives

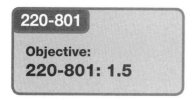

Flash memory is a type of memory that can retain its contents without electricity. It has no moving parts, so it is very durable. Standard flash memory is used in digital media players, memory cards for cameras and digital media devices, digital camcorders, and USB thumb drives.

Faster and higher-capacity forms of flash memory known as single-level cell (SLC) and multi-level cell (MLC) are used in solid state drives (SSDs), an emerging replacement for conventional hard disk drives.

Flash Memory Cards

Figure 12-14 compares the most common types of **flash memory** cards to each other. Table 12-3 lists the capacities and typical uses of the most common flash memory card types.

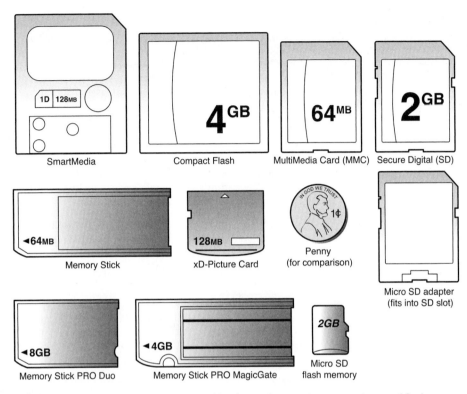

Figure 12-14   A U.S. penny compared in size to the most common types of flash memory cards.

Table 12-3   Flash Memory Card Capacities and Uses

Media Type	Common Capacity	Common Uses	Notes
SmartMedia (SM)	Up to 128MB	Digital cameras	Now obsolete.
CompactFlash (CF)	Up to 128GB	Digital SLR cameras; high-end point-and-shoot digital cameras	Check manufacturer's speed rating for best performance in burst mode.
MultiMedia Card (MMC)	Up to 4GB	Various devices	Largely replaced by SD and SDHC.
Memory Stick	Up to 128MB	Sony digital cameras and digital media devices	Older Sony point-and-shoot digital cameras and digital media devices; also PlayStation 3 (PS3).

Table 12-3 Continued

Media Type	Common Capacity	Common Uses	Notes
Memory Stick PRO MagicGate	Up to 4GB	Sony digital cameras and digital media devices, including PlayStation Portable	Recent Sony point-and-shoot digital cameras and digital media devices, including PlayStation Portable (PSP) and PS3.
Memory Stick PRO Duo	Up to 32GB	Sony digital cameras and digital media devices, including PlayStation Portable	Recent Sony point-and-shoot digital cameras and digital media devices, including PSP and PS3.
Secure Digital (SD)	Up to 2GB	Most models of point-and-shoot digital cameras; some digital SLR cameras; many flash memory–based media players	Has write-protect switch on left side of media. Can also be used in place of SDHC or SDXC memory.
Secure Digital High Capacity (SDHC)	Up to 32GB	Many recent models of point-and-shoot digital cameras, digital SLR cameras, and flash memory–based media players	SDHC media has the same physical form factor as SD; however, only devices made for SDHC can use SDHC. These devices are also compatible with SD. Check with device vendor for details.
Secure Digital Extended Capacity (SDXC)	Up to 128GB	Some high-performance digital SLR cameras	SDXC media has the same physical form factor as SD and SDHC; however, only devices made for SDXC media can use it.
miniSD	2GB	Mobile phones and cameras	Can be used in SD or SDHC slots with an optional adapter.
miniSDHC	32GB	Mobile phones and cameras	Can be used in SDHC slots with an optional adapter.
microSD	2GB	Various portable devices: mobile phones, video games, and expandable USB flash memory drives	Can also be used in place of microSDHC; can be used in SD or SDHC slots with an optional adapter.
microSDHC	32GB	Various portable devices: mobile phones, video games, and expandable USB flash memory drives	Device must support microSDHC; can be used in SDHC slots with an optional adapter.

Media Type	Common Capacity	Common Uses	Notes
xD-Picture Card	Up to 512MB (standard) Up to 2GB (Type M, Type M+, Type H)	Older FujiFilm and Olympus digital point-and-shoot cameras	Some cameras also support SD memory.

Flash Card Reader

To enable flash memory cards (refer to Figure 12-14 and Table 12-3) to be used with a computer, use a **card reader**. Figure 12-15 shows a typical external multislot card reader, and Figure 12-16 shows a typical internal multislot card reader. Most card readers assign a separate drive letter to each slot.

Figure 12-15   This multislot card reader supports a wide variety of flash memory cards and usually connects to a USB 2.0 port.

Figure 12-16   An internal card reader connects to an unused USB 2.0 port header on the motherboard.

> **NOTE**   Some printers and multifunction devices also include card readers. Some card readers built in to printers and multifunction devices are used only for printing, whereas others can be used to transfer files to and from the host computer.

When you insert a flash memory card containing files, Windows XP/Vista/7 might display an AutoPlay dialog providing various programs that can be used to view or use the files on the card (see Figure 12-17). If AutoPlay does not appear, open Computer/My Computer or Windows Explorer and navigate to the appropriate drive letter to use the files on the card.

Figure 12-17   A typical AutoPlay menu displayed by Windows 7 when a flash memory card containing photos is inserted into a card reader.

USB Flash Memory Drives

USB flash memory drives have largely replaced floppy drives for transfers of data between systems or for running utility programs. USB flash memory drives, like flash memory cards, use flash memory, a type of memory that retains information without a continuous flow of electricity. However, USB flash memory drives do not require a card reader.

USB flash memory drives are preformatted with the FAT16, FAT32, or exFAT (FAT64) file system and are ready to use. Simply plug one into a USB port, and it is immediately assigned a drive letter. You can copy, modify, and delete information on a USB flash memory drive, just as with a hard disk or floppy drive. A typical USB flash memory drive is shown in Figure 12-18.

Figure 12-18   A USB flash memory drive with a retractable connector.

SSD

A solid state drive (**SSD**) is a recent development in flash memory technology. Unlike conventional flash memory drives, an SSD is designed to emulate a hard disk, and you can use it in place of a hard disk in mobile devices such as netbooks and Ultrabooks as well as for high-performance laptops and desktops. An SSD (see Figure 12-19) uses a 2.5-inch form factor, but an optional 2.5-inch to 3.5-inch adapter enables it to be installed in a desktop computer.

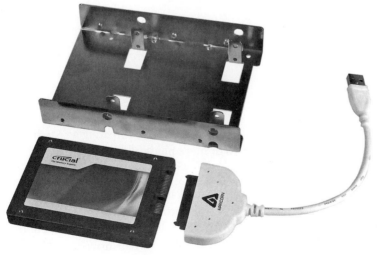

Figure 12-19   An SSD with optional data transfer cable and 2.5-inch to 3.5-inch bay adapter.

SSDs use one of two types of flash memory: multilevel cell (**MLC**) and single-level cell (**SLC**). MLC memory has lower performance than SLC and doesn't support as many write cycles, but it is much less expensive per GB than SLC memory. Almost all SSDs sold in the consumer space use MLC flash memory. The differences in performance for similarly sized drives result from the controller used, the firmware version in use, and whether the drive uses separate memory for caching or uses a portion of the SSD.

Although SSDs emulate hard disks, there are differences in their operation. Because unnecessary writing to flash memory causes premature failure, SSDs should not be defragmented, and newer SSDs use a feature known as TRIM to automatically deal-locate space used by deleted files and make it available for reuse. TRIM is supported by Windows 7, but older SSDs require you to use vendor-supplied utilities to perform this task.

Windows 7 is the first version of Microsoft Windows with integrated SSD support. When Windows 7 detects an SSD, it enables TRIM (if the drive supports this command), disables defragment, and disables other utilities such as ReadyBoost and SuperFetch that are designed for use with traditional hard disks.

> **TIP** An easy way to determine whether an SSD has been detected properly is to view its Windows Experience Index (WEI) score. An SSD should score 7.0 or above.

RAID

220-801

Objective:
220-801: 1.5

RAID (redundant array of inexpensive drives) is a method for creating a faster or safer single logical hard disk drive from two or more physical drives. The most common RAID levels include

- **RAID Level 0 (RAID 0)**—Two drives are treated as a single drive, with both drives used to simultaneously store different portions of the same file. This method of data storage is called striping. Striping boosts performance, but if either drive fails, all data is lost. Don't use striping for data drives.

- **RAID Level 1 (RAID 1)**—Two drives are treated as mirrors of each other; changes to the contents of one drive are immediately reflected on the other drive. This method of data storage is called mirroring. Mirroring provides a built-in backup method and provides faster read performance than a single drive. Suitable for use with program and data drives.

- **RAID Level 0+1 (RAID 10)**—Four drives combine striping plus mirroring for extra speed plus better reliability. Suitable for use with program and data drives.

- **RAID Level 5 (RAID 5)**—Three or more drives are treated as a logical array, and parity information (used to recover data in the event of a drive failure) is spread across all drives in the array. Suitable for use with program and data drives.

Most PCs with RAID support include support for Levels 0, 1, and 10. Table 12-4 provides a quick comparison of these types of RAID arrays.

Table 12-4   Comparisons of Common RAID Levels

RAID Level	Minimum Number of Drives Required	Data Protection Features	Total Capacity of Array	Major Benefit over Single Drive	Notes
0	2	None.	2 × capacity of either drive (if same size) OR 2 × capacity of smaller drive.	Improved read/write performance	Also called "striping"
1	2	Changes to contents of one drive immediately performed on other drive.	Capacity of one drive (if same size); OR capacity of smaller drive.	Automatic backup; faster read performance	Also called "mirroring"
10	4	Changes on one two-drive array are immediately performed on other two-drive array.	Capacity of smallest drive × number of drives / 2.	Improved read/write performance and automatic backup	Also called "striped and mirrored"
5	3	Parity information is saved across all drives.	(x-1) Capacity of smallest drive (x equals the number of drives in the array).	Full data redundancy in all drives; hot swap of damaged drive supported in most implementations	

Creating an ATA or SATA RAID Array

RAID **arrays** have been common for years on servers using SCSI-interface drives. However, a number of recent systems feature ATA RAID or SATA RAID host adapters on the motherboard. ATA and SATA RAID host adapter cards can also be retrofitted to systems lacking onboard RAID support. These types of RAID arrays are also referred to as hardware RAID arrays. RAID arrays can also be created through operating system settings and are sometimes called software RAID arrays. However, software RAID arrays are not as fast as hardware RAID arrays.

Motherboards that support only two drives in a RAID array support only RAID 0 and RAID 1. Motherboards that support more than two drives can also support RAID Level 0+1 (also known as RAID 10), and some support RAID 5 as well. RAID-enabled host adapters support varying levels of RAID.

NOTE   ATA or SATA RAID host adapters might also support non-RAID ATA or SATA host adapter functions. Check the system BIOS setup or add-on card host adapter setup for details.

An ATA or SATA RAID array requires

- **Two or more drives**—It's best to use identical drives (same capacity, buffer size, and RPMs). However, you can mix and match drives. If some drives are larger than others, the additional capacity will be ignored. Refer to Table 12-4. You can use standard hard disks, hybrid hard disks, or SSDs.

- **A RAID-compatible motherboard or add-on host adapter card**—Both feature a special BIOS, which identifies and configures the drives in the array.

Because RAID arrays use off-the-shelf drives, the only difference in the physical installation of drives in a RAID array is where they are connected. They must be connected to a motherboard or add-on card that has RAID support.

NOTE   Sometimes RAID connectors are made from a contrasting color of plastic compared to other drive connectors. However, the best way to determine whether your system or motherboard supports ATA or SATA RAID arrays is to read the manual for the system or motherboard.

After the drives used to create the array are connected to the RAID array's host adapter, restart the computer. If you are using the motherboard's RAID interface, start the system BIOS setup program, and make sure the RAID function is enabled (see Figure 12-20). Save changes and exit the BIOS setup program.

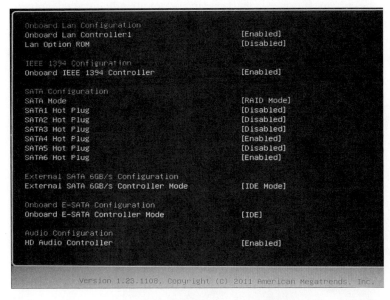

Figure 12-20   Enabling SATA RAID in a typical system BIOS.

When you restart the computer, watch for a prompt from the RAID BIOS to start the configuration process (see Figure 12.21).

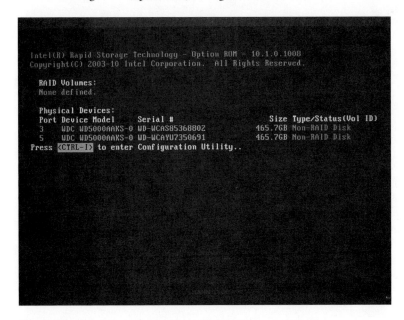

Figure 12-21   A typical prompt to start RAID array setup.

Specify the RAID setting wanted and any optional settings you want to use (see Figure 12.22). After the RAID array is configured, the drives are handled as a single physical drive by the system. If drivers for the array are not already installed, you need to install them when prompted by the computer. If you are installing Windows XP to a RAID array that is not recognized by Windows, you must provide driver files on a floppy disk. For Windows Vista and 7, you can provide driver files on USB or optical discs if necessary.

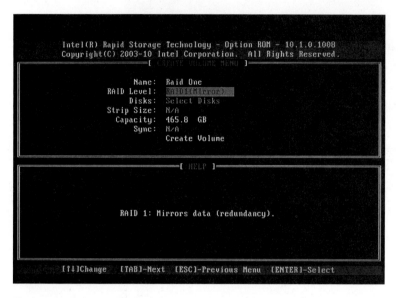

Figure 12-22   Preparing to create an SATA RAID1 array.

CAUTION   If one or more of the drives to be used in the array already contains data, back up the drives before starting the configuration process! Most RAID array host adapters delete the data on all drives in the array when creating an array, sometimes with little warning.

If you do not have RAID adapters in your system, you can create a software RAID volume, also known as a disk array, by using Windows. To learn how to create a software RAID volume, see "Disk Management" in Chapter 14, "Using and Managing Windows."

Optical Drives

220-801

Objective:
220-801: 1.5

Optical drives fall into three major categories:

- Those based on CD technology, including CD-ROM, CD-R (recordable CD), and CD-RW (rewritable CD)

- Those based on DVD technology, including DVD-ROM, DVD-ROM/ CD-RW combo, DVD-RAM, DVD-R/RW, DVD+R/RW, and DVD±R/RW

- Those based on Blu-ray technology, including BD-ROM, Combo BD-ROM/ DVD Super Multi, BD-R, and BD-RE

Internal CD and DVD drives typically connect via PATA or SATA. Internal Blu-ray drives connect via SATA. External drives connect via USB 2.0 or USB 3.0 ports.

To install an internal optical drive, you must remove the cover from the front of the 5.25-inch drive bay you plan to use.

Comparing CD, DVD, and Blu-ray Drives and Media

CD, **DVD**, and **Blu-ray** drives store data in a continuous spiral of indentations called pits and lands on the nonlabel side of the media from the middle of the media outward to the edge. All drives use a laser to read data; the difference between the storage capacities of Blu-ray, DVD, and CD is due to the difference in laser wavelength: Blu-ray, which has the highest capacity, uses a blue laser with a shorter wavelength than DVD or CD; DVD uses a red laser with a longer wavelength than Blu-ray but shorter than CD; CD, which has the lowest capacity, uses a near-infrared laser with the longest wavelength. The shorter the wavelength, the smaller the pits and lands, enabling more data to be stored in the same space.

Most CD, DVD, and Blu-ray drives are tray-loading, but a few use a slot-loading design. Slot-loading designs are more common in home and automotive electronics products.

CD-R and CD-RW drives use special media types and a more powerful laser than that used on CD-ROM drives to write data to the media. CD-R media is a write-once media—the media can be written to during multiple sessions, but older data cannot be deleted. CD-RW media can be rewritten up to 1,000 times. 80-minute CD-R media has a capacity of 700MB, whereas the older 74-minute CD-R media has a capacity of 650MB. CD-RW media capacity is up to 700MB, but is often less, depending on how the media is formatted.

Similarly, DVD-R and DVD+R media is recordable but not erasable, whereas DVD-RW and DVD+RW media uses a phase-change medium similar to CD-RW and can be rewritten up to 1,000 times. DVD-RAM can be rewritten up to 100,000 times, but DVD-RAM drives and media are less compatible with other types of DVD drives and media than the other rewritable DVD types, making DVD-RAM the least popular DVD format.

DVD Media Types

Here's more about the many members of the DVD family:

- **DVD-RAM**—A rewriteable/erasable media similar to CD-RW but more durable; it can be single sided (4.7GB) or double sided (9.4GB).

- **DVD-R**—A writeable/nonerasable media similar to CD-R; capacity of 4.7GB. Some DVD-RAM and all DVD-RW drives can use DVD-R media. DL media includes a second recording layer (capacity of 8.4GB).

- **DVD-RW**—A single-sided rewriteable/erasable media similar to CD-RW; capacity of 4.7GB. DVD-RW drives can also write to DVD-R media.

- **DVD+RW**—A rewritable/erasable media. Also similar to CD-RW but not interchangeable with DVD-RW or DVD-RAM; capacity of 4.7GB.

- **DVD+R**—A writeable/nonerasable media. Also similar to CD-R but not interchangeable with DVD-R; capacity of 4.7GB. DL media includes a second recording layer (capacity of 8.4GB).

So-called SuperMulti DVD drives can read and write all types of DVD media as well as CD media. Some early DVD+R/RW and DVD-R/RW drives cannot write to DL media.

Blu-ray Media Types

All Blu-ray drives are compatible with BD-ROM (read-only, Blu-ray media), such as the media used for Blu-ray movies. BD-R media is writeable/nonerasable. Thus, BD-R media is the Blu-ray equivalent of CD-R, DVD-R, or DVD+R. BD-RE media is rewritable and erasable, making it the Blu-ray equivalent of CD-RW, DVD-RW, or DVD+RW.

All single-layer standard size Blu-ray media has a capacity of 25GB; dual-layer Blu-ray media has a capacity of 50GB.

Drive Speed Ratings

Drive speeds are measured by an X-rating:

- When working with CD media, 1X equals 150KBps, the data transfer rate used for reading music CDs. Multiply the X-rating by 150 to determine the drive's data rate for reading, writing, or rewriting CD media.

- When working with DVD media, 1X equals 1.385MBps; this is the data transfer rate used for playing DVD-Video (DVD movies) content. Multiply the X-rating by 1.385 to determine the drive's data rate for reading, writing, or rewriting DVD media.

- When working with Blu-ray media, 1X equals 4.5MBps; this is the data transfer rate for playing Blu-ray movies. Multiply the X-rating by 4.5 to determine the drive's data rate for reading, writing, or rewriting Blu-ray media.

Note that Blu-ray drives are also compatible with CD and DVD media. Check the specifications for a particular drive to determine the specific types of media a drive supports and the maximum read/write/rewrite speeds for each media type.

Recording Files to Optical Discs

You can use the following methods to record files onto optical discs:

- Built-in recording features in Windows XP and later versions
- Third-party disc mastering programs
- Third-party drag-and-drop programs

All optical media must be formatted, but depending on how you write to the media, the formatting process might be incorporated into the writing process or require a separate step.

Recording CDs and DVDs in Windows XP

DVD-RAM drives are recognized as rewritable drives by all versions of Windows. However, recordable and rewriteable CD and DVD drives were treated as CD-ROM or DVD-ROM drives prior to Windows XP.

Windows XP provides rudimentary CD-R/RW recording capabilities with both CD-R/RW and rewritable DVD drives.

NOTE Commercial CD/DVD rewriting and mastering software such as Nero, Roxio Easy Media Creator, and others is highly recommended with Windows XP (and is required if you want to write to DVDs). Most rewritable drives sold at retail are equipped with some version of disc rewriting and mastering. However, some computer vendors have relied on the Windows XP recording feature to support their bundled CD-RW drives.

Windows XP's CD writing capability is automatically activated for any CD or DVD rewritable drive (although only CD-R/RW media is supported). To write files to the drive, insert a blank disc, drag files to the CD/DVD drive icon using Windows Explorer/My Computer, and click the CD/DVD drive icon. When the drive icon opens, files waiting to be written are listed. Click the task menu option **Write These files to CD** (see Figure 12-23).

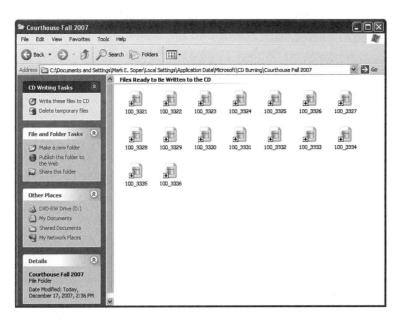

Figure 12-23 Preparing to write files to a CD using the Windows XP CD-writing wizard.

The files are written, albeit much more slowly than if you use a commercial CD-mastering or packet-writing program. When the files are written to disc, you are prompted to insert another disc or to close the wizard.

To erase files from a CD-RW disc, place the disc in the drive, open its icon in Windows Explorer/My Computer, select the file(s) to erase, and press the **Del** key to erase them.

NOTE   Because Windows XP doesn't format a CD-RW disc the same way a packet-writing (UDF disk format) program such as Drag to Disc, InCD, DLA, or the built-in DVD writing feature in Windows Vista and Windows 7 does, you cannot use a third-party program or Windows 7/Vista to erase files from a CD-RW disc written by Windows XP. You must use Windows XP to erase unwanted files. You can then reformat the media as wanted with a different program.

Creating Optical Discs in Windows Vista and 7

Windows Vista adds support for recordable and rewritable DVDs, and also adds additional functionality to the CD- or DVD-writing process. When you copy files to a recordable/rewritable CD or DVD drive using Windows Explorer, Send To, or other commands, Windows prompts you to insert a blank disc, and prompts you for a disc title. However, if you click the Show Formatting Options button, you can also choose how to format the disc (see Figure 12-24).

Which File System Is Best—and When

The default choice, **Live File System**, enables drag-and-drop file copying with both recordable and rewritable media, the ability to erase files when used with rewritable media, and support of individual file sizes more than 2GB. (2GB is the limit of the ISO 9660 file system used by the Mastered option.) However, Live File System discs (which use Universal Disc Format version 2.01 file system by default) might not be compatible with older operating systems and aren't suitable for use with CD or DVD drives in consumer and auto electronics systems. You can choose other Live File System (UDF) formats before the format process starts. See http://windows.microsoft.com/en-US/windows7/Which-CD-or-DVD-format-should-I-use for more information.

Use the Mastered option if you want to create a disc that can be read by virtually any drive on a PC, consumer electronics, or auto electronics device.

After selecting a format, click **Next** to continue. After the disc is formatted, Windows copies the files to the drive and displays a progress bar. At the end of the process, Windows displays the contents of the newly written disc.

If you use the Live File System, open Windows Explorer, right-click the disc, and select **Eject** so that the media will be prepared for use on other computers.

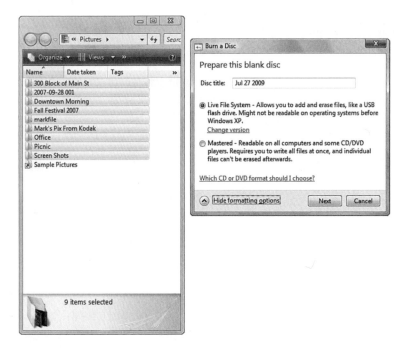

Figure 12-24   Selecting a disc format with Windows Vista's CD/DVD-writing wizard.

NOTE   When you insert a blank disc in Windows XP, Windows Vista, or Windows 7, you might have an AutoPlay dialog appear during the process. If you don't want to use any of the options on the AutoPlay menu, or you have already begun a process, close it.

Windows 7 includes all the CD and DVD writing features of Windows Vista and adds the ability to write a CD or DVD from an **ISO image** file (these files usually have the extension .iso) and support for writing to BD-R and BD-RE discs. However, you must use a third-party program if you want to create a video file on BD media. Figure 12-25 illustrates the Windows 7 Disc Image Burner.

Using Third-Party Optical Disc Mastering Programs

For more flexibility and the ability to save file lists for repeated burning at different times, consider a third-party disc mastering program. Some of the leading programs include Roxio Media Creator, Nero Multimedia Suite, ImgBurn (freeware), and CDBurner XP (freeware). These programs are sometimes bundled with rewriteable DVD and Blu-ray drives, or can be purchased or downloaded separately. Typical features include a wizard-based or menu-based burning process that makes it easier than with Windows to select the options needed, a preview option that shows you how much of a particular disc size will be used by your burning task, and options for creating audio discs for playback on a CD player.

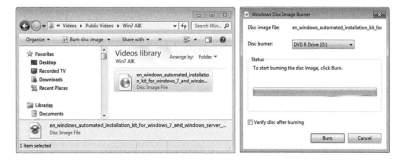

Figure 12-25 Burning an ISO image file to DVD with Disc Image Burner.

Using Third-Party Drag-and-Drop File Copying Programs

Some third-party disc mastering programs also include a drag-and-drop file copying utility. Examples include Roxio's Drag-to-Disc, Sonic's DLA (an improved version is known as Roxio Burn), and Nero's InCD. These utilities use the same UDF (Live File System) disc formats supported by Windows but provide more streamlined operation. For example, when you drag files to a disc prepared for drag-and-drop, the files are copied immediately.

These utilities are needed for Windows XP, which lacks true drag-and-drop capabilities, but are not needed with Windows Vista and Windows 7, which have integrated UDF support.

CAUTION   Because of differences in how different drag-and-drop programs function and the need to have UDF support installed in a computer that will be used with drag-and-drop media, you should test the capability of different computers to share (read and write) to media before implementing it in a production environment. A utility such as IsoBuster can read UDF media, even if the disc has problems.

Also, media that will be distributed outside an organization or home should be mastered. Mastered media can be read without the need to install a drag-and-drop program.

Floppy Drives

220-801

Objective:
220-801: 1.5

Floppy drives are now used primarily for bootable diagnostic disks and for the creation of bootable emergency or installation disks with Windows XP and older editions.

Floppy drives use flexible magnetic media protected by a rigid plastic case and a retractable shutter. There have been three different types of 3.5-inch floppy disk media used over time by PCs, although only the 1.44MB floppy disk is used currently.

Floppy Drive Capacities

Table 12-5 helps you distinguish between the different disk types.

Table 12-5   Physical Characteristics of 3.5-inch Floppy Media

Disk Type	Capacity	Write-Protect	Media Sensor	Typical Markings
3.5-inch DSDD	720KB	Open write-protect slider	N/A	—
3.5-inch DSHD	1.44MB	Open write-protect slider	Opposite write-protect slider	HD on disk shutter or jacket
3.5-inch DSED	2.88MB	Open write-protect slider	Opposite from write-protect slider and offset	ED on disk shutter or jacket

NOTE   Some older desktop and portable systems might use an LS-120 or LS-240 SuperDisk drive in place of a standard 1.44MB floppy drive. These drives can read and write 1.44MB and 720KB 3.5-inch floppy media but can also use high-capacity 3.5-inch media. The LS-120 SuperDisk uses 120MB media, and the LS-240 SuperDisk can use 120MB or 240MB media. These drives usually plug in to the ATA/ IDE (PATA) interface if internal, or the parallel or USB port if external.

5.25-inch floppy drives were used before 3.5-inch drives became commonplace, but they have been obsolete for some years and are seldom encountered today.

Floppy Disk Drive Hardware Configuration

Floppy disk drive hardware configuration depends on several factors, including

- **Correct CMOS configuration**—The system's BIOS configuration screen must have the correct drive selected for A: and B:. (Most recent systems with floppy drive support can support only one floppy drive.) The default on most recent systems is 1.44MB 3.5-inch, but because floppy drives are not detected, you need to verify this. You can also disable the floppy controller with the system BIOS program if you are not planning to use a floppy drive.

- **Correct cable positioning and attachment**—The position of the drive(s) on the cable determine which is A: and which is B:. If the cable is not oriented properly, the drive will spin continuously and the LED on the front of the drive will stay on. See Figure 12-26.

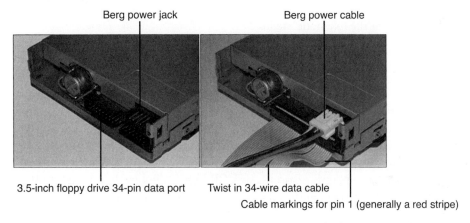

Berg power jack   Berg power cable

3.5-inch floppy drive 34-pin data port   Twist in 34-wire data cable

Cable markings for pin 1 (generally a red stripe)

Figure 12-26   A typical 3.5-inch 1.44MB floppy drive before (left) and after (right) attaching power and data cables. Note the twist in the data cable.

CAUTION   If you insert disks into a floppy drive while the data cable is reversed, the contents of the media can be damaged or the media can be rendered unusable. If you connect the power to a floppy drive incorrectly, the drive is damaged.

A 34-pin floppy disk drive data cable that supports drives A: and B: has wires numbered 10 to 16 twisted in reverse between the connectors for drive A: and drive B:. The drive beyond the twist is automatically designated as drive A:; the drive connected between the twisted and the untwisted end of the cable (which connects to the floppy controller) is automatically designated as drive B:. Older cables have two connectors for A: and for B:. The 34-pin connector is designed for 3.5-inch drives, whereas the edge connector is designed for 5.25-inch drives. The untwisted end of the cable is connected to the floppy header on the motherboard.

TIP If you need a floppy drive for only occasional use, you can connect an external floppy drive to the USB port. If you need to boot from an external floppy drive or need to load drivers from it during the installation of Windows, check the system BIOS setup program to verify that the drive is listed as a bootable device.

Maintaining Floppy Disks, Data, and Drives

You can protect the data on your floppy disks by following these recommendations; most of these suggestions also apply to higher-capacity magnetic removable media:

- Do not open the protective metal shutter on 3.5-inch disks or tape backups.

- Do not touch the magnetic media.

- Store disks away from sources of magnetism (CRT monitors, magnetized tools, unshielded speakers, and unshielded cables) or heat.

- Open the sliding write-protect hole on 3.5-inch disks to prevent the contents of the disk from being changed.

Floppy disk drives are a type of magnetic storage in which the read/write heads make direct contact with the media. This is similar to the way that tape drives work, and just like tape backup, music cassette, or VCR heads, a floppy disk drive's read/write heads can become contaminated by dust, dirt, smoke, or magnetic particles flaking off the disk's media surfaces. For this reason, periodic maintenance of floppy disk drives will help you avoid the need to troubleshoot drives that cannot reliably read or write data.

The following are some guidelines for cleaning a floppy disk drive:

- Whenever you open a system for any type of maintenance or checkup, review the condition of the floppy disk drive(s). Use compressed air to remove fuzz or hair from the drive.

- Approximately every 6 months, or more often in dirty or smoke-filled conditions, use a wet-type head-cleaning disk on the drive.

These cleaning kits use a special cleaning floppy disk that contains cleaning media in place of magnetic media, along with an alcohol-based cleaner. Add a few drops to the media inside the cleaning disk, slide it into the drive, and activate the drive with a command such as **DIR** or by using Windows Explorer; as the read/write heads move across the cleaning media, they are cleaned. Allow the heads to dry for about 1 hour before using the drive.

Tape Drives

220-801

Objective:
220-801: 1.5

Although **tape drive**s are primarily used by servers rather than desktops, they are also considered to be removable storage devices. Unlike disk-based removable storage, tape drives are used only for backup.

Tape drives use various types of magnetic tape. Their capacities are typically listed in two ways:

- Native (uncompressed) capacity
- Compressed capacity, assuming 2:1 compression

For example, a tape drive with a 70GB native capacity would also be described as having a 140GB compressed capacity. However, keep in mind that, depending on the data being backed up, you might be able to store more or (more typically) less than the listed capacity when using data compression.

NOTE Windows XP and Windows Vista include Removable Storage Manager (RSM). RSM supports tape backup drives that do not include drivers for Windows. RSM is enabled by default in Windows XP. However, it must be enabled in Windows Vista; use the Turn Windows Features On and Off setting in Control Panel. Windows 7 does not include RSM. To determine whether a particular tape drive is supported by drivers for Windows 7, check with the tape drive vendor.

Major types of tape drives include

- Travan (up to 40GB at 2:1 compression)
- DDS (up to 72GB at 2:1 compression)
- SLR (up to 140GB at 2:1 compression)

- VXA (up to 320GB at 2:1 compression)

- AIT (up to 800GB at 2:1 compression)

- DLT (up to 1.6TB at 2:1 compression)

- LTO Ultrium (up to 3TB [Generation 5] at 2:1 compression)

Most tape drives connect via SCSI interfaces, but some internal drives also connect via PATA or SATA interfaces, and some external tape drives use USB or FireWire interfaces. Most tape drives are also available in autoloader or tape library forms to permit backup automation, enabling unattended backup of drives that require multiple tapes.

Troubleshooting Hard Drives, SSDs, and RAID Arrays

220-802

Objective:
220-802: 4.3

Some of the common symptoms of problems with hard disk drives, SSDs, and RAID arrays include

- Read/write failure

- Slow performance

- Loud clicking noise

- Failure to boot

- Drive not recognized

- OS not found

- RAID not found

- RAID stops working

Use the following recommendations to help solve these problems.

NOTE   BSOD (also known as Blue Screen of Death or STOP errors) are discussed in Chapter 15, "Troubleshooting and Maintaining Windows."

Read/Write Failures

Read/write failures can take place for a number of reasons, including

- **Physical damage to the drive**—Dropping any magnetic storage drive can cause damage to read/write heads and platters. The drive may start to make noise or might not spin up at all.

- **Damaged cables**—PATA and SATA cables are often included with new motherboards and are inexpensive to purchase. Swapping cables is an easy first step that often solves the problem.

- **Damaged PATA or SATA host adapter on motherboard**—Most late-model motherboards have several SATA ports; if swapping an SATA cable doesn't solve the problem, use the original cable in a different SATA port on the motherboard.

- **Overheated hard disk**—The faster a hard disk turns (higher RPM), the more likely overheating can take place, especially if airflow is restricted. To prevent overheating, install a cooling fan in front of the 3.5-inch drive bays used for your hard disk(s) and make sure it pulls air into your PC. If you have two or more drives stacked on top of each other with limited airflow, move drives to other bays to improve airflow.

- **Overheated CPU or chipset**—Overheated CPU, chipset, or other components can cause read/write failures. Double-check case fans, the power supply fan, and the CPU and chipset's heat sinks. Remove dust and dirt from air intakes and fans. Remove loose or failed heat sinks, remove old thermal grease, and reassemble them with properly applied thermal grease.

Slow Performance

Although SATA, PATA, and SSD drives can all manifest slow performance, the causes and solutions for each type of drive vary widely.

To improve slow performance with SATA hard disks, look for these problems:

- **Reduced-performance configuration of 3Gbps or 6Gbps drives**—Some 3Gbps and 6Gbps SATA drives are jumpered to run at the next slower rate to enable compatibility with older host adapters. Remove the speed-reduction jumper when it is not needed; see drive documentation for details.

- **Using a 3Gbps cable with a 6Gbps drive and host adapter**—SATA cables made for 6Gbps drives can also be used with slower speeds.

- **SATA host adapter configured for IDE or emulation mode**—SATA host adapters can be configured by the system BIOS to run in IDE (emulation) mode, RAID mode, or AHCI mode. Use AHCI mode to enable full performance because this mode supports native command queuing (NCQ) and other advanced features.

- **SATA host adapter configured to run at reduced speed**—SATA host adapters on some systems can be configured to run at different speeds, such as 6.0Gbps, 3.0Gbps, or Auto. Select 6.0Gbps when using a 6.0Gbps drive and cabling. To enable the drive and host adapter to autonegotiate the correct speed, select Auto.

To improve slow performance with PATA hard disks, check for the following issues:

- **Incorrect cable type**—To achieve UDMA-66, 100, or 133 speeds with PATA drives, the 80-wire cable must be used. If a 40-wire cable is in use, replace it.

- **Drive configured to run at UDMA-33 speed**—Some older drives designed to run at UDMA-66 speeds might be configured (with a jumper block or by software) to run at lower speeds. Reconfigure the drive and be sure to use the 80-wire PATA cable to achieve the maximum speeds supported by the hard disk and host adapter.

- **Drive not configured to use IDE block mode**—Almost all PATA drives in use support IDE block mode, which enables the drive to read multiple sectors with a single command. If a PATA hard disk is manually configured in the system BIOS, IDE block mode might not be enabled. Enable IDE block mode manually, or configure the drive type as Auto in the system BIOS to have the drive's use of block mode be detected by the system.

- **Operating system not configured to use busmastering drivers**—A busmaster bypasses the CPU for data transfers between memory and the hard disk interface. This option is both operating system–specific and motherboard/host adapter–specific. If you have installed a new motherboard, busmastering drivers are provided on a driver CD or floppy disk or can be downloaded from the vendor. They are preinstalled on complete systems.

- **DMA transfers not enabled in Windows**—Busmastering drivers enable PATA hard disk host adapters to use DMA transfers. To enable DMA transfers after installing the correct busmastering drivers, check the properties sheet for the specific PATA host adapter used for a drive and enable DMA transfers. See the sidebar "Configuring DMA Transfers for PATA in Windows" for details.

- **PATA hard disk and optical drive on same cable**—For maximum performance, a PATA hard disk should be on a separate cable from PATA optical drives. On systems that have only one PATA host adapter but several SATA host adapters, upgrade to an SATA hard disk or use an adapter that enables PATA drives to connect to SATA host adapters. Configure the SATA adapter to run in IDE mode.

Configuring DMA Transfers for PATA in Windows

Before enabling DMA or UDMA mode, check the documentation for the drive to see if it supports this mode. Enabling DMA or UDMA on a drive that does not support it can have disastrous effects.

Step 1. Open the System Properties sheet.

Step 2. Open Device Manager.

Step 3. To determine which drives are connected to which host adapter, open the category containing the drives (Disk Drives for hard or removable-media drives or DVD/CD-ROM Drives for optical drives), and double-click the drive to open its Properties sheet. The location value visible on the General tab shows to which host adapter and device number the drive is connected. For example, location 0 (1) indicates the drive is connected to the primary host adapter (0) as the secondary device (1).

Step 4. Click the plus sign next to the IDE ATA/ATAPI Controllers category.

Step 5. Click the host adapter for which you want to adjust properties (primary or secondary IDE channel) to open its Properties sheet.

Step 6. Click **Advanced Settings**.

Step 7. To enable DMA for a particular drive, select **DMA** if available for the Transfer mode. If you need to disable DMA transfers (for example, for slow optical drives), select **PIO Only** (Windows XP) or clear the Enable DMA check box (Windows Vista/7).

Step 8. Click **OK**.

Step 9. Restart the computer as prompted.

For more information on why certain systems might not use DMA/UDMA transfers and why Windows sometimes disables DMA, see http://winhlp.com/node/10.

To improve slow performance with SSDs, look for the following issues:

- **Connecting the drive to a slow SATA host adapter**—Early SSDs were designed for 3Gbps SATA interfaces, but most recent models support the faster 6Gbps interface. When using an SSD on a system with a mixture of 3Gbps and 6Gbps SATA ports, be sure to use the 6Gbps ports.

- **The partition may be misaligned**—Windows 7 and Windows Vista automatically create the first partition on an SSD so that it is on a page boundary to provide maximum performance. However, if you do not use the entire SSD for a single partition, additional partitions might be misaligned (starting in the middle of a page rather than on a page boundary). Misaligned partitions cause slow read/write/reallocate performance. Instead of using Disk Management to create additional partitions, use the command-line program DISKPART and specify Align=1024 as part of the Create partition command. See http://support.microsoft.com/kb/300415 for the complete syntax.

- **The TRIM command is not enabled for the drive**—If the drive does not support TRIM, you must periodically run a utility provided by the drive vendor to reallocate deleted disk sectors. If the drive supports TRIM and you are using it with Windows 7, Windows needs to be optimized for use with SSDs.

- **Not optimizing the operating system for use with SSDs**—Although Windows 7 is designed to disable SuperFetch, defragment, and other services that can slow down SSD performance, it does not always detect an SSD as an SSD. Use the free SSD Tweak Utility (available online from many sources) to configure Windows 7/Vista/XP for maximum performance with SSDs. Using SSD Tweak can improve an SSD's Windows Experience Index rating significantly (in one example, from 5.9 to the maximum score of 7.9) as well as substantially improve real-world performance.

Noises Coming from Hard Disk

Hard disk drives are generally quiet. Loud noises coming from a drive can have at least two causes:

- **Loud clicking noises are typically caused by repeated re-reads of defective disk surfaces by the hard disk drive heads**—This is typically a sign of a failing drive. Replace the hard disk immediately after making a backup copy.

- **Humming noises can be caused by rapid head movement on a normally functioning hard disk**—This noise can be reduced or eliminated by enabling Automatic Acoustic Management (AAM), a feature of most recent hard disks. Some vendors provide a downloadable acoustic management tool. These reduce head speed to reduce noise, and may reduce drive performance as a result.

> **TIP**   If your drive vendor does not offer an acoustic management tool, you might be able to use the Hitachi Feature Tool (available from www.hgst.com/support/index-files/simpletech-legacy-downloads#FeatureTool) because it works with most Hitachi and many third-party hard disks.

Boot Failure

The primary hard disk is almost always the boot drive. Boot failures can have several causes. Check the following:

- **Boot sequence does not specify system hard disk, or lists system hard disk after other drives with nonbootable media**—Use the Boot Sequence dialog in the system BIOS to configure the hard disk as either the first boot device or as the second boot device after the optical drive. If a floppy drive is listed as the first boot device and the system is started with a nonbootable floppy, the system boot process will stop and display a boot error.

- **CMOS settings have been corrupted and system cannot find a bootable drive**—Reconfigure the CMOS settings, specify the system drive as a boot drive, and restart the system. Replace the battery if the settings continue to be corrupted.

- **PATA hard disk data cable is connected upside down**—Old 40-wire cables often lack keying, making it possible to connect the data cable incorrectly to either the drive or the motherboard. Many older systems send a spinup command to the hard disk at power-on and will not proceed with boot until the drive responds to the command. Make sure pin 1 on the cable (marked with a colored stripe) is connected to pin 1 on the drive and host adapter. Replace the unkeyed cable with a keyed 80-wire cable to prevent problems in the future.

> **NOTE**   To learn how to solve boot sector damage, corrupted boot.ini files, NTLDR Is Missing or NTDETECT.com errors, see Chapter 15.

Drive Not Recognized

Drive-recognition problems can involve problems with cabling, power, BIOS settings, or hard disk failure. If the hard disk is running (you can usually hear faint sounds from a working hard disk), check the following:

- **Bus-powered USB hard disk not recognized**—A bus-powered USB 2.0 hard disk needs 500mA of power to run (and some temporarily use more power to spin up). Some computers don't provide enough power in their root hubs (built-in USB ports) to support a bus-powered hard disk, and bus-powered hubs can provide only 100mA of power per port. Connect the drive to another port on a different root hub (each pair of USB ports is a root hub) or a self-powered USB hub, or use a Y-cable to pull power from two USB ports.

- **USB or FireWire drive not recognized**—If the data cable between the drive and the port is loose, the drive will not be recognized. Reconnect the cable to both the drive and the port and the drive should be recognized.

- **SATA, PATA, or SSD drive not recognized**—Loose or missing power or data cables causes this problem. Shut down the computer, disconnect it from AC power, and reconnect power and data cables. If you use Y-splitters or converters to provide power to some drives, keep in mind that these can fail.

- **PATA drives not recognized**—If you connect two PATA drives on a single cable and they are not properly jumpered, the system cannot recognize them. If you are using an 80-wire cable, both drives should normally be jumpered as cable select (CS or CSEL). However, if the system cannot properly identify the drives, replace the data cable. If the system still cannot recognize the drives, jumper the drive at the end of the cable as Master and the drive in the middle of the cable as Slave. This problem happens more often when the drives on the cable are from different vendors.

- **Single PATA drive not recognized**—If a single drive on a PATA cable is not recognized, make sure the drive is configured for single-drive operation. This might require removing the jumper. Check drive documentation for details.

Operating System Not Found

If the operating system is not found during boot, check the following:

- **Nonbootable disk in drive A:**—If the floppy drive is listed before the hard disk in the boot sequence and it contains a nonbootable disk, the computer displays an error message that it couldn't find the operating system. Remove the disk and restart.

- **Boot sequence doesn't list hard disk**—Restart the computer, start the BIOS setup procedure, and make sure the hard disk is listed as a bootable drive and is listed before options such as network boot.

- **Incorrect installation of another operating system**—Windows automatically sets up its own boot manager for access to more than one Windows version if you install the older version of Windows first followed by the later version. However, if you install a newer version first and install an older version later or install a non-Windows OS later, you cannot access the newer Windows version unless you install a custom boot manager.

RAID Not Found

RAID not found problems can result from the following:

- **RAID function disabled in system BIOS**—Reconfigure PATA and SATA ports used for RAID as RAID and restart the system.

- **Power or data cables to RAID drives disconnected**—Reconnect cables to RAID drive(s) and restart the system.

RAID Failure

A RAID failure is caused by the failure of one or more of the disk drives in the RAID array. Take the following steps if a single drive failure occurs:

- **RAID 0**—Determine which drive has failed. Replace it and follow the vendor's recommendations to re-create the array. Restore the latest backup. Any data that has not been backed up is lost.

- **RAID 1, RAID 10, and RAID 5**—Determine which drive has failed. Replace it. Follow the procedures provided by the RAID vendor to rebuild the array.

If both drives have failed in a RAID 0 or RAID 1 array, you must rebuild the array with new drives and restore the latest backup. Any data that has not been backed up is lost.

If two or more drives have failed in a RAID 10 or RAID 5 array, your recovery options might vary according to the exact configuration of the array. See the RAID vendor's procedures for details and recovery options.

Disk Surface and Data Recovery Tools

If read/write errors or other problems that could lead to data loss occur, become familiar with the following tools and techniques you can use to recover data and restore an ailing drive to health.

Using External Drive Enclosures and Docks

The easiest way to retrieve data from a drive you believe is working but is installed in a failed system is to move the drive into an external drive enclosure. These drive enclosures include a PATA or SATA interface internally and a USB 2.0, USB 3.0, eSATA, or FireWire interface externally. A bridge component converts one type of signal to the other. Figure 12-27 illustrates a typical external drive enclosure designed for SATA hard disks.

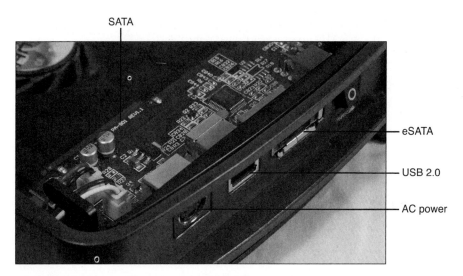

Figure 12-27   A typical external drive enclosure for SATA drives; this example connects to eSATA and USB ports.

When connected, a hard disk in an external drive enclosure is detected like any other external drive. Assuming the drive is working properly, the data on the drive can be copied to a different computer.

As an alternative to a drive enclosure, you can use an external drive dock. It has a slot on one side to allow an SATA hard disk (or a PATA hard disk in older dock models) to be plugged in for temporary access.

One limitation of drive enclosures and docks, especially when connected to USB ports, is that the PATA or SATA/USB bridge prevents low-level access to the drive for disk diagnostics programs supplied by the drive vendor.

Windows-Based Disk Tools

Windows includes the following disk tools: CHKDSK and FORMAT. (Although the CompTIA A+ Certification exam also lists FDISK, its functionality is now incorporated into Disk Management and DISKPART.) To learn more about using CHKDSK, see Chapter 15. To learn more about FORMAT and Disk Management, see Chapter 14.

Using Hard Disk Diagnostics

Most hard disk vendors provide diagnostic programs that can be used to test drives for errors. The latest versions of these programs can be obtained from the drive vendors' websites.

Typically, these programs offer a quick and a long test option. To determine whether a hard disk is functioning, run the quick test first (see Figure 12-28). If the drive passes, use the long test to determine whether the drive is working within specifications.

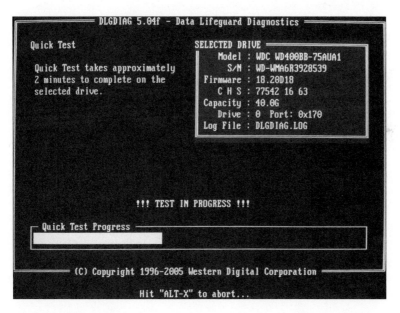

Figure 12-28 Performing a quick test on a Western Digital hard disk with vendor-supplied diagnostic software.

During the long test, defective areas on the drive can be replaced by spare capacity built in to the drive. Because defective areas on the disk might not be able to be moved to another location, drive vendors often recommend you perform a full backup before testing a hard disk.

Using Data Recovery Software

If you cannot restore a hard disk to health but do not have up-to-date backups of the data it contains, you might need to use data recovery software to attempt to locate and rescue your data.

CAUTION   To avoid data loss, never install a data recovery program on a drive that you are attempting to recover data from. And make sure you select a program that copies the data located to another drive. Because the need for data recovery is often caused by a failing drive, it's essential to make sure the data is safe after it is recovered.

There are three levels of data recovery software to consider:

- Do-it-yourself data recovery
- Commercial data recovery software
- Data recovery services

By booting with a Linux Live CD distribution (distro) that supports Windows file systems (most systems use NTFS), you can often recover your data by copying it to a different drive. The Knoppix Linux Live CD and Parted Magic distros are often used for this purpose.

Many vendors offer data recovery software, and most provide trial versions that you can use to preview your results. These programs work by bypassing normal disk structures, such as partitions and root directories, to access the disk contents directly.

If you cannot retrieve data with a bootable disc or with data recovery software, your last alternative is to use a data recovery service. These services can cost hundreds or thousands of dollars, but if you need to recover large amounts of customer data, accounting data, or line-of-business information, these services might be worth the money. These services can be performed remotely on drives that don't have physical damage to circuit boards or read-write heads, but some recovery services also use clean rooms that enable the safe dismantling of damaged drives so that defective read-write heads or other components can be replaced.

Exam Preparation Tasks

Review All the Key Topics

Review the most important topics in the chapter, noted with the Key Topic icon in the outer margin of the page. Table 12-6 lists a reference of these key topics and the page numbers on which each is found.

Table 12-6   Key Topics for Chapter 12

Key Topic Element	Description	Page Number
Table 12-1	Drive interface overview	503
Figure 12-1	PATA, SATA, floppy interfaces	504
Figure 12-2	PATA data cables	506
Figure 12-3	PATA jumper blocks	507
Figure 12-6	SATA and eSATA data cables	510
Figure 12-17	AutoPlay dialog	524
Figure 12-19	SSD	525
Table 12-4	RAID levels	527
List	DVD media types	532
List	Boot failure	547
List	Drive not recognized	548

Complete the Tables and Lists from Memory

Print a copy of Appendix A, "Memory Tables" (found on the CD), or at least the section for this chapter, and complete the tables and lists from memory. Appendix B, "Memory Tables Answer Key," also on the CD, includes completed tables and lists to check your work.

Define Key Terms

Define the following key terms from this chapter, and check your answers in the glossary.

AHCI, ATA, Blu-ray, cable select, card reader, CD, DVD, eSATA, flash memory, ISO image, Live File System, master, MLC, PATA, RPM, SATA, slave, SLC, SSD, tape drive

Complete Hands-On Lab

Complete the hands-on labs, and then see the answers and explanations at the end of the chapter.

Lab 12-1: Configure SATA Ports

Scenario: You are a technician working at a PC repair bench. Your client indicates that some of the SATA hard disks are not running as fast as expected.

Procedure:

Review Figure 12-29 to answer question 1.

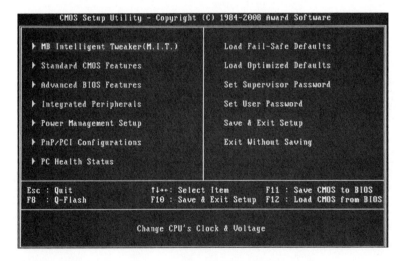

Figure 12-29   Main menu of a typical CMOS (BIOS) setup.

Question 1: From this menu (BIOS main menu), which option is most likely to access the SATA host adapter configuration menu?

Review Figure 12-30 to answer question 2.

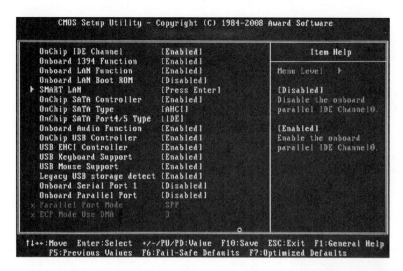

Figure 12-30 CMOS/BIOS dialog including SATA host adapter settings.

Question 2: From this menu, which SATA ports are not configured for best performance?

Question 3: What is the SATA BIOS setting needed for best performance?

Question 4: Which key would you press to saved changes and restart the computer?

Lab 12-2: Configure PATA Jumper Blocks

Scenario: You are a technician working at a PC repair bench. You are servicing a system with two PATA drives (hard drive and DVD drive), and users have been complaining of slow drive performance. The hard disk and DVD drive are designed to run at UDMA 66 or faster speeds. The system has two PATA host adapters.

What steps should you take to ensure best performance?

Procedure:

Use Figures 12-31 through 12-33 to answer the following questions.

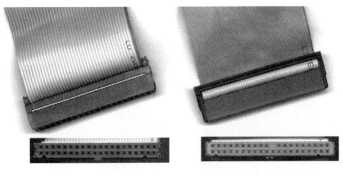

40-wire PATA data cable   80-wire PATA data cable

Figure 12-31   PATA cables.

Figure 12-32   Jumper settings on a hard drive.

Figure 12-33   Jumper settings on a DVD drive.

Question 1: The hard drive and DVD drive are connected to the same cable. It has 40 wires. You can also use an 80 wire cable (refer to Figure 12-31). What steps should you take to improve performance? (Choose all that apply.)

A: Change to 80 wire cable.

B: Change BIOS settings to UDMA.

C: Remove all drive jumpers.

D: Move the DVD drive to its own PATA host adapter.

E: Change drive jumpers.

Question 2: Looking at the drive in Figure 12-32, which jumper setting would you use for this drive based on the answers to Question 1?

Master (MA)

Slave (SL)

Cable Select (CS or CSEL)

Question 3: Looking at the drive in Figure 12-33, which jumper setting would you use for this drive based on the answers to Question 1?

Master (MA)

Slave (SL)

Cable Select (CS or CSEL)

Answer Review Questions

Answer these review questions and then see the answers and explanations at the end of the chapter.

1. Which of the following media types are used by a Super Multi DVD drive? (Select all that apply.)

    a. Blu-ray (BD)

    b. DVD+RW

    c. DVD-R DL

    d. LS-240 SuperDisk

2. Which of the following interfaces are typically used for internal hard disks on desktop PCs? (Select all that apply.)

    a. USB 3.0

    b. PATA

    c. eSATA

    d. SATA

3. Select the correct statement about PATA drives.

    a. PATA drives can use only 80-wire cables.

    b. PATA drives run at top speed when used with 40-wire cables.

    c. PATA UDMA133 drives are the only drives that require an 80-wire cable.

    d. PATA UDMA66 and faster drives require an 80-wire cable.

4. Select the correct statement about SATA drives.

    a. The slowest SATA drive runs at 1.0Gbps.

    b. SATA hard disks must use locking cables.

    c. SATA 3Gbps drives are compatible with slower SATA ports.

    d. SATA is used only by hard disk drives.

5. You have just installed an eSATA hard disk on your system by using an eSATA/SATA header cable. If you want to hot-swap the drive, which of the following configuration settings are needed in the system BIOS for the SATA port?

    a. Configure port for IDE mode.

    b. No changes needed in any event.

    c. Configure port for UDMA mode.

    d. Configure port for AHCI mode.

6. You have installed an SSD in a new Windows 7 system, and its performance is no faster than the hard disk it replaced. Which of the following steps should you perform to improve performance? (Choose all that apply.)

    a. Configure SATA port for IDE mode.

    b. Install new drivers in Windows.

    c. Upgrade drive to newest firmware version.

    d. Use tweaking utility for SSD drives.

7. You are upgrading a system with a tape backup drive from Windows XP to Windows 7. To ensure that existing tapes can be read by Windows 7, what else do you need to install?

    a. Removable Storage Manager for Windows 7.

    b. New drive firmware.

    c. Configure backup program to run in Windows XP compatibility mode.

    d. Windows 7 drivers for drive.

8. You need to install a RAID 1 array for a client. The client needs a minimum capacity of 500GB in the array and offers two available drives for possible use: 750GB and 1TB. Which of the following is the best solution?

    a. Use the 1TB drive and partition it into two drive letters to create the array.

    b. Can't be created with current drives; must purchase at least one additional hard disk with a 750GB or 1TB capacity.

    c. Partition both drives to have 500GB primary partitions, and use them in the array.

    d. Create a 750GB RAID 1 disk array using the hard disks.

9. You have used a bus-powered USB drive to make a backup copy of files you need to restore to a different system. When you plug the drive into a USB hub, it cannot be recognized. Which of the following is your best solution?

    a. Attach an AC adapter to the hub.

    b. Attach an AC adapter to the drive.

    c. Connect the drive directly to one of the USB ports on the computer.

    d. Use a longer USB cable between the drive and the hub.

10. Your client has a Windows XP computer with a Super Multi DVD drive. However, the user reports an inability to burn DVDs but can read DVD data discs. Which of the following could be accurate statements?

    a. DVD laser has failed.

    b. User needs to use third-party software to burn DVDs.

    c. Drive not designed to burn DVDs.

    d. User should install Windows Movie Maker to get better DVD support.

11. Your client wants to use an external hard disk to perform backups. Which of the following interfaces is the fastest?

    a. USB 2.0

    b. FireWire 800 (IEEE 1394b)

    c. eSATA 1.5Gbps

    d. USB 3.0

12. A computer's SATA RAID array is missing, and the onboard clock is slow. Which of the following steps should be taken to restore the system? (Choose all that apply.)

    a. Replace CMOS battery.

    b. Enable SATA RAID.

    c. Reset clock.

    d. Format hard disks.

Answers to Hands-On Lab

Lab 12-1: Configure SATA Ports

Answers:

Question 1: Integrated Peripherals. This CMOS/BIOS option is also used for access to USB, FireWire, and audio settings on most systems.

Question 2: Ports 5/6 are configured for IDE (emulation) mode, which prevents SATA drives connected to these ports from running at best performance.

Question 3: AHCI. This mode enables native command queuing (NCQ) and other features specific to SATA.

Question 4: F10 key.

Lab 12-2: Configure PATA Jumper Blocks

Answers:

Question 1: A, D, E. An 80-wire cable is needed to achieve UDMA66 or faster performance. The DVD drive should be on its own cable. Drive jumpers should be changed.

Question 2: Cable Select (CS); this setting is used on all drives (under normal circumstances) when connected to 80-wire PATA cables.

Question 3: Cable Select (CS); this setting is used on all drives (under normal circumstances) when connected to 80-wire PATA cables.

Answers and Explanations to Review Questions

1. **B, D.** Super Multi DVD drives can use any type of DVD recordable or rewriteable media as well as CD. LS-240 SuperDisk is an obsolete floppy disk type, and BD (Blu-ray) is a higher-capacity optical media than DVD.

2. **B, D.** PATA and SATA are the leading internal drive interfaces. USB 3.0 is a standard for external storage and other types of devices, while eSATA is an external variation of SATA.

3. **D.** PATA drives can use either 40-wire or 80-wire cables, but performance on newer drives is reduced when a 40-wire cable is used. UDMA133 drives are the fastest of the three drive classes that require the 80-wire cable.

4. **A.** SATA 3Gbps drives can be used with any speed of SATA port but might need to be jumpered to reduce performance to avoid data loss when used with 1.5Gbps ports (the slowest SATA speed). SATA is also used by DVD and Blu-ray drives.

5. **D.** AHCI mode enables hot-swapping. IDE mode forces the drive to emulate PATA drives (which can't be hot-swapped). UDMA mode is used by PATA drives, not SATA drives.

6. **C, D.** SSD drives don't require different drivers in Windows. IDE mode disables NCQ, TRIM, and other advanced features not supported by PATA drives. Firmware updates are essential to enabling SSD drives to run as fast as possible, and a tweaking utility for Windows helps ensure best performance.

7. **D.** Windows 7 does not include Removable Storage Manager (RSM) and RSM is not available for Windows 7. The only way to use a tape drive under Windows 7 is to install Windows 7-compatible drivers or to create a Windows XP VM and use the drive inside the VM to read data.

8. **D.** You must have two physical hard disks to create a RAID array. You can use different sizes of drives, but the array is limited to the size of the smaller drive in those cases. You don't need to partition the drives before creating the array.

9. **C.** A USB root hub (USB port on the computer) has the best chance of success. A USB hub that is bus powered usually doesn't have an AC adapter. In some cases, a shorter USB cable can transmit enough power from a USB root hub or self-powered hub to enable a bus-powered drive to work.

10. **B.** Windows XP can burn CDs, but not DVDs, in a DVD drive. If the DVD laser had failed, the drive could not read DVDs. A Super Multi DVD drive will burn DVDs. Windows Movie Maker for XP does not include DVD support.

11. **D.** USB 3.0 is the fastest (5Gbps) of the ports listed here. Note that some older backup programs don't support USB 3.0.

12. **A, B, C.** The slow clock is a symptom of a dead or dying CMOS battery. When system settings are lost, the RAID settings in the BIOS may be lost. However, the hard disks' contents are not affected.

This chapter covers the following subjects:

- **Installing Windows**—This section discusses the steps involved in preparing for and performing a full, upgrade, or multiboot installation of Windows XP, Vista, or 7, including minimum requirements, installation types, installation options, source media options, disk partitions, file systems, and alternative drivers.

- **Transferring User Data**—Learn the methods available for transferring user data before installing Windows.

- **Updating Windows**—This section covers the methods used to bring an installation of Windows up to date with Windows Update and with manual service pack installation.

- **Setting Up Recovery Partitions and Discs**—The chapter wraps up with a discussion of preparing recovery media for use if the system needs to be reset to its out-of-the-box condition.

This chapter covers the **CompTIA A+ 220-802 objectives 1.2 and 1.4**.

CHAPTER 13

Installing and Upgrading Windows

It's hard to estimate how many operating system installations a PC technician will do over the course of a career, but you can be assured that it will be a lot of installations. Because there are so many different hardware configurations in PCs today, almost every computer reacts differently to an installation or upgrade. In this chapter, you gain a foundation of knowledge about the possible installations and upgrades of Windows. Later, after you have installed several operating systems yourself, this foundation will help you build solid experience.

For this chapter, it is highly recommended that you try to get your hands on full version copies of Windows Vista, Windows 7, and Windows XP. You should also have a test computer so that you can run clean installations of these operating systems, as well as running the upgrade scenarios discussed in this chapter.

Foundation Topics

Installing Windows

220-802

Objective:
220-802: 1.2

Regardless of the Windows version (XP, Vista, or 7) or edition you need to install, you need to follow several steps to ensure a successful installation:

- Verify the target computer(s) can run the version and edition you plan to install.

- Choose the best boot method and installation method for a particular situation.

- Create suitable disk partitions for an installation.

- Choose the correct file system.

- Understand when and how to load third-party disk drivers.

- Understand the differences between workgroup and domain setups.

- Understand the significance of data/time/language region settings and when to change defaults.

> **NOTE**   To learn more about different versions and editions of Windows, see Chapter 14, "Using and Managing Windows."

Minimum and Recommended Hardware Requirements

Any system built in the last few years can easily achieve the hardware requirements needed for installing Windows Vista or Windows 7 and will far surpass the requirements of Windows XP. However, in the real world, digital dinosaurs that might not be fast enough or have enough free disk space to support some versions of Windows still roam the earth.

Table 13-1 lists the minimum requirements for Windows 7, Windows Vista, and Windows XP.

Table 13-1   Minimum Hardware Requirements for Windows 7, Vista, and XP

| Component | Windows Version | | |
	7	Vista	XP
Processor Speed	1GHz (x86 [32-bit] or x64 [64-bit] processor	800MHz	233MHz
RAM	1GB (32-bit) 2GB (64-bit)	512MB	64MB
Free disk space	16GB (32-bit) 20GB (64-bit)	15GB (20GB Partition)	1.5GB (2GB partition)
Video/graphics device	DirectX 9 graphics using WDDM v1.0 or higher driver	DirectX 9 graphics using WDDM v1.0 or higher driver; 128MB of RAM	Super VGA (800 × 600) or higher resolution
Other	DVD-ROM drive	CD-ROM or DVD-ROM drive	CD-ROM or DVD-ROM

NOTE   The specs in Table 13-1 are the minimum requirements. Microsoft recommends a 1-GHz processor for all versions of Vista, and 1GB of RAM plus a 40GB HDD for Vista Home Premium/Business/Ultimate. For additional information on Windows 7, see www.microsoft.com/windows/windows-7/products/system-requirements.

Windows 7 has higher requirements than Vista and has much higher requirements than XP. As a consequence, a system that might run Windows XP acceptably well might be too slow to run Windows Vista or Windows 7.

TIP   You might like to recycle old computer parts, but if the processor, hard disk size, and memory size of your PC barely meet the Microsoft requirements, prepare to be annoyed at how slowly your computer runs and how limited its capabilities are. You're much better off if your system greatly exceeds the minimums listed in Table 13-1.

You can use various types of system analysis programs and tools to verify that a system's hardware will be compatible with Windows 7, Windows Vista, or XP. If you are checking a computer that already has an operating system installed, use the following tools.

For Windows 7:

- Windows 7 Upgrade Advisor (runs on Windows XP SP2 or greater, Windows Vista, Windows 7): http://windows.microsoft.com/upgradeadvisor (see Figure 13-1)

- Windows 7 Compatibility Center: www.microsoft.com/windows/compatibility/windows-7/en-us/default.aspx

Figure 13-1   The Windows 7 Upgrade Advisor report on this system finds only one minor problem.

For Windows 7, Windows Vista, and Windows XP:

- **System Information**—You can access the Windows System Information tool by opening the Run/Search prompt and typing msinfo32.exe. See Figure 13-2.

- **Belarc Advisor**—Currently a free download, you can find this program at www.belarc.com/free_download.html. It's extremely quick and painless; all you need to do is double-click it after the download is complete. It automatically installs, looks for updates, and creates a profile of your computer that runs in a browser window. Here you can find all the hardware-related (and software-related) information on one screen. It also lists system security status.

- **SiSoftware Sandra 2012**—Powerful, flexible system reporting, benchmarking, and evaluation program. Available in limited-feature free and various commercial versions from www.sisoftware.co.uk/.

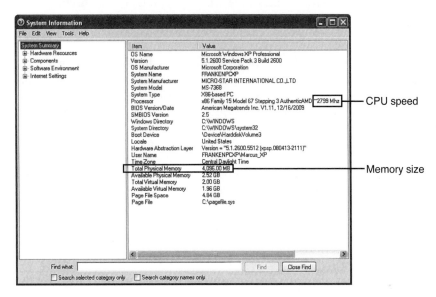

Figure 13-2 System Information shows that this computer has enough RAM and a fast enough processor to run Windows 7.

For computers without an installed operating system, use self-booting diagnostic programs such as

- #1-TuffTEST (available from www.tufftest.com/)
- PC Check (available from www.eurosoft-uk.com)
- Ultimate Boot CD (available from www.ultimatebootcd.com/index.html)

NOTE The Windows Vista DVD has a Check Compatibility Online option, but this is meant for upgrades as opposed to clean installations.

Boot Methods

You can use many methods to boot a system during the installation process:

- **Booting from the distribution DVD or CD**—Use this method to install Windows to an individual PC and to create a master PC from which disk images can be created.

- **Installing from the network (PXE)**—Use this method to install Windows to one or more systems that have working network connections. To use this method, network adapters must be configured to boot to a network location using the PXE boot ROM.

- **Booting from downloaded floppy disk images**—Use this method when a system cannot boot from a CD. You can download floppy disk boot images for Windows XP from the Microsoft website at http://support.microsoft.com/kb/310994 and use them when a system cannot boot directly to the CD-ROM. Note: There is no Microsoft supported floppy boot disk for Windows Vista or Windows 7.

- **Booting from USB thumb drive**—Use this method when installing from a DVD isn't feasible, such as installing Windows 7 to a netbook or other portable computer that lacks a DVD drive. For details, see http://windows.microsoft.com/en-us/windows7/installing-windows-7-on-a-netbook.

Types of Installation

You can install Windows in a variety of ways. The most common methods include

- As an upgrade to an existing version

- As a clean install to an empty hard disk or to the same partition as the current version

- To unused disk space (new partition) to permit multibooting the current or new version as needed

- As a repair installation to fix problems with the current installation

The preceding installation options typically use the original distribution media.

Large-scale or customized installations might use the following methods:

- Unattended installation

- Remote network installation

- Image deployment

This second group of installation options typically require the creation of an image file.

Upgrade Installation

To perform an upgrade installation of Windows, start the installation process from within your existing version of Windows. You can upgrade directly from Windows XP to Windows Vista, and from Windows Vista to Windows 7. An upgrade from Windows XP to Windows 7 involves backing up data and settings, performing a clean install of Windows 7, restoring data and settings, and restoring applications.

If you want to upgrade from Windows XP to Windows 7 without an intermediate upgrade to Windows Vista, you must use third-party utilities such as Laplink's PC Mover (www.laplink.com).

NOTE Although Microsoft does not offer a direct upgrade installation method for going from Windows XP to Windows 7, it does offer upgrade pricing on Windows 7 for Windows XP users.

The exact upgrade paths between Windows versions vary according to the Windows edition currently in use. You can upgrade to the equivalent or better edition of Windows but not a lower edition. For example, Windows XP Professional can upgrade to Windows Vista Business or Ultimate but not Home Premium. Windows Vista Business can upgrade to Windows 7 Professional or Ultimate but not Home Premium. The 32-bit versions can upgrade to 32-bit versions only; 64-bit versions can upgrade to 64-bit versions only.

Clean Install

Before starting a clean install process, check the following:

- Make sure the drive for installation is placed before the hard disk in the boot sequence. The system needs to boot from the Windows distribution media if you are installing to an empty hard disk. You can perform a clean install of Windows 7 from within an older version of Windows if you want to replace the older installation.

- If you will be installing to a drive that might require additional drivers (SCSI, SATA, RAID, or third-party host adapters on the motherboard or in an expansion slot), have the drivers available on floppy disk (Windows XP) or any type of removable media supported by the system (Windows Vista and 7). To learn more, see "Loading Alternative Third-Party Disk Drivers," later in this chapter.

If you are installing from CD or DVD media, after restarting the system with the CD or DVD media in place, press a key when prompted to boot from the CD or DVD.

During the installation process, be prepared to confirm, enter, select, or provide the following settings, information, media, or options when prompted:

- **Custom installation** (Windows Vista and 7).

- **Dialing information**—Only on systems with onboard dial-up modems.

- **Edition of Windows you are installing (Vista and 7 only)**—If you specify the incorrect version, the installation cannot be activated.

- **Location (home, work/office, or public: Vista and 7)**—The location information is used to configure Windows Firewall.

- **Network settings**—Windows XP treats IEEE 1394a (FireWire) ports as network ports, so if you plan to use these ports strictly for I/O devices, select custom network settings.

- **Partition location, partition type, and file system**—See "Partitioning" and "File System Types and Formatting" in this chapter for details.

- **Password and password hint**—Windows Vista and 7 prompt for a password, but only Windows 7 also prompts for a password hint. Windows XP prompts for an Administrator password.

- **Previous version CD if you are installing the Windows XP upgrade edition**— Windows Vista and 7 permit clean installs from an upgrade edition, but only if you do not activate the first installation and perform a reinstall over the first installation.

- **Product key**—Some installation processes enable you to skip this temporarily, but you must provide it before you can activate Windows.

- **Time, date, language, and region**—See "Time/Date/Language/Region Settings" in this chapter for details.

- **Time zone, time, and date**—U.S. editions of Windows default to Pacific time.

- **Username and company name**.

- **Workgroup or domain name**—See "Workgroup Versus Domain Setup," later in this chapter, for details.

NOTE The settings in the previous list are in alphabetical order, as Windows XP, Vista, and 7 prompt for this information at different points in the installation process.

At the end of the process, remove the distribution media. Windows is ready to download the latest updates and service packs.

Multiboot Installation

A multiboot installation of Windows enables you to choose from two or more operating systems when you start your computer. Windows XP, Windows Vista, and Windows 7 all support multiboot installations. If you want to use the multiboot support built in to Windows, follow these rules:

- **Install the oldest version of Windows first**—For example, if you want to multiboot Windows XP and Windows 7, install Windows XP first. If you want to multiboot Windows XP, Vista, and 7, install XP first as you would normally, then install Vista as noted next, and then install 7 as noted next.

- **You must install Windows 7 (or Windows Vista) into a separate disk partition than the previous operating systems, and the partition must be prepared as a primary partition**—For example, say you want to install Windows XP and Windows 7 to multiboot on a 500GB hard disk. First, install Windows XP to a primary partition that uses only a portion of the disk, and leave the rest of the drive unassigned. When you install Windows 7, you would create a new primary partition on the remainder of the drive and install to that partition.

- **If you want to install multiple editions of 7 and/or Vista as a multiboot, each installation must be to its own primary partition**—You can have up to four primary partitions on a hard disk. However, you can create primary partitions on more than one hard disk, so if you have two bootable hard disk drives, you could (theoretically) install up to eight different Windows editions.

- **Windows' multiboot support does not cover non-Windows operating systems such as Linux**—Use a third-part multiboot manager if you want to multiboot Windows and non-Windows operating systems, or if you need to install an older version of Windows to multiboot on a system that already has a newer Windows version installed.

TIP   If you need access to older Windows versions or non-Windows operating systems and don't want to reboot your system to switch between operating systems, use virtualization. Virtualization enables you to run operating systems in their own windows inside your primary operating system. To learn more, see "Virtualization" in Chapter 14.

Repair Installation

If a Windows operating system installation becomes corrupt, you can use a repair installation to restore working files and Registry entries without losing existing programs or information. Repair installations are available in Windows XP, Windows Vista, and Windows 7. You should make a backup copy of your data files (stored in \Documents and Settings\Username for each user of your PC) before performing a repair installation in case of problems.

> **NOTE**   The repair installation process is also known as an in-place upgrade.

To perform a repair install for Windows XP, do the following:

Preparations

Step 1.   If present, delete the Undo_guimode.txt file in \Windows\system32\.

Step 2.   The \Windows\system32\ folder also contains the following product activation files: wpa.dbl and wpa.bak. Copy these files to a storage device for safekeeping.

Step 3.   Disconnect USB devices other than the mouse and keyboard. They can be reconnected after the repair installation is complete.

Step 4.   Make a backup copy of each user's My Documents folder (which also stores My Pictures, My Music, and so on). Each user's My Documents folder is stored in a folder called \Documents and Settings\username. (Replace username with the actual user's name.)

Repair installation process

Step 1.   Boot the system with the Windows XP distribution media (CD or boot disks).

Step 2.   Press Enter when prompted to select the Setup option.

Step 3.   Accept the license agreement.

Step 4.   When your existing installation (usually stored at C:\Windows\) is located, you are prompted to repair it or install a new copy. Select this installation, and press R for repair.

The installation proceeds until completed.

If you performed a repair install of Windows XP original edition or Windows XP Service Pack 1, download and install Windows XP Service Pack 3, through automatic updates, Windows Update, or manually. This step is necessary because changes made by service packs are undone when you perform a repair installation of an earlier revision. This step is not necessary if you are performing a repair install from a CD containing Service Pack 3. However, in any event, you will want to check for updates with Windows Update.

Repair Installation Help and How-To

Many websites provide repair installation tutorials. Some of the most useful include Microsoft Knowledge Base article 315341, available at http://support.microsoft.com www.michaelstevenstech.com/XPrepairinstall.htm (includes important warnings) http://support.gateway.com/s/SOFTWARE/MICROSOF/7509595/Install/ Install06.shtml (includes illustrations)

To perform a repair installation of Windows Vista or Windows 7:

Step 1. Boot your computer normally (that is, to the Windows desktop).

Step 2. Insert your Windows disc.

Step 3. Start the setup program when prompted.

Step 4. Specify or accept the language, time and currency format, and keyboard layout, and click Next (see Figure 13-3).

Step 5. Click Install now.

Step 6. Accept the end-user licensing agreement.

Step 7. Select Upgrade as the installation option.

Step 8. The remainder of the installation proceeds as with a normal installation.

At the end of the installation, be sure to install the latest service pack and updates available for your version of Windows.

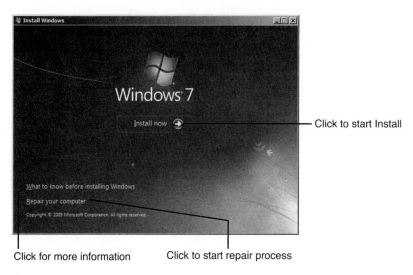

Click to start Install

Click for more information   Click to start repair process

Figure 13-3   Starting the Windows 7 installation from within Windows.

Unattended Installation

In an attended installation, you must provide information at various points during the process.

To create an unattended installation, you must create the appropriate type of answer file for the installation type. Windows 7 and Vista use the Windows **System Image Manager** (available from www.microsoft.com/download/), and Windows XP Professional includes the Setup Manager Utility (**Setupmgr.exe**) program to aid in the creation of an answer file.

In Windows XP the following files are created when you run Setupmgr.exe:

- **Unattend.txt**—Provides answers when you start the installation from a network share or from a command line.

- **Sysprep.inf**—Provides answers when running the Sysprep mini-setup on a target machine after copying the image file prepared with Sysprep.

- **Winnt.sif**—Copy this file to a floppy disk to use when booting the system from the Windows XP CD and starting the installation.

In Windows 7 and Vista, only the Unattend.xml file is created when you run the System Image Manager. This takes the place of all the previous files used by Windows XP.

NOTE   The Windows System Image Manager (SIM) for Vista and Windows 7 is part of the Windows Automated Installation Kit (AIK), which can be downloaded from Microsoft's website—search for Windows Automated Installation Kit (AIK).

Remote Network Installation

You can install Windows from a network drive by starting the computer with a network client and logging on to the server to start the process. If you want to automate the process, Windows 7, Vista, and XP can all be installed from a network drive automatically using either **Windows Deployment Services**, which can be installed on Windows Server 2008R2, Server 2008, and Server 2003, or the older **Remote Installation Services (RIS)** program, which can be installed on Windows Server 2003.

These two server-based programs work along with the Windows System Image Manager program (for Vista/7) or the Setup Manager Wizard found on the Windows XP CD-ROMs. These programs are used to create an answer file. The answer file provides the responses needed for the installation. In Windows Vista and Windows 7, there is a single answer file that is XML-based called Unattend. xml. In Windows XP the answer files are text-based—for example, Unattend.txt. For more information on how this works and the differences between Vista and XP, visit http://technet.microsoft.com/en-us/library/cc765993.aspx.

Image Deployment

Windows can be installed from a disk image of another installation. This process is called disk cloning. You can create a disk image with a variety of tools, including Norton Ghost, Acronis True Image, and others.

NOTE   You can burn a disc image file, which often has either an .iso or .img file name extension, to a recordable CD or DVD by using Windows Disc Image Burner in Windows 7.

However, if you plan to deploy a disk image to multiple computers, rather than as a backup of a single computer, you must consider special issues:

- **Hardware differences**—Traditional image cloning methods, such as those using Norton Ghost and Acronis True Image, were designed for restoration to identical hardware (same motherboard, mass storage host adapters, same BIOS configuration, same Hardware Abstraction Layer [HAL] and same

Ntoskrnl.exe [NT kernel] file). For organizations that have different types and models of computers, this poses a problem.

- **Same Security Identifier**—A cloned system is identical in every way to the original, including having the same Security Identifier (**SID**). This can cause conflicts in a network.

To overcome these problems, use the following tools and methods when creating a cloned system.

Instead of using programs such as Norton Ghost and Acronis True Image, use cloning programs designed to capture an image that can be deployed to different types of computers (laptops, desktops, and netbooks) with different hardware and software.

The free Microsoft ImageX utility (ImageX.exe) is part of the Windows Automated Installation Kit. Third-party tools, such as Symantec Ghost Solution Suite (www.symantec.com) and Acronis Snap Deploy (www.acronis.com), are also designed to create images that can be deployed to dissimilar hardware.

To fix problems with the SID and network settings, use the Sysprep utility from Microsoft to enable a system image created with ImageX or other imaging tools to make needed changes in SID and network settings after it has been transferred to a destination system. (Ghost Solution Suite and Snap Deploy include similar features.)

The Sysprep utility for Windows 7 and Vista is installed with the operating system and can be found by navigating to C:\Windows\System32\Sysprep. The Sysprep utility is available on full and OEM versions of the Windows XP Professional media at \SUPPORT\TOOLS\ in a cabinet file called DEPLOY.CAB. The most recent version of Sysprep for Windows XP can also be downloaded from the Microsoft website as part of the Windows XP Service Pack 3 Deployment Tools. See the following link for more information: http://support.microsoft.com/kb/936929.

Sysprep is installed on a system that will be used for cloning before it is cloned (see Figure 13-4). Select the mini-setup option shown in Figure 13-4, and a special mini-Setup Wizard starts on the cloned computer the first time it is run after cloning. Sysprep uses an answer file created with either the System Image Manager (SIM) or the Setup Manager (Setupmgr.exe) utilities described earlier. When Sysprep runs on the cloned system, it creates a unique SID and makes other changes as needed to the network configuration of the system. If the answer file does not have the answer needed by the setup program, you will be prompted to provide this information, such as the Windows license number (Product key).

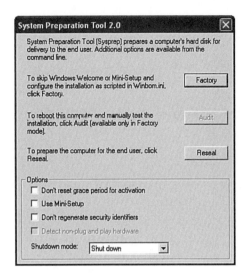

Figure 13-4 Starting the Sysprep 2.0 tool on a Windows XP system.

All cloning tools can work with a target drive that is the same size or larger than the original cloned system drive. Some can also work with a smaller drive; check documentation for details.

CAUTION   Do not use disk cloning to make illegal copies of Windows. You can use disk-cloning software legally to make a backup copy of your installation, but if you want to duplicate the installation on another PC, make sure you clone a system created with a multiple-computer license for Windows and make sure that you do not exceed the number of systems covered by that license, or make sure you have the correct license number (Product key) for each duplicate system. You can clone standalone computers or those connected to a workgroup (but not those that are members of a domain).

Time/Date/Language/Region Settings

Early in the installation process, Windows XP/Vista/7 prompt you to accept or change language, region, and keyboard settings. The defaults for these settings are based on the localized edition of Windows you are installing. For example, if you are installing a U.S. edition of Windows, the language is English, the region is the United States, and the keyboard layout is US. Make any changes needed before continuing. Figure 13-5 illustrates these settings in the Windows 7 installation program.

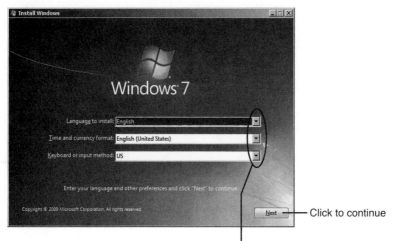

Open these menus to make changes if necessary

Figure 13-5   Windows 7 initial installation dialog when booting from the Windows 7 distribution media.

Later in the installation process, you are prompted to provide date, time, and time zone settings. As with language and region, the defaults are based on the localized edition of Windows you are installing. To ensure correct date and time information for files you create or modify and to receive accurate information for time-based information such as Windows Media Center's television guide, make any changes needed.

NOTE   You are prompted to accept or change these settings only in a clean install or multiboot install.

Partitioning

Whether Windows is being installed to an empty hard disk or to a hard disk that has unassigned space (for multibooting), at least one new hard disk partition must be created. To do this successfully, you need to understand the differences between

- Primary and extended partitions
- Extended partitions and logical disk drives
- Dynamic and Basic disks

Primary and Extended Partitions and Logical Drives

A hard disk cannot be used until it is prepared for use. There are two steps involved in preparing a hard disk:

- Creating partitions and logical drives

- Formatting partitions and logical drives (which assigns drive letters)

These steps must be performed during the Windows installation process if Windows is being installed to a new or empty hard disk, or after Windows is installed when new drives are added or connected to the computer.

A disk partition is a logical structure on a hard disk drive that specifies the following:

- Whether the drive can be bootable

- How many drive letters (one, two, or more) the hard disk will contain

- Whether any of the hard disk's capacity will be reserved for a future operating system or other use

Although the name "disk partition" suggests the drive will be divided into two or more logical sections, every hard disk must go through a partitioning process, even if you want to use the entire hard disk as a single drive letter. All versions of Windows support two major types of disk partitions:

- **Primary**—A primary partition can contain only a single drive letter and can be made active (bootable). Only one primary partition can be active. Although a single physical drive can hold up to four primary partitions, you need only one primary partition on a drive that contains a single operating system. If you install a new operating system in a multiboot configuration with your current operating system, you must install Windows Vista or Windows 7 to a different disk partition than the previous Windows version. If you want to use a non-Windows operating system along with your current operating system, it should be installed into its own primary partition.

NOTE Depending on the layout and contents of your current disk partitions, you might be able to shrink the size of existing partitions with Windows Disk Management (Windows Vista and 7 only) to make room for a new primary partition, or you might need to use third-party software such as Acronis Disk Director 11 or EASEUS Partition Master.

- **Extended**—An extended partition differs from a primary partition in two important ways:

  - An extended partition doesn't become a drive letter but can contain one or more logical drives, each of which is assigned a drive letter.

  - Neither an extended partition nor any drive it contains can be bootable.

Only one extended partition can be stored on each physical drive.

If the drive will be used by a single operating system, one of these three ways of partitioning the drive will be used:

- **Primary partition occupies 100% of the physical drive's capacity**—This is typically the way the hard disk on a system sold at retail is used and is also the default for disk preparation with Windows. This is suitable for the only drive in a system or an additional drive that can be used to boot a system but should not be used for additional drives in a system that will be used for data storage.

- **Primary partition occupies a portion of the physical drive's capacity, and the remainder of the drive is occupied by an extended partition**—This enables the operating system to be stored on the primary partition and the applications and data to be stored on one or more separate logical drives (drive letters created inside the extended partition). This is a common setup for laptops but requires the partitioning process be performed with different settings than the defaults. This configuration is suitable for the only drive or first drive in a multiple-drive system.

- **Extended partition occupies 100% of the physical drive's capacity**—The drive letters on the extended partition can be used to store applications or data but not for the operating system. An extended partition cannot be made active (bootable). This configuration is suitable for additional hard disk drives in a system (not the first drive); an extended partition can contain only one logical drive or multiple logical drives.

You can also leave some unpartitioned space on the hard disk for use later, either for another operating system or another drive letter.

Partitioning creates drive letters; formatting creates file systems on the drive letters created during partitioning. Figure 13-6 helps you visualize how these different partitioning schemes could be used on a typical hard disk.

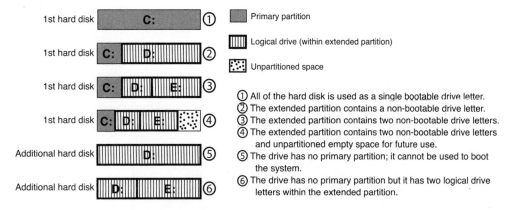

Figure 13-6 Typical disk partitioning schemes used for the first hard disk (first four examples) or an additional drive (last two examples).

After a disk is partitioned, the drive letters must be formatted using a supported file system.

Dynamic and Basic Disks

Windows supports two types of disks: basic and dynamic. A dynamic disk is more versatile than a basic disk because you can span two physical drives into a single logical drive, create striped or mirrored arrays, and adjust the size of a partition. However, during installation, Windows creates only basic disks.

NOTE   To learn more about working with disk drives in Windows after installation, see "Disk Management" in Chapter 14.

Creating Partitions During Windows XP Installation

If you install Windows XP to an empty hard disk, you will be prompted for a location:

- To use all the space in the disk, make sure that Unpartitioned Space is highlighted, and press Enter (see Figure 13-7).

- To use only part of the space, press C to Create Partition and specify the partition size on the next screen (see Figure 13-8). Press Enter after specifying the wanted size.

- To use an existing partition, arrow to that partition so that it becomes high-lighted, and press Enter. Be careful—whatever partition you select for the installation will be formatted.

- To delete a pre-existing partition, press D, press Enter at the next screen, and then press L to confirm.

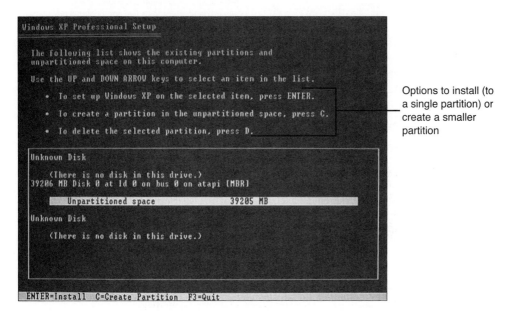

Options to install (to a single partition) or create a smaller partition

Figure 13-7   Partitioning options in the Windows XP installation program.

Creating Partitions During Windows Vista/7 Installation

If you install Windows Vista or Windows 7 to an empty hard disk, you will be prompted for a location:

- To use all the space in the disk, make sure that the disk and partition you want is highlighted, and click Next (see Figure 13-9).

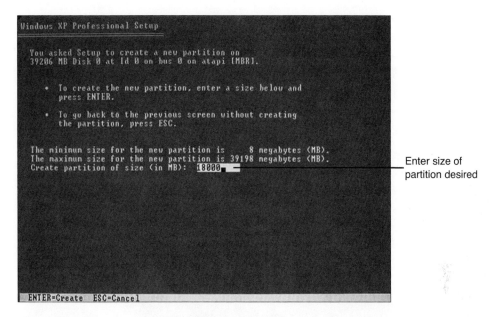

Figure 13-8 Creating an 18GB partition with the Windows XP setup program. You can create an extended partition and logical drives with the setup program or leave the rest of the disk empty until later.

Figure 13-9 Example of using an entire disk as one partition for the Windows Vista Installation.

- To use only part of the space, click Drive Options (Advanced), click New, specify the partition size, and click Apply (see Figure 13-10).

Figure 13-10 Specifying a partition size.

- To use an existing partition, highlight the wanted partition, and click Next. Be careful; whatever partition you select for the installation will be formatted, and all data on that partition will be erased.

You can also format partitions from here; they are automatically formatted as NTFS. In addition, you can extend existing partitions to increase the size of the partition but without losing any data.

File System Types and Formatting

Four different hard disk file systems are supported by Windows 7/Vista/XP:

- NTFS

- FAT32

- FAT16 (also known as FAT)

- exFAT (aka FAT64)

NOTE   CDFS is the file system used for CD media, such as the discs written with the Windows XP CD burning feature. Some external drives used for hard disk backup, such as ClickFree Automatic Backup drives, use a small CDFS partition for utility software.

Which file system should you use for the operating system installation? With Windows XP, most of the time you will use NTFS, unless you want to install to an existing FAT32 partition and do not want to lose data during the installation. The largest FAT32 partition that Windows can format during installation is 32GB; larger partitions must be formatted as NTFS. FAT16 is supported so that Windows can access other devices such as memory sticks or older hard drives, but chances are you won't come across it often. FAT16 drives are limited to 2GB if you want older operating systems such as Windows 9x or Me to also access them, or to 4GB if used only with Windows 2000 or XP.

NOTE   Keep in mind that much of the data security of Windows comes from the use of NTFS. If NTFS is not used to prepare a drive, encryption and compression are not available, nor is user-level or group-level access control. Windows Vista and Windows 7 can be installed only on NTFS drives.

After partitioning is complete in Windows XP, you need to format the partitions. Normally, you would select NTFS. Select FAT if the partition is under 32GB in size. If you specify FAT, the partition will be FAT16 if it is under 2GB in size and FAT32 if it is 2GB or larger.

Quick formatting is an option with all three versions of Windows discussed here. With new hard disks or existing drives known to be error-free, use quick formatting to quickly clear the areas of the hard disk that store data location records. If you choose the full format option, Windows must rewrite the disk structures across the entire disk surface. This can take many minutes with today's large hard disks.

NOTE   If you are concerned about the condition of a used hard disk you plan to re-use with Windows, use Windows CHKDSK if the drive has been formatted to check its state. You can also use the drive vendor's disk diagnostic utility program to verify the condition of a drive.

To learn more about file systems, see "Windows File Systems" in Chapter 14.

Windows XP offers the option to perform a quick format (saves time) or a regular format (takes longer but verifies the entire disk surface). Windows formats the partition with the file system you specify and continues the installation process.

Windows 7 and Windows Vista automatically format the partitions created by the partition process with NTFS.

Loading Alternative Third-Party Disk Drivers

If Windows does not detect your hard disks during installation, you must provide the drivers needed. The most likely situations in which this could occur include

- Using SATA or RAID onboard or add-on card host adapters in Windows XP

- Using third-party SATA or RAID onboard or add-on card host adapters in Windows Vista/7

- Using SCSI host adapters in Windows XP/Vista/7

What are the options you have for providing these drivers?

In Windows 7 and Vista, device drivers are added within the same screen where partitioning was done by clicking Load Driver (refer to Figures 13-9 and 13-10). These drivers can be installed from floppy disk, CD, DVD, or USB flash drive. Microsoft recommends that before you install, you check whether the devices you want to use are listed at the Windows 7 Compatibility Center: www.microsoft.com/windows/compatibility/windows-7/en-us/default.aspx.

If you click Load Driver and cannot supply a proper driver for Windows Vista or Windows 7, or if the computer cannot read the media where the driver is stored, you must exit the installation program.

In Windows XP, early in the installation process, the status line at the bottom of the screen displays a prompt to press F6 if you need to provide drivers for the drive that will be used for the installation (see Figure 13-11).

If you don't provide a driver when prompted and Windows cannot display your drive as an installation target, exit the installation program, restart it, and provide the driver when prompted. The driver must be provided on a floppy disk. Windows XP will not recognize a driver provided on a USB flash memory drive, CD, or DVD. Be sure to check your drive host adapters for hardware compatibility with Windows XP.

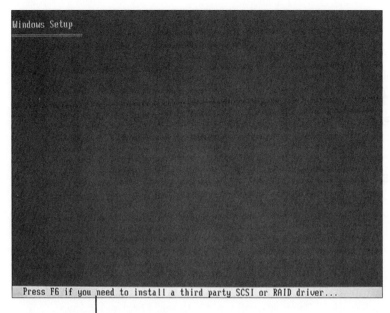

Prompt to install mass storage drivers

Figure 13-11   As soon as the Windows XP setup program starts, you have only a few moments to press F6 if you need to install a third-party SCSI or RAID driver (or Serial ATA driver).

Workgroup Versus Domain Setup

Windows can connect to either a workgroup (the default setting) or to a network managed by a domain controller. To learn more about these network types, see Chapter 16, "Networking."

Transferring User Data

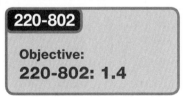

If a user will be using a new operating system, either on the same computer or on a new computer, you might need to move his files and settings to the new system. When doing so, make sure the destination computer has the latest service packs and updates and the same programs that are currently running on the original computer. Microsoft offers these free utilities for migrating data:

- **Windows Easy Transfer**—Copies files, photos, music, email, and settings (collectively known as the user state) to a Windows 7 or Windows Vista computer from a Windows XP, Windows Vista, or Windows 7 computer.

- **User State Migration Tool (USMT)**—This is a command-line tool that can be used to migrate user files and settings for one or more computers. The program can be downloaded from www.microsoft.com/downloads.

- **Files and Settings Transfer (FAST) Wizard**—This is the older version of Windows Easy Transfer and is installed by default on Windows XP. It is meant for transferring files and settings from a Windows XP, 2000, or 9x computer to a Windows XP computer but otherwise works in a similar fashion to Windows Easy Transfer.

NOTE   The objectives for 220-802 1.4 also mention "User Data Migration Tool (UDMT)." This tool was originally developed for Windows NT and Windows 2000 and has been replaced by USMT and Windows Easy Transfer.

Windows Easy Transfer

Windows Easy Transfer enables you to copy files, photos, music, email, and settings to a Windows 7 or Windows Vista computer; all this information is collectively referred to as *user state*. It is installed with Windows 7 and Vista and can be downloaded for Windows XP or for Windows Vista from http://windows.microsoft.com/en-us/windows7/products/features/windows-easy-transfer, where you can also learn more about how to use it.

When the program is installed, it is located in Start > All Programs > Accessories > System Tools after installation. Files and settings can be migrated over the network or by USB cable. The data can also be stored on media like a CD, DVD, or USB flash drive until the destination computer is ready (see Figure 13-12). Normally, you would start with the computer that has the files and settings that you want to transfer (the source computer). You can transfer the files and settings for one user account or all the accounts on the computer. All the files and settings will be saved as a single .MIG file (Migration Store). Then, you would move to the computer in which you want to transfer the files to (destination computer) and either load the .MIG file from CD, DVD, or USB flash drive or locate the file on the source computer through the use of a USB cable or network connection.

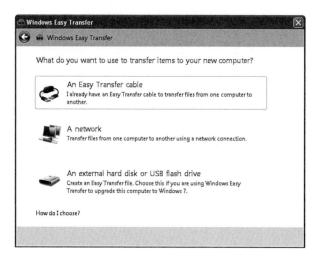

Figure 13-12   Selecting a transfer method with Windows Easy Transfer.

User State Migration Tool

The User State Migration tool (USMT) is a command-line tool that you can use to migrate user files and settings for one or more computers. USMT 4.0, which is designed for Windows 7, is part of the Windows Automated Installation Kit (Windows AIK) for Windows 7, which is available at www.microsoft.com/download/. Older versions of the USMT designed for use with Windows Vista (3.x) and Windows XP (2.6x) can be searched for at the same location.

NOTE   To learn more about Windows USMT 4.0, see http://support.microsoft.com/kb/2023591.

USMT uses two different tools: Scanstate.exe saves all the files and settings of the user (or users) on a computer, known as the user state, and loadstate.exe transfers that data to the destination computer(s). There are many options when using the scanstate and loadstate commands, including the ability to select which users are migrated and whether the store of data is uncompressed, compressed, or compressed and encrypted. By using scripting programs, the transfer of files to multiple computers can be automated over the network. For more information on how to transfer files and settings with USMT 4..0, see the following TechNet link: http://technet.microsoft.com/en-us/library/dd560801(WS.10).aspx.

Updating Windows

220-802

Objective:
220-802: 1.2

After Windows is installed, it should be updated with the latest drivers, hotfixes, and service packs. For individual PCs, the easiest way to perform these steps is to set up Windows Update for automatic updates.

Using Windows Update and Microsoft Update

To install additional updates for Windows through Windows Update, follow these steps:

Step 1. Click Start, All Programs, Windows Update.

Step 2. Vista and Windows 7 open the Windows Update window, where you can click the Install Updates button. Windows XP opens a web page where you can select Express or Custom installation of updates. Follow the prompts to install the latest version of the Windows Update software if necessary.

> **NOTE** Do not select Express or let Microsoft automatically install all updates if you do not want to use newer applications, such as Internet Explorer 9.

Step 3. Windows Update automatically scans for updates. Updates are divided into the following categories (Windows XP):

- **Critical Updates and Service Packs**—These include the latest service pack and other security and stability updates. Some updates must be installed individually; others can be installed as a group.

- **Windows Updates**—Recommended updates to fix noncritical problems certain users might encounter; also adds features and updates to features bundled into Windows.

- **Driver Updates**—Updated device drivers for installed hardware.

Windows Vista and Windows 7 have two categories:

- **Important**—Critical updates and service packs
- **Optional**—Driver updates and updates to Windows features

Step 4.   If you have selected an Express install or if you selected wanted updates, they are downloaded to your system and installed. You might need to restart your computer to complete the update process.

If you use Microsoft Office or other Microsoft applications as well as Microsoft Windows, Windows Update offers to install Microsoft Update, which provides a common update mechanism for both Windows and other Microsoft products. After you install Microsoft Update, it runs automatically whenever you run Windows Update. Keep in mind that Microsoft Office uses service packs as well.

Installing Service Packs Manually

Service packs for Windows and other Microsoft programs can include hundreds of updates, which means that they can be several hundred megabytes in size. If you need to install service packs on several computers, it can be faster and put less stress on the network's Internet connection to download and install them manually. All versions of Windows on the CompTIA A+ Certification exam have at least one service pack available.

> **NOTE**   Before downloading and installing a service pack, determine whether the service pack includes all previous service packs or if you need to install a service pack or other updates first.

To download and install a service pack for Windows manually, follow these steps:

Step 1.   Determine whether the system has any service packs installed. You should perform this check even if you have just installed Windows because you can install Windows with service packs included and newer Windows DVD/CDs contain a service pack. Right-click Computer/My Computer and select Properties to determine the current service pack. You can also use the command winver.exe in the Command Prompt to discern this information. Figure 13-13 illustrates a Windows 7 system with Service Pack 1 installed.

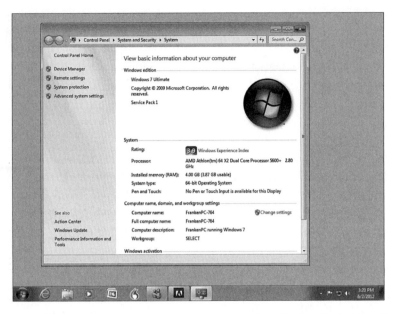

Figure 13-13   This Windows 7 Ultimate system has Service Pack 1 installed.

Step 2.   Go to http://windows.microsoft.com/ and follow the links provided for downloads for the version of Windows you need to update.

Step 3.   Review the release notes for the service pack to see whether it will cause any problems for your particular configuration, such as problems with networking, peripherals, CD/DVD mastering software, and so forth. Take the necessary actions as noted. (Some might require changes before you perform the service pack installation; others might take place afterward.)

TIP   To save the specific document referenced in the release notes so that you can follow up on the problem, use the Save as Web Archive option in Internet Explorer. This saves the entire web page (including graphics) as a single file with an .MHT extension. You can then view the file offline with Internet Explorer if necessary.

Step 4.   Select the correct language, and click the link.

Step 5.   Shut down real-time virus checkers.

Step 6.   Select the Manually Installing option to download the service pack from the Download Center.

Step 7. Click the link to download the service pack. Use Save As and when prompted, select a location to store the file with Network Installation.

Step 8. Open the file you downloaded in Step 7 to start the installation process.

Step 9. You should update your system backup media and back up your files before you install the service pack, and select the option to archive existing Windows files during the service pack installation.

Step 10. Restart the system when prompted.

> **TIP** In some cases, you might need to reinstall third-party applications or utilities after you install a service pack.

Service packs are large because they contain hundreds of updates and hotfixes. Hotfixes, which are solutions for specific problems experienced only by users with certain combinations of hardware and software, can also be downloaded individually. When a hotfix is deemed safe for all users, it will usually be distributed via Windows Update or Microsoft Update. However, it can also be downloaded manually or requested by the user. Hotfixes are listed as part of Help and Support (formerly Knowledge Base) articles about specific problems. See http://support.microsoft.com for Help and Support articles.

At one time, it was necessary to call Microsoft to request hotfixes that were not available for automatic downloading. Now, Microsoft provides a link on the Help and Support pages where you can make the request. Enter the wanted information and your email address, and a link to the requested hotfix will be emailed to you.

Setting Up Recovery Partitions and Discs

220-802

Objective:
220-802: 1.2

Most vendors no longer provide a full installation DVD/CD of Windows for computers with preinstalled Windows. Instead, a disk partition containing a special recovery image of the Windows installation is provided. Typically, you are prompted to burn the restore image to one or more DVDs or CDs.

NOTE   A recovery disc is also known as a system restoration disc. These special versions of Windows aren't standalone copies of Windows, meaning you can't use them to install Windows on another PC (unless the PC is identical to the one for which the disc was made).

Typically, you have limited choices when you want to restore a damaged installation with a recovery disc or recovery files on a disk partition. Typical options include

- Reformatting your hard disk and restoring it to just-shipped condition (causing the loss of all data and programs installed after the system was first used)

- Reinstalling Windows only

- Reinstalling support files or additional software

After you run the recovery disc to restore your system to its original factory condition, you need to activate your Windows installation again.

CAUTION   You might need the Windows Product key or your system's serial number to run the recovery disc program. Keep this information handy. Most systems with preinstalled Windows have a sticker with the Windows license key (Product key) somewhere on the system case.

If you want to restore your system, not to its original-out-of-the-box condition but to its most recent status, create an image and file backup of the system and update it frequently. See Chapter 15, "Troubleshooting and Maintaining Windows," for details.

Exam Preparation Tasks

Review All the Key Topics

Review the most important topics in the chapter, noted with the Key Topic icon in the outer margin of the page. Table 13-2 lists a reference of these key topics and the page numbers on which each is found.

Table 13-2 Key Topics for Chapter 13

Key Topic Element	Description	Page Number
Table 13-1	Minimum hardware requirements for Windows 7, Vista, and XP	567
Text	Boot methods	570
Text	Types of installation	570
Text	Unattended installation	576
Text	Remote network installation	577
Text	Image deployment	577
Text	Primary and extended partitions and logical drives	581
List	Four different hard disk file systems supported by Windows 7/Vista/XP	586
Text	Loading alternative third-party disk drivers	588
Text	Transferring user data	589
List	List of update categories (Windows XP)	592
List	List of update categories (Windows Vista/7)	593

Complete the Tables and Lists from Memory

Print a copy of Appendix A, "Memory Tables" (found on the CD), or at least the section for this chapter, and complete the tables and lists from memory. Appendix B, "Memory Tables Answer Key," also on the CD, includes completed tables and lists to check your work.

Define Key Terms

Define the following key terms from this chapter, and check your answers in the glossary.

> System Image Manager, Setup Manager Utility (Setupmgr.exe), Windows Deployment Services, Remote Installation Services (RIS), SID

Complete Hands-On Lab

Complete the hands-on labs, and then see the answers and explanations at the end of the chapter.

Lab 13-1: Selecting Installation Options for Windows 7

Scenario: You are a technician working at a PC setup bench. You are installing Windows 7 on a computer.

Procedure:

Step 1: Your client wants to set up the computer with a partition that uses only a portion of the space available on the hard disk. Review Figure 13-14, and select the correct option to proceed from those labeled A, B, C, and D.

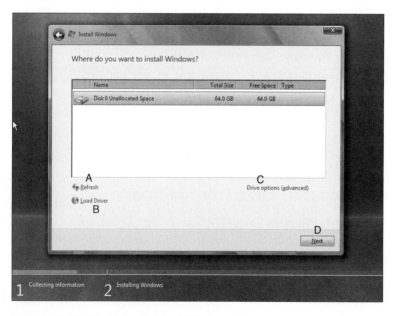

Figure 13-14   Preparing to install Windows 7.

Step 2: Review Figure 13-15. A size has been specified. Which of the options shown should be selected to continue? Choose from A, B, or C.

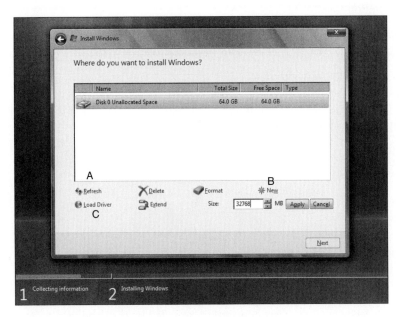

Figure 13-15 Choosing an installation option.

See the solution for this lab.

Answer Review Questions

Answer these review questions, and then see the answers and explanations at the end of the chapter.

1. You need to install the Windows 7 operating system on a client's computer. Upon arrival you notice that the system is an older model. What should you do first before trying to install the operating system?

   a. Format the hard drive.

   b. Verify the hard drive is large enough.

   c. Check the Windows 7 Compatibility Center.

   d. Run Chkdsk.

2. Which of the following are valid methods that can be used to install a Windows operating system? (Choose all that apply.)

   a. Distribution CD/DVD

   b. Network installation

   c. Drive imaging

   d. A recovery CD

3. You want to create an image for an unattended installation. Which of the following will be created for a Windows 7 install?

   a. Unattend.txt

   b. Winnt.sif

   c. Unattend.xml

   d. Sysprep.inf

4. You have just unpacked a system with a preinstalled copy of Windows 7 and no recovery disc. How can you create a recovery disc?

   a. Run Windows Backup.

   b. Use the recovery disc creation program provided by the vendor.

   c. Buy a full copy of Windows 7 to use as a spare.

   d. You must order a recovery disc from the vendor.

5. You are installing the Windows 7 operating system. You have a SCSI hard drive installed. Which of the following actions do you perform to install the device drivers?

   a. Press F6 when the operating system starts loading.

   b. Click on the Load Driver button where partitioning is done.

   c. Press F8 during boot.

   d. Click on the Load Windows 7 Drivers Only button.

6. You need to install a service pack on a group of older systems that are connected to a 768Kbps DSL gateway. Which is most likely to be the fastest way to install the service pack on all computers?

   a. Run Windows Update on all computers.

   b. Download the full service pack on all computers.

   c. Download the full service pack to one computer and burn a disc.

   d. Run Windows Update on one computer and clone the drive.

7. You have been asked to install Windows 7 on a computer currently running Windows XP. You first need to verify whether the system can run the new operating system. What is the minimum processor speed that will run Windows 7?

   a. 1000MHz

   b. 1.5GHz

   c. 800MHz

   d. 850MHz

8. You need to install Windows 7 on a computer currently running Windows XP. You need to verify that the upgrade will go smoothly. What should you do to determine whether this computer can run the Windows 7 operating system?

   a. Run the Windows 7 Upgrade Advisor.

   b. Check the HCL for computer specifications.

   c. Run the checkupgradeonly program.

   d. Run the 7 Upgrade Wizard.

9. You are the technician for your company. You are about to replace Windows XP with Windows 7. You need to prepare the computer for the upgrade. What should you do before attempting this upgrade? (Choose all that apply.)

   a. Install any new device drivers.

   b. Back up all important files.

   c. Download any application updates.

   d. Back up Internet Explorer favorites.

   e. Download any new device drivers, and download any application updates only.

10. You have a computer running the Windows XP operating system. You notice that the file system is FAT32. You are planning to upgrade to Windows Vista, which requires NTFS. At what point can you do this?

   a. Before the upgrade process begins.

   b. During the upgrade process.

   c. You cannot convert FAT32 to NTFS.

   d. After the upgrade process ends.

11. You need to back up files and settings on 20 computers running Windows XP before installing Windows 7. Which of the following programs will be the best choice?

    a. USMT 4.0

    b. Windows Easy Transfer

    c. NTBackup

    d. Norton Ghost

12. You need to create an image of Windows 7 that can be used for installations on laptops and desktops. Which of the following utilities should you use? (Choose all that apply.)

    a. ImageX

    b. Ghost

    c. Acronis True Image

    d. Sysprep

Answers to Hands-On Lab

Lab 13-1: Selecting Installation Options for Windows 7

Answers:

Step 1: C. Selecting Drive Options (Advanced) enables the user to choose the size of disk partition wanted for Windows.

Step 2: B. The size (32GB) has already been filled in. However, the partition will not be created until the user clicks New.

Answers and Explanations to Review Questions

1. **C.** When using the newer hardware, there would not be a problem; however, with older hardware, before you even try to install the operating system you should verify whether the computers are capable of running the new OS by checking the Windows 7 Compatibility Center.

2. **A, B, C, D.** All the listed methods are valid ways to install an operating system. The most common ways are to use the distribution CD or DVD, or the recovery disc that comes with your system. You can also install from a network share or by imaging the drive.

3. **C.** When creating an unattended installation disk for Windows 7, Unattend. xml is created as the answer file. The other files are created when setting up an unattended installation for older Windows versions.

4. **B.** Almost all systems preconfigured with Windows 7 include a utility to burn one or more recovery discs. Windows Backup can create an image of your system's current state but not its original condition. A Windows 7 install disc is just that—an install disc that must be installed to a system (it is not a backup of your installation). Order a recovery disc only if there is no way to make one or if the recovery partition was damaged or deleted.

5. **B.** In Windows 7, device drivers are added within the same screen where partitioning was done by clicking Load Driver. These could be drivers for SATA or SCSI controllers, or other special hard disk controllers. These drivers can come from floppy disk, CD, DVD, or USB flash drive.

6. **C.** A slow Internet gateway can make installing a service pack on a group of computers via Windows Update take many hours. It is faster to download a full copy of the service pack to only one computer, burn a disc, and install from the disc. Cloning the drive would clone the drive's entire contents, including device drivers, and is not suitable for this need.

7. **A.** Some older systems might require processor, memory, or hard disk upgrades to be qualified to run Windows 7. You should make sure your computer meets or exceeds these standards before you start the upgrade process.

8. **A.** Windows 7 Upgrade Advisor checks your existing hardware and software to determine whether it is compatible with 32-bit and 64-bit versions of Windows 7.

9. **B, C, D.** Before you replace Windows XP with Windows 7, you should also download any new device drivers or new application updates that you need. Create a folder for your updates on your system and uncompress them if necessary so that they can be used during the upgrade process. And, of course, back up any important files, email, and settings: For example, Internet Explorer favorites, your email program's blocked sender list, or download and run Windows Easy Transfer to back up the bulk of the files and settings on your computer.

10. **A.** Windows Vista does not support installation to a FAT32 drive and, the Vista installer does not have a file system conversion utility.

11. **A.** USMT 4.0 and Windows Easy Transfer are both designed to back up files and settings, but USMT 4.0 is scriptable and designed to work with multiple computers.

12. **A, D.** ImageX is designed to capture an image that can be used by different types of computers, and Sysprep prepares the image file for deployment.

This chapter covers the following subjects:

- **Windows Versions and Editions**—This section teaches you how to differentiate between Windows 7, Windows Vista, and XP. The graphical user interfaces (GUI) are different as well as the hardware requirements necessary to run each operating system.

- **Windows Features**—Discover essential Windows features such as Aero, gadgets, shadow copy, ReadyBoost, system restore, and user folders that vary from edition to edition.

- **Command-Line Tools**—Every technician needs to know how to open the Windows command prompt and use the command line. This section shows you how and what you can do with tools and commands such as Robocopy, Diskpart, and more.

- **Administrative Features**—Find out how to use Computer Management, services, and other features to help manage a Windows installation.

- **Disk Management**—In this section, you learn how to perform common (and not-so-common) tasks with the Disk Management tools and the features of each file system supported by Windows.

- **Run Line Utilities**—Windows 7, Windows Vista, and Windows XP feature programs such as DXDiag, MSInfo32, Regedit and others that are typically launched from the Run dialog. Learn when and how to use them.

- **Control Panel**—Although Windows 7, Vista, and XP all include the Control Panel, what you can do with its features can vary a lot. Discover the most important Control Panel utilities and how they work.

- **Client-Side Virtualization**—Virtualization turns a single physical PC into several virtual machines, and this section helps you understand the basics of the virtual machine revolution.

This chapter covers most of **CompTIA A+ 220-802 objectives 1.1, 1.3, 1.4, 1.5, and 1.9**.

CHAPTER 14

Using and Managing Windows

In Chapter 13, you learned the installation and update processes for Windows 7, Vista, and XP. Now, it's time to learn how to manage these operating systems. The emphasis is less on "what is a mouse" and much more about "when X goes wrong, which Windows feature should I use to fix it?"

Although Windows XP's days are numbered, it is still an important operating system in the Windows world, and much of this chapter is designed to help you understand how XP differs from its newer kin (Vista and 7).

Foundation Topics

Windows Versions and Editions

220-802

Objective:
220-802: 1.1

System requirements for different versions of Windows vary widely. Table 14-1 compares the hardware requirements for Windows 7, Vista, and XP.

Table 14-1   Minimum Hardware Requirements for Windows 7, Vista, and XP

	Windows Version		
Component	**7**	**Vista**	**XP**
Processor	1GHz	800MHz	233MHz
RAM	1GB (32-bit)	512MB	64MB
	2GB (64-bit)		
Free disk space	20GB	15GB (20GB partition)	1.5GB (2GB partition)
Video/Graphics device	DirectX 9 graphics using WDDM v1.0 or higher driver	DirectX 9 graphics using WDDM v1.0 or higher driver; 128MB of RAM	Super VGA (800 × 600) or higher resolution
Other	DVD-ROM drive	DVD-ROM or CD-ROM drive	CD-ROM or DVD-ROM

NOTE   The specifications in Table 14-1 are the *minimum* requirements. Microsoft recommends a 1GHz processor for all versions of Vista and 1GB of RAM plus a 40GB HDD for Vista Home Premium/Business/Ultimate. The Windows 7 hardware requirements vary according to whether a 32-bit or 64-bit version is being installed.

The terms x86 and x64 are important to understand: x86 refers to older CPU names that ended in an "86"—for example, the 80386 (shortened to just 386), 486, and so on. Generally, when people use the term x86, they are referring to 32-bit CPUs that allow for 4GB of address space. x64 (or x86-64) refers to newer 64-bit CPUs that are a superset of the x86 architecture. This technology can run 64-bit software as well as 32-bit software and can address a maximum of 1TB.

Windows 7, Vista, and XP come in 64- and 32-bit versions so that users from both generations of computers can run the software efficiently.

Windows XP Family

The Windows XP family includes the following editions:

- **Windows XP Home**—Includes all base features of Windows XP; available in 32-bit version only.

- **Windows XP Professional**—Adds support for corporate and enterprise features (domain networking, file and folder permissions, remote features, and centralized management). 32-bit version; 64-bit version available separately.

- **Windows XP Media Center Edition (XP MCE)**—The original edition was released in 2002; newer editions were released in 2004 and 2005. MCE 2005 was the first edition available to small system builders. All editions of XP MCE include the Windows Media Center, which is optimized for TV viewing and recording. Available in 32-bit version only.

- **Windows XP 64-bit Professional**—64-bit version of Windows XP Professional; most drivers supporting XP 64-bit can also be used with 64-bit editions of Windows Vista and Windows 7.

NOTE   Windows XP Edition N was created for the European Union and lacks Windows Media Player and Windows Movie Maker. Windows XP Edition K and KN were created for the South Korean market and lack Windows Media Player (KN) and Windows Messenger. These special editions were created to satisfy antitrust concerns. Similar customized editions were developed for Windows Vista and are also available for Windows 7.

Windows Vista Family

The Windows Vista family includes the following editions:

- **Windows Vista Home Basic**—Includes all base features of Windows Vista along with desktop window manager, Windows Movie Maker, Windows Photo Gallery, parental controls; 32-bit and 64-bit editions; widely used on netbooks. Maximum 8GB of RAM in 64-bit edition.

- **Windows Vista Home Premium**—Adds Windows Aero, glass effects, scheduled file backups, Windows Movie Maker HD, Windows Media Center, DVD authoring. 32-bit and 64-bit editions. Maximum 16GB of RAM in 64-bit edition.

- **Windows Vista Business**—Adds support for corporate and enterprise features (domain networking, file and folder permissions, remote features, and centralized management, scheduled image and file backups, shadow copy, fax and scan, and offline files), but omits Parental Controls, Windows Media Center, Windows Movie Maker, and DVD Maker. Games are hidden but can be exposed by using the Turn Windows Features On and Off feature in Control Panel. 32-bit and 64-bit editions. Maximum RAM 128GB or more in 64-bit edition.

- **Windows Vista Ultimate**—Combines all added features of Home Premium and Business editions, adds BitLocker full disk encryption for system drive, UNIX-based application subsystem, multiple language support, and support for downloadable Vista Ultimate Extras. 32-bit and 64-bit editions. Maximum RAM 128GB or more in 64-bit edition.

- **Windows Vista Enterprise**—Based on Vista Business but adds BitLocker, UNIX-based application subsystem, and multiple language support. 32-bit and 64-bit editions. Maximum RAM 128GB or more in 64-bit edition.

NOTE   For more information, see http://windows.microsoft.com/en-us/ windows-vista/products/compare?t1=tab05 and http://news.softpedia.com/news/ Windows-Vista-Home-Basic-Home-Premium-Business-Enterprise-and-Ultimate-Comparison-45570.shtml.

Windows 7 Family

The Windows 7 family includes the following editions:

- **Windows 7 Starter**—Includes all base features of Windows 7 (gadgets, DirectX 11, Windows Media Player 12, Action Center, Windows Update, image and file backups, and others). Widely used on netbooks. 32-bit only. 2GB memory limit.

- **Windows 7 Home Premium**—Adds ability to create a Homegroup, Internet TV, Windows Media Center, multiple monitor support, Aero, Windows Mobility Center, more. 32-bit and 64-bit editions. Maximum 16GB of RAM in 64-bit edition.

- **Windows 7 Professional**—Includes all base and Home Premium features. Adds support for corporate features (domain networking, file and folder permissions, remote features, and centralized management, network scheduled backup, shadow copy, group policy, offline folders, and more) and Windows XP Mode. (A virtualized version of Windows XP requires downloads of Windows Virtual PC as well as XP Mode files.) 32-bit and 64-bit editions. Maximum RAM 192GB in 64-bit edition.

- **Windows 7 Ultimate**—Includes all features of Professional, adds BitLocker and BitLocker-to-go disk encryption for all drives, UNIX-based application subsystem, multiple language support, support for bootable VHD images. 32-bit and 64-bit editions. Maximum RAM 192GB in 64-bit edition.

- **Windows 7 Enterprise**—Based on Windows 7 Ultimate but adds features oriented to enterprise and domain networking (diskless PCs, multiple virtual machines, DirectAccess, and AppLocker). Sold only through volume licensing through Microsoft Software Assurance. 32-bit and 64-bit editions. Maximum RAM 192GB in 64-bit edition.

NOTE   For more information, see http://windows.microsoft.com/en-US/windows7/products/compare.

Windows Features

220-802

Objective:
220-802: 1.1

Windows XP, Vista, and 7 include many different features that often vary by operating system version and edition. These include

- Aero and Aero Glass
- Sidebar
- Gadgets
- User Account Control (UAC)
- BitLocker full-disk encryption
- Shadow Copy

- System Restore

- ReadyBoost

- Compatibility mode

- Windows XP mode

- Windows Easy Transfer

- Administrative tools

- Windows Defender

- Windows Firewall

- Security Center

- Event Viewer

- File structure and paths

- Category view versus Classic view in Control Panel

The following sections take a closer look at these differences.

NOTE   For information about User Account Control (UAC) and BitLocker, see Chapter 17, "Security." For information about System Restore and Event Viewer, see Chapter 15, "Troubleshooting and Maintaining Windows." For more about Windows Easy Transfer, see Chapter 13, "Installing and Upgrading Windows." For information about Control Panel views, see "Control Panel" in this chapter.

Windows Desktop (Aero, Aero Glass, Sidebar, Gadgets)

One of the biggest differences between Windows XP and its successors Windows Vista and Windows 7 is the desktop. Introduced with Windows Vista, Aero features translucent windows, window animations, three-dimensional viewing of windows, and a modified taskbar. You can make modifications to the look of Aero by right-clicking the desktop and selecting **Personalization**. From here, you can modify things such as the window color and translucency of windows (Aero Glass). To disable **Windows Aero**, select **Windows Basic** or **Windows 7 Basic** from the Themes menu.

Figure 14.1 shows Aero Glass in the comparison of Windows 7 to Windows XP start menus.

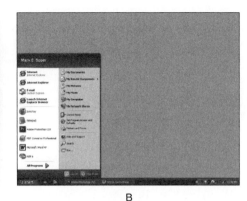

A   B

Figure 14-1   The Windows 7 Aero desktop and Start menu with gadgets (a) compared to the standard Windows XP Start menu (b).

Windows Vista also introduced the Windows Sidebar and small programs called gadgets. Gadgets are small programs such as clocks set for other time zones, slideshows, RSS newsfeeds, weather updates, and more. Windows Vista and Windows 7 include a number of gadgets and many more can be downloaded.

In Windows Vista, gadgets run only in the Windows Sidebar (see Figure 14-2), but in Windows 7, gadgets can run anywhere on the Windows desktop (refer to Figure 14-1). In both versions of Windows, gadgets can have different opacities and sometimes are available in different sizes.

Figure 14-2   The Windows Vista Aero desktop and Start menu.

Windows XP, Vista, and 7 can be configured to display a desktop and Start menu that emulate older Windows versions.

NOTE   To change only the Start menu to the Classic mode (Windows Vista and XP only), right-click the **Start** button, select **Properties**, and choose **Classic Start** menu. To change the Start menu and the desktop to the Classic mode, open the Display properties sheet, select **Themes**, and select **Windows Classic**. You can open the Display properties sheet from Control Panel or by right-clicking an empty area of the desktop and selecting **Properties**.

Shadow Copy

Windows Vista Business, Ultimate, and Enterprise, and Windows 7 Professional, Ultimate, and Enterprise include the Windows Shadow Copy feature. **Shadow Copy** stores previous versions of files in Windows restore points or in Windows Backup.

NOTE   By default, Windows creates restore points only for the system drive. To enable restore points for other drives, you must enable System Restore for those drives and specify Restore previous versions of files. See "Confirming System Restore Options," in Chapter 15 for more information.

If you overwrite a file with a newer one but want to return to the previous version of the file, follow this procedure:

Step 1.   Right-click the file in Windows Explorer.

Step 2.   Select **Properties**.

Step 3.   Click the **Previous Versions** tab.

Step 4.   Select the file version to restore. (If none are listed, no shadow copies are available.) If the file location is listed as Backup, insert the last disk in the backup media set, or attach the backup drive that contains the old version of the file.

Step 5.   Click **Restore** (see Figure 14-3).

Step 6.   To confirm the restoration, click **Restore**. The previous version replaces the current version.

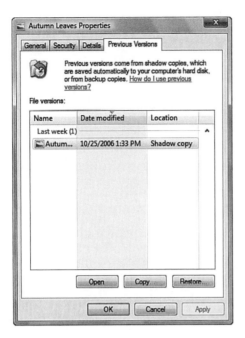

Figure 14-3   Using Shadow Copy to restore an earlier version of a file.

ReadyBoost

Windows **ReadyBoost** is a feature included in Windows Vista and Windows 7 to help improve hard disk read performance. ReadyBoost requires

- A USB flash memory drive connected to a USB 2.0 or 3.0 port or a flash memory card in a USB 2.0 or 3.0–compatible card reader.

- 256MB or more of free space. (Best performance is reached when free space equals or exceeds system RAM.)

- Sufficient performance to speed up disk reads; USB drives fast enough for ReadyBoost are sometimes sold in packages marked ReadyBoost-compatible.

When you connect a flash memory drive or card to your system, click Speed Up My System (see Figure 14-4) from the AutoPlay menu.

If the drive performs fast enough for ReadyBoost, the next dialog displays options for using the drive. If the drive is empty (as in Figure 14-5), you can dedicate the entire drive for use with ReadyBoost. Otherwise, you can select Use This Device and specify how much of the drive's free space to use. Click Apply, and then OK to use the settings.

Figure 14-4   Windows 7 displays ReadyBoost on the AutoPlay menu for a flash memory drive.

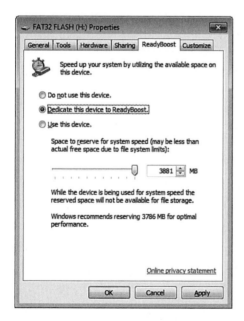

Figure 14-5   Dedicating an empty flash drive for ReadyBoost.

If the flash memory drive or card is removed, no data is lost but Windows will no longer benefit from the cache memory, and hard disk read performance will be lower.

Compatibility Mode

Most commercial business applications should run properly on Windows 7/Vista/ XP as well as on older versions of Windows. However, some commercial and custom applications designed for older versions of Windows and some games might not run properly on Windows 7/Vista/XP.

To enable applications written for older versions of Windows to run properly on Windows 7/Vista/XP, you can use the Program Compatibility Wizard built in to Windows or the Compatibility tab located on the executable file's properties sheet to run the program in a selected compatibility mode.

Program Compatibility Wizard in Windows 7

To start the program in Windows 7, click Start, Control Panel, Programs, Run Programs Made for Previous Versions of Windows.

After the wizard starts, click **Next** on the opening screen, and select the program that doesn't work properly. To try recommended compatibility settings, click **Try Recommended Settings**, and click **Start the Program**. If the program runs properly, click **Next** and then **Yes**.

If the program doesn't run properly, click **No, Try Again**, and answer questions about the problems you noticed (see Figure 14-6). From the answers you select, Windows selects settings to try (see Figure 14-7) and prompts you to run the program. After you find settings that work, Windows uses them every time you run the program.

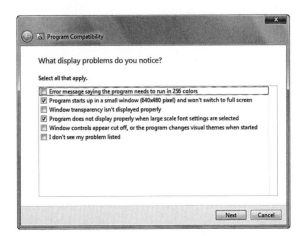

Figure 14-6 Answering questions about problems with an older program with Windows 7's Program Compatibility Wizard.

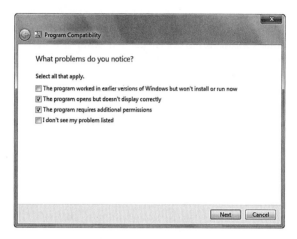

Figure 14-7   Based on your answers, Windows 7's Program Compatibility Wizard selects settings to help your older program run properly.

Program Compatibility Wizard in Windows XP and Vista

To start the wizard in Windows XP, click Start, All Programs, Accessories, Program Compatibility Wizard. To start the wizard in Windows Vista, click Start, Control Panel, Programs, Use an Older Program with This Version of Windows.

After the wizard starts, you can select from programs already installed on your computer, select the current program in the CD-ROM drive, or browse to the program manually. After you select a program, you can select the version of Windows the program worked best under (see Figure 14-8).

On the next screen, you can select one or more of the following options to aid compatibility:

- **256 Colors**—Many older Windows programs can't run under 16-bit or higher color depths.

- **640 × 480 Screen Resolution**—Many older Windows programs use a fixed screen size and can't run properly on a high-resolution screen.

- **Disable Visual Themes**—Many older Windows programs were created before visual themes were common.

After selecting the options, test the program (which applies the settings you selected and runs the program). After you close the program, Windows switches back to its normal screen settings if necessary, and you can decide whether to use these settings for your software or try others. You can choose whether to inform Microsoft of your settings, and the settings you chose for the program are used automatically every time you run the program.

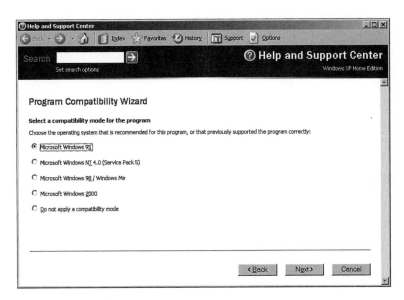

Figure 14-8   Using the Program Compatibility Wizard to run an older Windows program under Windows XP as Windows 95 would run it.

Keep in mind that the Program Compatibility Wizard won't work with all old Windows programs; in particular, the wizard should not be used with antivirus, disk, or system utilities that are not compatible with the Windows version in use. Instead, replace outdated applications with updated versions made for the version of Windows in use.

As an alternative to the Program Compatibility Wizard, you can apply the same settings by using the Compatibility tab on an executable file's properties sheet (see Figure 14-9) with XP, Vista, and 7. Use this method if you already know the appropriate settings to use.

NOTE   Microsoft periodically offers Application Compatibility Updates through Windows Update. These updates improve Windows compatibility with older applications. If you can't get an older program to work with Windows now, it might be able to work in the future. To see which programs are affected by a particular Application Compatibility Update, click the Details button on the listing in Windows Update.

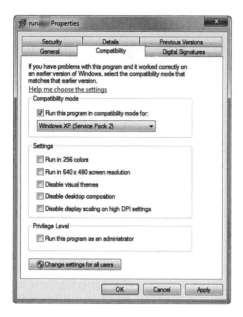

Figure 14-9   Using the Compatibility tab to specify compatibility settings in Windows 7.

Windows XP Mode

Windows 7 Professional, Ultimate, and Enterprise support a virtualization environment called **Windows XP Mode**. This mode enables users of these versions of Windows 7 to use a virtualization-ready edition of Windows XP Professional within a virtualization program called Windows Virtual PC. Programs installed in Windows XP Mode can be run from the Windows 7 start menu as well as from Windows XP Mode. To download **Windows Virtual PC** and Windows XP Mode, go to www.microsoft.com/windows/virtual-pc/download.aspx. To learn more about virtualization, see "Client-Side Virtualization" later in this chapter.

Administrative Tools

Windows XP, Vista, and 7 all include a Control Panel folder called Administrative Tools. This folder provides shortcuts to a variety of management, configuration, and troubleshooting tools:

- **Component Services**—Used by developers and administrators to configure and administer Component Object Model (COM) components

- **Computer Management**—Manages local and remote computers, including viewing system events, managing services, configuring hard disk storage, and others

- **Data Sources (ODBC)**—Moves data between different types of databases using Open Database Connectivity (ODBC)

- **Event Viewer**—Displays the contents of system logs for errors, program start and stop, and other significant events.

- **iSCSI Initiator**—Configures devices on storage networks that use Internet Small Computer System Interface (iSCSI) connections

- **Local Security Policy**—Views and edits Group Policy security settings

- **Performance Monitor**—Monitors performance of CPU, memory, hard disk, and network

- **Print Management**—Manages and administers network printers and print servers

- **Services**—Manages background services (print spooler, search, others)

- **System Configuration**—Starts MSConfig, which helps troubleshoot problems with Windows

- **Task Scheduler**—Schedules programs and tasks

- **Windows Firewall with Advanced Security**—Creates rules and other advanced firewall settings for local and remote computers on the network

- **Windows Memory Diagnostic**—Tests computer RAM to verify proper functioning before the Windows desktop appears

- **Windows PowerShell Modules**—Runs Windows PowerShell, a powerful scripting language

NOTE   To learn more about Computer Management, see "Computer Management (MMC)" in this chapter. To learn more about Event Viewer, see "Using Event Viewer" in Chapter 15. To learn more about local security policy and Windows Firewall with Advanced Security, see Chapter 17. To learn more about Performance Monitor (System Monitor in Windows XP), see "Performance Monitor/System Monitor" in this chapter. To learn more about Print Management, see "Print Management" in this chapter. To learn more about Services, see "Services (Services.msc)" in this chapter. To learn more about System Configuration, see "Using MSConfig" in Chapter 15. To learn more about Task Scheduler, see "Task Scheduler" in this chapter.

File Structure and Paths

In Windows XP, Windows Vista, and Windows 7, file and path structures vary both by operating system version and by whether a 32-bit or 64-bit version of Windows is in use.

Windows XP File Structure and Paths

In Windows XP, user folders are stored in the path

> C:\Documents and Settings*UserName*\\

Folders include My Documents, Desktop, Cookies, Start Menu, User Data, and hidden folders. Folders for user-generated files, such as My Music, My Pictures, My Videos, and so on, are stored as subfolders of My Documents.

Windows Vista File Structure and Paths

In Windows Vista, user folders are stored in the path

> C:\Users*UserName*\\

Folders such as Documents, Downloads, Favorites, Music, Pictures, Videos, and so on are stored as subfolders of ..\UserName\.

Windows 7 File Structure and Paths

In Windows 7, user folders and libraries are stored in the path

> C:\Users*UserName*\\

Libraries (My Documents, My Music, My Pictures, and My Videos) as well as folders such as Desktop, Download, Favorites, Saved Games and so on are stored as subfolders of ..\UserName\.

Libraries are a new folder structure in Windows 7 that permit multiple folders containing related material to be viewed as a single logical folder. For example, by default, the user's Documents library includes the user's My Documents or Documents folder and the shared Public Documents folder. Libraries can be modified by adding other folders, such as a folder on an external drive or a network folder. All local folders in a library are backed up by Windows Backup when the library is selected for backup.

32-Bit Versus 64-Bit File Structure and Paths

In Windows XP and in 32-bit versions of Windows Vista and Windows 7, all program files are stored in a subfolder of C:\Program Files\. However, in 64-bit editions of Windows Vista and Windows 7 (as well as Windows XP Professional 64-bit edition), C:\Program Files\ is used for 64-bit programs and drivers. 32-bit programs are stored in C:\Program Files (x86)\.

Command-Line Tools

220-802

Objective:
220-802: 1.3

Windows XP, Vista, and 7 contain a number of command-line tools for systems operation and management. These include Taskkill, Shutdown, Tasklist, Make Directory, Remove Directory, Change Directory (MD, RD, CD), delete a file (DEL), Format, Copy, Xcopy, Robocopy, Diskpart, and Help.

NOTE SFC and CHKDSK are discussed in Chapter 15. Objective 1.3 refers to KILL and TLIST, but these have been superseded by TASKKILL and TASKLIST.

Starting a Command-Prompt Session with CMD.EXE

Although most computer users won't use the command prompt often, technicians use it frequently because it enables you to

- Recover data from systems that can't boot normally.

- Reinstall lost or corrupted system files.

- Print file listings (believe it or not, you can't do this in Windows Explorer or My Computer/Computer!).

- Copy, move, or delete data.

- Display or configure certain operating system settings

You can start a command-prompt session in Windows by clicking the **Command Prompt** option in the Start menu; it's usually located in the Accessories menu on most versions of Windows. However, it's faster to use the Run command or Search box:

- **In Windows XP**—Click **Start** > **Run**. Then, type **cmd** and click **OK**.

- **In Windows 7/Vista**—Click **Start**, type **cmd** in the Search box, and then press **Enter** or press **Ctrl+Shift+Enter** to run in elevated mode. (It might be necessary for some commands.) You can also right-click cmd and select **Run as Administrator** to run in elevated mode.

Figure 14-10 shows a typical command prompt session in Windows 7.

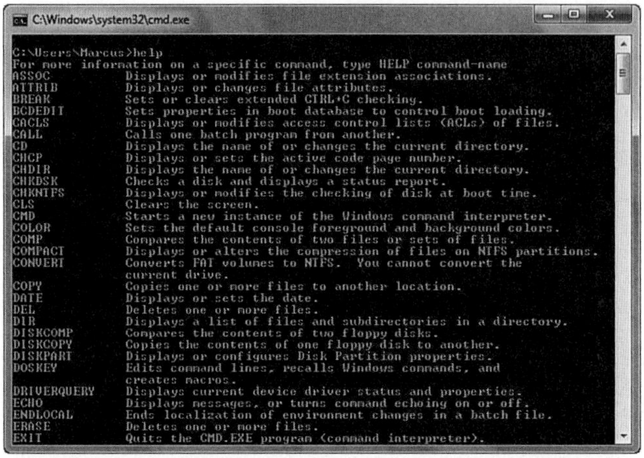

Figure 14-10   Using the **Help** command to view a list of command prompt commands in Windows 7.

Internal Commands Overview

Command-prompt tools include both **internal commands** (commands included in cmd.exe) and **external commands** (programs run from a command-prompt session). Cmd.exe contains the internal commands listed in Table 14-2. Windows Vista and 7's Recovery Environment command prompt fully support the commands listed in Table 14-2. However, Windows XP's Recovery Console supports only some commands as noted.

Table 14-2   Major Internal Commands

Internal Command	Supported in XP Recovery Console	Category	Use	Example
DATE	—	System management	Views system current date and allows it to be changed	**DATE**
TIME	—	System management	Views system current time and allows it to be changed	**TIME**
COPY	Yes	Disk management	Copies one or more files to another folder or drive	**COPY *.* A:**
DEL	Yes	Disk management	Deletes one or more files on current or specified folder or drive	**DEL *.TMP**

Internal Command	Supported in XP Recovery Console	Category	Use	Example
ERASE	Yes	Disk management	Same as **DEL**	**ERASE *.TMP**
DIR	Yes	Disk management	Lists files on current or specified folder or drive	**DIR *.EXE**
MD (MKDIR)	Yes	Disk management	Makes a new folder (subdirectory)	**MD TEMP**
CD (CHDIR)	Yes	Disk management	Changes your current location to the specified folder (subdirectory)	**CD TEMP**
RD (RMDIR)	Yes	Disk management	Removes an empty folder	**RD TEMP**
RENAME (REN)	—	Disk management	Renames a file	**REN joe.txt jerry.txt**
VER	—	System management	Lists the version of operating system in use	**VER**
VOL	—	Disk management	Lists the current volume label and serial number for the default drive	**VOL**
SET	—	System management	Used to set options for a device or program; **SET** without options displays all current **SET** variables	**SET TEMP=C:\ TEMP**
PROMPT	—	System management	Sets display options for the command prompt	**PROMPT=$P $G** (displays drive letter followed by greater-than sign)
PATH	—	System management	Sets folders or drives that can be searched for programs to be run	**PATH=C:\ DOS;C:\ WINDOWS**
ECHO	—	Batch files	Turns on or off the echo (display) of commands to the screen	**ECHO OFF**
CLS	Yes	Batch files, system management	Clears the screen of old commands and program output	**CLS**
TYPE	Yes	System management	Views text files onscreen	**TYPE AUTOEXEC.BAT**

> **TIP**   To get help for any internal or external command-prompt function or program, type the program name followed by **/?**. For example, **DIR /?** displays help for the **DIR** command.

Using Wildcards to Specify a Range of Files

Command-prompt functions and utilities can be used to operate on a group of files with similar names by using one of the following **wildcard** symbols:

- **?** replaces a single character.
- ***** replaces a group of characters.

For example, **DIR *.EXE** displays files with the .EXE extension in the current folder (directory). **DEL MYNOVEL??.BAK** removes the following files: MYNOVEL00.BAK, MYNOVEL01.BAK, but not MYNOVEL.BAK.

COPY

The **COPY** command copies files from one drive and folder to another folder and drive. The folder specified by **COPY** must already exist on the target drive. **COPY** does not work with files that have the system or hidden file attributes; to copy these files, use **XCOPY32** or **ROBOCOPY** instead.

The syntax for **COPY** in Windows 7/Vista/XP is

```
COPY [/D] [/V] [/N] [/Y | /-Y] [/Z] [/L] [/A | /B ] source [/A | /B]
     [+ source [/A | /B] [+ ...]] [destination [/A | /B]]
```

The following is an explanation of the options:

source	Specifies the file or files to be copied
/A	Indicates an ASCII text file
/B	Indicates a binary file
/D	Enables the destination file to be created decrypted
destination	Specifies the directory and/or filename for the new file(s)
/V	Verifies that new files are written correctly
/N	Uses short filename, if available, when copying a file with a non-8dot3 name

/Y	Suppresses prompting to confirm you want to overwrite an existing destination file
/-Y	Causes prompting to confirm you want to overwrite an existing destination file
/Z	Copies networked files in restartable mode
/L	If the source is a symbolic link, copies the link to the target instead of the actual file the source link points to

The switch **/Y** may be preset in the COPYCMD environment variable. This may be overridden with **/-Y** on the command line. The default is to prompt on overwrites unless the **COPY** command is being executed from within a batch script.

To append files, specify a single file for destination but multiple files for source (using wildcards or file1+file2+file3 format).

Here are some examples:

- **COPY *.* A:**—Copies all files in the current folder to the current folder on the A: drive

- **COPY *.TXT C:\Mydocu~1**—Copies all .txt files in the current folder to the Mydocu~1 folder on the C: drive

- **COPY C:\WINDOWS\TEMP*.BAK**—Copies all *.bak files in the \Windows\Temp folder on drive C: to the current folder

- **COPY C:\WINDOWS*.BMP D:**—Copies all .bmp files in the \Windows folder on drive C: to the current folder on drive D:

XCOPY

The **XCOPY** command can be used in place of **COPY** in most cases and has the following advantages:

- **Faster operation on a group of files**—**XCOPY** reads the specified files into conventional RAM before copying them to their destination.

- **Creates folders as needed**—Specify the destination folder name in the **XCOPY** command line, and the destination folder will be created if needed.

- **Operates as backup utility**—Can be used to change the archive bit from on to off on files if wanted to allow **XCOPY** to be used in place of commercial backup programs.

- **Copies files changed or created on or after a specified date**—Also useful when using **XCOPY** as a substitute for commercial backup programs.

The options for **XCOPY.EXE** in Windows 7/Vista/XP include the following:

source	Specifies the file(s) to copy.
destination	Specifies the location or name of new files.
/A	Copies only files with the archive attribute set; doesn't change the attribute.
/M	Copies only files with the archive attribute set; turns off the archive attribute.
/D:*m-d-y*	Copies files changed on or after the specified date. If no date is given, copies only those files whose source time is newer than the destination time.
/EXCLUDE: *file1*[+*file2*] [+*file3*]	Specifies a list of files containing strings. Each string should be in a separate line in the files. When any of the strings match any part of the absolute path of the file to be copied, that file will be excluded from being copied. For example, specifying a string like \ obj\ or .obj excludes all files underneath the directory obj or all files with the .obj extension, respectively.
/P	Prompts you before creating each destination file.
/S	Copies directories and subdirectories except empty ones.
/E	Copies directories and subdirectories, including empty ones. Same as **/S /E**. May be used to modify **/T**.
/V	Verifies each new file.
/W	Prompts you to press a key before copying.
/C	Continues copying even if errors occur.
/I	If destination does not exist and copying more than one file, assumes that destination must be a directory.
/Q	Does not display filenames while copying.
/F	Displays full source and destination filenames while copying.
/L	Displays files that would be copied.
/G	Enables the copying of encrypted files to destination that does not support encryption.
/H	Copies hidden and system files.
/R	Overwrites read-only files.

/T	Creates directory structure but does not copy files. Does not include empty directories or subdirectories.
/T /E	Includes empty directories and subdirectories.
/U	Copies only files that already exist in destination.
/K	Copies attributes. Normal Xcopy resets read-only attributes.
/[LB]	Copies using the generated short names.
/O	Copies file ownership and ACL information.
/X	Copies file audit settings (implies /O).
/Y	Suppresses prompting to confirm you want to overwrite an existing destination file.
/-Y	Causes prompting to confirm you want to overwrite an existing destination file.
/Z	Copies networked files in restartable mode.
/B	(Vista/7 only) Copies the symbolic link itself versus the target of the link.
/J	(Vista/7 only) Copies using unbuffered I/O. Recommended for very large files.

XCOPY can be used to "clone" an entire drive's contents to another drive. For example, the following copies the entire contents of D: drive to H: drive:

```
XCOPY D:\   H:\   /H /S /E /K /C /R
```

This command copies all files from drive D.'s root folder (root directory) and subfolders to drive H.'s root folder and subfolder, including system and hidden files, empty folders and subfolders, file attributes. This will continue even if errors are detected and will overwrite read-only files.

ROBOCOPY.EXE

ROBOCOPY.EXE is a robust file-copying utility included in Windows Vista and 7 that can be used in place of XCOPY.EXE. ROBOCOPY.EXE has several advantages over XCOPY.EXE, including the capability to tolerate pauses in network connections, to mirror the contents of the sources and destination folders by removing files as well as copying files, to perform multithreaded copies for faster copying on multicore PCs, to log copy processes, and others.

Robocopy is included in Windows 7 and Windows Vista. Windows XP users can obtain Robocopy by downloading the Windows Server 2003 Resource Kit Tools from the Microsoft Download center.

The syntax for Robocopy for Windows 7, Windows Server 2008, and Windows Server 2008 R2 is available from http://technet.microsoft.com/en-us/library/cc733145(WS.10).aspx.

ROBOCOPY.EXE uses much different syntax than XCOPY.EXE and has had syntax changes over its different editions. For these reasons, you might prefer to run it by means of a GUI such as the Robocopy GUI available at http://technet.microsoft.com/en-us/magazine/2006.11.utilityspotlight.aspx (see Figure 14-11) or third-party GUIs available online.

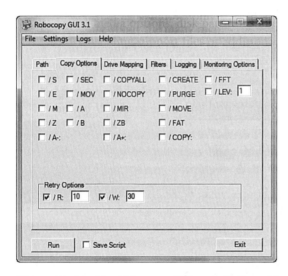

Figure 14-11   The Robocopy GUI available from Microsoft TechNet provides a convenient click-to-select interface for setting Robocopy's many option switches.

NOTE   Microsoft TechNet has also introduced RichCopy as an alternative to Robocopy GUI. To learn more, see http://technet.microsoft.com/en-us/magazine/2009.04.utilityspotlight.aspx.

MKDIR, CHDIR, and RMDIR (MD, CD, and RD)

You can make, change to, or remove folders (directories) with the following commands, as shown in Table 14-3.

Table 14-3   Folder Management Commands

Command	Abbreviation*	Use	Example
MKDIR	**MD**	Creates a folder (directory)	**MKDIR \Backups** Makes the folder Backups one level below the root folder of the current drive
CHDIR	**CD**	Changes to a new folder	**CHDIR \Backups** Changes to the \Backups folder
RMDIR	**RD**	Removes a folder (if empty)	**RMDIR \Backups** Removes the \Backups folder (if empty)

Abbreviations are not supported in Windows XP Recovery Console but can be used in Windows Vista/7 Recovery Environment command prompt.

Folders (directories) can be referred to in two ways:

- Absolute
- Relative

An absolute path provides the full path to the **directory** (folder). For example, to change to the folder \Backups\Word from the folder \My Documents on the same drive, you would use the command **CHDIR\Backups**.

NOTE   You can't use the **CHDIR** command to change to a different drive and folder. It works only on the current drive.

A relative path can be used to change to a folder one level below your location. For example, to change to the folder \Backups\Word from the folder \Backups, you would use the command **CHDIR Word** (or just **CD Word**). No backslash is necessary.

To change to the root folder from any folder, use **CHDIR** (or just **CD**). To change to the folder one level higher than your current location, use **CHDIR..** (or just **CD..**).

Format/Format.exe

In Windows, the Format command is used primarily to re-create the specified file system on a floppy disk, removable-media disk, or a hard disk. In the process, the contents of the disk are overwritten.

Format appears to "destroy" the previous contents of a hard disk, but if you use Format on a hard disk by mistake, third-party data recovery programs can be used to retrieve data from the drive. This is possible because most of the disk surface is not changed by Format when a quick format option is selected.

Windows Vista and Windows 7 overwrite the entire surface of a disk with zeros if the quick format option is not selected. Windows XP checks the drive for errors when quick format is not selected but data might still be recoverable.

If the Quick Format or Safe Format option is used, the contents of the disk are marked for deletion but can be retrieved with third-party data recovery software.

> **NOTE**   The hard disk format process performed by the Format command (which creates the file system) is sometimes referred to as a high-level format to distinguish it from the low-level format used by hard drive manufacturers to set up magnetic structures on the hard drive. When floppy disks are formatted with the Full or Unconditional options, Format performs both a low-level and high-level format on the floppy disk surface.

Using Format with Floppy, USB Flash, and Removable-Media Drives

Although floppy disks, USB flash memory drives, and removable-media drives are preformatted at the factory, Format is still useful as a means to

- Erase the contents of a disk quickly, especially if it contains many files or folders.
- Place new sector markings across the disk.
- Create a bootable disk that can be used to run MS-DOS programs.

Formatting Floppy and Hard Disks with Windows Explorer

You can use Windows Explorer to format both hard drives and floppy disks. Right-click the drive you want to format, select **Format**, and the Format options for Windows display, as shown in Figure 14-12.

Windows Vista and 7 also offer the exFAT (FAT64) file system option for hard disks and high-capacity flash drives. Windows Vista and 7 do not offer the compression option on the Format menu, but if you want to compress the drive after formatting it, you can do so from the General tab of the drive's properties sheet.

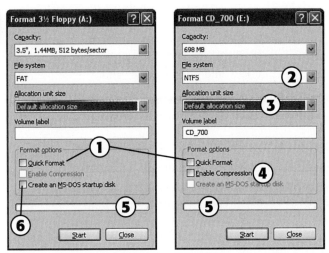

1. Reduces format time, but doesn't check for disk errors
2. Select FAT (FAT16), FAT32, or NTFS
3. Unless you have a specific requirement for a non-standard allocation unit size, use the Default Allocation Size setting
4. Compression available with NTFS file system only
5. Status bar indicates progress of format
6. Option available in Windows XP only; creates a bare-bones MS-DOS boot disk without optical drive or memory management software

Figure 14-12   The Windows XP Explorer Format menu for a floppy disk (left) and hard disk (right).

> **NOTE**   Writeable optical media must also be formatted before it can be used. To learn more about the format options used with these types of media, see Chapter 12, "Storage Devices."

Using FORMAT.EXE

The **FORMAT.EXE** command deletes all existing files and folders from a system. It overwrites the current contents of the target drive unless the **/Q** (Quick Format) option is used. When **/Q** is used, only the file allocation table and root folder are overwritten. To retrieve data from a drive that has been formatted, you must use third-party data-recovery software.

In Windows 7/Vista/XP, **FORMAT.EXE** includes a variety of options for use with floppy disks, hard disks, removable-media and optical drives, and USB flash memory drives. These include the following:

volume	Specifies the drive letter (followed by a colon), mount point, or volume name.
/FS:*filesystem*	Specifies the type of the file system (FAT, FAT32, or NTFS; Windows 7 and Vista SP2 also support exFAT).
/V:*label*	Specifies the volume label.
/Q:	Performs a quick format.

/C	NTFS only: Files created on the new volume will be compressed by default.
/X:	Forces the volume to dismount first if necessary. All opened handles to the volume would no longer be valid.
/R:*revision*	(7/Vista only) UDF only: Forces the format to a specific UDF version (1.20, 1.50, 2.00, 2.01, 2.50). The default revision is 2.01.
/D	(7/Vista only) UDF 2.50 only: Metadata will be duplicated.
/A:*size*	Overrides the default allocation unit size. Default settings are strongly recommended for general use. NTFS supports 512, 1024, 2048, 4096, 8192, 16K, 32K, 64K. FAT supports 512, 1024, 2048, 4096, 8192, 16K, 32K, 64K, (128K, 256K for sector size > 512 bytes). FAT32 supports 512, 1024, 2048, 4096, 8192, 16K, 32K, 64K, (128K, 256K for sector size > 512 bytes). (Vista/7 only) exFAT supports 512, 1024, 2048, 4096, 8192, 16K, 32K, 64K, 128K, 256K, 512K, 1M, 2M, 4M, 8M, 16M, 32M.
/P:*passes*	(Vista/7 only) Zero every sector on the volume passes times. This switch is not valid with /Q.
/S:*state*	(Vista/7 only) Where "state" is either "enable" or "disable" Short names are enabled by default

Floppy disk format options

/F:*size*	Specifies the size of the floppy disk to format (1.44).
/T:*tracks*	Specifies the number of tracks per disk side.
/N:*sectors*	Specifies the number of sectors per track.

Note that the FAT and FAT32 files systems impose the following restrictions on the number of clusters on a volume:

FAT: Number of clusters <= 65526

FAT32: 65526 < Number of clusters < 4177918

FORMAT immediately stops processing if it decides that the preceding requirements cannot be met using the specified cluster size. NTFS compression is not supported for allocation unit sizes above 4096.

Diskpart

Diskpart is a disk management program included in Windows XP, Vista, and 7. It can be used to perform disk partitioning and management commands that are not included in Computer Management's Disk Management module.

When you run Diskpart, a new window opens with a Diskpart> prompt. Only Diskpart commands can be entered in the window:

ACTIVE	Mark the selected partition as active.
ADD	Add a mirror to a simple volume.
ASSIGN	Assign a drive letter or mount point to the selected volume.
ATTRIBUTES	Manipulate volume or disk attributes.
ATTACH	Attaches a virtual disk file.
AUTOMOUNT	Enable and disable automatic mounting of basic volumes.
BREAK	Break a mirror set.
CLEAN	Clear the configuration information, or all information, off the disk.
COMPACT	Attempts to reduce the physical size of the file.
CONVERT	Convert between different disk formats.
CREATE	Create a volume, partition, or virtual disk.
DELETE	Delete an object.
DETAIL	Provide details about an object.
DETACH	Detaches a virtual disk file.
EXIT	Exit DiskPart.
EXTEND	Extend a volume.
EXPAND	Expands the maximum size available on a virtual disk.
FILESYSTEMS	Display current and supported file systems on the volume.
FORMAT	Format the volume or partition.
GPT	Assign attributes to the selected GPT partition.
HELP	Display a list of commands.
IMPORT	Import a disk group.
INACTIVE	Mark the selected partition as inactive.

LIST	Display a list of objects.
MERGE	Merge a child disk with its parents.
ONLINE	Online an object that is currently marked as offline.
OFFLINE	Offline an object that is currently marked as online.
RECOVER	Refresh the state of all disks in the selected pack. Attempt recovery on disks in the invalid pack, and resynchronize mirrored volumes and RAID5 volumes that have stale plex or parity data.
REM	Does nothing. This is used to comment scripts.
REMOVE	Remove a drive letter or mount point assignment.
REPAIR	Repair a RAID-5 volume with a failed member.
RESCAN	Rescan the computer looking for disks and volumes.
RETAIN	Place a retained partition under a simple volume.
SAN	Display or set the SAN policy for the currently booted OS.
SELECT	Shift the focus to an object.
SETID	Change the partition type.
SHRINK	Reduce the size of the selected volume.
UNIQUEID	Display or set the GUID partition table (GPT) identifier or master boot record (MBR) signature of a disk.

Figure 14-13 demonstrates two Diskpart commands:

```
Select disk x
Detail disk
```

Figure 14-13   Using Diskpart to determine details about the selected disk.

Diskpart shows that the selected disk drive is the boot drive, contains the pagefile, and is used to store crashdump information.

> **TIP** To learn more about using Diskpart, see http://support.microsoft.com/kb/300415 and http://technet.microsoft.com/en-us/library/cc766465(v=ws.10).aspx. Diskpart commands can be included in scripts.

DEL

The **DEL** command is an internal command (that is, a command built in to CMD. EXE) used to delete files. The syntax for **DEL** (or **ERASE**, which can be used interchangeably with **DEL**) is

```
DEL [/P] [/F] [/S] [/Q] [/A[[:]attributes]] names
```

```
ERASE [/P] [/F] [/S] [/Q] [/A[[:]attributes]] names
```

names	Specify a list of one or more files or directories. Wildcards may be used to delete multiple files. If a directory (folder) is specified, all files within the directory (folder) will be deleted.
/P	Prompt for confirmation before deleting each file.
/F	Force deleting of read-only files.
/S	Delete specified files from all subdirectories.
/Q	Quiet mode; do not ask if okay to delete on global wildcard.
/A	Select files to delete based on attributes.
attributes	**R** Read-only files.
	S System files.
	H Hidden files.
	A Files ready for archiving.
	I Not content indexed Files.
	L Reparse Points.
	- Prefix meaning not.

If Command Extensions are enabled, **DEL** and **ERASE** change as follows. The display semantics of the **/S** switch are reversed in that it shows you only the files that are deleted, not the ones it could not find.

For example, the following deletes all *.bak files in the current folder:

```
del *.bak
```

The following deletes all temp files in the C:\Temp\ folder and its subfolders:

```
del c:\temp\*.tmp /s
```

NOTE   File deletions at the command prompt bypass the Windows Recovery Bin. However, files deleted with **DEL (ERASE)** can be retrieved with third-party disk data recovery tools.

Tasklist

Tasklist.exe is a command-line utility for Windows XP Professional, Windows Vista, and Windows 7. Use Tasklist to learn about 32-bit tasks running on the current system or on a remote system. When you use the simple command **Tasklist**, it displays a list of all running tasks on the current system. However, **Tasklist** supports many option switches:

```
TASKLIST [/S system [/U username [/P [password]]]]
         [/M [module] | /SVC | /V] [/FI filter] [/FO format] [/NH]
```

Tasklist displays a list of currently running processes on either a local or remote machine.

Parameter list:

/S *system*	Specifies the remote system to connect to.
/U [*domain*]*user*	Specifies the user context under which the command should execute.
/P [*password*]	Specifies the password for the given user context. Prompts for input if omitted.
/M [*module*]	Lists all tasks currently using the given exe/dll name. If the module name is not specified, all loaded modules are displayed.
/SVC	Displays services hosted in each process.
/V	Displays verbose task information.
/FI *filter*	Displays a set of tasks that match a given criteria specified by the filter.

/FO *format*	Specifies the output format. Valid values: TABLE, "LIST", "CSV".
/NH	Specifies that the Column Header should not be displayed in the output. Valid only for TABLE and CSV formats.
/?	Displays this help message.

You can use filters to customize the output:

```
Filter Name        Valid Operators           Valid Value(s)
-----------        ---------------           -------------------------
   STATUS          eq, ne                    RUNNING |
                                             NOT RESPONDING | UNKNOWN
   IMAGENAME       eq, ne                    Image name
   PID             eq, ne, gt, lt, ge, le    PID value
   SESSION         eq, ne, gt, lt, ge, le    Session number
   SESSIONNAME     eq, ne                    Session name
   CPUTIME         eq, ne, gt, lt, ge, le    CPU time in the format
                                             of hh:mm:ss.
                                             hh - hours,
                                             mm - minutes, ss - seconds
   MEMUSAGE        eq, ne, gt, lt, ge, le    Memory usage in KB
   USERNAME        eq, ne                    User name in [domain\]user
                                             format
   SERVICES        eq, ne                    Service name
   WINDOWTITLE     eq, ne                    Window title
   MODULES         eq, ne                    DLL name
```

NOTE WINDOWTITLE and STATUS filters are not supported when querying a remote machine.

Here are some examples to try:

```
TASKLIST
TASKLIST /M
TASKLIST /V /FO CSV
TASKLIST /SVC /FO LIST
TASKLIST /M wbem*
TASKLIST /S system /FO LIST
TASKLIST /S system /U domain\username /FO CSV /NH
TASKLIST /S system /U username /P password /FO TABLE /NH
TASKLIST /FI "USERNAME ne NT AUTHORITY\SYSTEM" /FI "STATUS eq running"
```

Figure 14-14 uses Tasklist to displays programs that use the kernel32.dll module.

Key Topic

```
C:\Windows\system32\cmd.exe

C:\Users\Marcus>tasklist /m kernel32.dll

Image Name                   PID Modules
========================= ======== =============================================
taskhost.exe                3152 kernel132.dll
dwm.exe                     3224 kernel132.dll
explorer.exe                3404 kernel132.dll
msseces.exe                 4156 kernel132.dll
E_IATIEKA.EXE               4220 kernel132.dll
sidebar.exe                 3428 kernel132.dll
HelpPane.exe                3332 kernel132.dll
WMUindow.exe                5040 kernel132.dll
vpc.exe                     1792 kernel132.dll
cmd.exe                     6660 kernel132.dll
conhost.exe                 2316 kernel132.dll
notepad.exe                 5726 kernel132.dll
tasklist.exe                1400 kernel132.dll

C:\Users\Marcus>
```

Figure 14-14   Using **Tasklist /m kernel32.dll** to see the programs that use the kernel32.dll file.

TIP   To see information about both 32-bit and 64-bit tasks on a 64-bit Windows system, download the free Process Explorer utility from the Microsoft TechNet Sysinternals site: http://technet.microsoft.com/en-us/sysinternals/bb896653.

Tasklist can create a .CSV (comma separated value) list of tasks (as well as a table or list). A CSV file can be opened with Microsoft Excel or other spreadsheet programs, and can be imported into most database programs.

Taskkill

Taskkill is a command-line utility for Windows XP, Vista, and 7. **Taskkill** is used to shut down a task on a local or remote system. It is a companion utility to **Tasklist** and shares some of its syntax:

```
TASKKILL [/S system [/U username [/P [password]]]]
         { [/FI filter] [/PID processid | /IM imagename] } [/T] [/F]
```

Taskkill is used to terminate tasks by process id (PID) or image name.

Parameter List:

/S *system*	Specifies the remote system to connect to.
/U [*domain*]*user*	Specifies the user context under which the command should execute.
/P [*password*]	Specifies the password for the given user context. Prompts for input if omitted.
/FI *filter*	Applies a filter to select a set of tasks. Allows "*" to be used; for example, imagename eq acme*.

/PID *processid*	Specifies the PID of the process to be terminated. Use TaskList to get the PID.
/IM *imagename*	Specifies the image name of the process to be terminated. Wildcard '*' can be used to specify all tasks or image names.
/T	Terminates the specified process and any child processes that were started by it.
/F	Specifies to forcefully terminate the process(es).
/?	Displays this help message.

You can use filters to select certain tasks only:

Filter Name	Valid Operators	Valid Value(s)
STATUS	eq, ne	RUNNING | NOT RESPONDING | UNKNOWN
IMAGENAME	eq, ne	Image name
PID	eq, ne, gt, lt, ge, le	PID value
SESSION	eq, ne, gt, lt, ge, le	Session number.
CPUTIME	eq, ne, gt, lt, ge, le	CPU time in the format of hh:mm:ss. hh - hours, mm - minutes, ss - seconds
MEMUSAGE	eq, ne, gt, lt, ge, le	Memory usage in KB
USERNAME	eq, ne	User name in [domain\]user format
MODULES	eq, ne	DLL name
SERVICES	eq, ne	Service name
WINDOWTITLE	eq, ne	Window title

NOTE These rules apply when running **TaskKill**:

1. Wildcard * for **/IM** switch is accepted only when a filter is applied.

2. Termination of remote processes will always be done forcefully (**/F**).

3. "WINDOWTITLE" and "STATUS" filters are not considered when a remote machine is specified.

The following are some examples of using Taskkill:

```
TASKKILL /IM notepad.exe
TASKKILL /PID 1230 /PID 1241 /PID 1253 /T
TASKKILL /F /IM cmd.exe /T
TASKKILL /F /FI „PID ge 1000" /FI „WINDOWTITLE ne untitle*"
TASKKILL /F /FI „USERNAME eq NT AUTHORITY\SYSTEM" /IM notepad.exe
TASKKILL /S system /U domain\username /FI "USERNAME ne NT*" /IM *
```

The task is killed as soon as the command is issued. When a command is successful, Taskkill reports that the task has been killed.

Administrative Features

Windows contains a number of administrative features designed to help you manage operations and users. The following sections discuss many of these components, including

- Computer management
- Performance Monitor/System Monitor
- Services (Services.msc)
- Task Scheduler
- Print Management
- Task Manager

Computer Management (MMC)

This component of Windows 7/Vista/XP has been mentioned a few times already, but it's worth mentioning again. Instead of hunting around for different utilities in different places in Windows, it's simpler to use the **Computer Management** console window because it has most of the tools you need in one organized two-pane (XP) or three pane (7/Vista) window system. Here are the ways to open Computer Management:

- Click **Start**; then right-click **Computer/My Computer** and select **Manage**.

- Navigate to Start, All Programs, Administrative Tools, Computer Management.

- Open the Run prompt (Windows+R) and type **compmgmt.msc** (a personal favorite).

In Computer Management, you find the Event Viewer, Device Manager, Local Users and Groups, Services, and disk tools such as Disk Management.

Computer Management is an example of the Microsoft Management Console (MMC). This is a blank console that uses various snap-in console windows. MMC saves the consoles you snap in and remembers the last place you were working, and this becomes a valuable and time saving tool.

To open it, open the **Run** program (Windows XP) or click the Search box (Windows 7, Vista) and type **MMC**. This opens a new blank MMC. Then, to add console windows, go to **File** and then **Add/Remove Snap-in** (or press **Ctrl+M**). From there, click the **Add** button to select the consoles you want, such as Computer Management, Performance Logs and Alerts, or ActiveX Controls. You also can change the "mode" in which the user works when accessing the MMC—for example, Author mode, which has access to everything, and User mode, which has various levels of limitation. When you are finished, save the MMC and consider adding it as a shortcut within the desktop or in the Quick Launch area and maybe add a keyboard shortcut to open it. The next time you open it, it remembers all the console windows you added and starts you at the location you were in when you closed the program. By default, Windows 7 and Vista include version 3.0 of the MMC, and Windows XP includes Version 2.0. However, you can download version 3.0 for Windows XP from http://technet.microsoft.com. Just search for "Microsoft Management Console 3.0 for Windows XP."

Performance Monitor/System Monitor

The Windows 7/Vista Performance Monitor and Windows XP System Monitor can be used to determine whether more RAM should be added to a computer.

- To access the Windows 7/Vista Performance Monitor, open the Run prompt, type **perfmon.exe**, and press **Enter**. Windows 7 opens the Performance Monitor window. In Windows Vista, the Reliability and Performance Monitor window opens. In either case, you must then click the **Performance Monitor** node.

■ To access the Windows XP System monitor, open the Run prompt, type **perfmon.exe**, and press **Enter**. This opens the Performance console window. Click the **System Monitor** node.

Many different types of performance factors can be measured with these programs. This is done by measuring objects. Objects include physical devices, such as the processor and memory, and software, such as protocols and services. The objects are measured with counters. For example, a common counter for the processor is % Processor Time.

To see whether additional RAM is needed in a system, select the object called **Paging File**; then select the counters **% Usage** and **Pages/Sec**, as shown in the following steps:

Step 1.   Click the + sign, or right-click in the table beneath the graph and select **Add Counters**.

Step 2.   Select **Paging File** as the Performance Object, and then choose **% Usage**. In Windows 7 and Vista, this is shown as a drop-down menu within the object.

Step 3.   Click **Add**.

Step 4.   Select **Memory** as the Performance Object, and then choose **Pages/Sec**. In Windows 7 and Vista, this is shown as a drop-down menu within the object. In XP, it might be added already.

Step 5.   Click **Add**.

Step 6.   Click **Close** (XP) or **OK** (7, Vista), and then run normal applications for this computer.

If the Performance Monitor/System Monitor indicates that the Paging File % Usage is consistently near 100% or the Memory Pages/Sec counter is consistently higher than 5, add RAM to improve performance. Figure 14-15 shows an example of adequate memory within Windows XP's System monitor.

Services (Services.msc)

Many of Windows 7/Vista/XP's core functions are implemented as services, including features such as the print spooler, wireless network configuration, DHCP client service, and many more. Services can be run automatically or manually and are controlled through the Services node of the Computer Management Console. To open the Computer Management Console, right-click **My Computer/Computer** and select **Manage**. Then, expand the Services and Applications node, and click **Services**.

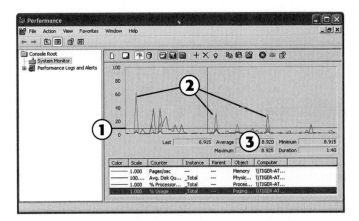

1. Paging file % usage
2. Memory page/second
3. Current average for
   selected counter

Figure 14-15   This Windows XP system has adequate memory at this time, as indicated by the low levels of usage of the Paging File % Usage and Memory Pages/Sec counters.

You can also access the Services dialog from the Services applet in Control Panel's Administrative Tools folder or by running Services.msc from the Run line dialog; opening Services in these ways displays the dialog shown in Figure 14-16. The Services dialog lists each service by name, and provides a description, status message, and startup type, and whether the service is for a local system or network service.

Figure 14-16   The Services dialog.

To view the properties for a particular service, double-click the service listing. The General tab of the properties sheet, as shown in Figure 14-17, displays the service name, description, path to executable file, startup type, and status. You can also stop, pause, or resume a service from this dialog, as well as from the Services dialog.

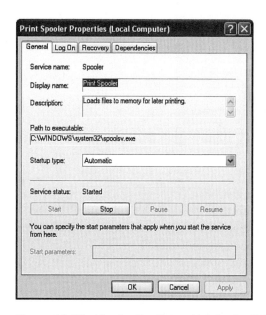

Figure 14-17   Viewing the General tab for the Print Spooler service.

Use the Log On tab if you need to configure the service to run for a specific user, the Recovery tab to specify what to do if the service fails, and the Dependencies tab to see what other services work with the specified service.

If a system cannot perform a task that uses a service, go to the Services dialog and restart the service. If a service prevents another task from running (for example, a third-party wireless network client might not run if the Windows XP Wireless Zero Configuration service is running), go to the Services dialog and stop the service.

NOTE   For more information about specific Windows services, I recommend The Elder Geek's Windows Services Guide (Windows XP version at www.theeldergeek. com/services_guide.htm; Windows 7 version at www.theeldergeek.com/windows_7/ windows_7_services.htm) or the Answers That Work list of "Task List Programs" at www.answersthatwork.com/Tasklist_pages/tasklist.htm.

Task Scheduler

Windows XP, Vista, and 7 all include the capability to run a task on a specified schedule. In Windows XP, this feature is called Scheduled Tasks; in Windows Vista and 7, it is called Task Scheduler.

Create a Task in Windows XP

To create a task in Windows XP, follow this procedure:

Step 1. Open Control Panel in Classic Mode.

Step 2. Click **Scheduled Tasks**.

Step 3. Double-click **Add Scheduled Task**.

Step 4. Click **Next**.

Step 5. Select a program to run, and click **Next**.

Step 6. Enter a name for the task.

Step 7. Select an interval (daily, weekly, monthly, one-time only, when my computer starts, or when I log on), and click **Next**.

Step 8. Select a start time, frequency, and day of the week, and click **Next**.

Step 9. Enter the username and password; confirm the password, and click **Next**.

Step 10. Review the settings for the task (see Figure 14-18) and click **Finish**.

Step 11. The task is saved in the Scheduled Tasks folder. You can edit or delete tasks in this folder as needed.

NOTE To specify advanced settings, click the check box in Step 10 before clicking **Finish**.

Create a Task in Windows Vista and 7

To create a basic task in Windows Vista or 7, follow this procedure:

Step 1. Open Control Panel in Small Icons or Large Icons mode.

Step 2. Open the Administrative Tools folder.

Step 3. Double-click **Task Scheduler**.

Figure 14-18 Reviewing a Backup task created with the Windows XP Scheduled Tasks Wizard.

NOTE You can also run Task Scheduler from the Run or Search box as **taskschd.msc /s.**

Step 4. Click **Create Basic Task** in the Actions menu.

Step 5. Enter a name for the task and a description, and click **Next**.

Step 6. Select an interval (daily, weekly, monthly, one-time only, when my computer starts, when I log on, or when a specific event is logged), and click **Next**.

Step 7. Specify when to start the task and recurrence, and whether to synchronize across time zones; then click **Next**.

Step 8. Specify what to do (start a program, send an email, or display a message), and click **Next**. The following steps assume that Start a Program has been selected.

Step 9. Select a program or script to run, add options (arguments), and specify where to start the program or script. Click **Next**.

Step 10. Review the settings for the task (see Figure 14-19) and click **Finish**.

The task is saved in the Task Scheduler library (see Figure 14-20). You can edit or delete tasks in this folder as needed.

NOTE   Some tasks need to be configured for Windows 7 or Windows Vista. To see this option and other settings you might need to adjust, click the check box in Step 10 before clicking **Finish**.

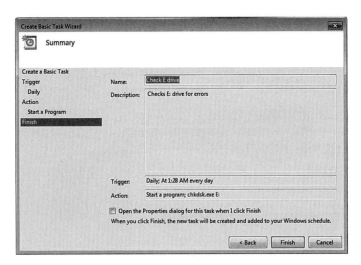

Figure 14-19   Reviewing a Disk Check task created with the Windows 7 Task Scheduler.

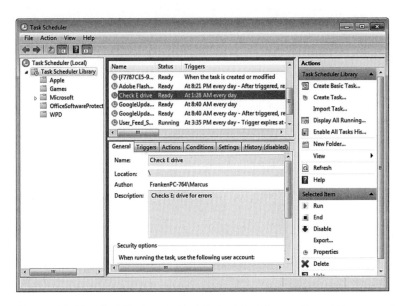

Figure 14-20   The Windows 7 Task Scheduler Library after adding a new task.

Print Management

Print Management is a utility included in Windows Vista and Windows 7 for managing printers connected to the computer or on a network. It is also available for Windows XP.

NOTE   To obtain Print Management for Windows XP SP2 and above, download pmcmgmt.exe from the Microsoft Download page for "Windows Server 2003 R2 Administration Tools Pack."

To start print management from Windows Vista and Windows 7, open the Administrative Tools folder in Control Panel, and double-click **Print Management**. The Print Management console opens (see Figure 14-21). From it, you can view print servers and connected printers, manage jobs, manage printer ports and forms, and perform other tasks.

Figure 14-21   The Windows 7 Print Management console.

Task Manager

The **Task Manager** utility provides a useful real-time look into the inner workings of Windows and the programs that are running. There are several ways to display the Task Manager including

- Right-click the taskbar and select **Task Manager**.

- Press **Ctrl+Shift+Esc**.

- Open the Run or Search box and type **taskmgr**.

- Press **Ctrl+Alt+Del** and select **Task Manager** from the Windows Security dialog. (Note: This works only in Windows XP if you have turned off the Welcome Screen option.)

The Task Manager tabs include

- **Applications**—Shows running applications

- **Processes**—Program components in memory

- **Performance**—CPU, memory, pagefile, and caching stats

- **Networking**—Lists network utilization by adapter in use

- **Users**—Lists current users

- **Services**—Lists services and their status (Windows Vista and Windows 7)

Use the Applications tab to determine whether a program has stopped responding; you can shut down these programs by using the **End Task** button.

Use the Processes tab to see which processes are consuming the most memory. Use this dialog along with the System Configuration Utility (MSConfig) to help determine whether you are loading unnecessary startup applications; MSConfig can disable them to free up memory. If you are unable to shut down a program with the Applications tab, you can also shut down its processes with the Processes tab, but this is not recommended unless the program cannot be shut down in any other way.

Use the Performance tab to determine whether you need to install more RAM memory or need to increase the computer's paging file size. Use the Networking tab to monitor the performance of the computer's connection to the network. Use the Services tab to see the services currently running on a system. Figure 14-22 illustrates these tabs on a Windows 7 system with a dual-core processor.

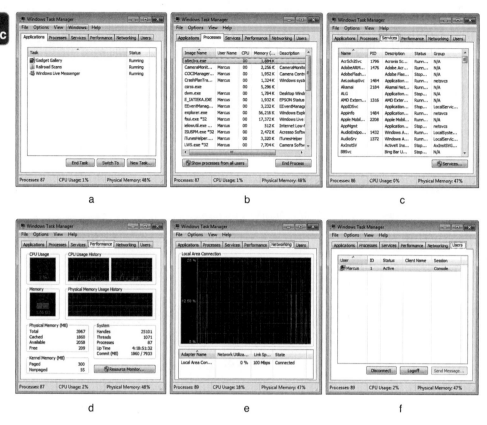

a   b   c

d   e   f

Figure 14-22   The Windows 7 version of the Windows Task Manager.

Disk Management

The **Disk Management** snap-in of the Computer Management console is the
GUI-based application for analyzing and configuring hard drives. You can do a lot
from here, as shown in Table 14-4. Try some of the configurations listed on a test
computer. All you need is one or two drives with unpartitioned space.

Table 14-4   Disk Configuration Options Available in Disk Management

Configuration	Steps
Initialize a new disk.	A secondary hard disk installed in a computer might not be seen by Windows Explorer immediately. To make it accessible, locate the disk (for example Disk 1), right-click **Disk 1** or **Disk 2**, and so on, and select **Initialize Disk**.
Create a primary partition (Windows XP).	1. Right-click a disk's unallocated space (shown with a black header) and select **New Partition**, as shown in Figure 14-23. 2. Click **Next** for the wizard, and then select **Primary Partition**. 3. Select the amount of unallocated space you want for the partition, and click **Next**. 4. Select a drive letter. 5. Choose whether you want to format at this point. 6. Review the summary screen, and if it is correct, click **Finish**. Note: For computers with limited resources, it is recommended that you wait to format until after the partition is created.
Create an **extended partition** (Windows XP).	1. Right-click a disk's unallocated space (shown with a black header) and select **New Partition**, as shown in Figure 14-23. 2. Click **Next** for the wizard, and then select **Extended Partition**. 3. Select the amount of unallocated space you want for the partition, and click **Next**. 4. Review the summary screen, and if it is correct, click **Finish**.
Create a **logical drive** (Windows XP).	This can be done only within an extended partition that has already been created. 1. Right-click the extended partition (shown with a green header) and select **New Logical Drive**, as shown in Figure 14-24. 2. Click **Next** for the wizard. You will notice that your only option is Logical drive. Click **Next**. 3. Select the amount of unallocated space you want for the partition and click **Next**. 4. Select a drive letter. 5. Choose whether you want to format at this point. 6. Review the summary screen, and if it is correct, click **Finish**.
Format a partition/logical drive (Windows XP).	1. Right-click the primary partition or logical drive and select **Format**. 2. In the Format x: window, select the file system and whether to do a quick format. If it is a new drive, you can select quick format. However, if the drive was used previously, you might want to leave this option unchecked. *All data will be erased during the format procedure.*

Table 14-4 Continued

Configuration	Steps
Make a partition active.	Right-click the primary partition and select **Mark Partition** as **Active**. You can have up to four primary partitions on a hard disk, but only one of them can be active.
Convert a basic disk to dynamic.	To change the size of a partition in Windows XP, to create simple and spanned volumes, or to implement RAID, the hard disk(s) need to be converted to dynamic. It's highly recommended that you back up your data before attempting this configuration. 1. Right-click the hard disk where it says Disk 0 or Disk 1, and select **Convert to Dynamic Disk**. 2. In the ensuing window, you can select multiple disks to switch over to dynamic. This can also be done in Windows Vista and Windows 7; however, in Vista and 7 you now have the option to extend a partition, as shown later in this table.
Create and Format a Partition (Vista and 7).	Windows Vista and 7 simplify the process of creating and formatting a partition. To create a partition on unallocated space 1. Right-click unallocated space on a drive. (With a new drive. the entire drive will be listed as unallocated.) 2. Select **New Simple Volume**. 3. Click **Next**. 4. To use the entire space for a volume (drive letter), click **Next**. To use only part of the space, specify the amount of space to use (in MB), and then click **Next**. 5. Select the drive letter to install, and click **Next**. (You can also select the option to not assign a drive letter or to mount the drive in an empty NTFS folder on an existing drive.) 6. Specify the file system (NTFS is default), the volume name, and whether to use a quick format or prepare the drive as compressed. Click **Next**. 7. Review all options, and click **Finish** (see Figure 14-25). Note: Windows Vista/7 can use extended partitions but cannot create them with Disk Management. If you need to set up an extended partition with logical drives, use the command-line program Diskpart.exe.

Configuration	Steps
Extend a partition (Vista and 7 only).	Windows Vista and 7 enable you to extend the size of a partition (volume) or shrink it within the Disk Management utility. It's highly recommended that you back up your data before attempting this configuration.
	1. Right-click the volume to be extended.
	2. Select **Extend Volume**. (Remember that a volume is any section of the hard drive with a drive letter.)
	3. Click **Next** for the wizard, and select how much space you'd like to add to the partition.
	4. Select any other disks (with unpartitioned space) to combine with the first disk to create a spanned partition, and click **Next**.
	5. Click **Finish** at the summary screen.
	A reboot is not required, and this process should finish fairly quickly. This process can also be done using the Diskpart command.
Create a **drive array**.	1. Start with at least two hard drives. (Any data on the drives will be deleted, so back them up first!)
	2. Right-click the first drive to add to your array, and select the array type. (See the note following the table.)
	3. Select the other drive to add to your array, and click **Add**. Click **Next**.
	4. Assign a drive letter or mount point. Click **Next**.
	5. Select the option to format the volume and name it. Click **Next**.
	6. Review your settings. Click **Finish**.
	7. Click **Yes** to convert the drives to dynamic disks (required for arrays). The array is created.

NOTE Windows Disk Management supports three types of disk arrays: a spanned array includes two or more hard disks of any size that are treated as a single unit. A striped array includes two hard disks (preferably of the same size) with data striped across them. A mirrored array includes two hard disks (preferably of the same size) with the contents of one drive mirrored on the other. Windows XP also supports a RAID-5 volume (also known as a striped volume with parity), which uses three or more drives. A RAID-5 array cannot be created with Disk Management with Windows Vista or Windows 7.

Spanned is equivalent to "just a bunch of disks" or JBOD mode on a hardware RAID adapter. Striped is equivalent to RAID 0 on a hardware RAID adapter. Mirrored is equivalent to RAID 1 on a hardware RAID adapter. Windows Disk Management's disk arrays are slower than some hardware RAID arrays (the amount depends on the hardware RAID host adapter in the comparison) but can be set up with standard non-RAID PATA or SATA host adapters.

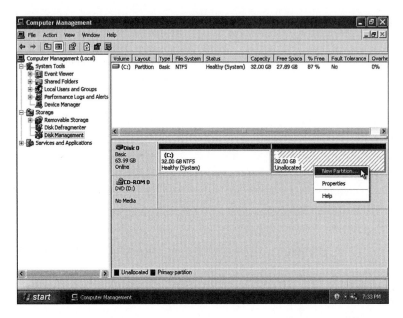

Figure 14-23   Creating a partition from Unallocated Disk Space with Windows XP.

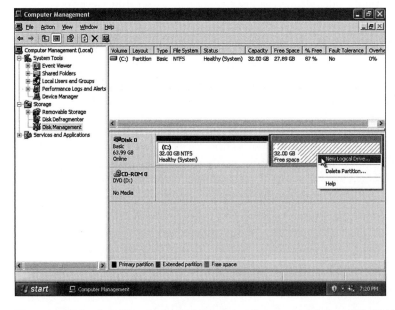

Figure 14-24   Creating a logical drive from within an extended partition with Windows XP.

Figures 14-23 and 14-24 illustrate the process of using Disk Management to create a partition and a logical drive with Windows XP.

Figure 14-25 illustrates the process of creating a simple volume with Windows 7.

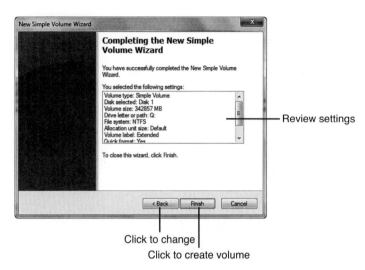

Figure 14-25   Preparing to create a new simple volume with Windows 7.

In Figure 14-23, you also can see the disks at the top of the window and their status. For example, the C: partition is healthy. It also shows the percentage of the disk used and other information, such as whether the disk is currently formatting, whether it's dynamic, or whether it has failed. In some cases, you might see "foreign" status. This means that a dynamic disk has been moved from another computer (with another Windows operating system) to the local computer, and it cannot be accessed properly. To fix this and be able to access the disk, add the disk to your computer's system configuration. To add a disk to your computer's system configuration, import the foreign disk. (Right-click the disk, and then click **Import Foreign Disks**.) Any existing volumes on the foreign disk become visible and accessible when you import the disk. For more information on the plethora of disk statuses, see the Microsoft TechNet article, "Disk Status Descriptions," at http://technet.microsoft.com/en-us/library/cc738101(WS.10).aspx.

To learn more about disk partition types, see "Partitioning," in Chapter 13.

Mount Points and Mounting a Drive

You can also "mount" drives in Disk Management. A **mounted drive** is a drive mapped to an empty folder within a volume that has been formatted as NTFS. Instead of using drive letters, mounted drives use drive paths. This is a good solution for when you need more than 26 drives in your computer because you are not limited to the letters in the alphabet. Mounted drives can also provide more space for temporary files and can enable you to move folders to different drives if space runs low on the current drive. To mount a drive, follow these steps:

Step 1.   Right-click the partition or volume you want to mount, and select **Change Drive Letters and Paths**.

Step 2.   In the displayed window, click **Add**.

Step 3.   Browse to the empty folder you want to mount the volume to, and click **OK** for both windows.

As shown in Figure 14-26, the DVD-ROM drive has been mounted within a folder on the hard drive called Test. The figure shows the Properties window for the folder Test. It shows that it is a mounted volume and shows the location of the folder (which is the mount point) and the target of the mount point, which is the DVD drive containing a Windows Vista DVD. To remove the **mount point**, go back to Disk Management, right-click the mounted volume, and select **Change Drive Letters and Paths**; and then select **Remove**. Remember that the folder you want to use as a mount point must be empty and must be within an NTFS volume.

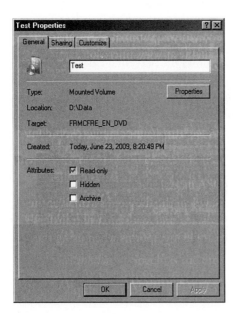

Figure 14-26   Empty NTFS folder acting as a mount point.

Windows File Systems

What exactly is a **file system**, anyway? A file system describes how data and drives are organized. In Windows, the file system you choose for a hard disk affects the following:

- The rules for how large a logical drive (drive letter) can be and whether the hard disk can be used as one big drive letter, several smaller drive letters, or must be multiple drive letters.

- How efficiently a system stores data; the less wasted space, the better.

- How secure a system is against tampering.

- Whether a drive can be accessed by more than one operating system.

The term *file system* is a general term for how an operating system stores various types of files. Windows supports three different file systems for hard drives, FAT32, NTFS, and exFAT, and supports FAT for floppy disks.

FAT32

FAT32 was introduced in 1995 and is supported by Windows 7, Vista, and XP, although NTFS is preferred. **FAT32** has the following characteristics:

- The 32-bit file allocation table, which allows for 268,435,456 entries (2^{32}) per drive. Remember, an entry can be a folder or an allocation unit used by a file.

- The root directory can be located anywhere on the drive and can have an unlimited number of entries, which is a big improvement over FAT.

- FAT32 uses an 8KB allocation unit size for drives as large as 16GB.

- The maximum logical partition size allowed is 2TB (more than 2 trillion bytes). Some hard disk drives now on the market are as large as 3TB.

NOTE Windows 7, Vista, and XP can't create a FAT32 partition larger than 32GB. However, if the partition already exists, they can use it.

You can use FAT32 to format hard disks, flash memory, and removable media drives. However, FAT32 is recommended for hard disks *only* if the hard disk must also be accessed by dual-booting with an older version of Windows—for example, Windows 95, 98, or Me, which do not support NTFS.

> **NOTE**   If you want to store scheduled backups on a hard disk with Windows Vista or 7, you must use a backup hard disk that uses the NTFS file system.

exFAT (FAT64)

exFAT (also known as FAT64) is a newer file system designed to enable mobile personal storage media to be used seamlessly on mobile and desktop computers. exFAT enables Windows 7, Vista, XP, and CE (portable edition of Windows) to have file system support parity. It is designed to be as simple as FAT32, but with many improvements in capacity and scalability.

exFAT is also called FAT64 because it supports 64-bit addressing. exFAT's main features include

- Support for volumes (drive letters) larger than 32GB (theoretical maximum for FAT32 in Windows XP). 512TB is the recommended maximum volume size, but the theoretical volume size is 64ZB.

- Recommended and maximum file sizes also increase to 512TB and 64ZB, respectively.

- Improvements in file system structure for better performance with flash media and for movie recording.

- Support for Universal Time Coordinate (UTC) date stamps.

exFAT support is included in Windows 7, Windows Server 2008 and 2008 R2, and Windows Vista SP1 and above. To add exFAT support to Windows XP SP2 and SP3, Windows XP x64 edition, Windows Server 2003 SP2 and SP1, download the appropriate driver from the links at http://support.microsoft.com/kb/955704. To find information about non-Microsoft operating systems that support exFAT, see http://en.wikipedia.org/wiki/ExFAT.

NTFS

The New Technology File System (**NTFS**) is the native file system of Windows 7, Vista, and XP. As implemented in Windows 7, Vista, and XP, NTFS has many differences from FAT32, including

- **Access Control**—Different levels of access control by group or user can be configured for both folders and individual files.

- **Built-in compression**—Individual files, folders, or an entire drive can be compressed without the use of third-party software.

- **A practical limit for partition sizes of 2TB due to BIOS issues (see the following note)**—The same as with FAT32, although partitions theoretically can reach a maximum size of 16 exabytes (16 billion billion bytes. 1 exabyte = 1.1529215 × 1018 bytes).

- **Individual Recycle Bins**—Unlike FAT32, NTFS includes a separate recycle bin for each user.

- **Support for the Encrypting File System (EFS)**—EFS enables data to be stored in an encrypted form. No password and no access to files!

- **Support for mounting a drive**—Drive mounting enables you to address a removable-media drive's contents, for example, as if its contents are stored on your hard disk. The hard disk's drive letter is used to access data on both the hard disk and the removable media drive.

- **Disk quota support**—The administrator of a system can enforce rules about how much disk space each user is allowed to use for storage.

- **Hot-swapping**—Removable-media drives that have been formatted with NTFS (such as USB, Jaz, Orb, and others) can be connected or removed while the operating system is running.

- **Indexing**—The Indexing service helps users locate information more quickly when the Search tool is used.

NOTE If you want to boot from a 3TB or larger hard disk, you must use a 64-bit version of Windows 7 or later on a system that has an EFI or UEFI (Extensible Firmware Interface or Unified Extensible Firmware Interface) BIOS. EFI and UEFI support the GPT partition table. 3TB drives can be used on older systems by splitting the drive into partitions no larger than 2.2TB each.

3TB and larger hard disks also use a new low-level format scheme known as Advanced Format (4KB sectors rather than 512-byte sectors). If you are planning to move legacy partitions to these drives, you will want to use an alignment tool to realign the drive for maximum performance. See www.pcworld.com/article/235088/everything_ you_need_to_know_about_3tb_hard_drives.html and http://msdn.microsoft.com/ en-us/windows/hardware/gg463524 for more information.

Follow these steps to determine what file system was used to prepare a Windows hard drive:

Step 1. Open Windows Explorer.

Step 2. Right-click the drive letter in the Explorer Window, and select **Properties**.

The Properties sheet for the drive lists FAT32 for a drive prepared with FAT32 and NTFS for a drive prepared with NTFS (see Figure 14-27).

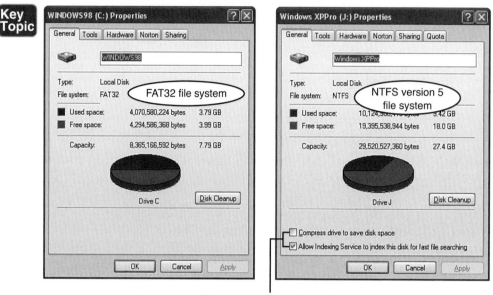

Disk compression and indexing
features available with NTFS 5

Figure 14-27 A hard disk formatted with FAT32 (left) and a hard disk formatted with NTFS version 5 (right).

Converting a Drive's File System with CONVERT.EXT

Windows includes the command-line program **CONVERT.EXE**, which is designed to help you convert a drive from a FAT file system to NTFS.

To convert a drive's file system using Convert.exe, follow these steps:

Step 1.   Open a command-prompt window. (On Windows Vista and 7, open the command prompt window in elevated mode.)

Step 2.   Type **Convert x: /fs:ntfs** and press **Enter**. For example, to convert f:, type **Convert f: /fs:ntfs**.

To see advanced options for Convert, type **convert /?**.

Run-Line Utilities

220-802

Objective:
220-802: 1.4

Windows contains a variety of run-line utilities you can use for system management. A run-line utility is a program you can start by using the Run dialog. You can also start these utilities by using Windows Desktop Search in Windows Vista and 7 or by opening the program's icon from Windows Explorer (My Computer). The most significant ones for the purposes of the A+ Certification exams include

- **SERVICES.MSC**—Views Windows Services
- **MMC**—Starts Microsoft Management Console
- **Notepad**—Opens Notepad text editor/viewer
- **Explorer**—Starts Windows Explorer
- **MSInfo32**—Starts Windows System Information
- **DXDiag**—Starts DirectX Diagnostic
- **MSConfig**—Starts System Configuration utility
- **Regedit**—Launches Registry Editor
- **CMD**—Opens the command prompt

These run-line utilities not otherwise covered are discussed in the following sections.

NOTE SERVICES.MSC is discussed earlier in this chapter. See "Services (Services. MSC)." MMC is discussed earlier in this chapter. See "Computer Management Console (MMC)." MSConfig, REGEDIT, and CMD are discussed in Chapter 15. MSTSC (Remote Desktop Connection) is discussed in Chapter 16, "Networking."

Notepad

Notepad is a simple plain-text editor; however, it has several uses in system management:

- Creating batch files and scripts. When saving a batch file or script, use quotes around the filename and extension thus: "myscript.scr" or "mybatch.bat"

- Viewing text-based reports.

- Editing HTML files.

Notepad is the default program for opening up .txt (plain-text) files.

To open a text file with a different extension in Notepad

Step 1.   Right-click the file in Windows Explorer.

Step 2.   Select **Open With**.

Step 3.   Choose **Notepad**.

Windows Explorer

Windows Explorer is the file-management utility used by Windows (see Figure 14-28 and Figure 14-29). Windows can use Explorer to view both local drive/network and Internet content. In Windows XP, it integrates tightly with My Computer and Internet Explorer. However, in Windows 7 and Windows Vista (and in Windows XP systems using Internet Explorer 7 or higher), **Windows Explorer** launches a new process when connecting to Internet sites.

By default, Windows Explorer doesn't display hidden and system files unless the View options are changed; see the section "Folder Options," later in this chapter, for details.

Windows Explorer can be started in any of the following ways in Windows:

- From the Start menu, click Start, All Programs, Accessories, Windows Explorer.

- Open the **Run** prompt (Windows XP) or click the **Search** box (Windows 7, Vista), type **Explorer**, and press **Enter**.

- Open My Computer (XP) or Computer (7, Vista) to start Explorer automatically.

Path to current location   Click to change view

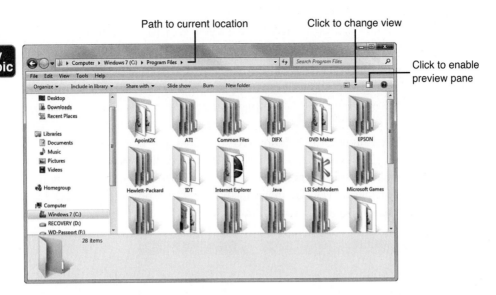

Click to enable
preview pane

Figure 14-28   Windows Explorer in Windows 7; the Explorer bar uses a "breadcrumb" motif to indicate the current location and the path to that location.

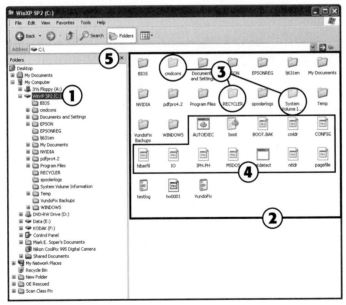

1. Selected object (C: drive)
2. Contents of C: drive (default large icons view)
3. Hidden and system folders
4. Hidden and system files
5. Click to switch to Common Tasks View

Figure 14-29   Windows Explorer in Windows XP; the current object's name appears in the Address bar.

TIP   To view the contents of a particular drive with Windows Explorer, type **Explorer x:** into the Run prompt or Search box (replace x with the actual drive letter) and press **Enter**.

Common Tasks View in Windows XP

When you start My Computer in Windows XP, the Common Tasks view shown in Figure 14-30 displays by default. The Common Tasks view displays the properties of the selected object and displays a preview when available. However, the most significant feature is the changeable task pane in the upper-left portion of the display. In Windows Vista, this has been replaced by Favorite Links.

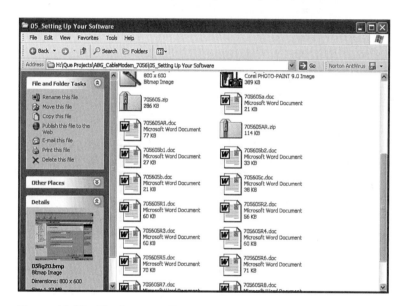

Figure 14-30   The Common Tasks view of a folder in Windows XP.

As shown in Figure 14-30, the Details pane at the lower left displays a preview of the selected file as well as its properties. The File and Folder Tasks task pane at the upper left changes its name and contents to provide task options suitable for the folder or selected object.

The contents and name of the task pane change according to the characteristics of the selected or displayed object. For example, click My Computer and the task pane is titled System Tasks, with a choice of options such as View System Information, Add or Remove Programs, or Change a Setting. The contents of Other Places also changes to display related objects.

> **TIP**   To switch between Common Tasks and Classic view, click the Folders icon on the toolbar.

Windows Vista Favorite Links View

Windows Vista uses the Favorite Links view, as shown in Figure 14-31, in place of Windows XP's Common Tasks view. Favorite Links provides shortcuts to the current user's Documents, Pictures, and Music folders, and searches for recently changed files, saved searches, and the system's Public folder (replaces Windows XP's Shared Folders). Click the up or down pointer below Favorite Links to toggle Folders on/off. The right pane lists the contents of the current location. Common tasks have been moved to a menu strip above the panes.

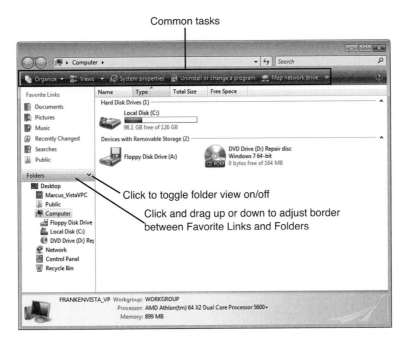

Figure 14-31   The Favorite Links view in Windows Vista provides shortcuts to the most common locations.

Windows 7 Explorer View

Windows 7 groups shortcuts to a wide variety of locations in its left pane (see Figure 14-32). The Favorites section includes shortcuts to the current user's desktop, downloads folder, and recently visited objects (folders and libraries). The Libraries section includes shortcuts to the current user's Documents, Music, Pictures, and Videos libraries. If the computer is part of a homegroup network (a new type of network for Windows 7 computers only), the Homegroup section lists other computers in the homegroup. The Computer section lists all connected drives. The Network section lists all computers on the network. The right pane lists the contents of the current location. As in Windows Vista, common tasks have been moved to a menu strip above the panes.

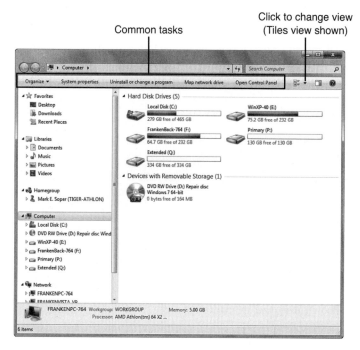

Figure 14-32   Windows 7's Explorer view provides a scrolling pane with access to libraries, local and network locations, and homegroup computers.

Displaying Objects in Files and Folders (Windows XP)

You can display objects such as files and folders in several ways within Windows Explorer. In Windows XP, choose from the following options:

- **Tiles**—The default; similar to Large Icons view in earlier Windows versions.

- **Icons**—Displays more objects onscreen without scrolling vertically; might require the user to scroll horizontally to view multiple columns; similar to Small Icons view in earlier Windows versions.

- **List**—Displays more objects onscreen than large icons in a single column.

- **Details**—The same size of icons used by Small or List, plus size and last-modified date details (see Figure 14-33A).

- **Thumbnails**—Displays a thumbnail (small-sized graphic) sample of previewable files and folders (.BMP, .JPG, and some other graphics file formats and folders containing these files) in the selected folder and uses large-tiled icons for nonpreviewable files. Thumbnail view can be used in any folder.

- **Filmstrip**—Displays a larger preview of the selected graphic file at the top of the right window and smaller thumbnails below it. You can use buttons below the large preview to rotate the graphic or to move to another graphic. This view is available in the My Pictures folder or other folders that contain digital photos in formats recognized by Windows Preview, such as .TIF or .JPG (see Figure 14-33B).

A   B

Figure 14-33   Comparing the Details and Filmstrip views of a folder containing digital photos (Windows XP). The task pane lists Picture Tasks such as printing photos or copying items to a recordable/rewritable CD.

Displaying Objects in Files and Folders (Windows Vista and Windows 7)

Windows Vista and Windows 7 offer the following options:

- **Small icons**—Similar to Icons view in Windows XP

- **Medium, Large, and Extra Large icons**—Different-sized thumbnails of supported file types

Windows 7 also includes the following:

- **Content**—Lists medium icons (thumbnails) along with their creation dates

To change the view for the current folder, use the Views button or the View pull-down menu.

Windows Vista also incorporates the Stacks view, which groups files according to what is specified by the user. You can click the stacks to filter the files shown in Windows Explorer. You also have the ability to save searches as virtual folders or search folders. Another new addition to Windows Explorer in Vista is the Details pane, which displays information relating to the currently selected file or folder.

Libraries (Windows 7)

When you open Windows Explorer in Windows 7, the default view shows your libraries (see Figure 14-34). A **library** includes the contents of the current user's documents, music, pictures, or videos folder, but also includes the contents of the corresponding public folder and can display the contents of any other local or network folder the user adds to the library. In any Windows Explorer view in Windows 7, click **Organize** to display file, folder, and layout options and to view properties for the currently selected object.

To learn more about libraries, see "File Structure and Paths," earlier in this chapter.

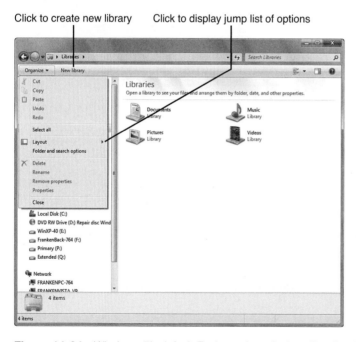

Click to create new library   Click to display jump list of options

Figure 14-34   Windows 7's default Explorer view displays libraries. In this example, the Organize menu has been opened.

My Computer (Computer)

My Computer (known as Computer in Windows 7/Vista) is integrated tightly with Windows Explorer. My Computer is still available on all versions of Windows but many users prefer to use Windows Explorer due to its additional functionality. My Computer provides access to the following features and utilities:

- Open My Computer to view the local drives on your system, available network drives, the Control Panel folder, and imaging devices (see Figure 14-35). In Windows XP, use the System Tasks left pane menu to open the System properties sheet (View system information), Add or Remove Programs (runs Add or Remove Programs applet from Control Panel), or Change a Setting (opens Control Panel). In Windows 7/Vista, similar options are listed just below the navigation bar (see Figure 14-36).

- Right-click the My Computer icon or the My Computer option in the Start menu to choose options such as Properties (which opens the System properties sheet), Manage (which opens the Computer Management Console), Windows Explorer, Search/Find, drive mapping, and creating shortcuts.

Figure 14-35 My Computer window and available System Tasks in Windows XP.

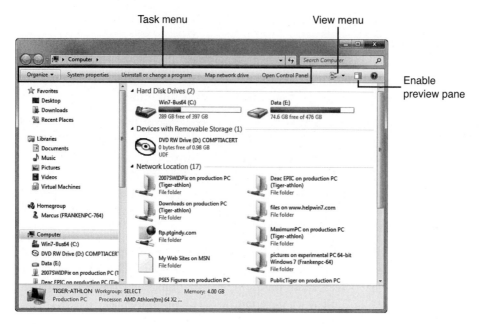

Figure 14-36   Computer window and available tasks in Windows 7.

MSInfo32 (System Information)

MSInfo32.exe, also known as System Information, displays a great deal of information about the computer hardware and Windows installation in a system. The System Summary (Figure 14-37) provides basic information about the Windows installation and hardware configuration. To dig deeper, open the nodes in the left pane. Figure 14-38 lists loaded program modules.

Use the Find window to locate specific information. Use the File menu to save the report or to export it as a text file.

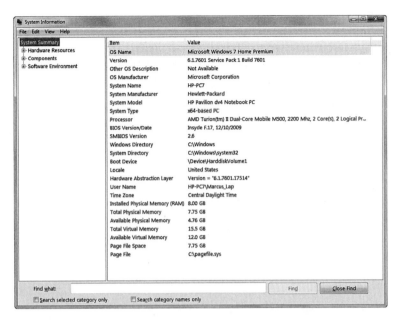

Figure 14-37   MSInfo32 system summary. Click a subnode (left pane) for more detailed information about system hardware, components, or software environment.

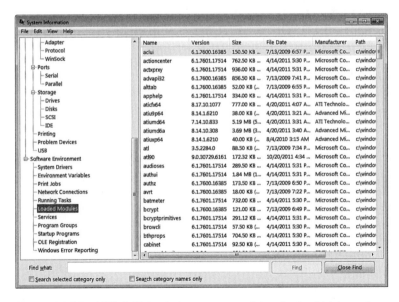

Figure 14-38   MSInfo32 loaded program modules display (right pane).

DXDiag (DirectX Diagnostics)

DXDiag.EXE displays and troubleshoots DirectX components in Windows. Use it to determine the version of DirectX on your system and to test DirectX components (see Figure 14-39).

> **NOTE**   DirectX is Microsoft Windows's 3D gaming application programming interface (API).

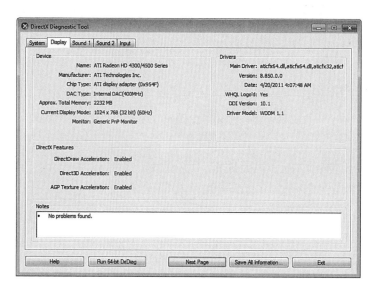

Figure 14-39   DXDiag's Display tab verifies proper video card operation on this system.

> **NOTE**   If DXDiag finds problems with your system, download updated drivers for any problem devices. If you need to download replacement DirectX files for version 9.0x or earlier, use the link in DXDiag's Help menu. To repair problems with DirectX 10.0 or above, use Windows Update or perform a repair installation of Windows Vista or Windows 7 followed by running Windows Update.

Control Panel

220-802

Objective:
220-802: 1.5

The **Control Panel** is the major starting point for adjusting the hardware and user interface settings in Windows. Although Windows XP, Vista, and 7 all feature the Control Panel, there are many differences between these versions of Windows in how the Control Panel is accessed, how items are placed in categories, and the contents of the Control Panel itself.

All three versions of Windows have Control Panel entries for the following:

- Internet options
- Display
- User accounts
- Folder options
- System
- Security Center (part of Action Center in Windows 7)
- Windows Firewall
- Power options
- Printers

Other important Control Panel features vary from version to version. These include

- Add/Remove Programs (XP)
- Programs and Features (Vista/7)
- Automatic Updates (XP)
- Tablet PC Settings (Vista/7)
- Pen and Input Devices (Vista)
- Problem Reports and Solutions (Vista, 7)
- Devices and Printers (7)
- HomeGroup (7)
- Action Center (7)

Items not discussed elsewhere are covered in the following sections of this chapter.

NOTE   Internet and Networking options are discussed in Chapter 16. User accounts, Security Center, and Windows Firewall are discussed in Chapter 17. Printing options are discussed in Chapter 11, "Printers."

Starting Control Panel

You can open the Control Panel from the Start button, Computer/My Computer, or the left window pane of Windows Explorer. (Note: If you're using the Classic Start menu in Windows XP, you must click **Start, Settings, Control Panel.**) With Windows Vista and 7, you can also configure Control Panel as a right-pane menu item.

Open any Control Panel icon or link to see current settings and make adjustments for the devices it controls. If the Classic view is used for the Control Panel folder in Windows XP, double-click an icon to open it. If Web view is used in Windows XP, a single click opens an icon. Single click is the default for Windows Vista and 7.

Category and Icon Views

The Control Panel's default view is known as Category view. When you click a category icon, it displays various available tasks. Figures 14-40, 14-41, and 14-42 show the Windows 7, Vista, and XP versions of the Control Panel configured for the default view.

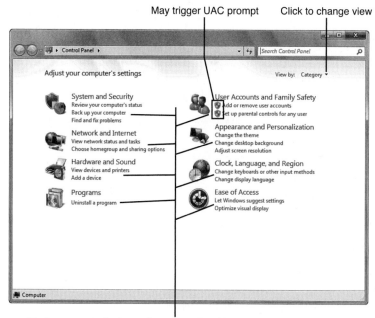

Figure 14-40   The Windows 7 Control Panel in its default Category view.

Figure 14-41   The Windows Vista Control Panel in its default Category view.

Switches Control Panel to Classic view

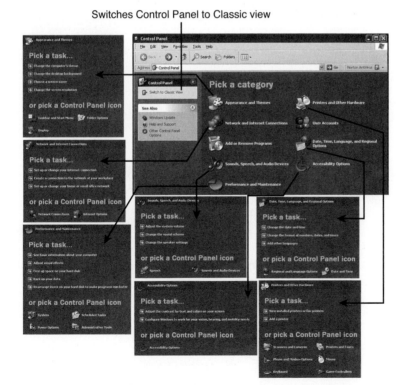

Figure 14-42   The Windows XP Control Panel in its default Category view, and the submenus triggered by each icon.

If you're a Windows newcomer, you might prefer the Category view's task-oriented design. However, if you're already familiar with Control Panel, you'll probably prefer to see each individual applet. This option is known as the Classic View in Windows XP and Vista, and the All Control Panel Items view (available in Large or Small Icons variations) in Windows 7. Figures 14-43, 14-44, and 14-45 show Windows 7, Vista, and XP versions of the Control Panel configured to display individual applets.

Figure 14-43   The Windows 7 Control Panel in its alternative All Control Panel Icons (small icons) view.

NOTE   Switching to a view that displays all applets is sometimes necessary to locate applets not part of a category. You can also use the Search tool to locate an applet by name.

For the exam, you must know how to open the Control Panel and how to access some of the Control Panel functions by way of Properties sheets, which are located in various areas of Windows.

Figure 14-44   The Windows Vista Control Panel in its alternative Classic View.

Figure 14-45   The Windows XP Control Panel in its alternative Classic View.

Shortcuts to Control Panel Functions

Some Control Panel functions can be accessed through properties sheets. For example, the following list explains how to access the Control Panel by right-clicking:

- **Computer/My Computer** and select **Properties** to open the System Window.

- **Taskbar** and select **Properties** to open the Taskbar and Start Menu Properties window.

- **Desktop** in Windows XP and select **Properties** to open the Display window.

- **Desktop** in Windows Vista and select **Personalize**. The Personalize menu performs the same functions as the Desktop properties window in Windows XP.

- **Desktop** in Windows 7 and choose one of the following: **Personalize, Screen Resolution**, or **Gadgets** options to configure various display properties).

- **Network** in Windows Vista and Windows 7 and select **Properties** to open the Network and Sharing Center window.

- **My Network Places** in Windows XP and select **Properties** to open the Network Connections window.

Display Options

Depending on the version of Windows you use, there may be several different Control Panel applets to use to configure settings. Table 14-5 provides a reference to these.

Table 14-5   Configuring Display Settings in Windows XP, Vista, and 7

| Display Setting | Control Panel Setting/Tab | | |
	XP	Vista	7
Resolution	Display/Settings	Personalization	Display
Color depth (number of colors)	Display/Settings	Personalization	Display Advanced/Monitor
Screen saver	Display/Screen Saver	Personalization	Personalization
Background	Display/Desktop	Personalization	Personalization
Theme	Display/Theme	Personalization	Personalization
Windows Color	Display/Desktop	Personalization	Personalization
Add additional displays	Display/Settings	Personalization	Display

Folder Options

By default, Windows Explorer prevents users from seeing information such as

- File extensions for registered file types; for example, a file called LETTER. DOCX displays as LETTER because Microsoft Word is associated with .docx files

- The full path to the current folder

- Files or folders with hidden or system attributes, such as the AppData folder

- The Windows folder

Concealing this information is intended to make it harder for users to "break" Windows, but it makes management and troubleshooting more difficult.

As an alternative to using the Folder Options applet in Control Panel, you can use this procedure:

Step 1.   Open Windows Explorer.

Step 2.   Click **Tools** on the menu bar, **Folder Options**, and select the **View** tab. If you use the Folder Options applet in Control Panel, select the **View** tab.

NOTE   In Windows Vista and Windows 7, the Menu Bar is hidden by default. To show it temporarily, press **Alt+T** (which in this case brings up the Tools menu). To show it permanently, click the **Organize** button, **Layout**, and then **Menu Bar**.

Step 3.   Select the options you want (see Figure 14-46). The following changes are recommended for experienced end users:

- Enable the Display the Full Path in the Title Bar option. (In Vista and 7, this works only if you are using the Classic theme.)

- Disable the Hide Extensions for Known File Types option.

If you are maintaining or troubleshooting a system, I also recommend you change the following:

- Enable the Show Hidden Files and Folders setting.

- Disable the Hide Protected Operating System Files setting.

- You should probably change these settings back to their defaults before you return the system to normal use.

Step 4.   Click **OK** to close the Folder Options window.

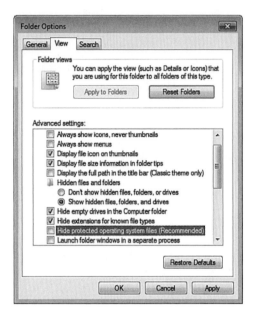

Figure 14-46   The Windows Explorer Folder Options, View tab in Windows 7 after selecting recommended options for use by technicians and experienced end users.

System

Use the System applet (System properties sheet) to view

- Windows version

- 32-bit or 64-bit edition

- Processor model number and clock speed

- Windows Experience Index (WEI) (Vista and 7 only)

You can also use the System applet to change

- Computer name

- Workgroup name

- Domain name

- System protection settings (System Restore)

- Hardware profiles

- Remote settings

- Performance and virtual memory settings

For more about computer, workgroup, and domain settings, see Chapter 16. For more about System Restore, see Chapter 15.

Hardware Profiles (Windows XP)

Windows XP supports the creation of hardware profiles to enable or disable support for hardware in situations such as a laptop being docked or undocked. To create a new hardware profile, follow this procedure:

Step 1.   Log in to Windows XP as an administrator.

Step 2.   Open the System applet (properties sheet).

Step 3.   Click the **Hardware** tab.

Step 4.   Click Hardware Profiles.

Step 5.   Select the current hardware profile (Profile 1 Current) and click **Copy**.

Step 6.   Enter a name for the new hardware profile, and click **OK**.

Step 7.   When the hardware your computer connects to changes (docked, undocked, and so on), select the new profile, and use Device Manager to enable or disable devices for that profile.

NOTE   Windows Vista and Windows 7 do not include support for hardware profiles. However, you can use command-line programs to stop and start unwanted services. See www.microsoft-questions.com/microsoft/Windows-Vista/31409673/ what-to-do-in-lieu-of-hardware-profiles.aspx for an example.

Virtual Memory Settings

If you run short of money, you can borrow some from the bank (assuming your credit's in decent shape). However, there's a penalty: interest. Similarly, if your system runs short of memory, it can borrow hard disk space and use it as virtual memory. The penalty for this type of borrowing is performance: **Virtual memory** is much slower than real RAM memory. However, you can adjust how your system uses virtual memory to achieve better performance.

TIP   To minimize the need to use virtual memory, increase the physical memory (RAM) in a 32-bit Windows system to at least 3GB and on a 64-bit Windows system to at least 4GB. The largest amount of usable RAM on a 32-bit Windows system is 3.25GB; 64-bit Windows systems can use 4GB or more.

When additional RAM is added to a computer running Windows, it is automatically used first before the paging file.

The performance of the **paging file** can be improved by

- Setting its minimum and maximum sizes to the same amount.

- Moving the paging file to a physical disk (or disk partition) that is not used as much as others.

- Using a striped volume for the paging file. A striped volume is an identical area of disk space stored on two or more dynamic disks referred to as a single drive letter. Create a striped volume with the Windows Disk Management tool. If a RAID 0 (striped) disk array is available, use it instead of a striped volume for even better paging file performance.

- Creating multiple paging files on multiple physical disks in the system.

- Moving the paging file away from the boot drive.

To adjust the location and size of the paging file in Windows, follow these steps:

Step 1.   From the System Properties window, click the **Advanced** tab (Windows XP) or click **Advanced System Settings** under Tasks (Windows Vista, Windows 7).

Step 2.   Click the **Settings** button in the Performance Options (Performance in 7/Vista) box.

Step 3.   Click the **Advanced** tab, and then the **Change** button.

Step 4.   Specify the initial and maximum sizes you want to use for the paging file and its location (see Figure 14-47). Click **Set** and then click **OK** to finish. (In 7/Vista, you must deselect the **Automatically Manage Paging File Size** check box first.)

Step 5.   If you make any changes to size or location, you must restart the computer for the changes to take effect.

Power Options

Windows XP, Vista, and 7 offer power management settings, but Windows XP's version is a great deal different than Vista's and 7's power management. With all three versions of Windows, you can manage power options from an applet in the Control Panel. If a Power options icon is available in the notification area of the Windows taskbar, you can use it to view the current power option setting and select a different one.

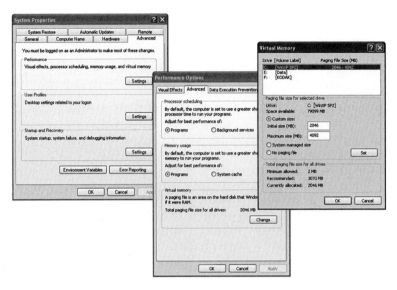

Figure 14-47   The Virtual Memory dialog enables you to set the size and location of virtual memory (Windows XP version shown).

Windows XP Power Schemes

Windows XP refers to power settings as power schemes. Windows XP includes six different settings, but these settings work in different ways, depending on whether the computer is running on AC power or on battery power. In Table 14-6, the times listed are for periods of inactivity: Touch the keyboard, move the mouse, start a print job, and so on, and the clock starts over.

Table 14-6   Windows XP Power Schemes

Power Scheme	Display Off	Hard Disk Off	Standby	CPU on AC**	CPU on Battery**
Home/Office Desk	20 minutes	Never	Never	High	Varies with load
Portable/Laptop	15 minutes	30 minutes	20 minutes	Varies with load	Varies with load
Presentation	Never	Never	Never	Low	Low to lower
Always on	20 minutes	Never	Never	High	High
Minimal Power Management*	15 minutes	Never	Never	Varies with load	Varies with load
Max Battery	15 minutes	Never	20 minutes	Varies with load	Low to lower

*Disables timed hibernation

**Assumes variable CPU performance features enabled (Intel Enhanced Speed Step, AMD Cool 'n' Quiet)

To change a power scheme, select it, make the wanted changes, click **Save As**, and give it a different name. Figure 14-48 shows how this process works.

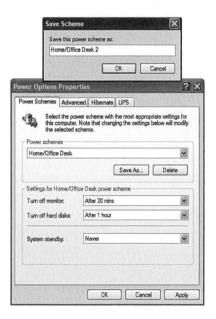

Figure 14-48   Saving changes to the Home/Office Desk power scheme as Home/Office Desk2.

Use the Advanced tab to specify whether to put the power icon in the notification area, whether to prompt for a password when resuming from standby, and to configure the power button to put the computer in standby, to shut down the computer, to ask the user what to do, or to do nothing. On a laptop or portable computer, this tab also has a setting for what to do when the laptop's lid is closed: hibernate, stand by, or do nothing.

Use the Hibernate tab to enable or disable hibernation. It also lists the amount of space the hibernation file, hiberfil.sys, uses.

Use the UPS tab to see the status of your battery backup (if any) and to manage its settings.

NOTE   For systems running Windows XP SP2 or SP3, use the command-line POWERCFG.EXE program to control additional power settings. To learn more, see http://support.microsoft.com/kb/324347. The article was originally written for Windows Server 2003 but also applies to these versions of Windows.

Windows Vista/7 Power Settings

Windows Vista and Windows 7 offer three standard power plans (some portable vendors might offer additional plans in systems with pre-installed Windows):

- **Balanced**—Default plan

- **High performance**—Fastest CPU performance, brightest screen, and shortest battery life

- **Power saver**—Reduces CPU performance and screen brightness more than with Balanced plan for longest battery life

Desktop computers hide Power Saver by default; laptop computers hide High Performance by default. To see these and other plans, click **Show Additional Plans**.

> **NOTE** To sleep or hibernate the computer, select **Sleep** or **Hibernate** from the Start menu. If Hibernate is not available, this option might be disabled in the system BIOS.

To change a plan, click **Change Plan Settings**. You can change the display of and sleep settings for each plan, and to change additional settings, click **Change Advanced Power Settings**. You can change power settings for

- Hard disk shutoff timing

- Desktop backgrounds

- Wireless adapters

- Sleep timings

- USB ports and devices

- Power buttons and lid

- PCI Express devices

- CPU performance and cooling

- Display shutoff timings

- Multimedia idle time and screen quality

- Internet Explorer JavaScript timing frequency

To create a new **power plan**, click **Create a Power Plan** from the Power Options dialog. From the Create a Power Plan dialog, follow these steps:

Step 1.   Select a plan to use as the basis for your plan.

Step 2.   Enter a plan name, and click **Next**.

Step 3.   Specify timings for the display and sleep, and click **Create**.

To change additional settings, click **Change Plan Settings**, select the custom plan, and change other settings. See Figure 14-49.

Figure 14-49   Editing a custom power plan in Windows 7.

NOTE   To learn more about a system's power management features, use the command-line POWERCFG.EXE program to control additional power settings. PowerCFG for Windows Vista and 7 uses different syntax than the Windows XP version. To learn more, see http://support.microsoft.com/kb/980869.

Add/Remove Programs (Windows XP)

The Windows XP version of Control Panel includes the Add/Remove Programs applet. Use this feature to change or remove a program, add a new program, add or remove Windows components, and specify program access and defaults. Figure 14-50 shows how you can repair a program installation, and by clicking the Show Updates box, you can see when updates for a particular program (Microsoft .NET Framework 2.0 Service Pack 2 in this example) were installed.

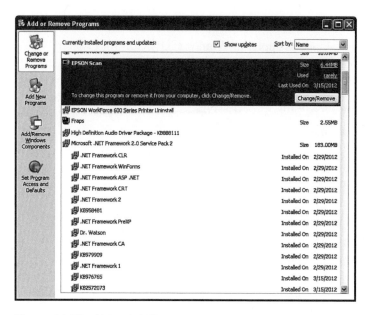

Figure 14-50   Using Add/Remove Programs in Windows XP.

Programs and Features (Windows Vista/7)

Programs and Features is the Windows Vista/7 counterpart to Add/Remove Programs in Windows XP. Use it to uninstall or change a program, to turn Windows features on and off (Figure 14-51), and to view installed updates.

Figure 14-51   Turning Windows 7 features on and off.

Automatic Updates (Windows XP)

You can use the Automatic Updates applet in Windows XP's Control Panel to configure Windows Update. The default setting is to check for updates daily at 3:00 a.m. and install them automatically, but you can select these options instead:

- Check on a specified day of the week (weekly).

- Check at a different time.

- Download updates and notify you when they are ready to install.

- Notify you of updates, but don't download them automatically.

- Turn off Automatic Updates.

For systems that can be rebooted, the default is a good choice. However, for systems that need to be available at all times, downloading updates for installation later or notifying you of updates are better choices. Disabling automatic updates is useful for organizations that use centralized patch management to push out updates after testing and verification.

Tablet PC Settings (Windows Vista/7)

Windows Vista and Windows 7 include Tablet PC Settings in Control Panel. In Windows Vista, the dialog includes the following tabs:

- **General**—Selects right or left-handedness, menu location, and tablet calibration

- **Handwriting recognition**—Personalization (providing handwriting samples to improve recognition) and Automatic Learning (for handwriting and typing) options

- **Display**—Selects menu location

- **Other**—Links to the Input Panel Settings dialog

In Windows 7, there are only two tabs:

- **Display**—Selects where to display the menu

- **Other**—Specifies right or left handedness and links to the Pen and Touch Control Panel

Pen and Input Devices (Windows Vista)

Windows Vista uses the Pen and Input Devices applet in Control Panel to set up how a pen works on a Tablet PC or an add-on tablet. Tabs include

- **Pen options**—Set double-tab speed and spatial tolerance, press and hold gestures, and gestures for starting the Tablet PC input panel.

- **Pointer options**—Configure dynamic feedback and pen cursors.

- **Flicks**—Configure pen gestures to navigate and edit.

Windows 7 uses the Pen and Touch Control Panel for similar configuration settings.

Problem Reports and Solutions (Windows Vista, and 7)

Windows Vista uses Problem Reports and Solutions to provide a convenient way to view and manage problem reports and receive solutions. The main pane lists problems caused by Microsoft and third-party programs along with any current solutions to install.

The left pane provides additional options: check for new solutions, view problems to check, view problem history, change tool settings, and clear solution and problem history.

NOTE   In Windows 7, this functionality is part of the Maintenance section of Action Center.

Devices and Printers

Windows 7 includes the new Devices and Printers folder to make access to managing the most common devices in (or connected to) your computer easier to perform. You can launch Devices and Printers from the Hardware and Sound category of Control Panel or add it to your Start menu.

Devices and Printers is divided into two sections. The upper section contains icons for connected devices, and the lower section contains icons for printers, faxes, and all-in-one units. To manage a device, right-click it, and choose from the options listed. The options available for each device vary with the device selected.

For example, if you right-click the computer icon, you can AutoPlay removable-media drives; browse files; eject drives; configure network, sound, mouse, keyboard, and region and language settings; and view and configure system properties, power options, device installation settings, and Windows Update (see Figure 14-52). Right-click a display, and you can access the Display settings dialog. Right-click a mouse, and you can access the Mouse properties dialog.

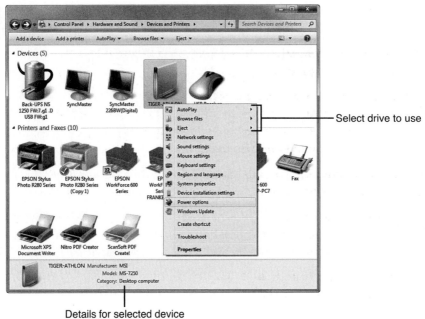

Figure 14-52   Using Devices and Printers to manage a computer's components.

To learn more about managing printers, faxes, and multifunction devices with Devices and Printers, see Chapter 11.

HomeGroup (Windows 7)

Windows 7 includes the new HomeGroup feature as part of its network functionality. HomeGroup enables the creation of an easy to manage but secure home or home office network, provided it contains only Windows 7 or Windows 8 PCs. HomeGroup can coexist with traditional wired or wireless workgroup networking, enabling systems that are part of a homegroup to also be in a network with computers running other operating systems.

NOTE   To learn more about HomeGroup, see Chapter 16.

Action Center (Windows 7)

Windows 7's **Action Center** combines several system management and trouble-shooting functions that were formerly separate in Windows XP and Windows Vista into a single interface. Action Center's main window features two sections: Security and Maintenance. These sections are collapsed unless there is an issue to attend to. In those cases, the section is expanded and displays a yellow or red bar (see Figure 14-53) next to the action item.

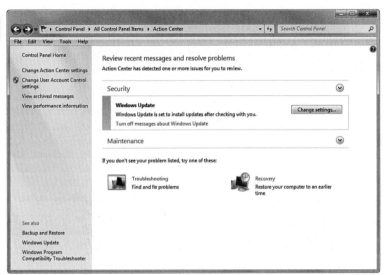

Figure 14-53   The new Problem Reports and Solutions tool.

Click the down arrow to expand the category. The Security section lists the status of Windows Update, Windows Firewall, virus and spyware protection, Internet security settings, UAC, and network access protection.

The Maintenance section provides options for reviewing problems, checking for solutions, and reviewing the system's reliability history; and monitors Windows Backup and troubleshooting.

Action Center is also the home of Windows 7's Troubleshooters for programs, hardware and sound, network and internet, appearance and personalization, and system and security features.

Client-Side Virtualization

220-802

Objective:
220-802: 1.9

Microsoft and third-party vendors such as VirtualBox and VMware have offered
virtualization solutions for some time. What is virtualization? Virtual machines
enable a single computer to run two or more operating systems at the same time
using the same hardware.

There are several categories of virtualization: host/guest, hypervisor, server-hosted,
and client-side.

Host/Guest Virtualization

In this type of virtualization, a PC or workstation runs a standard operating system
and a virtualization machine manager (VMM) that runs inside the operating system;
each virtual machine (VM) is a guest operating system. Connections to hardware
(networking, display, printing, and so on) are passed from the guest operating system
to the virtualization program to the host computer's operating system.

This type of virtualization is often used for client-side virtualization. However,
client-side virtualization can also be centrally managed from the standpoint of the
creation and management of VM images, although the images are being run locally.

Hypervisor

A hypervisor is a VMM that runs directly on the hardware. It does not need to run
inside an operating system. Hypervisor-based virtualization (sometimes referred
to as bare-metal virtualization) is therefore faster than host/guest virtualization
and, because the hypervisor uses few computer resources (memory, CPU), more
computer resources can be made available to each VM.

This type of virtualization can be used for servers and thin client virtualization.
Often referred to as virtual desktop infrastructure (VDI), this type of virtualization
runs VMs on its own hardware and uses the network to interface with thin clients
who interact with the VMs via the network. This type of virtualization, although
easy to manage, is not suitable for multimedia-intensive software and requires the
client to stay connected to the network at all times.

Examples of client-side host/guest virtualization include Windows Virtual Machine and Virtual PC 2007 from Microsoft, VirtualBox, VMware Workstation, and others.

Examples of hypervisor virtualization include Hyper-V from Microsoft, VMware ESX and ESXi, Citrix XenServer, and others.

Features and Benefits of Virtual Machines

The savings over two or more physical workstations can be significant in terms of space, cooling, peripheral hardware (displays, mice, keyboards, printers, and desks).

Virtual machines enable help desk and support specialists to run older operating systems without changing computers and without rebooting their systems. Virtual machines enable a single PC to run 32-bit and 64-bit versions of the same operating system so that applications that run better in 32-bit mode can be run without the need for a separate computer. Each virtual machine on a computer can perform different tasks at the same time, enabling more work to be done with less hardware investment.

System images can be centrally created, modified, and managed for easier instal-lation. Because the VMM acts as a translator between the VM and the actual computer hardware, there are fewer problems due to differences in system hardware.

Resource Requirements

A computer that will be used for virtualization needs to be designed with fast multicore processors and as much RAM as possible given the limitations of the motherboard and VMM (or host operating system). For this reason, it's better to use 64-bit processors and a 64-bit-compatible VMM (and host operating system if a hypervisor is not being used). 64-bit operating systems or VMMs avoid the 4GB RAM limit imposed by 32-bit architecture.

Processors selected for a virtualization system should also feature hardware-assisted virtualization. The system BIOS must also support this feature and must be enabled in the system BIOS. Otherwise, VMs will run much more slowly.

If several VMs will be run at the same time, the use of two or more displays is highly recommended.

Emulator Requirements

Although a VM must interface with the hardware, it does not do so directly; instead, it uses emulation to communicate with the hardware. For example, regardless of the actual display hardware on a VM under Windows Virtual PC, the video card in the virtualized environment is a standard VGA card. It lacks 3D acceleration and support for SLI or CrossFire multi-GPU standards. This "dumbing down" in emulation is typical of VMs.

Some VMMs restrict a virtual machine's access to some types of hardware. For example, Virtual PC 2004 and 2007 could not use USB ports for storage devices. Before adopting a particular VMM, make sure you determine whether the hardware you plan to use inside the VM will work.

Security Requirements

Because a single physical computer can house two or more VMs, knowing which computers in an organization are using VMs is a vital first step in securing a virtualized environment. Although host/guest VMMs don't include security features, most hypervisors do.

Other factors to consider include change management, securing virtual switches and other virtualized components; and using the security and management features either available in the organization's choice of VMMs or in third-party products made for virtualization.

NOTE   For more information, see http://searchsecurity.techtarget.com/magazineContent/Virtualization-security

Exam Preparation Tasks

Review All the Key Topics

Review the most important topics in the chapter, noted with the Key Topic icon in the outer margin of the page. Table 14-7 lists a reference of these key topics and the page numbers on which each is found.

Table 14-7 Key Topics for Chapter 14

Key Topic Element	Description	Page Number
Figure 14-1	Windows XP and 7 Start menus	611
Text	Windows XP file structure and paths	620
Text	Windows Vista file structure and paths	620
Text	Windows 7 file structure and paths	620
Text	32-bit versus 64-bit file structure and paths	620
List	Start command-line prompt in Windows XP, Vista, and 7	621
Figure 14-12	Formatting floppy and hard disk in Windows Explorer	631
Figures 14-13	Using Diskpart	634
Figures 14-14	Using Tasklist	638
Figure 14-16	Using Services	643
Figure 14-22	Task Manager in Windows 7	650
Figure 14-27	Determining a file system on a drive	660
Figures 14-28, 14-29	Windows Explorer (7, and XP)	663
List	Shortcuts to Control Panel functions	678
List	System properties sheet	680
Figure 14-52	Devices and printers	690
Figure 14-53	Action Center	691

Complete the Tables and Lists from Memory

Print a copy of Appendix A, "Memory Tables" (found on the CD), or at least the section for this chapter, and complete the tables and lists from memory. Appendix B, "Memory Tables Answer Key," also on the CD, includes completed tables and lists to check your work.

Define Key Terms

Define the following key terms from this chapter, and check your answers in the glossary.

Action Center, Computer Management, Control Panel, CONVERT.EXE, COPY, directory, Disk Management, Diskpart, drive array, Dynamic disk, exFAT (FAT64), Extended partition, external command, FAT32, internal command, Library, Windows 7 , Logical drive, mount point, mounted drive, NTFS, Paging file, Power plan, Primary partition, ReadyBoost, ROBOCOPY, Shadow Copy, Simple volume, Task Manager, Theme, virtual memory, virtualization, wildcard, Windows Aero, Windows Explorer, Windows Virtual PC, Windows XP Mode, XCOPY

Complete Hands-On Lab

Complete the hands-on labs, and then see the answers and explanations at the end of the chapter.

Lab 14-1: Open and Use the Command Prompt

Scenario: You are a technician on a service call. The system can be booted only from the Windows Vista or Windows 7 Recovery Environment emergency disc. Perform the following commands:

1. Connect an external hard disk to the system's USB port.

2. Create a folder called MyUser on the external hard disk.

3. Transfer the contents of a particular user's Documents and Pictures folders to an external hard disk.

Procedure: Boot the system with the Recovery Environment emergency disc. Open the command prompt. The external hard disk is the next available drive letter (probably E: or F: on typical systems). Determine which drive letter is being used for the external hard disk. Determine which commands to use to create the folder and copy the files needed to the drive.

Lab 14-2: Using Microsoft Management Console

Scenario: You are a technician on a service call. You need to check the status of hard disks and services. What is the procedure for this?

Answer Review Questions

Answer these review questions, and then see the answers and explanations at the end of the chapter.

1. Which of the following technologies is the graphical user interface used by default in Windows Vista and Windows 7?

   a. Windows PowerGUI

   b. Windows Aero

   c. Windows GUI version II

   d. Windows PowerShell

2. You are the PC technician for your company. You are upgrading your computers to Windows 7. There are certain users who have older applications that will run only in Windows XP. Which combination of products will enable you to run these programs with support for USB storage devices?

   a. Windows 7 Professional, Virtual PC 2007, Windows XP as a VM

   b. Windows 7 Professional, Windows Virtual PC, Windows XP Mode

   c. Program Compatibility Wizard

   d. None of the above

3. You are working on a computer using Windows XP. You need to back up the current user's pictures. Which of the following locations is the most likely location for the user's My Pictures folder?

   a. C:\Users\

   b. C:\Program Files (x86)

   c. C:\Documents and Settings*Username*\My Documents

   d. Homegroup

4. You need to copy files from one folder to another folder on the same computer. Which of the following command-line utilities will enable you to do this with a single command?

   a. **XCOPY**

   b. Drag and drop

   c. **COPY**

   d. **DISKPART**

5. You are setting up an external drive for use with scheduled backups in Windows 7. The drive uses the FAT32 file system. Which of the following should you do to make the drive ready to use?

   a. Nothing.

   b. Use Disk Management.

   c. Use CONVERT.EXE.

   d. Format.

6. You need to create a list of 32-bit services that can be imported into Microsoft Excel for analysis. Which of the following programs should you use?

   a. Taskkill.exe

   b. Services.msc

   c. Explorer.exe

   d. Tasklist.exe

7. You need to shut down a service that is interfering with another program. Which of the following can you use to perform this task? (Choose all that apply.)

   a. Taskkill.exe

   b. Services.msc

   c. Task Manager

   d. All the above

8. You have just set up a procedure to run every Wednesday evening with Windows 7. Where will you find this task?

   a. Documents library

   b. Task Scheduler library

   c. Windows\System32 folder

   d. C:\Temp folder

9. A client's system drive (which is formatted as NTFS) is running low on space, but there isn't time to take the computer out of service to install a larger hard disk. Which of the following procedures would enable you to add an external drive that will be used by Windows as if it's part of the C: drive?

    a. Format an external drive as NTFS and assign it to a library.

    b. Use the CONVERT.EXE utility.

    c. Run the Mount Drive subroutine in Disk Management.

    d. Use Change Drive Letters and Paths to assign the drive to an empty folder on the system drive.

10. You are using the Windows Vista/7 Recovery Environment's command prompt to copy files from a system that won't start. Assuming you've logged into c:\, which of the following commands can copy all files, folders, and subfolders, including empty subfolders, from the current location to the TEST folder on an external drive?

    a. xcopy *.* f:\ test /T

    b. xcopy *.* f:\ test /S

    c. xcopy *.* f:\ test /E

    d. xcopy *.* f:\ test \ T

11. You are providing some phone support for your clients. The secondary display on a computer running Windows Vista is not displaying a picture. The clients have already verified the display is connected to the computer and turned on. Which of the following options is most likely to make the secondary display available?

    a. Display Properties

    b. Screensaver

    c. Personalization

    d. Display Theme

12. You are contacted by a client that is having problems because her computer is running slowly. You need to run a utility to see whether the system needs to have more memory installed. Which of the following utilities should you use?

    a. Performance Monitor

    b. System Performance Wizard

    c. Memory Tasks Wizard

    d. System Configuration Utility

13. What is the minimum processor requirement for Windows 7?

    a. 133MHz

    b. 233MHz

    c. 800MHz

    d. 1GHz

14. What is the minimum RAM requirement for Windows 7 32-bit version?

    a. 256MB

    b. 512MB

    c. 1024MB

    d. 2048MB

15. You need to configure several hardware components on a computer running Windows 7. Which of the following Control Panel options provides quick access to most computer hardware?

    a. Device Manager

    b. Computer Management

    c. Devices and Printers

    d. Action Center

Answers to Hands-On Lab

Lab 14-1: Open and Use the Command Prompt

Answer: Use **DIR E:** to view the contents of drive E:. An error message displays if there is no drive present. Repeat with the next available drive letter (F:, and so on) until you locate the hard disk. Enter **C:** from the command prompt to change to C: drive. Use **CD** commands to change to the folder containing the user's Documents and Pictures folders:

```
CD\ (changes to root folder)
CD\Users\Username
```

Use **Xcopy** to copy the contents to a folder you specify on Drive F: (replace F: with drive letter actually used by external hard disk).

```
Xcopy Documents\*.* F:\MyUser\ /E
Xcopy Pictures\*.* F:\MyUser\ /E
```

Lab 14-2: Using Microsoft Management Console

Answer: Open the Microsoft Management Console, and use the Storage node to see the layout and sizes of the hard disks in the system. Open the Services node, and view the properties of some of the services.

Answers and Explanations to Review Questions

1. **B.** Windows Aero is the default desktop in Windows Vista and Windows 7. It features translucent windows, window animations, three-dimensional viewing of windows, and a modified taskbar. You can make modifications to the look of Aero by right-clicking the desktop and selecting Personalize. Then select Windows Color and Appearance. There you can modify features such as the transparency of windows. Note: Aero is not available in Windows Vista Home Basic or Windows 7 Starter.

2. **B.** To enable applications that will not run on any operating system newer than Windows XP to run on a Windows 7 computer, use XP Mode under Windows Virtual PC. Windows Virtual PC supports XP Mode (a virtualized copy of Windows XP Professional), whereas the older Virtual PC 2007 does not (and does not work with USB-connected storage devices).

3. **C.** Folders such as My Pictures are stored under the My Documents folder in Windows XP. Later versions of Windows place documents, pictures, and music folders at the same level.

4. **A.** The **XCOPY** command copies folders and files and is run from the command line.

5. **C.** Windows Backup requires the use of a hard disk drive using NTFS for scheduled backups. CONVERT.EXE is designed to convert the file system from FAT32 to NTFS without deleting files.

6. **D.** The TASKLIST.EXE program has an option to create a CSV (.csv) listing of 32-bit services. The file can be imported into Microsoft Excel.

7. **D.** TASKKILL.EXE, Services.msc, and Task Manager can all be used to shut down a service.

8. **B.** The Task Scheduler Library stores all scheduled tasks in Windows 7.

9. **D.** By using Change Drive Letters and Paths, you can mount an external hard disk into an empty folder on an NTFS drive. Windows views the external drive's capacity as an extension of the host drive's capacity.

10. **C.** **/E** is needed to copy the files, directories, subdirectories, including empty subdirectories. **/S** will copy files, directories, and subdirectories but not empty subdirectories. If you add **/T** to the end, you will get just the empty directories copied. **\T** is not a valid switch.

11. **C.** In Windows Vista, Personalization is used the same way that the Display properties were used in Windows XP. In Windows 7, Display properties would be used for this task.

12. **A.** You can use the performance monitor by going to the Run command (Windows XP) or Search box (Windows Vista, 7) and typing **perfmon**. This utility can help you diagnose memory bottlenecks.

13. **D.** Windows 7 requires at least a 1GHz processor, although faster processors will improve performance.

14. **C.** 1024MB (1GB) of RAM is the minimum needed for the 32-bit version of Windows 7. However, 2048MB (2GB) is the minimum needed for the 64-bit version of Windows 7.

15. **C.** Devices and Printers enables you to browse drives, set device settings, and view problem devices when used to view your computer.

This chapter covers the following subjects:

- **STOP (Blue Screen of Death) Errors**—Discover what a BSOD is, typical causes, how to diagnose one, and how to specify whether a system restarts if a BSOD occurs or stays on.

- **Boot Failures**—Boot failures can cause problems with any version of Windows, but Windows XP, Vista, and 7 provide different tools for dealing with them. Learn what causes boot failures and how to restore an unbootable system back to operation.

- **Other Windows Problems**—From a system that won't shut down to a system that can 't boot normally (and more), find out what Windows tools and features you can use to find the cause and solve the problem.

- **Windows Diagnostic and Repair Tools**—A closer look at System File Checker, Defrag, Registry Editor, Recovery Console, Windows Recovery Environment, and other Windows features designed for troubleshooting and system repair.

- **Maintaining Windows**—How to schedule and perform Windows best practices to help a system run reliably.

This chapter covers **CompTIA A+ 220-802 objectives 1.7 and 4.6.**

CHAPTER 15

Troubleshooting and Maintaining Windows

When Microsoft Windows stops working, so does the computer and its users. This chapter is designed to help you understand common Windows-related problems and to master the tools and techniques necessary to solve them.

Because prevention is better than a cure, this chapter also discusses best practices for Windows maintenance and how to use the tools available from Microsoft and others to achieve these goals.

Foundation Topics

STOP (Blue Screen of Death) Errors

220-802

Objective:
220-802: 4.6

STOP errors (also known as Blue Screen Of Death or **BSOD** errors) can occur either during startup or after the system is running. The BSOD nickname is used because the background is normally blue (or sometimes black) with the error message in white text. Figure 15-1 displays a typical BSOD.

Key Topic

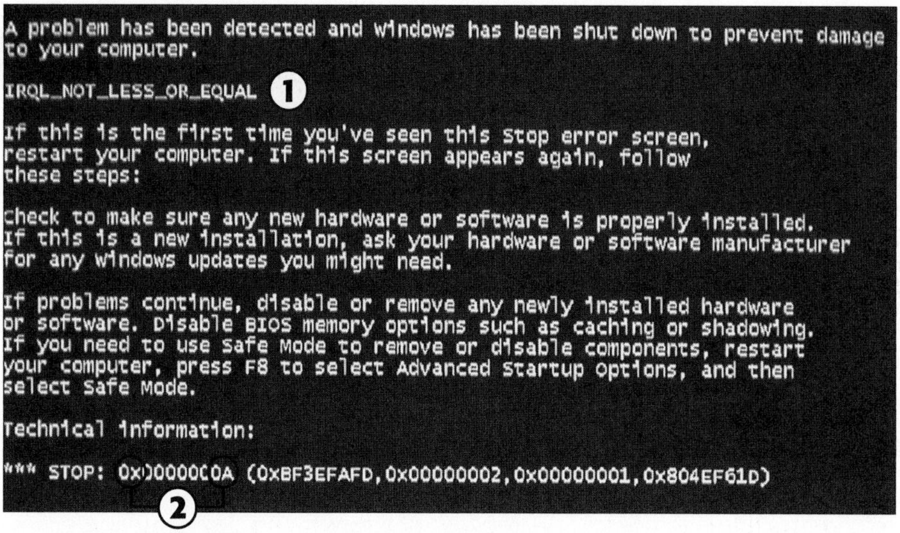

A problem has been detected and windows has been shut down to prevent damage to your computer.

IRQL_NOT_LESS_OR_EQUAL ❶

If this is the first time you've seen this stop error screen, restart your computer. If this screen appears again, follow these steps:

Check to make sure any new hardware or software is properly installed. If this is a new installation, ask your hardware or software manufacturer for any windows updates you might need.

If problems continue, disable or remove any newly installed hardware or software. Disable BIOS memory options such as caching or shadowing. If you need to use Safe Mode to remove or disable components, restart your computer, press F8 to select Advanced Startup options, and then select Safe Mode.

Technical information:

*** STOP: 0x0000000A (0xBF3EFAFD,0x00000002,0x00000001,0x804EF61D) ❷

1. Enter this text as shown to look up the error by name
   at http://support.microsoft.com or third-party websites.
2. STOP errors are often listed as 0x followed by the last
   two digits in the error code, such as 0x0A in this example.

Figure 15-1 A typical STOP (BSOD) error. You can look up the error by name or by number.

NOTE   Regardless of when a STOP/BSOD error occurs, your system is halted by default. To restart the computer, you must turn off the system and turn it back on. But, before you do that, record the error message text and other information so that you can research the problem if it reoccurs. It is possible for the system to restart on its own. For more information on this, see the next section, "Causes of BSOD Errors."

Causes of BSOD Errors

BSOD errors can be caused by any of the following:

- **Incompatible or defective hardware or software**—Start the system in Safe Mode and uninstall the last hardware or software installed. Acquire updates before you reinstall the hardware or software. Exchange or test memory. Run **SFC /scannow** to check for problems with system files.

- **Registry problems**—Select Last Known Good Configuration as described later in this chapter and see whether the system will start.

- **Viruses**—Scan for viruses and remove them if discovered.

- **Miscellaneous causes**—Check the Windows Event Viewer and check the System log. Research the BSOD with the Microsoft Help and Support website.

Researching Causes and Solutions

To determine the exact cause of the error, you must do the following:

Step 1.   Record the exact error message before restarting the computer.

Step 2.   Research the error at the Microsoft Help and Support website (http://support.microsoft.com) if the BSOD keeps happening.

TIP   Unfortunately, you can't take a screen capture of a BSOD for printing because a BSOD completely shuts down Windows. However, if you have a digital camera handy, it makes a great tool for recording the exact error message. Just be sure to use the correct range setting to get the sharpest picture possible (normal or closeup, often symbolized with a flower icon). Turn off the flash on the camera, and use ISO 400 or Hi ISO to enable handheld shooting in dim light.

BSOD and Spontaneous Shutdown and Restart

Windows can be configured to automatically restart if a STOP error occurs. When a STOP (BSOD) error happens on a system configured to restart automatically, the system will seem to spontaneously shut down and restart. This problem is sometimes referred to as an Auto Restart Error.

If a system needs to be available at all times and STOP/BSOD errors are rare, it might be preferable to configure the system to restart automatically. (Different versions of Windows enable or disable this option by default.) To change this option, follow these steps:

Step 1.   Open the System Properties window. With Windows 7 and Windows Vista, click **Advanced System Settings**.

Step 2.   Click the **Advanced** tab.

Step 3.   Click **Settings** under the Startup and Recovery section.

Step 4.   To enable auto restart, click the empty check box for **Automatically Restart** under the System Failure section (see Figure 15-2). To disable auto restart if it is already enabled, clear this check box.

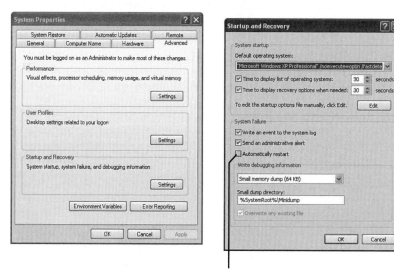

Click the empty checkbox to enable auto restart;
clear it (as shown here) to disable auto restart.

Figure 15-2   The Automatically Restart check box on the Startup and Recovery dialog determines whether a STOP error halts or restarts the system.

To enable diagnosis of a STOP/BSOD error when auto restart is enabled, make sure the Write an Event to the System Log option is enabled (refer to Figure 15-2). When a STOP error is saved to the System Log, it is listed with the type set as Information (not as Error, as you might expect). To find the event, search for events with the source listed as Save Dump. The STOP error will be listed thus:

```
The system has rebooted from a bugcheck. The bugcheck was (error
number).
Look up the error number to find the solution.
```

When a stop error occurs, Windows writes debugging information to the hard drive for later analysis with programs such as Dumpchk.exe; this debugging information is essentially the contents of RAM.

The default setting in Windows XP is to write only a portion of the contents of RAM, known as a Small Memory Dump; this is written to %systemroot%\ Minidump as shown in Figure 15-2. Or you could configure Windows to do a Kernel memory dump, which is the default in Windows Vista and 7.

The Kernel memory dump is saved as the file %systemroot\MEMORY.DMP, which is larger than the minidump file. This is where the phrase "My computer Just Took a Dump…" comes from! For more information on how to analyze the debugging information resulting from these stop errors, see the following link: http://support.microsoft.com/kb/315263.

Boot Failures

220-802

Objective:
220-802: 4.6

Boot failures can be caused by incorrect boot configuration in the BIOS, corrupt or missing boot files, and missing driver files. The solutions for these problems vary with the version of Windows in use.

Windows 7/Vista Boot Errors

Windows 7/Vista uses the bootmgr and BCD files during the startup process. If these files are corrupted or missing, you will see corresponding error messages:

- **BOOTMGR is missing**—This message displays if the bootmgr file is missing or corrupt. This black screen will probably also say Press Ctrl+Alt+Del to Restart; however, doing so will probably have the same results.

- **The Windows Boot Configuration Data file is missing required information**— This message means that either the Windows Boot Manager (Bootmgr) entry is not present in the **Boot Configuration Data** (BCD) store or that the Boot\BCD file on the active partition is damaged or missing. Additional information you might see on the screen includes File: \ Boot\BCD, and Status: 0xc0000034.

There are two ways to repair a missing BOOTMGR file:

- Boot to the System Recovery Options, and select the **Startup Repair** option. This should automatically repair the system and require you to reboot.

- Boot to the System Recovery Options, and select the Command Prompt option. Type the command **bootrec /fixboot**, as shown in Figure 15-3.

NOTE   A hard drive's lifespan is not infinite. In some cases, it is not possible to repair this file and unfortunately the hard drive will need to be replaced.

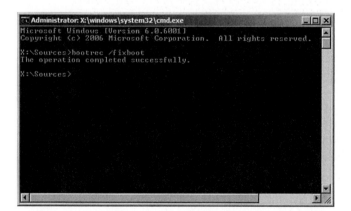

Figure 15-3   Repairing BOOTMGR.exe from the Windows Recovery Environment's command prompt. Windows Recovery Environment is a feature of Windows Vista and Windows 7.

To repair the BCD store, use this three-step process:

Step 1.   Boot to the System Recovery Options and select the Startup Repair option. This should automatically repair the system and require you to reboot. If not, move on to the second method.

Step 2.   Boot to the System Recovery Options and select the Command Prompt option. Type **bootrec /rebuildbcd**. If the Bootrec.exe tool runs successfully, it presents you with an installation path of a Windows directory. To add the entry to the BCD store, type **Yes**. A confirmation message appears that indicates the entry was added successfully. Restart the system.

Step 2b.   If the Bootrec.exe tool can't locate any missing Windows installations, you must remove the BCD store and then re-create it. To do this, type the following commands in the order in which they are presented. Press **Enter** after each command.

```
Bcdedit /export C:\BCD_Backup
ren c:\boot\bcd bcd.old
Bootrec /rebuildbcd
```

These steps usually work, but if they don't the BCD store can be rebuilt manually. You can find more information on this process at the following links:

- **Windows Vista**—http://support.microsoft.com/kb/927391

- **Windows 7**— http://support.microsoft.com/kb/2004518

NOTE   If you want to install two versions of Windows in a multiboot configuration, install the older version first. For example, install Windows XP first, followed by Windows 7 or Windows Vista.

Various issues can happen if you attempt to dual boot an older operating system that you installed after Windows Vista or Windows 7 was installed. For example, Vista or Windows 7 may cease to boot after the second operating system is installed. This could mean that the master boot record was overwritten, along with other issues. Several steps are involved to repair this problem. The initial command in this process, which will restore the MBR and the boot code that transfers control to the Windows Boot Manager program, is X:\ boot\Bootsect.exe /NT60 All. X is the drive where the installation media exists. See the following Microsoft Help and Support link for more information on how to manually create an entry into the BCD store for the new operating system and how to troubleshoot this further: http://support.microsoft.com/kb/919529.

Windows XP Boot Errors

Windows XP uses the NTLDR, **Boot.ini**, NTDETECT.COM, and Ntoskrnl.exe files during the startup process. If these files are corrupted or missing, you will see corresponding error messages:

- **NTDETECT failed**—This message displays if the NTDETECT.COM file is missing or corrupted.

- **NTLDR is missing**—This message displays if the NTLDR file is missing or corrupted.

- **Invalid boot.ini**—This message displays if the boot.ini file is missing or corrupted. The system might boot anyway, particularly if there is only disk partition on the first hard disk. However, if the system is configured as a dual boot or if Windows is not installed on the first disk partition, you must re-create or recopy the file to enable your system to boot.

- **Ntoskrnl.exe is missing**—This message displays if Windows cannot find the file. If the boot.ini file is invalid, fixing it could fix this problem as well.

Restoring a Missing NTLDR File

To restore a missing NTLDR file from the Windows XP CD, use this command after starting the Recovery Console. (If you didn't boot from the Windows XP CD, be sure it is in your system's CD or DVD drive.)

Type **copy d:\i386\ntldr c:** and press the **Enter** key. (Replace d: with the drive letter used by your Windows XP CD-ROM.)

Restoring a Missing NTDETECT.COM File

To restore a missing NTDETECT.COM file from the Windows XP CD, use this command after starting the Recovery Console. (If you didn't boot from the Windows XP CD, be sure it is in your system's CD or DVD drive.)

Type **copy d:\i386\ntdetect.com c:** and press the **Enter** key. (Replace d: with the drive letter used by your Windows XP CD-ROM.)

Restart your system after copying either or both files as needed.

Re-creating the Boot.ini File with Bootcfg

To re-create the boot.ini file, use these commands from the Recovery Console:

Step 1.   Type **bootcfg /rebuild** and press the **Enter** key.

Step 2.   When bootcfg finds your Windows installation, it lists the installation and prompts you thus: Add installation to boot list? (Yes/No/All). Type **Y** and press the **Enter** key.

Step 3.   When prompted to Enter Load Identifier:, type the name of your operating system (for example, **Windows XP Pro**) and press **Enter**.

Step 4.   When prompted to Enter OS Load Options:, type **/Fastdetect** and press **Enter**.

Step 5.   Remove the Windows XP CD and type **exit**. Press **Enter**. Your system restarts.

For more information, see http://support.microsoft.com/kb/330184.

Reinstalling the Ntoskrnl.exe File

If repairing or re-creating the boot.ini file does not resolve a problem with Ntoskrnl.exe, you need to reinstall the file from the Windows XP CD. The file is stored in compressed form, and you will need to use the Recovery Console and its Expand command to restore the file from the CD. For details, see http://support.microsoft.com/kb/314477/.

Missing Operating System Error

An Operating System Not Found or Missing Operating System error can be caused by incorrect or missing hard disk settings in the system BIOS or by problems with the hard disk's master boot record (MBR).

Before attempting to repair the MBR, restart the computer, enter the BIOS setup program, and check the following:

- Make sure the system drive is correctly identified in the system BIOS.
- Make sure the system drive is listed before other bootable drives in the boot sequence or boot order menu.

Save any changes needed, and restart the computer. If the same error is displayed, restart the computer with the Windows installation media.

With Windows XP, start the Recovery Console and use the Fixmbr command to repair the boot sector.

With Windows Vista or 7, start the Windows Recovery Environment and use Startup Repair.

Missing Graphical Interface

Windows can be started without a graphical user interface (**GUI**) by selecting the Command Prompt Only option from the Advanced Startup menu. To restore the GUI, simply restart Windows normally.

To learn more, see "Safe Mode and Advanced Startup Menu," later in this chapter.

GUI Fails to Load

If the display's vertical refresh setting in Windows is out of range, you can see BIOS boot information, such as the splash screen or the summary of onboard components, but you will not see the Windows GUI. Your display might provide a warning of an incorrect vertical refresh rate setting when it's time to load the Windows desktop.

To solve this problem, restart Windows in VGA mode, open the Advanced Display properties sheet, and select the correct refresh rate (typically 60Hz for LCD or LED panels or integrated LCD or LED displays; 60Hz or higher for CRTs). Restart the system normally.

Other Windows Problems

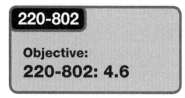

220-802

Objective:
220-802: 4.6

Other problems with Microsoft Windows, including shutdowns, devices that won't start, missing DLL files, services that won't start, incompatible programs, slow system performance, Safe Mode, and files that won't open, can also be solved through the use of various Windows features and utilities.

To learn more about the utilities and features discussed in the following sections, see the "Windows Tools" and "Run-Line Utilities" sections later in this chapter.

Improper Shutdowns

Some startup programs or services might prevent Windows from shutting down properly. Use MSConfig to perform a **clean boot** to see whether Windows can shut down correctly. If so, reenable services and programs with MSConfig until you determine which service or program is causing a problem.

For details, see http://support.microsoft.com/kb/929135.

Device Fails to Start

A device that fails to start is displayed in Device Manager with an error icon, typically a black exclamation mark on a yellow field. When you view the properties sheet for the device, it displays This Device Cannot Start. (Code 10).

Update the drivers using the Drivers tab. If this does not resolve the problem, see http://support.microsoft.com/kb/943104 for more information.

Missing DLL Message

A dynamic link library (**DLL**) file is a binary file used by Windows or a program. An error message indicating a missing DLL might indicate one of the following problems:

- File deletion or renaming
- Damage from virus or malware

Before attempting to fix the problem, check your system for viruses and malware and resolve any detected infections.

If the file is a Windows system DLL, use SFC (System File Checker) to check your Windows files and reinstall a replacement.

If the file appears to be part of an application, use the Repair option in Add/Remove Programs (XP) or Uninstall or Change a Program (Vista/7) to repair the program. If this option doesn't work or is not available, uninstall and reinstall the program.

Services Fail to Start

Many Windows features, such as the print spooler, wireless network configuration, Windows Search, and others, are run as services. Services are managed through the Services and Applications branch of Computer Management.

A service might not start for the following reasons:

- Hardware used for the service is not present. For example, wireless network configuration will not run automatically if a wireless adapter is not installed.
- Other services that are used by the service are not running. In this case, an error such as The Dependency Service or Group Failed to Start appears.

- The service requires login information that has not been provided.

- The service has stopped due to previous errors and is not configured to restart automatically.

To learn how to manage services, see "Services.MSC" later in this chapter.

Compatibility Error

Programs written for older versions of Windows might trigger a This Program Has Known Compatibility Issues error dialog when you try to run them. The dialog box lists the program name and location and the program developer and provides you with three choices:

- **Check for Solutions Online**—Choose this option to see whether an updated program or a patch is available.

- **Run Program**—Windows will run the program, but it is not likely to work.

- **Cancel**—Windows will not run the program.

Get an updated version of the program, either by selecting the **Check for solutions…** option or by manually searching for and downloading an update.

Slow System Performance

Slow system performance can be caused by many issues, including the following:

- **System not configured for maximum performance**—To solve this problem, set the Power setting to Office/Desk (Windows XP) or High Performance (Windows 7/Vista) using the Power options icon in the notification area or the Power options in Control Panel.

- **Drive containing paging file and temporary files is nearly full or badly fragmented**—The paging file and temporary files are normally stored on C: (system) drive. If this drive has less than 15% free space, performance can suffer. Use Disk Cleanup in drive properties to remove unwanted files, check the drive for errors, and defragment it. If you have more available space on a different drive, use the Advanced tab in System properties to change the location of the paging file and temp files.

- **System is overheating and CPU is running at reduced speed**—Remove dust and dirt on the CPU and system fans. Check for adequate airflow through the system.

Boots to Safe Mode

If Windows does not shut down properly (such as because of a crash, lockup, or power failure), it displays the option to start in Safe Mode the next time the computer starts. You can accept this option or elect to start the system in Normal mode.

Even if you don't believe there are serious problems with the system, it is usually best to start the system in Safe Mode and then perform the shutdown/restart procedure from the Windows desktop. If there are no serious problems with the system, it usually restarts correctly.

File Fails to Open

If a file can be opened from the File, Open menu in an application but not from Windows Explorer, the file extension is not associated with a program. In this situation, you might not see an error message, or you might see an error message such as

> This File Does Not Have a Program Associated with It for Performing This Action. Create an Association in the Folder Options Control Panel. (Windows XP)

> This File Does Not Have a Program Associated with It for Performing This Action. Please Install a Program, or if One Is Already Installed, Create an Association in the Default Programs Control Panel. (Windows Vista, 7)

Use the appropriate Control Panel utility to create or edit an association. You can also use the methods described in this article for Windows XP, which are similar for Windows 7 and Vista: http://support.microsoft.com/kb/307859.

Windows Diagnostic and Repair Tools

220-802

Objective:
220-802: 4.6

Windows XP, Vista, and 7 contain a wide variety of diagnostic and repair tools you can use to solve problems with systems you manage.

Commands marked with an asterisk (*) must be run from within a command-prompt session in elevated mode. For details, see "Starting a Command-Prompt Session with CMD.EXE" in Chapter 14, "Using and Managing Windows." The tools are

- **Sfc***—System File Checker is used to check system files and replace damaged or invalid files with the correct versions.

- **MSConfig**—System Configuration is used to display and configure boot options and as a convenient way to access other troubleshooting programs.

- **Defrag**—Defragments files to improve file access speed, especially on a drive that has frequent changes to its contents and doesn't have a lot of unused space.

- **REGSVR32***—Registers or unregisters DLL files and ActiveX components.

- **REGEDIT**—Views and edits Windows Registry contents.

- **Event Viewer**—Displays event logs for troubleshooting or management purposes.

- **Safe Mode and other advanced boot options**—Special boot options that can be used when the system won't boot normally; press F8 repeatedly when starting the system until the boot options window is shown.

- **Device Manager**—Displays driver, resource, and version information for hardware devices.

Tools specific to Windows XP include

- **Recovery Console**—A limited command-line environment that can be run from the Windows XP CD or from the startup menu (if it was preinstalled or installed by the user).

- **Fixboot and Fixmbr**—Two utilities available from the Windows XP Recovery Console for fixing boot problems.

- **Automated System Recovery (ASR)**—A special backup routine that can be used to restore an unbootable system; the user must then reinstall applications and restore data files to complete the recovery process.

Tools specific to Windows Vista/7 include

- **Windows Recovery Environment (WinRE)**—Provides access to Startup Repair, System Restore, full-featured command prompt and run-line utilities, Windows memory diagnostics, and Complete PC restore (restores image backup). Can be run from a hidden recovery partition, from the Windows distribution media, or from a repair disc. WinRE is an example of a preinstallation environment.

- **Windows Repair Discs**—Enables the user to run WinRE from a bootable CD or DVD. Can be created with Windows Vista SP1 or higher and with any release of Windows 7.

The following sections discuss how to use these tools to solve the problems discussed earlier in this chapter as well as others you might encounter in your daily work.

Using System File Checker (SFC)

System File Checker (SFC) is a Windows 7/Vista/XP utility that checks protected system files (files such as .DLL, .SYS, .OCX, and .EXE, as well as some font files used by the Windows desktop) and replaces incorrect versions or missing files with the correct files.

Use SFC to fix problems with Internet Explorer or other built-in Windows programs caused by the installation of obsolete Windows system files, user error, deliberate erasure, virus or Trojan horse infections, and similar problems.

To run SFC, open the command prompt and type **SFC** with the appropriate switch. A typical option is **SFC /scannow**, which scans all protected files immediately (Figure 15-4).

Figure 15-4   SFC /scannow reports that corrupt files were repaired (Windows 7).

Another is **SFC /scanonce**, which scans all protected files at the next boot. If SFC finds that some files are missing and replacement files are not available on your system, you will be prompted to reinsert your Windows distribution disc so that the files can be copied to the DLL cache. Other options include **/scanboot**, which scans all protected files every time the system starts; **/revert**, which returns the scan setting to the default; and **/purgecache** and **/cachesize=x**, which enable a user to delete the file cache and modify its size. For more information, see http://support.microsoft.com/kb/310747.

Using MSConfig

The Microsoft System Configuration Utility, Msconfig, enables you to selectively disable programs and services that run at startup. If your computer is unstable, runs more slowly than usual, or has problems starting up or shutting down, using Msconfig can help you determine whether a program or service running when the system starts is at fault. To start Msconfig:

Step 1.   Click **Start**, **Run** (Windows XP) or click **Start** to open the Windows Desktop Search pane.

Step 2.   Type **msconfig** and press **Enter**.

All versions of Msconfig have a multitabbed interface used to control startup options. The General tab (see Figure 15-5) enables you to select from Normal, Diagnostic (clean boot) or Selective Startup. (You choose which items and services to load.) Use the Boot tab (see Figure 15-6) to specify how to boot a Windows Vista or 7 system. (This tab is called Boot.ini in Windows XP's version of MSConfig.)

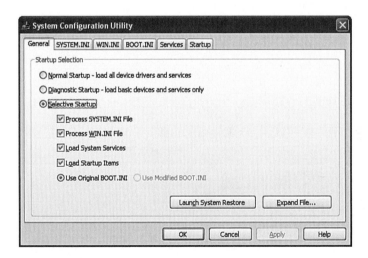

Figure 15-5   Msconfig's General tab (Windows XP).

Use the Services tab to disable or reenable system services. Use the Tools tab to launch System Restore, Computer Management, and other management tasks.

NOTE   The Tools tab is added to Windows XP SP2's version of MSConfig by installing the MSConfig update available from http://support.microsoft.com/kb/906569. This update is included in Windows XP SP3.

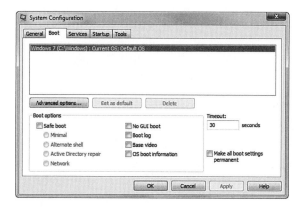

Figure 15-6   Msconfig's Boot tab (Windows 7).

The Windows XP version of MSConfig also includes the following tabs:

- System.ini (manages legacy hardware settings)
- Win.ini (manages legacy software and configuration settings)

Using REGSVR32

If a program stops working after another program was installed or removed, some program components might have been replaced or disabled. The Microsoft command-line tool Regsvr32 is used to reregister .dll or .ocx files used by applications.

To use Regsvr32.exe, open a command prompt as administrator. Go to the folder containing the file(s) you need to reregister.

The basic syntax to register a program file with Regsvr32 is

```
Regsvr32 filename.ext
```

For example, to reregister a file called jscript.dll in the current folder, use the following:

```
Regsvr32 jscript.dll
```

NOTE   To learn more about Regsvr32, see http://support.microsoft.com/kb/249873. TechRepublic has a helpful article on using Regsvr32 at http://articles.techrepublic.com/ 5100-6270-1054872.html.

Using REGEDIT

Under most normal circumstances, the **Registry** will not need to be edited or viewed. However, Registry editing might be necessary under the following circumstances:

- To view a system setting that cannot be viewed through normal interfaces.

- To add, modify (by changing values or data), or remove a Registry key that cannot be changed through normal Windows menus or application settings. This might be necessary to remove traces of a program or hardware device that was not uninstalled properly or to allow a new device or program to be installed.

- To back up the Registry to a file.

To start Regedit, open the Run or Windows Desktop Search window, type **regedit**, and press **Enter**. Changes made in Regedit are automatically saved when you exit; however, you might have to log off and log back on or restart the system for those changes to take effect.

CAUTION   The Registry should never be edited unless a backup copy has been made first because there is no Undo option for individual edits and no way to discard all changes when exiting Regedit.

Editing the Windows Registry is even more difficult because Registry keys can be expressed in decimal, hexadecimal, or text. When editing the Registry, be sure to carefully follow the instructions provided by a vendor.

Figure 15-7 shows the Registry in Windows Vista with a modification being made to the MenuBar color, which isn't accessible within normal Windows display menus. Figure 15-8 shows the Registry in Windows XP, viewing the uninstall folder for Mozilla Firefox.

Making Changes to the Registry by Importing a Text File

Some changes to the Registry are performed by importing a text file into the Registry. See the "Let Me Fix It Myself" section at http://support.microsoft.com/kb/950505 for an example of importing a user-created Registry key into the Registry.

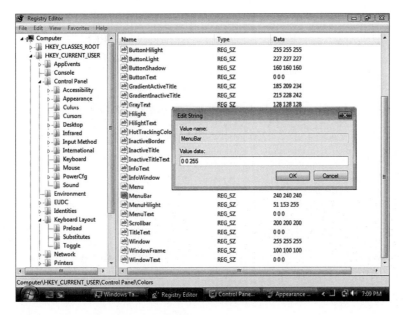

Figure 15-7   Using Regedit (Windows Vista).

Figure 15-8   Using Regedit (Windows XP).

Backing Up the Registry Before Editing

Always back up the Registry before editing it. Follow these steps to back up part or all the Registry to a text file:

Step 1. Start Regedit.

Step 2. To make a partial backup, highlight the section of the Registry you want to back up.

Step 3. Click **File**.

Step 4. Select **Export**.

Step 5. Select a location to store the Registry backup.

Step 6. Enter a name for the backup.

Step 7. Click **All** to back up the entire Registry. Click **Selected Branch** to back up only the Registry branch you selected in Step 2.

Step 8. Click **Save**.

Using Event Viewer

Windows XP, 7, and Vista all store system events, warnings, and errors in various event logs. Although these events can be viewed from Computer Management Console (refer to Figure 15-10), it is easier to view them with Event Viewer. Event Viewer can be run from the Run window (XP), with Windows Desktop Search (Vista, 7), from the Tools tab in MSConfig, or from Administrative Tools.

Use the Overview and Summary window (Vista, 7) or the branches of the Event Viewer or Computer Management Console to locate log message you need to read. Look for Error messages (marked with a white X on a red circle) first and then Warnings (yellow triangle). In Windows 7 and Vista, click **View All Instances of This Event** to view only those events. Frequent errors or warnings that point to the same program or device can indicate a serious problem (see Figures 15-9 and 15-10). You might need to update drivers for a problem device, obtain a software update for a problem program, or remove the device or program and replace it with a different one to resolve the problems.

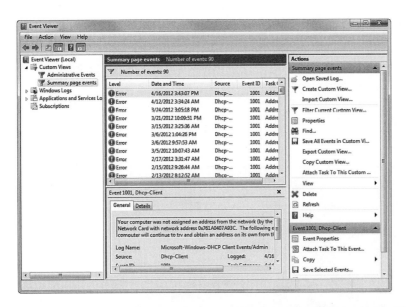

Figure 15-9   Viewing a series of errors involving the DHCP-client with the Windows 7 Event Viewer.

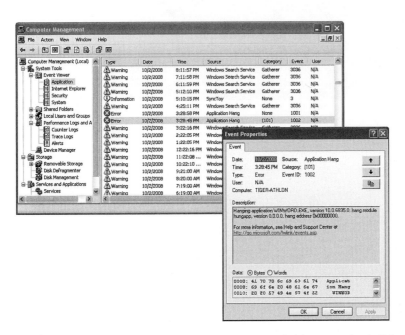

Figure 15-10   Viewing an error message in the Application event log in Windows XP's Computer Management Console.

Using Safe Mode and Other Advanced Boot Options

If you cannot start Windows but don't see an error message, the problem could be caused by a driver or startup program, video driver problems, or problems with the system kernel. Windows offers various advanced boot options to help you correct startup problems. To access these startup options, Press **F8** repeatedly right after the BIOS POST begins to display the Windows Advanced Boot Options menu (which you may also see referred to as advanced startup options) as shown in Figure 15-11.

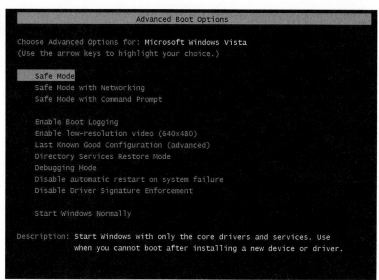

Figure 15-11   Windows Vista Advanced Boot Options menu.

Various editions of Windows offer the following startup options as part of the Advanced Boot Options menu:

- **Repair Your Computer (Vista, 7 only)**—Runs the Windows Recovery Environment (WinRE).

- **Safe Mode**—Starts the system with a minimal set of drivers; can be used to start System Restore or to load Windows GUI for diagnostics.

- **Safe Mode with Networking**—Starts the system with a minimal set of drivers and enables network support.

- **Safe Mode with Command Prompt**—Starts the system with a minimal set of drivers but loads command prompt instead of Windows GUI.

- **Enable Boot Logging**—Creates an ntbtlog.txt file.

- **Enable low-resolution video (640 × 480)**—Uses a standard VGA driver in place of a GPU-specific display driver, but uses all other drivers as normal. (This is called Enable VGA Mode in Windows XP.)

- **Last Known Good Configuration**—Starts the system with the last configuration known to work; useful for solving problems caused by newly installed hardware or software.

- **Directory Services Restore Mode**—Used to restore a domain controller's active directory (Windows Server). Even though it is listed, it is not used in Windows 7/Vista/XP.

- **Debugging Mode**—An advanced diagnostics tool that enables the use of a debug program to examine the system kernel for troubleshooting.

- **Disable automatic restart on system failure (Vista and 7 only)**—Prevents Windows from automatically restarting if a STOP (BSOD) error causes Windows to fail. Choose this option only if Windows is stuck in a loop where Windows fails, attempts to restart, and fails again.

- **Disable driver signature enforcement (Vista and 7 only)**—Allows drivers containing improper signatures to be installed.

- **Start Windows Normally**—Can be used to boot to regular Windows. This option is listed in case a user inadvertently presses F8 but does not want to use any of the Advanced Boot Options.

If Windows 7 or Vista fails to start properly and then restarts automatically, they normally display the Windows Error Recovery screen and give you the following options: Safe Mode, Safe Mode with Networking, Safe Mode with Command Prompt, Last Known Good Configuration, and Start Windows Normally. This means that Windows has acknowledged some sort of error or improper shutdown and offers a truncated version of the Advanced Options Boot menu.

Table 15-1 lists typical problems and helps you select the correct startup option to use to solve the problem.

Table 15-1   Using the Windows Advanced Boot Options Menu

Problem	Startup Option to Select	Notes
Windows won't start after you install new hardware or software.	Last Known Good Configuration	Resets Windows to its last-known working configuration; you need to reinstall hardware or software installed after that time.
Windows won't start after you upgrade a device driver.	Safe Mode	After starting the computer in this mode, open the Device Manager, select the device, and use the Rollback feature to restore the previously used device driver. Restart your system.
Windows won't start after you install a different video card or monitor.	Enable low-resolution video (640 × 480) / Enable VGA Mode	Most video cards should be installed when your system is running in VGA Mode. If a video error occurs, use this option, and then the Display Properties window to select a working video mode before you restart.
Windows can't start normally, but you need access to the Internet to research the problem or download updates.	Safe Mode with Networking	You can use Windows Update and the Internet, but some devices won't work in this mode. This mode also uses 640 × 480 resolution but retains the color settings normally used.
Windows doesn't finish starting normally, and you want to know what device driver or process is preventing it from working.	Enable Boot Logging	This option starts the computer with all its normal drivers and settings and also creates a file called ntbtlog.txt in the default Windows folder (usually C:\ Windows). Restart the computer in Safe Mode, and open this file with Notepad or WordPad to determine the last driver file that loaded. You can update the driver or remove the hardware device using that driver to restore your system to working condition.
Windows is loading programs you don't need during its startup process.	Boot computer in Normal Mode (or Safe Mode if the computer won't start in Normal Mode); click Start, Run or Start Search; and then type MSConfig.	Use this program to disable one or more startup programs, and then restart your computer. You can also use it to restore damaged files or to start System Restore to reset your computer to an earlier condition.

It is important to note that the Last Known Good Configuration option will be helpful only before a successful logon occurs. After a user logs on, that becomes the Last Known Good logon. It is recommended that you attempt to repair a computer with Advanced Boot Options *before* using Windows 7 or Vista's System Recovery Options, or Windows XP's Recovery Console.

Using Device Manager

Windows Device Manager is used to display installed device categories and specific installed devices, and to troubleshoot problems with devices.

To use Device Manager in Windows 7/Vista, follow these steps:

Step 1.   Click **Start**, right-click **Computer**, and select **Properties**. This displays the System window.

Step 2.   Click the **Device Manager** link on the left side under Tasks.

To use Device Manager in Windows XP:

Step 1.   Open the System Properties window in the Control Panel, or right-click **My Computer** and select **Properties**.

Step 2.   Click the **Hardware** tab and select **Device Manager**.

NOTE   There are two other options for opening Device Manager. The first is by using the Search box within the Start menu. Just type **device manager**, and then click the link for Device Manager that appears in the results box. The second is from the Computer Management console window. It opens the same way in Windows 7, Vista, and XP. To open this, right-click **Computer (My Computer** in XP), and select **Manage**. This displays the Computer Management window; from there, click **Device Manager** in the left window pane. Get in the habit of using Computer Management. It has lots of common settings in one location. Another way to open Computer Management is by going to the Run prompt or Windows Desktop Search, typing **compmgmt.msc**, and pressing **Enter**.

To view the devices in a specific category, click the plus (+) sign next to the category name, as shown in Figure 15-12. If a particular category contains a device with problems, the category automatically opens when you start Device Manager.

Figure 15-12 Device Manager with selected categories expanded.

NOTE   Different systems will have different categories listed in Device Manager because Device Manager lists only categories for installed hardware. For example, the system shown in Figure 15-12 has a battery backup, so it has a Batteries category.

To see more information about a specific device, double-click the device to open its properties sheet. Device properties sheets have a General tab and some combination of other tabs:

- **General**—Displays device type, manufacturer, location, status, troubleshoot button, and usage. Applies to all devices.

- **Properties**—Device-specific settings. Applies to multimedia devices.

- **Driver**—Driver details and version information. Applies to all devices.

- **Details**—Technical details about the device (added in Windows XP SP2 and newer versions). Applies to all devices.

- **Policies**—Optimizes external drives for quick removal or performance. Applies to USB, FireWire (IEEE 1394), and eSATA drives.

- **Resources**—Hardware resources such as IRQ, DMA, Memory, and I/O port address. Applies to I/O devices.

- **Volumes**—Drive information such as status, type, capacity, and so on. Click Populate to retrieve information. Applies to hard disk drives.

- **Power**—Power available per port. Applies to USB root hubs and generic hubs.

- **Power Management**—Specifies device-specific power management settings. Applies to USB, network, keyboard, and mouse devices.

Figure 15-13 illustrates some of these tabs.

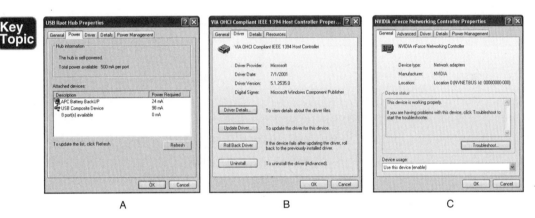

Figure 15-13   Selected Device Manager tabs: the Power tab for a USB hub (A); the Driver tab for an IEEE-1394 port (B); and the General tab for an network controller (C).

If your computer has devices that are malfunctioning in a way that Device Manager can detect, or has devices that are disabled, they will be displayed as soon as you open Device Manager. For example, in Figure 15-14 the Ports (COM and LPT) category displays a malfunctioning port, COM2, indicated by an exclamation mark (!) in a yellow circle. (Windows XP version; Vista/7 use an exclamation mark [!] in a yellow triangle.) The parallel printer port, LPT1, has been disabled, as indicated by a red X. (Windows XP version; Vista/7 use a down-arrow icon.) If the malfunctioning or disabled device is an I/O port, such as a serial, parallel, or USB port, any device attached to that port cannot work until the device is working properly.

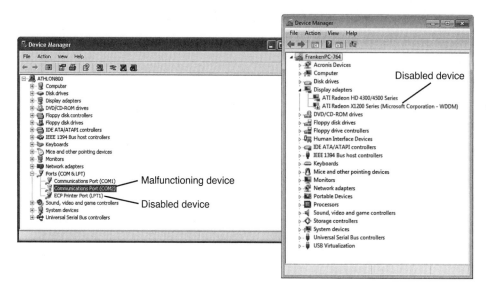

Figure 15-14   Windows XP (left) and Windows 7 (right) Device Manager windows displaying a malfunctioning and two disabled devices.

Not every problem with a device shows up in Device Manager, but most problems with resource conflicts or drivers display here.

To troubleshoot problems with a device in Device Manager, open its Properties sheet by double-clicking the device. Use the General tab shown in Figure 15-15 to display the device's status and to troubleshoot a disabled or malfunctioning device.

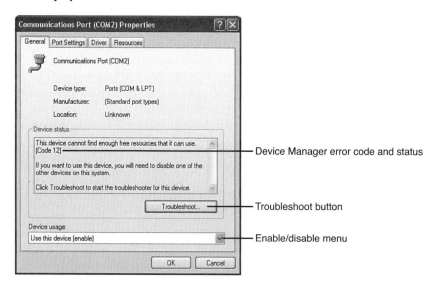

Figure 15-15   A problem device's General properties. If the device's General Properties sheet lacks a solution button, look up the Device Manager error code and take appropriate action manually.

When you have a malfunctioning device such as the one in Figure 15-15, you have several options for resolving the problem:

- Look up the Device Manager code to determine the problem and its solution (see Table 15-2 for a few examples).

- Click the **Troubleshoot** button (if any) shown on the device's General Properties tab; the button's name and usage depends on the problem. Table 15-2 lists a few examples, their meanings, and the solution button (if any).

- Manually change resources (applies primarily to older systems that don't use ACPI power management). If the nature of the problem is a resource conflict, you can click the **Resources** tab, change the settings, and eliminate the conflict if possible.

- Manually update drivers. If the problem is a driver issue but an Update Driver button isn't available, open the **Driver** tab and install a new driver for the device.

Table 15-2 Examples of Some Device Manager Codes and Solutions

Device Manager Code Number	Problem	Recommended Solution
Code 1	This device is not configured correctly.	Update the driver.
Code 3	The driver for this device might be corrupted, or your system might be running low on memory or other resources.	Close some open applications. Uninstall and reinstall the driver. Install additional RAM.
Code 10	Device cannot start.	Update the driver. View Microsoft Help and Support article 943104 for more information.
Code 12	This device cannot find enough free resources that it can use. If you want to use this device, you need to disable one of the other devices on this system.	You can use the Troubleshooting Wizard in Device Manager to determine where the conflict is, and then disable the conflicting device. Disable the device.
Code 22	The device is disabled.	Enable the device.

> **NOTE** For a comprehensive discussion of Device Manager error codes, see these resources:
>
> - For Windows XP, see http://support.microsoft.com/kb/310123.
>
> - For Windows Vista or Windows 7, see "Error Codes in Device Manager" at http://technet.microsoft.com/en-us/library/cc771355.aspx.

If the device has a conflict with another device, you might be able to change the settings in the device's Properties page/Resources tab (see Figure 15-16). If the device is a legacy (non-PnP) device, you might need to shut down the system and reconfigure the card manually before you can use Device Manager to reset its configuration in Windows.

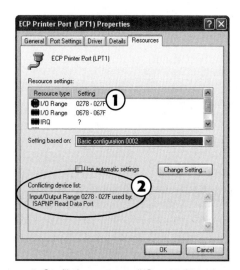 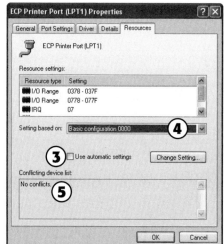

1. Conflicting resource (I/O port address)
2. Conflicting device
3. Can solve most configuration conflicts when selected
4. Selects from various preconfigured settings
5. Conflict resolved

Figure 15-16   The parallel port's current configuration (left), conflicts with another port. By selecting another configuration (right), the conflict is resolved.

You can also use the Device Manager to disable a device that is conflicting with another device. To disable a device, follow these steps:

For Windows Vista/7:

Step 1. Click the plus (+) sign next to the device category containing the device.

Step 2. Double-click the device, click the **Driver** tab, and select **Disable**.

For Windows XP:

Step 1. Click the device and select **Properties**.

Step 2. Click the **General** tab; look for the Device Usage display at the bottom of the window. Click the menu and select **Do Not Use This Device (disable)**. Refer to Figure 15-15. If you prefer to solve the problem with the device, click the **Troubleshoot** button.

Depending on the device, you might need to physically remove it from the system to resolve a conflict. To use the Device Manager to remove a device, follow these steps:

Step 1. Click the plus (+) sign next to the device category containing the device.

Step 2. Double-click the device and select **Uninstall**.

Step 3. Shut down the system and remove the physical device.

or

Step 1. Double-click the device and select **Properties**.

Step 2. Click the **Driver** tab, and click the **Uninstall** button.

Step 3. Shut down the system and remove the physical device.

If a device malfunctions after a driver update, roll back the driver. Use the Roll Back Driver button on the Driver tab to return to the preceding driver version.

Using Windows XP Recovery Console

The Windows XP **Recovery Console** is a special command-line interface designed for copying files and performing disk repairs. Use Recovery Console when the system cannot start from the hard disk because of missing or corrupted boot files, or when other types of missing system files prevent the computer from starting in Safe Mode.

To start Windows XP's Recovery Console, you have two options:

- **Option 1**—Boot your system with the Windows XP CD, and run the Recovery Console as a repair option.

- **Option 2**—While the system is working properly, install the Recovery Console from the Windows XP CD-ROM. It appears automatically as a startup option when you restart your computer.

To start Recovery Console from the Windows XP CD, follow these steps:

Step 1. Start the system with the Windows XP CD.

Step 2. When prompted, press **R** to start the Recovery Console.

To log in to Recovery Console:

Step 1. Select the installation to log in to. (Do this by pressing the number that corresponds to the operating system.)

Step 2. Enter the administrator password for the system.

To copy Recovery Console from the Windows XP CD:

Step 1. Windows is running; insert the Windows CD into the CD or DVD drive.

Step 2. Click **Start**, **Run**.

Step 3. At the Run prompt, type *x*:**\i386\winnt32.exe /cmdcons** where *x* is the drive letter for the CD or DVD drive, and press the **Enter** key.

Step 4. To confirm the installation, click **Yes** in the Windows Setup dialog box describing Recovery Console.

Step 5. Shut down the computer. The next time that you start your computer, Microsoft Windows Recovery Console appears on the startup menu. Select it to start Recovery Console.

> **NOTE** For Windows XP Professional x64 Edition, the path to use in Step 3 is *x*:**\amd64\ winnt32.exe /cmdcons**.

The Recovery Console contains some of the same commands that are available in the normal command-line interface, along with additional commands that are necessary only for repairing the installation.

CAUTION   The Recovery Console permits access to only the following locations:

- The root folder (root directory)
- The %SystemRoot% (Windows) folder and its subfolders
- The Cmdcons folder
- Removable-media drives such as CD and DVD drives

In other words, you cannot use the Recovery Console to access files not stored in these folders, such as users' data files.

Table 15-3 lists Recovery Console commands and uses.

Table 15-3   Recovery Console Commands

Command	Uses
Attrib	Changes file/folder attributes.
Batch	Executes the commands specified in the text file.
Bootcfg	Boot file (boot.ini) configuration and recovery. Can also rebuild a lost boot.ini.
ChDir (Cd)	Displays the name of the current folder or changes the current folder. Requires quotes around folder names with spaces.
Chkdsk	Checks a disk and displays a status report. Use the **/r** option to repair bad sectors.
Cls	Clears the screen.
Copy	Copies a single file to another drive or folder. Automatically uncompresses files from the Windows CD during the copy process. Can't copy to removable media.
Delete (Del)	Deletes a single file.
Dir	Displays a list of files and subfolders in a folder. Lists file/folder attributes for each item listed.
Disable	Disables a system service or a device driver. Helpful if Ntbtlog.txt (the bootlog) indicates a service or device driver is preventing the system from starting.
Diskpart	Manages partitions on your hard drives. Can be used in interactive mode or with optional switches to add or remove partitions.
Enable	Starts or enables a system service or a device driver.
Exit	Exits the Recovery Console and restarts your computer.

Table 15-3 Continued

Command	Uses
Expand	Extracts a file from a compressed (.cab) file, or file with an underscore at the end of the extension (for example .DL_) from the CD to the hard disk.
Fixboot	Writes a new partition boot sector onto the specified partition. Often used with Fixmbr.
Fixmbr	Repairs the master boot record of the specified disk. Often used with Fixboot.
Format	Formats a disk with options for file system and quick format.
Help	Displays a list of the commands you can use in the Recovery Console.
Listsvc	Lists the services and drivers available on the computer.
Logon	Logs on to a Windows installation.
Map	Displays the drive letter mappings. Useful if run before using Fixboot or Fixmbr to make sure you work with the correct disk or drive letter.
Mkdir (Md)	Creates a directory.
More	Displays a text file.
Net Use	Connects a network share to a drive letter.
Rename (Ren)	Renames a single file.
Rmdir (Rd)	Deletes a directory.
Set	Displays and sets environment variables. Can be used to enable copying files to removable media, use of wildcards, and other options within the Recovery Console if the system security settings are adjusted.
Systemroot	Sets the current directory to the systemroot directory of the system you are currently logged on to.
Type	Displays a text file.

Commands in the Recovery Console often have different options and more limitations than the same commands used at a normal command prompt. Use Help and the command-specific help (/?) to determine what options you can use in the Recovery Console, even if you're familiar with how the command works from a command prompt.

TIP If you need to recover users' files from a Windows XP system that cannot boot, even in Safe Mode, consider these alternatives:

- Create a BartPE CD or DVD from the same version of Windows, and use its file manager to copy files or perform data recovery. Get more information on BartPE from www.nu2.nu/pebuilder/.

- Install the drive into another computer and use the other computer's operating system to access the drive.

Using Fixboot and Fixmbr to Fix Boot Problems

Windows XP's Recovery Console includes the command **Fixmbr** to fix boot problems on an NTFS-based drive. If the drive is FAT-based, first use **Fixboot** followed by **Fixmbr**. To rewrite the boot sector on a FAT-based drive, type **Fixboot** and press **Enter**. To repair the master boot record with an NTFS-based drive, type **Fixmbr** and press **Enter**. (If you boot from a different drive letter than the default Windows drive or a different hard disk than normal, you can specify the hard disk drive letter or drive number with these commands.)

Because damaged MBRs can be caused by a computer virus, you should test systems with an up-to-date antivirus program before using either of these commands. If a boot-sector virus is located by an antivirus program, the program's own disk-repair options should be used first. Don't forget that many BIOS programs come with the option to scan the boot sector for viruses. If you have this functionality in your motherboard's BIOS, consider using it!

If this is unsuccessful, you can use the appropriate repair tool to attempt to fix the MBR.

Using Automated System Recovery to Restore a Windows XP Installation

Windows XP Professional does not include a true disaster-recovery backup program. However, the **Automated System Recovery** (ASR) option in NTBackup does enable you to restore the system state (user accounts, hard disk configuration, network configuration, video settings, hardware configuration, software settings, and operating system boot files).

To create an ASR backup with Windows XP Backup (NTBackup), follow these steps:

Step 1. After starting backup, switch to Advanced Mode (if NTBackup starts in Wizard mode) and click the **Automated System Recovery Wizard** button (see Figure 15-17).

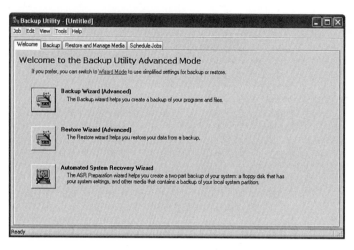

Figure 15-17   Preparing to start the ASR Wizard.

Step 2.   When the Automated System Recovery Preparation Wizard's opening dialog appears, click **Next** to continue.

Step 3.   Select where to store the backup, and click **Next**.

Step 4.   Click **Finish** to complete the wizard. The backup starts. Provide a floppy disk when prompted to store configuration files.

The floppy disk created by the ASR Wizard contains three files that store information about storage devices (asr.sif), Plug and Play (PnP) information (asrpnp.sif), and a list of system state and critical files that were backed up (setup.log).

To restore a system with ASR, you need the following:

- The Windows XP Professional distribution CD

- The ASR backup

- The ASR floppy disk

- A supported floppy drive

If the computer does not have provision for a floppy drive connected to a floppy drive controller, a few USB floppy drives are supported. The USB floppy drives that Microsoft supports for installing Windows XP (and for ASR) are listed in Microsoft Help and Support article 916196, available at http://support.microsoft.com/kb/916196.

Follow this procedure:

Step 1.   Boot the system with the Windows XP Professional CD.

Step 2.   Press **F2** when prompted to start Automated System Recovery.

Step 3.   Insert the ASR floppy disk.

Step 4.   Provide backup files when prompted.

After completing the ASR restore, you need to reinstall your applications and restore your most recent backup to return your system to service.

To learn more about Windows XP Backup, see "Using Windows Backup for XP," later in this chapter.

Using Windows Recovery Environment

Windows Recovery Environment (WinRE) is a set of tools included in Windows 7 and Windows Vista. It takes the place of the Recovery Console used in Windows XP. Also known as System Recovery Options, WinRE's purpose is to recover Windows from errors that prevent it from booting. These are three possible ways to access WinRE:

- **Option 1**—Booting to the Windows 7 or Vista DVD

- **Option 2**—Booting to the Windows 7 or Vista SP2 System Repair CD

- **Option 3**—Booting to a special partition on the hard drive that has WinRE installed

The first option is more common with an individual computer that has Windows 7 or Vista installed; for example, if you performed a clean installation with the standard Windows 7 or Vista DVD and made no modifications to it. To start WinRE, make sure that the DVD drive is first in the boot order of the BIOS, boot to the Windows 7 or Vista DVD (as if you were starting the installation), choose your language settings, and click **Next**. Then select **Repair Your Computer**, which you can find at the lower-left corner of the screen.

CAUTION   Important! Do not select **Install Now**. That would begin the process of reinstalling Windows on your hard drive.

The second option uses a CD created by the Windows 7 or Windows Vista SP2 user. To create a System Repair CD, open the Backup and Restore Center in Control Panel, click the Create a System Repair disc link, and follow the prompts to insert a blank writable CD and label it. You must use a disc made from a 32-bit Windows 7 repair disc to repair a 32-bit installation, and a 64-bit Windows 7 repair disc to repair a 64-bit system.

On Windows Vista, the third option is used by OEMs (original equipment manufacturers) so that users can access WinRE without having to search for, and boot off of, a Windows Vista DVD. These OEMs (computer builders and system integrators) will preinstall WinRE into a special partition on the hard drive, separate from the operating system, so that the user can boot into it at any time. Compare this to the older Recovery Console that was installed into the same partition as the operating system. On Windows 7, the Windows installation program automatically installs WinRE in a special partition.

To access WinRE that has been preinstalled, press **F8** to bring up the Advanced Boot Options menu, highlight **Repair Your Computer**, and press **Enter**. If you don't see Repair Your Computer in the Advanced Boot Options menu, then it wasn't installed to the hard drive, and you must use option 1 or 2 as appropriate. Note that you can still use option 1 even if WinRE was installed to the hard drive; for example, in a scenario in which the hard drive installation of WinRE has failed.

NOTE   The process to install WinRE to the hard drive in Windows Vista is a rather complicated one and is not covered on the A+ exam. However, if you are interested, this link gives the basics of installing WinRE on Windows Vista: http://blogs.msdn.com/winre/archive/2007/01/12/how-to-install-winre-on-the-hard-disk.aspx.

Regardless of which option you selected, at this point a window named System Recovery Options should appear, prompting you to select an operating system to repair. Most users have only one listed. Highlight the appropriate operating system in need of repair and click **Next**. That displays the options at your disposal, as shown in Figure 15-18. Table 15-4 describes these options in more depth.

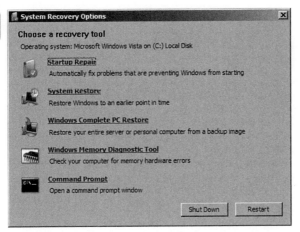

Figure 15-18   Windows Vista System Recovery Options window. (Most options are the same in Windows 7.)

Table 15-4   Description of the Windows 7 and Vista System Recovery Options

System Recovery Option	Description
Startup Repair	When clicked, this automatically fixes certain problems, such as missing or damaged system files that might prevent Windows from starting correctly. When you run Startup Repair, it scans your computer for the problem and then tries to fix it so that your computer can start correctly. If Startup Repair cannot fix all startup problems the first time you run it, you can run it up to four additional times.
System Restore	This restores the computer's system files to an earlier point in time. It's a way to undo system changes to your computer without affecting your personal files, such as email, documents, or photos. Note: If you use this command when the computer is in Safe Mode, you cannot undo the restore operation. However, you can run it again and choose a different restore point if one exists.
System Image Recovery (Windows 7 only)	This restores the contents of a hard disk from an image backup performed with the Windows 7 backup program.
Windows Complete PC Restore (Windows Vista only)	This restores the contents of a hard disk from a backup performed with Windows Complete PC Backup (an image backup). This feature is included only with Vista Business, Ultimate, and Enterprise.

Table 15-4 Continued

System Recovery Option	Description
Windows Memory Diagnostic Tool	Scans the computer's memory for errors.
Command Prompt (replaces the Recovery Console in XP)	Advanced users can use the command prompt to perform recovery-related operations and run other command-line tools for diagnosing and troubleshooting problems. Puts the user into a directory called X:\ Sources. Offers many additional options compared to the Recovery Console in Windows XP. The command prompt in Windows 7 and Vista enables you to copy or batch copy files in both directions between the computer and external USB drives with command-line programs such as Robocopy. Also, you can access any folder on the system, including users' data files.

Maintaining Windows

220-802

Objective:
220-802: 1.7

Although Windows XP, Vista, and especially Windows 7 provide an excellent collection of troubleshooting tools and techniques, it's much better to avoid problems in the first place. The following sections help you master the best practices necessary to maintain healthy Windows installations.

Best practices for Windows maintenance include

- Creating scheduled backups

- Performing scheduled disk checks

- Scheduling defragmentation

- Scheduling Windows updates and patches

- Creating system restore points on a regular basis

- Checking for firmware updates on a regular basis

- Updating antivirus and antimalware programs and scanning on a scheduled basis

NOTE   For information about Windows Update and Microsoft Update (which provide updates to Windows, drivers, and applications), see Chapter 13, "Installing and Upgrading Windows." For information about antivirus and antimalware programs, see Chapter 17, "Security."

Using Windows Backup for XP

Windows XP includes a backup program (**NTBackup**) that can be run from the Windows GUI or from the command line.

NOTE   The Microsoft Backup utility (NTBACKUP) for Windows XP Home Edition must be installed manually from the \ValueAdd\MSFT\NTBACKUP folder on the Windows XP Home Edition CD.

You can start NTBackup in the following ways:

- From the System Tools submenu of the Start menu's Accessories submenu.
- From the command line (ntbackup.exe; for command-line options, open **Help and Support Center**, and type **ntbackup** into the Search box).
- From the Tools menu of the drive properties sheet; choose **Backup Now**.

NTBackup supports backups to a wide variety of drive types, including tape drives; floppy disk drives; removable-media drives such as Zip, Jaz, and Rev drives; and external hard disks. A backup can be saved to a rewritable CD or DVD drive as long as the backup fits on a single disc; however, the backup file must be created first because it cannot be burned directly to the disc during the backup process.

During the backup process, you can specify the following:

- Which drive(s) to back up
- Which files to back up—whether to select all data files or new and changed files only
- Whether to back up the Windows Registry (part of system state data)
- Where to create the backup—to tape drive, floppy disk, another hard disk, or a removable-media drive
- Whether to replace an existing backup on the backup medium or to append the backup to existing backup files

- When and how often to run the backup—scheduled backups are an important part of best practices

- How to run the backup—whether to use data compression, protect the backup with a password, verify the backup, and use volume shadow copy (which enables open files to be backed up)

NTBackup can be run in interactive mode as shown in Figure 15-19, or in wizard mode as shown in Figure 15-20.

Figure 15-19   Preparing to create a backup to an external hard disk with NTBackup in interactive mode.

NTBackup in Windows XP is also used to perform an Automated System Recovery (ASR) backup/restore to rebuild a Windows installation after a system failure, as discussed earlier in this chapter.

NOTE   If you need to restore backup files created with NTBackup to a system running Windows Vista, download and install Windows NT Backup Restore Utility from the Microsoft download website. This utility also requires that you enable Removable Storage Management, and supports tape backups as well as other backup media types.

A similar utility for Windows 7 and Windows Server 2008 R2 is available from http://support.microsoft.com/kb/974674. It does not support tape drives.

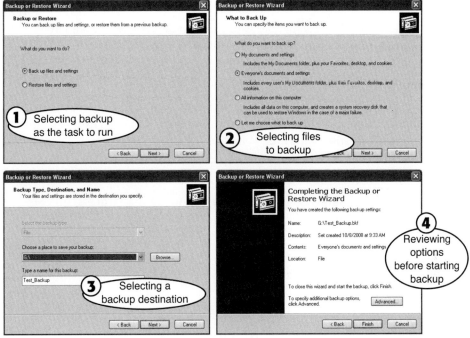

Figure 15-20   Running NTBackup in wizard mode.

Creating an Image Backup for a Windows XP System

As noted in the previous section, NTBackup does not create a system image. To create an **image backup** of a system running Windows XP, you must use a third-party backup utility. Two of the most popular image backup utilities include

- **Norton Ghost (Symantec)**—Creates image and file-by-file backups.

- **Acronis True Image Home Edition**—Creates image and file-by-file backups. Also has options for restoring images to dissimilar hardware and integration with cloud-based backup.

> **NOTE**   Seagate and Western Digital have licensed Acronis True Image as the basis for Seagate Disc Wizard and Acronis True Image WD Edition. These utilities are also used for cloning drives and installing new disk drives. Although they don't include incremental or differential backups, you can manually restore backed-up files with drag and drop. See the Seagate (www.seagate.com) and Western Digital (www.wdc.com) websites for details.

Using Windows Vista's Backup and Restore Center

Backup and Restore Center is the successor to Windows XP's NTBackup. It can back up individual files to writeable CD or DVD, high-capacity removable media such as Iomega REV, external hard disk, or a network location (in Business, Ultimate, and Enterprise only).

The Complete PC Backup program also found in Backup and Restore Center can create an image of your system to one or more writeable DVDs, an external hard disk, or a network location. However, Windows Vista backup programs do not support tape drives.

NOTE Complete PC Backup is available only in Windows Vista Business, Enterprise, and Ultimate editions.

Figure 15-21 illustrates Backup and Restore Center on Windows Vista Ultimate.

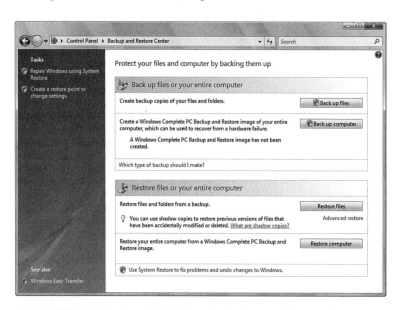

Figure 15-21   Windows Vista Ultimate's Backup and Restore Center.

NOTE Before Backup and Restore Center is configured for the first time, it is listed as Backup Status and Configuration.

During the file backup process, you specify the types of files to back up, as shown in Figure 15-22, and when to perform scheduled backups after the first backup is completed. The file backup process backs up data files and program settings but not Windows files, program files, or a system image. Use Complete PC Backup (if available) or a third-party image backup program to create a system image backup.

Windows Vista stores its file backups as .zip files that can be opened by Windows Explorer as well as by Backup and Restore Center.

Figure 15-22   Specifying the file types to back up with Windows Vista's Back Up Files.

Creating an Image Backup with Complete PC Backup for Windows Vista

Complete PC Backup is the successor to Windows XP's Automated System Recovery. However, unlike ASR, it backs up an entire image of your system to the removable media of your choice, for example DVD, or to an external hard disk. To create a backup of your PC with Vista's Complete PC Backup, follow these steps:

Step 1.   Start the Complete PC Backup program by going to Start > All Programs > Accessories > System Tools > Backup Status and Configuration.

Step 2.   Click the **Complete PC Backup** button.

Step 3.   Click **Create a Backup Now** and follow the directions. Have media ready that can hold an image of your operating system, such as writable DVD or an external hard disk. Be ready; this will be a sizeable image that might require multiple DVDs. If your system drive uses more than 20GB of space, consider using an external hard disk for backup.

To restore a system from the backup, follow these steps:

Step 1.   Insert the installation disc or the System Repair disc, connect the external hard disk where the backup resides (if you used an external hard disk), and then restart the computer. (Make sure that the DVD drive is listed first in the BIOS boot order.)

Step 2.   Press any key when prompted to boot off of the DVD.

Step 3.   Verify or select your language settings, and then click **Next**.

Step 4.   Click **Repair Your Computer**.

Step 5.   Select the operating system you want to repair (usually there will be only one), and then click **Next**.

Step 6.   From the System Recovery Options menu, click **Windows Complete PC Restore**, and then follow the instructions. If you used DVDs to store the backup image, insert the last DVD of the backup set when prompted to do so. Restart the system when prompted.

NOTE   If you are restoring a 64-bit system using a 32-bit Complete PC backup or a 32-bit system using a 64-bit Complete PC backup and have more than one operating system installed, do not select an operating system. If an operating system is selected by default, clear the selection by clicking a blank area of the window, and then click Next.

Using Windows 7's Backup and Restore

All editions of Windows 7 include Backup and Restore (see Figure 15-23). The backup function can create both an image and a file backup in a single operation. By default, a backup includes a system image, files in libraries, and personal folders for all users.

During the configuration process before the initial backup, you can specify the drives to include in the system image, the files to be backed up (see Figure 15-24), and when to perform scheduled backups. To perform scheduled backups, you must use a drive formatted with the NTFS file system (or a network location with Professional, Ultimate, and Enterprise editions). When you run scheduled backups after the initial backup, the backup image is updated and changed, and new files are also backed up.

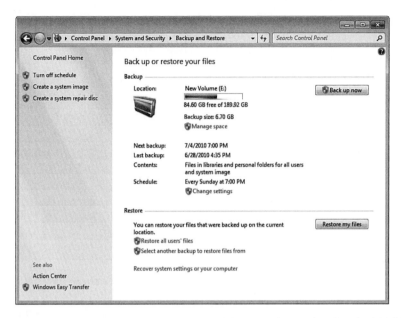

Figure 15-23 Windows 7's Backup and Restore after performing the initial file and image backup.

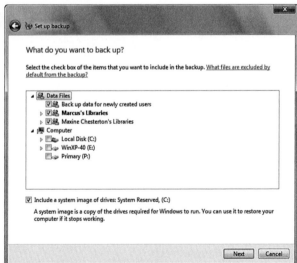

Figure 15-24 Selecting files and drives to be backed up by Window 7 Backup and Restore.

To manage the space used by the backup image and delete older backups, click the **Manage Space** link, as shown in Figure 15-23.

By default, Windows 7 backup performs an image backup of your system as well as a file backup of files in the users' libraries. It backs up an entire image of your system to the removable media of your choice, for example DVD. You can also choose to create an image backup only. To create an image backup of your PC with Windows 7's Backup and Restore, follow these steps:

Step 1.   Start the image backup process by going to **Start** > **Control Panel** > **Back Up Your Computer**.

Step 2.   Click **Create a System Image**.

Step 3.   Select a destination. Although you can use recordable or rewritable DVDs, consider using an external hard disk, especially if you have a system drive with more than 20GB in use.

Step 4.   Click **Next**.

Step 5.   Click **Start Backup**.

Step 6.   At the end of the image backup, you are prompted to create a system repair disc (a single writable CD or DVD is required). Click **Yes** to create the disc, or **No** if you already have one. If you select **No**, skip to Step 8.

Step 7.   If you answered **Yes** in Step 6, follow the prompts to make the disc and label it.

Step 8.   Click **Close** to end the backup process.

Restoring a System Image with Backup and Restore

To restore a system from the image backup, follow these steps:

Step 1.   Connect the backup drive containing your image, insert the installation disc or system repair disc, and then restart the computer. (Make sure that the DVD drive is listed first in the BIOS boot order.)

Step 2.   Press any key when prompted to boot off of the DVD or CD. If you are booting from the Windows 7 DVD, go to Step 3. If you are booting from the system repair disc, go to Step 5.

Step 3.   Choose your language settings, and click **Next**.

Step 4.   Click **Repair Your Computer**. Go to Step 6.

Step 5.   Click **Next**.

Step 6.   Select **Restore Your Computer Using a System Image That You Created Earlier**.

Step 7.   To restore the most recent system image, click **Next**.

Step 8.   Click **Next** to continue.

Step 9.   Click **Finish**.

Backup Versus File Copy Utilities

When considering whether to use a backup program or file copy to make copies of a file, consider the following:

- Backups are typically compressed; file copies performed with COPY/ XCOPY/ROBOCOPY or with drag and drop from the Windows GUI generally are not.

- Backups can span a large file onto two or more separate pieces of supported media; COPY/XCOPY/ROBOCOPY and drag and drop from the Windows GUI cannot subdivide a large file.

- Backups must be restored by the same or compatible program; files copied by COPY/XCOPY/ROBOCOPY or drag and drop can be retrieved by Windows Explorer and standard Windows programs.

- Backups created by NTBackup can be stored to tape, floppy disk, or other types of removable storage such as Zip drives (but not rewritable CD or DVD) as well as external hard disks; backups created by Windows Vista and 7's Backup can be stored on recordable or rewritable CD or DVD or external hard disks; COPY/XCOPY/ROBOCOPY can work only with drives that can be accessed through a drive letter or a UNC (Universal Naming Convention) network path. However, COPY/XCOPY/ ROBOCOPY and drag and drop from the Windows GUI can be used with CD-RW and CD-R media that have been formatted for UDF (drag-and-drop) file copying. Note that third-party backup utilities can use rewriteable CD and DVD media as well as other types of media.

If you want to retrieve the information at any time, use drag and drop from the Windows GUI or copy, xcopy.exe, or robocopy.exe (Windows 7 and Vista only) from the command prompt. However, if you need to back up large files or an entire system image, want to save space and don't mind restoring the files with a specific program, use NTBackup (XP), Backup and Restore Center (Vista), Backup and Restore (7), or a third-party backup program.

CHKDSK.EXE

Windows includes the CHKDSK.EXE program to check disk drives for errors. It can be run from the Windows GUI, as shown in Figure 15-25, or from the command line.

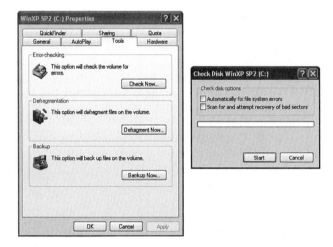

Figure 15-25   Windows C: Properties Sheet and Check Disk Window after the Check Now button has been clicked.

> **TIP**   It's no coincidence that Check Now is listed before Defragmentation and Backup in the Windows disk Tools menu. You should check the drive for errors first before you perform a defrag or backup operation.

As Figure 15-25 shows, you can also select whether to automatically fix file system errors and attempt the recovery of bad sectors with CHKDSK. If you select the option to automatically fix file system errors on the system drive, CHKDSK will be scheduled to run at the next restart. This is necessary because CHKDSK requires exclusive access to the drive. CHKDSK performs a three-phase test of the drive after the system is rebooted but before the Windows desktop appears. The results are reported after the Windows desktop appears.

You can also run CHKDSK from the command prompt. For options, type **CHKDSK /?** from the command prompt. In Windows Vista and 7, you need to run this command in elevated mode using either of these methods:

- Click **Start, All Programs, Accessories, Command Prompt**. Right-click **Command Prompt**, and select **Run as Administrator**. Click **Continue** at the permission window.

- Click **Start** and type **cmd**. Then press **Ctrl+Shift+Enter** to execute cmd.exe in elevated mode. Click **Continue** at the permission window.

NOTE By default, CHKDSK runs automatically at boot time if a drive is dirty (has errors); to adjust this behavior, run CHKDSK with appropriate options from the command prompt. Use **CHKDSK /?** to see the options you can use.

If you want to run CHKDSK on a schedule, use the Task Scheduler in Windows XP or Scheduled Tasks in Windows Vista/7.

Defrag

Over time, a hard disk becomes fragmented as temporary and data files are created and deleted. When a file can no longer be stored in a contiguous group of allocation units, Windows stores the files in as many groups of allocation units as necessary and reassembles the file when it is next accessed. The extra time needed to save and read the file reduces system performance. Windows includes a disk defragmentation tool to help regain lost read/write performance.

Defragment can be run in the following ways:

- From the Accessories menu's System Tools submenu (Disk Defragmenter)

- From a drive's properties sheet's Tools tab (Defragment Now)

- From the command line: **defrag** (type **defrag /?** for options)

Use Windows XP's Task Scheduler to set up a defragment schedule. Windows 7's Disk Defragmenter utility includes its own scheduling tool. To maintain the best possible disk performance, schedule defragmentation on a regular basis. (Weekly is recommended.)

The Windows 7/XP defragmenter features an Analyze button that determines whether defragmentation is necessary (see Figure 15-26). There is no Analyze button in Vista; however, Defrag will analyze the disk automatically before defragmenting. If you want more control over Vista's defragment feature, use Vista's command-line defrag.exe utility. For details, see http://support.microsoft.com/kb/942092.

TIP The narrower the colored stripes visible in the Estimated Disk Usage Before Defragmentation display, the more fragmented the drive is.

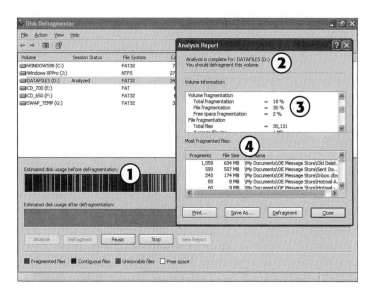

1. Visual display of drive fragmentation
2. Indicates whether defragmentation is necessary
3. Fragmentation of tested drive
4. The most fragmented files on the tested drive

Figure 15-26   Disk Defragmenter's analysis indicates this drive needs to be defragmented.

System Restore and Restore Points

Have you ever wanted a time machine so that you could go back before you installed a bad driver or troublesome piece of software? Windows 7, Vista, and XP feature a "time machine" called System Restore.

System Restore enables you to fix problems caused by a defective hardware or software installation by resetting your computer's configuration to the way it was at a specified earlier time. The configuration is stored in a file called a **restore point**. The driver or software files installed stay on the system, and so does the data you created, but Registry changes made by the hardware or software are reversed, so your system works the way it did before the installation. Restore points can be created by the user with System Restore and are also created automatically by the system before new hardware or software is installed. Restore points in Windows Vista and Windows 7 also store older versions of data files created by the Windows Shadow Copy service.

TIP   Before you make changes to your system configuration , create a restore point so that you can easily reverse the changes if they are not satisfactory.

Creating a Restore Point (7, Vista)

To create a restore point in Windows 7 or Vista, follow these steps:

Step 1.   Right-click **Computer** and select **Properties**. This opens the System Properties window.

Step 2.   Click the **System Protection** task, which opens the System Protection tab on the System properties sheet.

Step 3.   Click the **Create** button. This opens the System Protection window.

Step 4.   Type a name for the restore point, and click **Create**. The computer's current hardware and software configuration is stored as a restore point.

Creating a Restore Point in Windows XP

To create a restore point in Windows XP, follow these steps:

Step 1.   Click **Start, All Programs, Accessories, System Tools, System Restore**. This opens the System Restore window (see Figure 15-27).

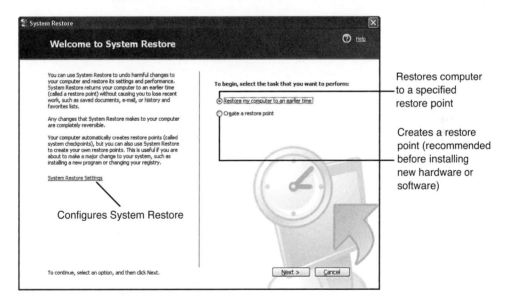

Figure 15-27   The main menu of the System Restore program in Windows XP.

Step 2.   Click **Create a Restore Point** and click **Next**.

Step 3.   Type a descriptive name for the restore point, such as **Before I installed DuzItAll Version 1.0** and click **Create**. The computer's current hardware and software configuration is stored as a restore point.

Restoring Your System to an Earlier Condition (Vista, 7)

Follow these steps to restore your system to an earlier condition in Windows 7 and Vista:

Step 1.   Open the System Protection tab again, and this time click the **System Restore** button. This opens the System Restore window.

Step 2.   Click either Recommended Restore or Choose a Different Restore Point.

Step 3.   The Recommended Restore point dialog asks you to confirm. If you are choosing a different restore point, you will need to select the appropriate one and confirm.

Step 4.   The system initiates the restore and automatically restarts.

Windows 7 and Vista also enable you to undo a system restore if it did not repair the problem.

If you cannot boot the system, you can also run System Restore from the Windows Recovery Environment.

Restoring Your System to an Earlier Condition (XP)

To restore your system to an earlier condition in Windows XP, follow these steps:

Step 1.   Navigate to the same location you did when creating a restore point.

Step 2.   Click Restore My Computer to an Earlier Time, and click Next.

Step 3.   Select a date from the calendar. (Dates that have restore points are in bold text.)

Step 4.   Select a restore point and click **Next** (see Figure 15-28).

Step 5.   Close any open programs, and save your work before you click **Next** to start the process; Windows shut downs and restarts.

Step 6.   The system initiates the restore and automatically restarts.

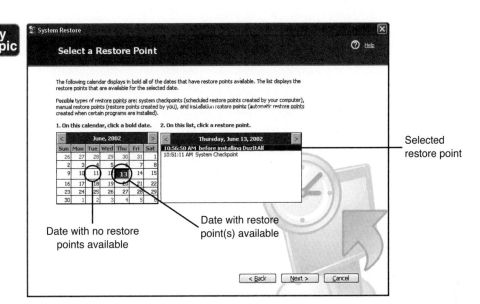

Figure 15-28   Choosing a restore point with Windows XP's System Restore.

Configuring System Restore Options

If System Restore is not available, it might be turned off. Within Windows 7 and Vista, you can enable or disable System Restore on any volume from the System Properties window/System Protection tab. Simply check or uncheck any volume that you want to enable or disable. Within Windows XP, the state of System Restore affects all drives; you can only turn the utility on and off. This is done from the System Properties window/System Restore tab. You can also change the amount of disk space it uses here.

What to Try Before Using System Restore

Be aware that System Restore is not necessarily the first step you should try when troubleshooting a computer. Simply restarting the computer has been known to "fix" all kinds of issues. It's also a good idea to try the Last Known Good Configuration. You can access this within the Windows Advanced Boot Options menu by pressing **F8** when the computer first boots. Also, if System Restore doesn't seem to work in normal mode, attempt to use it in Safe Mode. Safe Mode is another option in the Windows Advanced Boot Options menu.

Be wary of using System Restore if you're fighting a computer virus or malware infection. If you (or the system) create a restore point while the system is infected, you could re-infect the system if you revert the system to that restore point. To prevent re-infection, most antivirus vendors recommend that you disable System Restore (which eliminates stored restore points) before removing computer viruses.

Firmware Updates

Unlike other Windows best practices, Windows does not include a built-in utility for firmware updates. (Driver updates are handled by Windows Update.) To locate firmware updates for systems and devices you manage, use the following techniques.

- Enable the Intel Management Engine (found on systems that use Intel vPro technology) and use a distribution tool to roll out updates to supported systems. Lenovo, Symantec, and others support this technology.

- Create a list of systems you support, and check the vendors' websites for firmware updates.

- Firmware updates also improve the performance of DVD and Blu-ray drives, laser printers, and other devices. Be sure to list these devices, and check the vendors' websites for firmware updates.

- Before performing a firmware update, determine whether the update is necessary. Install a firmware update only if it is needed to permit necessary memory or CPU upgrades, resolve stability and reliability problems, improve media compatibility, or improve similar benefits.

Exam Preparation Tasks

Review All the Key Topics

Review the most important topics in the chapter, noted with the Key Topic icon in the outer margin of the page. Table 15-5 lists a reference of these key topics and the page numbers on which each is found.

Table 15-5 Key Topics for Chapter 15

Key Topic Element	Description	Page Number
Figure 15.1	STOP (BSOD) error	706
List	Windows Vista/7 boot errors	710
List	Windows XP boot errors	712
Figure 15-4	Using System File Checker	719
List	Backing up the Registry	724
Figure 15-11	Vista Advanced Boot options	726
Figure 15-12	Windows Device Manager	730
Figure 15-13	Device Manager tabs	731
List	Starting Recovery Console in Windows XP	735
List	Restoring a system with ASR	740
List	Starting Windows recovery environment	741
Figure 15-18	System recovery environment	743
Figure 15-20	Running NTBackup in Wizard mode	747
Figure 15-24	Selecting files and drives for backup with Windows 7 Backup and Restore	751
Figure 15-28	Choosing a restore point with Windows XP's System Restore	759

Complete the Tables and Lists from Memory

Print a copy of Appendix A, "Memory Tables" (found on the CD), or at least the section for this chapter, and complete the tables and lists from memory. Appendix B, "Memory Tables Answer Key," also on the CD, includes completed tables and lists to check your work.

Define Key Terms

Define the following key terms from this chapter, and check your answers in the glossary.

Automated System Recovery, Boot Configuration Data, Boot.ini, BSOD, clean boot, DLL, GUI, image backup, NTBackup, Recovery Console, Registry, restore point, STOP errors, System Restore, Windows Recovery Environment

Complete Hands-On Lab

Complete the hands-on labs, and then see the answers and explanations at the end of the chapter.

Lab 15-1: Check System Protection Settings

Scenario: You are a technician on a service call. The client wants to know whether the system is configured to automatically restart in the event of a BSOD and if System Restore is enabled.

Procedure: Note the version of Windows you used, the steps to arrive at the correct dialogs, and how these settings were configured.

Lab 15-2: Using Event Viewer

Scenario: You are a technician on a service call. The client reports erratic system performance over the past 24 hours.

Procedure: Note the version of Windows you used, the steps to arrive at the correct dialogs, and what you discovered.

Lab 15-3: Using Device Manager

Scenario: You are a technician on a service call. The client reports an installed device no longer works.

Procedure: Note the version of Windows in use. Identify how you arrived at the correct dialog. Note any devices that are not working. Note the error code for each device. Resolve the error. Note the procedure you followed to resolve the error.

Answer Review Questions

Answer these review questions, and then see the answers and explanations at the end of the chapter.

1. Which of the following are accurate statements about STOP errors? (Choose all that apply.)

   a. You need to stop the computer and reboot it.

   b. The computer always freezes an error message onscreen until you turn it off.

   c. The computer cannot function properly until the error is resolved.

   d. The error is displayed on a red background.

2. You are working on a computer running the Windows 7 operating system. You get a boot error. What option would you use first to recover your system to normal?

   a. NTBACKUP

   b. System Restore

   c. ASR Disk

   d. WinRE

3. You are working on a computer running the Windows XP operating system. You receive a boot error that the NTLDR is missing or corrupt. Which of the following could you use to restore the file?

   a. Copy and paste from the CD.

   b. The Recovery Console.

   c. The NTBACKUP program.

   d. Use the advanced boot options.

4. You have just set up a new user's computer that is running the Windows XP operating system. This user wants to make sure that the computer's system state can be restored if a failure occurs. What system recovery option would you want to set up?

   a. Automated System Recovery

   b. Emergency Repair Disk

   c. No option available

   d. Complete PC Backup

5. You are contacted by a customer who is running a preinstalled copy of Windows 7. The client wants to be able to boot the system if the operating system fails. Where should the client look for the option to create an emergency disc?

   a. MSCONFIG

   b. Backup and Restore

   c. System Properties

   d. Action Center

6. Which of the following gives you the ability to recover an operating system if you have a system boot failure? (Choose all that apply.)

   a. WinRE

   b. Last Known Good Configuration

   c. Recovery Console

   d. All these options are correct.

7. A client needs help with an application that cannot find some of its DLL files. The DLL files are in the correct folder for the application. Which of the following programs or procedures should be used to solve the problem?

   a. Regsvr32

   b. Last Known Good Configuration

   c. Recovery Console

   d. System Restore

8. A computer cannot boot normally but can boot in Safe Mode. Which of the following startup options will enable you to download needed updates to get the computer working properly again?

   a. Safe Mode

   b. Safe Mode with Networking

   c. Recovery Console

   d. WinRE

9. A computer has stopped working after several hardware and software changes were made to it on the previous day before you were called. What is the fastest and most reliable way to restore the computer to good working order?

   a. Restore the most recent system backup.

   b. Boot to the Last Known Good Configuration.

   c. Edit the system Registry.

   d. Use System Restore.

10. You are working as a desktop technician for your company. You have been asked to create a way to protect all users' documents in case they are deleted. Which of the following should you do?

   a. Create system restore points on all computers.

   b. Schedule backups.

   c. Save all data to a removable drive.

   d. Send all documents to a remote location.

11. You are the desktop technician for your company. After some programs that affect system startup were installed on a particular system, it is running slower. Which of the following programs can you use to view startup programs and services and to set up a clean boot environment for diagnostics?

   a. System Restore

   b. MSConfig

   c. Sysinfo32

   d. WinRE

12. Which of the following are programs that you as a technician can use to create an image backup on a computer running Windows XP?

   a. System Restore

   b. NTBACKUP

   c. Norton Ghost

   d. Acronis True Image

Answers to Hands-On Lab

Lab 15-1: Check System Protection Settings

Answer: Open the System properties sheet to check these options. Disable automatic restarts, and make sure that System Restore is enabled. Be sure to note other information requested as part of the question.

Lab 15-2: Using Event Viewer

Answer: Open the Event Viewer, and review errors over the past 24 hours and over the last week. Do you see the same programs, procedures, or devices listed repeatedly? Check with Microsoft or vendor websites for updates or known problems. Be sure to note other information requested as part of the question.

Lab 15-3: Using Device Manager

Answer: Open Device Manager and view the properties for the device. If an error code is listed, check the error code, and follow the recommendations to solve the problem. Be sure to note other information requested as part of the question.

Answers to Review Questions

1. **B, C.** A STOP (BSOD) error stops the system from working. Until the problem that causes the STOP error is resolved, the system will not work properly. Blue Screen of Death (BSOD), the unofficial name for a STOP error, comes from the fact that the error is almost always displayed in white text on a blue screen. Depending on how the system is configured, it might leave the message onscreen until you shut off the computer, or it might restart immediately.

2. **D.** WinRE is a set of tools included in Windows 7, Windows Vista, and Windows Server 2008. It takes the place of the Recovery Console used in Windows XP. Also known as System Recovery Options, WinRE's purpose is to recover Windows from errors that prevent it from booting.

3. **B.** The Windows Recovery Console is a special command-line interface designed for copying files and performing disk repairs. It is used by Windows XP.

4. **A.** The Automated System Recovery (ASR) option in NTBackup enables you to restore the system state (user accounts, hard disk configuration, network configuration, video settings, hardware configuration, software settings, and operating system boot files). However, you must reinstall programs and restore data files from a backup.

5. **B.** Open Backup and Restore in Control Panel to find the option to create an Emergency Repair Disc. This disc can be used to boot the system into the Windows Recovery Environment (WinRE). WinRE can be used to repair a system that can't boot and for other system restoration and repair options.

6. **D.** All the listed options are valid for recovering an operating system if the system will not boot. WinRE is the Windows 7 and Vista Recovery Environment, which has several options to repair boot failure. The Last Known Good Configuration is one of the Advanced Boot Options that can be accessed by pressing F8 in any version of Windows. You can install the Recovery Console from the Windows XP CD-ROM. After it's installed, it becomes part of the boot selection in the boot.ini file.

7. **A.** The Regsvr32.exe program is run from the command line to reregister "lost" DLLs that are present on the system but not listed in the Registry.

8. **B.** Safe Mode with Networking loads a limited group of features, like Safe Mode does, but it also loads networking services. Use this option when you need to connect to a network or to the Internet to download updates or for other purposes.

9. **D.** By choosing a restore point just prior to the recent hardware and software changes, you can quickly restore the system to good working order. To determine which change caused problems, install each change one at a time, and restart the system as prompted. B (Last Known Good Configuration) will not work because the system was probably rebooted at least once during the hardware and software installations.

10. **B.** You should always have some sort of backup schedule for your user documents to prevent permanent loss of their data. The backup tools in Windows XP, Vista, and 7 can all be scheduled to run at a specified time.

11. **B.** MSConfig displays startup programs and services and has an option to selectively disable some items or all items for a clean boot.

12. **C, D.** Modern image backup programs, such as recent versions of Norton Ghost and Acronis True Image, make it possible to restore an entire computer to an earlier state. They can also be used to create incremental backups, enabling the image backup program to work as both an image and file/folder backup.

This chapter covers the following subjects:

- **Network Models**—This section defines the client/server and peer-to-peer networking models and explains the differences between the two. This portion also briefly describes the four network topologies you should know for the exam and gives an introduction to LANs and WANs.

- **Internet Connectivity Technologies**—This section demonstrates how to install modems and make dial-up connections, and it defines services such as ISDN, DSL, cable, and satellite. It also talks about LAN connectivity to the Internet.

- **TCP/IP**—In this section, you learn the basics about the Transmission Control Protocol/Internet Protocol (TCP/IP) suite.

- **TCP and UDP Ports**—This section briefly covers the differences between TCP and UDP, and the port numbers you should know for the exam.

- **Cable and Connector Types**—This section defines twisted pair cable, coaxial, fiber-optic, and the different connectors each cable uses.

- **Networking Tools**—This section briefly defines the various tools used to cable a network.

- **Network Types**—Here you find out about the types of wired network technologies.

- **Wireless Networking Standards**—This section defines wireless networking standards and protocols such as 802.11a/b/g and n and Bluetooth.

- **Switches and Hubs**—This section covers the differences between a hub and a switch.

- **Building a Small Office/Home Office Network**—This section demonstrates how to install and configure network interface cards and network clients and configure TCP/IP, and it covers IPv4/IPv6 addressing concepts. It also delves into setting up and using shared resources, configuring the web browser, and functionality of multifunction network devices.

- **Using Network Command-Line Tools**—You have to know how to use ping, ipconfig, tracert, and more commands for the exam. Learn it here!

- **Network and Internet Troubleshooting**—This section describes what to do in the event of a network failure or loss of access to resources and printers.

This chapter covers the **CompTIA A+ 220-801 objectives 2.1 through 2.10** and **CompTIA A+ 220-802 objectives 1.6 and 4.5**.

CHAPTER 16

Networking

A network is a group of computers, peripherals, and software that are connected to each other and can be used together. Special software and hardware are required to make networks work.

Two or more computers connected together in the same office are considered a **LAN (local area network)**. LANs in different cities can be connected to each other by a **WAN (wide area network)**. The Internet represents the world's largest network, connecting both standalone computers and computers on LAN and WAN networks all over the world.

This chapter discusses wired and wireless networking technologies, TCP/IP, network devices, and Internet connectivity options. It also goes into depth on how to create your own small office/home office (SOHO) network and how to troubleshoot networks.

Foundation Topics

Network Models

> **220-801**
>
> **Objectives:**
> **220-801: 2.8, 2.9**

Computer networks come in all forms and are organized in a variety of ways. You should understand the organizational differences between client/server networks and peer-to-peer networks, the design differences of the various network topologies, types of networks such as LAN and WAN, and the common devices you will encounter in today's computer networks.

Client/Server Versus Peer-to-Peer

As the network features found in Windows suggest, there are two major network models:

- Client/server
- Peer-to-peer

It's important to understand the differences between them as you prepare for the exams and as you work with networks.

Client/Server

Most departmental and larger networks are **client/server** networks, such as the one illustrated in Figure 16-1. The networks are often controlled by Windows Server 2008, or Windows Server 2003.

The roles of each computer in a client/server network are distinctive, affecting both the hardware used in each computer and the software installed in each computer. A client/server environment has many advantages, including centralized administration, better sharing capabilities, scalability, and possibly increased security.

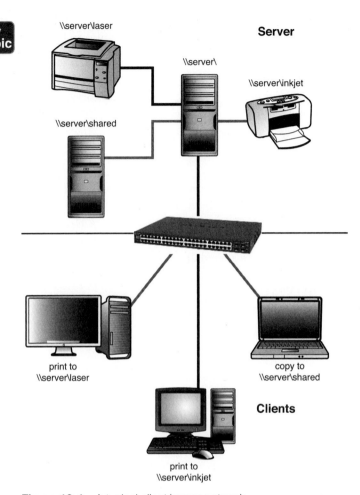

Figure 16-1 A typical client/server network.

Servers

A **server** is a computer on the network that provides other computers (called clients or workstations) access to resources, such as disk drives, folders, printers, modems, scanners, and Internet access. Because these resources can be used by different computers over the network, they are called *shared* resources.

Servers can also be used for different types of software and tasks. For example, application servers run tasks for clients, file servers store data and program files for clients, and mail servers store and distribute email to clients.

Servers typically have more powerful hardware features than PCs, such as SCSI or SATA RAID arrays or network-attached storage for hard disk storage, larger amounts of RAM, hot-swap power supplies, and server-optimized network adapters. However, because servers are not operated by an individual user, they often use low-performance integrated or PCI video and might be managed remotely rather than with a keyboard or monitor connected directly to the server.

Clients

A **client** is a computer that uses the resources on a server. Typical examples of operating systems used by client computers include Windows 7, Vista, and XP (as well as Linux and Mac OS). Depending on the network operating system in use, clients and servers can be separate machines or a client can act as a server and a server can act as a client. Clients can refer to servers either by assigning drive letters to shared folders (see the section "Setting up Shared Resources," later in this chapter) or by using a Universal Naming Convention (UNC) path name to refer to the server, as shown earlier in Figure 16-1. See "The Universal Naming Convention (UNC)" later in this chapter.

Peer-to-Peer

The network features built in to Windows allow for peer servers: Computers can share resources with each other, and machines that share resources can also be used as client workstations. As with client/server networking, resources on peer servers can be accessed via universal naming convention (as shown earlier in Figure 16-1) or by mapping drive letters and printer ports on a client to server resources.

As Figure 16-2 shows, if mapped drive letters and printer ports are used in a **peer-to-peer** network, the same resource will have a different name, depending on whether it's being accessed from the peer server (acting as a workstation) itself or over the network. In Figure 16-2, the system on the top shares its external hard disk drive with the system on the bottom, which refers to the shared hard disk drive as F:\ . The system on the bottom shares its printer with the system on the top, which has mapped the shared printer to LPT2.

The peer server loads file and printer-sharing software to make printers and drives or folders available to others. Because a peer server is also used as a workstation, it is equipped in the same way as a typical workstation or standalone PC.

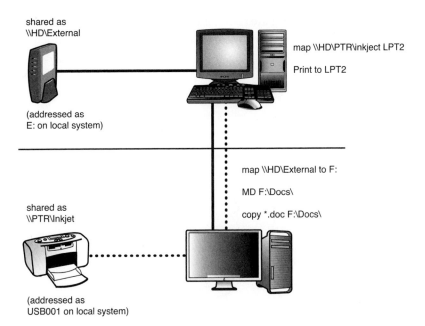

shared as
\\HD\External

map \\HD\PTR\inkject LPT2

Print to LPT2

(addressed as
E: on local system)

map \\HD\External to F:

MD F:\Docs\

shared as
\\PTR\Inkjet

copy *.doc F:\Docs\

(addressed as
USB001 on local system)

Figure 16-2   A simple two-station peer-to-peer network, in which each computer acts as a peer server to the other.

LANs and WANs

It's important to know how networks are classified. The two most common terms are local area network (LAN) and wide area network (WAN). But you should also know what a MAN and PAN are. Let's begin with LAN and WAN.

A LAN is a group of computers and other devices usually located in a small area: a house, a small office, or a single building. The computers all connect to one or more switches, and a router allows the computers access to the Internet.

A WAN is a group of one or more LANs over a large geographic area. Let's say a company had two LANs, one in New York and one in Los Angeles. Connecting the two would result in a WAN. However, to do this would require the help of a tele-communications company. This company would create the high-speed connection required for the two LANs to communicate quickly. Each LAN would require a router to connect to each other.

A smaller version of a WAN is known as a metropolitan area network (MAN), also known as a municipal area network. This is when a company has two offices in the same city and wants to make a high-speed connection between them. It's different from a WAN in that it is not a large geographic area, but it is similar to a WAN in that a telecommunications company is needed for the high-speed link.

On a slightly different note, a personal area network or PAN is a smaller computer network used for communication by smartphones, PDAs, and other small computing devices. Take this to the next level by adding wireless standards such as Bluetooth and you get a wireless PAN, or WPAN. These networks are ad-hoc, meaning that no one is the controlling device or server.

Network Topologies

The physical arrangement of computer, cables, and network devices is referred to as a network topology. There are four different types of network topologies (see Figure 16-3):

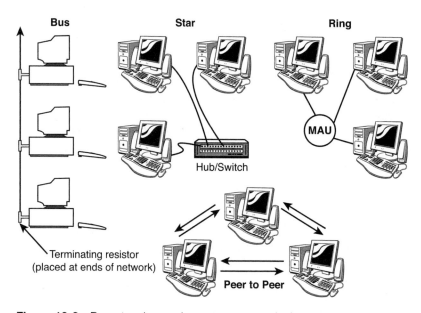

Figure 16-3 Bus, star, ring, and peer-to-peer topologies compared.

- **Bus**—Computers in a bus topology share a common cable. Connections in this topology are made largely with coaxial 10BASE2 and 10BASE5 cables.

- **Star**—Computers in a **star topology** connect to a central hub or switch (wired) or access point (wireless). This topology is used by 10BASE-T (10Mbps Ethernet), 100BASE-T (Fast Ethernet), and 1000BASE-T (Gigabit Ethernet) Ethernet networks and by Wireless Ethernet (Wi-Fi) when configured for the default infrastructure mode.

- **Ring**—Computers in a ring topology either connect as a physical ring, for example FDDI networks, or a logical ring, as is the case with Token Ring networks.

- **Peer-to-peer (Mesh)**—Computers in a peer-to-peer or mesh topology can connect directly to every other computer. This topology is used by computers with multiple network adapters, Wireless Ethernet (Wi-Fi) when configured for peer-to-peer mode, and Bluetooth.

The network goes down if a single computer on a bus-topology network fails, but the other network types stay up if one or more computers fail.

You might also hear of hybrid topologies. This is when one or more of the previous types of topologies are combined. A couple examples of this include the star-bus, when two star networks are connected by a single cable, usually between the switches of each star, and a hierarchical star, which is when multiple star networks are all connected to one master switch.

Network Devices

To allow communication between computers we need to put some other devices in place. For example, hubs, switches, and access points connect computers on the LAN. Routers and firewalls enable connectivity to other networks and protect those connection points. There are 10 types of devices you should know for the A+ exams; let's start with basic connectivity of computers on the LAN that use the Ethernet standard.

Hub

The **hub** is the original connecting devices for computers on the LAN. It creates a simple shared physical plant that all computers use to send data. It's a basic device that has multiple ports, usually in intervals of four. This device broadcasts data out to all computers. The computer that it is meant for accepts the data; the rest drop the information. Because of this broadcasting and sharing, this device allowed only two computers to communicate with each other at any given time. In the days of 10Mbps and 100Mbps networks it was common to have a hub. But for a decade, the hub has given way to the switch.

Switch

The **switch** is similar to the hub in appearance, but when it comes to sending data it works differently. Each port on the switch works independently allowing more than one concurrent session. The switch sends information to the specific computer that it was meant for, and that computer only; it does this by identifying the MAC address of each computer. In today's networks, the switch is king and is common in 100Mbps, 1000Mbps, and 10Gbps networks. Hubs and switches both work within the Ethernet standard, which is the most common networking standard used today; it was ratified by the IEEE and is documented in the 802.3 set of standards.

> **NOTE**   A **repeater** is used to carry the signals even farther than normal.

Wireless Access Point (WAP)

While hubs and switches deal with wired networks, the **WAP** deals with wireless connections. It is also based on Ethernet, but now we are talking about the IEEE 802.11 group of standards, which define wireless LANs (WLANs). Wireless access points act as a central connecting point for computers equipped with wireless network adapters; like switches, the WAP identifies each computer by its MAC address.

Bridge

The bridge is a device that can either connect two LANs together or separate them into two sections. There are wired and wireless bridges that are more commonly used today to increase the size of networks.

Network Attached Storage (NAS)

A NAS is a device that contains multiple hard drives (often hot-swappable) that connect directly to the network. Data can be stored to and retrieved from these devices by way of mapped network drives, and of course exploring the network. They offer high-speed access with no operating system to slow things down. Basic examples of NAS devices for home use might have one or two drives, and much more advanced examples for corporate use have many hard drives and incorporate RAID functionality.

Modem

Now, let's move outside the LAN and talk about Internet and wide area network connectivity. The term **modem** is a conjunction of the words *modulate* and *demodulate*. It is a device that allows a computer (or in rare cases multiple computers) access to the Internet by changing the digital signals of the computer to analog signals used by a typical land-based phone line. These are slow devices and are usually used only if no other Internet option is available. However, they might be used in server rooms as a point of remote administration as well.

Internet Appliance

The term *Internet appliance* refers to any device that enables easy connectivity to the Internet. Historically, that was usually its only function and was often implemented in the form of handheld devices. Nowadays, some people refer to tablets such as Apple's iPad as an Internet appliance, though the iPad is not limited to that singular purpose. On a side note, some technicians refer to Internet appliances as any device that allows connectivity to the Internet. We talk more about iPads and other similar Internet appliances in Chapter 10, "Mobile Devices."

Router

The **router** enables these connections with individual high-speed interconnection points. A common example would be an all-in-one device or multifunction network device that might be used in a home or small office. These devices route signals for all the computers on the LAN out to the Internet. Larger organizations use more advanced routers that can make connections to multiple various networks as well as the Internet.

Firewall

A firewall is any hardware appliance or software application that protects a computer from unwanted intrusion. In the networking world we are more concerned with hardware-based devices that protect an entire group of computers such as a LAN. When it comes to small offices and home offices, firewall functionality is usually built into the router. In larger organizations it is a separate device. The firewall stops unwanted connections from the outside and can block basic networking attacks.

VoIP Phones

Voice over Internet Protocol (VoIP) is a collection of technologies, devices, and protocols that allow voice communication over IP-based networks. VoIP phones are the Internet telephony devices that a person would use to make conversations. These devices connect directly to the Ethernet network and communicate on the network just like a computer. All of the words you speak are converted and encapsulated into packets that are sent across the network. It is a cheaper method of telephony, but there can be sound quality and latency issues if they are not configured properly.

Internet Connectivity Technologies

220-801

Objectives:
220-801: 2.7

One of the best reasons to create a network of any size is to provide access to the Internet. The many types of connectivity technologies that can be used for Internet access are discussed in the following sections.

TIP   As you review the following sections, try to determine which type of Internet connections you use at home and at your workplace.

Modems and Dial-Up Internet Connectivity

Until the late '90s, **dial-up networking (DUN)** was the most common way for home and small businesses to connect to the Internet. Dial-up connections are often referred to as *analog* connections because the device used to make the connection is an analog modem, which connects to the Internet through an ordinary telephone line. Every time you connect to the Internet with a dial-up modem, you are making a network connection.

Modem Technologies and Types

A modem sending data modulates digital computer data into analog data suitable for transmission over telephone lines to the receiving modem, which demodulates the analog data back into computer form. Modems share two characteristics with serial ports:

- Both use serial communication to send and receive information.

- Both often require adjustment of transmission speed and other options.

In fact, most external modems require a serial port to connect them to the computer; some external modems use the USB port instead.

NOTE   Properly used, the term *modem* (modulator-demodulator) refers only to a device that connects to the telephone line and performs digital-to-analog or analog-to-digital conversions. However, other types of Internet connections such as satellite, wireless, DSL, and cable Internet also use the term *modem*, although they work with purely digital data. When used by itself in this book, however, *modem* refers only to dial-up (telephone) modems.

Modems come in six types:

- **Add-on card**—Add-on card modems for desktop computers, such as the one shown in Figure 16-4, fit into a PCI expansion slot.

- **External**—External modems plug into a serial or USB port.

- **PC Card**—PCMCIA (PC Card) modems are sometimes built in a combo design that also incorporates a 10/100 Ethernet network adapter.

- **Motherboard-integrated**—Many recent desktop computers have integrated modems, as do many notebook computers.

- **Mini-PCI card**—Some older-model computers that appear to have built-in modems actually use modems that use the mini-PCI form factor and can be removed and replaced with another unit.

- **Mini-PCIe card**—Many late-model notebook computers that appear to have built-in modems actually use modems that use the mini-PCIe form factor and can be removed and replaced with another unit.

To learn more about expansion slots, see "Expansion Slots" in Chapter 2, "Motherboards and Processors." To learn more about mini-PCI cards, see "Mini-PCI" in Chapter 9, "Laptop and Notebook Computers."

Although some high-end add-on card and PC Card modems have a hardware universal asynchronous receiver transmitter (UART) or UART-equivalent chip, most recent models use a programmable digital signal processor (DSP) instead. Modems with a DSP perform similarly to UART-based modems but can easily be reprogrammed with firmware and driver updates as needed. Low-cost add-on card and PC Card modems often use host signal processing (HSP) instead of a UART or DSP. HSP modems are sometimes referred to as Winmodems or soft modems because Windows and the computer's processor perform the modulation, slowing down performance. HSP modems might not work with some older versions of Windows or non-Windows operating systems.

External modems, such as the one shown in Figure 16-5, must be connected to a serial or USB port. Serial port versions require an external power source (USB modems are usually powered by the USB port or hub), but the portability and front-panel status lights of either type of external modem make them better for business use in the minds of many users.

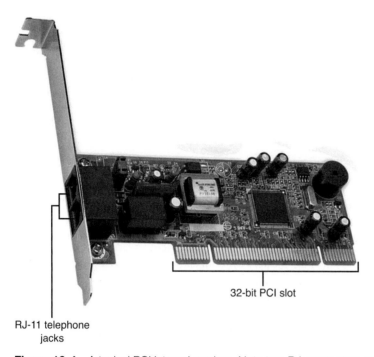

32-bit PCI slot

RJ-11 telephone
jacks

Figure 16-4   A typical PCI internal modem. Note two RJ connectors on the rear of the modem:
They enable you to plug a phone into the modem, so you can use the modem or your telephone.

Key
Topic

1. Status/activity lights
2. RJ-11 connector for
   telephone pass-through
3. RJ-11 telephone cable
4. Power cable
5. 9-pin serial cable
6. Reset switch

Figure 16-5   A typical external modem that connects to a serial port. Note the reset switch,
which enables the user to reset the modem without turning off the computer.

A typical PC Card modem is shown in Figure 16-6. The modem pictured here uses a dongle, a proprietary cable that attaches to one end of the PC Card to enable the modem to plug into a standard telephone jack or telephone line. If the dongle is lost or damaged, the modem can't be used until the dongle is replaced. Some PC Card modems use an integrated or pop-out RJ-11 jack instead of a dongle (it's one less thing to lose or break as you travel). To learn more about PC Card modems, see "PCMCIA (PC Card, CardBus)" in Chapter 9.

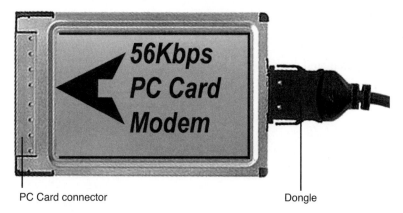

PC Card connector   Dongle

Figure 16-6   A typical PC Card modem that uses a dongle (right). Many recent PC Card modems feature integrated or pop-out RJ-11 jacks instead of a dongle.

There have been various standards for analog modems used to make dial-up connections. Before the advent of so-called "56K" standards, the fastest dial-up connection possible was 33.6Kbps. Virtually all modems in recent systems or available for purchase support either the ITU v.90 or v.92 standards.

NOTE   Although v.90 and v.92 modems are all designed to perform downloading at up to 56Kbps, FCC (Federal Communications Commission) regulations limit actual download speed to 53Kbps. Speeds greater than 33.6Kbps apply only to downloads from Internet service providers (ISPs) and their special modems. If you make a direct connection between two PCs, the fastest speed you can have in either direction is just 33.6Kbps (if both modems can run at least that fast).

Analog Modem Installation

The method used for physical installation of the modem varies with the modem type. To install a PCI modem, follow these steps:

Step 1.   Take ESD precautions. (See Chapter 18, "Operational Procedures and Communication Methods," for details.)

Step 2.   Open the system and locate an empty slot of the appropriate type.

Step 3.   Remove the screw holding the slot cover in place.

Step 4.   Remove the slot cover.

Step 5.   Install the modem into the slot and fasten it into place with the screw previously used to secure the slot cover.

Step 6.   Connect an RJ-11 telephone cable running from the telephone jack in the wall to the line connection.

Step 7.   If desired, plug a telephone into the Telco jack.

Step 8.   Close the system and restart it.

Step 9.   Install drivers as required.

CAUTION   You can drive yourself crazy trying to make a connection with your modem if you plug the RJ-11 telephone cord into the wrong jack. There are actually three ways to make this mistake:

- Plugging in the RJ-11 cord to the phone jack instead of the line or telco jack on the modem

- Plugging in the RJ-11 cord to the slightly larger RJ-45 jack used for 10/100/1000 Ethernet networking

- Plugging in the RJ-11 cord to a HomePNA network card (which also has two RJ-11 jacks) instead of the modem

If you use the now-rare (and obsolete) HomePNA network, check the network documentation for the correct way to connect your network card and your modem to the telephone line.

To install a PC Card modem, use these steps:

Step 1.   Insert the PC Card modem into an empty PC Card slot of the appropriate type (Type II or Type III; see Chapter 9 for details).

Step 2.   After the operating system indicates the modem has been detected, attach the dongle (if appropriate).

Step 3.   If the dongle has an RJ-11 plug, connect it to the telephone wall jack.

Step 4.   For modems with a pop-out RJ-11 jack, release the jack.

Step 5.   Connect an RJ-11 telephone cable between the RJ-11 connector on the PC Card or dongle and the wall jack.

Step 6.   Install drivers as required.

To install an external modem, follow these steps:

Step 1.   Connect the modem to a USB or serial port as appropriate.

Step 2.   Connect the modem to AC power and turn it on (if necessary).

Step 3.   If the modem is not detected automatically, use the operating system's modem dialog in the Control Panel to detect the modem and install its drivers.

See Chapter 9 for more information about mini-PCI modems.

Dial-Up Internet Service Providers

An Internet service provider (ISP) provides a connection between the user with an analog (dial-up) modem (or other connectivity device) and the Internet. ISPs that provide dial-up access have several modems and dial-up numbers that their customers can access. The ISP's modems are connected to the Internet via high-speed, high-capacity connections.

An ISP can be selected from many different sources:

- National companies
- Local or regional providers
- Specialized providers such as those that provide filtered, family-friendly access

Choose an ISP based on its rates, reliability, or special services (such as content filtration or proprietary content) that are appropriate to your needs.

Creating a Dial-Up Connection

Windows Vista and Windows 7 create dial-up networking (DUN) connections within the Network and Sharing Center window. Windows XP creates DUN connections within the same window that stores other types of network connections.

NOTE If an ISP provides customized setup software, the software usually creates an icon for you in the folder used for DUN connections. This icon contains the settings needed to make your connection.

Requirements for a Dial-Up Internet Connection

All ISPs must provide the following information to enable you to connect to the Internet:

- Client software, including the preferred web browser, dial-up information, and TCP/IP configuration information

- Dial-up access telephone numbers

- Modem types supported (33.6Kbps, 56Kbps, v.90, v.92)

- The username and initial password (which should be changed immediately after first login)

Even if the client software provided by the ISP configures the connection for you, you should record the following information in case it is needed to manually configure or reconfigure the connection:

- **The dial-up access telephone number**—This might be different for different modem speeds. Users with a 56Kbps modem should know both the standard (33.6Kbps) and high-speed access numbers if different numbers are used.

- **The username and password**—Windows often saves this during the setup of a DUN connection, but it should be recorded in case the system must be reconfigured or replaced.

- **The TCP/IP configuration**—This is set individually for each dial-up connection through its properties sheet.

To determine this information, right-click the icon for the connection and select **Properties**.

For more information, see "TCP/IPv4 Configuration" later in this chapter.

ISDN Internet Connectivity

ISDN (Integrated Services Digital Network) was originally developed to provide an all-digital method for connecting multiple telephone and telephony-type devices, such as fax machines, to a single telephone line and to provide a faster connection for teleconferencing for remote computer users. A home/small office-based connection can also provide an all-digital Internet connection at speeds up to 128Kbps. Line quality is a critical factor in determining whether any particular location can use ISDN service. If an all-digital connection cannot be established between the customer's location and the telephone company's central switch, ISDN service is not available or a new telephone line must be run (at extra cost to you!).

NOTE   The telephone network was originally designed to support analog signaling only, which is why an analog (dial-up) modem that sends data to other computers converts digital signals to analog for transmission through the telephone network. The receiving analog modem converts analog data back to digital data.

ISDN Hardware

To make an ISDN connection, your PC (and any other devices that share the ISDN connection) needs a device called an ISDN terminal adapter (TA). A TA resembles a conventional analog modem. Internal models plug into the same PCI, ISA, and PC Card slots used by analog modems, and external models use USB or serial ports. External TAs often have two or more RJ-11 ports for telephony devices, an RJ-45 port for the connection to the ISDN line, and a serial or USB port for connection to the computer. For more information about these ports, see Chapter 6, "I/O and Input Ports and Devices."

Setting Up an ISDN Connection

ISDN connections (where available) are provided through the local telephone company. There are two types of ISDN connections:

- Primary Rate Interface (PRI)
- Basic Rate Interface (BRI)

A PRI connection provides 1.536Mbps of bandwidth, whereas a BRI interface provides 64Kbps (single-channel) or 128Kbps (dual-channel) of bandwidth. BRI is sold to small businesses and home offices; PRI is sold to large organizations. Both types of connections enable you to use the Internet and talk or fax data through the phone line at the same time.

A direct individual ISDN connection is configured through the network features of Windows with the same types of settings used for an analog modem connection. Configuring a network-based ISDN connection is done through the network adapter's TCP/IP properties window. For more information, see "TCP/IPv4 Configuration," later in this chapter.

TIP   Most telephone companies have largely phased out ISDN in favor of DSL, which is much faster and less expensive for Internet connections.

Broadband Internet Services (DSL, Cable, Satellite)

Broadband Internet service is a blanket term that refers to the following Internet access methods: digital subscriber line (DSL), cable, and satellite. All these methods provide bandwidth in excess of 300Kbps, and current implementations are two-way services, enabling you to use your telephone while accessing the Internet.

> **NOTE** Other types of broadband Internet service, including direct wireless (using microwave transceivers) and power line, are not part of the A+ Certification exam domains, but you might encounter them in some areas.

DSL

DSL can piggyback on the same telephone line used by your telephone and fax machine, or it can be installed as a distinctly separate line. Either way, DSL requires a high-quality telephone line that can carry a digital signal. For home use, DSL is designed strictly for Internet access. But for business use, DSL can be used for additional services and can be used in site-to-site scenarios between organizations.

When it comes to connection speed, DSL leaves BRI ISDN in the dust. There are two major types of DSL: **ADSL (Asynchronous DSL)** and **SDSL (Synchronous DSL)**. Their features are compared in Table 16-1.

Table 16-1 Common DSL Services Compared

Service Type	Supports Existing Telephone Line	User Installation Option	Typical Downstream Speeds	Typical Upstream Speeds	Typically Marketed To
ADSL	Yes	Yes	384Kbps to 24Mbps	128Kbps to 3.3Mbps	Home, small business
SDSL	Not typical	No	384Kbps to 2.0Mbps	Same as downstream speed	Larger business and corporate

> **NOTE** *Downstream* refers to download speed; *upstream* refers to upload speed. SDSL gets its name from providing the same speed in both directions; ADSL is always faster downstream than upstream.

A device known as a *DSL modem* is used to connect your computer to DSL service. DSL modems connect to your PC through the RJ-45 (Ethernet) port or the USB port. The rear of a typical DSL modem that uses an Ethernet (RJ-45) connection is shown in Figure 16-7.

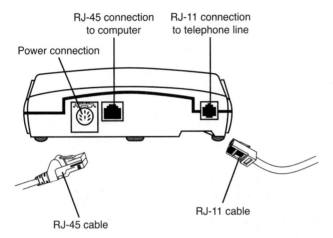

Figure 16-7   The rear of a typical DSL modem with a power port (top left), RJ-45 data port to the PC (top center), and an RJ-11 telephone line port (top right). The RJ-45 cable is shown at bottom left, and the RJ-11 cable is shown at bottom right.

As Figure 16-7 indicates, DSL uses the same telephone lines as ordinary telephone equipment. However, your telephone can interfere with the DSL connection. To prevent this, in some cases a separate DSL line is run from the outside service box to the computer with the DSL modem. However, if your DSL provider supports the self-installation option, small devices called *microfilters* are installed between telephones, answering machines, fax machines, and other devices on the same circuit with the DSL modem. Microfilters can be built in to special wall plates but are more often external devices that plug into existing phone jacks, as shown in Figure 16-8.

Some DSL connections are configured as an always-on connection similar to a network connection to the Internet. However, many vendors now configure the DSL connection as a PPPoE (point-to-point protocol over Ethernet) connection instead. A PPPoE connection requires the user to make a connection with a username and password.

NOTE   Windows 7, Vista, and XP have native support through their Network Connection wizards. With older versions of Windows, the vendor must provide setup software.

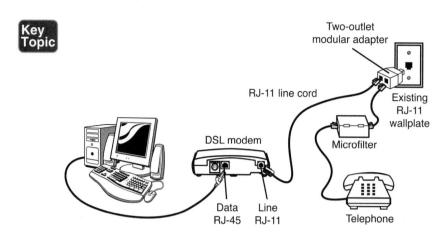

Figure 16-8   A typical self-installed DSL setup. The DSL vendor supplies the DSL modem (center) and microfilters that attach between telephones and other devices and the wall outlet (right).

Cable Internet

Cable Internet service piggybacks on the same coaxial cable that brings cable TV into a home or business. A few early cable ISPs used internal cable modems, which supported one-way traffic. (The cable was used for downloads, and a conventional telephone line was used for uploads and page requests.) Virtually all cable Internet service today is two-way and is built upon the fiber-optic network used for digital cable and music services provided by most cable TV vendors.

Cable Internet can reach download speeds anywhere from 2Mbps up to 50Mbps or faster. Upload speeds are typically about 10% of upload speed, but vary by vendor.

NOTE   You can have cable Internet service without having cable TV.

Some cable TV providers use the same cable that carries cable TV for cable Internet service, while others run a separate cable to the location. When the same cable is used for both cable TV and cable Internet service, a splitter is used to provide connections for cable TV and Internet. The splitter prevents cable TV and cable Internet signals from interfering with each other. One coaxial cable from the splitter goes to the TV or set-top box as usual; the other one goes into a device known as a *cable modem*. Almost all cable modems are external devices that plug into a computer's 10/100/1000 Ethernet (RJ-45) or USB port. Figure 16-9 shows a typical cable Internet connection.

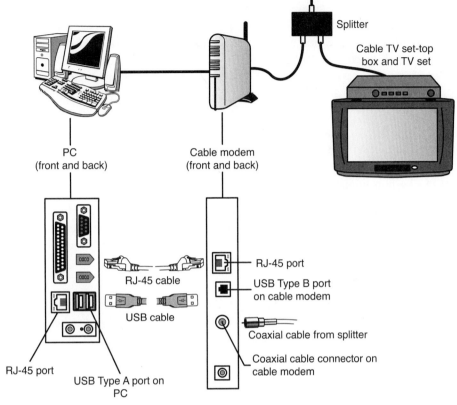

Figure 16-9   A typical cable modem and cable TV installation. The cable modem can be connected to the computer through an RJ-45 cable or a USB cable.

A cable Internet connection can be configured through the standard Network properties sheet in Windows or with customized setup software, depending on the ISP.

Satellite

Satellite Internet providers, such as HughesNet (previously known as DirecWAY, and before that as DirecPC), StarBand, and WildBlue use dish antennas similar to satellite TV antennas to receive and transmit signals between geosynchronous satellites and computers. In some cases, you might be able to use a dual-purpose satellite dish to pick up both satellite Internet and satellite TV service.

NOTE   Geosynchronous satellites orbit the Earth's equator at a distance of more than 22,000 miles (approximately 35,000 kilometers). Because of their orbits and altitudes, they remain in the same location in the sky at all times. In the Northern Hemisphere, you need an unobstructed view of the southern sky to make a connection. In the Southern Hemisphere, you need an unobstructed view of the northern sky to make a connection.

Satellite Internet services use external devices often called *satellite modems* to connect the computer to the satellite dish. They connect to the USB or Ethernet (RJ-45) port in a fashion similar to that used by DSL or cable modems.

The FCC requires professional installation for satellite Internet service because an incorrectly aligned satellite dish with uplink capabilities could cause a service outage on the satellite it's aimed at. Setup software supplied by the satellite vendor is used to complete the process.

NOTE   Satellite connections can also be made between buildings to allow for the high-speed exchange of data. In this scenario, a satellite dish would need to be installed on each building, and they would need to be in direct line of sight of each other. Internet access can also be offered in this manner.

Fiber-Optic

Instead of using a copper connection to the home or business the way dial-up, DSL, or cable Internet do, some companies offer fiber-optic connections direct to the home. Fiber-optic cables can run at much higher data transfer rates than copper-based cables. One example where this is evident is Verizon FIOS, which can be used to bundle various services but especially offers much faster download speeds, from 3 Mbps to 150 Mbps. Upload speeds are typically less, as they are in most Internet services, generally from 1Mbps to 35Mbps.

Cellular

It's also possible to connect to the Internet directly through your cellular phone or smartphone even if no Wi-Fi access point is available. This is usually done through the Global System for Mobile Communications (GSM). You might have heard of the terms 2G, 3G, and currently 4G. These refer to the different generations (and speeds) of GSM. Most cellular devices are equipped with a 3G antenna, which can achieve a maximum theoretical download speed of 56Mbps, though this is rarely accomplished in reality due to signal strength, location, and so on. 4G technology has peak requirements of 100Mbps. As of the writing of this book, not all cellular devices are equipped with a 4G antenna, and 4G coverage is limited mostly to urban areas.

WiMAX

The Worldwide Interoperability for Microwave Access (WiMAX) is a wireless technology that offers high-speed connections within the 4G range, but over much larger distances than a standard Wi-Fi access point could, on average 50 kilometers. So, if your organization is within 50km of an urban area, it might be able to connect its LAN to the Internet at high-speed in a completely wireless fashion. There are individual WiMAX modems for laptops and PCs and gateway devices for entire LANs. For an optimal connection, these gateways (or routers) will usually be placed on a window sill facing where the signal is coming from.

LANs and Internet Connectivity

A LAN is an ideal way to provide Internet access to two or more users. However, a LAN by itself cannot connect to the Internet. Two additional components must also be used with a LAN to enable it to connect to the Internet:

- **An Internet access device**—This could be a dial-up modem, but more often a broadband connection such as DSL, cable, or satellite is used.

- **A router**—This device connects client PCs on the network to the Internet through the Internet access device. To the Internet, only one client is making a connection, but the router internally tracks which PC has made the request and transmits the data for that PC back to that PC, enabling multiple PCs to access the Internet through the network.

NOTE   As an alternative to a router, some small networks use a gateway, which is a PC configured to share its Internet connection with others on the network. Windows 2000 and later versions support this feature, known as Internet Connection Sharing. Note that wireless access devices known as gateways actually resemble routers.

TCP/IP

> **220-801**
>
> **Objective:**
> **220-801: 2.3**

TCP/IP is short for Transport Control Protocol/Internet Protocol. It is a multi-platform protocol used for both Internet access and local area networks. Though there are other networking protocols, TCP/IP is by far the most common and is used by all major operating systems including Windows 7/Vista/XP and Linux.

TCP/IP actually is a suite of protocols used on the Internet for routing and transporting information. The following sections discuss some of the application protocols that are part of the TCP/IP suite, as well as some of the services and technologies that relate to TCP/IP.

HTTP/HTTPS

Hypertext Transfer Protocol (HTTP) is the protocol used by web browsers, such as Internet Explorer, Firefox, and Chrome, to access websites and content. Normal (unsecured) sites use the prefix http:// when accessed in a web browser. Sites (**HTTPS**) that are secured with various encryption schemes are identified with the prefix https://.

> **NOTE** Most browsers connecting with a secured site will also display a closed padlock symbol onscreen.

SSL

Secure Socket Layers (SSL) is an encryption technology used by secured (https://) websites. To access a secured website, the web browser must support the same encryption level used by the secured website (normally 128-bit encryption) and the same version(s) of SSL used by the website (normally SSL version 2.0 or 3.0).

TLS

Transport Layer Security (TLS) is the successor to SSL. SSL3 was somewhat of a prototype to TLS and was not fully standardized. TLS was ratified by the IETF in 1999. However, many people and companies might still refer to it as SSL.

HTML

Hypertext Markup Language (HTML) is the language used by web pages. An HTML page is a specially formatted text page that uses tags (commands contained in angle brackets) to change text appearance, insert links to other pages, display pictures, incorporate scripting languages, and provide other features. Web browsers, such as Microsoft Internet Explorer and Firefox, are used to view and interpret the contents of web pages, which have typical file extensions such as .HTM, .HTML, .ASP (Active Server pages generated by a database), and others.

You can see the HTML code used to create the web page in a browser by using the View Source or View Page Source menu option provided by your browser. Figure 16-10 compares what you see in a typical web page (top window) with the HTML tags used to set text features and the underlined hyperlink (bottom window). The figure uses a different text size and shading to distinguish tags from text, and so do most commercial web-editing programs used to make web pages.

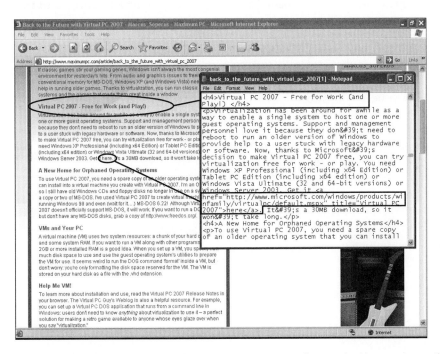

Figure 16-10   A section of an HTML document as seen by a typical browser uses the HTML tags shown in Notepad for paragraphs (<P>) titles (<H4>, </H4>), and hyperlinks (<A HREF>, </A>).

Tags such as <P> are used by themselves, and other tags are used in pairs. For example, <A HREF...> is used to indicate the start of a hyperlink (which will display another page or site in your browser window), and </A> indicates the end of a hyperlink.

> **NOTE** The World Wide Web Consortium (http://www.w3c.org) sets the official standards for HTML tags and syntax, but major browser vendors, such as Microsoft and Netscape, often modify or extend official HTML standards with their own tags and syntax.

FTP

File Transfer Protocol (FTP) is a protocol used by both web browsers and specialized FTP programs to access dedicated file transfer servers for file downloads and uploads. When you access an FTP site, the site uses the prefix ftp://.

Windows contains ftp.exe, a command-line FTP program; type **FTP**, press **Enter**, and then type **?** at the FTP prompt to see the commands you can use.

FTP sites with downloads available to any user support anonymous FTP; if any credentials are required, it's typically the user's email address as a password (the username is preset to anonymous). Some FTP sites require the user to log in with a specified username and password.

> **TIP** Although you can use Windows' built-in FTP client for file uploads and downloads with both secured and unsecured FTP sites, you should consider using third-party FTP products such as FileZilla (http://filezilla-project.org/) or WS_FTP Pro (http://www.ipswitchft.com/Products/WS_Ftp_Pro/). These programs enable you to create a customized setup for each FTP site you visit and will store passwords, server types, and other necessary information. They also enable faster downloads than typical web browsers running in ftp:// mode.

Telnet

Telnet enables a user to make a text-based connection to a remote computer or networking device and use it as if he were a regular user sitting in front of it, rather than simply downloading pages and files as he would with an http:// or ftp:// connection.

Windows contains a command-line Telnet program. To open a connection to a remote computer, enter a command such as

```
telnet a.computer.com
```

To use other commands, open a command prompt, type **telnet** and press the **Enter** key. To see other commands, type **?/help**.

SSH

Secure Shell (SSH) allows data to be exchanged between computers on a secured channel. This protocol offers a more secure replacement to FTP and Telnet. The Secure Shell server housing the data you want to access would have port 22 open. Several other protocols use SSH as a way of making a secure connection. One of these is Secure FTP (SFTP). Regular FTP can be insecure. SFTP combats this by providing file access over a reliable data stream, generated and protected by SSH.

DNS

The **domain name system (DNS)** is the name for the network of servers on the Internet that translate **domain names,** such as www.informit.com, and individual host names into their matching IP addresses. If you manually configure an IP address, you typically provide the IP addresses of one or more DNS servers as part of the configuration process.

If you want a unique domain name for either a website or email, the ISP that you use to provide your email or web hosting service often provides a registration wizard you can use to access the domain name registration services provided by various companies such as VeriSign.

A domain name has three major sections, from the end of the name to the start:

- The top-level domain (.com, .org, .net, and so on).

- The name of the site.

- The server type; www indicates a web server, ftp indicates an FTP server, mail indicates a mail server, and search indicates a search server.

For example, Microsoft.com is located in the .com domain, typically used for commercial companies. Microsoft is the domain name. The Microsoft.com domain has the following servers:

- www.microsoft.com hosts web content, such as product information.

- support.microsoft.com hosts the Microsoft.com support website, where users can search for Knowledge Base (KB) and other support documents.

- ftp.microsoft.com hosts the File Transfer Protocol server of Microsoft.com; this portion of the Microsoft.com domain can be accessed by either a web browser or an FTP client.

Many companies have only WWW servers, or only WWW and FTP servers.

NOTE   Some small websites use a folder under a domain hosted by an ISP: www.ispname.com/~smallsitename.

DHCP

The **Dynamic Host Configuration Protocol (DHCP)** is used to automatically assign IP addresses to hosts. These hosts could be computers, printers, servers, routers, and so on. In most SOHO networks a router uses DHCP to assign IP addresses to the client computers. However, your ISP also uses DHCP to assign an IP address to you; usually your router gets this. The DHCP service makes life easier for the network administrator by automatically assigning IP addresses, subnet masks, gateway addresses, DNS servers, and so on. If you get your address from a DHCP server, you are getting your address assigned dynamically, and it could change periodically. However, some computers require a static address, one that is assigned by the network administrator manually. It is better in many situations for servers and printers to use static addresses, so you know exactly what the address is, and so it won't change.

Email

All email systems provide transfer of text messages, and most have provisions for file attachments, enabling you to send documents, graphics, video clips, and other types of computer data files to receivers for work or play. Email clients are included as part of web browsers and are also available as limited-feature freely downloadable or more-powerful commercially purchased standalone email clients. Some email clients, such as Microsoft Outlook, are part of application suites (such as Microsoft Office) and also feature productivity and time-management features.

TIP   Users who travel away from corporate networks might prefer to use a web-based email account, such as Hotmail or Gmail, or use Outlook Web Access to get access to email from any system with a properly configured web browser.

To configure any email client, you need

- The name of the email server for incoming mail

- The name of the email server for outgoing mail

- The username and password for the email user

- The type of email server (POP3, IMAP, or HTTP)

Some email clients and servers might require additional configuration options.

To access web-based email, you need

- The website for the email service

- The username and password

The following sections describe three email protocols: SMTP, POP3, and IMAP.

SMTP

The **Simple Mail Transfer Protocol (SMTP)** is used to send email from a client system to an email server, which also uses SMTP to relay the message to the receiving email server.

POP

The Post Office Protocol (POP) is the more popular of two leading methods for receiving email (IMAP is the other). In an email system based on POP, email is downloaded from the mail server to folders on a local system. POP is not a suitable email protocol for users who frequently switch between computers because email might wind up on multiple computers. The **POP3** version is the latest current standard. Users that utilize POP3 servers to retrieve email typically use SMTP to send messages.

> **TIP**   For users who must use POP3-based email and use multiple computers, a remote access solution, such as Windows Remote Desktop or a service such as GoToMyPC, is recommended. A remote access solution enables a user to remotely access the system that connects to the POP3 mail server so she can download and read email messages, no matter where she is working.

IMAP

The **Internet Message Access Protocol (IMAP)** is an email protocol that enables messages to remain on the email server so they can be retrieved from any location. IMAP also supports folders, so users can organize their messages as desired.

To configure an IMAP-based email account, you must select IMAP as the email server type and specify the name of the server, your username and password, and whether the server uses SSL.

Remote Desktop

To facilitate connections to remote computers and allowing full remote control, Microsoft uses the Remote Desktop program, which is based off the Remote Desktop Protocol (RDP). This works in three ways. First, users can be given limited access to a remote computer's applications such as Word or Excel. Second, administrators can be given full access to a computer so that they can troubleshoot problems from another location. Third, another part of the program known as Remote Assistance allows users to invite a technician to come and view their desktop in the hopes that the technician can fix any encountered problems. These invitations can be made via email or by Windows Messenger. The RDP port, 3389, is also used by Microsoft Terminal Services, which is the server-based companion of Remote Desktop.

SNMP

Simple Network Management Protocol (SNMP) is used as the standard for managing and monitoring devices on your network. It manages routers, switches, and computers and is often incorporated in software known as a network management system or NMS. The NMS is the main software that controls everything SNMP-based; it is installed on a computer known as a manager. The devices to be monitored are known as managed devices. The NMS installs a small piece of software known as an agent that allows the NMS to monitor those managed devices.

SMB

Server Message Block (SMB) provides access to shared items such as files and printers. They are actual packets that authenticate remote computers through what are known as *interprocess communication mechanisms*.

LDAP

Lightweight Directory Access Protocol (LDAP) is used to access and maintain distributed directories of information such as the kind involved with Microsoft domains. Microsoft refers to this as *directory services*.

TCP and UDP Ports

220-801

Objective:
220-801: 2.4

For two computers to communicate, they must both use the same protocol. For an application to send or receive data, it must use a particular protocol designed for that application and open up a port on the network adapter to make a connection to another computer. For example, let's say you want to visit www.google.com. You would open a browser and type http://www.google.com. The protocol being used is HTTP, short for Hypertext Transfer Protocol, which makes the connection to the web server: google.com. The HTTP protocol would select an unused port on your computer (known as an outbound port) to send and receive data to and from google.com. On the other end, google.com's web server will have a specific port open at all times ready to accept sessions. In most cases the web server's port is 80, which corresponds to the HTTP protocol. This is known as an *inbound port*.

Transmission Control Protocol (TCP) sessions are known as connection-oriented sessions. This means that every packet that is sent is checked for delivery. If the receiving computer doesn't receive a packet, it cannot assemble the message and will ask the sending computer to transmit the packet again. No one packet is left behind.

User Datagram Protocol (UDP) sessions are known as *connectionless sessions*. UDP is used in streaming media sessions. In these cases if a packet is dropped, it is not asked for again. Let's say you were listening to some streaming music and you heard a break in the song or a blip of some kind. That indicates some missing packets, but you wouldn't want those packets back because by the time you get them you would be listening to a totally different part of the music stream.

It's expected to lose packets in UDP streams, but not when making TCP connections. Both TCP and UDP utilize ports to make connections. Remember, it's the inbound ports that you are concerned with. For example, an FTP server that stores files for customers needs to have inbound port 21 open by default. Table 16-2 displays some common protocols and their default corresponding inbound ports.

Table 16-2   Common Protocols and Their Ports

Protocol	Port Used
FTP	21
SSH	22
Telnet	23
SMTP	25
DNS	53
HTTP	80
POP3	110
IMAP	143
HTTPS	443
RDP	3389

TIP   Know these protocols and their corresponding port numbers for the exam.

Cable and Connector Types

220-801

Objectives:
220-801: 2.1, 2.2

There are four major types of network cables:

- Unshielded twisted pair (UTP)

- Shielded twisted pair (STP)

- Fiber-optic

- Coaxial

Network cards are designed to interface with one or more types of network cables, each of which is discussed in the following sections.

NOTE   Serial (RS-232) null modem and parallel (LPT) crossover cables can be used with direct parallel or direct serial connections (also known as direct cable connection), which are special types of two-station networking included in Windows that use standard network protocols but do not use network cards.

Infrared (IR) ports built in to many notebook computers can also be used with direct serial connection.

UTP and STP Cabling

UTP cabling is the most common of the major cabling types. The name refers to its physical construction: four twisted pairs of wire surrounded by a flexible jacket.

UTP cable comes in various grades, of which Category 5e (Cat5e) and Category 6 are the most common of the standard cabling grades. These are suitable for use with both standard 10BASE-T and Fast Ethernet networking and can also be used for Gigabit Ethernet networks if it passes compliance testing.

STP cabling was originally available only in Cat4, which was used by the now largely outdated IBM Token-Ring Networks. STP uses the same RJ-45 connector as

UTP but includes a metal shield for electrical insulation between the wire pairs and the outer jacket. It's stiffer and more durable, but also more expensive and harder to loop through tight spaces than UTP. Type 1 STP cable used by older token-ring adapters has a 9-pin connector. STP cabling is also available in Cat5, Cat5e, and Cat6 for use with Ethernet networks. It is used where electromagnetic interference (EMI) prevents the use of UTP cable.

Figure 16-11 compares the construction of STP and UTP cables.

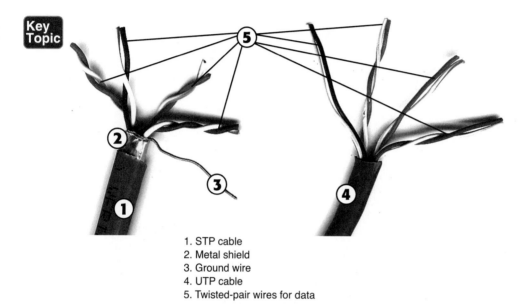

1. STP cable
2. Metal shield
3. Ground wire
4. UTP cable
5. Twisted-pair wires for data

Figure 16-11   An STP cable (left) includes a metal shield and ground wire for protection against interference, while a UTP cable (right) does not.

Table 16-3 lists the various types of UTP and STP cabling in use and what they're best suited for.

Table 16-3   Categories and Uses for UTP and STP Cabling

Category	Network Type(s) Supported	Supported Speeds	Cable Type, Notes
1	Telephone, DSL, HomePNA	Up to 100Mbps (HomePNA)	UTP; one wire pair
2	LocalTalk	Up to 4Mbps	UTP; obsolete; one wire pair
3	10BASE-T Ethernet	Up to 10Mbps	UTP; obsolete; Replace with Cat5, Cat5e, or Cat6; four wire pairs
4	Token ring	Up to 16Mbps	Shielded twisted pair (STP); one wire pair

Category	Network Type(s) Supported	Supported Speeds	Cable Type, Notes
5	10BASE-T, 100BASE-T,	Up to 100Mbps	UTP, STP; four wire pairs
5e	10BASE-T, 100BASE-T, 1000BASE-T	Up to 1000Mbps	Enhanced version of Cat5; available in UTP, STP; four wire pairs
6	10BASE-T, 100BASE-T, 1000BASE-T	Up to 1000Mbps	Handles higher frequencies than Cat5/5e; available in UTP, STP
7	10BASE-T, 100BASE-T, 1000BASE-T	Up to 1000Mbps	Uses 12-connector GG45 connector (backward-compatible with RJ-45); available in UTP, STP

TIP Memorize Category 3 through 6 for the exam.

UTP and STP cable can be purchased in prebuilt assemblies or can be built from bulk cable and connectors.

NOTE The de facto standard for wire pairs in both UTP and STP cables is the EIA-568B standard. You can create a crossover cable by building one end to the EIA-568B standard and the other end to the older EIA-568A standard. See http://www.incentre.net/content/view/75/2/ for a color-coded diagram.

Figure 16-12 compares Ethernet cards using UTP (or STP), thin coaxial, and thick coaxial cables and connectors to each other.

The connector used by Ethernet cards that use UTP or STP cable is commonly known as an RJ-45 connector. *RJ* stands for registered jack; the RJ-45 has eight contacts that accept eight wires, also known as *pins*. It resembles a larger version of the RJ-11 connector used for telephone cabling. UTP cabling runs between a computer on the network and a hub or switch carrying signals between the two. The hub or switch then sends signals to other computers (servers or workstations) on the network. When a computer is connected to a hub or switch, a straight-through cable is used. This means that both ends of the cable are wired the same way. If a computer needs to be connected directly to another computer, a crossover cable, which has a different pin configuration on one end, is used. Keep in mind that between the computer and the hub or switch, other wiring equipment might be involved, for example, RJ-45 jacks, patch panels, and so on. UTP and STP cable can be purchased in prebuilt form or as bulk cable with connectors, so you can build the cable to the length you need. Figure 16-13 compares RJ-11 and RJ-45 connectors.

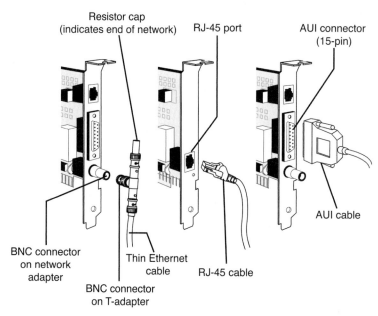

Figure 16-12   Combo UTP/BNC/AUI Ethernet network cards (left and right) compared with a UTP/STP-only Ethernet card (center) and cables.

Figure 16-13   RJ-11 connector (left) compared to RJ-45 connector (right).

NOTE   Although RJ-45 is the common name for the UTP Ethernet connector, this is a misnomer; the proper name is 8P8C (8 position, 8 contact). Don't confuse it with the RJ-45S connector, an eight-position connector used for telephone rather than computer data. An RJ-45S jack has a slightly different shape than the connector.

Fiber-Optic Cabling

Fiber-optic cabling transmits signals with light rather than with electrical signals, which makes it immune to electrical interference. It is used primarily as a backbone between networks. Fiber-optic cable comes in two major types:

- **Single-mode**—Has a thin core (between 8 and 10 microns) designed to carry a single light ray long distances

- **Multi-mode**—Has a thicker core (62.5 microns) than single-mode; carries multiple light rays for short distances

Fiber-optic cabling can be purchased prebuilt, but if you need a custom length, it should be built and installed by experienced cable installers because of the expense and risk of damage. Some network adapters built for servers are designed to use fiber-optic cable. Otherwise, media converters are used to interconnect fiber-optic to conventional cables on networks.

NOTE   When Ethernet is run over fiber-optic cables, the letter *F* is used in place of *T* (twisted pair) in the name. For example, 10BASE-F is 10Mbps Ethernet running on fiber-optic cable, 100BASE-F is 100Mbps Ethernet running on fiber-optic cable, and so on.

Coaxial Cabling

Coaxial cabling is the oldest type of network cabling; its data wires are surrounded by a wire mesh for insulation. Coaxial cables, which resemble cable TV connections, are not popular for network use today because they must be run from one station directly to another rather than to or from a hub/switch.

Coaxial cabling creates a bus topology; each end of the bus must be terminated, and if any part of the bus fails, the entire network fails.

The oldest Ethernet standard, 10BASE5, uses a very thick coaxial cable (RG-8) attached to a NIC through a transceiver that uses a so-called "vampire tap" to connect the transceiver to the cable. This type of coaxial cable is also referred to as Thick Ethernet or Thicknet.

Thin Ethernet, also referred to as Thinnet, Cheapernet, or 10BASE2 Ethernet was used for low-cost Ethernet networks before the advent of UTP cable. The coaxial cable used with 10BASE2 is referred to as RG-58. This type of coaxial cable connects to network cards through a T-connector that bayonet-mounts to the rear of the network card using a BNC connector. The arms of the *T* are used to connect two cables, each running to another computer in the network.

If the workstation is at the end of a network, a terminating resistor is connected to one arm of the *T* to indicate the end of the network (refer to Figure 16-12). If a resistor is removed, the network fails; if a station on the network fails, the network fails.

Two other types of coaxial cable are common in cable Internet, satellite Internet, and fixed wireless Internet installations:

- **RG-59**—Used in older cable TV or satellite TV installations; 75-ohm resistance. Also used by the long-obsolete Arcnet LAN standard.

- **RG-6**—Uses same connectors as RG-59 but has a larger diameter with superior shielding; used in cable TV/Internet, satellite TV/Internet, and fixed wireless Internet/TV service; 75-ohm resistance. These are also known as *F connectors*.

Plenum and PVC

The outer jacket of UTP, STP, and coaxial cable is usually made of PVC (polyvinyl chloride), a low-cost durable vinyl compound. Unfortunately, PVC creates dense poisonous smoke when burned. If you need to run network cable through suspended ceiling or air vents, you should use more expensive plenum cable, which produces less smoke and a lower level of toxic chemicals when burned.

Connector Types

Most coaxial cables, including RG-58, RG-59, and RG-6, use a BNC (Bayonet Neill-Concelman) connector. RG-58 uses a T-adapter to connect to a 10BASE2 Ethernet adapter. RG-11 (Thicknet) cable is connected to an Ethernet card by means of an external transceiver, which attaches to the AUI port on the rear of older Ethernet network cards. The transceiver attaches to the cable with a so-called "vampire tap."

10BASE-T, 100BASE-T, and 1000BASE-T Ethernet cards using copper wire all use the RJ-45 connector shown in Figure 16-13, as do newer token-ring, some ISDN, and most cable Internet devices. DSL devices often use the RJ-11 connector shown in Figure 16-13, as do dial-up modems.

To attach a cable using RJ-11 or RJ-45 connectors to a network card or other device, plug it into the connector so that the plastic locking clip snaps into place; the cable and connector will fit together only one way. To remove the cable, squeeze the locking clip toward the connector and pull the connector out of the jack. Some cables use a snagless connector; squeeze the guard over the locking clip to open the clip to remove the cable.

Fiber-optic devices and cables use one of several connector types. The most common include (see Figure 16-14)

- **SC**—Uses square connectors

- **LC**—Uses square connectors, similar to SC

- **ST**—Uses round connectors

- **FC**—Uses a round connector

If you need to interconnect devices that use two different connector types, use adapter cables that are designed to match the connector types and other characteristics of the cable and device.

SC cable   FC cable   ST cable

Figure 16-14 SC, FC, and ST fiber-optic cable connectors compared.

Networking Tools

220-801

Objective:
220-801: 2.10

If you plan on building a physical network, you need to stock up on some key networking tools. These tools aid you when running, terminating, and testing cable. For this short section, let's imagine a scenario where you are the network installer and are required to install a wired network for 12 computers.

To start, you should check with your local municipality for any rules and regulations for running networking cable. Some municipalities require a person to have an electrician's license. But most only require an exemption of some sort that anyone can apply for at the town or county seat. Due to the low-voltage nature of network wiring (for most applications), some municipalities have no rules regarding this. But in urban areas you need to apply for a permit and have at least one inspection done when you are finished with the installation.

Permits and regulations aside, let's say that in this scenario you have been cleared to install 12 wired connections to computers (known as drops) and have diagrammed where the cables will be run and where they will terminate. All cables will come out of a wiring closet where you will terminate them to a small patch panel. On the other end, they will terminate at in-wall RJ-45 jacks near each of the computers. Let's discuss each of the tools that you will use to complete this job.

The first tool you should have is a good, sharp cutting tool. You need to make a clean cut on the end of the network cable; scissors will not do. Either cut pliers or other cable cutting tools will be necessary. Klein is an excellent manufacturer of these types of tools.

The second tool is a wire stripper. This tool is used to strip a portion of the plastic jacket off of the cable exposing the individual wires. At this point you can separate the wires and get ready to terminate them.

The third tool is a punch down tool. This device punches the individual wires down into the 110 IDC clips of an RJ-45 jack and the patch panel. This "punching down" of the wires is the actual termination.

The last tool necessary for the job is a cable testing tool. You have a few options here. The best option is a proper network cable tester. This device will have LAN testing unit that you can plug in to a port on the patch panel and a terminator that you plug in to the other end of the cable in the corresponding RJ-45 jack. This tool tests each wire in the cable and makes sure that every one is wired properly. Another option is the tone and probe kit (referred to in the CompTIA objectives as "toner probe"). This kit consists of two parts: a tone device, which connects to one end of the network cable and when turned on, sends a tone along the length of the cable; and a probing device, also known as an inductive amplifier, that can pick up the tone anywhere along the cable length and at the termination point. This tool is not as good as a proper network cable tester because it only tests one of the pairs of the wires. However, it is an excellent tool for finding individual phone lines and is more commonly used for that. You can also use a multimeter to do various tests of individual lines, but it usually is not necessary if you own the other tools mentioned.

At this point, the cables have been run, terminated on both ends, and tested. The only other thing you need is patch cables. The patch cables connect the various ports of the patch panel to a switch and the RJ-45 jacks to the computers. Before connecting the patch cables you should test them with a patch tester. This device has two RJ-45 jacks; you plug each end of the patch cable and press the button to make sure each wire on each connection makes a proper connection. Usually, you would buy patch cables for $2 or $3 each. However, you can make them yourself. You would have to purchase cable, as well as RJ-45 plugs. The plugs are attached to the cable ends with an RJ-45 crimping tool.

Another tool every PC tech should have in his kit is a loopback plug. This connects directly to the RJ-45 port of a PC's network adapter. It simulates a network and tests whether the network adapter and TCP/IP are functioning properly.

That's about it for networking tools. For the A+ exam you should know the basic purposes of wire cutters, wire strippers, punchdown tools, cable testing tools, and loopback plugs.

Network Types

> **220-801**
>
> Objective:
> **220-801: 2.8**

The A+ Certification exam expects you to be familiar with the key features of wired Ethernet network types.

The oldest network in common use today is Ethernet, also known as IEEE-802.3. Most recent wired Ethernet networks use unshielded twisted pair (UTP) cable, but older versions of Ethernet use various types of coaxial cable.

NOTE   Ethernet uses the Carrier Sense Multiple Access/Collision Detect (CSMA/CD) method of transmission access. Here's how it works: A station on an Ethernet network can transmit data at any time; if two stations try to transmit at the same time, a collision takes place. Each station waits a random amount of time and then retries the transmission.

Table 16-4 lists the different types of Ethernet networks and their major features.

Table 16-4   Wired Ethernet Networks

Network Type	Cable and Connector Type	Also Known As	Maximum Speed	Network Topology Supported	Maximum Distance Per Segment
10BASE-T	UTP Cat3 cable with RJ-45 connector	Ethernet	10Mbps	Star	100 meters
100BASE-TX	UTP Cat5, 5e, or 6 cable with RJ-45 connector	Fast Ethernet	100Mbps	Star	100 meters
1000BASE-T	UTP Cat5e or 6 cable with RJ-45 connector	Gigabit Ethernet	1000Mbps	Star	100 meters

For more information about cables and connectors, refer to "Cable and Connector Types," and for more information about network topologies, see "Network Topologies," both earlier in the chapter.

NOTE   Fiber-optic cables can also be used for Ethernet signaling. They are particularly common for long cable runs with Fast and Gigabit Ethernet.

Wireless Network Standards

220-801

Objectives:
220-801: 2.5, 2.6

There are several wireless network standards you should know for the exam. The main one that you should really concentrate on is Wireless Local Area Networks or WLAN. It is also referred to as Wi-Fi and wireless Ethernet. But you should also understand the basics of Bluetooth, IrDA, and cellular.

Wireless Ethernet

Wireless Ethernet, also known as IEEE 802.11, is the collective name for a group of wireless technologies compatible with wired Ethernet; these are referred to as wireless LAN (WLAN) standards. Wireless Ethernet is also known as Wi-Fi, after the Wireless Fidelity (Wi-Fi) Alliance (www.wi-fi.org), a trade group that promotes interoperability between different brands of Wireless Ethernet hardware.

Table 16-5 compares different types of Wireless Ethernet to each other.

Table 16-5   Wireless Ethernet Standards

Wireless Ethernet Type	Frequency	Maximum Speed	Interoperable With
802.11a	5GHz	54Mbps	Requires dual-mode (802.11a/b or 802.11a/g) hardware; 802.11n networks supporting 5GHz frequency
802.11b	2.4GHz	11Mbps	802.11g
802.11g	2.4GHz	54Mbps	802.11b, 802.11n
802.11n	2.4GHz (standard)	Up to 600Mbps	802.11b, 802.11g
	5GHz (optional)	(300Mbps max. is typical)	(802.11a on networks also supporting 5GHz frequency)

NOTE   Wi-Fi–certified hardware is 802.11-family Wireless Ethernet hardware that has passed tests established by the Wi-Fi Alliance. Most, but not all, 802.11-family Wireless Ethernet hardware is Wi-Fi–certified.

Wireless Ethernet hardware supports both the star (infrastructure) network topology, which uses a wireless access point to transfer data between nodes, and the peer-to-peer topology (ad-hoc), in which each node can communicate directly with another node.

TIP   Additional information on Wireless Ethernet can be found in the section "Wireless Ethernet (WLAN) Configuration," later in the chapter.

Bluetooth

Bluetooth is a short-range low-speed wireless network primarily designed to operate in peer-to-peer mode (known as ad-hoc) between PCs and other devices such as printers, projectors, smartphones, mice, keyboards, and other devices. Bluetooth runs in virtually the same 2.4GHz frequency used by IEEE 802.11b, g, and n wireless networks but uses a spread-spectrum frequency-hopping signaling method to help minimize interference. Bluetooth devices connect to each other to form a personal area network (PAN).

Some systems and devices include integrated Bluetooth adapters, and others need a Bluetooth module connected to the USB port to enable Bluetooth networking.

Bluetooth version 1.2 offers a data transfer rate of 1Mbps. Version 2 is 3Mbps. Newer versions of Bluetooth can go faster, but they do so by combining with 802.11 WLAN technologies. Bluetooth is divided into classes, each of which has a different range. Table 16-6 shows these classes, their ranges, and the amount of power their corresponding antennae use to generate signal.

Table 16-6   Bluetooth Classes

Class	mW	Range
Class 1	100 mW	100 meters (328 ft.)
Class 2	2.5 mW	10 meters (33 ft.)
Class 3	1 mW	1 meter (3 ft.)

As you can see, Class 1 generates the most powerful signal, and as such has the largest range. The most common Bluetooth devices are Class 2 devices with a range of 10 meters. Examples of this include portable printers, headsets, and computer dongles.

Infrared

Infrared is a short-range, low-speed, line-of-sight network method that can be used to connect to other PCs, PDAs, or Internet kiosks. Infrared networking is based on the **Infrared Data Association (IrDA)** protocol. Some laptops include an integrated IrDA port. IrDA can also be used for printing to printers that include an IrDA port or are connected to an IrDA adapter.

If you want to use a computer that does not have IrDA support with infrared networking, you can add an IrDA adapter. Many desktop motherboards include integrated IrDA support. To enable IrDA support, connect a header cable (available from various third-party sources) to the IrDA port and configure the system BIOS to provide IrDA support. On many systems with integrated IrDA support, one of the COM ports can be switched between its normal mode and IrDA support.

To add IrDA support to computers that don't include an IrDA port, use a third-party IrDA module that connects to the USB port.

Cellular

Digital cellular phone networks can be used for Internet access and remote networking, a feature that is extremely useful to mobile workers. To enable a laptop to use a cellular network for data access, you need to connect a cellular modem to your PC and purchase the appropriate data access plan from a wireless carrier.

Cellular modems can be connected to USB ports or installed into CardBus or ExpressCard slots. They can be purchased separately or as a bundle with a data access plan. If you purchase a cellular modem separately, make sure it supports the data access method used by your wireless carrier.

VoIP

Voice over IP (VoIP) is an increasingly popular method for providing home and business telephone access. VoIP routes telephone calls over the same TCP/IP network used for LAN and Internet access. Companies such as Vonage, Skype, AT&T, Verizon, and others provide VoIP services.

To add VoIP service to an existing Ethernet network, you can use either an analog telephone adapter (ATA) or a VoIP router. An ATA enables you to adapt standard telephones to work with VoIP services. It plugs into your existing router. A VoIP router can be used as a replacement for an existing wired or wireless router. Typical VoIP routers support most or all of the following features:

- **Quality of Service (QoS) support**—This feature prioritizes streaming media, such as VoIP phone calls and audio or video playback, over other types of network traffic.

- **One or more FXO ports**—An FXO port enables standard analog telephones to be used in VoIP service.

- **Real-time Transport Protocol/Real-time Transport Control Protocol (RTP/RTCP)**—Supports streaming media, video conferencing, and VoIP applications.

- **Session Initiation Protocol (SIP) support**—A widely used VoIP signaling protocol also used for multimedia distribution and multimedia conferences.

Switches and Hubs

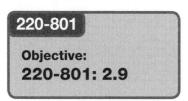

220-801

Objective:
220-801: 2.9

Hubs connect different computers with each other on an Ethernet network based on UTP or STP cabling. A hub has several connectors for RJ-45 cabling, a power source, and signal lights to indicate network activity. Most hubs are stackable, meaning that if you need more ports than the hub contains, you can connect it to another hub to expand its capabilities.

A hub is the slowest connection device on a network because it splits the bandwidth of the connection among all the computers connected to it. For example, a five-port 10/100 Ethernet hub divides the 100Mbps speed of Fast Ethernet among the five ports, providing only 20Mbps of bandwidth to each port for Fast Ethernet and 10/100 adapters, and only 2Mbps per port for 10BASE-T adapters. A hub also broadcasts data to all computers connected to it.

A switch resembles a hub but creates a dedicated full-speed connection between the two computers that are communicating with each other. A five-port 10/100/1000 switch, for example, provides the full 10Mbps bandwidth to each port connected to a 10BASE-T card and a full 100Mbps bandwidth to each port connected to a Fast Ethernet or 10/100 card. If the network adapters are configured to run in full-duplex mode (send and receive data simultaneously) and the switch supports full-duplex (most modern switches do), the Fast Ethernet bandwidth on the network is doubled to 200Mbps and the 10BASE-T bandwidth is doubled to 20Mbps. Switches can be daisy-chained in a manner similar to stackable hubs, and there is no limit to the number of switches possible in a network.

Building a Small Office/Home Office Network

220-801

Objectives:
220-801: 2.6

220-802

Objectives:
220-802: 1.6

You will be building, configuring, and troubleshooting small office/home office (SOHO) networks quite often. A lot goes into this type of network including installing network interface cards, setting up a SOHO router, configuring TCP/IP, setting up shared resources, and configuring browsers. Let's start with installing network interface cards.

Installing Network Interface Cards

Although many recent computers include a 10/100 or 10/100/1000 Ethernet port or a Wireless Ethernet (WLAN) adapter, you sometimes need to install a network interface card (NIC) into a computer you want to add to a network.

PCI and PCI Express

To install a Plug and Play (PnP) network card, follow this procedure:

Step 1. Turn off the computer and remove the case cover.

Step 2. Locate an available expansion slot matching the network card's design. (Most use PCI, but some servers and workstations might use PCI-X or PCI Express.).

Step 3. Remove the slot cover and insert the card into the slot. Secure the card in the slot.

Step 4. Restart the system and provide the driver disk or CD-ROM when requested by the system.

Step 5. Insert the operating system disc if requested to install network drivers and clients.

Step 6. The IRQ, I/O port address, and memory address required by the card will be assigned automatically.

Step 7. Test for connectivity (check LED lights, use a command such as ping, and so on), and then close the computer case.

USB

Although USB network adapters are also PnP devices, you may need to install the drivers provided with the USB network adapter before you attach the adapter to your computer. After the driver software is installed, the device will be recognized as soon as you plug it into a working USB port.

NOTE   If you are using a wireless USB adapter, you can improve signal strength by using an extension cable between the adapter and the USB port on the computer. Using an extension cable enables you to move the adapter as needed to pick up a stronger signal.

Most USB network adapters are bus powered. For best results, they should be attached to a USB port built in to your computer or to a self-powered hub. Most recent adapters support USB 3.0, which provides full-speed support for 100BASE-TX (Fast Ethernet) and 1000BASE-T (gigabit Ethernet) signal speeds.

PC Card/CardBus

PC Card network adapters work with both the original 16-bit PC Card slot and the newer 32-bit CardBus slot. However, CardBus cards work only in CardBus slots.

Both PC Card and CardBus cards are detected and installed by built-in support for these adapters in Windows XP and newer versions.

Some PC Card and CardBus network adapters often require that a dongle be attached to the card to enable the card to plug in to a network port. See Chapter 9 for details.

Configuring Network Interface Cards

Although PCI, USB, PC Card, CardBus network adapters, and integrated adapters support PnP configuration for hardware resources, you might also need to configure the network adapter for the type of media it uses, for the speed of the connection, and with Wireless Ethernet adapters, the security settings that are used on the wireless network.

Hardware Resources

Typical network interface card hardware resource settings include

- IRQ
- I/O port address range

If the workstation is a diskless workstation, a free upper memory address must also be supplied for the boot ROM on the card. A few older network cards also use upper memory blocks for RAM buffers; check the card's documentation.

Media Type

Most recent Ethernet cards are designed to use only UTP Cat3 or greater network cabling. However, some older cards were also designed to use 10BASE5 (Thicknet) or 10BASE2 (Thinnet) cabling. Cards that are designed to use two or more different types of cabling are known as combo cards and during card configuration, you need to select the type of media that will be used with the card. This option is also known as the Transceiver Type option. Depending on the card's drivers, you might need to make this setting through the card's command-line configuration program or the card's properties sheet in Windows Device Manager.

NOTE   Some network adapters designed for use with UTP cable can automatically sense when the cable is not connected. Windows 7 and Vista automatically display if a network adapter is connected or not. Windows XP might display an icon in the system area, but it depends on the type of card. To enable notification in Windows XP, open the Network Connections window, right-click the connection, select **Properties**, and make sure the option **Show Icon in Notification Area When Connected** is enabled.

Full/Half-Duplex

If the hardware in use on an Ethernet, Fast Ethernet, or Gigabit Ethernet network permits, you can configure the network to run in full-duplex mode. Full-duplex mode enables the adapter to send and receive data at the same time, which doubles network speed over the default half-duplex mode (where the card sends and receives in separate operations). Thus, a 10BASE-T-based network runs at 20Mbps in full-duplex mode; a 100BASE-T-based network runs at 200Mbps in full-duplex mode; and a 1000BASE-T-based network runs at 2000Mbps in full-duplex mode.

To achieve full-duplex performance on a UTP-based Ethernet network, the network adapters on a network must all support full-duplex mode, and be configured to use full-duplex mode with the device's setup program or properties sheet, and a switch must be used in place of a hub.

Wireless Ethernet (WLAN) Configuration

Wireless Ethernet requires additional configuration compared to wired Ethernet, as shown in Table 16-7. To connect to a wireless network, use the built-in Windows wireless network locator within the Network and Sharing Center, the third-party wireless locator that accompanies the wireless adapter, or a program such as NetStumbler.

Most home and small-business networks using encryption use a pre-shared key (PSK). When a pre-shared key is used, both the wireless router or access point and all clients must have the same PSK before they can connect with each other. WPA and WPA2 also support the use of a RADIUS authentication server, which is used on corporate networks.

Table 16-7   Wireless Ethernet Configuration Setting

Setting	What the Setting Does
Service Set Identifier (SSID)	Names the network. Windows XP, Vista, and 7 can detect SSIDs from unsecured networks and from secured networks that broadcast their SSIDs.
Channel	Specifies a channel for all stations to use. On wireless access points (WAPs), this is between 1 and 11. If you have multiple WAPs, consider using 1, 6, and 11, so that the channels do not overlap. This option is required for ad-hoc (peer-to-peer) configurations and if the vendor's own software is used to configure the network. Windows Wireless Zero Configuration service determines the channel to use automatically.
Wireless Equivalent Privacy (WEP)	Enable to prevent access by unauthorized users. Use this setting in place of WPA only if some hardware does not support WPA. WEP is not supported by 802.11n wireless network hardware. If WEP or WPA security is disabled (the default with most hardware), anybody can get on the network if they know or detect the SSID.
WEP Encryption Strength	Use the highest setting supported by both WEP and adapters for best security. Small-office home-office hardware might use 64-bit; business-market hardware often uses 128-bit encryption.
WEP Key	Use 10 alphanumeric characters for 64-bit encryption; use 26 characters for 128-bit encryption. All network devices must use the same WEP key and encryption strength if WEP is enabled.
Wi-Fi Protected Access (WPA)	Enable to prevent access by unauthorized users. WPA is much more secure than WEP. Disable this option and use WEP to secure your network only if some equipment on the network does not support WPA. A driver or firmware upgrade might be necessary on some older equipment to enable WPA support. Currently the latest version is WPA2, which is more secure than WPA.

Setting	What the Setting Does
WPA Key	WPA can use a variable-length alphanumeric key up to 63 characters. (Some WPA-compliant hardware might not work with a 63-character key.)
WPA Encryption Type	■ Temporal Key Integrity Protocol (TKIP) is a 128-bit encryption protocol that was developed for WPA to address weaknesses within WEP, but without the need to replace older equipment. This is the original version of WPA. ■ Advanced Encryption Standard (AES) is a 128–256-bit encryption protocol used in several technologies including wireless networking. It can be used exclusively or in conjunction with TKIP and is the recommended option. WPA using AES is often referred to as WPA2.
Wi-Fi Protected Setup (WPS)	This is a standard used by many router manufacturers to make connecting to a wireless network easier for the user. It usually consists of an 8- to 10-digit PIN and is located on the bottom of the router. It can also be viewed within the router's firmware. There have been several problems with WPS, and most manufacturers recommend that you disable it within the firmware.

TCP/IPv4 Configuration

The TCP/IPv4 protocol, although it was originally used for Internet connectivity, is currently the most important network protocol for LAN as well as larger networks; in most modern business networks, TCP/IP v4 and v6 are used side by side. To connect with the rest of a TCP/IP-based network, each computer or other device must have a unique IP address. If the network connects with the Internet, additional settings are required.

There are two ways to configure a computer's TCP/IP settings:

■ Server-assigned IP address

■ Static IP address

Table 16-8 compares the differences in these configurations.

Table 16-8   Static Versus Server-Assigned IP Addressing

Setting	What It Does	Static IP Address	Server-Assigned IP
IP address	Identifies computer on the network	Unique value for each computer	Automatically assigned by DHCP server
DNS configuration	Identifies domain name system servers	IP addresses of one or more DNS servers, host name, and domain name must be entered	Automatically assigned by server
Gateway	Identifies IP address of device that connects computer to Internet or other network	IP address for gateway must be entered; same value for all computers on network	Automatically assigned by server
WINS configuration	Maps IP addresses to NetBIOS computer names; used with Windows NT 4.0 and earlier versions	IP addresses for one or more WINS servers must be entered if enabled	Can use DHCP to resolve WINS if necessary

All versions of Windows default to using a server-assigned IP address. As Table 16-8 makes clear, this is the preferable method for configuring a TCP/IP network. Use a manually assigned IP address if a Dynamic Host Configuration Protocol (DHCP) server (which provides IP addresses automatically) is not available on the network—or if you need to configure a firewall or router to provide different levels of access to some systems and you must specify those systems' IP addresses.

NOTE   Routers, wireless gateways, and computers that host an Internet connection shared with Windows's Internet Connection Sharing or a third-party sharing program all provide DHCP services to other computers on the network.

To configure TCP/IP in Windows, access the Internet Protocol Properties window; this window contains several dialogs used to make changes to TCP/IP. Note that these dialogs are nearly identical in Windows XP, Vista, and 7. To open the General tab of the Internet Protocol Properties window, open Network Connections, right-click the network connection, select **Properties**, click **Internet Protocol (TCP/IP)** in the list of protocols and features, and click **Properties**.

TCP/IP Configuration with a DHCP Server

Figure 16-15 shows the General tab as it appears when a DHCP server is used.

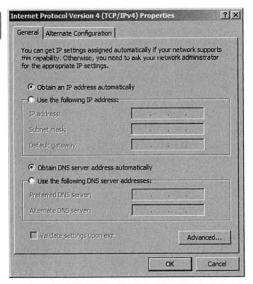

Figure 16-15   The General tab is configured to obtain IP and DNS server information automatically when a DHCP server is used on the network.

NOTE   To determine the IP address, default gateway, and DNS servers used by a system using DHCP addressing, open a command prompt and enter the **ipconfig /all** command.

To learn more about using ipconfig, see "Using Ipconfig," later in this chapter.

TCP/IP Alternate Configuration

The Alternate Configuration tab shown in Figure 16-16 is used to set up a different configuration for use when a DHCP server is not available or when a different set of user-configured settings is needed, as when a laptop is being used at a secondary location. By default, automatic private IP addressing (APIPA) is used when no DHCP server is in use. APIPA assigns each system a unique IP address in the 169.254.x.x range. APIPA enables a network to perform LAN connections when the DHCP server is not available, but systems using APIPA cannot connect to the Internet.

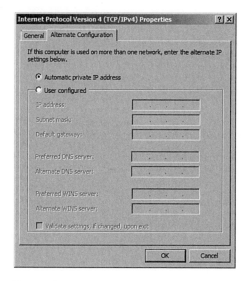

Figure 16-16   The Alternate Configuration tab is used to set up a different IP configuration for use on another network or when no DHCP server is available.

You can also use the Alternate Configuration tab to specify the IP address, subnet mask, default gateway, DNS servers, and WINS servers. This option is useful if this system is moved to another network that uses different IP addresses for these servers.

TCP/IP User-Configured IP and DNS Addresses

When a DHCP server is not used, the General tab is used to set up the IP address, subnet mask, default gateway, and DNS servers used by the network client. (The information shown in Figure 16-17 is fictitious.)

TCP/IP User-Configured Advanced Settings

Click the Advanced button shown in Figure 16-17 to bring up a multitabbed dialog for adding or editing gateways (IP Settings), DNS server addresses (DNS), adjusting WINS resolution (WINS), and in Windows XP, adjusting TCP/IP port filtering (Options). These options can be used whether DHCP addressing is enabled or not. Figure 16-18 shows these tabs.

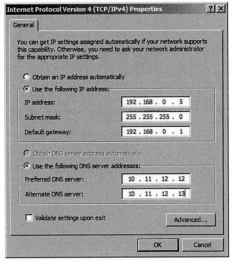

Figure 16-17   The General tab of the TCP/IP properties sheet when manual configuration is used.

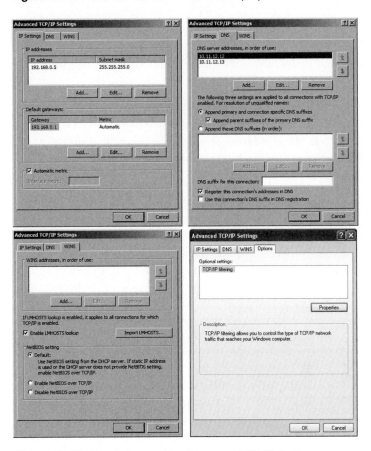

Figure 16-18   The tabs used for Advanced TCP/IP Settings.

Understanding IP Addressing, Subnet Masks, and IP Classes

An IPv4 address consists of a group of four numbers that each range from 0 to 255, for example: 192.168.1.1. IP addresses are divided into two sections: the network portion, which is the number of the network the computer is on, and the host portion, which is the individual number of the computer. Using the IP address we just mentioned as an example, the 192.168.1 portion would typically be the network number, and .1 would be the host number. A subnet mask is used to distinguish between the network portion of the IP address and the host portion. For example, a typical subnet mask for the IP address we just used would be 255.255.255.0. The 255s correspond to the network portion of the IP address. The 0s correspond to the host portion, as shown in Table 16-9.

Table 16-9   An IP Address and Corresponding Subnet Mask

IP Address/Subnet Mask	Network Portion	Host Portion
192.168.1.1	192.168.1	1
255.255.255.0	255.255.255	0

The subnet mask is also used to define subnetworks, if subnetworking is being implemented.

Both computers and other networked devices, such as routers and network printers, can have IP addresses, and some devices can have more than one IP address. For example, a router typically has two IP addresses—one to connect the router to a LAN and the other that connects it to the Internet, enabling it to route traffic from the LAN to the Internet and back.

IP addresses are divided into three major categories: Class A, Class B, and Class C, which define ranges of IP addresses. Class A is designated for large corporations, ISPs, and government. Class B is designated for midsized corporations and ISPs. Class C is designated for small offices and home offices. Each class of IP address uses a default subnet mask, as shown in Table 16-10.

Table 16-10   Internet Protocol Classification System

Class	First Octet Range	Starting IP	Ending IP	Default Subnet Mask
Class A	1–127	0.0.0.0	127.255.255.255	255.0.0.0
Class B	128–191	128.0.0.0	191.255.255.255	255.255.0.0
Class C	192–223	192.0.0.0	223.255.255.255	255.255.255.0

NOTE The 127 network is reserved for testing. This is known as the loopback, for example, 127.0.0.1. The usable starting IP for Class A is actually 1.0.0.0.

In any given network, the first and last addresses are reserved and cannot be assigned to computers or other hosts. For example, in the 192.168.1.0 network, 192.168.1.1 through 192.168.1.254 can be assigned, but 192.168.1.0 is reserved for the network number, and 192.168.1.255 is reserved for something called the broadcast.

Each number in an IP address is called an *octet*. An octet is an eight-bit byte. This means that in the binary numbering system the number can range from 00000000–11111111. For example, 255 is actually 11111111 when converted to the binary numbering system. Another example: 192 equals 11000000.

NOTE To convert numbers from decimal to binary and vice versa use the Windows calculator. Press Windows+R to bring up the Run prompt; then type **calc**. This runs the Windows Calculator. From there, click **View** on the menu bar and select **Scientific**. Now you will notice radio buttons on the upper left that allow you to change between numbering systems. Simply type any number, and then select the numbering system you want to convert it to.

In a Class A network, the first octet is the network portion of the IP address, and the three remaining octets identify the host portion of the IP address. Class B networks use the first and second octets as the network portion and the third and fourth octets as the host portion. Class C networks use the first three octets as the network portion and the last octet as the host portion of the IP address. Table 16-11 gives one example IP address and subnet mask for each Class.

Table 16-11 Internet Protocol/Subnet Mask Examples for Classes A, B, and C

Class	IP Address/Subnet Mask	Network Portion	Host Portion
Class A	10.0.0.1	10	0.0.1
	255.0.0.0	255	0.0.0
Class B	172.16.0.1	172.16	0.1
	255.255.0.0	255.255	0.0
Class C	192.168.1.100	192.168.1	100
	255.255.255.0	255.255.255	0

See a pattern? The size of the network portion increases in octets, and the host portion decreases as you ascend through the classes. As time goes on, you will see more patterns like this within TCP/IP.

You should know the difference between public and private IP addresses. A public IP is one that faces the Internet and can be seen by any computers that connect to the Internet. For example, for google.com to have a properly functioning web server, the web server needs to have a public IP address. If it didn't, no one would be able to connect to it. Private IP addresses are hidden from sight; usually they are behind a firewall. If your computer has an IP address on the 192.168.0 or 192.168.1 networks, it is a private IP, and you most likely have a router that is protecting your IP from the Internet. Each IPv4 class has its own range of private IP addresses:

- **Class A**—Uses the entire 10 network, from 10.0.0.0 to 10.255.255.255

- **Class B**—Uses the range 172.16.0.0 through 172.31.255.255

- **Class C**—Uses the range 192.168.0.0 through 192.168.255.255

Computers on a LAN normally are be given private IPs, whereas servers on the Internet use public IPs.

WINS Configuration

Windows Internet Naming Service (WINS) matches the NetBIOS name of a particular computer to an IP address on the network; this process is also called *resolving* or *translating* the NetBIOS name to an IP address. WINS requires the use of a Window Server that has been set up to provide the resolving service. If WINS is enabled, the IP addresses of the WINS servers must be entered.

If the IP address is provided by a DHCP server, or if a WINS server is used, you need to enter the correct WINS settings (refer to Figure 16-18).

The network administrator will inform you of the correct settings to use on this dialog.

Gateway

A *gateway* is a computer or device (such as a router) that provides a connection between a LAN and a wide area network (WAN) or the Internet. Computers that use a LAN connection to connect to the Internet need to enter the IP address or addresses of the gateways on this tab (refer to Figure 16-17) if the computer doesn't use DHCP to obtain an IP address.

DNS Configuration

The Internet uses the domain name system (DNS) to map domain names, such as www.microsoft.com, to their corresponding IP address or addresses. A computer using the Internet must use at least one DNS server to provide this translation service. Use the DNS Configuration tab to set up the computer's host name, domain name, and DNS servers (refer to Figure 16-17) if the computer doesn't use DHCP to obtain an IP address.

NOTE   Most ISPs and networks have at least two DNS name servers to provide backup in case one fails. Be sure to enter the IP addresses of all DNS servers available to your network. In Windows, these are referred to as preferred and alternate DNS servers.

IPv6 Addressing

IP version 6 enables a huge increase in the number of available IP addresses for computers, smartphones, and other mobile devices. Windows Vista and 7 include IPv6. IPv6 uses 128-bit source and destination IP addresses (compared to 32-bit for IPv4), features built-in security, and provides better support for Quality of Service (QoS) routing, which is important to achieve high-quality streaming audio and video traffic.

IPv6 addresses start out as 128-bit addresses that are then divided into eight 16-bit blocks. The blocks are converted into hexadecimal, and each block is separated from the following block by a colon. Leading zeros are typically suppressed, but each block must contain at least one digit.

Here is a typical IPv6 address:

> 21DA:D3:0:2F3B:2AA:FF:FE28:9C5A

A contiguous sequence of 16-bit blocks set to zero can be represented by :: (double-colon). This technique is also known as *zero compression*. To determine the number of zero bits represented by the double colon, count the number of blocks in the compressed address, subtract the result from 8, and multiply the result by 16. An address can include only one zero-compressed block.

Here is an IPv6 address that does use the double colon:

> FF02::2.

There are two blocks (FF02 and 2). So, how many zero bits are represented by the double colon? Subtract 2 from 8 (8-2=6, then multiply 6 by 16 (6 × 16=96). This address includes a block of 96 zero bits.

The loopback address on an IPv6 system is 0:0:0:0:0:0:0:1, which is abbreviated as ::1. Thus, if you want to test your network interface in Windows Vista/7 where IPv6 is enabled by default, you can type ping ::1.

IPv6 supports three types of addresses: unicast, multicast, and anycast. There are five types of unicast addresses:

- Global unicast addresses are used in the same way as IPv4 public addresses. The first three bits are set to 001, followed by 45 bits used for the global routing prefix; these 48 bits are collectively known as the public topology. The subnet ID uses the next 16 bits, and the interface ID uses the remaining 64 bits.

- Link-local addresses correspond to the Automatic Private IP address (APIPA) address scheme used by IPv4 (addresses that start with 169.254). The first 10 bits are set to FE80 hex, followed by 54 zero bits, and 64 bits for the Interface ID. Using zero compression, the prefix would thus be FE80::/64. As with APIPA, link local addresses are not forwarded beyond the link.

- Site-local addresses correspond to IPv4 private address spaces (10.0.0.0/8, 172.16.0.0/12, and 192.168.0.0/16).

- Special addresses include unspecified addresses (0:0:0:0:0:0:0:0 or ::), which are equivalent to IPv4's 0.0.0.0 and indicate the absence of an IP address; loopback address (0:0:0:0:0:0:0:1 or ::1) is equivalent to the IPv4 loopback address of 127.0.0.1.

- Compatibility addresses are used in situations in which IPv4 and IPv6 are both in use. In the following examples, w.x.y.z are replaced by the actual IPv4 address. An IPv4-compatible address (0:0:0:0:0:0:w.x.y.z or ::w.x.y.z) is used by nodes that support IPv4 and IPv6 communicating over IPv6. An IPv4-mapped address (0:0:0:0:0:FFFF:w.x.y.z or ::FFFF:w.x.y.z) represents an IPv4-only node to an IPv6 node. A 6to4 address is used when two nodes running both IPv4 and IPv6 connect over an IPv4 routing. The address combines the prefix 2002::/16 with the IPv4 public address of the node. ISATAP can also be used for the connection; it uses a locally administered ID of ::0:5EFE:w.x.y.z (w.x.y.z could be any unicast IPv4 address, either public or private); Teredo addresses are used for tunneling IPv6 over UDP through Network Address Translation (NAT); they use the prefix 3FFE:831F::/32.

Both IPv4 and IPv6 support multicasting, which enables one-to-many distribution of content such as Internet TV or other types of streaming media. IPv6 multicast addresses begin with FF.

Anycast addressing sends information to a group of potential receivers that are identified by the same destination address. This is also known as one-to-one-to-many association. Anycast addressing can be used for distributed services, such as DNS or other situations in which automatic failover is desirable. IPv6 uses anycast addresses as destination addresses that are assigned only to routers. Anycast addresses are assigned from the unicast address space.

To see the IPv4 and IPv6 addresses assigned to a Windows Vista or 7 PC using both IPv4 and IPv6, use the command-line ipconfig utility. Here's an example of the output from a system using a wireless Ethernet adapter:

```
Wireless LAN adapter Wireless Network Connection:
    Connection-specific DNS Suffix  . :
    Link-local IPv6 Address . . . . . : fe80::5cf1:2f98:7351:b3a3%12
    IPv4 Address. . . . . . . . . . . : 192.168.1.155
    Subnet Mask . . . . . . . . . . . : 255.255.255.0
    Default Gateway . . . . . . . . . : 192.168.1.1
```

For more information, see http://technet.microsoft.com/en-us/library/dd392266(WS.10).aspx.

Setting Up Shared Resources

Sharing resources with other network users requires the following steps:

Step 1.   Install and/or enable File and Printer sharing.

Step 2.   Select which drives, folders, or printers to share.

Step 3.   Set permissions.

> **NOTE** Windows XP uses NTFS security permissions only on NTFS-formatted drives and only if simple file sharing is disabled.

The following sections cover performing these processes manually. However, the Network Setup Wizard can also perform these steps for you.

Installing File and Printer Sharing

By default, File and Printer Sharing is installed in Windows. However, if you need to add it, File and Printer Sharing can be installed through the network connection's properties sheet. For Windows 7/Vista/XP, follow this procedure:

Step 1.   Open the Local Area Connection properties sheet.

Step 2.   Click the **Install** button.

Step 3.   Click the **Service** icon.

Step 4.   Click the **Add** button.

Step 5.   Select **File and Printer Sharing for Microsoft Networks** and click **OK**.

Step 6.   Restart the computer.

Figure 16-19 illustrates a typical Windows 7 network properties sheet after File and Printer Sharing is installed. The check box indicates this feature is enabled.

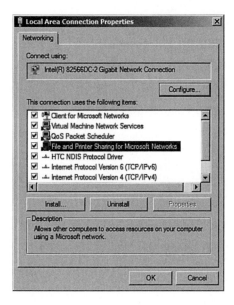

Figure 16-19   This network connection has File and Printer Sharing for Microsoft Networks installed and enabled.

Shared Folders and Drives

A shared folder or drive can be accessed by other computers on the network. Shares can be provided in two ways:

- On a client/server-based network, or a peer-to-peer network with peer servers that support user/group permissions, shares are protected by lists of authorized users or groups. Windows 7, Vista, and XP support user/group access control. However, Windows XP supports user/group access control only when the default simple file sharing setting is disabled.

- A peer-to-peer network whose peer servers do not support user/group access control might only offer options for read-only or full access (as with Windows XP using its default simple file sharing setting).

When user/group-based permissions are used, only members who belong to a specific group or are listed separately on the access list for a particular share can access that share. After users log on to the network, they have access to all shares they've been authorized to use without the need to provide additional passwords. Access levels include full and read-only and, on NTFS drives, other access levels, such as write, create, and delete. Let's show the various ways to share data starting with Windows XP and then moving on to Windows 7/Vista.

Sharing a Folder Using Simple File Sharing

To share a folder or drive in Windows XP with simple file sharing enabled, follow these steps:

Step 1. Right-click the folder or drive and select **Sharing and Security**.

Step 2. If you right-click a drive, Windows XP displays a warning. Click the link to continue.

Step 3. Click the box **Share This Folder on the Network** to share the folder in read-only mode. To share the folder in read/write mode, click the box **Allow Network Users to Change My Files**. Click **OK**.

Figure 16-20 illustrates sharing a folder or drive when simple file sharing is enabled.

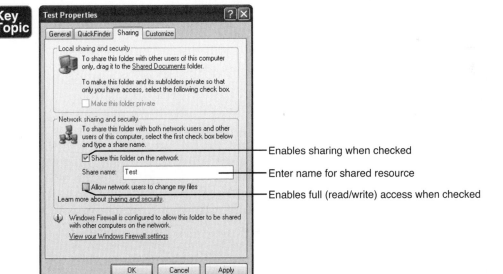

Figure 16-20 Setting up a network share in Windows XP using the default simple file-sharing option.

Sharing a Folder with User/Group Permissions in Windows XP

If you want to set up user/group permissions on Windows XP, you must first disable simple file sharing.

Step 1.   Open My Computer or Windows Explorer.

Step 2.   Open the Tools menu and click **Folder Options**.

Step 3.   Click the **View** tab.

Step 4.   In the Advanced Settings portion of the dialog, scroll down to **Use Simple File Sharing (Recommended)** and clear the check box.

Step 5.   Click **Apply** and then **OK**.

After simple file sharing is disabled, you can share a folder and control access with user/group permissions on any drive that uses the NTFS file system.

After simple file sharing is disabled, use this procedure to share a folder or drive:

Step 1.   Right-click the folder or drive and select **Properties**.

Step 2.   Click the **Sharing** tab (see Figure 16-21).

Step 3.   Click **Share This Folder** and specify a share name. (The default share name is the name of the drive or folder.) Add a comment if desired.

Step 4.   Specify the number of users or use the default (10).

Step 5.   Click **Permissions** to set folder permissions by user or group.

Step 6.   Click **Caching** to specify whether files will be cached on other computers' drives and how they will be cached.

NOTE   If you need to convert a drive from a FAT-based file system to NTFS, you can use the command-line convert program. For example, if you were to convert the C: drive, the syntax would be

convert c: /FS:NTFS

Step 7.   Click **OK**.

See "Operating System Access Control" in Chapter 17, "Security," for details.

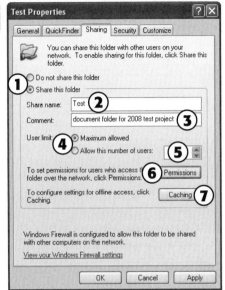

1. Enables/disables sharing
2. Share name
3. Comment (optional)
4. Specifies user limit
5. Specifies maximum number of users (1-10)
6. Configures permissions
7. Controls caching of offline files by other users

Figure 16-21   Setting up a network share in Windows XP when simple file sharing is disabled.

Sharing a Folder with User/Group Permissions in Windows Vista or Windows 7

To share a folder in Windows Vista or 7, follow these steps:

Step 1.   Ensure that file sharing is enabled. This is done by navigating to **Start, Control Panel** and double-clicking the **Network and Sharing Center** icon. In Windows Vista, click the down arrow next to File Sharing and select the **Turn on File Sharing** radio button. (This window is also where you would enable printer sharing.) To access this dialog in Windows 7, click **Change Advanced Sharing Settings** after opening the Network and Sharing Center.

Step 2.   Click **Start**; then click **Computer**.

Step 3.   In the Computer window, navigate to a folder that you want to share.

Step 4.   Right-click the folder that you want to share; then click **Share**. The File Sharing window is now displayed.

Step 5.   If you have enabled password-protected sharing, use the File Sharing window and select which users will have access to the shared folder and select their permission levels. To allow all users, select the **Everyone** group within the list of users. If you disabled password-protected sharing, use the File Sharing window and select the **Guest** or **Everyone** account. This is the equivalent of simple file sharing in Windows XP.

Step 6.   When you are done configuring permissions, click **Share** and then click **Done**.

Shared Printers

To set up a printer as a shared printer, follow these steps:

Step 1.   Open the Printers or Printers and Faxes folder.

Step 2.   Right-click a printer and select **Sharing**.

Step 3.   Select **Share This Printer** and specify a share name. (In Windows Vista, you must click the Sharing tab first.)

Step 4.   Click **Additional Drivers** to select additional drivers to install for other operating systems that will use the printer on the network. Supply driver disks or CDs when prompted.

Administrative Shares

Administrative shares are hidden shares that can be identified by a $ on the end of the share name. These shares cannot be seen by standard users when browsing to the computer over the network; they are meant for administrative use. All the shared folders including administrative shares can be found by navigating to **Computer Management** > **System Tools** > **Shared Folders** > **Shares**. Note that every volume within the hard drive (C: or D:, for example) has an administrative share (for example, C$ is the administrative share for the C: drive). Although it is possible to remove these by editing the Registry, it is not recommended because it might cause other networking issues. You should be aware that only administrators should have access to these shares.

Setting Up the Network Client

The client in both peer-to-peer networks and dedicated server networks is a computer that uses shared resources. To access shared resources, a client computer needs

- Network client software
- The name of the network and server(s) with shared resources
- The printer drivers for the network printers

To install network client software in Windows, open the Properties sheet of the appropriate network connection. To change the name of the network that the computer is a member of, open the System Properties window and click the **Computer Name** tab.

In Windows XP, My Network Places is used to locate shared resources and to provide passwords; in Windows 7 and Vista, it is simply called Network. Printers is used to set up access to a network printer in all versions of Windows. My Network Places, Network, and Printers can be accessed from the Start menu or from within Windows Explorer.

Installing Network Client Software

Windows 7, Vista, and XP incorporate network client software for Microsoft Networks.

If you need to install additional network clients, such as for NetWare, in Windows XP, follow this procedure:

Step 1. Open the Network Connections icon in Control Panel or right-click **My Network Places** and select **Properties**.

Step 2. Right-click the connection you want to modify and select **Properties**.

Step 3. Click the **Install** button.

Step 4. Click the **Client** icon.

Step 5. Select the client you want to add.

Step 6. Click **OK**.

NOTE Windows 7 and Vista do not support Novell NetWare by default.

Installing a Network Printer

Follow this procedure to install a network printer:

Step 1. Open the Printers and Faxes (or Printers) folder.

Step 2. Click **Add a Printer** (or **Add Printer**). In some cases, you might need to click anywhere in the white area and select **Add Printer**.

Step 3. Click **Next** (Windows XP), and then select Network Printer. In Windows 7 and Vista, click the button to add a network printer. It tries to search for a printer automatically. To bypass this, click **The Printer I Want Isn't Listed**.

Step 4.   You can browse for the printer on a workgroup network, use Active Directory to search for a printer on a domain-based network, or enter its name (\\server\printername). You can also specify the printer's URL. Click **Next**.

Step 5.   After the printer is selected, specify whether you want to use the new printer as the default printer. Click **Next**.

Step 6.   Specify whether you want to print a test page. Printing a test page allows you to verify whether the correct print driver has been installed.

Step 7.   Click **Finish** to complete the setup process. Provide the Windows CD or printer setup disk if required to complete the process.

Using Shared Resources

With any type of network, the user must log on with a correct username and password to use any network resources. With a dedicated server, such as Windows Server 2008, a single username and password is needed for any network resource the user has permission to use. On a peer-to-peer network using user/group permissions, you must configure each peer server with a list of users or groups. In either case, you must then specify the access rights for each shared folder.

Information can be copied from a shared drive or folder if the user has read-only access; to add, change, or delete information on the shared drive or folder, the user needs full access.

Network printing is performed the same way as local printing after the network printer driver software has been set up on the workstation.

You can identify shared resources with Windows by using Explorer or My Computer/Computer. On a Windows XP system that is sharing resources with other users, a shared drive, folder, or printer will use a modified icon with a hand, indicating that it is being shared (see Figure 16-22). In Windows Vista, there will be a small icon of two users indicating a share. In Windows Vista and Windows 7, the easiest way to see shared resources on a local or remote computer is to open the Network dialog and click the computer (see Figure 16-23).

NOTE   On Windows 7 computers belonging to a homegroup, sharing is configured through the Homegroup option in Network and Sharing Center.

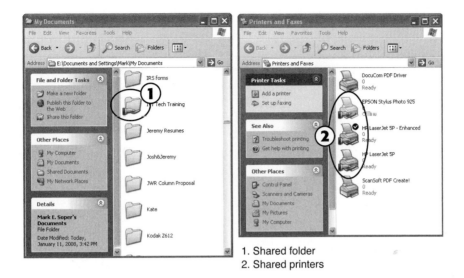

1. Shared folder
2. Shared printers

Figure 16-22   Viewing a shared folder and shared printers in Windows XP.

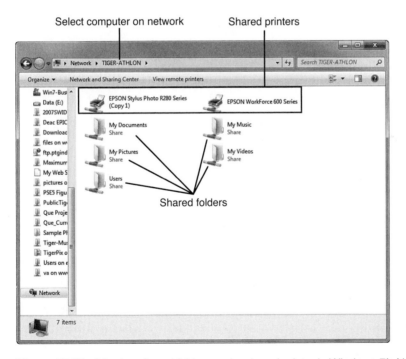

Select computer on network   Shared printers

Shared folders

Figure 16-23   Viewing shared folders and a shared printer in Windows 7's Network dialog.

To use a shared resource on a peer server that uses share-level security, the user must provide the correct password for any password-protected share. To use a shared resource on a network that uses user/group permissions, the user must log on to the network. The administrator of the server or network has already assigned access levels and permissions to each user or group, so the user can immediately begin using shared resources as permitted.

Shared drives and folders can be referred to by a Universal Naming Convention (UNC) name, a fully qualified domain name (FQDN), or a mapped drive letter. Each of these is explained in the following sections.

The Universal Naming Convention

The Universal Naming Convention (UNC) is designed to enable users to access network resources such as folders or printers without mapping drive letters to network drives or specifying the type of device that stores the file or hosts the printer. A UNC name has the following structure in Windows:

\\servername\share name\path\filename

A typical UNC path to a document would resemble

\\Tiger1\O\NetDocuments\this_doc.doc

A typical UNC path to a shared printer on the same system would resemble

\\Tiger1\Printername

What does this mean in plain English?

- **\\Tiger1** is the server.

- **\O** is the share name.

- **\NetDocuments** is the path.

- **\this_doc.doc** is the document.

- **\Printername** is the printer.

UNC enables files and printers to be accessed by the user with 32-bit and 64-bit Windows applications. Because only 23 drive letters (maximum) can be mapped, UNC enables network resources beyond the D–Z limits to still be accessed.

To display the UNC path to a shared folder with Windows XP, right-click the share in My Network Places (Network in Windows 7/Vista) and select **Properties**. The Target field in the dialog lists the UNC path.

Some Windows applications display the UNC path to a file even if the file was accessed through a mapped drive letter, and other Windows applications refer to the UNC path or mapped drive letter path to the file, depending on how the file was retrieved.

Offline Files and Folders

You use offline files to access the information stored in shared network folders, even when the network copies are unavailable. You do this simply by choosing the network files to make available offline, which automatically creates a copy of the network files on the local computer. Windows automatically synchronizes the offline files and opens them whenever the network versions are unavailable.

You might use offline files and folders to protect them from network outages, to work with the files while you are away from the main office, and to boost efficiency when working with a slow connection.

Offline files and folders are available in Windows 7 Professional, Ultimate and Enterprise, Windows Vista Business, Ultimate and Enterprise, and Windows XP Professional.

To enable offline files and folders in Windows 7, access the Control Panel and open the Sync Center. Then click the **Manage Offline Files** link. A dialog box named Offline Files will appear. Click the **Enable Offline Files** button and click **OK**. Then, in Windows Explorer, locate the network folder or file that you want to make available offline, right-click it, and select **Always Available Offline**. This synchronizes the contents of the folder or file to a special location within Windows 7 on the local machine, enabling its use even when the local computer is away from the network. When this is selected, the folder or file will show a Sync icon on top of it telling you that it is set up to work as an offline folder or file. If the folder or file is not necessary as an offline item anymore, simply disable it at the network share, or turn off offline files in the Sync Center. You can also view a list of offline files and folders in the Offline Files dialog box in the Sync Center.

In Windows Vista, go to the Control Panel and access the Offline Files icon. Then continue in the same manner listed for Windows 7 previously.

In Windows XP, turn on offline files by opening My Computer or Windows Explorer. Then, on the Tools menu click **Folder Options**. Click the **Offline Files** tab and select **Enable Offline Files**, and then click **OK**. To make a file or folder available offline, locate the network folder or file; then right-click it, select **Make Available Offline,** and click **Next**. Then, select **Automatically Synchronize the Offline Files when I log On and Log Off My Computer**, and click **Next**. Finally, create a shortcut if you want to.

Fully Qualified Domain Names (FQDNs)

TCP/IP networks that contain DNS servers often use FQDNs to refer to servers along with, or in place of, UNC names. The structure of an FQDN is

> Name-of-server.name-of-domain.root-domain

For example, a server called "charley" in the informit.com domain would have an FQDN of

```
charley.informit.com
```

If you want to access the shared Docs folder on charley.informit.com, you would refer to it as

```
\\charley.informit.com\Docs
```

You can also use the IP address of the server in place of the servername. If 192.10.8.22 is the IP address of charley.informit.com, you can access the Docs folder with the following statement:

```
\\192.10.8.22\Docs
```

You can use either UNCs or FQDNs along with the Net command-line utility (discussed later) to view or map drive letters to shared folders.

Mapped Drives

Windows enables shared folders and shared drives to be mapped to drive letters on clients. In Windows Explorer and My Computer (Computer in Windows 7/Vista), these mapped drive letters show up in the list along with the local drive letters. A shared resource can be accessed either through Network/My Network Places (using the share name) or through a mapped drive letter.

Drive mapping has the following benefits:

- A shared folder mapped as a drive can be referred to by the drive name instead of a long Universal Naming Convention path (see Universal Naming Convention," earlier in this chapter for details).

- If you still use MS-DOS programs, keep in mind that mapped drives are the only way for those programs to access shared folders.

To map a shared folder to a drive in Windows 7/Vista/XP, follow this procedure:

Step 1. Click the shared folder in Network (7/Vista) or My Network Places (XP).

Step 2. Click **Tools, Map Network Drive**. (Note: In Windows 7/Vista, the menu bar might be hidden. To show it use the Alt+T shortcut. Alternatively, you can right-click the shared resource and select **Map Network Drive**.)

Step 3.   Select a drive letter from the list of available drive letters; only drive letters not used by local drives are listed. Drive letters already in use for other shared folders display the UNC name of the shared folder.

Step 4.   Click the **Reconnect at Login** box if you want to use the mapped drive every time you connect to the network. This option should be used only if the server will be available at all times; otherwise, the client will receive error messages when it tries to access the shared resource.

Step 5.   Click the **Connect Using Different Credentials** box if you want to use a different username/password to connect to the shared resource. (Not in Windows XP.) See Figure 16-24.

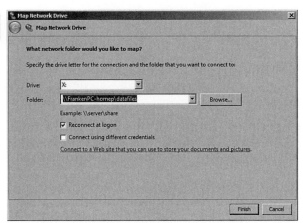

Figure 16-24   The Map Network Drive dialog can be used to create a temporary or permanent drive mapping.

Step 6.   Click **Finish**.

Shared folders can be accessed by either their mapped drive letters or by their folder names in Windows Explorer.

Browser Installation and Configuration

A web browser, such as Microsoft Internet Explorer, Mozilla Firefox, or Google Chrome, is the main interface through which you navigate the Internet. Internet Explorer is a standard component of Windows. Updates and newer versions can be downloaded manually from the Microsoft website or via Windows Update. Other browsers can be downloaded in compressed form and installed manually.

Depending on how you connect with the Internet, you might need to adjust the browser configuration.

Typical options you might need to change include

- **Proxies for use with LAN-based or filtered access**—Users who access the Internet through a local area network might be doing so through a proxy server. A proxy server receives a copy of the website or content the user wants to look at and checks it for viruses or unapproved content before passing it on. The proxy server information is set through the browser's configuration menu (for example, Internet Options in Internet Explorer).

- **Automatic dial up for convenience**—Internet Explorer and most other browsers can also be set to dial up the Internet automatically whenever you start the browser to make Internet access easier. This option is useful for dial-up connections.

- **Email configuration**—Most browsers include an email client; the settings for the email server and other options must be made to allow email to be seen and replied to within the browser.

- **Disable graphics**—Users with extremely slow connections who view primarily text-based pages can disable graphics for extra speed.

- **Security settings for Java**—Advanced features, such as Java and ActiveX, make sites more interactive, but might also pose a security risk; these features can be limited or disabled through the Security menu.

You can also adjust default colors and fonts and the default start page.

Generally, you should use all the features possible of the browser unless you have speed or security concerns that lead you to disable some features.

Setting Up Your Browser to Use Your Internet Connection

In most cases, users want the Internet to be available as soon as they open their web browser. Because some users have dial-up connections and some networks use proxy servers to provide firewall protection or content filtering, you might need to adjust the browser configuration to permit Internet access.

To view or adjust the browser configuration for Internet Explorer, follow this procedure:

Step 1.   Open Internet Explorer.

Step 2.   Click **Tools, Internet Options**.

Step 3.   Click the **Connections** tab.

Step 4.   If the Internet connection uses a dial-up modem, select the correct dial-up connection from those listed and choose **Always Dial** (to start the connection when the browser is opened) or **Dial Whenever a Network Connection Is Not Present**. Click **Set Default** to make the selected connection the default.

Step 5. If the Internet connection uses a network, click **Never Dial a Connection**, and click **LAN Settings** to check network configuration.

Step 6. Ask the network administrator if you should use Automatically Detect Settings or whether you should specify a particular automatic configuration script.

Step 7. Click **OK** to save changes at each menu level until you return to the browser display.

If a proxy server is used for Internet access, it must be specified by server name and port number (see Figure 16-25):

Step 1. From the Connections tab, click **LAN settings**.

Step 2. From the Local Area Network (LAN) Settings window, you have two options underneath Proxy Server. If a single proxy server address and port number is used for all types of traffic, click the **Use a Proxy Server** check box and enter the address and port number. However, if different proxy servers or ports will be used, click the **Use a Proxy Server** check box and click the **Advanced** button.

Step 3. Specify the correct server and port number to use.

Step 4. Click **OK** to save changes at each menu level until you return to the browser display.

Enabling/Disabling Script Settings

Some networks use a separate configuration or logon script for Internet access. To specify a script with Internet Explorer, click **Tools, Internet Options, Connections, LAN Settings, Use Automatic Configuration Script**. Enter the URL or filename of the script and click OK.

> **TIP** You can also configure Internet Explorer to automatically detect the settings if your network is configured to provide them. However, if you enable this option and the network is not configured to provide them, Internet Explorer will not be able to connect to the Internet.

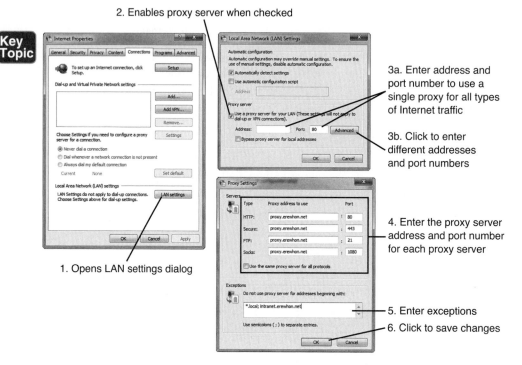

Figure 16-25   Configuring proxy server settings in Internet Explorer 8.

Configuring Browser Security Settings

You can configure Internet Explorer's default security settings for Java, ActiveX, and other potentially harmful content through the Internet Options Security tab. Open the Internet Options tab with Control Panel, or click **Tools**, **Settings**, **Internet Options** within Internet Explorer.

Depending on the version of Internet Explorer, there will be four or five default security settings: High, Medium-High, Medium, Medium-Low, and Low. High blocks almost all active content and prevents websites from setting cookies (small text files that can track website usage). Medium (the default) enables some active content but blocks unsigned ActiveX controls. Medium-Low blocks unsafe content but downloads other content without prompts, and Low has no safeguards.

Each setting is matched to a web content zone. By default, all sites not in other zones are placed in the Internet zone, which uses Medium-High security (Medium on older versions of Internet Explorer). The local Intranet zone uses Medium-Low security by default (medium in older versions). Trusted sites use Medium security by default (Low in older versions); restricted sites use High security by default.

To add or remove sites on the local Intranet, Trusted, or Restricted site list, select the zone and click Sites.

By default, local Intranet sites include all local sites, all sites that don't use a proxy server, and all UNC network paths. Remove check marks to restrict these options. Click Advanced to add or remove a specific site or to require a secured server. Trusted or Restricted sites display the Add/Remove dialog box immediately.

> **NOTE**   Click **Custom** from the main **Security** tab to adjust the default settings for any security level. If the settings of any zone are misconfigured, one can return to default settings for an individual zone or reset security of all zones by clicking the **Reset All Zones to Default Level** button.

Multifunction Network Device Configurations

Your SOHO network wouldn't be complete without a multifunction network device. These are usually just referred to as routers—it's much simpler! But the device does much more than route information to the Internet. It often has a built-in 4-port switch (or possibly more ports), acts as a firewall, and has some additional functionality that we'll detail now.

NAT

Network address translation (NAT) is the process of modifying IP addresses as information crosses a router. Generally, this functionality is built into a router. It hides an entire IP address space on the LAN, for example, 192.168.0.1 through 192.168.0.255. Whenever an IP address on the LAN wishes to communicate with the Internet, the IP is converted to the public IP of the router, for example, 68.54.127.95, but it will be whatever IP address was assigned to the router by the ISP. This way, it looks like the router is the only device making the connection to remote computers on the Internet, providing safety for the computers on the LAN. It also allows a single IP to do the work for many IP addresses in the LAN.

Port Forwarding

This method is used to forward external visitors through the router to a specific computer. Instead of opening up the entire LAN, port forwarding directs particular traffic where you want it to go. A basic example would be if you were to set up an FTP server internally on your LAN. The FTP server might have the IP address 192.168.0.250 and have port 21 open ready to accept file transactions; or, you could use a different inbound port if you want. Clients on the Internet that want to connect to your FTP server would have to know the IP address of your router, so for example the clients would connect with an FTP client using the IP 68.54.127.95 and port 21. Once you create the appropriate port forwarding rule, the router would then see these packets and forward them to 192.168.0.250:21, or whatever port you choose. Now, many ISPs block this type of activity, but it becomes a common and important method in larger networks.

DMZ

A **demilitarized zone (DMZ)** is an area that is not quite on the Internet and not quite part of your LAN. It's a sort of middle ground that is for the most part protected by a firewall, but particular traffic will be let through. It's a good place for web servers, email servers, and FTP servers because these are services required by users on the Internet. The beauty of this is that the users will not have access to your LAN—if it is configured correctly of course.

MAC Filtering

The media access control (MAC) address of your network adapter is what identifies it on most LANs. An example of a MAC address would be 00-12-23-A4-B1-F8. This hexadecimal number is burned into the PROM chip of the network adapter. MAC filtering is a technique used to secure the multifunction network device by only allowing computers with specific MAC addresses. These addresses are added to a list in the router's firmware. Any other computers that attempt to connect through normal means will be denied access. Aside from disabling the SSID and using encryption, this is one of the most common ways of securing a router.

Using Network Command-Line Tools

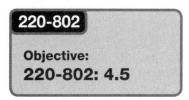

220-802

Objective:
220-802: 4.5

Windows contains several command-line tools for troubleshooting and configuring the network. These include the following:

- **Net**—Displays and uses network resources
- **Ping**—Tests TCP/IP and Internet connections
- **Tracert**—Traces the route between a specified website or IP address and your PC

- **NSLookup**—Displays detailed information about DNS

- **IPConfig**—Displays detailed TCP/IP configuration about your Windows 7/Vista/XP system

- **Netstat**—Displays Protocol statistics and current TCP/IP network connections

- **NBTSAT**—Displays protocol statistics and current TCP/IP connections using NBT (NetBIOS over TCP/IP)

The following sections describe these tools.

Using the Net Command

Windows includes the **Net** command for use in displaying and using network resources from the command line. Some of the **Net** commands you can use include

- **Net Help**—Displays help for a **Net** option; for example, use **Net Help View** for help with the **Net View** command.

- **Net Use**—Maps a network drive to a shared resource on the network; for example, **Net Use Q: \\Tiger1\shared**. In this example, Q: will behave just like any other drive letter such as C:, D:, and so on. The only difference is that it will redirect to another computer on the network.

- **Net View**—Displays other hosts on the network.

- **Net Helpmsg errorcode#**—Displays the meaning of any Microsoft error code.

To display a complete list of **Net** commands, type **Net /? |More** from the command prompt.

Using Ping

Windows can use the **Ping** command to test TCP/IP, check for connectivity to other hosts on the network, and check the Internet connection for proper operation. **Ping** is a more reliable way to check an Internet connection than opening your browser because a misconfigured browser could cause you to think that your TCP/IP configuration is incorrect.

To use **Ping** to check connectivity with another host on the network, follow this procedure:

Step 1.   Open a command-prompt window.

Step 2.   Type **Ping IPaddress** or **Ping servername** to ping another host on the network; then press **Enter**. For example, to ping a router, typical syntax would be **Ping 192.168.1.1**.

To use **Ping** to check your Internet connection, follow this procedure:

Step 1.   Start your Internet connection. If you use a LAN to connect to the Internet, you might have an always-on connection.

Step 2.   Open a command-prompt window.

Step 3.   Type **Ping IPaddress** or **Ping servername** and press **Enter**. For example, to ping a web server called www.erewhon.net, type **Ping www.erewhon.net**.

By default, Ping sends four data packets from your computer to any IP address or servername you specify. If your TCP/IP connection is working properly, you should see a reply from each ping you sent out indicating how quickly the signals traveled back from the target and the IP address or URL of the target. Note that some websites and servers are configured to ignore pings as a security measure. The replies indicate that the host is alive. Any other message would indicate a problem; for example, the "Request timed out" or "Destination host unreachable" messages would require further troubleshooting. Keep in mind that if the local computer is configured incorrectly, you might not be able to "ping" anything! Also watch for the amount of time the ping took to reply back. A longer latency time could indicate network congestion. Conversely, the lower the time in milliseconds (ms), the faster your connection. Connection speeds vary a great deal due to various factors, such as Internet network congestion, server speed, and the number of relays needed to transfer your request from your computer to the specified server. To check relay information, use the **Tracert** command.

Using Tracert

The **Tracert** command is used by Windows to trace the route taken by data traveling from your computer to an IP address or website you specify. By default, Tracert checks up to 30 hops between your computer and the specified website or IP address. To use **Tracert** to check the routing, follow this procedure:

Step 1.   Start your Internet connection. If you use a LAN to connect to the Internet, you might have an always-on connection.

Step 2.   Open a command-prompt window.

Step 3.   Type **Tracert IP address** or **Tracert servername** and press **Enter**. For example, to trace the route to a web server called www.erewhon.tv, type **Tracert www.erewhon.tv**. **Tracert** displays the IP addresses and URLs of each server used to relay the information to the specified location, as well as the time required.

To see help for the **Tracert** command, type **Tracert** without any options and press the **Enter** key.

Using NSLookup

NSLookup is a command-line tool used to determine information about the DNS. When **NSLookup** is run without options, it displays the name and IP address of the default DNS server before displaying a DNS prompt. Enter the name of a website or server to determine its IP address; enter the IP address of a website or server to determine its name. Enter a question mark (?) at the prompt to see more options; type exit, and then press **Enter** to exit the program.

Using Ipconfig

The **IPConfig** command-line utility is used to display the computer's current IP address, subnet mask, and default gateway (see Figure 16-26). **Ipconfig** combined with the **/all** switch will show more information including the DNS server address and MAC address, which is the hexadecimal address that is burned into the ROM of the network adapter.

TIP   If you're having problems seeing other computers on the network or connecting to the Internet on a network that uses server-assigned IPv4 addresses, type **IPConfig /release** and press **Enter**; then type **IPConfig /renew** and press **Enter** to obtain a new IP address from the DHCP server on your network. The comparable commands for releasing/renewing an IPv6 address are **IPConfig /release6** and **IPConfig /renew6**.

Using Netstat

Most commonly **netstat** is used to show the current connections to a remote computer. Let's say you connected to google.com and went into the Command Prompt and typed **netstat**. You would get several results, one of which would look similar to this:

```
TCP    192.168.0.5:49732    google.com:80        Established
```

The **netstat** command shows only TCP connections. If you were interested in seeing both TCP and UDP connections, you could use the command **netstat –a**. And to see the information in numerical format, use **netstat –n**. This displays IP addresses instead of domain names as shown here:

```
TCP    92.168.0.5:49732    74.125.113.106:80        Established
```

Netstat can also be used to show the network adapter's Ethernet statistics with the **netstat –e** command. Check out the other various switches by typing **netstat /?**.

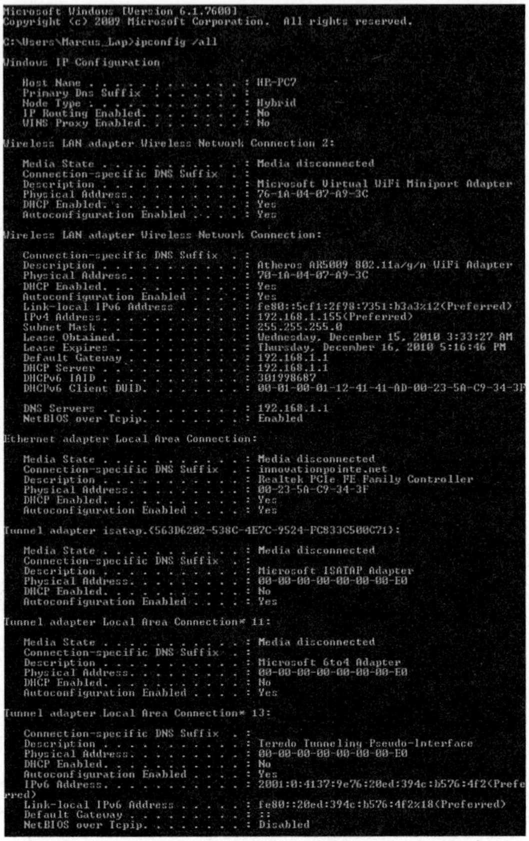

Figure 16-26 IPConfig /all displays complete information about your TCP/IP configuration.

Using NBTSTAT

NBTSTAT can be used to show the services running on the local computer or a remote computer. It calls this the name table. For example, you could find out what services are running, what the computer's name is, and what network it is a part of by typing **netstat –a 192.168.0.5** (or whatever your local IP is). The results would be similar to the following:

```
Computer1           <00>      Unique          Registered

Workgroup           <00>      Group           Registered

Computer1           <20>      Unique          Registered
```

The computer and network names are easy to see: Computer1 and Workgroup. But also notice that there are numbers in alligators such as <00> and <20>. These are the services mentioned previously. <00> is the workstation service, the service that allows your computer to redirect out to other systems to view shared resources. <20> is the server service that allows your computer to share resources with other systems. Check out the other various switches by typing **nbtstat /?**.

Network and Internet Troubleshooting

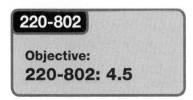

Use this section to prepare for troubleshooting questions involving network hardware and software on the A+ Certification exams and in your day-to-day work as a computer technician.

Can't Access Network Resources

If an error message such as Duplicate Computer Name or Duplicate IP Address is displayed during system startup, open the Network icon and change the name of the computer or the system's IP address. Contact the network administrator for the correct name or IP address settings to use. Apply this same method if your computer is showing an APIPA address on the 169.254.0.0 network. This usually happens if the computer is unable to obtain an IP address from the DHCP server.

Significant Drops in Network Performance

Significant drops in network performance and slow network speeds can be traced to a variety of causes, including

- Damage to cables, connectors, hubs, and switches

- Expanding network capacity with hubs in place of switches

- Connecting high-speed NICs to low-speed hubs or switches

- RFI/EMI interference with wireless networks

If network usage patterns remain constant but some users report lower performance, check cables, connectors, and other network hardware for physical damage. Dry, brittle, and cracked cables and connectors can generate interference, which forces network stations to retransmit data because it wasn't received correctly. Replace damaged cables and connectors.

Use diagnostic programs supplied with the network adapter if the same brand and model of adapter is used by multiple computers. These diagnostics programs send and receive data and provide reports of problems.

If all the users connected to a single hub or switch report slowdowns, check the hub or switch. Replace a hub with a switch to see an immediate boost in performance. Continue to use switches to add capacity.

Make sure that computers with Fast Ethernet (10/100) hardware are connected to dual-speed switches to get the benefits of 100Mbps performance. 10/100 cards will run at 10Mbps if connected to 10Mbps switches. Enable full-duplex mode if the cards and switches support it to boost performance to 20Mbps (with 10BASE-T) or 200Mbps (with 10/100 cards running Fast Ethernet).

Make sure that computers with Gigabit Ethernet (10/100/1000) hardware are connected to Gigabit Ethernet switches to get the benefits of 1000Mbps performance.

On the wireless side of things, watch out for low radio frequency (RF) signal. This is usually due to the distance of the wireless adapter from the wireless access point. Or, there could be obstructions that cause interference. Radio frequency interference (RFI) is closely related to EMI, and RFI/EMI interference can have a big impact on wireless network (WLAN) performance. For the A+ exam, some things to consider include cordless phone and microwave usage. Because these devices can also inhabit the 2.4GHz frequency range used by 802.11b, g, and n networks, they can interfere with the network signal. Because 2.4GHz cordless phones use spread-spectrum technology to help avoid eavesdropping, it is not possible to configure these phones to use a particular 2.4GHz channel.

To help avoid interference from other wireless networks, configure your 2.4GHz wireless network to use one of the non-overlapping channels (1, 6, or 11). Some anecdotal evidence suggests that channel 11 is less likely to receive RFI from 2.4GHz cordless phones.

You should also consider using cordless phones that use frequencies that will not interfere with 2.4GHz or 5GHz wireless networks, such as phones using DECT (1.9GHz) or DECT 6.0 (6.0GHz) frequency bands.

To avoid interference from microwave ovens or other microwave devices, make sure the oven or device is not physically near any wireless devices.

Unattended PC Drops Its Network Connection

Incorrect settings for power management can cause stations to lose their network connections when power management features, such as standby mode, are activated.

Check the properties for the network adapter to see whether the adapter can be set to wake up the computer when network activity is detected.

All Users Lose Network Connection

If the network uses a bus topology, a failure of any station on the network or of termination at cither end of the network will cause the entire network to fail. Check the terminators first, and then the T-connectors and cables between computers. If you suspect that a particular computer is the cause of the failure, move the terminator to the computer preceding it in the bus topology. Repeat as needed to isolate the problem. Replace cables, connectors, or network cards as needed to solve the problem.

If the network uses a star topology, check the power supply going to the hub, switch, or wireless access point, or replace the device.

If only the users connected to a new hub or switch that is connected to an existing hub or switch lose their network connection, check the connection between the existing hub or switch and the new one. Most hubs and switches have an uplink port that is used to connect an additional hub or switch. You can either use the uplink port or the regular port next to the uplink port, but not both. Connect the computer using the port next to the uplink port to another port to make the uplink port available for connecting the new hub or switch.

If the uplink port appears to be connected properly, check the cable. Uplink ports perform the crossover for the user, enabling you to use an ordinary network cable to add a hub or switch.

TIP If you use a crossover cable, you must connect the new hub or switch through a regular port, not the uplink port.

Users Can Access Some Shared Resources But Not Others

Users who need to access shared resources on a network using user/group permissions must be granted permission to access resources; different users are typically allowed different access levels to network resources. Contact the network or system administrator for help if a user is prevented from using a resource; the administrator of the network or peer server needs to permit or deny access to the user.

Can't Print to a Network Printer

Problems with network printing can also come from incorrect print queue settings and incorrect printer drivers.

When you configure a network printer connection, you must correctly specify the UNC path to the printer. For example, if the printer is shared as LaserJ on the server Xeon3, the correct UNC path to specify in the printer properties sheet would be

   \\Xeon3\LaserJ

TIP   If a shared printer connected to a Windows system is available at some times, but not at other times, open the printer's properties sheet and adjust the Scheduling Option settings. See Chapter 11, "Printers," for details.

Ping and Tracert Work, But User Can't Display Web Pages with Browser

If Ping and Tracert receive output from the specified websites but the web browser cannot display web pages on those or other sites, the browser configuration might be incorrect.f

If the browser doesn't use the correct configuration for the connection type, no pages will be displayed. With dial-up Internet connections, either the user must manually open the connection or the browser should be set to dial the connection. If a proxy server or special network configuration is needed, this must be configured in the browser.

See "Setting Up Your Browser to Use Your Internet Connection," earlier in this chapter for details.

Overview of Creating a Small Office/Home Office Network

Use the following information to help you understand the "big picture" of creating a Small Office/Home Office (SOHO) network that can be used to share an Internet connection and provide shared resources:

Step 1.   Decide on the type of Internet connection you will use. For best performance, use a cable or DSL connection with at least 6Mbps minimum download speed. Choose higher speeds to enable more users to share the connection with acceptable performance.

Step 2.   Determine how users will connect to the network: wired Ethernet, wireless Ethernet, or a mixture of wired and wireless devices.

Step 3.   Select a cable or DSL modem (depending on your connection type) and a router. You have more flexibility if you use separate modem and router devices.

Step 4. Have the cable or DSL modem installed by the ISP (or order a self-install kit from the ISP; a self-install kit contains the modem and other hardware needed for installation). You can also purchase cable modems at computer and electronics stores.

Step 5. Place the router where it will be most convenient for connections, such as a wiring closet or shelf. Make sure the modem and the router can connect to each other via a suitable network cable (CAT5e or better quality). If you plan to connect with wireless clients, try to choose a central location for the router.

Step 6. Configure the router to connect to the modem and, if you are using wireless clients, select the most appropriate wireless security settings.

Step 7. Connect each client to the router. If you are using wireless Ethernet, you must configure each client to use the same SSID, encryption type, and encryption key as those you used when setting up the router.

Step 8. Configure each client to be part of the same workgroup.

Step 9. Set up file and printer sharing on each client that has resources you want to share.

Step 10. Test the Internet connection on each client.

Step 11. Test the ability to access shared resources. Depending on the version(s) of Windows in use, you might need to set up additional user accounts on systems with shared resources or change password settings to enable remote users to access shared resources.

Exam Preparation Tasks

Review All the Key Topics

Review the most important topics in the chapter, noted with the key topics icon in the outer margin of the page. Table 16-12 lists a reference of these key topics and the page numbers on which each is found.

Table 16-12   Key Topics for Chapter 16

Key Topic Element	Description	Page Number
Figure 16-1	A server with three workstations, each of which is using a different shared resource.	771
Figure 16-5	A typical external modem that connects to a serial port.	780
Figure 16-8	A typical self-installed DSL setup.	788
Figure 16-9	A typical cable modem and cable TV installation.	789
Table 16-2	Common Protocols and their Ports	800
Figure 16-11	An STP cable (left) includes a metal shield and ground wire for protection against interference, while a UTP cable (right) does not.	802
Table 16-3	Categories and Uses for UTP and STP Cabling	802
Figure 16-13	RJ-11 connector (left) compared to RJ-45 connector (right).	804
Figure 16-14	SC, FC, and ST fiber-optic cable connectors compared.	807
Table 16-4	Wired Ethernet Networks	810
Table 16-5	Wireless Ethernet Standards	811
Table 16-6	Bluetooth Classes	812
Table 16-7	Wireless Ethernet Configuration Settings	818
Table 16-8	Static Versus Server-Assigned IP Addressing	820
Figure 16-15	The General tab is configured to obtain IP and DNS server information automatically when a DHCP server is used on the network.	821
Figure 16-17	The General tab of the TCP/IP properties sheet when manual configuration is used.	823
Table 16-9	An IP Address and Corresponding Subnet Mask	824
Table 16-10	Internet Protocol Classification System	824

Key Topic Element	Description	Page Number
Figure 16-20	Setting up a network share in Windows XP using the default simple file-sharing option.	831
Figure 16-21	Setting up a network share in Windows XP when simple file sharing is disabled.	833
Figure 16-24	The Map Network Drive dialog can be used to create a temporary or permanent drive mapping.	841
Figure 16-25	Configuring proxy server settings in Internet Explorer 8.	844

Complete the Tables and Lists from Memory

Print a copy of Appendix A, "Memory Tables," (found on the CD), or at least the section for this chapter, and complete the tables and lists from memory. Appendix B, "Memory Tables Answer Key," also on the CD, includes completed tables and lists to check your work.

Define Key Terms

Define the following key terms from this chapter, and check your answers in the glossary.

LAN, WAN, client, server, client/server, peer-to-peer, modem, DUN, DSL, ADSL, SDSL, TCP/IP, HTTP, HTTPS, SSL, TLS, HTML, FTP, DNS, domain name, SMTP, POP3, IMAP, 802.11a, 802.11b, 802.11g, 802.11n, IrDA, VoIP, SSID, WAP, WEP, WPA, star topology, repeater, hub, switch, router, WINS, DHCP, LDAP, DMZ

Complete Hands-On Labs

Complete the hands-on labs, and then see the answers and explanations at the end of the chapter.

Lab 16-1: Select the Appropriate Type of Cable

Scenario: You are required to recommend three different types of cabling that will best suit each environment.

Cable Type #1:

The customer requires a cable that is resistant to EMI, is easy to install, and will work with their current 1000Mbps network. Write down the type of cable you would use and why.

_____

_____

_____

Cable Type #2:

The customer requires a cable that is fire-resistant and will work with their 100Mbps network. Final request, it must be cheap! Write down the type of cable you would use and why.

_____

_____

_____

Cable Type #3:

The customer requires a cable that is completely resistant to EMI and will work as a backbone cable between switches at 10Gbps. Write down the type of cable you would use and why.

_____

_____

_____

Lab 16-2: Select the Appropriate IP Networks

Scenario: A customer asks you to create a new IP network within the Class B private range. It must include a gateway that uses the first available address on the network. Write down the IP network you would use and the IP address of the gateway.

_____

_____

Lab 16-3: Select the Network Option and Appropriate Ports

Scenario: A customer needs you to set up an area where you can install an FTP server, HTTP server, and POP3 email server using the default protocols. This area must be between the LAN and the Internet. Write down the network type where the servers will be placed and the ports you would use.

_____

_____

Lab 16-4: Install an Appropriate Wireless Network

Scenario: A customer wants you to install a wireless network that complies with the fastest current WLAN standard and uses the best wireless encryption currently available on a typical wireless router. Write down your information below.

_____

_____

_____

Answer Review Questions

Answer these review questions and then see the answers and explanations at the end of the chapter.

1. The Windows operating system uses two major types of networks. Which of the following are the two?

   a. Client/server

   b. Node server

   c. Peer-to-peer

   d. IP network model

2. One reason for implementing a network is to share the Internet. Which of the following methods can connect a network to the Internet? (Choose all that apply.)

   a. Dial-up modem

   b. ISDN modem

   c. DSL modem

   d. Cable modem

3. You are a technician for your company. You have been asked to determine which protocols are in use. You discover that the company is using TCP/IPv4. Which of the following network protocols might you also find on the network? (Choose all that apply.)

   a. TCP/IPv6

   b. ISP

   c. NetBEUI

   d. IEEE

4. Which of the following technologies are part of the TCP/IP suite? (Choose all that apply.)

   a. HTTP/HTTPS

   b. SSL

   c. TLS

   d. Ethernet

5. You have been asked to recommend a network topology to use in a new network. Which of the following are valid network topologies?

   a. Bus

   b. Star

   c. Ring

   d. Mesh

   e. All of these options are correct.

6. The company you work for is using the oldest and most commonly used network today, Ethernet. Which of the following is another name for Ethernet?

   a. IEEE 1394

   b. IEEE 802.11b

   c. IEEE 802.3

   d. IEEE 802.11g

7. You have been asked by your company to create and install a network. You have decided that you are using Category 5e. Which of the following is the most common type of cable used by Cat5e? (Choose all that apply.)

    a. STP

    b. Coaxial

    c. UTP

    d. Thin-net

8. Which of the following devices would you need if a client asks you to connect his computer to a network? (Choose two.)

    a. A network interface card

    b. A wireless card

    c. An AGP adapter card

    d. A BNC connector

9. You are installing a network interface card. You have been instructed to configure the network card to send and receive data at the same time. Which of the following settings will you need to configure the network card to complete what has been asked of you?

    a. Half duplex

    b. Full duplex

    c. Super duplex mode

    d. Single duplex mode

10. You have been asked by your company to upgrade all hubs to switches. How would this upgrade change the existing network?

    a. The network will be slower.

    b. There is no difference in speeds.

    c. A switch creates a dedicated full speed connection.

    d. You do not need to have NIC cards.

11. You have been asked by a company to analyze their network. You find several hubs and switches within the network. Which of the following additional devices might you find in this network?

   a. Routers

   b. Bridges

   c. Repeaters

   d. VLAN technology

12. You have been contacted by a client who is having problems connecting to the Internet. Where would be a good place to start the troubleshooting process?

   a. File and Print Sharing

   b. Run the Ping command-line utility

   c. Configure the DHCP server

   d. TCP/IP configuration

13. You have been contacted by a client who is unable to access network printers and other shared resources. Which of the following should you verify is installed and enabled?

   a. Client services

   b. System monitor

   c. File and print sharing

   d. TCP/IP protocol

14. What is the name of the service that must be installed on a Windows computer to resolve host names to IP addresses?

   a. DNS

   b. TCP/IP

   c. HTTP

   d. PING

15. You need to connect to a server to use shared resources. Which of the following are ways to connect to the server? (Choose two.)

   a. Use the UNC path of the resource you need access to.

   b. Contact the network administrator for help.

   c. Use the map network drive tool.

   d. Just walk over to the server and do what you need.

16. Which of the following programs enables a user to browse the Internet? (Choose two.)

    a. Internet Explorer

    b. Firefox

    c. Windows Explorer

    d. The command prompt

17. A user with your company is having connectivity problems. You need to diagnose the problem as soon as possible. You call the client and walk her through finding the IP address. What should you do next?

    a. Run ipconfig /release.

    b. Run ipconfig /flushdns.

    c. Ping the IP address of the client's computer.

    d. Walk her through how to ping the server.

18. A user is unable to access the network. Which of the following could cause this to happen? (Choose all that apply.)

    a. Damage to cables.

    b. A faulty network card.

    c. The boot files are corrupt.

    d. Connecting a high-speed NIC to a low-speed port.

19. Which port is used by the DNS protocol?

    a. 21

    b. 25

    c. 53

    d. 80

    e. 110

    f. 3389

20. Which of the following technologies offers wireless 4G connection speeds up to 50km away from a city's transmitting station?

    a. Fiber optic

    b. WiMAX

    c. Cable Internet

    d. WLAN

21. What type of tool would you use to terminate a wire to a RJ-45 jack?

    a. Wire stripper

    b. Cable tester

    c. Punchdown tool

    d. Tone and probe

Answers to Hands-On Labs

Lab 16-1: Select the Appropriate Type of Cable

Answers:

Cable Type #1:

The cable should be Category 6 shielded twisted pair (STP). STP is resistant to EMI. Category 6 is easier to install than fiber optic and works best with 1000Mbps networks as compared to Cat 5 or Cat 5e.

Cable Type #2:

The cable should be plenum-rated Category 5e. Plenum-rated cable is fire-resistant. Cat 5e is the cheapest viable option that meets 100Mbps speeds. (Category 5 would also work, but could be difficult to find and won't be much cheaper.)

Cable Type #3:

The cable should be Multimode optical fiber. Fiber-optic cabling is completely resistant to EMI. Multimode can do 10Gbps over distances as much as 300 meters. That is plenty to connect our two switches.

Lab 16-2: Select the Appropriate IP Networks

Answer: The network should be within the private Class B range: 172.16.0.0 through 172.31.0.0. For this answer we'll use 172.16.0.0. The gateway should use the IP address 172.16.0.1 because that is the first available address for that network.

Lab 16-3: Select the Network Option and Appropriate Ports

Answer: The network type you should implement is a demilitarized zone (DMZ). This is neither on the LAN nor on the Internet; it is an area between the two so to speak. The ports you should use are FTP = 21, HTTP = 80, and POP3 = 110.

Lab 16-4: Install an Appropriate Wireless Network

Answer: The WLAN standard you should use is 802.11n, which is currently the fastest option at a maximum of 600Mbps. The wireless encryption type you should use is WPA2 with AES, as of the writing of this book, the most powerful encryption you can use on a typical wireless router.

Answers and Explanations to Review Questions

1. **A, C.** The Windows operating system uses two types of networks. One is a client/server network, meaning that client computers need to contact a domain controller to work. A peer-to-peer network is used in smaller networks where the expense is a factor, no centralized administration is necessary, or if the organization doesn't have the resources to support a client/server network.

2. **A, B, C, D.** Although the older dial-up modems are going by the wayside, they are still used. The newer technologies such as an ISDN, cable, and DSL more commonly connect today's networks to the Internet.

3. **A, C.** Although most current networks use TCP/IPv4, you can also find the TCP/IPv6 and in some situations you might even find the older NetBEUI protocol (Network BIOS Extended User Interface).

4. **A, B, C.** The TCP/IP protocol suite includes many protocols including the Hypertext Transfer Protocol (HTTP), HTTP Secure (HTTPS), Secure Sockets Layer (SSL), and its successor Transport Layer Security (TLS). Ethernet is a network architecture commonly used, upon which TCP/IP runs.

5. **E.** Bus, star, ring, and mesh topologies are used in the field today. You can use these techniques to supply network connectivity to your client computers.

6. **C.** The oldest network in common use today is Ethernet, also known as IEEE-802.3. IEEE 1394 refers to the PC version of FireWire cable. 802.11b and 802.11g are wireless networking technologies.

7. **C.** UTP cable comes in various grades, of which Category 5e is the most common of the standard cabling grades. Category 5e cabling is suitable for use with both standard 10BASE-T and Fast Ethernet networking, and can also be used for Gigabit Ethernet networks if it passes compliance testing. STP is a form of cabling also available in Cat5e but is used only when shielding from EMI/RFI is necessary, as it is more expensive, bulkier, and harder to work with than UTP.

8. **A, B.** Although many recent computers include a 10/100 or 10/100/1000 Ethernet port or a wireless Ethernet adapter, you might need to install a network interface card (NIC) into a computer you want to add to a network. For desktops, the card would be installed into a PCIe x1 or a PCI slot; for laptops, the card would be installed into an ExpressCard or CardBus slot. A USB network adapter could be used by both types of computers.

9. **B.** If the hardware in use on an Ethernet, Fast Ethernet, or Gigabit Ethernet network permits, you can configure the network to run in full-duplex mode. Full-duplex mode enables the adapter to send and receive data at the same time, which doubles network speed over the default half-duplex mode.

10. **C.** A switch resembles a hub but creates a dedicated full-speed connection between the two computers communicating with each other. By doing this it upgrades the speed of the existing network.

11. **A, B, C.** Hubs or switches are the only connectivity equipment needed for a workgroup LAN. However, if the network needs to span longer distances than those supported by the network cabling in use or needs to connect to another network, additional connectivity equipment is needed. A repeater is used to carry the signals even farther than normal. You can also use a bridge to connect two networks together. A router can be used to connect two or more networks.

12. **B.** Ping is a command-line utility used to check Internet connectivity. Ping is already included in Windows.

13. **C.** On a Windows operating system, to be able to share printers and resources with other users, you must make sure that the file and print services are installed and enabled in the Properties window of a network connection.

14. **A.** DNS is the Domain Name System. The DNS service must be installed on a computer to resolve host names or domain names to their corresponding IP addresses. TCP/IP is the Transmission Control Protocol/Internet Protocol suite. HTTP is the Hypertext Transfer Protocol. PING is a command used to test whether other computers are available on the network.

15. **A, C.** The Universal Naming Convention (UNC) is designed to enable users to access network resources, such as folders or printers, without mapping drive letters to network drives or specifying the type of device that stores the file or hosts the printer. If you are using a Windows operating system, you can also use the map network drive tool and provide the UNC path.

16. **A, B.** A web browser, such as Microsoft Internet Explorer or Mozilla Firefox, is the main interface through which you navigate the Internet. Internet Explorer is a standard component of Windows. Updates and newer versions can be downloaded manually from the Microsoft website or via Windows Update. Other browsers can be downloaded in compressed form and installed manually.

17. **C.** After you have discerned the IP address of the client's computer, ping that IP address to see whether it is alive. If you get replies, then the client computer has network connectivity. If your ping times out, then you will need to troubleshoot the issue further.

18. **A, B.** If a user reports that he or she cannot connect to the network, check cables, connectors, and other network hardware. A disconnected cable is a common culprit. A faulty connector or network card could also be the cause. Replace any damaged cables and connectors.

19. **C.** The Domain Name System (DNS) uses port 53 by default. Port 21 is used by FTP. Port 25 is used by SMTP. Port 80 is used by HTTP. Port 110 is used by POP3. Port 3389 is used by RDP.

20. **B.** WiMAX can send information over much larger distances than WLAN standards, up to 50 kilometers. It offers high-speed connections in the 4G range. Fiber-optic is a type of wired connection that uses glass or plastic fibers to transmit data over light. Cable Internet is a copper-based wired technology. WLAN stands for wireless local area network and refers to the 802.11 standards such as a, b, g, and n.

21. **C.** You use a punchdown tool to terminate individual network wires to RJ-45 jacks and patch panels. A wire stripper is used to remove the PVC jacket from the network cable. The cable tester is used to test the network run from end to end. A tone and probe kit is used to test telephone connections from end to end and can test individual pairs of wires on a network cable.

This chapter covers the following subjects:

- **Security Fundamentals**—This section covers the mindset you should have when securing a computer. File systems, authentication, and how to protect against malware are all dealt with in this section.

- **Data and Physical Security**—This section describes encryption types, the Local Security Policy, backups, password management, and much more.

- **Securing Wireless Networks**—This section talks about wireless encryption and maximizing security on wireless devices.

- **Securing Wired Networks**—This section discusses how to secure wired Ethernet networks from intruders and eavesdroppers.

- **Access Control Purposes and Principles**—Windows uses an Access Control Model to set what users have rights to what resources. User Account Control (UAC), NTFS permissions, and auditing are also described.

- **Data Destruction/Disposal Techniques**—In this section you will learn how to recycle, dispose of, or destroy hard drives and other data storing devices.

- **Installing, Configuring, and Troubleshooting Security Features**—This section demonstrates how to secure the BIOS, configure a firewall, and set up a secure wireless connection.

This chapter covers **CompTIA A+ 220-802 objectives 1.8, 2.1 through 2.6, and 4.7**.

CHAPTER 17

Security

Some of the more significant changes to the 2012 A+ Certification exams include a shift of all security topics to the second exam, 220-802; plus, additional security objectives in general. It's not surprising, however. With widespread reports of security breaches, identity theft, and lost hardware, understanding how to secure an individual's computers and networks is an important skill.

The A+ 220-802 exam includes objectives measuring your understanding of security as it relates to both individual computer and network environments. Mastering these objectives will help you pass the exams and will also help you handle the increasing challenges of computer security in the real world.

Foundation Topics

Security Fundamentals

220-802

Objective:
220-802: 2.3

Security is more than a set of techniques; it is a mindset. The information your clients or company stores on computers can be highly damaging to those organizations or to society at large if it falls into the wrong hands. When you understand that fact, you understand why the security techniques discussed in the following sections are necessary to protect that information.

Secure and Insecure File Systems

The decisions made about the file system used to set up a computer have a big impact on how secure that computer will be against intruders. Windows 7, Vista, and XP are all designed to use the New Technology File System (NTFS) as the default file system. NTFS was designed from the start as a much more secure file system than the FAT file systems used on previous operating systems.

NTFS supports the creation of user and group accounts with different levels of access to folders and files and the use of the Encrypted File System (EFS) for user-specific encryption of individual files and folders (EFS support varies by Windows version). FAT file systems, such as FAT12 (floppy disks), FAT16 (small hard disks), and FAT32 (large hard disks), do not support user and group accounts, nor do they include file/folder encryption. Consequently, NTFS should be used whenever possible. Note that Windows Vista and Windows 7 cannot be installed on a drive that uses a FAT file system. However, Windows XP can be installed on drives that use FAT.

NOTE Windows includes the command-line Convert.exe utility for converting FAT and FAT32 file systems to NTFS. Once converted, drives cannot be changed back to FAT unless a third-party utility is used.

Authentication Technologies

Authentication is a general term for any method used to verify a person's identity and protect systems against unauthorized access. It is a preventative measure that can be broken down into four categories:

- Something the user knows, for example, a password or PIN

- Something the user has, for example, a smart card or other security token

- Something the user is, for example, the biometric reading of a fingerprint or retina scan

- Something the user does, for example, writing a signature

The devices used to authenticate a user, such as smart cards, biometrics, key fobs, and other products, are often referred to as *authentication technologies*.

Username/Password/PIN

Username/password or personal identification number (PIN) authentication technologies can take many forms. Some examples include

- **An authentication server on a network maintains a list of authorized users and passwords**—Only users with a recognized username and password (credentials) are allowed to access the network's resources.

- **A keypad lock on an entrance into a secure area can store a list of authorized PINs**—Only users with a recognized PIN can enter the secure area.

These technologies can be used in conjunction with other methods for additional security, such as a smart card or biometric reading.

Smart Cards

A smart card is a credit-card–sized card that contains stored information and might also contain a simple microprocessor or a radio-frequency identification (RFID) chip. Smart cards can be used to store identification information for use in security applications, stored values for use in prepaid telephone or debit card services, hotel guest room access, and many other functions. Smart cards are available in contact, contactless, or proximity form factors. Key fobs containing RFID chips work similarly to proximity-based smart cards.

A smart card–based security system includes smart cards, card readers that are designed to work with smart cards, and a back-end system that contains a database that stores a list of approved smart cards for each secured location. Smart card-based security systems can also be used to secure individual personal computers.

To further enhance security, smart card security systems can also require the user to input a PIN or security password as well as provide the smart card at secured check-points, such as the entrance to a computer room.

Biometrics

Biometrics refers to the use of biological information, such as human body characteristics, to authenticate a potential user of a secure area. The most common type of biometric security system for PCs is fingerprint-based, but other methods include voice measurements and eye retina and iris scans.

NOTE   The best type of authentication system is one that uses two or more of the previous methods. This is known as *multifactor authentication*. An example of this would be a person using a smart card and typing a username and password to gain access to a system. The combination of the password and the physical token makes it very difficult for imposters to gain access to a system.

Protection Against Viruses and Malware

Protection against viruses and malware is necessary for every type of computing device, from portable PC to server. Computer protection suites that include anti-virus, antimalware, anti-adware, and antiphishing protection are available from many vendors, but some users prefer a "best of breed" approach that uses the best available products in each category.

These programs can use some or all of the following techniques to protect users and systems:

- Real-time protection to block infection
- Periodic scans for known and suspected threats
- Automatic updating on a frequent (usually daily) basis
- Renewable subscriptions to obtain updated threat signatures
- Links to virus and threat encyclopedias
- Inoculation of system files
- Permissions-based access to the Internet
- Scanning of downloaded files and sent/received emails

When attempting to protect against viruses and malware, the most important thing to remember is to keep your antimalware application up to date. The second most important item is to watch out for unknown data, whether it comes via email, USB flash drive, or elsewhere.

Software Firewalls

A software firewall is a program that examines data packets on a network to determine whether to forward them to their destination or block them. **Firewalls** can be used to protect against inbound threats only (one-way firewall) or against both unauthorized inbound and outbound traffic; this type of firewall is often referred to as a *two-way* firewall. The standard firewall in Windows XP, Windows Vista, and Windows 7 is a one-way firewall. However, many third-party firewall programs, such as Zone Alarm, are two-way firewalls.

NOTE   Firewalls for Windows Vista and Windows 7 can also be used in two-way mode by modifying their configuration through the Windows Firewall with Advanced Security Microsoft Management Console (MMC) snap-in. For details, see http://technet.microsoft.com/en-us/library/cc732283(WS.10).aspx.

A software firewall can be configured to permit traffic between specified IP addresses and to block traffic to and from the Internet except when permitted on a per-program basis.

Corporate networks sometimes use a proxy server with a firewall as the sole direct connection between the Internet and the corporate network and use the firewall in the proxy server to protect the corporate network against threats.

Data and Physical Security

220-802

Objectives:
220-802: 2.1, 2.2

Even if the computer network is secure, a PC and its information are not completely secure if data and physical security issues are overlooked. The following sections help you understand how to ensure that these potential security risks are dealt with properly.

Data Access Local Security Policy

The Local Security Policy window provides access to a variety of policies that can be used to protect data residing on the system. In Windows 7/Vista/XP this can be accessed by navigating to the **Start** menu and then choosing **Control Panel**. Verify that you are in Classic view (known in Windows 7 as Large Icons or Small Icons), double-click **Administrative Tools**, and then double-click **Local Security Policy**. Alternatively, you can press **Windows+R** to open the Run prompt, and type **secpol.msc**.

These policies include

- **Enable auditing**—Open the Local Policies section of the Security Settings dialog, click Audit Policy, and change the policies listed from No Auditing (default) to auditing success and failure. To audit user access to files, folders, and printers, make sure Audit Object Access is configured to audit Success and Failure to access; to specify a file, folder, or printer to audit, use the object's Auditing tab (located in the Advanced dialog of the object's Security tab). For details, see Microsoft Help and Support article 310399 at http://support.microsoft.com/. This function is available on Windows XP only if Simple File Sharing is disabled. Success and Failure information is stored in the Event Viewer's Security logfile.

- **Shutdown: Clear Virtual Memory Pagefile**—The pagefile might store passwords and user information. By enabling this option, you can prevent this information from being used to compromise the system.

- **Take ownership of files or other objects**—This setting is located in Security Settings, Local Policies, User Rights Assignments. By default, this is set to the Administrators group, but to reduce the chance of ownership changes by unauthorized persons, modify this to just one account, for example, the primary account on the computer.

- **Turn on Ctrl+Alt+Del**—The actual name of this policy is "Interactive logon: Do not require Ctrl+Alt+Del." By disabling this policy, the actual Ctrl+Alt+Del screen will appear before logging in, a valuable security feature that can deter would-be hackers from getting into the system and accessing its data.

TIP For other security settings, see the Windows XP security checklists at LabMice.net (http://labmice.techtarget.com/articles/winxpsecuritychecklist.htm) and the Computer Protection Program at the Berkeley Lab (http://www.lbl.gov/cyber/systems/wxp-security-checklist.html).

Encryption Technologies

Microsoft includes two types of built-in encryption with some of their versions of Windows. The Encrypting File System (dependent on an NTFS-formatted volume) is used to encrypt individual files and folders. BitLocker is used to encrypt an entire disk.

Encrypting File System

Windows XP Professional and certain Windows Vista and Windows 7 editions (Windows Vista Business, Enterprise, and Ultimate; Windows 7 Professional, Enterprise, and Ultimate) all include support for EFS (Encrypting File System). **EFS** can be used to protect sensitive data files and temporary files and can be applied to individual files or folders. (When applied to folders, all files in an encrypted folder are also encrypted.)

EFS files can be opened only by the user who encrypted them, by an administrator, or by EFS keyholders (users who have been provided with the EFS certificate key for another user's account). Thus, they are protected against access by hackers.

Files encrypted with EFS are listed with green filenames when viewed in Windows Explorer or My Computer (Windows XP) or Computer (Windows 7/Vista). Only files stored on a drive that uses the NTFS file system can be encrypted.

To encrypt a file, follow this process:

Step 1.   Right-click the file in Windows Explorer or My Computer or Computer and select **Properties**.

Step 2.   Click the **Advanced** button on the General tab.

Step 3.   Click the empty **Encrypt Contents to Secure Data** check box.

Step 4.   Click **OK**.

Step 5.   Click **Apply**. When prompted, select the option to encrypt the file and parent folder or only the file as desired and click **OK**.

Step 6.   Click **OK** to close the properties sheet.

To decrypt the file, follow the same procedure, but clear the Encrypt Contents to Secure Data check box in Step 3.

NOTE   To enable the recovery of EFS encrypted files in the event that Windows cannot start, you should export the user's EFS certificate key. For details, see the Microsoft TechNet article "Data Recovery and Encrypting File System (EFS)" at http://technet.microsoft.com/en-us/library/cc512680.aspx.

BitLocker Encryption

To encrypt an entire disk, you need some kind of full disk encryption software. Several currently are available on the market; one developed by Microsoft for Windows Vista and Windows 7 is called BitLocker—available only on the Ultimate and Enterprise editions. This software can encrypt the entire disk which, after complete, is transparent to the user. However, there are some requirements for this including

- A Trusted Platform Module (TPM): a chip residing on the motherboard that actually stores the encrypted keys.

  or

- An external USB key to store the encrypted keys. Using BitLocker without a TPM requires changes to Group Policy settings.

  and

- A hard drive with two volumes, preferably created during the installation of Windows. One volume is for the operating system (most likely C:), which will be encrypted; the other is the active volume that remains unencrypted so that the computer can boot. If a second volume needs to be created, the BitLocker Drive Preparation Tool can be of assistance and can be downloaded from Windows Update.

BitLocker software is based on the Advanced Encryption Standard (AES) and uses a 128-bit encryption key.

Starting with Windows Vista SP1, BitLocker can be used to encrypt internal hard disk volumes other than the system drive. For example, if a hard disk is partitioned as C: and D: drives, BitLocker could encrypt both drives.

In Windows 7, BitLocker functionality is extended to external USB drives (including flash drives) with BitLocker To Go. Windows 7 also simplifies BitLocker and BitLocker To Go configuration: Simply right-click a drive and select Enable BitLocker to start the encryption process. During the process, you are prompted to specify a password or a SmartCard for credentials to access the drive's contents.

To enable access to the contents of BitLocker To Go USB drives on Windows Vista and Windows XP, Microsoft now offers the BitLocker To Go Reader. Download it from the Microsoft website.

Backups

Securing backups prevents them from being misused by unauthorized users. Some backup applications include an option to password-protect the backup files so they can be restored only if the user provides the correct password. If you use a backup program that does not support password protection (such as Windows XP's integrated NTBackup.exe or Windows Vista's and Windows 7's Windows Backup), you must physically secure the backup media or drive to prevent it from access by unauthorized users.

Data Migration

The process of migrating data from one system to another, such as during the replacement of an old system by a new system, provides another potential security risk if the data migration is not performed in a secure manner.

If possible, perform the data migration with a direct network or USB connection between the old and new computers. If this is not possible, make sure you use a migration program that can password-protect the migration file. The Files and Settings Transfer Wizard in Windows XP and the Windows Easy Transfer program in Windows Vista and Windows 7 automatically provide a password after collecting information from the old computer. This password must be used on the new computer before the migration file can be accessed.

If you use other migration programs, check their documentation to determine whether and how password protection is provided.

Data and Data Remnant Removal

After data is migrated to the new computer, the old computer should be cleared of data or data remnants. If the computer will no longer be used, you can use a full-disk scrubbing program to wipe out the entire contents of the hard disk, including the operating system. For details, see the section "Data Destruction/Disposal Techniques," later in this chapter.

However, if the computer will still be in use with its current operating system, you can use software that overwrites only data files and "empty" disk space (no-longer-allocated disk space that might still contain recoverable files). Programs such as Microsoft Sysinternals SDelete, Norton Wipe Info (included as part of Norton System Works and Norton Utilities), McAfee Shredder (included in various McAfee programs), and others offer options to wipe files and folders, "empty" disk space, or an entire disk drive.

Password Management

PC users should use passwords to secure their user accounts. Through the local security policy and group policy in Windows, you can set up password policies that require users to do the following:

- Change passwords periodically (Local Policies, Security Options)

- Be informed in advance that passwords are about to expire (Account Policies, Password Policy)

- Enforce a minimum password length (Account Policies, Password Policy)

- Require complex passwords (Account Policies, Password Policy)

- Prevent old passwords from being reused continually (Account Policies, Password Policy)

- Wait a certain number of minutes after a specified number of unsuccessful logins has taken place before they can log in again (Account Policies, Account Lockout Policy)

To make these settings in Local Security Settings, open the Security Settings node and navigate to the appropriate subnodes (shown in parentheses in the preceding list). In Group Policy (gpedit.msc), navigate to

- Computer Configuration, Windows Settings, Security Settings, Account Policies, Password Policy

- Computer Configuration, Windows Settings, Security Settings, Account Policies, Account Lockout Policy

- Computer Configuration, Windows Settings, Security Settings, Local Policies, Security Options as appropriate

Locking a Workstation

You should lock your computer whenever you are not at the keyboard. The ability to lock the computer depends on each user being assigned a password. You can use the following methods to lock a computer:

- To lock the computer automatically after the screen saver is enabled, do the following, depending on which Windows operating system you are running:

  - In Windows XP, select the **On Resume, Password-Protect** check box. This option is located on the Display properties sheet's Screen Saver tab.

- In Windows Vista and Windows 7, select the **On Resume, Display Logon** Screen check box. This option is located in the Screen Saver Settings window, which can be accessed from Control Panel, Personalization.

- To lock the computer immediately, press **Windows key+L** on your keyboard or press **Ctrl+Alt+Del** and select **Lock Computer**.

To log back on to the computer, provide your username and password or just your password (if your username is already displayed) when prompted.

Even if the person doesn't lock the system, it can be configured to automatically lock after a certain period of time, or a screen saver with a login option can be configured within the Screen Saver Settings dialog box. In this case the On Resume, Display Logon Screen option should be checked.

Incident Reporting

In addition to enabling auditing of local security policy settings and checking the audit logs periodically, organizations should also set up and follow procedures for reporting security-related incidents. These could include the following:

- Repeated attempts to log in to password-protected accounts

- Unlocked doors to areas that should be secure, such as computer or server rooms, backup media storage, or network wiring closets

- Unknown clients detected on wireless networks

- Viruses and malware detected on clients or servers

- Unauthorized access in the form of denial-of-service (DoS) and other malicious attacks, remote access Trojans (RATs), and the detection of unrecognized network sniffers

Organizations have varying procedures when it comes to incident reporting. One common process for incident reporting and response includes the identification and containment of problems, and then evidence gathering and further investigation. Afterward, the process will usually include procedures for the eradication of threats and the recovery from them. Finally, documentation and monitoring procedures are common to attempt to avoid the same issues in the future.

Social Engineering

Social engineering is a term popularized by the career of successful computer and network hacker Kevin Mitnick, who used a variety of methods to convince computer users to provide access to restricted systems. Some of these methods include

- **Pretexting**—Pretending to be from the company's help desk, telephone, or Internet provider or an authorized service company and asking the user to provide login credentials to enable routine maintenance to be performed or to solve an urgent computer problem.

- **Phishing**—Setting up bogus websites or sending fraudulent emails that trick users into providing personal, bank, or credit card information. A variation, phone phishing, uses an interactive voice response (IVR) system that the user has been tricked into calling to trick the user into revealing information.

- **Trojan horse**—Malware programs disguised as popular videos or website links that trap keystrokes or transmit sensitive information.

- **Baiting**—Leaving physical media (such as a CD, DVD, or USB drive) that appears to be confidential information lying around. The media autoruns when inserted and can deliver various types of malware, including backdoor access to a company's computer network.

- **Tailgating**—When an unauthorized person attempts to accompany an authorized person into a secure area by following them closely and grabbing the door before it shuts. This is usually done without the authorized person's consent. If the authorized person is knowingly involved it is known as *piggybacking*.

- **Shoulder surfing**—When a person attempts to view physical documents on a user's desk or electronic documents displayed on the monitor, by actually looking over the user's shoulder. While this might sound ludicrous, you would be surprised how many people have had their confidential documents, passwords, and PINs compromised in this manner. Shoulder surfers either act covertly, looking around corners, using mirrors or binoculars, or they might introduce themselves to the user and make conversation in the hopes that the user will let his or her guard down.

Although antivirus and antiphishing programs and features in the latest web browsers can stop computer-based social engineering exploits, pretexting can only be stopped by users who refuse to be gulled into letting down their guard. Teach users to do the following:

- Ask for ID when approached in person by somebody claiming to be from the help desk, the phone company, or the service company.

- Ask for a name and supervisor name when contacted by phone by someone claiming to be from the help desk, the phone company, or the service company.

- Provide contact information for the help desk, phone company, or authorized service companies and ask users to call the authorized contact person to verify that the service call or phone request for information is legitimate.

- Log in to systems themselves and then provide the tech the computer, rather than giving the tech login information.

- Change passwords immediately after service calls.

- Report any potential social engineering calls or in-person contacts, even if no information was exchanged. Social engineering experts can gather innocuous-sounding information from several users and use it to create a convincing story to gain access to restricted systems.

Physical Security

In some ways, nothing beats physical security. For example, no matter how great the computer hacker, a computer simply cannot open a physical keyed lock. So having locking doors is the first step in protecting an investment, whatever it might be. The door locking system might also incorporate proximity-based access cards, or smart cards. Some organizations combine these types of door security with a biometrics system that, for example, analyzes a person's thumbprint. Finally, documents and passwords should be physically protected. This is generally accomplished by locking the documents in a secure area and by implementing a clean-desk policy.

Doors

This might sound a bit silly, but don't forget to lock the doors! So many people forget to do this that some organizations have written policies explaining how, when, and where to lock doors. Aside from main entrances, you should also always lock server rooms, wiring closets, labs, and other technical rooms when not in use.

Now, the question is how are the locks controlled? Some security analysts will tell you that nothing beats a physical door lock that uses a key. In this day and age of software and encryption, a lot of hackers have a more difficult time with keyed locks. The concept of a physical item that you need to carry around can't be denied. It should be documented who has the keys to server rooms and wiring closets. Locks should be changed out and rotated with other locks every so often. This keeps things dynamic and harder to guess at. Another type of lock is the cipher lock, which uses a punch code to unlock the door. These physical methods might be used by them-selves or combined with an electronic system.

The most common electronic entry system is the cardkey system. These use proximity-based door access cards that you simply press against a transmitter next to the door handle. While these are common, they are not the best option. But because they are inexpensive compared to other systems, you see them often. Other electronic systems use key cards that incorporate a photo ID (a worker's badge), or magnetic stripe, barcode, or a radio-frequency identification (RFID) chip. Each of these can contain information about the identity of the user. These don't have to be cards either; they can come in smaller form factors such as key fobs, which can be attached right to a user's keychain.

Moving on to the next level of security, let's talk briefly about the smart card. These cards have a nano-processor and can actually communicate with the authentication system. Examples of these include the Personal Identity Verification (PIV) card used by U.S. government employees and contractors, and the Common Access Card (CAC) used by Department of Defense (DoD) personnel. These cards identify the owner, authenticate them to areas of the building and to computers, and can digitally sign and encrypt files and email with the RSA encryption algorithm. Due to the fact that these are physical items a user carries with them to gain access to specific systems, they are known as *tokens*. A token might also display a code that changes, say, every minute or so. If a person wants access to a particular system, such as an accounting or other confidential area, the person would have to type the current code that is shown on the token into the computer. This is a powerful method of authentication but can be expensive as well.

Some organizations design what is known as a *mantrap*: an area with two locking doors. A person might get past a first door by way of tailgating, but might have difficulty getting past the second door, especially if there is a guard in between the two doors. If the person doesn't have proper authentication, he will be stranded in the mantrap until authorities arrive.

Biometrics

A biometric security system uses a reader or scanner to analyze physical characteristics of a person to authenticate her. The information is digitized into a series of match points. The system also includes a database that stores the match points of approved users and software that determines whether the information coming from the reader or scanner matches a user in the database. To prevent identity theft, biometric information is usually encrypted.

Biometrics are increasingly being used to prevent unauthorized access to desktop and laptop PCs. Many laptop and portable PCs now include fingerprint readers and biometric software, and USB-based fingerprint readers can be added to desktop and laptop PCs. Some fingerprint readers require users to swipe the finger across the reader, while others use a pad that the user pushes, similar to the way a finger-print is placed on an ink pad. Although the fingerprint (and thumbprint) is the most common, biometric readers may also scan a person's retina. This is more common in intelligence agencies, prisons, and even in some banks.

Protecting Data Physically

Confidential documents should never be left sitting out in the open. They should either be properly filed in a locking cabinet or shredded and disposed of if they are no longer needed. Passwords should not be written down and definitely not left on a desk or taped to a monitor where they can be seen. Many organizations implement a clean desk policy that states users must remove all papers from their desk before leaving for lunch, breaks, or at the end of the day. Anything that shows on the computer screen can be protected in a variety of ways. To protect data while the person is working, you can install a privacy filter, which is a transparent cover for PC monitors and laptop displays. It reduces the cone of vision, usually to about 30 degrees, so that only the person in front of the screen can see the content. Many of these are also antiglare, helping to reduce eye stress of the user. Also, the user should lock the computer whenever he leaves the workstation. Windows can also be auto-matically set to lock after a certain amount of time, even if the user forgets to do so manually.

Securing Wireless Networks

220-802

Objective:
220-802: 2.5

Wireless networks have become important to businesses of all sizes as well as indi-vidual users. However, they also represent a significant potential vulnerability if they are not properly secured. The following sections help you understand how the different encryption methods work and the additional steps that must be taken to completely secure a wireless network.

WEP and WPA Encryption

An encrypted wireless network relies on the exchange of a passphrase between the client and the wireless access point (WAP) or router before the client can connect to the network. There are three standards for encryption: WEP, WPA, and WPA2.

Wireless equivalent privacy (WEP) was the original encryption standard for wireless Ethernet (Wi-Fi) networks. It is the only encryption standard supported by most IEEE 802.11b-compliant hardware. Unfortunately, WEP encryption is not strong enough to resist attacks from a determined hacker. There are several reasons this is true, including key length (64-bit WEP uses a 10-character hex key, and 128-bit WEP uses a 26-character hex key) and the use of unencrypted transmissions for some parts of the handshaking process. Because WEP encryption is not secure, it should not be used to "secure" a wireless network.

As a replacement to WEP, **Wi-Fi Protected Access (WPA)** was developed a few years ago. It is available in two strengths: WPA (which uses TKIP encryption) and the newer, stronger WPA2 (which uses AES encryption). WPA and WPA2's encryption is much stronger than WEP, supports a key length from 8 up to 63 alphanumeric characters (enabling the use of punctuation marks and other characters not permitted with WEP) or 64 hex characters, and supports the use of a RADIUS authentication server in corporate environments.

NOTE In some environments, WPA and WPA2 are both referred to as WPA, so the encryption method selected during wireless security configuration determines whether WPA or WPA2 has been chosen.

Because all clients and WAPs or wireless routers on a wireless network must use the same encryption standard, use the strongest standard supported by all hardware.

Ideally, all wireless networks should be secured with WPA2 (WPA has been cracked, although cracking WPA is much harder than cracking WEP). However, the use of WPA2 encryption might require upgraded drivers for older network adapters and upgraded firmware for older WAPs or wireless routers. Wi-Fi Certified adapters and WAPs or wireless routers must support WPA2 as of March 13, 2006.

TIP There are various ways to create a strong passphrase for use with a WPA or WPA2 network. Some vendors of WAPs and wireless routers include a feature sold under various brand names that is compliant with the Wi-Fi Protected Setup standard (also known as Easy Config). If this cannot be used on some hardware, you can obtain a dynamically generated strong passphrase at Gibson Research Corporation's Perfect Passwords website: https://www.grc.com/passwords.htm.

Copy and paste the passphrase provided into Notepad or another plain-text editor and then copy or paste it into the configuration dialog for a WAP, wireless router, and wireless client as needed.

Access Point Configuration for Maximum Security

Configuring your wireless network with the strongest possible encryption (and using a strong WPA or WPA2 passphrase) is just the beginning of true wireless network security. The following sections discuss other changes to the default configuration of a WAP or wireless router to help improve security.

DHCP Versus Static IP Addresses

By default, almost all WAPs and wireless routers are configured to act as DHCP servers; that is, they hand out IP addresses to all computers they're connected to. This is a convenience, but if you want to limit access to the Internet for certain computers or log activity for computers by IP address, this setting should be disabled and static IP addresses should be assigned instead, using each client's IP configuration dialog. Make sure you assign an IP address range supported by the router. For details, see "TCP/IPv4 Configuration" in Chapter 16, "Networking."

Even if you don't want to disable DHCP, you will probably want to adjust the number of IP addresses that the WAP or wireless router will assign. A good rule of thumb is to configure the router to assign the number of addresses equal to the number of clients that will connect to the router at any one time. If additional portable clients connect from time to time, add those to the number. In many cases, the result is that you need to greatly reduce the default number of DHCP addresses the router is configured to provide.

Figure 17-1 illustrates a typical wireless router's DHCP configuration dialog.

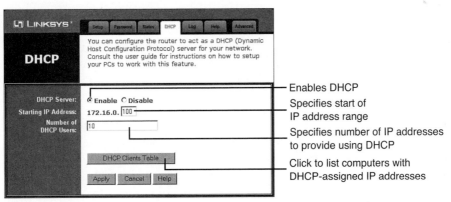

Figure 17-1   Specifying a range of IP addresses for DHCP on a Linksys router.

Changing the SSID

The **Service Set Identifier (SSID)** can provide a great deal of useful information to a potential hacker of a wireless network. All wireless networks must have an SSID, and by default, WAPs and wireless routers typically use the manufacturer's name or the device's model number as the default SSID. If a default SSID is broadcast by a wireless network, a hacker can look up the documentation for a specific router or the most common models of a particular brand and determine the default IP address range, the default administrator username and password, and other information that would make it easy to attack the network.

To help "hide" the details of your network and location, a replacement SSID for a secure wireless network should not include any of the following:

- Your name

- Your company name

- Your location

- Any other easily identifiable information

An SSID that includes a sports team popular in the area or obscure information (such as the name of your first pet) would be a suitable replacement.

Figure 17-2 shows a typical WAP or wireless router Basic Setup dialog that includes this and other configuration options discussed later in this chapter.

Disabling SSID Broadcast

In addition to changing the default SSID for a WAP or wireless router, you can disable SSID broadcast. This is widely believed to be an effective way to prevent your wireless network from being detected and is so regarded by the A+ Certification exams (see Figure 17-2 for a typical dialog).

CAUTION   Although disabling SSID broadcast prevents casual bandwidth snoopers from finding your wireless network, Microsoft does not recommend disabling SSID broadcasting as a security measure. According to a TechNet white paper, "Non-broadcast Wireless Networks with Microsoft Windows," available at http://technet.microsoft.com, wireless client systems running Windows transmit ("advertise") the names of non-broadcast (also known as hidden) wireless networks they are configured to connect to. This information can be used by wireless network hacking programs to help launch an attack against the network.

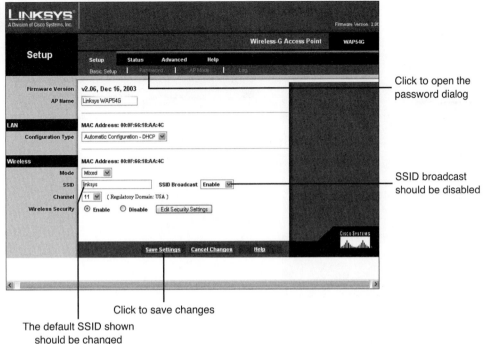

Figure 17-2 Preparing to change the default wireless settings on a Linksys router.

MAC Address Filtering

Every network adapter—whether it's built in to a PC, an add-on card, or built in to a specialized device such as a media adapter or a networked printer—has a unique identification known as the media access control address or MAC address. The MAC address (sometimes known as the physical address) is a list of six two-digit hexadecimal numbers (0–9, A–F). The MAC address is usually found on a label on the side of the network adapter, as shown in Figure 17-3. Depending on the device, the MAC address might be labeled MAC, MAC address, or ID No. Many devices that have integrated network adapters also list their MAC address on a label. Note that MAC addresses are sometimes listed as 12 digits rather than in six groups of 2 digits.

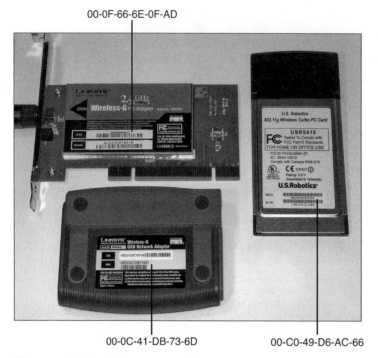

00-0F-66-6E-0F-AD

00-0C-41-DB-73-6D   00-C0-49-D6-AC-66

Figure 17-3 Typical locations for MAC addresses on wireless adapters.

To determine the MAC address for an adapter already installed in a PC, or the MAC address for an integrated adapter for a system running Windows XP, Windows Vista, or Windows 7, run the Ipconfig.exe command with the /all switch: ipconfig /all. The physical address (MAC address) is listed for each adapter in the computer (see Figure 17-4).

With most wireless routers and WAPs, you can specify the MAC addresses of devices on your network (see Figure 17-5). Only these devices can access your network; some routers can also be configured to block a list of specified MAC addresses from accessing the network.

Ethernet adapter

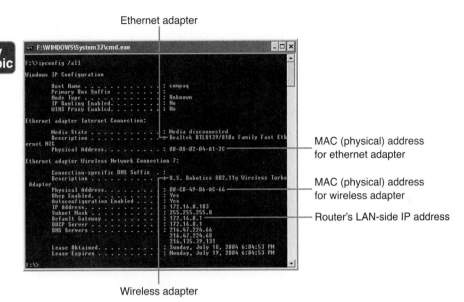

MAC (physical) address
for ethernet adapter

MAC (physical) address
for wireless adapter

Router's LAN-side IP address

Wireless adapter

Figure 17-4   Using ipconfig /all to determine MAC addresses for installed network adapters.

Enables MAC address filtering

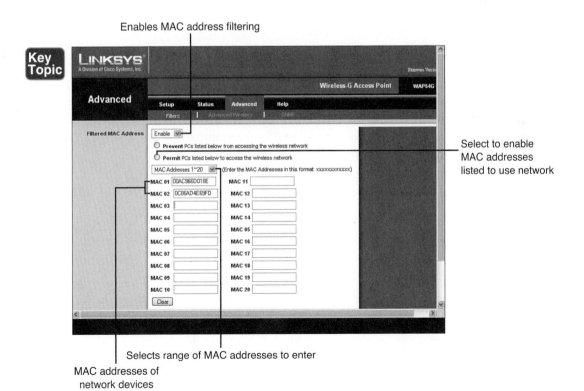

Select to enable
MAC addresses
listed to use network

Selects range of MAC addresses to enter

MAC addresses of
network devices

Figure 17-5   Configuring a Linksys WAP54G WAP to use MAC address filtering.

MAC address filtering can be a useful way to block casual hackers from gaining access to a wireless (or wired) network. However, keep in mind that it is possible to use software to change the MAC address of a network device (a feature sometimes referred to as *MAC address cloning*), and that MAC addresses are not encrypted and can be detected by software used to hack networks. Thus, MAC address filtering alone should not be relied on to stop serious attacks.

Changing Default Administrator User Password

As mentioned previously, the documentation for almost all WAPs and wireless routers lists the default administrator password and the documentation can be readily downloaded in PDF or HTML form from the vendors' websites. Because an attacker could use this information to "take over" the device, it's a good idea to change the default.

Most routers use the Administration or Management dialog for the password and other security settings.

> **TIP** To further secure the router or WAP, configure the device so it can be managed only with a wired Ethernet connection.

Updating Access Point Firmware

Most vendors issue firmware updates for each model of WAP and wireless router. These updates solve operational problems and might add features that enhance Wi-Fi interoperability, security, and ease of use. To determine whether a WAP or wireless router has a firmware update available, follow these steps:

Step 1.   View the device's configuration dialogs to see the current firmware version (refer to Figure 17-4).

Step 2.   Visit the device vendor's website to see whether a newer version of the firmware is available. Note that you must know the model number and revision of the device. To find this information, look on the rear or bottom of the device.

Step 3.   Download the firmware update to a PC that can be connected to the device with an Ethernet cable.

Step 4.   Connect the PC to the device with an Ethernet cable.

Step 5.   Navigate to the device's firmware update dialog.

Step 6.   Follow instructions to update the firmware.

Firewall Features

By default, most WAPs and wireless routers use a feature called Network Address Translation (NAT) to act as a simple firewall. NAT prevents traffic from the Internet from determining the private IP addresses used by computers on the network. However, many WAPs and wireless routers offer additional firewall features that can be enabled, including

- Access logs

- Filtering of specific types of traffic

- Enhanced support for VPNs

See the router documentation for more information about advanced security features.

WAP Placement and Radio Levels

When configuring and/or troubleshooting wireless connections, think about WAP location. The placement of the access point plays a big part in a strong signal. Generally, it should be placed in the middle of an office to offer greatest coverage while reducing the chance of outsiders being able to connect to the device. The antennae on the access point should also be set at a 90-degree angle to each other. Keep the device away from any forms of electrical interference such as other wireless devices, speakers, CRTs, and any devices that use a lot of electricity. Another thing to watch out for is radio power levels. These can be modified within the access point. If set too low, clients at the perimeter of the building will not be able to gain access. If set too high, computers located in neighboring businesses will be able to attempt access.

Securing Wired Networks

220-802

Objective:
220-802: 2.6

Many of the things mentioned in the "Securing Wireless Networks" section can be applied to wired networks as well, including using static addresses instead of dynamic for particular devices, changing the default administrator password to something complex, enabling MAC filtering, and updating the firmware of the router. The most important of these is that password. The best passwords have

14 characters or more and include uppercase and lowercase letters, numbers, and special characters. Also, passwords should be changed every month or two. For some help creating complex passwords, check out the following links:

- https://www.microsoft.com/security/pc-security/password-checker.aspx

- http://www.passwordmeter.com/

Simply type in a password and the program shows you its strength.

Copper-based cabling is susceptible to eavesdropping, wiretapping, crosstalk, EMI, and RFI. One way to defend against these is to use shielded twisted pair (STP) cable. Another is to use fiber-optic cable, which is the most resistant to all of these because it uses light instead of electricity to send data.

Another thing to watch out for, and it might seem kind of simple, are visible network wires and unused network jacks. Network cables should be routed in the walls and ceiling out of sight. If they are not visible, it cuts down on the chances of someone tapping into the network. RJ-45 jacks that currently don't have a computer connected to them should be noted. In the wiring closet, disconnect those network drops at the patch panel by removing the patch cable that leads to the switch. This way, a person can't just sit down, plug into a network jack, and attempt to hack the network. On some switches you can also disable ports within the firmware.

Access Control Purposes and Principles

220-802

Objective:
220-802: 1.8

Controlling access to files, folders, printers, and physical locations is essential for system and network security. The following sections discuss the purposes and principles of access control.

Operating System Access Control

Operating system access control in Windows XP, Vista, and 7 requires the use of the NTFS file system. To use access control in Windows XP Professional, the default Simple File Sharing setting must also be disabled.

User, Administration, and Guest Accounts

There are three standard account levels in Windows:

- **Limited (known as Standard user accounts in Windows Vista and Windows 7)**—Limited accounts have permission to perform routine tasks. However, these accounts are blocked from performing tasks that involve systemwide changes, such as installing hardware or software. (Windows Vista and Windows 7 permit Standard user accounts to perform UAC-restricted tasks, such as adding hardware, if they can provide an administrator password.)

- **Administrator**—Users with an administrator account can perform any and all tasks.

- **Guest**—The guest account level is the most limited. A guest account cannot install software or hardware or run already-existing applications and cannot access files in shared document folders or the Guest profile. The Guest account is disabled by default. If it is enabled for a user to gain access to the computer, that access should be temporary and the account should be disabled again when the user no longer requires access.

When a user is created using the Users applet in Windows, the user must be assigned a limited (Standard) or Administrator account. Guest accounts are used for visitors.

User Account Control

User Account Control (UAC) is a security component of Windows Vista and Windows 7 that keeps every user (besides the actual Administrator account) in standard user mode instead of as an administrator with full administrative rights— even if they are a member of the administrators group. It is meant to prevent unauthorized access, as well as avoid user error in the form of accidental changes. With UAC enabled, users perform common tasks as non-administrators and, when necessary, as administrators, without having to switch users, log off, or use Run As.

Basically, UAC was created with two goals in mind:

- To eliminate unnecessary requests for excessive administrative-level access to Windows resources

- To reduce the risk of malicious software using the administrator's access control to infect operating system files

When a standard end-user requires administrator privileges to perform certain tasks such as installing an application, a small pop-up UAC window appears notifying the user that an administrator credential is necessary. If the user has administrative rights and clicks Continue, the task will be carried out, but if the user does not have sufficient rights, the attempt will fail. Note that these pop-up UAC windows will not appear if the person is logged on with the actual Administrator account

In Windows Vista, turning UAC on and off can be done by going to **Start**, **Control Panel**, **User Accounts and Family Safety**. Then select **User Accounts** and **Turn User Account Control On or Off**. From there, UAC can be turned on and off by checking or unchecking the box. If a change is made to UAC, the system will need to be restarted. Note that if you are using the Classic View in the Control Panel, User Accounts and Family Safety is bypassed.

In Windows 7, UAC offers a range of settings. To adjust UAC settings, go to **Start**, **Control Panel**, **System and Security**, **Action Center**. Then select **Change User Account Control** settings. The default setting, **Notify Me Only When Programs Try to Make Changes to My Computer**, enables UAC to protect your computer against unauthorized changes by programs. The **Always Notify** option works similarly to the default UAC setting in Windows Vista, as it displays notifications when either the user or a program attempts to makes changes to the computer. The **Never Notify** option, which turns off UAC notifications, works similarly to turning off UAC in Windows Vista. The **Notify Me Only Ehen Programs Try to Make Changes to My Computer (Do Not Dim My Desktop)** option should be used only if the computer takes a long time to dim the desktop and bring up the UAC prompt.

Groups

Users in Windows XP, Vista, and 7 can be assigned to different groups, each with different permissions. The Local Policy (local PCs) and Group Policy (networked PCs connected to a domain controller) settings can restrict PC features by group or by PC. Aside from the Administrator, User, and Guest groups (whose corresponding accounts were explained previously), there is one additional group you should know for the exam: the Power Users group. Power users have more permissions than standard users, but fewer permissions than administrators. Power users can install drivers, run noncertified programs, and in general modify computerwide settings. Because of this, members of the Power Users group might be able to expose the computer to security risks such as running a Trojan horse program or executing a virus. Be especially careful which users are added to the Power Users and Administrators groups. Because the Power Users group can be a security risk, Microsoft has decreased the amount of "power" these users have in Windows Vista. For example, power users can no longer customize file associations the way they did in Windows XP. Windows 7 maintains support for the Power Users group only for compatibility with legacy applications. Power users on Windows Vista or Windows 7 may need to run some applications with the Run as Admin option and provide administrator credentials when prompted by UAC.

Principle of Least Privilege

The principle of least privilege basically says that a user should only have access to what is required. If a person needs to update Excel files and browse the Internet, that person should not be given administrative access. You might think of this as common sense, but it should not be taken lightly. When user accounts are created locally on a computer and especially on a domain, great care should be taken when assigning users to groups. Also, many programs when installed ask who can use and make modifications to the program; often the default is "all users." Some technicians just click Next when hastily installing programs, without realizing that the user now has full control of the program, something you might not want. Just remember, keep users on a need-to-know basis; give them access only to what they specifically need, and no more.

Permissions Actions, Types, and Levels

Permissions for folders, files, and printers are assigned via the Security tab of the object's properties sheet. Folder and file permissions vary by user type or group and can include the following:

- **Full control**—Complete access to contents of file or folder. When Full Control is selected, all of the following are selected automatically.
- **Modify**—Change file or folder contents.
- **Read & Execute**—Access file or folder contents and run programs.
- **List Folder Contents**—Display folder contents.
- **Read**—Access a file or folder.
- **Write**—Add a new file or folder.

Each permission has two settings: Allow or Deny. Generally, if you want a user to have access to a folder, you would add them to the list and select **Allow** for the appropriate permission. If you don't want to allow them access, normally you simply wouldn't add them. But in some cases, an explicit Deny is necessary. This could be because the user is part of a larger group that already has access to a parent folder, but you don't want the specific user to have access to this particular subfolder. This leads us to permission inheritance.

Permission Inheritance and Propagation

If you create a folder, the default action it takes is to inherit permissions from the parent folder. So any permissions that you set in the parent will be inherited by the subfolder. To view an example of this, locate any folder within an NTFS volume (besides the root folder), right-click it and select **Properties**, access the **Security** tab, and click the **Advanced** button. Here you see an enabled check box named **Inherit from Parent the Permission Entries that apply to Child Objects** toward the bottom of the window. This means that any permissions added or removed in the parent folder will also be added or removed in the current folder. In addition, those permissions that are being inherited cannot be modified in the current folder. To make modifications to the permissions you would need to deselect the **Inherit from Parent the Permission Entries that apply to Child Objects** check box. When you do so, you have the option to copy the permissions from the parent to the current folder or remove them entirely. So by default, the parent is automatically propagating permissions to the subfolder, and the subfolder is inheriting its permissions from the parent.

You can also propagate permission changes to subfolders that are not inheriting from the current folder. To do so, select the **Replace Permission Entries on All Child Objects** with entries shown here that apply to the Child Objects check box. This might all seem a bit confusing; just remember that folders automatically inherit from the parent unless you turn inheriting off—and you can propagate permission entries to subfolders at any time by selecting the **Replace** option.

Moving and Copying Folders and Files

Moving and copying folders will have different results when it comes to permissions. Basically, it breaks down like this:

- If you *copy* a folder on the same, or to a different volume, the folder inherits the permissions of the parent folder it was copied to (target directory).

- If you *move* a folder to a different location on the same volume, the folder retains its original permissions.

Components

Use the Security tab on a printer's properties sheet to restrict access to the printer. To restrict access to other components, such as optical drives, use Local Policy or Group Policy settings.

Restricted Spaces

This may simply be referred to as preventing users from accessing restricted spaces, such as computer or server rooms or LAN wiring closets, and using physical access restriction devices, such as smart cards or key fobs.

Auditing and Event Logging

Windows XP, Vista, and 7 all support auditing and event logging, both of which enable you to find out what issues affecting security might be taking place on a particular computer.

Event logs are enabled by default, while auditing of files, folders, and printers must be enabled by the system administrator. When auditing is enabled, success and failure entries for audited devices are stored in the Security log.

To view event logs in these versions of Windows, follow these steps:

Step 1.   Right-click **My Computer** (XP) or **Computer** (Vista, 7) and select **Manage**. The Computer Management console opens.

Step 2.   Expand the Event Viewer node. In Windows XP and Windows Vista it contains four subnodes: Application, Internet Explorer, Security, System. In Windows Vista and Windows 7, click the Windows Logs subnode to see these subnodes; these versions of Windows also include a Forwarded Events subnode.

Step 3.   Select the desired node to see events (see Figure 17-6).

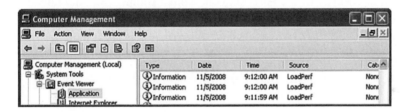

Figure 17-6   Viewing the Application Event Log.

Step 4.   To view details of a particular event, double-click the event (see Figure 17-7).

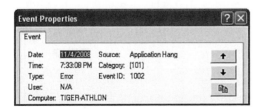

Figure 17-7   Viewing the details of an application hang in the Application Event log.

To enable auditing, see the section "Data Access Local Security Policy," earlier in this chapter.

Periodically, event logs should be cleared. Before clearing these logs, you might want to archive their contents. To learn how to archive event logs in Windows XP, see Microsoft Help and Support article 308427 at http://support.microsoft.com. To archive event logs in Windows Vista or 7, click **Save All Events As** and select the appropriate format for your needs (Event files, XML files, tab delimited text, or CSV text).

Data Destruction/Disposal Techniques

220-802

Objective:
220-802: 2.4

Even after a computer has reached the end of its useful life, the hard disk it contains represents a potential security risk. To prevent confidential company or client information from being accessed from a computer that is being disposed of for resale, recycling, or deconstruction for parts, you can use one of the following methods:

- Remove the hard disk(s) and destroy their platters with a drill, hammer, or other device; then recycle the scrap. Using this method when preserving the hard disk as a working device is not necessary.

- Overwrite the hard disk(s) with a program that meets or exceeds recognized data-destruction standards such as the U.S. Department of Defense 5220.22-M (7 passes) or Peter Gutman's 35-pass maximum security method. These programs destroy existing data and partition information in such a way as to prevent data recovery or drive forensics analysis. Use this method when maintaining the hard disk as a working device is important (such as for donation or resale). A variety of commercial and freeware programs can be used for this task, which is variously known as disk scrubbing, disk wiping, or drive wiping.

- Other tools such as electromagnetic degaussers and permanent magnet degaussers can also be used to permanently purge information from a disk.

External hard disks should also be handled in one of these ways when being disposed of. USB flash drive and floppy disks that contain sensitive information can be physically destroyed or can be bulk-erased to prevent information from being recovered. To protect information on optical media, shredding is recommended.

Remember that formatting a disk (or disc) is not enough. Regardless of whether it is a standard format (done by the operating system) or a low-level format (done by the BIOS), to truly sanitize a drive you need to use one of the preceding methods.

Installing, Configuring, and Troubleshooting Security Features

220-802

Objectives:
220-802: 2.1, 4.7

The following sections help you understand how to set up and configure major security features.

BIOS Security Features

Several common BIOS features can be used to help prevent unauthorized access to the computer. These include

- **Boot sector virus protection**—Enable this feature to prevent boot sector viruses and malware from infecting the system hard drive. If the BIOS doesn't have this feature, you will need to boot from USB, floppy disk, or optical media to remove boot sector viruses.

- **Boot sequence**—Place the system hard drive first in the boot order to prevent unauthorized users from booting from a floppy disk, CD, DVD, or USB device.

- **BIOS setup password**—Enable this feature to prevent unauthorized users from altering BIOS setup information.

NOTE In the event that the setup password is mislaid, the CMOS chip used to store BIOS settings can be reset with a jumper on the motherboard or by removing the battery for several minutes.

- **BIOS HDD password**—On a semi-related note, many laptops come equipped with drive lock technology: an HDD password. If enabled, it prompts the user to enter a password for the hard drive when the computer is first booted.

If the user of the computer doesn't know the password for the hard drive, the drive will lock and the OS will not boot. An eight-digit or similar hard drive ID usually associates the laptop with the hard drive that is installed. On most systems this password is clear by default, but if the password is set and forgotten, it can usually be reset within the BIOS. Some laptops come with documentation clearly stating the BIOS and drive lock passwords.

If you are unable to boot from CD, DVD, USB device, or floppy disk to perform PC maintenance or troubleshooting, change the boot sequence to place removable media earlier in the boot order than the system hard drive.

If the BIOS setup program is protected by a password and the password is lost, you can clear the password on most desktop systems by using the BIOS clear jumper on the motherboard or by removing the battery for several seconds.

CAUTION   Some laptops use the password to permanently restrict access to only the password holder. In such cases, the password cannot be bypassed. See the documentation for your laptop or portable system before applying a BIOS password to determine whether this is the case.

For details, see Chapter 3, "BIOS."

Software Firewalls

Software firewalls, such as the firewalls incorporated in Windows XP SP2 and SP3, Windows Vista, and Windows 7, can be configured to permit specified applications to pass through the firewall, to open specific ports needed by applications, or to block all traffic. Whenever possible, it's easier to permit traffic by application rather than by UDP or TCP port numbers.

To enable the Windows Firewall in Windows XP SP2/SP3 while permitting exceptions, click **On** (recommended) and leave the Don't Allow Exceptions check box cleared (see Figure 17-8). To block all incoming traffic (recommended when the computer is used in a public location, such as a hotel or restaurant), click the **Don't Allow Exceptions** check box.

To enable the Windows Firewall in Windows Vista or Windows 7 while permitting exceptions, select **Home** (Vista, 7), **Work** (7), or **Office** (Vista) network locations when prompted after setting up a new network connection. The location setting also can be changed with the Network and Sharing Center. To configure the Windows Firewall for Don't Allow Exceptions, select the network location as **Public Network**. Figure 17-9 shows the Set Network Location dialog used by Windows 7 (Windows Vista's is similar).

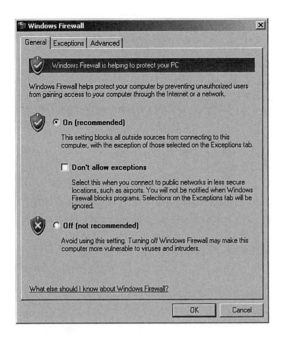

Figure 17-8   The Windows Firewall's General tab (Windows XP).

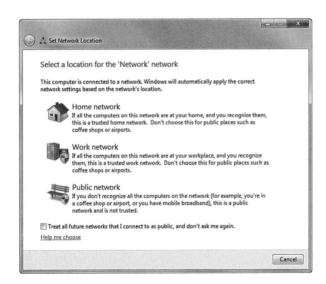

Figure 17-9   Setting a network location in Windows 7 (shown) or Windows Vista configures the Windows Firewall.

Turn off the Windows Firewall only if directed by an installer program or if you prefer to use a third-party firewall.

Configuring Exceptions

In Windows XP SP2/SP3, click the **Exceptions** tab to view programs that are permitted to access your computer (checked programs). To access the tabbed Windows Firewall interface in Windows Vista, click the **Change Settings** link. You can then click the **Exceptions** tab to see checked programs.

With either version of Windows, click **Add Program** to add a program or **Add Port** to add a TCP or UDP port number to the list of Exceptions.

To revoke an exception temporarily, clear the check box. To remove the program or port from the list of Exceptions, select the program or port and click **Delete**. Use **Edit** (Windows XP only) to change the program, port number, or scope (list of IP addresses) for the selected item. In Windows 7, click **Allow a Program or Feature Through Windows Firewall** to view checked programs. Windows 7's version of Windows Firewall provides separate settings for Home/Work and Public networks (see Figure 17-10).

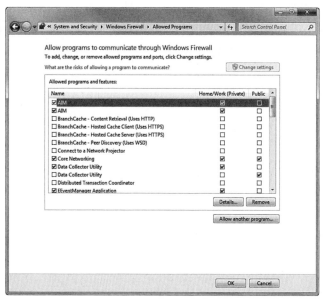

Figure 17-10   Windows 7 provides separate settings for allowed programs based on the network location.

In Windows XP SP2/SP3 and Windows Vista, use the Advanced tab (see Figure 17-11) to specify which connections are protected by Windows Firewall, to set up a security log, to set up ICMP for messaging between networked computers, and to reset Windows Firewall's defaults.

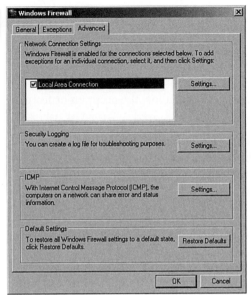

Figure 17-11 The Windows Firewall's Advanced tab (Windows XP).

In Windows 7, the Advanced Settings link opens a dialog that enables Windows Firewall to be configured to block unauthorized outbound as well as inbound traffic and to use user-defined firewall rules.

Troubleshooting Software Firewalls

If users are unable to connect to shared folders on your system, or if you are unable to use programs that require inbound connections, you might have one of the following situations:

- **Your firewall is configured to block all connections (No Exceptions setting)**— In Windows XP, turn the Windows Firewall on but clear the **No Exceptions** check box. In Windows Vista and Windows 7, select the **Home, Work**, or **Office** network location as appropriate.

- **A Windows Firewall is blocking x program dialog has appeared**—Click **Unblock** to permit the program access to your system.

- **Your firewall does not have an exception set up for the program**—With the Windows Firewall in Windows XP and Windows Vista, open the Exceptions dialog and make sure the program that is being blocked is listed and is checked. Click an empty check box to reenable an exception. Use **Add Program** to add the program. To enable Windows Firewall to permit access to your computer's shared files and printers, File and Printer Sharing must be on the Exceptions list and the exception must be enabled. In Windows 7, click the **Allow a Program or Feature Through Windows Firewall** task, click **Change Settings**, and click **Allow Another Program**. Choose the program from the list of programs, or use **Browse** to locate the program manually and click **Add**. Use the **Allow a Program or Feature Through Windows Firewall** to specify which network locations will allow the program or feature to run.

- **You might have two firewalls (Windows Firewall and a third-party firewall or two third-party firewalls) running and one or both of them are blocking connections**—Turn off one of the firewall programs and configure the other one properly.

- **You did not open the correct TCP or UDP ports for a program**—Generally, it's easier to set up exceptions by adding a program. However, in some cases, you might need to use Add Port to set up the exceptions needed. Be sure to specify each of the port numbers and the correct port type for each port number.

Ports are usually the culprit when it comes to firewall troubleshooting. If a person cannot ping your computer, yet you can access the network and the Internet, and people need to access your system remotely, consider checking the ports of your firewall.

Wireless Network Configuration

After configuring a WAP or wireless router to provide WEP, WPA, or (preferably) WPA2 encryption, you must configure wireless clients with the same encryption information. You can set up clients manually or automatically. Note that each wireless client connecting to a WAP or wireless router must use the same encryption standard and passphrase and specify the SSID used by the WAP or wireless router.

You can configure a client in the following ways:

- Use Microsoft Connect Now. This technology, supported by most recent WAPs and wireless routers, enables Windows to set up clients automatically.

- Create a USB flash drive that includes configuration information on one computer, and use it to set up other clients.

- Configure each client manually.

The following sections describe in more detail the steps to configure a wireless client in Windows XP, Windows Vista, and Windows 7.

Configuring a Wireless Client with Windows XP SP2/SP3

Windows XP SP2 and SP3 include a Wireless Network Setup Wizard. This wizard can be used to set up a brand-new wireless network or to add a client to an existing wireless network. To run the wizard, in Windows XP SP2/SP3 follow this procedure:

Step 1.   Click **Start, All Programs, Accessories, Communications, Wireless Networking** wizard. At the introductory screen, click **Next** to continue.

Step 2.   In the Create a Name for Your Wireless Network dialog (see Figure 17-12), enter the service set identifier (SSID) you want to use for your network. You can create an SSID up to 32 characters.

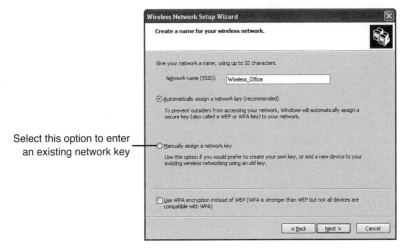

Select this option to enter an existing network key

Figure 17-12   Creating an SSID and selecting network encryption with the Windows XP SP2 Wireless Network Setup Wizard.

Step 3.   Select whether you want to automatically assign a network key (default) or manually assign a network key. Use the manual option if you are adding your system to an existing network. If you use the manual option, you are prompted to enter your wireless network's existing WEP or WPA key later (see Step 6).

Step 4.   By default, the wizard uses WEP encryption; to use WPA encryption, click the **Use WPA Encryption** check box. Click Next to continue. Note that you see an error dialog onscreen if your network hardware is already connected to your system and it does not support WPA. Click **OK** to continue.

Step 5.   If you select the default "automatic" option shown in Figure 17-12, you can select from two options to save your settings: a USB flash (keychain) drive or manual network setup. The USB flash memory drive option can be used by any devices that support Microsoft Connect Now. Such devices automatically read the XML-format network setup files from the USB flash memory drive when the drive is connected to the device.

Step 6.   If you select the option to enter a network key yourself, you see the dialog shown in Figure 17-13. Enter the network key and then reenter it. Click Next to continue.

Figure 17-13   Entering a WEP key manually with the Windows XP Wireless Network Setup Wizard.

Step 7.   On the following screen, select the option to store the network settings to a USB flash drive or to configure the network manually.

Step 8.   If you selected the option to store the network settings on a USB flash drive, insert the drive when prompted. Click **Next**. A dialog displays the setup files as they are transferred to the flash drive.

Step 9.   Follow the instructions shown in Figure 17-14 to transfer the settings from the USB flash drive to your wireless access point (or router) and other network client PCs and devices. Click **Next** to continue.

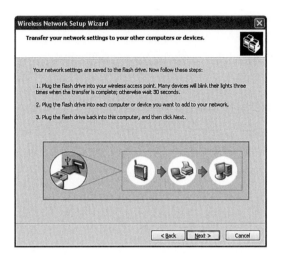

Figure 17-14   How to transfer settings to other computers and devices.

Step 10.   At the end of the process, the wizard displays a "completed successfully" dialog. If you transferred settings to other devices using the USB flash memory drive (Step 9), the devices are listed by name.

Step 11.   Click the **Print Network Settings** button to open the settings in Notepad (see Figure 17-15).

Figure 17-15   Using Notepad to view, save, or print your settings.

Step 12. Click **File**, **Save As** and name the file to create a backup of your settings, or click **File**, **Print** to make a printout that you can use to manually enter the settings on your wireless access point, router, or other network clients.

Configuring a Wireless Client with Windows Vista

The wireless client configuration process in Windows Vista is performed when you connect to a wireless network. Follow these steps:

Step 1. Click **Start**, **Control Panel**, **Connect to the Internet**.

Step 2. Select the network you want to connect to.

Step 3. Click **Connect**.

Step 4. If you selected a secured network in Step 2, enter the security key (passphrase) when prompted. If you selected an unnamed network (a network that does not broadcast its SSID), enter the SSID when prompted.

Step 5. To save the network for reuse, make sure the Save This Network check box is checked. To connect automatically when the network is in range, make sure the Start This Connection Automatically check box is checked. To disable either feature, clear the check box.

Step 6. Click **Next** to start the connection.

Step 7. Click **Browse the Internet Now** to open your web browser.

Step 8. Click **Close** to close the wizard.

Step 9. When prompted, select the network location (Home, Office, Public) to set up the Windows Firewall.

NOTE Connections marked with the Windows security shield are unsecured.

Configuring a Wireless Client with Windows 7

The wireless client configuration process in Windows 7 is performed when you connect to a wireless network. Follow these steps:

Step 1. Click Start, Control Panel, View Network Status and Tasks.

Step 2. Click Connect to a Network.

Step 3. A list of wireless networks appears. Select the network you want to connect to.

Step 4.   To save the network for reuse, make sure the Connect Automatically box is checked.

Step 5.   Click Connect (see Figure 17-16).

Figure 17-16   Connecting to an unsecured wireless network in Windows 7.

Step 6.   If you selected a secured network in Step 3, enter the security key (passphrase) when prompted. If you selected Other Network (a network that does not broadcast its SSID), enter the SSID when prompted.

Step 7.   If prompted, click **Additional Log On Information May Be Required**. When your browser opens, provide the authorization needed.

Step 8.   When prompted, select the network location (**Home**, **Work**, **Public**) to set up the Windows Firewall.

> **NOTE**   If you need to set up a wireless router with Windows 7, open the Network and Sharing Center and select **Set Up a New Connection or Network**. With Windows Vista, open the Network and Sharing Center and select **Set Up a Connection or Network**.

Troubleshooting Wireless Clients

If you are unable to connect to a wireless network, check the following settings:

- **You might have selected the wrong SSID from the list of available wireless networks**—If you did not change the default SSID for your WAP or wireless router to a custom name, you might be trying to connect to the wrong wireless network. If you are entering the SSID for a non-broadcast network, double-check your spelling, punctuation, and capitalization.

- **If the network is encrypted, you might have selected the wrong encryption type or entered the wrong passphrase**—Be sure to select the same encryption type and enter the same passphrase as those used on the WAP or wireless router. This step is not necessary when using WCN-based routers in Windows Vista SP2 or Windows 7.

- **If you are connecting directly to another wireless device using an ad-hoc connection with Windows XP, you might have specified the wrong channel**—Both devices in an ad-hoc connection must use the same channel. Windows Vista and Windows 7 automatically determine the correct channel for ad-hoc connections.

- **If you have not connected to the network before and you are not using a dual-channel (2.4GHz and 5GHz) wireless adapter, you might not have the correct adapter for the network**—This is much more likely if you have an 802.11a (5GHz) wireless adapter, as there are relatively few wireless networks using this standard.

- **If you have not connected to an 802.11n network before and you are using an 802.11g wireless adapter, the network might be configured to permit only 802.11n clients**—To permit both 802.11g and 802.11n clients to connect to an 802.11n network, make sure the network is set as mixed rather than N-only. See the router or WAP documentation for details.

Unused Wireless Connections

As you make connections to wireless networks, Windows XP, Windows Vista, and Windows 7 can store the connections for reuse. Periodically, you should review this list of connections and delete connections you no longer need. By removing unused connections, you prevent your system from connecting to wireless networks that might not be secure.

To view the list of stored connections in Windows XP, follow these steps:

Step 1.   Open My Network Places.

Step 2.   Click **View Network Connections** in the Network Tasks pane.

Step 3.   Right-click your wireless network connection and select **Properties**.

Step 4.   Click the **Wireless Networks** tab. Your connections are listed.

Step 5. To delete an unused connection, select it and click **Remove** (see Figure 17-17).

Step 6. Repeat Step 5 until you have deleted all of the unused connections you no longer need.

Step 7. Click **OK** to close the dialog.

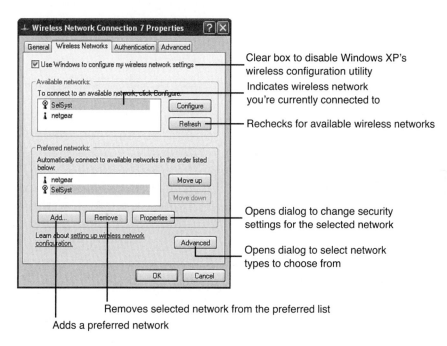

Figure 17-17 Windows XP's Wireless Networks dialog lists the connections you have made to various networks.

To view the list of stored connections in Windows Vista or Windows 7, follow these steps:

Step 1. Open Control Panel.

Step 2. Click **Network and Internet**.

Step 3. Open Network and Sharing Center.

Step 4. Click **Manage Wireless Networks** in the Tasks pane. Your connections are listed.

Step 5. To delete an unused connection, select it and click **Remove** (see Figure 17-18).

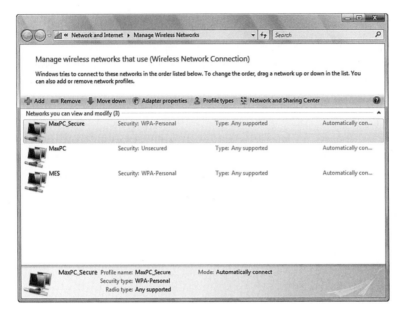

Figure 17-18   Windows Vista's Wireless Networks dialog lists the connections you have made to various networks.

Step 6.   Repeat Step 5 until you have deleted all of the unused connections you no longer need.

Step 7.   Click the close button (red X) to close the dialog.

File Systems (Converting from FAT32 to NTFS)

Windows XP can be installed on either FAT32 or NTFS file systems. However, the FAT32 file system lacks the security and user/group permissions features of NTFS. Windows Vista and Windows 7 can be installed only on NTFS file systems. In addition, the scheduled backup feature in these operating systems requires the use of a backup location formatted as NTFS.

To convert a FAT32 drive to NTFS so you can use NTFS's security and user/group permissions features, use the command-line Convert.exe program:

Step 1.   Click **Start**, **Run**.

Step 2.   Enter **cmd.exe** and click **OK** to open a Windows command prompt session.

Step 3.   To convert drive C:, enter **convert c: /fs:ntfs**.

Malicious Software Protection

Windows XP, Windows Vista, and Windows 7 include Windows Defender, which provides real-time and scan-based protection against malware types such as Trojan horses and worms. However, for complete protection, you also need to install an antivirus program.

To determine whether antivirus, antimalware, and firewall programs are running properly and are up to date with Windows XP or Windows Vista, open the Security Center in Control Panel (see Figure 17-19). It reports the status of both Microsoft and third-party security programs.

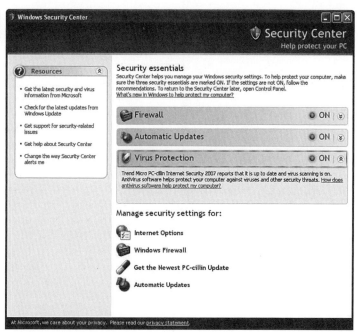

Figure 17-19   The Windows XP Security Center.

TIP   When you install third-party security programs that support Security Center, you will be asked whether you want Security Center or the third-party security program to report potentially dangerous conditions. To avoid duplicate warnings, select the option to use Security Center to provide warnings.

Windows 7 replaces Security Center with Action Center, which also monitors maintenance activities such as Defrag. Open Action Center to determine the status of antivirus, antimalware, the firewall, and any maintenance issues that need to be taken care of. Note in Figure 17-20 that the Windows 7 firewall is off and that the Action Center is prompting the user to update drivers and set backups. If a computer in the field shows any of these messages, be sure to take action in the form of preventative security measures and the appropriate maintenance.

Figure 17-20   The Windows 7 Action Center.

Types of Malware and Infection Methods

Malware is a combination of the words *malicious* and *software*. It is any type of software that is used to disrupt computers and gain unauthorized access to systems, networks, and data. Malware types and infection methods you should understand for the A+ Certification exams include

- **Viruses and worms**—A **virus** is a program that infects files in an operating system; it wreaks havoc on the system by rewriting those files so that they do what the programmer of the virus wants. Viruses can replicate but usually only if the user executes them (unknowingly). **Worms** are similar but can self-replicate; no user intervention is required. Both of these are commonly sent to the unsuspecting user through email or might be found on removable media such as a USB flash drive. Viruses can also hijack a browser and cause it to be redirected to undesirable websites. If your browser suddenly accesses strange sites, a full scan will be necessary. Viruses can also cause slow system performance. Viruses might also be the culprit for Internet connectivity issues because they modified the DNS server or gateway address. Computer lockups can also be attributed to viruses and can cause Windows updates to fail.

- **Trojan horses**—Programs that purport to be useful utilities or file converters but actually install various types of harmful programs on your computer, including spyware, remote access, and rootkits.

- **Rootkits**—A concealment method used by many types of malware to prevent detection by normal antivirus and antimalware programs. If you find renamed files, especially system files, this could be an indicator of a rootkit. Another indicator is file permission changes (for example, access denied) and files that suddenly go missing.

- **Spyware**—Software that spies on system activities and transmits details of web searches or other activities to remote computers. If you get multiple unwanted pop-up windows when browsing the Internet, it's a good indicator of spyware. Some pop-up windows will show fake security alerts in the hopes that you will click on something that will lead to a purchase such as rogue or fake antivirus software (or perhaps will lead to more malware). Spyware can possibly cause slow system performance.

- **Remote access**—Programs that enable unauthorized control of your system; can be used to set up networks of compromised computers known as *botnets*.

- **Adware**—Software that displays pop-up ads and banners related to your web searches and activities.

- **Grayware**—General term for dialers, joke programs, adware, and spyware programs.

- **Spam**—This is unwanted email sent by unknown entities. It could be benign, in the form of a person who wants to sell you something ridiculous, or it could be malevolent—for example, a person from another country asking for personally identifiable information. Attackers often try to hijack a person's email by cracking their password. Once the attacker can access the person's email server, he can use it to send out spam, and the unknowing user takes the blame. This is also common in web-based email systems; thus, it becomes all the more important to use extremely strong passwords with these systems.

Windows Defender

Windows Defender is a Microsoft program that protects computers in real time from threats such as spyware and other undesirable software. It also can be used to scan for various types of malware. It is built in to newer versions of Windows, can be downloaded from the Internet for older versions, and is available in 32-bit and 64-bit versions. It can be updated automatically and disabled if a computer has other third-party antimalware installed.

Windows Defender is located in the Control Panel, but you also can start it by clicking **Start** and typing **Windows Defender** in the Search box. In Windows 7, if Windows Defender is off, you can turn it on simply by opening it using one of the methods mentioned previously and clicking the **Click Here To Turn It On** link. To turn it off, go to **Tools** > **Options** > **Administrator** and deselect the **Use This Program** check box.

To quickly search a computer for unwanted malware, click the **Scan** option near the top of the Windows Defender screen. You also can schedule scans to occur periodically by clicking the down arrow located to the right of the Scan link.

To update Windows Defender, click the **Tools** link, then **Options**, and select **Automatic Scanning**. From there, you can set the time, frequency, and type of scan that Windows Defender will perform.

More Tools That Can Defend Against Malware

We talked about antivirus software, antispyware, and antimalware in general, but there are some tools that can aid you when affected with malware.

In Windows XP understanding of the Recovery Console is crucial. This tool offers you that unprotected command-line access to the operating system where you can replace compromised system files. In Windows 7/Vista, the Windows Recovery Environment (WinRE) has the same functionality, but it is known simply as the Command Prompt. This is one of many System Recovery Options available. Another one of these options that can help to revert a system back to before it was compromised is System Restore. And in any Windows OS, use the Event Viewer to discern what has been compromised. For more information about these tools see Chapter 15, "Troubleshooting and Maintaining Windows."

Best Practices for Malware Removal

When a system becomes infected, it can be a nightmare. But if you think logically and apply a few basic rules, you will escape the dreadful situation intact.

First, you need to identify what is happening. The symptoms will give you a good indication of what type of malware has occurred. Once you have identified what is happening, you need to quarantine the infected system or systems. Disconnect them from the network and get ready to repair!

How much fixing you do depends on the scope of the problem. If a computer has a single virus, then a simple virus scan (while in Safe Mode) and quarantine of the file will do the trick. It's also recommended that you disable System Restore while you do this. However, if the malware really has its hooks in the system, it could get more difficult. Full virus scans might not uncover all the problems. You might need to run a System Restore (after turning it back on of course) to bring the system back to a time before it was infected. However, even older restore points can become infected. When you get to the point where full antivirus scans, System Restores, in-depth reconfigurations of the system, and even other tools such as HijackThis or other third-party tools don't work, you might have to consider backing up the data and reinstalling the OS and applications. In the end, this might be a faster solution than trying to repair a compromised system. In some cases, you will be under a deadline and the customer needs the data from the infected computer quickly and can't wait for you to remove all of the malware. In these cases, you should remove the hard drive and connect it to another computer by way of an external dock or with a USB to SATA adapter kit. Then copy the required data to the second computer for the customer to use. Once the customer is satisfied in that respect, you can continue trying to "heal" the compromised computer.

Regardless of the outcome, you should install and/or update the antivirus software and schedule automated scans and updates to occur frequently. Then enable System Restore once again and create a restore point. Finally, train the end-user in ways that he or she can keep the system malware free as shown in the next section.

Training Users in Malware Protection

Users should be educated in how to do the following:

- Keep antivirus, antispyware, and antimalware programs updated.

- Scan systems for viruses, spyware, and malware.

- Understand major malware types and techniques.

- Scan removable-media drives (CDs, DVDs, USB drives, and floppy disks) for viruses and malware.

- Disable autorun (the steps for this are shown later).

- Configure scanning programs for scheduled operation.

- Respond to notifications when viruses, spyware, or malware have been detected.

- Quarantine suspect files.

- Report suspect files to the help desk and to the software vendor.

- Remove malware.

- Disable antivirus when needed (such as during software installations) and to know when to reenable antivirus.

- Use antiphishing features in web browsers and email clients.

If you disable autorun, a CD or DVD won't automatically start its autorun application (if it has one), and any embedded malware won't have a chance to infect the system before you scan the media. To disable autorun in Windows 7, complete the following steps:

Step 1. Click **Start** and in the search field type **gpedit.msc**. This opens the Local Group Policy Editor

Step 2. Navigate to **Computer Configuration** > **Administrative Templates** > **Windows Components** > **AutoPlay Policies**.

Step 3. Double-click the **Turn Off Autoplay** setting. This displays the Turn Off AutoPlay configuration window.

Step 4. Click the **Enabled** radio button and click **OK**. You are actually enabling the policy named "Turn off Autoplay."

This turns off all AutoPlay and AutoRun features. Use this sparingly on laptops that do presentations, as these computers might require AutoPlay.

Exam Preparation Tasks

Review All the Key Topics

Review the most important topics in the chapter, noted with the key topics icon in the outer margin of the page. Table 17-1 lists a reference of these key topics and the page numbers on which each is found.

Table 17-1 Key Topics for Chapter 17

Key Topic Element	Description	Page Number
Figure 17-1	Specifying a range of IP addresses for DHCP on a Linksys router	885
Figure 17-2	Preparing to change the default wireless settings on a Linksys router	887
Figure 17-4	Using ipconfig /all to determine MAC addresses for installed network adapters	889
Figure 17-5	Configuring a Linksys WAP54G WAP to use MAC address filtering	889
Figure 17-10	Windows 7 exceptions	902
Figure 17-11	The Windows Firewall's Advanced tab (Windows XP)	903
Figure 17-19	The Windows XP Security Center	913
Figure 17-20	The Windows 7 Action Center	914

Define Key Terms

Define the following key terms from this chapter, and check your answers in the glossary.

> biometrics, malware, virus, worm, Trojan horse, spyware, rootkit, social engineering, phishing, shoulder surfing, tailgating, firewall, WEP, WPA, SSID, EFS, UAC

Complete Hands-On Labs

Complete the hands-on labs, and then see the answers and explanations at the end of the chapter.

Lab 17-1: Hard Drive Security and Disposal

Scenario: You are required to install a new hard drive to a customer's laptop. You should implement whole disk encryption. You are also required to remove the old drive and sanitize the drive so that data cannot be retrieved from it and so that it can be used again.

Procedure:

Specify what you would do to implement whole disk encryption on the drive.

_____

_____

_____

Explain how you would sanitize the drive.

_____

_____

_____

Lab 17-2: Secure a Customer's Wireless Network

Scenario: You are tasked with securing a customer's SOHO wireless network. The customer wants several security mechanisms but doesn't know the correct terminology for them. Each of the items the customer wants is listed in the procedure area in the customer's own words. You must recommend each security method and decide where you will implement it—for example, on a router, a WAP, or a computer OS. Use the latest and greatest options available to you.

Procedure:

Scramble the wireless data so that eavesdroppers won't be able to decode it.

_____

_____

Make it so people can't see the name of the wireless network.

_____

_____

Disallow all computers access except the ones desired.

_____

_____

Answer Review Questions

Answer these review questions and then see the answers and explanations at the end of the chapter.

1. Which type of authentication technology uses a credit-card–sized device that stores information about the user?

   a. Smart card

   b. Credit card

   c. Keyless entry

   d. Biometrics

2. What technology uses human body characteristics as a way of allowing users into a secured area?

   a. Smart card

   b. Biometrics

   c. PIN number

   d. Keyless entry

3. What are special products that can protect you from viruses and malware?

   a. Antivirus software

   b. Malware protection

   c. Phishing protection

   d. All of these options are correct.

4. Which of the following can help protect your computer from inbound and outbound attacks?

   a. Gateway

   b. Router

   c. Software firewall

   d. Hub

5. What are the three standards for encryption of wireless networks?

   a. WEP

   b. WPA

   c. WAP

   d. WPA2

6. To prevent a hacker from obtaining useful information about a wireless network, what should you change from the manufacturer's defaults? (Choose all that apply.)

   a. Reset the default password.

   b. Change the SSID name.

   c. Hide the SSID name.

   d. All of these options are correct.

7. Windows XP, Windows Vista, and Windows 7 come with which type of encryption technology?

   a. NAT

   b. EFS

   c. User account

   d. WEP

8. You are using a computer with Windows 7 Enterprise installed. You need to encrypt the entire disk for security purposes. What technology will allow you to do this?

   a. IPsec

   b. EFS

   c. BitLocker

   d. L2TP

9. When attackers ask questions to obtain information, what is this type of attack called?

   a. Social engineering

   b. System hacking

   c. Spam

   d. Spyware

10. You are working on a Windows 7 computer. You keep getting messages from the operating system asking you for permissions. What is the name of this feature?

    a. User State Migration

    b. User Account Control

    c. User State Control

    d. User Account Information

11. Your company has a desktop that has a BIOS password assigned. The user who was in charge of the computer has left the company. What would you need to do to resolve this issue?

    a. Use a password reset CD.

    b. Reset the BIOS to the defaults.

    c. You cannot do this.

    d. Remove the jumper from the motherboard.

12. You receive a call from a customer for whom you have just installed a wireless router. They tell you that they cannot connect to the router for Internet access. Which of the following solutions would you have them try?

    a. Reset the device to default.

    b. Turn the router off and back on.

    c. Make sure they are using the same passphrase to connect to the router.

    d. Tell them to rerun the wireless network setup wizard.

13. Which of the following is a method used when removing boot sector viruses?

    a. Boot the computer with peripheral devices connected to it.

    b. Boot from a USB flash drive, floppy disk, or CD-ROM prior to scanning.

    c. Set the BIOS boot order to hard drive first.

    d. Perform a standard hard drive format.

14. Which of the following symptoms is an indication that an operating system has been compromised by malware?

    a. The computer intermittently shows a blue screen.

    b. The screen is dimmer than usual.

    c. The browser has been redirected away from the default website.

    d. When you type certain keys, you see numbers instead of the expected letters.

15. You are troubleshooting a customer's computer that has been infected with hundreds of viruses. The customer has mission-critical data on the computer that needs to be recovered in 30 minutes. What should you do?

    a. Remove the hard drive and copy the critical data to another system using an external hard drive dock.

    b. Reformat the hard drive and recover the data from a recent backup.

    c. Add a second drive to the system and copy the critical files to that drive.

    d. Update the antivirus software and run a complete virus scan.

Answers to Hands-On Labs

Lab 17-1: Hard Drive Security and Disposal

Answer:

Part 1: You should verify that the laptop has a trusted platform module (TPM) on the motherboard. If not, the encryption key can be stored on a USB flash drive. Then, once Windows is installed to the new drive, enable BitLocker encryption to encrypt the entire drive.

Part 2: You should overwrite the disk with a program that meets or exceeds standards for data destruction such as Peter Gutmann's 35-pass security method. Or, you could opt to use magnetic or electromagnetic degaussers to purge the information.

Lab 17-2: Secure a Customer's Wireless Network

Answer:

Part 1: You should implement wireless encryption. WPA2 and AES are the best options for most SOHO router/wireless access points.

Part 2: Once all the necessary computers are connected to the wireless network, you should disable the SSID.

Part 3: Enable MAC filtering. To do this, you need to either scan the network for MAC addresses or go to each computer and type ipconfig /all. All of the MAC addresses then need to be entered into the router. MAC filtering should be set to "Turn MAC filtering on, and allow computers listed to access the network."

Answers and Explanations to Review Questions

1. **A.** A smart card contains user information and when used with a PIN to secure workstations gives you better security.

2. **B.** Biometrics is a technology that can use fingerprints, voice, and retina scans as an authentication method.

3. **D.** All of the listed products can help in the prevention of viruses, malware, and phishing scams. These need to be turned on and kept up to date to be effective.

4. **C.** A software firewall is a program that examines data packets on a network to determine whether to forward them to their destination or block them. Firewalls can be used to protect against inbound threats only (one-way firewall) or against both unauthorized inbound and outbound traffic.

5. **A, B, D.** The three standards are WEP, WPA, and WPA2. All are used to encrypt data on wireless networks.

6. **D.** All wireless routers come with default SSID names and passwords. You should change these, and hide the SSID name, to prevent a hacker from looking up the information about what type of WAP you are using.

7. **B.** Windows 7, Vista, XP, and 2000 have a built-in encryption protocol called the Encrypting File System. Once applied, it can be accessed only by the user who created it and the administrator or the EFS key holders.

8. **C.** Windows 7 Enterprise includes the option to use BitLocker Drive Encryption, which can encrypt an entire hard disk drive without a user's knowledge.

9. **A.** Social engineering is a simple and easy way to get information from someone inside a company. By simply calling on the phone and pretending to be someone else, hackers can get information that should not be given out. Training users is the best way to prevent this kind of attacks.

10. **B.** User Account Control (UAC) is a security component of Windows 7 that keeps every user (besides the actual Administrator account) in standard user mode instead of as an administrator with full administrative rights even if they are a member of the administrators group.

11. D. If the BIOS setup program is protected by a password and the password is lost, you can clear the password on most desktop systems by using the BIOS clear jumper on the motherboard or by removing the battery for several seconds.

12. C. After configuring a WAP or wireless router to provide WEP, WPA, or (preferably) WPA2 encryption, you must configure wireless clients with the same encryption information. You can set up clients manually or automatically. Note that each wireless client connecting to a WAP or wireless router must use the same encryption standard and passphrase and specify the SSID used by the WAP or wireless router.

13. B. When removing boot sector viruses, you should boot from a USB flash drive, floppy disk, or CD-ROM disc prior to scanning. Boot sector viruses can also be removed by the BIOS if the feature is available and enabled. You wouldn't want the hard drive listed first in the boot order because you need to boot from the removable media to start the scan. You should remove peripheral devices before running these types of scans. Formatting the hard drive will definitely remove the virus, as well as the OS, data, and a host of other things you could lose your job over.

14. C. If the browser has been redirected away from the default website that is configured, you can bet that some type of malware has compromised the system, most likely a virus. If the computer shows a blue screen once in a while, it could mean that a driver or hardware is failing, causing a stop error. If the screen is dimmer than usual, especially on a laptop, it could mean that the system is running in battery mode. If you type certain keys and see numbers instead of expected letters, it probably means that you are working on a laptop and the Number Lock is on.

15. A. Hundreds of viruses is a disaster. You won't be able to fix the problem in 30 minutes. You should remove the hard drive and connect it externally to another computer with a dock or USB to SATA hard drive adapter. Then copy the data to that other computer. If you have ever restored data from backup, you know it can be a time-consuming process. Hundreds of viruses usually requires a reformat, but that can wait until after the data has been recovered to the other computer. Adding a second drive to the infected system will not help. This is because the operating system is still infected and will be difficult to use properly. It's too late to update the antivirus software and run a complete virus scan. Maybe, if you had more time, but in this scenario you need to get the data as fast as possible.

This chapter covers the following subjects:

- **Computer Safety**—In this section you learn how to prevent electrostatic discharge (ESD) and work safely with computers.

- **Environmental Controls**—Here you find out how to control the environment and protect against issues that are out of your control.

- **Incident Response and Documentation**—In this section we discuss some basic first response procedures and how to document problems when they occur utilizing the concept of chain of custody.

- **Communication Methods and Professionalism**—In this final section, you read about how to talk to and treat customers, focusing on respect for the customer. After all, this is where all PC repair business comes from!

This chapter covers the **CompTIA A+ 220-801 objectives 5.1, 5.2, 5.3, and 5.4**.

CHAPTER 18

Operational Procedures and Communications Methods

This chapter is all about safety, the environment, response procedures, and professional behavior. When you build and repair PCs you should carefully consider the safety of your computer components. More important is your own personal safety. Computer components are expensive, and your well-being is priceless. By employing smart safety precautions you protect your investment and yourself. Thinking bigger, the environment is a factor in the well-being of a computer. Some parts of the environment you can manipulate; others you need to take preventative measures against. However, no matter how much you plan, incidents will occur. By responding quickly and effectively to problems, and documenting everything that happens, you ensure that issues are solved quickly and efficiently. Finally, whenever working with a customer, it's important to be professional and courteous; it's even more important to be able to communicate with the customer successfully.

Foundation Topics

Computer Safety

220-801

Objective:
220-801: 5.1

Computer safety is about keeping the computer you are working on safe from failure, but it is also about protecting yourself while working with computers and other technology. The three concepts we focus on in this section are how to prevent electrostatic discharge, how to work with electricity safely, and how to protect your personal and physical safety.

ESD

Electrostatic discharge (ESD) is the silent enemy of computer equipment. Because of this it is often disregarded, almost as a fairytale! But it's real and has been the bane of many a computer component. The human body builds up static electricity all the time, even if you are just sitting at your desk. And the dryer the atmosphere is, the easier static electricity can build. Without protection, that static electricity will seek to discharge to anything else that has a different electric potential, especially metallic items; or let's say for example—circuit boards. That's right, if you were sitting at your desk and picked up a $200 PCI Express x16 video card, static will discharge from you to the component, possibly damaging it. This damage could cause a complete failure, or it could cause intermittent issues that can be difficult to troubleshoot. Make things easier for yourself and employ antistatic measures at all times. It just might save you $200—or more.

When working on computers, you can equalize the static electricity playing field in a lot of ways including the following:

- **Use an antistatic wrist strap**—This is the number one method. A general purpose antistatic wrist strap will go for about $7 and is the number one best investment you can make. Put the wrist strap on and connect the other end's alligator clip to some kind of ground, for example, the unpainted portion of a computer case. Always use an antistatic wrist strap.

- **Touch the chassis of the computer**—This is the number two method. When working on a computer, touch an unpainted portion of the case with both hands before installing or uninstalling a component. Do this every time before you touch a component. If no other antistatic options are available to you, this will be your last resort. But don't let it be; always carry your antistatic strap with you!

- **Use antistatic bags**—When you remove a component from the computer, immediately place it in an antistatic bag and put it off to the side. Parts should never be lying around without their antistatic bag! Bubble wrap bags do not constitute antistatic protection, make sure they are proper antistatic bags.

NOTE   Remember to keep the computer unplugged. Disconnect the power or hit the kill switch on the back of the computer (if there is one) before working on the system. You might not know whether the AC outlet is wired properly. Regardless, by simply disconnecting the power, you eliminate any chance of a shock.

- **Handle components properly**—If you are sitting at your desk without any ESD protection, there is really no reason to be handling components, so don't. Only handle components when you are fully protected. When you do handle components, try to hold them at the edge. For example, when installing RAM, hold the module at the sides. This inhibits any direct handling of the chips, contacts, and other circuitry. Adapter cards should either be held by the metal plate, or by the edge of the fiberglass board, but never the contacts. When you handle components, stay stationary. Don't shuffle your feet or move any more than you have to to install or remove the component.

- **Remove jewelry, and wear protective clothing**—Remove and jewelry before working on a computer. You don't want this to come into contact with any components. Consider wearing clothes that are tighter fitting so that there is no chance of anything contacting the computer components. In some labs you might see technicians wearing antistatic nylon jumpsuits. For the average person, rubber-soled shoes can also help to prevent ESD.

- **Use an antistatic mat**—A computer can be placed on an antistatic mat. The alligator clip of the mat is then fastened to the unpainted chassis of the computer case just like the antistatic strap. Some people use a second mat and stand on it, connecting that mat to the case as well.

- **Raise the humidity**—Computers work best at 40% to 50% humidity. If your computer room or lab has a humidity control, consider increasing the humidity as this will decrease friction and ultimately lead to less ESD.

- **Work in a noncarpeted area**—Carpet is the ultimate gatherer of static electricity. Never work on a computer in a carpeted area. Or, if you have no choice, consider the antistatic mat on the floor solution mentioned earlier.

- **Keep away from devices that use electricity**—Try to steer clear of mechanized tools such as battery operated screw guns. Watch out for vacuums as well. Keep anything that is AC powered far away from the computer. Keep battery operated devices away as well unless it's your trusty multimeter.

Of course, there are plenty of other ways to protect against ESD, but for the exam remember the first three, they are the most important.

You might see more advanced antistatic straps that connect to an actual ground, which could be a grounding strip, or a special dedicated AC outlet (which uses the ground wire only). These might be found in more sophisticated labs, but don't try to get smart. *Do not* attempt to connect your general all-purpose antistatic strap to the grounding plug of an AC outlet. If the outlet is not wired properly you could be electrocuted. Consider that fair warning. Use the tool as it was intended. Attach the other end of the antistatic strap to the case of the computer.

Electrical Safety

Electricity is a hazard to computers and to humans. Approach any encounter with electricity with great caution. One snap decision is all it takes to ruin your day, so take it slow and consider the ramifications of your actions carefully.

First, let's talk about protecting yourself. Before working with any AC outlet or plugging a computer or other device into an outlet, test it. Use your trusty AC receptacle tester to find out whether the outlet is wired properly. If it is not, stop what you are doing and notify your supervisor and/or building management so that they can contact a licensed electrician to fix the problem. Remember that most receptacle testers display a double yellow if the outlet is wired properly, but not all. Check the chart on the tester to identify the different lighted options. Improperly wired outlets are a common cause of computer failure. For example, if the hot and the neutral are reversed, there can be no proper grounding, even if the ground wire is connected properly. In this case, or if the ground wire is not connected, the system is a sitting duck, just waiting for a surge that could fry power supplies, hard drives, optical discs, and even the guts of the computer.

Okay, let's say the receptacle tester gave you positive results. The next step is to check the outlet with your multimeter. You want to find out whether the power is *clean*. In America this means a voltage close to 120 V AC that does not fluctuate. An AC outlet that fluctuates more than 1 or 2 volts or so is a good indicator of dirty power. This will require you to install a line conditioner or UPS between the

AC outlet and the computer. Unchecked dirty power damages tens of thousands of components every year in the United States alone, and that is a conservative estimate.

Moving on, let's assume that the outlet is supplying clean power. You still want to protect the computer from surges. Use a decent surge suppressor (also known as a surge protector) and make sure that all computer equipment is plugged into it. Surge suppressors are rated in joules. The more the better. Keep in mind that a well-used surge suppressor will last a couple of years before it needs to be replaced. This is because the metal-oxide varistors inside the device that protect from surges deteriorate over time. Dispose of used surge suppressors according to your local municipal code.

Watch how many computers you connect to your surge suppressor. Add the combined wattage or volt-amp ratings of the devices you want to plug in to the surge suppressor and compare that to the maximum that the surge suppressor can support. Usually a surge suppressor can handle two basic computers and two monitors. But watch out for high-powered devices. These should get their own surge suppressor, for example, laser printers. And never plug a laser printer into a UPS; the way the UPS manipulates electricity could cause damage to the laser printer.

You should also know several electrical conditions for the exam, and how to protect against them, as shown in Table 18-1.

Table 18-1   Electrical Conditions and Protective Measures

Type of Electrical Condition	Description	Protective Measure
Power surge	A short increase in AC voltage, say from 120 volts to 130 volts or higher	Surge suppressor
Dirty power	When AC voltage continuously fluctuates, for example, between 113 and 130 volts AC	Line conditioner or uninterruptible power supply (UPS)
Sag	An unexpected short decrease in voltage	Line conditioner or UPS
Brownout	Larger voltage drop than a sag, could cut the voltage supply in half	UPS
Blackout	Total loss of power for an extended period of time	UPS or generator

Let's talk a little about electrical fire safety. The safest measures are preventative ones. Buildings should be outfitted with smoke detectors and fire extinguishers. The proper type of fire extinguisher for an electrical fire is a Class C extinguisher. CO2-based BC fire extinguishers are common and relatively safe to humans, but they can cause damage to computers. If equipment needs to be protected more, then an ABC Halotron extinguisher should be used. Server rooms and data centers often are protected by a larger special hazard protection system that uses the FM-200 clean agent system. This clean agent won't cause damage to servers and other expensive equipment.

If you see an electrical fire, use the proper extinguisher to attempt to put it out. If the fire is too big for you to handle, the number one thing to do is dial 911. Then evacuate the building. Afterward, you can notify building management, your supervisor, or other facilities people.

Hopefully you will never come near a live electrical wire. But if you do, you want to attempt to shut off the source. Do not attempt to do this with your bare hands, and make sure that your feet are dry and that you are not standing in any water. Use a wooden stick, board, or rope. If this is not possible, contact your supervisor or building management so they can shut down power at another junction. If you find an apparently unconscious person underneath a live wire, do not touch the person! Again, attempt to move the live wire with a wooden stick or similar object. Never use anything metal, and do not touch anything metal while you are doing it. After moving the wire, call 911 and contact your superiors immediately. While waiting, attempt to administer first aid to the person.

Physical Safety

When considering personal physical safety you should think about: using caution with heavy items, avoiding hot and dangerous components, and creating a cable management plan.

Lifting heavy items incorrectly can cause many types of injuries. As a general rule, if an item is heavier than one quarter of your body weight, you should ask someone else to help. When lifting items, stand close to the item, squat down to the item by bending the knees, grasp the item firmly, keep the back straight and slowly lift with the legs, not the back. Be sure no to twist the body and keep the item close to the body. This helps to prevent back injuries. When moving items, it is best to have them stored at waist level so that minimal lifting is necessary. The Occupational Safety & Health Administration (OSHA) has plenty of guidelines and recommendations for physical safety at the workplace. Their website is http://www.osha.gov/.

Be careful when handling components that might be hot. The best method is to wait when dealing with hot items such as a laser printer's fuser, a burned out power supply, or a CPU or hard drive that needs to be replaced. To be safe, before replacing items, wait 15 minutes for them to cool. Servers and networking equipment can get hot as well, even if they are stored in a climate controlled room. Take great care when working with these devices. Also, be careful with items that hold a charge. As far as the A+ certification goes, if a device has the possibility of holding a charge, you should not open it. This includes power supplies and CRT monitors. These types of electronics can be recycled in most municipalities. Programs might include curb-side pickup, drop-off centers, or recycling events. Usually these are free. There are also many donation programs for equipment that still functions.

Cable management is even more important outside the computer than it is inside. We talked about routing power cables and data cables inside the PC so that the computer would have good circulation. But cables outside the computer can be a trip hazard. Any external USB cables should be routed in a way that they won't interfere with the normal activity of employees. More importantly, network cables should be stationary and routed away from walking areas. Your municipality will have rules governing how networking and telecommunication wires should be installed. In fact, many municipalities require a license to install any of these cables. If you need to run network cables for new computers, check your local regulations first and see whether you are even allowed to do it yourself. If so, make sure that cables do not pose trip hazards and are not run near any electrical devices or wires if at all possible.

Environmental Controls

> **220-801**
>
> **Objective:**
> **220-801: 5.2**

Environmental factors vary greatly from one organization to the next. For the exam you need to know how and why to control temperature and humidity, what an MSDS is and how to use it, and how to deal with dust and debris when it comes to computers.

Temperature, Humidity, and Air

You should be aware of the temperature and humidity measurements in your building. You also should be thinking about airborne particles and proper ventilation. Collectively, OSHA refers to this as "air treatment," the removal of air contaminants and/or the control of room temperature and humidity. Although there is no specific government policy regarding this, there are recommendations, including a temperature range of 68 to 76 degrees Fahrenheit (20 to 24 degrees Celsius) and a humidity range of between 20% and 60%. Remember, the higher the humidity, the less chance of ESD, but it might get a bit uncomfortable for your co-workers; they might not want to work in a rainforest, so a compromise will have to be sought. If your organization uses air handlers to heat, cool, and move the air, it will be somewhat difficult to keep the humidity much past 25% or 30% anyway.

That brings us to ventilation. An organization should employ the use of local exhaust (to remove contaminants generated by the organization's processes) and introduce an adequate supply of fresh outdoor air through natural or mechanical ventilation. As far as air treatment goes, organizations should use filtration devices, electronic cleaners, and possibly chemical treatments activated with charcoal or other sorbents (materials used to absorb unwanted gases). Most filtration systems use charcoal and HEPA filters. These filters should be replaced at regular intervals. Air ducts and dampers should be cleaned regularly, and ductwork insulation should be inspected now and again.

If there still is a considerable amount of airborne particles, portable air filtration enclosures can be purchased that also use charcoal and HEPA filters, or possibly utilize ultraviolet light to eliminate particles. These are commonly found in PC repair facilities due to the amount of dust and dirt sitting in PCs that are waiting for repair. Some organizations even foot the bill for masks or even respirators for their employees. Many PC workbenches are equipped with a compressed air system and vacuum system. This way, the PC tech can blow out the dust and dirt from a computer, and vacuum it up at the same time. Otherwise, it is usually best to take the computer outside, unless it is very windy.

Material Safety Data Sheet (MSDS)

A **material safety data sheet (MSDS)** is a document that gives information about particular substances, such as the toner in a laser printer's toner cartridge. Products that use chemicals are required to have an MSDS. The MSDS includes the following information:

- Proper treatment if a person comes into contact with the substance or ingests it

- Procedures on how to deal with spills

- Procedures on how to dispose of the substance properly

- How and where to store the substance

TIP MSDS personal protection ratings are designed to inform the consumer of the safe way to handle the material. The recommendations for ratings A–D are as follows:

Rating A: Safety glasses

Rating B: Safety glasses and gloves

Rating C: Safety glasses, gloves, and apron

Rating D: Face shield, eye protection, gloves, and apron

Most companies have their MSDS documents online. For example, if you were to access www.hp.com/go/ecodata (or do a search for "HP MSDS"), you would find all the MSDS documents for Hewlett Packard's various inkjet cartridges, toner cartridges, batteries, and so on. MSDS documents are usually in PDF format so be sure to have Adobe Acrobat Reader or other PDF reader installed.

Generally, substances that contain chemicals should be stored in a cool, dry place, away from sunlight. "Cool" means the lower end of the OSHA guideline, about 68 degrees F (20 degrees C). Often, this will be in a storage closet away from the general work area and outside the air filtration system. This also allows the items to be stored in a less humid area. As far as disposal, basically, any substance with an MSDS should not be thrown away when it is finished with. It will usually be recycled according to the document's procedures. This could be through the local municipality (in the case of batteries), or by returning items directly to the manufacturer or vendor (in the case of ink/toner cartridges). CRTs and just about any circuit board contain lead, which is an extreme risk when introduced to a water system. Even though the Restriction of Hazardous Substances (RoHS) directive has been able to greatly reduce the amount of lead in circuit boards, you never know how old a board you are dealing with might be or what other toxic substances are within those boards. And CRTs are simply boxes of toxicity. Handle these with care and do not dispose of them in the trash. An organization could be heavily fined, and possibly shut down, for placing these items in the garbage, so be sure to recycle these items properly as well.

It's important to know what to do if someone is adversely affected by a product that has chemicals. A person might have skin irritation from coming into contact with toner particles or a cleaner that was used on a keyboard or mouse. As a technician, your job is to find out how to help the person. If you do not have direct access to the MSDS, contact your facilities department or building management. Perhaps the cleaning crew uses a particular cleaning agent that you are not familiar with, and only the facilities department has been given the MSDS for this. It's better to review all MSDS documents and be proactive, but in this case, you probably won't have access to the document. Collaborate with the facilities department to get the affected person the proper first aid and, if necessary, take the person to the emergency room. Finally, remove the affected device if it is a keyboard or mouse, for example. Replace it with a similar device until you can get the original device cleaned properly.

Incident Response and Documentation

```
220-801

Objective:
220-801: 5.4
```

How you follow-up on an incident is a good measure of your capability to an organization. Incident response is the set of procedures that any investigator follows when examining a technology incident. How you first respond, how you document the situation, and your ability to establish a chain of custody are all important to your investigating skills.

First Response

When you first respond to an incident, your first task is to identify exactly what happened. You must first recognize whether this is a simple problem that needs troubleshooting or an incident that needs to be escalated. For example, if you encounter a person who has prohibited content on a computer, this can be considered an incident, and as part of **first response**, you will be expected to escalate the issue to your supervisor, reporting on exactly what you have found. Copyrighted information, malware, inappropriate content, and stolen information could all be considered prohibited. So before you *do* anything, you should report what you have found to the proper channels, and then make sure the data and affected devices are preserved. This often means making a backup of the computer's image. However, this will depend on your organization's policies. You might be told to leave everything as is and wait for a computer forensics expert, or a security analyst; it depends on the scenario. The idea here is that the scene be preserved for that other person so that he or she can collect evidence.

Documentation

You want to document everything that you find, and anything that happens after that. If your organization doesn't have any other methodology, write it down! When you leave the scene you will be required to divulge any and all information to your supervisor. If you were able to fix the problem and no other specialists were required, the documentation process will continue through to the completion of the task and beyond when you monitor the system. You should also document any processes, procedures, and user training that might be necessary for the future.

Chain of Custody

If you are required to preserve evidence, one way of doing this is to set up a **chain of custody**. This is the chronological documentation or paper trail of evidence. It should be initiated at the start of any investigation. It documents who had custody of the evidence all the way up to litigation (if necessary). It also verifies that the evidence has not been modified or tampered with.

As a PC tech, you will usually not get too involved with investigations. But you should know the basic concepts of first response, documentation, and chain of custody for the exam, and in the case that you find yourself in a situation where you have found prohibited content or illegal activities.

Communication Methods and Professionalism

220-801

Objective:
220-801: 5.3

Passing the A+ Certification exams isn't an end in itself—it is designed to help start (or advance) your Information Technology (IT) career. In most IT careers, how you deal with customers, whether they're people you see day after day in your company or clients you might see only once or twice, can have as much of an impact on your career progress as your knowledge of hardware, software, firmware, and operating systems. The following sections help you master the "soft skills" you need to move up in the computing world.

How to Interact with to Customers

According to pop-culture references like the *Dilbert* comic strip and innumerable others, computer techs are incapable of relating to "normal" people in either social or professional situations. Unfortunately, these comic stereotypes are based on a lot of real-world data. Here's how to reverse the stereotype, one customer interaction at a time:

- **Use proper language**—Speak clearly and in a simple, concise manner. Use proper English and no slang. Avoid computer jargon and acronyms such as "WPA2" or "TCP/IP." They often confuse the customer.

- **Be punctual**—This is probably the most important thing when it comes to customer relationships. If you have to be late, contact the customer. You might also consider contacting your supervisor depending on how late you are.

- **Listen to the customer**—Mind your manners! Don't interrupt the customer. Listen carefully to what the person has to say about the problem she is experiencing. This should offer clues as to the reason for the problem. Even if the customer admits to being a nontechnical person or even a technophobe, listen carefully. Be respectful and culturally sensitive. If a person has an accent and is hard to understand, concentrate harder, and ask the person to repeat anything that you didn't understand.

- **Clarify the problem**—Ask the customer open-ended questions to further identify what the issue is and narrow the scope of the problem. After you think you understand what the problem is, you should always clarify by repeating the problem back to the customer. Restate the issue to verify everyone's understanding of the problem.

- **Set and meet expectations**—When you understand what the problem is, state how you plan to fix it and how long it will take. Create a timeline, and communicate your status with the customer often. If applicable, offer different repair or replacement options and allow the customer to select the one that fits his needs best. Provide and organize proper documentation of any services and products you offer. After the job is complete, document what happened and follow up with the customer at a later date to verify that they are still satisfied.

- **No matter how difficult the problem, *maintain a positive attitude and tone of voice***—Your job is to make possible the seemingly impossible. As discussed earlier in this chapter, abundant resources are available from Microsoft, hardware vendors, and numerous forums and newsgroups to help you solve problems.

- **No matter how tough the problem (or the customer), *avoid arguing with customers and drop the defensive attitude too***—Your job is to solve the customer's problem. To do that, you need to work *with* the customer. Get it? Got it? Good!

- **No matter how many times you've seen the same problem, *do not minimize customers' problems***—Sure, you might have seen a couple of dozen instances of drive failure, for example, but keep in mind that every person with a dead drive has lost valuable personal or business data—maybe even enough of a loss to wipe out a business. You wouldn't want your handyman or mechanic acting as if your house or car problems were trivial—don't act as if your customers' problems are trivial, either.

- **No matter how incorrect their actions or poor their judgment, *avoid being judgmental of your customers, and while you're at it, drop the insults and name-calling*—**Declaring "war" on your customers just adds to everyone's stress level and doesn't get you any closer to a solution. Even if the customer decides to call your ancestry or intelligence into question, avoid responding in kind. "Fight the real enemy"—the computer problem!

- **Don't let your cell phone, the big game on the big-screen TV, or the view out the corner office window get between you and a solution: *avoid distractions and/or interruptions when talking with customers*—**Stay focused on what your customer is telling you, and the solution will be easier to find. Don't talk with other co-workers while interacting with customers. Stay away from personal interruptions unless an emergency.

How to Treat Customers' Property

The old Aretha Franklin song said it best: "R-E-S-P-E-C-T." Whether you are servicing a device in person, or speaking to a customer over the phone, be respectful. Here's how:

- **Don't use customer equipment for personal tasks—**Make personal phone calls with your own phone (you do have a cell phone, don't you?).

- **Don't go poking around their hard disk or mobile device folders unless it's necessary to solve the problem—**This becomes especially important if you come into contact with confidential information on a computer desk, at a printer, or within computer files. Ask the customer to move the confidential items to another area where you will not be able to see them. Do not look at or touch the confidential materials. This could include bank statements, accounting information, legal documents, and other top secret company information.

- **Don't "test" the printer by printing personal information—**Use your own printer to print your resume or a pinup of your favorite movie star, sports figure, or car.

- **If you need to reset the resolution on the display for testing, change it back when you're done—**Ditto with any other changes necessary for troubleshooting.

- **Don't make the customers sorry they called you or your company for help—**Customers who become ex-customers have a way of helping potential customers call somebody else for help.

So in general, remember to listen to the customer, use proper language, be positive, be on time, avoid distractions, keep calm, and meet expectations. If you can do all of these things while happily solving problems for the customer, they'll want you back!

Exam Preparation Tasks

Review All the Key Topics

Review the most important topics in the chapter, noted with the key topics icon in the outer margin of the page. Table 18-2 lists a reference of these key topics and the page numbers on which each is found.

Table 18-2   Key Topics for Chapter 18

Key Topic Element	Description	Page Number
Bulleted list	Antistatic methods	930
Table 18-1	Electrical Conditions and Protective Measures	933
Bulleted list	Customer interaction methods	939

Complete the Tables and Lists from Memory

Print a copy of Appendix A, "Memory Tables" (found on the CD), or at least the section for this chapter, and complete the tables and lists from memory. Appendix B, "Memory Tables Answer Key," also on the CD, includes completed tables and lists to check your work.

Define Key Terms

Define the following key terms from this chapter, and check your answers in the glossary.

electrostatic discharge (ESD), cable management, material safety data sheet (MSDS), first response, chain of custody

Complete Hands-On Labs

Complete the hands-on labs, and then see the answers and explanations at the end of the chapter.

Lab 18-1: Select the Appropriate Power Protection Equipment

Scenario: You are required to provide power protecting equipment for one personal computer and monitor, one server, and a laser printer. Select the best options for each.

Procedure:

1. Circle the best power protecting option for the personal computer and monitor.

   surge suppressor   line conditioner   UPS

2. Circle the best power protecting option for the server.

   surge suppressor   line conditioner   UPS

3. Circle the best power protecting option for the laser printer.

   surge suppressor   line conditioner   UPS

4. Explain your reasoning for why you selected each of these.

   _____

   _____

Answer Review Questions

Answer these review questions and then see the answers and explanations at the end of the chapter.

1. What are the best ways of avoiding ESD? (Select the three best answers.)
   a. Antistatic strap
   b. Remove jewelry
   c. Antistatic bags
   d. Antistatic spray
   e. Lower the humidity
   f. Touch the case

2. You are installing a new computer and are ready to plug it in. What should you do first? (Select the two best answers.)
   a. Plug a lamp into the outlet to see if it works.
   b. Test the AC outlet with a receptacle tester.
   c. Test the voltage supply with a multimeter.
   d. Switch the computer's power supply to 115 V.

3. A customer is worried about intermittent blackouts, especially in the summer when there are lightning storms. The customer wants to protect his server from shutting down without warning. What should you propose to the customer?

   a. To install a line conditioner

   b. To install a new electrical panel

   c. To install a UPS

   d. To install a gas generator

4. You walk into the server room and see a person lying on the floor with a live electrical wire draped over. What should you do first?

   a. Run out and call 911.

   b. Grab the wire and fling it off the person.

   c. Grab the person and drag them out from under the wire.

   d. Grab a piece of wood and use it to move the wire off the person.

5. You need to move a computer desk so that you can run some network cabling behind it. What should you do first?

   a. Move the desk quickly so that no one notices.

   b. Take confidential documents and place them in the drawer.

   c. Ask a co-worker to help you.

   d. Contact the local municipality to see if you are allowed to run network cable.

6. You see a network cable run between two cubicles where people walk back and forth. What should you do first?

   a. Install a cable runner.

   b. Call 911.

   c. Call building management.

   d. Disconnect the cable and remove it.

7. Most of your co-workers have desks near large windows. One cold day you get many complaints that it is too cold. What should you do?

   a. Set the temperature to 80 degrees F so that the building will warm up faster.

   b. Tell your co-workers to wear a sweater.

   c. Increase humidity to 50%.

   d. Set the temperature to 24 degrees C to combat the cold.

8. A co-worker complains that after the cleaning crew has come through, the keyboard irritates his hands and leaves some green residue. What should you do?

   a. Call the fire department.

   b. Contact the facilities department.

   c. Contact the manufacturer of the keyboard.

   d. Call OSHA and complain.

9. Which of the following can be defined as a chronological paper trail? (Select the best answer.)

   a. First response

   b. Forensic analysis

   c. Chain of custody

   d. Documentation

10. You have been contacted by a client. You arrive at her location and find that she is unable to work on her computer due to a malfunction. You need to find out what has happened. What should you do first?

    a. Walk in and tell the user you will handle it from here.

    b. Learn as much as possible when speaking to the client.

    c. Tell the client you will have to run some tests.

    d. Look to see whether anything has come unplugged.

11. You are sent out on a tech call. You arrive at the client's desk. He seems to know what the problem is during the interview. Which of the following should you *not* do during the interview?

    a. Use clear, concise statements.

    b. Allow the customer to complete statements.

    c. Use tech jargon to make you look smarter.

    d. Listen to the customer until he is finished.

12. A client is having problems with his computer. He is under a tremendous amount of stress and is very hostile. What should you do to prevent a confrontation with him?

    a. Tell the client to leave the area while you work.

    b. Tell him you don't have to listen to him talk like that and leave.

    c. Avoid having a defensive attitude.

    d. Call your supervisor and have her speak with the customer.

13. You are at the home of one of your main customers. Since she knows and trusts you, she leaves you alone to work. Which of the following should you *not* do while at her home? (Choose all that apply.)

    a. Look around her hard drive.

    b. Print personal information.

    c. Use her equipment for your personal tasks.

    d. Make her sorry she called you.

14. You have been notified to work on a client's workstation. You ask who it is. and you find out it is someone who is very difficult to deal with. What should you do when you arrive at the client's desk?

    a. Go in knowing you will be confronted by the client.

    b. Take your time in getting to their desk.

    c. Try your best to smile.

    d. Maintain a positive attitude.

15. A customer explains an issue to you. You think you understand what the problem is. What should you do first?

    a. Troubleshoot the problem with a smile.

    b. Tell the customer you will have the problem fixed in no time.

    c. Set and meet expectations.

    d. Clarify the problem.

16. You are fixing a customer's PC when a very important customer calls about a server problem. What should you do?

    a. Stop troubleshooting the PC and find out what the problem is.

    b. Tell the current customer that you have to leave.

    c. Tell the other customer that someone will get back to them shortly.

    d. Hang up the phone; you shouldn't allow interruptions.

Answers to Hands-On Labs

Lab 18-1: Select the Appropriate Power Protection Equipment

Answer:

1. Surge suppressor.

2. UPS.

3. Line conditioner.

4. The best option for the computer and monitor is a surge suppressor. It is the cheapest of the three items, and personal computers generally don't require anything further. The best option for the server is a UPS. The UPS provides battery backup in the case that the power fails. Most servers will be connected to a UPS because of the crucial and possibly real-time data they possess. The best option for the laser printer is the line conditioner. Also, it should be the only device plugged into that line conditioner because of the laser printer's high current draw. A surge protector or power strip would be okay if no other devices were plugged into them, though the line conditioner allows the printer to be protected from dirty power. Do not plug laser printers into a UPS, it could damage them.

Answers and Explanations to Review Questions

1. **A, C, F.** You should always wear an antistatic strap, touch the unpainted chassis of the computer case, and use antistatic bags. These are the three best ways to eliminate ESD. However, removing jewelry and using antistatic sprays are also good ideas. You should raise the humidity, not lower it, to increase moisture and reduce friction and static.

2. **B.** Before connecting a system to an outlet, test that outlet with a receptacle tester. This will verify whether it is wired properly. Afterward, you can test the voltage supply with a multimeter, especially if you suspect dirty power (perhaps you have seen some lights flickering while you were working). Plugging something else into the outlet is a waste of your time. It might work, but that doesn't tell you whether the outlet is wired properly. Check the voltage setting on the back of the power supply when you are ready to plug it in. By the way, many power supplies today will autosense the voltage and automatically select 115 or 230 as necessary.

3. **C.** You should propose the installation of an uninterruptible power supply (UPS). In the case of a blackout, the UPS provides temporary power to the server and can also be programmed to signal the server to shut down gracefully. Line conditioners help even out dirty, fluctuating power. A new electrical panel would be a great expense, and still wouldn't help with blackouts! A gas generator is used to supply power for a longer term than a UPS. It probably won't turn on in time to stop the server from shutting down without warning. Also, it can be a much more expensive investment.

4. **D.** The first thing you should do is get a wooden stick, rope, or something similar (every server room should have one), and use it to *carefully* move the wire off the person. In reality, the first thing you should do is to breathe, and not make any rash decisions, because in the heat of the moment, you might think a bit less clearly than you are right now. Anyway, after the wire is removed, you should call 911 and then attempt to offer first aid to the victim. DO NOT ever touch a live wire or anything that the live wire is coming into contact with.

5. **C.** Always ask for help when moving large heavy items. Or call the facilities department or building management for assistance. Moving the desk by yourself (even if you do it quickly) makes injury possible. If you see confidential items you should ask the owner to move them. Check with your local municipality about wiring codes and exemptions before you start any work.

6. **A.** For now, the first thing you should do is install a cable runner over the cable. FloorTrak is one type of cable runner. Or you could use duct tape or similar tape to minimize trip hazards temporarily. Afterward, you should inform your supervisor or building management of the trip hazard so that it can be rerouted according to your cable management policy. An emergency hasn't happened yet so there is no need to call 911. You shouldn't disconnect a network cable without knowing what it does and without permission.

7. **D.** You should increase the temperature to between 68 and 76 degrees F (20 to 24 degrees C). This is the recommended range. Setting the temperature to a higher number such as 80 will not make the equipment heat the building any faster! You could tell your co-workers to put on a sweater, but don't expect any cheer from them at the company holiday party. Increasing the humidity will not increase the temperature.

8. **B.** Contact the facilities department and see whether they have the MSDS for the cleaner. You and/or the facilities department should then treat the irritation according to the MSDS. If this does not work, and the problem gets worse, bring the co-worker to the emergency room. Remove the keyboard from the work environment.

9. **C.** The chain of custody is required to preserve evidence. It is the chronological documentation of evidence that verifies nontampering. First response is when you first encounter an issue and recognize whether it is a simple problem that needs troubleshooting, or something that needs to be escalated. If the problem needs to be escalated it could require forensic analysis by an expert. The chain of custody is a type of documentation.

10. **B.** You should always gather as much information as possible before you start working on the client's computer. You should also document the details so that in the future you have this information readily available.

11. C. Avoid using jargon, abbreviations, and acronyms. Explain what you mean in plain language. Remember, if you can't explain a problem or solution in everyday language, you don't understand it either.

12. **C.** No matter how tough the problem (or the customer), avoid arguing with customers—and drop the defensive attitude, too. Your job is to solve the customer's problem. To do that, you need to work *with* the customer.

13. **A, B, C, D.** You must learn to respect other people's property. You should never use customers' equipment for personal tasks or look at their personal information, such as documents or pictures.

14. **D.** No matter how difficult the customer might seem, maintain a positive attitude and tone of voice. Your job is to make possible what is seemingly impossible. As discussed in this chapter, abundant resources are available from Microsoft, hardware vendors, and numerous forums and newsgroups to help you solve problems.

15. **D.** Always repeat the problem back to the customer. Clarify it so that everyone is on the same page and there is no mistake. After, you should set expectations, and then go ahead and troubleshoot the issue. Never tell the customer that you will have the problem fixed in no time. Most problems are worse than they seem; it's a good way of sticking your foot in your mouth!

16. **C.** Tell the second customer that someone will get back to them shortly. If you cannot complete your current job quickly, then call your supervisor to have another technician sent to the second customer. Don't stop to find out exactly what the second customer's problem is; stay focused on the current job, and definitely don't leave the current customer, regardless of who is calling you. Every customer is important. You really shouldn't allow interruptions, but if you were to answer the phone, don't just hang up! Tell the person you or someone else will get back to them shortly.

Glossary

104-key keyboard Keyboard layout with Windows and right-click keys added to the old 101-key layout.

802.11a A wireless Ethernet standard that uses 5GHz radio signals and provides performance at rates from 6Mbps up to 54Mbps. It is not compatible with other 802.11-based wireless networks unless dual-band access points are used.

802.11b A wireless Ethernet standard that uses 2.4GHz radio signaling for performance from 2Mbps to 11Mbps. It is compatible with 802.11g-based wireless networks but not with 802.11a-based networks unless dual-band access points are used.

802.11g A wireless Ethernet standard that uses 2.4GHz radio signaling for performance up to 54Mbps. It is compatible with 802.11b-based wireless networks but not with 802.11a-based networks unless dual-band access points are used.

802.11n A wireless Ethernet standard that uses 2.4GHz and 5-GHz radio signaling for performance up to 600Mbps.

A

AC Alternating current; the type of electrical current used to run homes and businesses.

AC'97 version 2.3 audio An analog audio codec standard that supports 96kHz sampling and 20-bit stereo playback. Most implementations support jack sensing.

accelerometer A combination of hardware and software that measures velocity in mobile devices; accelerometers detect rotation, shaking of the device, and so on.

Action Center Windows 7 Control Panel utility that provides one-stop access for security, maintenance, troubleshooting, and recovery options.

active heat sink Heat sink with attached fan.

ADSL   Asymmetric Digital Subscriber Line. A form of DSL that enables faster downloads than uploads. Can be provided over high-quality existing phone lines and is well suited for residential and small-business use.

Advanced RISC Machine (ARM)   In mobile devices, a 32-bit reduced instruction set computing architecture designed for low-power consumption and simplicity.

AGP (Accelerated Graphics Port)   A 32-bit I/O bus used for video, provides for a direct connection between the video card and memory.

AHCI   Advanced Host Controller Interface; SATA setup option in BIOS that supports native command queueing (NCQ) and all other advanced features.

AMR (Audio Modem Riser)   A riser card and slot designed to support surround audio and soft modem on some motherboards.

ATA   AT Attachment; a family of standards for PATA and (in ATA-7 and above) SATA interfaces.

ATX (Advanced Technology Integrated)   Motherboard form factor with integrated port cluster at left rear of board, basis for most mid-size to full-size desktop systems.

audio mini-jack   3.5mm (1/8 inch) jacks used for stereo and surround audio, microphones, and line in/line out connections.

Automated System Recovery   ASR; special backup option in NTBackup (Windows XP) that enables a bootable Windows installation to be restored from a backup.

B

battery backup   A device that provides temporary power to connected units until they can be shut down; UPS and SPS devices are two different types of battery backups.

Belarc System Advisor   A third-party ActiveX web-based program that identifies the computer's operating system, hardware, Windows version, and security status.

biometrics   Biometrics fall into the category of "something a person is." Examples of bodily characteristics that are measured include fingerprints, retinal patterns, iris patterns, and even bone structure.

BIOS   Basic Input Output System. It controls and tests basic computer hardware at the beginning of the boot procedure.

BitLocker   A full disk encryption feature available in the Enterprise and Ultimate editions of Windows Vista and Windows 7.

Blu-ray   An optical medium originally developed for HD movies; capacity of 25GB single-layer and 50GB in dual-layer; also referred to as BD.

Boot Configuration Data   BCD; the configuration information used by Windows Vista and Windows 7 to determine how to start (boot) the system.

Boot.ini   The configuration information used by Windows XP to determine how to start (boot) the system.

BSOD   Blue Screen of Death. So named because the error message is in white text against a blue background. *See* STOP errors.

bus speeds   Speeds of various buses on motherboards (PCI, PCIe, memory, and so on).

bus-powered hub   Receives power from upstream USB port; limits power to 100mA per device.

C

cable management   The act of controlling where cables are installed. They should be kept out of walkways, off the floor, and away from anywhere a person might move about.

cable select   A PATA jumper setting that enables the 80-wire cable to determine primary and secondary drives.

CAD/CAM   Computer aided drafting/computer aided manufacturing.

calibration   Adjustments to improve print quality on inkjet or color laser printers.

card reader   A single-slot or multislot device for reading from and writing to flash memory cards.

CardBus   32-bit version of PC Card add-on card used in laptops.

CCFL backlight   Backlight for conventional LCD displays.

CD   Compact disc; the oldest optical disc format; DVD and BD drives can also use CD media.

chain of custody   The chronological documentation or paper trail of evidence that might be used in a court of law.

chip creep   Socketed chips working their way out of sockets over time due to heating/cooling.

chipset   Support chips on a motherboard (northbridge or memory controller hub; southbridge or I/O controller hub) that provide interface between onboard components and expansion slots and CPU.

clean boot   Starting Windows without startup services or programs.

client   Computer that uses shared resources on network.

client/server   Network using dedicated servers such as Novell NetWare or Windows Server.

CMOS   Complimentary Metal-Oxide Semiconductor. Refers to low-power chip design; it's also a common term for Real-Time-Clock/Non-Volatile RAM chip (RTC/NVRAM).

CNR   Communications Network Riser. Riser slot and card for soft modem and network adapter on some motherboards.

COM   *See* serial port.

Computer Management   Windows XP/Vista/7 interface for managing tasks, events, users, performance, storage, and services. Snap-in for the Microsoft Management Console (MMC).

continuous reboots   Symptom of Power Good power supply problem or STOP (BSOD) error if system is configured to restart on BSOD.

Control Panel   A Windows feature that sets Windows hardware options. It can be accessed from the Start or Start, Settings menu in most versions of Windows.

CONVERT.EXE   Windows command-line utility for converting a FAT32 drive to NTFS.

COPY   Windows internal command for copying files between one location and another.

CPU (central processing unit)   An electronic circuit that can process data and execute computer programs (Core i7, Phenom II, and so on).

CPU fan connector   Connection on motherboard to power CPU fan and monitor speed.

CPU-Z   A third-party CPU identification program that provides extensive technical information on a CPU's features and revision level.

CRT   Cathode ray tube. A monitor's picture tube, a large vacuum tube that displays information.

custom system configuration   A computer configuration that is not a stock or standard configuration to better fit the computer to a specified task.

D

daisy-chaining   Connecting multiple devices through a single port; used by EPP and ECP parallel-port modes and SCSI.

DC   Direct current; the type of electrical current supplied by batteries or by a PC's power supply.

DDR SDRAM   Double Data-Rate Synchronous Dynamic Random Access Memory. Double Data-Rate SDRAM. A faster form of SDRAM used by many high-performance video cards and motherboards.

DDR2 SDRAM   Double-Double Data-Rate SDRAM (DDR2 SDRAM) is the successor to DDR SDRAM. DDR2 SDRAM runs its external data bus at twice the speed of DDR SDRAM, enabling faster performance.

DDR3 SDRAM   Double Data-Rate Three SDRAM (DDR3 SDRAM) is the successor to DDR2 SDRAM. DDR3 SDRAM runs its external data bus at twice the speed of DDR2 SDRAM, enabling faster performance. DDR3 SDRAM also uses lower voltages than DDR2 and supports higher memory capacities.

dead short   Short circuit on the motherboard that makes the system appear to be dead.

degaussing   To demagnetize a CRT display. Degaussing removes color fringing and distortions onscreen. Some monitors automatically degauss the CRT when the monitor is turned on, and others offer a degaussing button or menu option to degauss on demand.

device ID   Method of indicating different devices attached to a SCSI host adapter; each device must use a unique device ID#, which is set on each device.

Device Manager   A Microsoft Windows utility that displays detailed information about the computer hardware in the system, including status and driver information.

DHCP   Dynamic Host Configuration Protocol. Provides IP addresses as required; allows a limited number of IP addresses to service many devices that are not connected at the same time.

digital camera   A camera that uses a digital image sensor instead of film. Most use flash memory cards for storage.

DIMM   Dual Inline Memory Module. These are available in 168-pin, 184-pin, and 240-pin versions. *Dual* refers to each side of the module having a different pinout.

direct thermal   Thermal printing technology in which the printhead heats the paper.

directory   Older term for a folder in Windows.

Disk Management   Windows XP/Vista/7 interface for managing hard drive storage. Can also manage removable-media and tape drives in Windows XP and Vista.

diskpart   Window command-line utility for creating and managing disks, partitions, and volumes.

DisplayPort   Primarily used to transmit video but can also send audio and USB signals as well. Designed as a replacement to VGA and DVI.

DLL   Dynamic Link Library. Binary files used by Windows and Windows programs.

DMZ   Demilitarized zone. In network computing it is a subnetwork that provides external services. It is often between the LAN and the Internet but is controlled by the organization that also controls the LAN.

DNS   Domain name service or domain name server. Translates domain names into IP addresses.

docking station   Enables laptop computers to use devices not built in, such as card slots, high-end audio and video ports, and others; requires a proprietary, dedicated external bus connector.

domain name   Unique alphanumeric identifier for websites.

DRAM   Dynamic Random Access Memory. Dynamic RAM. The slowest type of RAM, which requires frequent electrical refreshes to keep contents valid.

drive array   Two or more drives used as a single logical unit.

DSL   Digital Subscriber Line. A type of broadband Internet service that uses telephone lines to carry Internet traffic at speeds as high as 768Kbps or more while allowing you to use your phone for normal functions at the same time. Two major types of DSL are ADSL and SDSL. See those entries for details.

DualView   Windows standard for supporting extended desktop or cloned desktop with external video port on laptop computers.

DUN   Dial-up networking. Using an analog (phone line) modem to connect to other computers.

DVD   Digital versatile disc; the most common optical disc format.

DVI   Digital Visual Interface. Replaced DFP as the standard for support of LCD displays on desktop computers. DVI-D is for digital displays only; DVI-I supports digital and analog displays. Sometimes this is also referred to as Digital Video Interface.

dye sublimation   Thermal printing technology in which dye is released as a gas onto the page.

Dynamic disk   Windows disk storage type that permits drive spanning, striping, mirroring, and fault-tolerant volumes.

E–F

ECC   Error correction code. Advanced memory that can correct errors and requires special chipsets. It is used primarily in servers.

EFS   Encrypting File System. The encryption subset of NTFS.

electrostatic discharge (ESD)   The release of static electricity when two objects with varying electrical potentials come into contact with each other.

eSATA   External SATA, a version of SATA for use with external drives.

exFAT (FAT64)   File system designed to support high-capacity removable storage media, such as flash drives.

expansion slots   Slots in the motherboard for video, network, mass storage, and other types of cards. Types include PCIe, PCI, and others.

ExpressCard   High-performance replacement for CardBus; available in 34mm-wide (/34) and 54mm-wide (/54) versions.

Extended partition   Windows disk partition that can be divided into one or more logical drives. Cannot be made bootable.

external command   Programs run from the command line, such as XCOPY.EXE.

FAT32   32-bit file allocation table. FAT method is optionally available with Windows 7, Vista, and XP, and 2000. It allows for drive sizes up to 2TB (terabytes).

firewall   A network device or software that blocks unauthorized access to a network from other users. Software firewalls, such as the Windows Firewall, Zone Alarm, and Norton Internet Security, are sometimes referred to as personal firewalls. Routers can also function as firewalls.

FireWire 400   *See* IEEE 1394.

FireWire 800   *See* IEEE 1394.

firmware   A middle ground between hardware and software, it is a software program that has been written for read-only memory (ROM).

first response   When the first technician arrives at the incident scene and identifies what happened.

flash memory   Memory that retains its contents without electricity.

FlexATX   Small version of ATX motherboard designed for low-profile or small form factor systems.

Fn key   Special key on laptop keyboards that, when pressed, enables other keys to perform an additional task, such as adjusting screen brightness, toggling the Windows desktop to an external display, and so on.

form factor   Physical size and shape of motherboard, power supply. *See* www.formfactors.org for specifications for common motherboard and power supply standards.

front-panel connectors   Connections on front or side of motherboard for power switch, indicator lights, reset, and other features from the front of the computer.

FTP   File Transfer Protocol. File transfer to or from a special server site on the World Wide Web.

G

generic hub   USB hub that plugs in to a USB port or USB root hub.

geotracking   The practice of tracking and recording the location of a mobile device over time.

global positioning system (GPS)   A worldwide system of satellites that provide information concerning the whereabouts of mobile devices and anything else with a GPS receiver.

GUI   Graphical user interface. Windows is a GUI.

gyroscope   In addition to the accelerometers, this adds the measurements of pitch, roll, and yaw to mobile devices, just like in the concept of flight dynamics.

H

hardware   Objects in a computer that are tangible; can be physically installed or removed.

hardware-assisted virtualization   Features in CPU and BIOS that enable virtualization to perform faster.

HD Audio   An Intel standard for High Definition Audio (also known as HAD or Azalia). It supports 192kHz 32-bit sampling in stereo and 96kHz 32-bit sampling for up to eight channels.

HDMI   High-Definition Multimedia Interface. A compact audio/video interface for transmitting uncompressed digital data.

header cable   Connects to motherboard header pins connected to integrated I/O ports.

heat sink   Device that draws heat away from a component (CPU, GPU, and memory).

Hi-Speed USB   USB 2.0 ports and devices.

HID   Human interface device; mouse or keyboard.

home server PC   A PC optimized to provide file, print, and backup services on a home or SOHO network.

HTML   Hypertext Markup Language. A standard for markup symbols that enables hyperlinking, fonts, special text attributes, graphics, and other enhancements to be added to text files for display with web browsers such as Microsoft Internet Explorer, Mozilla Firefox, and Google Chrome. The official source for HTML standards is the World Wide Web Consortium (W3C), but both Microsoft and Netscape have added proprietary features to the HTML dialects they understand.

HTTP   Hypertext Transfer Protocol. The basis for hyperlinking and the Internet; it is interpreted by a web browser program.

HTTPS   Hypertext Transfer Protocol over Secure Sockets Layer. HTTPS connections are often used for payment transactions on the World Wide Web and for sensitive transactions in corporate information systems.

hub   Central connecting point for UTP-based forms of Ethernet. A hub broadcasts messages to all computers connected to it and subdivides the bandwidth of the network among the computers connected to it. *See* switch. Also refers to a device used to enable multiple USB devices to connect to a single USB port.

hyperthreading (HT Technology)   Intel CPU technology that enables a single processor core to work with two execution threads at the same time.

I

IEEE 1394   A high-speed serial connection. IEEE 1394a (FireWire 400) runs at 400Mbps and IEEE 1394b (FireWire 800) runs at 800Mbps. i.LINK is Sony's name for a four-wire version of IEEE-1394a.

i.LINK   *See* IEEE 1394.

imaging device   How Microsoft Windows identifies devices such as digital cameras or scanners in My Computer/Computer.

IMAP   Internet Message Access Protocol. Second most common protocol used to download email.

image backup   System backup that stores all information on the system including the operating system, programs, settings, and data. Most recent image backup programs also support restoration of individual files.

impact printer   Print technology that uses a multipin printhead and an inked ribbon to make an image.

inkjet printer   Print technology that sprays fine droplets of ink on the page.

integrated GPU   GPU (graphics processing unit) incorporated in the CPU.

integrated I/O ports   Ports built in to the motherboard port cluster or internal headers such as parallel, serial, USB, and others.

internal command   Windows command-line operations built in to the Windows command interpreter, CMD.EXE, such as COPY, DEL, and DIR.

Internet pass-through   When a mobile device connects to a PC to use the PC's Internet connection.

inverter   Converts DC current into AC current to power CCFL backlight in LCD displays.

I/O port   A generic term for ports used for input or output, such as USB, parallel, serial, SCSI, PS/2 mouse and keyboard, and FireWire. Storage device ports (PATA, SATA, and eSATA) are not categorized as I/O ports.

IrDA   Infrared Data Association. Defines physical specifications and communications protocol standards for the short-range exchange of data over infrared, used in personal area networks (PANs).

ISO image   A single file that contains the layout of an optical disc.

J–K

jailbreaking   The process of removing limitations on Apple devices, giving the user root access and allowing a person to install unauthorized software.

jumper   Group of two or three pins on a motherboard or card; used for configuration.

jumper block   Fits across two jumper pins to enable or disable a feature.

KVM switch   Keyboard-video-mouse; a device that enables a single keyboard, video display, and mouse to work with two or more computers.

L

LAN Local area network. A network in which the components connect through network cables; if a router is used, the network is a WAN.

Land grid array (LGA) Intel CPU socket technology that uses small metal lands in the CPU socket instead of pins on the CPU.

laser printer Type of nonimpact page printer that quickly produces quality text and images. Most use the electrophotographic (EP) printing process.

LCD Liquid crystal display. Type of screen used on portable computers and on flat-panel desktop displays.

LDAP Lightweight Directory Access Protocol. Maintains distributed directory information services. Examples include email and Microsoft Active Directory.

LED A LED refers to a LED (light-emitting diode)-backlit LCD display. It is similar to an LCD display but uses LED backlighting instead of a cold cathode fluorescent lamp (CCFL).

Level 1 (L1) cache Cache memory read by CPU first when new memory information is needed; smallest cache size.

Level 2 (L2) cache Cache memory read by CPU if L1 cache does not have wanted information; much larger than L1 cache.

Level 3 (L3) cache Cache memory read by CPU if L2 cache does not have wanted information; much larger than L2 cache; used on high-performance CPUs.

LGA1155 LGA socket used by second- and third-generation Core i-series processors; 1155 lands.

LGA1156 LGA socket used by first-generation Core i-series processors; 1156 lands.

LGA1366 LGA socket used by Extreme Core i7 CPUs; 1366 lands.

LGA775 First LGA socket from Intel; used by late-model Pentium 4, Pentium D, others; 775 lands.

Library A Windows 7 feature that enables multiple locations to be viewed in a single Windows Explorer window.

liquid cooling Cooling system for CPU, GPU, and other components that replaces air cooling with heat blocks, a heat exchanger, and liquid-filled hoses; used for extreme overclocking.

Live File System   Microsoft's implementation of the Universal Disc Format (UDF) for writing to recordable or rewriteable CD or DVD media in Windows Vista and Windows 7.

Logical drive   Drive created inside of an extended partition.

LPT   *See* parallel port.

M

malware   Malicious software, or malware, is software designed to infiltrate a computer system and possibly damage it without the user's knowledge or consent. Malware is a broad term used by computer people to include viruses, worms, Trojan horses, spyware, rootkits, adware, and other types of unwanted software.

master   Jumper setting for primary PATA drive on a 40-wire cable.

material safety data sheet (MSDS)   A document that contains information about substances that contain chemicals. It explains how to treat a person who comes in contact with the substance.

MIDI   Musical Instrument Digital Interface. A standard developed for the storage and playback of music based on digital sampling of actual musical instruments.

Mini-ITX   VIA Tech-originated ultra-compact motherboard design; used in computing appliances (media servers, and so on).

MLC   Multi Level Cell; faster but more expensive than SLC flash memory; used in SSDs.

Mobile Device Management (MDM)   Software that secures, manages, and monitors multiple mobile devices from a central location.

modem   Short for modulate-demodulate, this device converts digital computer information into analog form and transmits it via telephone system to another computer.

motherboard   The logical foundation of the computer; all components connect to it.

mount point   Empty NTFS folder used to mount a drive.

mounted drive   A drive accessed through an empty NTFS folder.

Multicore   Processor with two or more cores; some desktop processors have as many as eight cores.

multimeter   An electrical testing device that can test amperage, AC and DC voltage, continuity, and other items.

multitouch touchscreens   A display that can sense the presence of two or more contact points. Common in Apple and Android mobile devices.

N–O

nozzle check   Inkjet printer maintenance option that uses all nozzles to print a pattern that indicates whether some nozzles are clogged.

NTBackup   Windows XP's integrated backup program.

NTFS   New Technology File System. Preferred file system for Windows XP, Vista, and 7.

null-modem   Serial cable that has transmit and receive wires crossed at one end; used for data transfer.

OLED   OLED displays use organic light-emitting diodes based on organic compounds that emit light.

overclocking   Running CPU, memory, and other components at faster-than-normal speeds. May require adjustments to component voltage and improved air cooling or a switch to liquid cooling.

P–Q

paging file (virtual memory)   The file stored on the hard drive used by the paging process as virtual memory, also known as a swap file. In Windows it is a file called pagefile.sys.

parallel port   I/O port that enables data-transfer method sending 8 bits or multiples of 8 in a single operation; quite often a DB25F port. Also known as LPT port.

passive heat sink   Heat sink that relies on outside air flow for cooling.

PATA   Parallel ATA; term used for drives that use the 40-pin interface formerly known as IDE or ATA-IDE.

PC card   16-bit PCMCIA card used in older laptops.

PC99 system design guide   A series of computer specifications originally developed by Intel and Microsoft in the late 1990s. Most of its recommendations are obsolete, but the port color coding it contains continues to be followed by the industry.

PCI (Peripheral Component Interconnect)   32-bit I/O bus providing a shared 33-MHz or 66-MHz data path between the CPU and peripheral controllers.

PCI Express (PCIe)   A high-speed set of serial bus communication channels used by adapter cards.

PCI-X   Workstation/server version of PCI used for network and mass storage cards; provides faster performance than PCI.

peer-to-peer   Network in which some or all of the client PCs also act as peer servers.

phishing   The attempt to gain information such as personally identifiable information and credit cards using email or other electronic communications.

pin grid array (PGA)   CPU socket design in which pins in the rear of the CPU are inserted into holes in socket and clamped into place.

plasma   Type of display that uses small cells that contain ionized gas.

pointing device   General term for any mouse-type device.

pointing stick   Generic term for IBM/Lenovo TrackPoint, Toshiba AccuPoint, or other eraser-head pointing devices located in the middle of the keyboard.

POP3   Post Office Protocol 3. Email protocol used by client computers to download or receive email.

port replicator   Provides a single connection for various types of I/O ports for portable computers; the port replicator is connected to the external devices and is then connected to the portable computer through an external proprietary expansion bus or through a USB port.

POST   Power-On Self Test. BIOS test of basic hardware performed during cold boot.

Power plan   Windows Vista/7 power management setting.

power supply   Converts high-voltage AC to low-voltage DC.

Primary partition   Bootable disk partition created with Disk Management in Windows XP or with Diskpart (XP, Vista, and 7).

print queue   List of print jobs waiting to be sent to the printer.

print spooler   Windows service responsible for receiving print jobs and sending them to the printer.

printer preferences   Printer settings such as quality, paper type, monochrome or color; details vary with printer.

printer properties   Printer management options such as sharing, port usage, security, spooling options, and availability.

PS/2 port   A 6-pin Mini-DIN port used for mice or keyboards.

R

RAM   Random Access Memory. Volatile memory whose contents can be changed.

Rambus   Also known as RDRAM, Rambus Dynamic Random Access Memory. Rambus Dynamic RAM. A high-speed, narrow-channel (8-bit) wide memory technology designed to work with 1GHz+ processors, better than other memory technologies such as SDRAM or DDR SDRAM. RDRAM is supported by some Intel chipsets for the Pentium III and the first Intel Pentium 4 chipsets but is two to four times more expensive than DDR SDRAM. Most tests do not show a clear-cut practical advantage to RDRAM over DDR SDRAM. Rambus is now obsolete.

Rambus RDRAM Module   A memory module using Direct Rambus memory (RDRAM) chips. Kingston Technology has copyrighted the name RIMM for its Rambus RDRAM modules, but Rambus RDRAM modules are often referred to as RIMMs, regardless of their actual manufacturer.

ReadyBoost   Windows Vista/7 feature that uses flash memory as a disk cache.

Recovery Console   Windows XP repair feature.

refresh rate   Rate at which electron guns in the monitor's CRT repaint the picture onscreen; also called vertical refresh rate. It is measured in hertz (Hz).

registry   Database of all hardware, software, and system settings in Windows.

Remote Installation Services (RIS)   Program run by Windows Server 2003 that enables remote installation of operating systems. RIS was later replaced with Windows Deployment Services.

repeater   Amplifies a network signal to enable it to run over longer cable than normal; hubs or switches also act as repeaters.

resolution   The number of dots per inch (dpi) supported by a scanner or printer, or the number of pixels supported by a display.

restore point   File that stores configuration information for the system. Created automatically. Used by System Restore. Also stores older versions of data files in Windows Vista and Windows 7.

RGB   Stands for red, green, and blue. These are the three additive primary colors used in electronic systems and monitors.

ROBOCOPY   Windows XP/Vista/7 file copying utility with mirroring and logging capabilities.

root hub   Hosts USB ports on a PC.

rootkit   Malware designed to gain administrative-level control of a computer.

router   Device that routes data from one network to another. Often integrated with wireless access points and switches.

RPM   Revolutions per minute.

RS-232   *See* serial port.

S

SATA   Serial ATA; this version of ATA uses thin data and power cables to transmit data serially at rates of 1.5Gbps, 3.0Gbps, and 6.0Gbps.

screen calibration   A program on a mobile device that verifies the three axes (left to right, up and down, and back to front) are calibrated properly.

screenlocks   A pattern drawn on the display, a PIN (passcode), or a password, used to make a mobile device inaccessible to other people.

SCSI   Small Computer System Interface. A flexible interface usable for hard and optical drives, scanners, and other devices. Narrow SCSI interfaces enables daisy-chaining of 7 devices to a single port. Wide SCSI enables daisy-chaining of up to 15 devices to a single port.

SDRAM   Synchronous DRAM. Fast RAM synchronized to the motherboard's clock speed; current types include 66MHz, 100MHz, and 133MHz.

SDSL   Synchronous DSL. A type of DSL connection in which upload and download speeds are the same. SDSL connections are marketed to business rather than to home users and almost always require a newly installed circuit to the location and professional installation. *See also* DSL, ADSL.

self-powered hub   Uses AC adapter; provides full power specified for USB port type(s) supported.

serial port   A serial communication physical interface (also known as COM port) through which information transfers in or out one bit at a time. The RS-232 standard is commonly used to transmit data through DB-9 ports.

server   Computer that shares drives and other resources over a network. Peer servers can also be used as workstations; dedicated servers provide services to other computers such as file, print, email, and so on.

Setup Manager Utility (Setupmgr.exe)   A Windows XP tool that enables you to create answer files for unattended installations.

Shadow Copy   Windows Vista/7 feature that uses restore points to store older versions of files.

shoulder surfing   Direct observation techniques used to gain information about a user, document, or computer system.

SID   Security identifier. A unique name assigned to an object such as a user or computer.

SIMM   Single Inline Memory Module. Has a single row of 30 or 72 edge connectors on the bottom of the module. *Single* refers to both sides of the module having the same pinout.

Simple volume   Windows Vista and 7 disk structure similar to a primary partition but resizable. Up to four simple volumes can exist on a drive; the fourth volume will be created as an extended partition containing one or more logical drives.

SiSoftware Sandra   A third-party system analysis program that provides extensive technical information on a computer's hardware.

slave   Jumper setting for secondary PATA drive on a 40-wire cable.

SLC   Single level cell; flash memory type most often used in SSDs.

Small Outline Rambus Module   A compact version of the standard Rambus module for use in notebook computers.

SMTP   Simple Mail Transfer Protocol. A common Internet standard for uploading or sending email.

social engineering   The act of obtaining confidential information by manipulating people.

Socket 940   AMD PGA socket; requires registered memory; 940 pins.

Socket AM2   AMD PGA socket; supports CPUs with dual-channel DDR2 memory controller; 940 pins.

Socket AM2+   AMD PGA socket; enhanced version of AM2; supports CPUs with L3 cache; 940 pins.

Socket AM3   AMD PGA socket; supports CPUs with dual-channel DDR2 or DDR3 memory controller; 941 pins.

Socket AM3+   AMD PGA socket; supports CPUs with up to eight cores; 942 pins.

Socket FM1   AMD PGA socket; supports APUs (AMD term for CPU with integrated GPU); 905 pins.

SODIMM   Small Outline DIMM. A compact version of the standard DIMM module, available in various pinouts for use in notebook computers and laser/LED printers.

software   Anything that can be stored electronically, known as data, instructions, programs, or applications.

sound card   An add-on card designed for digital sound recording and playback. Plugs into a PCI or PCIe x1 slot.

SPDIF   Sony/Philips Digital Interface; digital audio standard for interfacing sound cards or onboard sound hardware to a digital amplifier.

spyware   A type of malware that collects computer and user information without the owner's consent or knowledge.

SRAM   Static Random Access Memory. Static RAM. RAM based on transistors; requires electricity far less often; too expensive and bulky to use as main RAM but popular for use as Cache RAM.

SSD   Solid state drive; a hard drive that uses flash memory instead of magnetic storage platters.

SSID   Service set identifier is a user-friendly name that identifies the wireless network. It is usually set on a SOHO router device.

SSL   Secure Sockets Layer. Predecessor of TLS. Used for securing online transactions.

standard thick client   A computer used to run locally stored and locally processed applications.

star topology   Network topology in which a central hub or switch is connected to individual workstations with separate cables. This topology is used by Ethernet networks that use UTP cables. Wireless networks also use this topology but substitute a wireless access point in place of a hub or switch and radio waves in place of cables.

STOP errors   Also known as Blue Screen of Death. An error that forces the system to halt until resolved. Systems can be configured to restart automatically after a STOP error or to leave it onscreen.

SVGA   Super Video Graphics Array or Super VGA. May refer to 800x600 VGA resolution or to any VGA display setting that uses more than 16 colors or a higher resolution than 640x480.

S-Video   S-Video (known as Separate Video) is an analog video standard used in many VCR and DVD products for input and output of video signals. Many recent video cards use S-video for their TV outputs. Can be down-converted to composite video by using an adapter.

SuperSpeed USB   USB 3.0 ports and devices.

surge suppressor   A device that absorbs overvoltage conditions such as spikes and surges to prevent damage to connected devices.

switch   Network device that sets a direct path for data to run from one system to another; can be combined with a router or wireless access point; faster than a hub because it supports the full bandwidth of the network at each port, rather than subdividing the bandwidth among active ports as a hub does.

synchronization   The matching up of files and other data between one computing device and another.

system fan connectors   Connectors on the motherboard that provide power and speed monitoring to case fans and sometimes the power supply fan.

System Image Manager   A Windows 7 and Vista tool that enables you to create answer files for unattended installations. Takes the place of Windows XP's Setup Manager Utility.

System Information   A Microsoft Windows application that displays information about a computer's operating system, hardware, and environment (MSInfo32.exe).

system lockups   System is completely unresponsive; usually caused by overheating leading to corrupted memory contents.

System Restore   Windows feature that enables a system to be returned to a previous condition.

T

tailgating   Also known as piggybacking. When a person tags along behind another person to gain entry to a restricted area.

tape drive   A drive that makes backups of a system or selected files with magnetic tape.

Task Manager   Windows XP/Vista/7 interface for viewing and managing running programs, processes, services, and other information.

TCP/IP   Transmission Control Protocol/Internet Protocol. The Internet's standard network protocol that is now becoming the standard for all networks.

termination   Device placed at the end of the SCSI daisy-chain or a switch setting on the last device on a SCSI daisy-chain.

theme   Windows term for the combination of desktop wallpaper, color scheme, and sound effects.

thermal compound   A material sandwiched between a device and a heat sink to provide the best possible heat transfer from the device to the heat sink.

thermal transfer   Thermal printer technology that uses a heated wax or resin ribbon.

thin client   A computer used to access network stored and processed applications.

touchpad   Most common type of pointing device installed in laptops. All emulate mice, but some recent models also support multitouch.

TLS   Transport Layer Security. Successor of SSL. A cryptographic protocol that provides security and data integrity for communications over networks such as the Internet.

Trojan horse   A file or program that appears to be legitimate but is used to steal information or gain backdoor access to a computer.

TV tuner   A device that can receive analog or digital TV from over-the-air or cable TV sources for live playback or storage for later viewing.

U–V

UAC   User Account Control. A security component of Windows 7 and Vista that controls how users gain access to resources.

Universal Serial Bus (USB)   High-speed replacement for older I/O ports USB 1.1 has a peak speed of 12Mbps. USB 2.0 has a peak speed of 480Mbps; USB 2.0 ports also support USB 1.1 devices. USB 2.0 devices can be plugged into USB 1.1 devices but run at only USB 1.1 speeds. USB 3.0 runs at 5Gbps; supports older USB devices at the native speeds of those devices.

VGA   Video Graphics Array. First popular analog video standard; basis for all current video cards.

video capture   The process of capturing live video from analog or digital sources and storing it as a computer file.

video card   A video card (also known as display adapter or graphics card) is an expansion card that generates video signal and displays it on a monitor.

virtual memory   Disk space used as a substitute for RAM.

virtualization   Creating an environment in which operating systems or applications run on a software-created simulation of a computer rather than directly on the computer hardware itself.

virus   Computer program designed to infect a computer and make unwanted modifications to the operating system. If executed, the virus can replicate itself; in this way it resembles a Trojan horse that can also replicate itself to other computers.

VoIP   Voice over Internet Protocol. Delivery of voice communications over IP networks such as the Internet.

W–Z

WAN   Wide area network. Network that spans multiple cities, countries, or continents. Network sections might be linked by leased line, Internet backbone, or satellite feed; routers connect LANs to WANs and WAN segments to each other.

WAP   Wireless Access Point. A device that enables connectivity between computers with wireless network adapters to create a wireless network.

webcam   A video camera designed for live chat sessions. Resolutions range from sub-VGA to 1080p HD.

WEP   Wired equivalent privacy. An older wireless network security standard, succeeded by WPA.

Wi-Fi tethering   When a mobile device shares its Internet connection with other Wi-Fi capable devices.

wildcard   Characters used as variables in command-line operations such as DIR, DEL, or COPY and in searches. * = any characters and ? = any single character.

Windows 7   Microsoft's seventh-generation desktop operating system.

Windows Aero   Windows Vista/7 3D desktop with translucent windows.

Windows Deployment Services   Program run by Windows Server 2008 and 2008 R2 that enable remote installation of operating systems.

Windows Explorer   File management interface for Windows desktop.

Windows Recovery Environment   Windows Vista and 7 replacement for Recovery Console. Collection of automatic and user-operated repair and diagnostic tools for fixing problems with systems that won't start.

Windows Virtual PC   Virtualization environment supported in Windows 7 Professional, Ultimate, and Enterprise. Required by Windows XP Mode.

Windows XP Mode   Virtualized installation of Windows XP Professional; runs under Windows Virtual PC.

WINS   Windows Internet Name Service. Method sometimes used by server versions of Windows to dynamically match NetBIOS computer names to their IP addresses (NetBIOS name resolution).

worm   A computer worm is a self-replicating type of malware similar to a virus but without the need for a user to execute it. It often uses a network to spread itself.

WPA   Wi-Fi Protected Access. A security protocol developed by the Wi-Fi Alliance to secure wireless networking. Takes the place of WEP. Uses the TKIP encryption protocol.

WPA2   Wi-Fi Protected Access version 2. A security protocol developed by the Wi-Fi Alliance to secure wireless networking using the AES encryption protocol. Takes the place of WPA.

WXGA   Wide XGA. A common widescreen graphics resolution for laptops and some displays.

x64   64-bit extension to x86 processor architecture; backward compatible; supports more than 4GB of RAM.

x86   32-bit processor architecture used by AMD and Intel CPUs.

XCOPY   Command-line utility for copying files and folders.

XGA   eXtended Graphics Array. 1024 × 768 display standard that is a minimum requirement for most Windows programs.

Index

Symbols and Numerals

A

E

F

G

H

Q

U

X - Z

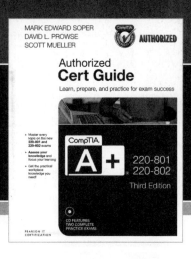

MARK EDWARD SOPER
DAVID L. PROWSE
SCOTT MUELLER

AUTHORIZED

Authorized
Cert Guide
Learn, prepare, and practice for exam success

CompTIA
A+
220-801
220-802
Third Edition

Safari
Books Online

FREE
Online Edition

Your purchase of *CompTIA A+ 220-801 and 220-802 Authorized Cert Guide* includes access to a free online edition for 45 days through the **Safari Books Online** subscription service. Nearly every Pearson IT Certification book is available online through **Safari Books Online**, along with thousands of books and videos from publishers such as Addison-Wesley Professional, Cisco Press, Exam Cram, IBM Press, O'Reilly Media, Prentice Hall, Que, Sams, and VMware Press.

Safari Books Online is a digital library providing searchable, on-demand access to thousands of technology, digital media, and professional development books and videos from leading publishers. With one monthly or yearly subscription price, you get unlimited access to learning tools and information on topics including mobile app and software development, tips and tricks on using your favorite gadgets, networking, project management, graphic design, and much more.

Activate your FREE Online Edition at
informit.com/safarifree

STEP 1:   Enter the coupon code: EVQKQZG.

STEP 2:   New Safari users, complete the brief registration form.
            Safari subscribers, just log in.

If you have difficulty registering on Safari or accessing the online edition,
please e-mail customer-service@safaribooksonline.com

Addison Wesley   Adobe Press   ALPHA   Cisco Press   FT Press FINANCIAL TIMES   IBM Press   Microsoft Press   New Riders   O'REILLY

Peachpit Press   PRENTICE HALL   que   Redbooks   SAMS   SAS Publishing   vmware PRESS   WILEY   wrox